R Thayer
6/93

Portraits in the Collection of the

Virginia Historical Society

A CATALOGUE

Portraits in the Collection of the Virginia Historical Society

A CATALOGUE

COMPILED BY

Virginius Cornick Hall, Jr.

PUBLISHED FOR THE VIRGINIA HISTORICAL SOCIETY

UNIVERSITY PRESS OF VIRGINIA · CHARLOTTESVILLE

THE UNIVERSITY PRESS OF VIRGINIA
Copyright © 1981 by the Virginia Historical Society

First published 1981

Frontispiece: William Byrd (Portrait II)

Library of Congress Cataloging in Publication Data

Virginia Historical Society, Richmond.
  Portraits in the collection of the Virginia Historical Society.

  Includes index.
    1. Virginia—Biography—Portraits—Catalogs. 2. Virginia
Historical Society, Richmond—Catalogs. I. Hall,
Virginius Cornick, 1932– II. Title.
F225.V87 1980   704.9'42'0740155451   80–14079
ISBN 0–8139–0813–2

PRINTED IN THE UNITED STATES OF AMERICA

CONTENTS

ILLUSTRATIONS

PLATES

FIGURES

viii

PREFACE

I T HAS BEEN thirty-five years since Alexander Wilbourne Weddell's *Portraiture in the Virginia Historical Society* was published. During those years the Society's collection has grown from approximately 125 portraits to more than 600. The time has clearly come for an up-to-date catalogue.

In the earlier work, "portraiture" was broadly defined—so broadly as to include the allegorical likenesses of "Sincerity" and "Hope" and the racehorse Argyle. While the present work restricts "portraits" to actual persons, it remains broad and roomy in the matter of media. Both two- and three-dimensional likenesses are included: oils, watercolors, pastels, sketches in pencil, ink, and charcoal, silhouettes, cameos, reliefs, and portrait sculpture. It excludes readily reproducible likenesses such as prints and photographs. A plaster life (or death) mask of Robert E. Lee, included in Weddell's book, has likewise been excluded, on the grounds of its having been created without benefit of an interpretive intermediary. In this respect it would appear to be less a portrait than a historic relic—like Lenin in Red Square or the casts of Pompeii's incinerated citizens.

Although the vast majority of portraits owned by the Society depict Virginians born and bred, the collection also includes some "outlanders": Englishmen, Frenchmen, a Spanish queen, and various Confederate officers from other states. By reason of their service to Virginia as governors, adventurers, diplomats, or soldiers, or on the strength of other, more tenuous, Virginia connections, their presence in the Society's galleries is appropriate. It will also be observed that the majority of the portraits represent males. This does not reflect a deliberately chauvinistic collecting policy, for almost without exception the Society's portraits have come as gifts. Thus, chance rather than design has shaped the portrait collection, though it cannot be denied that design has sometimes lent a helping hand.

The arrangement of the catalogue is alphabetical, with husbands and wives appearing in a single entry if both are represented in the collection. If only the wife is represented, she appears under her maiden name if she was portrayed before her marriage and under her married name if the portrait was painted after her marriage. Cross-references lead the user from maiden names to married names. The biographical sketches were compiled from the sources indicated and from reference materials in the Society's library. Catlin's group portrait of the Virginia Convention of 1829–30 includes the likenesses of 101 persons. These portraits, though small, are accurate and in some cases are the only surviving portrait of the person depicted. For this reason cross-references to the picture have been placed under the names of all the persons thus portrayed. Portraits that have been deposited with the Society but which are not the Society's property (a few of which have long been exhibited in the Society's rooms) will not be found in the pages of this catalogue.

In the portrait entries the artist's name is provided only if the work is signed or if there are compelling reasons for making an attribution. A similarly conservative approach has governed the dating of portraits. Dimensions are given in both inches and centimeters, height before width.

The compiler acknowledges with gratitude the assistance of all members of the staff of the Virginia Historical Society, but in particular Mrs. Kenneth W. Southall, until her recent retirement the Curator of Special Collections. Staff members at the Virginia State Library, the Valentine Museum, the Virginia Museum of Fine Arts, the National Portrait Gallery in Washington, D.C., and the National Portrait Gallery in London, the Jones Memorial Library in Lynchburg, the New-York Historical Society, and the Columbia Historical Society have responded graciously to my inquiries, as have the Director of University Communications at the College of William and Mary and the Superintendent of the Presbyterian Burying Ground in Lynchburg. Mrs. Ralph T. Catterall of Richmond, who graciously consented to scrutinize the manuscript, has contributed immeasurably to the compiler's peace of mind. The introduction to this volume is an expanded version of an article first published in the magazine *Antiques* (November 1979) and is here used with its permission. The color photographs that illustrated the article (the work of the Helga Studio) were subsequently presented to the Society by the magazine *Antiques* for use in this catalogue—a generous gift for which the Society is warmly grateful. Photographs for the remaining color plates and all the black-and-white illustrations were made by Mr. George Nan of Richmond, who for many years has done the Society's exacting photographic work with skill, patience, and good humor.

1. John Melville Jennings

THIS VOLUME IS DEDICATED TO

JOHN MELVILLE JENNINGS
Director of the Virginia Historical Society, 1953–1978

The twenty-five years during which John Melville Jennings served as director of the Virginia Historical Society were the greatest years the Society enjoyed since its founding in 1831. He came to the Society from the library of the College of William and Mary where, under the tutelage of the distinguished Virginia bibliographer Earl Gregg Swem, he learned both to appreciate and care for books. After three years as the Society's librarian he was elevated to the directorship.

Mr. Jennings's vast knowledge of Virginia history and of the men and women who moved through it, especially their family relationships, was a tremendous asset. An expert bibliographer, he made wise decisions for the acquisition of books and manuscripts. A man of unfailing personal charm, he created innumerable ties with Virginians, inside and outside the state, who enriched the Society with gifts of books, portraits, papers, and funds.

Endowed with great administrative ability, Mr. Jennings assembled and trained an exceptional staff. His detailed knowledge of the Society's finances never failed to amaze those responsible for the fiscal aspects of the organization's operations. A literary style at once graceful and to the point characterized his correspondence, his annual reports, and *An Occasional Bulletin*, the newsletter he wrote and saw through the press twice annually for eighteen years. The talents and abilities he possessed in such abundant measure were widely recognized, and with recognition came honors and opportunities; but his first loyalty remained always with the Virginia Historical Society. Good taste and modesty distinguished all that he did, and his gracious manner and antique Virginia accent shed luster over all.

More than any other person, John Melville Jennings is responsible for the eminent position that the Virginia Historical Society enjoys today among the historical societies of the United States.

ABBREVIATIONS AND SHORT TITLES

The Beverley Family. John McGill. *The Beverley Family of Virginia: Descendants of Major Robert Beverley (1641–1687) and Allied Families.* Columbia, S.C., 1956.

Biographic Catalogue. United Confederate Veterans. Virginia Division. R. E. Lee Camp No. 1. *Biographic Catalogue of the Portraits in the Confederate Memorial Institute, "The Battle Abbey."* Richmond, 1929.

Biographical Directory. United States Congress. *Biographical Directory of the American Congress, 1774–1971.* Washington, D.C., 1971.

The Cabells and Their Kin. Alexander Brown. *The Cabells and Their Kin: A Memorial Volume of History, Biography, and Genealogy.* Richmond, 1939.

Confederate Military History. Clement Anselm Evans, ed. *Confederate Military History: A Library of Confederate States History.* Atlanta, 1899.

CMA Archives. Confederate Memorial Association Archives. In the Manuscripts Division of the Virginia Historical Society.

DAB. Dictionary of American Biography. New York, 1928–37.

DNB. Dictionary of National Biography. Oxford, Eng., 1921–22.

Eminent and Representative Men. Eminent and Representative Men of Virginia and the District of Columbia in the Nineteenth Century. Madison, Wis., 1893.

Encyclopaedia Britannica. The Encyclopaedia Britannica. Chicago, 1947.

Encyclopedia Americana. The Encyclopedia Americana. New York, 1974.

Encyclopedia of Virginia Biography. Lyon Gardiner Tyler, ed. *Encyclopedia of Virginia Biography.* New York, 1915.

Family of Early. Ruth Hairston Early. *The Family of Early Which Settled upon the Eastern Shore of Virginia and Its Connection with Other Families.* Lynchburg, Va., 1920.

Generals in Gray. Ezra J. Warner. *Generals in Gray: Lives of the Confederate Commanders.* Baton Rouge, La., 1959.

History of Virginia. P. A. Bruce et al. *History of Virginia.* Chicago and New York, 1924.

Lee of Virginia. Edmund Jennings Lee. *Lee of Virginia, 1642–1892: Biographical and Genealogical Sketches of the Descendants of Colonel Richard Lee.* Philadelphia, 1895.

Memorial, Virginia Military Institute. Charles Duy Walker. *Memorial, Virginia Military Institute: Biographical Sketches of the Graduates and Elèves of the Virginia Military Institute Who Fell during the War between the States.* Philadelphia, 1875.

Men of Mark in Virginia. Lyon Gardiner Tyler, ed. *Men of Mark in Virginia.* Washington, D.C., 1906–9.

National Cyclopaedia. The National Cyclopaedia of American Biography. New York, 1892–1906.

Occasional Bulletin. Virginia Historical Society, Richmond. *An Occasional Bulletin.* Richmond, 1960—.

Overwharton Parish. George Harrison Sanford King. *The Register of Overwharton Parish, Stafford County, Virginia, 1723–1758, and Sundry Historical and Genealogical Notes.* Fredericksburg, Va., 1961.

The Page Family. Richard Channing Moore Page. *Genealogy of the Page Family in Virginia. Also a Condensed Account of the Nelson, Walker, Pendleton, and Randolph Families.* 2d ed. New York, 1893.

Por946.25. Virginia Historical Society portrait accession number.

Portraits and Miniatures. Charles Coleman Sellers. *Portraits and Miniatures by Charles Willson Peale.* Philadelphia, 1952.

Portraits and Statuary. Ray O. Hummel, Jr., and Katherine M. Smith. *Portraits and Statuary of Virginians Owned by the Virginia State Library, the Medical College of Virginia, the Virginia Museum of Fine Arts, and Other State Agencies.* Richmond, 1977.

Portraiture. Alexander Wilbourne Weddell. *Portraiture in the Virginia Historical Society, with Notes on the Subjects and Artists.* Richmond, 1945.

The Randolphs. Hamilton James Eckenrode. *The Randolphs: The Story of a Virginia Family.* Indianapolis and New York, 1946.

The Randolphs of Virginia. Robert Isham Randolph. *The Randolphs of Virginia: A Compilation of the Descendants of William Randolph of Turkey Island and His Wife Mary Isham of Bermuda Hundred.* Chicago, 1936.

Richmond Portraits. Valentine Museum, Richmond. *Richmond Portraits in an Exhibition of Makers of Richmond, 1737–1860.* Richmond, 1949.

Seldens of Virginia. Mary Selden Kennedy. *Seldens of Virginia and Allied Families.* New York, 1911.

SHS Papers. Southern Historical Society. *Southern Historical Society Papers.* Richmond, 1876–1959.

Tyler's Quart. *Tyler's Quarterly Historical and Genealogical Magazine.* Richmond, 1920–52.

University of Virginia. Paul Brandon Barringer. *University of Virginia: Its History, Influence, Equipment, and Characteristics, with Biographical Sketches and Portraits of Founders, Benefactors, Officers, and Alumni.* New York, 1904.

The University Memorial. John Lipscomb Johnson, ed. *The University Memorial: Biographical Sketches of Alumni of the University of Virginia Who Fell in the Confederate War.* Baltimore, 1871.

VHS Archives. Virginia Historical Society Archives. In the Manuscripts Division of the Virginia Historical Society.

VHS Mss1 W435a. Virginia Historical Society manuscript call number.

VMHB. Virginia Historical Society, Richmond. *Virginia Magazine of History and Biography.* Richmond, 1893—.

Virginia and Virginians. Robert Alonzo Brock. *Virginia and Virginians: Eminent Virginians.* Richmond and Toledo, 1888.

Virginia Genealogies. Horace Edwin Hayden. *Virginia Genealogies: A Genealogy of the Glassell Family of Scotland and Virginia, Also of the Families of Ball, Brown, Bryan, Conway, Daniel, Ewell, Holladay, Lewis, Littlepage, Moncure, Peyton, Robinson, Scott, Taylor, Wallace, and Others, of Virginia and Maryland.* Wilkes-Barre, Pa., 1891.

Virginia Historical Portraiture. Alexander Wilbourne Weddell. *A Memorial Volume of Virginia Historical Portraiture, 1585–1830.* Richmond, 1930.

Virginia House. Alexander Wilbourne Weddell. *A Description of Virginia House in Henrico County, near Richmond, Virginia, the Home of Mr. & Mrs. Alexander Wilbourne Weddell.* Richmond, 1947.

W. & M. Quart. *William and Mary Quarterly: A Magazine of Early American History, Institutions, and Culture.* Williamsburg, Va., 1892—.

Portraits in the Collection of the
Virginia Historical Society
A CATALOGUE

INTRODUCTION

IN 1854 William Maxwell (1784–1857), corresponding secretary of the Virginia Historical Society, paid a diplomatic call on the aged Mrs. J. A. M. Chevallié of Richmond. Maxwell did not arrive empty-handed: he gave the old lady an orange. It can be assumed that he also paid her some pretty compliments, for he was an attractive man not lacking the social graces. She, in turn, gave him four Charles Willson Peales! They still hang in the Society's rooms.

The Virginia Historical Society had been in existence twenty-three years when Maxwell charmed the pictures off Mrs. Chevallié's walls. It had been organized late in 1831, four days after Christmas, when a group of citizens under the leadership of Jonathan Peter Cushing (1793–1835), president of Hampden-Sydney College, gathered in the Old Hall of the House of Delegates in Richmond to approve a constitution, elect officers, and draw up an address to acquaint the public with the Society's objectives. Among the founders were Governor John Floyd, James Ewell Heath, Conway Robinson, George Tucker, and John Hampden Pleasants, all of them persons of more than local distinction. Richmond's first citizen, John Marshall, chief justice of the United States, was the logical choice for president of the new organization, and was duly elected.

In its early years the Virginia Historical and Philosophical Society, as it was then known, addressed itself to both history and the natural sciences. Although its principal interest soon became historical rather than scientific, it was not until after the Civil War that it abandoned the natural sciences altogether, shortened its name, and put its mineral specimens in storage. From the outset the Society solicited books and manuscripts for its library, relics and curiosities for its cabinet. Portraits, however, were not mentioned in the Society's early list of desiderata and appear to have been largely overlooked. When James Herring (1794–1867), compiler of *The National Portrait Gallery of Distinguished Americans*, approached the executive committee in 1836 (VHS Archives, folio G1-1836) requesting assistance in the compilation of a second volume and access to the Society's "collection of pictures," there was little help forthcoming. Eleven years later, when a fine portrait bust of John Marshall, the Society's first president, became available, the Society's officers failed to secure it, though—cold comfort—the details of the lost opportunity survive in the archives. The bust in question was executed by one of America's pioneer sculptors, John Frazee (1790–1852). He sculpted the original, commissioned by the Boston Athenaeum, in 1834, just a year before the chief justice's death; subsequently he made at least three replicas, one of which he hoped to place in Richmond. In a letter to Conway Robinson, a founder-member of the Society, Frazee wrote:

The Bust is of the finest Carara Marble, and will, when finished, be a beautiful work, equal to any of those I have previously made, and there are three of them; one in the Boston Athenaeum, another in the Council Chamber of our City Hall here [in New York], and a third in the Supreme Court Room at New Orleans. They have all given the highest satisfaction to the purchasers, and are greatly admired. For each of those I was paid $500. and I ask the same price for the one I am finishing. It will take me some 5 or 6 weeks yet to complete it; meanwhile I would be glad to learn from either yourself or Mr. Stanard, as to whether the sale of it at Richmond can be effected. I think you may find with some of the family connections of Judge Marshall, a copy, in plaster, from my original model, as he purchased 10 copies which he told me he should distribute with his kindred & friends. [VHS Archives, folio C42-1847]

In response, Robinson noted that "efforts are now making to resuscitate the Virginia Historical Society of which Chief Justice Marshall was the first president, and I am disposed to think the most practicable course here for obtaining a marble bust of the chief justice will be for a number of gentlemen to subscribe for it and present it to the Society" (VHS Archives, folio C42-1847). Although the Society let Frazee's portrait bust get away, the following year, in 1848, it received its first painting: a three-quarter-length portrait by Charles Willson Peale (1741–1827), identified by the donor as the marquis de Lafayette (1757–1834). With this splendid canvas as its foundation piece, the Society began collecting.

Shortly after the receipt of the Peale, Thomas Sully (1783–1872), an early friend of the Society, donated a replica of his portrait of Patrick Henry and an idealized picture of the Indian princess Pocahontas. Two other Sully portraits, presented by the treasurer, Jaquelin P. Taylor, came to the collection about the same time: one of President James Madison after Gilbert Stuart and one of the celebrated jurist Edmund Pendleton (1721–1803), copied from the only known life portrait, a miniature. It should be noted in passing that the miniature, the work of William Mercer (1773–1850), the deaf-mute son of General Hugh Mercer, was acquired a hundred and ten years later, in 1960. These canvases were joined in short order by Chester Harding's (1792–1866) full-length portrait of Governor William Branch Giles (1762–1830) painted at the Virginia Convention of 1829–30, John Wollaston's portrait of Peyton Randolph (1721?–1775), president of the Continental Congress, and Peale's Arthur Lee (1740–1792). Arthur Lee's portrait had not hung for many months in the Society's rooms before the artist George P. A. Healy wrote from Chicago to say that he was "to sail from New York early in Oct. for Paris where I am to paint a large picture for Congress of Franklin & the other American commissioners treating with Louis XVI" and needed a photograph of the Society's portrait of Lee, together with "the color of the eyes, complexion, etc. etc." (VHS Archives, folio G1-1856). The Society complied with the artist's request, but the painting, a copy of his celebrated earlier canvas, was evidently never completed.[1]

---

[1] The original study for the picture, completed about 1847, is now in the collection of the American Philosophical Society. The larger version, commissioned by Louis Philippe for the Palace of Versailles, was completed by the artist after the abdication of his royal patron in 1848. It won a medal at the Paris Universal Exposition in 1855 and was eventually destroyed in the great Chicago fire of 1871.

These and more than a dozen other canvases, originals and copies, found their way to the Society's rooms during the years before the outbreak of the Civil War. Here they were examined in 1858 by no less an authority than Rembrandt Peale, then visiting Richmond. George Wythe Randolph, an officer of the Society, recalled the visit in a letter to his niece:

> Rembrandt Peale the Painter is here. . . . I took the old fellow to the Historical Society rooms. He recognized at once the old French portraits and those of George Washington. He said the two last were by his father and he thought the others were probably his. The Painting of Queen Ann he pronounced a splendid Godfrey Kneller, one of the most beautiful he had ever seen and very valuable. The Frenchman in purple & gold is the Chevalier de Luzerne, the first French Minister to this country, the other two he was not certain about, but promised to ascribe. [George Wythe Randolph to Mary Randolph, Richmond, May 3, 1858, University of Virginia Library, Edgehill-Randolph Papers]

The Peale portraits thus authenticated were Mrs. Chevallié's collection. As for Kneller's portrait of Queen Anne, it was one of several that vanished during the Civil War. Its loss is the more regrettable in the light of a recent suggestion that it may have been the official portrait of the queen at one time displayed in the Governor's Palace in Williamsburg and known to have been sold at auction with other palace furnishings after Lord Dunmore's departure in 1775.

Another portrait caught the eye of Hugh Blair Grigsby at much the same time. Writing to William H. Macfarland, a vice-president of the Society, Grigsby, benefactor and member of the executive committee, reported:

> I saw in the gallery of my friend Dr. Swann of Philadelphia a magnificent painting of William of Orange, the good king William of England, and the king more beloved in the Colony than any other king who ever filled the English throne. He is represented as large as life sitting at a table. The painting was executed from life by Vollevins just before William left Holland at the Revolution. An undoubted original, and splendidly executed, it is in fine order. Now I am anxious to procure this painting for William and Mary College. The original cost must have been 500 guineas, but Dr. Swann, who is a Virginian, is ready to let me have it at $300, and of this sum we can possibly raise one hundred dollars in Norfolk. Can the other alumni of the old college residing in Richmond make out the remainder? If you cannot, and William and Mary cannot secure possession, I must try for the Historical Society, for surely such a painting ought to be owned in Virginia. [VHS Archives, folio G1-1857]

If the portrait was in fact secured for William and Mary, it was probably destroyed shortly thereafter in one of two fires, in 1859 and 1862, that the college sustained. No such portrait belongs to the college now, nor is there any record of its having come by default to the Virginia Historical Society.

In the turmoil of the war years the portrait of Queen Anne was but one of the Society's portraits to disappear; others were destroyed together with books and manuscripts in the evacuation fire that razed much of Richmond in 1865; still others were recovered and returned to the Society at the close of hostilities. Thomas T. Giles, charged with retrieving the Society's scattered possessions, reported to the executive committee in 1870: "Notwithstanding all the disadvantages under which it has labored from its origin, and notwithstanding the calamities and disasters of the late war, the Society still has in its possession a large amount of very valuable property, consisting of about 6000 volumes of Books, a numerous collection of Pamphlets, a Mass of Manuscripts, and 36 Portraits, and a considerable number of relics and Geological specimens, much of which, if lost, could never be restored" (March 10, 1870, VHS Archives, folio C3). Although some of the collections were recovered, it was not easy to replace the endowment that had been invested with greater patriotism than prudence in Confederate bonds. Despite a shortage of funds that persisted for the next three-quarters of a century, the Society's doors remained open to scholars; the publications program, initiated in 1833, continued active; and most important, gifts of books, manuscripts, and museum objects arrived in increasing numbers. Desperately poor in terms of cash and capital (for it had been organized as an independent organization, receiving no support from public revenues), the Society assembled during those lean years historical resources that were enormously varied and valuable. Additions to the portrait collection, however, were few immediately after the war. In fact, between 1870 and 1881 the collection dwindled from thirty-six to twenty-eight portraits, a shrinkage due in all probability to the withdrawal of various deposited items. Letters in the Society's archives document one such withdrawal. On February 20, 1874, Miss Fannie B. Nelson of Yorktown wrote Anthony M. Keiley, mayor of Richmond and member of the Society's executive committee:

> May I trouble you to ask of the Historical Society the return of the pictures which they have in charge belonging to the Nelson family. They were sent to Richmond for safety on the evacuation of Yorktown by the Confederate forces and are the portraits of Gen. Nelson's Father, Mother, and Grand Mother. There are three separate pictures but only one has a frame & one has a rent in it, said to have been made by British soldiers in revolutionary times running their swords through them as they were packed to be sent away. They are of little value save as relics to the family, but to the family they are held very precious, therefore I beg the favor of you to have them sent as soon as you can without inconvenience to yourself. [VHS Archives, folio G1-1874]

It will be observed in passing that the well-known Yankee propensity for doing battle with portraits had British antecedents. In the same proportion as officer-ancestors outnumber enlisted ancestors, so apparently do the portraits slashed by enemy bayonets outnumber those damaged in spring cleaning. Mayor Keiley forwarded Miss Nelson's letter to the Society's corresponding secretary, Thomas Hicks Wynne. He, in turn, wrote Charles G. Barney, saying, "I do not know how this Society obtained the pictures in question and I have heard that you know all about them, I beg you will give all the information you possess." Barney did indeed know all about them and replied the same day:

In the year 1861 word was sent to me (then the Treasurer of the Society) that there was a wagon before the Historical building containing some Portraits, and the only information I could then obtain was that our troops were leaving Yorktown, and it was thought best to send them to the Society for safe keeping. I took charge of them, and when the rooms containing the books and Pictures were wanted by the Government the Portraits were taken to my own house where they remained until after the war, and then were called for by the Society, and to them I delivered the same. Subsequently I learned that Col. Boulware directed these portraits to be sent to the Historical Society. The Portraits are now in the rooms of the Society. [VHS Archives, folio G1-1874]

The Society's executive committee at its next meeting authorized Keiley to oversee the return of the portraits to the Nelsons.

Throughout the last two decades of the century portrait acquisitions were reported with heartening frequency in the minutes of the executive committee's monthly meetings: the charming group portrait of the children of Philip Grymes; a portrait of Martha Washington's father, John Dandridge (1700–1756) of New Kent County; Peter Cardelli's bust of James Madison, modeled from life shortly after his retirement from the presidency; a George Washington by Charles Willson Peale; and a portrait by Cephas Thompson (1775–1852) of the Society's vice-president and corresponding secretary William Maxwell—he who so beguiled Mrs. Chevallié. Indeed, although still occupying rooms in the Westmoreland Club, the Society expressed itself publicly well pleased with its situation, singling out the portraits for particular notice. In the *Richmond Dispatch* of June 1, 1887, it announced that "the present rooms of the Society, enjoyed by the liberality of the Westmoreland Club, are handsomely and thoroughly furnished with new cases and other essential conveniences, and the valuable assemblage of portraits of those distinguished and revered in the annals of Virginia have been put in perfect order, canvas and frame. The exhibit is fairly an honor and an ornament to Richmond and the State, and must attract and gratify all visitors" (VHS Archives, liber A4, p. 78).

Adequate quarters, long a pressing need, at last became available in 1893 when the Lee House in downtown Richmond was acquired to house the library, museum, and offices. Here, and later in the annex which was added to the structure, there was sufficient space for all the portraits. Assembled under one roof and properly exhibited, they served public notice that the Society not only was actively collecting Virginia portraiture but was in a position to care for the likenesses entrusted to its care. The quality of the acquisitions made during the first three decades of the present century indicates that the message was being heard: Thomas Sully's striking portrait of founder-member Conway Robinson (1805–1884); Andrew Nicolson (1763–1819) by Saint-Mémin; a fine Zachary Taylor; yet another *pater patriae*, this one the work of Charles Peale Polk (1767–1822); the early eighteenth-century likenesses of George Eskridge (d.1735) and his lady of Westmoreland County; a full-length portrait of the Right Reverend James Madison (1749–1812), first Episcopal bishop of Virginia; a bust by the black sculptor Eugene

Warburg (1825–1861) of John Young Mason (1799–1859), minister to France and vice-president of the Virginia Historical Society; a miniature of James Blair (1655–1743), colonial Virginia's cantankerous commissary; a magnificent collection of eighteenth-century portraits of members of the Randolph family; and numerous portraits dating from the second half of the nineteenth century and later.

Acquisitions of such distinction helped focus attention on portraiture and the Society's growing collection. A well-publicized exhibition helped even more. In 1929 Alexander Wilbourne Weddell, shortly to become a member of the Society's executive committee and from 1943 to 1948 its president, organized, under the Society's auspices, an extensive exhibition of early Virginia portraits drawn not only from the Society's collection but from public and private collections in this country and abroad. The paneled rooms of the Weddells's residence, a Tudor priory recently transplanted from England to a commanding site overlooking the James River in a western suburb of Richmond, provided a congenial setting for the exhibition. Even more impressive was the 556-page catalogue, *A Memorial Volume of Virginia Historical Portraiture, 1585–1830* (Richmond, 1930), a massive, full-morocco-bound volume which reproduced, full page, every portrait in the exhibit, and remains the standard work on the subject. A considerably less ambitious catalogue, *Portraiture in the Virginia Historical Society*, describing the approximately 125 items then comprising the collection, appeared in 1945. Through unanticipated circumstances the volume was outdated almost as soon as it came off the press. A few months after its publication the Society's portrait holdings almost tripled in size.

This astonishing growth came about as a result of a merger concluded in 1946 between the Virginia Historical Society and the Confederate Memorial Association. Through it the Society gained title to the Association's handsome neoclassical building known as Battle Abbey in the western part of Richmond (greatly enlarged in 1958 and since that time the Society's headquarters) and the Association's library and picture collection. The portraits, more than 200 in number, depict Virginia's Civil War veterans, from the monumental figures of Lee, Jackson, and Stuart to the gunners and private soldiers, painted in later life, who manned the batteries. If the rank of the subjects is diverse, so too is the artistic ability of those who recorded their features, extending as it does from the highly competent William Garl Brown (1823–1894) and William Ludwell Sheppard (1833–1912) to various self-taught local painters. The collection thus acquired is a remarkable pictorial archive, the largest of its kind in existence.

Financial solidarity, an elusive objective for more than a century, was achieved, at least to a degree, with the receipt in 1948 of substantial legacies from the estates of Mr. and Mrs. Alexander Wilbourne Weddell. Since that time, in the enjoyment of a firmer financial position, the Society has increased its usefulness to the scholarly community by further developing its research collections and providing services commensurate with the quality of the materials it holds. It has concurrently evolved into a center for the study of Virginia portraiture, its long-standing concern with the likenesses of Virginians and their limners having led to the development of extensive photographic files and related documentation. In this field, the principal challenge to researchers stems not from the Wollastons, the Hesseliuses, the Saint-Mémins, but from the obscure artists, both itinerant and untraveled, who are known to have worked in the Old Dominion. Thus, when a portrait is acquired that is firmly attributed to a minor artist previously unrepresented in the collection, it is welcomed with an enthusiasm that often has little to do with its intrinsic merit.

Portrait accessions since 1948 have been more numerous than at any time in the Society's previous history—apart from the en bloc acquisition of 1946—and of comparable quality. They include likenesses of six generations of the Wormeley family of Rosegill in Middlesex County, the finest piece being Robert Edge Pine's superb "leaving picture" of Ralph Wormeley (1745–1809); a group of mid-eighteenth-century Fitzhugh family portraits, the work of John Hesselius (1728–1778); Richmond's founder, William Byrd (1674–1744) of Westover; Governor Sir Edmund Andros (1637–1714), whose remarkably sour countenance may well have a bearing on his perennial unpopularity in the colonies; John Baylor (1705–1772), horseman par excellence of Newmarket, Caroline County; Matthew Pratt's three-quarter-length portraits of James Balfour (d.1775) and his wife; life portraits by Joseph Wood (ca.1778–1830) of James and Dolley Madison; and a group portrait of the delegates to the Virginia Constitutional Convention of 1829–30, executed by George Catlin (1796–1872), best known for his later scenes of the American West. To the cabinet of miniatures have been added likenesses of Governor Alexander Spotswood (1676–1740) and his lady; Virginia's giant of the Revolution, Peter Francisco (1760–1831); the only surviving life portrait of Benjamin Harrison (1726–1791), signer of the Declaration of Independence; and portraits in miniature of numerous other Virginians whose influence was felt in more restricted circles. To this sampling of early portraits should be added scores of later likenesses acquired during the same period: Lady Astor as seen by Jo Davidson, Siegfried Joseph Charoux, and Edith Leeson Everett; Pierre Troubetzkoy's canvas of his wife, the novelist Amélie Rives Troubetzkoy; the Jonniaux portraits of Mr. and Mrs. Weddell and of Edmund Randolph Williams—portraiture of a quality to hold its own in any assemblage of twentieth-century works.

From tentative beginnings the Society's collection has grown in size and in quality over the past century and a half to rank among the major collections in the South. Approximately six hundred likenesses now comprise the collection; of these only a portion can be exhibited in the Society's galleries at any one time. All, however, are available for study, and all have been photographed to meet an increased demand for their illustrative use in books and periodicals. Interest in the Society's portrait holdings is greater now than it was a decade ago. It is substantially greater than it was in 1945 when the last portrait catalogue was published. The purpose of the present catalogue is to help satisfy this greater interest, to acquaint an inquiring public with the richness of the collection, and to share it, albeit imperfectly, with those persons who are unable to inspect the originals in the rooms of the Virginia Historical Society.

CATALOGUE OF
PORTRAITS

Mark Alexander, 1792–1883
See The Convention of 1829–30

Daniel Allen, 1728–1807

Daniel Allen, son of James and Anne (Anderson) Allen of Hanover County, was born on October 12, 1728. A devout Presbyterian, he was a member of Samuel Davies's congregation in Hanover County; soon after Davies left Virginia, Allen with his four brothers removed to Cumberland County where he was instrumental in the establishment of Guinea Church. He married, first, Anna Harrison, and by her had ten children; he married, second, on February 21, 1775, Joanna (Read) Hill, widow of Joseph Hill. At Mountain View, his residence in Cumberland County, he raised his large family, one of whom, Cary, went to Kentucky in 1791 as a missionary, dying four years later at the early age of twenty-eight. Daniel Allen remained in Cumberland for the rest of his life. In a letter dated March 7, 1794, he

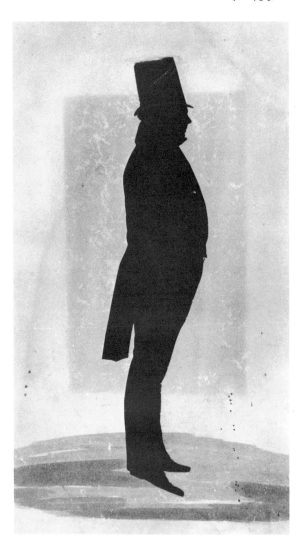

Daniel Allen

stated, "I am now sixty-five years old, a planter, and never was but a little over one hundred miles from home in my life. . . . I feel now like I never could give up to the foolish fashions and customs of the world. I remain a stranger." He died in 1807.

William Henry Foote, *Sketches of Virginia, Historical and Biographical*, 2d ser. (Philadelphia, 1855), pp. 223–35; Alfred James Morrison, *College of Hampden Sidney Dictionary of Biography, 1776–1825* (Hampden-Sydney, Va., 1921), pp. 67–68; Marie Oliver Watkins, *Tearin' through the Wilderness* (Charleston, W.Va., 1957), p. 127.

ARTIST UNIDENTIFIED

Silhouette: 9 in. (22.9 cm.) in height, mounted on cardboard 11 x 6½ in. (27.9 x 16.5 cm.)

Presented in 1965 by William Munford Ellis Rachal of Richmond. Por965.24

Jessup Lightfoot Allen, 1863–1912

Born on September 16, 1863, in Richmond, the youngest child of William and Frances Augusta (Jessup) Allen (qq.v.) of Claremont, Surry County, the subject attended the Preparatory Boys Department of Georgetown University, D.C., but information about his subsequent career has not been found. He died at Atlantic City, New Jersey, on January 15, 1912, survived by his wife, Ray (Shelton) Allen (d. 1960); he is buried in Hollywood Cemetery, Richmond.

Portraiture, p. 19; Richmond *Times-Dispatch*, Jan. 17, 1912, p. 2; VHS Archives, liber A9, pp. 214, 230, and liber B9, p. 148.

ATTRIBUTED TO JOHN ADAMS ELDER. 1868

Oil on canvas: 22 x 17½ in. (55.9 x 44.5 cm.)

Presented in 1942 by the subject's widow, Ray (Shelton) Allen (Mrs. Jessup Lightfoot Allen) of Atlantic City, New Jersey. Por942.13

This portrait, depicting the subject as a child, is thought to have been painted at the same time and by the same artist as the signed, dated portraits of the subject's two brothers, John and William Allen (qq.v.).

John Allen, 1857–1904

John Allen was born on September 17, 1857, at Claremont, Surry County, the second son of William and Frances Augusta (Jessup) Allen (qq.v.). No information has been found about his career. He died in Florida on June 16, 1904, and is buried in Hollywood Cemetery, Richmond. His wife and three children, Bertha, Potter, and William, survived him. Portraits of the subject's brothers, William and Jessup Lightfoot Allen (qq.v.), are also owned by the Society.

Encyclopedia of Virginia Biography, 5: 639; VHS Archives, liber A12, p. 266.

By JOHN ADAMS ELDER. Signed. Dated 1868

Oil on canvas: 22½ x 17 in. (57.2 x 43.2 cm.)

Presented in 1950 by Bertha P. Allen (Mrs. John Allen) of Albuquerque, New Mexico. Por950.18

The portrait is framed as an oval; the date is hidden by the spandrel.

William Allen, 1815–1875
Frances Augusta (Jessup) Allen, 1832–1905 (Mrs. William Allen)

William Griffin Orgain, son of Richard Griffin Orgain and Martha Armistead (Edlow) Orgain, changed his name to William Allen, thus fulfilling a condition by which in 1831 he inherited Claremont, Surry County, from his great-uncle William Allen. He became through this inheritance a man of wealth, reputedly owning 800 slaves and 30,000 acres of land, including not only Claremont, a seat of the Allen family since the seventeenth century, but also Curles Neck, in Henrico County, and Jamestown Island. He married on December 22, 1852, Frances Augusta Jessup, born in 1832, the eldest child of James and Catherine (Shriver) Jessup of Brockville, Canada. They became the parents of three daughters and three sons, William, John, and Jessup Lightfoot Allen (qq.v.), whose portraits are in the Society's collection. During the Civil War, William Allen commanded the Jamestown Heavy Artillery and served as commander of the port of Jamestown. On his Curles Neck plantation Cyrus H. McCormick gave an early demonstration of his harvesting machinery. Allen died in 1875 and is buried at Claremont; his wife died in Philadelphia on January 28, 1905, and is buried in Hollywood Cemetery, Richmond.

Encyclopedia of Virginia Biography, 5: 637–39; Mary A. Stephenson, *Old Homes in Surry & Sussex* (Richmond, 1942), pp. 30–31; John Bennett Boddie, *Southside Virginia Families* (Redwood City, Calif., 1955–56), 1: 4; James D. Kornwolf, *The Surry County, Virginia, 1776 Bicentennial Committee Guide to the Buildings of Surry* (Surry, Va., 1976), pp. 44–47; *Portraiture*, p. 19; VHS Archives, liber A9, pp. 214, 230, liber A12, p. 266, and liber B9, p. 148; *W. & M. Quart.*, 1st ser., 8 (1899–1900): 110–15.

Portrait I. William Allen

ATTRIBUTED TO LOUIS MATHIEU DIDIER GUILLAUME

Oil on canvas: 23½ x 19¾ in. (59.7 x 50.2 cm.) (oval)

Presented in 1950 by Bertha P. Allen (Mrs. John Allen) of Albuquerque, New Mexico. Por950.15

William Allen, 1815–1875

Frances Augusta (Jessup) Allen

Portrait II. Frances Augusta (Jessup) Allen

By LOUIS MATHIEU DIDIER GUILLAUME. Signed

Oil on canvas: 26¾ x 22 in. (68 x 55.9 cm.) (oval)

Presented in 1950 by Bertha P. Allen (Mrs. John Allen) of Albuquerque, New Mexico. Por950.16

William Allen, 1855–1917

Born January 13, 1855, at Claremont, Surry County, the eldest son of William and Frances Augusta (Jessup) Allen (qq.v.), the subject received his early education in Richmond and in 1865 entered the school of the Reverend Edmund Wood in Montreal, Canada. In 1875 he graduated from Georgetown University, D.C., and entered the University of Virginia law school. He began practice in Richmond in 1877, later forming a partnership with Bernard Peyton; in 1892 he removed to New York where he continued the practice of his profession. He was appointed in September 1901 a referee in bankruptcy for the Southern District of New York. William Allen died in New York and was buried in Hollywood Cemetery, Richmond, on April 14, 1917. His wife, whom he married in 1878, was Mary Houstoun (Anderson) Allen, daughter of General Robert Houstoun Anderson of Savannah, Georgia; known as "Mrs. Willie Allen," she was in her day one of Richmond's foremost social belles. Portraits of the subject's brothers, John and Jessup Lightfoot Allen (qq.v.), are also in the Society's collection.

Encyclopedia of Virginia Biography, 5: 637–39; *University of Virginia*, 2: 140–41; VHS Archives, liber A12, p. 266.

By JOHN ADAMS ELDER. Signed. Dated 1868

Oil on canvas: 22½ x 17 in. (57.2 x 43.2 cm.)

Presented in 1950 by Bertha P. Allen (Mrs. John Allen) of Albuquerque, New Mexico. Por950.17

The portrait is framed as an oval; the artist's signature and date are hidden by the spandrel. The back of the canvas bears stenciling: "R. Wendenburg, 808 Main Street, Richmond, Va."

James Markham Marshall Ambler, 1848–1881

Naval surgeon and Arctic explorer, James Markham Marshall Ambler was born in Fauquier County on December 30, 1848, son of Dr. Richard Cary Ambler and Susan (Marshall) Ambler. During the last months of the Civil War he enlisted, a youth of sixteen, in the 12th Virginia Cavalry. After graduating from Washington College (now Washington and Lee University) in 1867, he commenced the study of medicine at the University of Maryland. In April 1874 he was commissioned an assistant surgeon in the United States Navy, assigned first to the North Atlantic fleet and later to the training ship *Minnesota*; he was transferred in 1877 to the Norfolk Naval Hospital. Asked to serve as surgeon on the ill-fated expedition to the Arctic on the *Jeannette*, he agreed, sailing with the ship on July 8, 1879. With the loss of the ship in June 1881 the survivors sought to reach land in three boats. Adrift in Arctic waters, Ambler and his companions suffered acutely from cold and hunger; in time the boats became separated. Some weeks later Ambler and a dozen others reached land, but after struggling overland for more than a month, he succumbed at last to hunger and exposure. He died on October 30, 1881. His remains were later recovered and brought to his birthplace for burial.

DAB.

By WILLIAM LUDWELL SHEPPARD. Signed. 1895? Oil on canvas: 30 x 25 in. (76.2 x 63.5 cm.). Inscribed on the back: "James M. Ambler Surgeon USN perished on the Jeannette Expedition to Polar Seas Painted by Wm. L. Sheppard 1895[?] from photo taken 1879 and description."

Presented in 1978 by Jacqueline (Johnston) Gilmore (Mrs. J. Spencer Gilmore) of Richmond. Por978.10

Archer Anderson, 1838–1918

Born at Old Point Comfort on October 15, 1838, at the home of his grandfather, Dr. Robert Archer, the subject was the son of Joseph Reid Anderson and Sarah (Archer) Anderson. Entering the University of Virginia before he was sixteen years old, he received his Master of Arts degree in two years, then

Archer Anderson (Portrait II)

traveled and studied in Europe for two years before returning to the university to study law. In August 1859 at the embassy in Paris he married Mary Anne Mason, daughter of John Young Mason (q.v.), American minister to France. He served throughout the Civil War, seeing action at Sharpsburg, the Chickamauga campaign, Drewry's Bluff, and Bentonville. In February 1865 he was made adjutant general of the Army of Tennessee under General Joseph E. Johnston. After the war he settled in Richmond where for more than fifty years he was intimately associated with the management of the Tredegar Company, iron manufacturers. On the death of his father, the founder of the corporation, in 1892, he was elected to succeed him as president. He died January 4, 1918, survived by his wife, three sons, and three daughters. Colonel Anderson became a member of the Society's executive committee in 1868.

Egbert Giles Leigh, *An Appreciation of Colonel Archer Anderson* (Richmond, 1918); Lawrence Buckley Thomas, *The Thomas Book* (New York, 1896), p. 556d; *Biographic Catalogue*; *VMHB* 56 (1948): 238.

Portrait I

BY EDITH LEESON EVERETT

Oil on canvas: 30 x 25 in. (76.2 x 63.5 cm.)

Presented to the R. E. Lee Camp, Confederate Veterans, in 1926; acquired by the Virginia Historical Society in 1946 through merger with the Confederate Memorial Association. Por946.102

Portrait II

BY JOHN WYCLIFFE LOWES FORSTER. Signed

Oil on canvas: 40 x 30 in. (101.6 x 76.2 cm.)

Presented in 1947 by the subject's grandchildren: Francis Deane Williams, Jr., Frances Leigh Williams, and Mary Mason (Williams) Holt (Mrs. Henry Winston Holt) of Richmond. Por947.22

Henry Watkins Anderson, 1870–1954

Son of William Watkins Anderson and Laura (Marks) Anderson, the subject was born at Hampstead, Dinwiddie County, on December 20, 1870. As secretary to William L. Wilson, president of Washington and Lee University, he was enabled to study law at the university, receiving his Bachelor of Laws degree in 1898. Removing to Richmond, he became associated with the firm of Staples and Munford, to which he was shortly admitted as a partner. In 1901, in association with Edmund Randolph Williams (q.v.), he formed a partnership with Beverley B. Munford and Eppa Hunton, Jr., under the name of Munford, Hunton, Williams and Anderson; he con-

tinued with this firm until his death. During World War I Anderson was chairman of an American Red Cross mission to Rumania and commissioner of the American Red Cross in the Balkan States. A participant in much important litigation, he served variously as United States government trustee for the Armour and Swift interests 1921; special assistant to the attorney general of the United States 1922–23; United States agent on the Mexican Claims Commission 1924–26; counsel for the receivers of the Seaboard Air Line Railway 1931–32; and member of the National Commission of Law Observance and Enforcement 1929–31. He was proposed in the state Republican convention in 1920 as a nominee of the party for the vice-presidency and was Republican candidate for governor of Virginia in 1921. One of the original trustees of the Virginia Museum of Fine Arts, he became its president in 1947. Anderson was a member of the Virginia Historical Society. He died, unmarried, in Richmond, on January 7, 1954.

Men of Mark in Virginia, 2d ser., 1: 57–59; Virginia State Bar Association, *Proceedings* 65 (1954): 115–17; *VMHB* 54 (1946): 171.

BY ALFRED JONNIAUX. Signed. 1945

Oil on canvas: 40 x 30 in. (101.6 x 76.2 cm.)

Presented by the subject in 1946. Por946.24

John Thomas Anderson, 1804–1879
Cassandra Morrison (Shanks) Patton Anderson, 1807–1887 (Mrs. John Thomas Anderson) with Her Children

Son of William and Anne (Thomas) Anderson (qq.v.) of Walnut Hill, Botetourt County, John Thomas Anderson was born on April 15, 1804. He attained early eminence at the bar, managed large business interests, including an iron manufactory in Botetourt County, and was appointed by Andrew Jackson to the board of visitors of West Point Military Academy. He took an active part in public life, representing his county in the Virginia House of Delegates 1827–31, 1859–65 and in the state Senate 1834–42; he was a delegate to the State Constitutional Convention of 1850–51. His wife was Cassandra Morrison (Shanks) Patton Anderson; the couple had two children, a daughter, Mary, who died young, and a son, Joseph Washington Anderson (q.v.). The family resided at Mount Joy, Botetourt County, not far from Buchanan. John Thomas Anderson was a prominent member of the Presbyterian church, serving as a ruling elder for over twenty-five years. Gravestones in the churchyard of the Presbyterian church at Fincastle record Anderson's death on August 27, 1879, and his wife's on January 1, 1887.

Robert Douthat Stoner, *A Seed-bed of the Republic* (Roanoke, Va., 1962), p. 272; Anne Lowry Worrell, *Over the Mountain Men: Their Early Court Records in Southwest Virginia* (Baltimore, 1962), p. 65; Lawrence Buckley Thomas, *The Thomas Book* (New York, 1896), p. 556a; *VMHB* 70 (1962): 237.

Portrait I. John Thomas Anderson

ARTIST UNIDENTIFIED

Oil on canvas: 29³/4 x 25 in. (75.6 x 63.5 cm.)

Presented in 1961 by E. W. Morehouse of Princeton, New Jersey. Por961.32

Portrait II. Cassandra Morrison (Shanks) Patton Anderson with Mary and Joseph Washington Anderson

ARTIST UNIDENTIFIED. Ca. 1838

Oil on canvas: 40¹/2 x 33 in. (102.9 x 83.8 cm.)

Presented in 1961 by E. W. Morehouse of Princeton, New Jersey. Por961.33

Mrs. Anderson's portrait dates from about 1838, judging from the age of the baby she holds in her lap, Joseph Washington Anderson (q.v.), who was born in 1836 and appears in the portrait to be no more than two years old.

Joseph Washington Anderson, 1836–1863

Born in Fincastle on December 19, 1836, son of John Thomas Anderson and Cassandra Morrison (Shanks) Patton Anderson (qq.v) of Mount Joy, Botetourt County, the subject entered the University of Virginia in 1855. The day following his graduation in 1859 he married Susan W. Morris of Charlottesville, youngest daughter of Dr. J. M. Morris of Louisa County. Although educated for the practice of law, Anderson retired from the bar after only one year to devote himself to agricultural pursuits. In 1861 he entered the Confederate service as captain of an infantry company, later transferring to the artillery. In the spring of 1862 he served under General E. Kirby Smith in Kentucky and Tennessee; the following December he was ordered to Vicksburg and shortly thereafter was promoted to major. At the battle of Baker's Creek, midway between Jackson and Vicksburg, Anderson fell mortally wounded. He died in the early hours of May 17, 1863, his remains being later removed from the battlefield by his father for reinterment at Fincastle. He was survived by his wife and two children.

The University Memorial, pp. 383–99; *Confederate Veteran* 19 (1911): 116; *VMHB* 70 (1962): 237; Lawrence Buckley Thomas, *The Thomas Book* (New York, 1896), p. 556a.

Joseph Washington Anderson (Portrait I)

Portrait I

ARTIST UNIDENTIFIED. Ca. 1850

Oil on canvas: 36 x 28³/4 in. (91.4 x 73 cm.)

Presented in 1961 by E. W. Morehouse of Princeton, New Jersey. Por961.34

Joseph Washington Anderson is here depicted at perhaps fourteen years of age, taking his ease with a canine companion in the shade of a tree, his straw hat cast aside. If his age is correct, the portrait was painted around 1850. He also appears as a baby in the portrait of his mother, Cassandra Morrison (Shanks) Patton Anderson (Mrs. John Thomas Anderson) (q.v.).

Portrait II

See John Thomas Anderson, 1804–1879 (Portrait II)

Mary Anderson

See John Thomas Anderson, 1804–1879 (Portrait II)

Richard Heron Anderson, 1821–1879

A native South Carolinian, General Anderson was born at Hill Crest, Sumter County, on October 7, 1821, son of Dr. William Wallace Anderson and Mary Jane (Mackenzie) Anderson. A graduate in the West Point class of 1842, he saw action in the

Mexican War. On the secession of South Carolina he was commissioned brigadier general in the Confederate army; he was placed in command of Charleston and later transferred to the Army of Northern Virginia. He saw action at Seven Pines, Second Manassas, Sharpsburg, Fredericksburg, Chancellorsville, and Gettysburg. With the disabling of General Longstreet, Anderson assumed command of Longstreet's corps, leading it in the numerous battles of the summer and autumn of 1864. At Longstreet's return, Anderson, now a lieutenant general, was put in charge of a portion of the Richmond defenses and later participated in the battle of Sayler's Creek. After Appomattox he returned to South Carolina to devote himself to agriculture. His efforts, however, met with scant success, so he later accepted a post with the South Carolina Railroad. He died on June 26, 1879, survived by his second wife, Martha (Mellette) Anderson, his first wife, Sarah (Gibson) Anderson, having died in 1872.

Generals in Gray; *SHS Papers* 39 (1914): 146–52; *Biographic Catalogue*; Cornelius Irvine Walker, *The Life of Lieutenant General Richard Heron Anderson* (Charleston, S.C., 1917).

By JOHN P. WALKER. Signed. Dated 1922

Oil on canvas: 30 x 25 in. (76.2 x 63.5 cm.)

Acquired in 1946 through merger with the Confederate Memorial Association. Por946.164

William Anderson, 1764–1839
Anne (Thomas) Anderson, 1770–1848 (Mrs. William Anderson)

A native of Delaware, William Anderson was born on June 2, 1764. He moved at an early age with his parents, Robert and Margaret (Neeley) Anderson, to Botetourt County, which was his home for the rest of his life. He joined the Revolutionary forces at age sixteen, seeing action at Cowpens and King's Mountain. During the War of 1812, although fifty years of age, Colonel Anderson raised his own company of troops and served on the Eastern Shore of Virginia and at Norfolk. On March 15, 1793, he was appointed surveyor of Botetourt, a post he held for many years. Later he was appointed engineer of public improvements and commissioner for the construction of the turnpike from Covington to Charleston. He represented Botetourt County in the Virginia House of Delegates for the session 1831–32. In 1796 he married Anne Thomas, daughter of Francis and Grace (Metcalf) Thomas of Montevue, near Frederick, Maryland. The couple resided at Walnut Hill, Botetourt County, and became the parents of four daughters and four sons, among them John Thomas Anderson (q.v.) and Joseph Reid Anderson, father of Archer Anderson (q.v.). Colonel Anderson died on September 13, 1839, and is buried in the churchyard of the Fincastle Presbyterian Church, which he had served as an elder for many years; Mrs. Anderson died on July 23, 1848.

Robert Douthat Stoner, *A Seed-bed of the Republic* (Roanoke, Va., 1962), pp. 270–71; William Henry Foote, *Sketches of Virginia, Historical and Biographical*, 2d ser. (Philadelphia, 1855), pp. 584–86; Stephen F. Cocke, *A Funeral Sermon on the Death of Col. William Anderson* (Richmond, 1840); Lawrence Buckley Thomas, *The Thomas Book* (New York, 1896), pp. 147–48, 556a-b; *VMHB* 70 (1962): 237.

William Anderson, 1764–1839

Portrait I. William Anderson
ARTIST UNIDENTIFIED
Oil on canvas: 30 x 25 in. (76.2 x 63.5 cm.)
Presented in 1961 by E. W. Morehouse of Princeton, New Jersey. Por961.30

Portrait II. Anne (Thomas) Anderson
ARTIST UNIDENTIFIED
Oil on canvas: 30 x 25 in. (76.2 x 63.5 cm.)
Presented in 1961 by E. W. Morehouse of Princeton, New Jersey. Por961.31

William Anderson, b. 1788
See The Convention of 1829–30

Sir Edmund Andros, 1637–1714

Andros, who served five years as governor of Virginia, was born on December 6, 1637, son of Amice and Elizabeth (Stone) Andros, members of the feudal aristocracy of Guernsey. He commenced his colonial career in 1666 as a major in a regiment of foot sent to protect the West Indies from the Dutch. In 1674 he was appointed governor of the province of New York, being rewarded for his services there with a knighthood four years later. On the accession of James II, Sir Edmund was appointed governor of the Dominion of New England, an area that included all English North American settlements between Maryland and Canada (except Pennsylvania). Although

Sir Edmund Andros

he led successful military operations against both Indians and pirates, his too-vigorous enforcement of the Navigation Acts, his conservative financial policies, and his interference with the settlers' lands did little to endear him to the colonists. On learning of the flight of James II and the landing in England of William of Orange, the people of Boston seized the governor on April 18, 1689, and sent him to England for trial. Acquitted, he returned to America as governor of Virginia, a post he held from 1692 to 1697. His administration was not tranquil; his violent disputes with the Reverend James Blair (q.v.) on such matters as clergy salaries and prerogatives and the affairs of the College of William and Mary led to his resignation. On his return to England he became in 1704 lieutenant governor of Guernsey. Two years later he retired from public service, spending the rest of his life in London. He died on February 27, 1714, and is buried at St. Anne's, Soho.

DAB; *DNB*; *Occasional Bulletin*, no. 13 (1966): 9–11; *VMHB* 75 (1967): 240.

By MARY BEALE

Oil on canvas: 30 x 25 in. (76.2 x 63.5 cm.)

Acquired in 1966 with funds contributed for the purpose by Langbourne Meade Williams of Rapidan. Por966.23

William S. Archer, 1843–1930

Born on July 12, 1843, at Mount St. Bernard, Goochland County, son of Peter Jefferson Archer and Martha (Michaux) Archer, the subject received his education at Hanover Academy. In 1861 he left school to join Company F, 49th Virginia Infantry, seeing action with that unit at the Seven Days battles, Second Manassas, and the Wilderness campaign. At the war's end he made his home in Richmond, where he was employed by the Chesapeake and Ohio Railway for twenty-seven years. During the latter part of his life he was active in Confederate organizations and served for some years as commander of the R. E. Lee Camp Soldiers' Home. He died in Richmond on June 18, 1930, and is buried in Hollywood Cemetery. His wife, Mary (McIlwaine) Archer, from Petersburg, predeceased him; he was survived by five children.

Richmond Times-Dispatch, June 19, 1930, p. 19; *Biographic Catalogue*; *VMHB* 45 (1937): 315.

By JOHN P. WALKER. Signed. Dated 1913

Oil on canvas: 20 x 16 in. (50.8 x 40.6 cm.)

Acquired in 1946 through merger with the Confederate Memorial Association. Por946.190

Lewis Addison Armistead, 1817–1863

Armistead, a native of New Bern, North Carolina, was born on February 18, 1817, son of General Walker Keith Armistead and Elizabeth (Stanley) Armistead. Following in the steps of his father, he was admitted to West Point in 1834, but he was dismissed in 1836, allegedly for breaking a mess-hall plate over the head of Jubal Anderson Early (q.v.). Three years later he was appointed to the regular army; he saw service with the 6th Infantry in the Mexican War and was twice brevetted for gallantry. In Confederate service Armistead first commanded the 57th Virginia Infantry in western Virginia and North Carolina. Upon his appointment as brigadier general, April 1, 1862, he was placed in command of a brigade in what later became Pickett's Division, leading it from the Peninsular campaign to Gettysburg. On the third day of Gettysburg he was mortally wounded while leading his men in an assault;

he died in a federal field hospital on July 5, 1863, and is buried in St. Paul's churchyard, Baltimore. He was survived by a son, Walker Keith Armistead, the only child of his marriage in 1844 to Cecelia Matilda Lee Love, daughter of Richard H. Love and Eliza Matilda (Lee) Love.

DAB; *Generals in Gray*; *SHS Papers* 37 (1909): 144–51; *Lee of Virginia*, p. 327; Virginia Armistead Garber, *The Armistead Family, 1635–1910* (Richmond, 1910), p. 68; *W. & M. Quart.*, 1st ser., 6 (1897–98): 169; *Biographic Catalogue*.

ARTIST UNIDENTIFIED

Oil on canvas: 30 x 25 in. (76.2 x 63.5 cm.)

Presented to the R. E. Lee Camp, Confederate Veterans, in 1909; acquired by the Virginia Historical Society in 1946 through merger with the Confederate Memorial Association. Por946.77

Turner Ashby, 1828–1862

Born on October 23, 1828, at Rose Bank, Fauquier County, the residence of his parents, Colonel Turner and Dorothy (Green) Ashby, the subject received a private education and later engaged in agricultural pursuits near his birthplace. Learning of John Brown's raid, Ashby gathered a group of mounted men and rode to Charles Town, but found that Brown was already in prison. With Virginia's secession from the Union he again gathered and led a troop of horsemen which in June 1861 was incorporated into the 7th Virginia Cavalry. Scouting and outpost duty occupied him until the spring of 1862, when he led Jackson's cavalry in the Shenandoah campaign. His brilliant performance in the Valley led to his promotion to brigadier general on May 23, 1862. During Jackson's subsequent retreat up the Valley, Ashby was killed, on June 6, 1862, fighting a rearguard action several miles south of Harrisonburg. He is buried in Stonewall Cemetery, Winchester. General Ashby was not married.

DAB; *Generals in Gray*; *Biographic Catalogue*.

BY LLOYD FREEMAN

Oil on canvas: 30¼ x 25 in. (76.8 x 63.5 cm.)

Presented to the R. E. Lee Camp, Confederate Veterans, in 1899 by James A. Moncure and his brother, nephews of the subject; acquired by the Virginia Historical Society in 1946 through merger with the Confederate Memorial Association. Por946.47

The portrait was rejected by the R. E. Lee Camp Portrait Committee on June 26, 1899, "because of lack of artistic merit." It was returned to the artist, and on July 28, 1899, the chairman of the Portrait Committee reported that "he had seen Artist Freeman & at his request went to his studio to see his oil portrait of Genl. Turner Ashby—that it has been improved since it was taken from this room, & he thought it was as good in point of merit as we could hope for it to be made by him." The portrait was accepted at the meeting of August 4, 1899.

VHS Mss, R. E. Lee Camp, Portrait Committee, Minute book, pp. 55, 60.

Nancy Witcher (Langhorne) Shaw Astor, Viscountess Astor, 1879–1964

The subject was born in Danville on May 19, 1879, daughter of Chiswell Dabney Langhorne and Nancy Witcher (Keene) Langhorne. The family later resided in Richmond and at Mirador, Albemarle County. Her first marriage, in 1897, to Robert Gould Shaw of Boston, ended in divorce. In 1906 she married, second, in England, Waldorf Astor, son of William Waldorf Astor, first Viscount Astor. The couple resided at Cliveden in Buckinghamshire. When her husband succeeded to the title in 1919, thereby becoming ineligible to sit in the House of Commons, Nancy Astor stood for election herself, becoming in 1919 the first woman member of Parliament. She represented Plymouth, Sutton division, from 1919 to 1945, and was later elected mayoress of Plymouth. Lady Astor championed such causes as temperance, women's and children's welfare, and opposition to socialism; as a leader of the so-called Cliveden set, she was accused of advocating appeasement of Hitler in the years before World War II. She maintained close ties with Virginia throughout her life, returning frequently to visit family and friends. She died on May 2, 1964, and is buried at Cliveden. Lady Astor had one son by her first marriage and four sons and a daughter by her second. She was a member of the Virginia Historical Society.

Elizabeth Coles Langhorne, *Nancy Astor and Her Friends* (New York, 1974); Maurice Collis, *Nancy Astor, an Informal Biography* (New York, 1960); *Encyclopedia Americana*; *Occasional Bulletin*, no. 16 (1968): 3–5 (Portraits I and II reproduced) and no. 26 (1973): 4–5 (Portrait III reproduced).

Portrait I

BY SIEGFRIED JOSEPH CHAROUX. Signed

Bronze bust: 21 in. (53.3 cm.) in height

Presented in 1967 by the subject's son, the Honourable David Astor of London, England. Por967.21

Portrait II

BY JO DAVIDSON. Signed

Bronze bust: 18 in. (45.7 cm.) in height

Presented in 1967 by the subject's son, the Honourable David Astor of London, England. Por967.22

2. Nancy, Lady Astor (Portrait III)

Portrait III   *See* Plate 2

BY EDITH LEESON EVERETT

Oil on canvas: 47 x 30 in. (119.4 x 76.2 cm.)

Presented by the artist. Received by the Society in 1972. Por972.23

A portrait in oils of Lady Astor by Robert Ossory Dunlop came into the Society's custody in 1962; its receipt was twice noted in the Society's publications. The year after its acquisition the portrait was released to the subject's family.

Occasional Bulletin, no. 6 (1963): 10–11 (portrait reproduced); *VMHB* 71 (1963): 239.

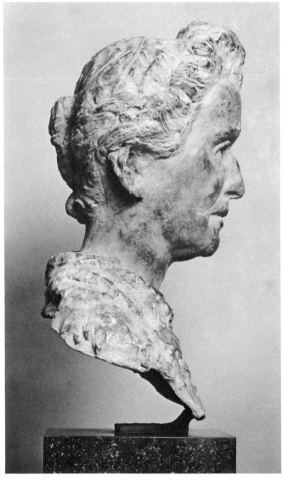

Nancy, Lady Astor (Portrait I)

Ann Mary (Wetzel) Aulick, 1759–1834   (Mrs. Charles Aulick)

Although the subject's parents have not been identified, they may have been related to Christopher Wetzel of Winchester. Born in Germany on April 4, 1759, she came to Virginia, settled in Winchester, and married Charles Aulick. The couple were the parents of eleven children. Charles Aulick died in

1812. Six years later his widow moved to Centerville, Indiana, with her second husband, Samuel P. Booker, who became one of the town's most successful merchants. The subject died in 1834.

Corcoran Gallery of Art, *Jacob Frymire, American Limner* (Washington, D.C., 1975), pp. 32–33 (portrait reproduced); VHS Mss2 B6443 a1; *VMHB* 64 (1954): 238; *Antiques* 116 (1979): 1136 (portrait reproduced).

BY JACOB FRYMIRE. 1805

Oil on canvas: 29 x 24¼ in. (73.7 x 61.6 cm.). The original inscription, "Painted by J. Frymier [*sic*] March 17th 1805," was copied on the back after the painting was relined.

Received in 1953 as a bequest of Mrs. Therese Study Porter of Evanston, Illinois, a great-granddaughter of the subject. Por955.18

Ann Mary (Wetzel) Aulick

George William Bagby, 1828–1883

Author, editor, and humorist, Bagby was born in Buckingham County, on August 13, 1828, the eldest son of George and Virginia (Evans) Bagby. He spent his early years in Lynchburg, attended a boarding school in Prince Edward Courthouse, and graduated from the University of Pennsylvania in 1849 with a degree in medicine. The success of a series of articles from his pen published in the *Lynchburg Virginian* led him to withdraw from medicine and turn to a literary career. In 1860, having previously worked as a newspaper correspondent in Washington, he moved to

Richmond to become editor of the *Southern Literary Messenger*. His service in the Confederate army was of brief duration owing to ill health, but he remained active as a newspaper correspondent throughout the war. At the close of hostilities he turned to popular lecturing, enjoying considerable success with "The Old Virginia Gentleman," "The Virginia Negro," and lectures on similar themes. His humorous articles and essays, such as *What I Did with My Fifty Millions* (1874) and *Meekins's Twinses* (1877), were greatly admired locally, though the topical nature of his writings precluded a widespread popularity. Dr. Bagby was corresponding secretary of the Virginia Historical Society, 1859–68. He died in Richmond on November 29, 1883, survived by his widow, Lucy Parke (Chamberlayne) Bagby, daughter of Lewis Webb Chamberlayne and Martha Burwell (Dabney) Chamberlayne. Dr. and Mrs. Bagby had ten children.

DAB; *VMHB* 56 (1948): 237.

By GEORGE BAGBY MATTHEWS. Signed (initials). Dated October 1877

Charcoal on paper: 23 x 18 in. (58.4 x 45.7 cm.) (oval)

Presented in 1947 by Ellen Matthews Bagby of Richmond. Por947.23

Briscoe Gerard Baldwin, 1789–1852
See The Convention of 1829–30

George Balfour, 1771–1830
See James Balfour, d. 1775

James Balfour, d. 1775, with His Son
Mary Jemima Balfour, d. 1785
(Mrs. James Balfour)

James Balfour, agent for the English mercantile house of Hanbury and Company, came to Virginia around 1741. Although he resided in Elizabeth City County and served that county as justice of the peace in 1762, 1766, and 1767, he also held land in Brunswick County. In 1766 he was residing at Little England, an estate of one hundred acres near Hampton; the same year he visited London and while there participated in debates on the repeal of the Stamp Act. He later formed a mercantile partnership with Daniel Barraud under the name Balfour and Barraud. In the conflict preceding the Revolution he supported the American cause, being one of the signatories to the "Association" drawn up in Williamsburg on June 22, 1770. His death was reported in the *Virginia Gazette* of April 14, 1775. He was survived by his wife, Mary Jemima Balfour, who lived until 1785, by a daughter, Charlotte, and a son, George, who is depicted, as a child, in his father's portrait. George Balfour (1771–1830) became a physician, entered the medical staff of the United States Army in 1792, served with Anthony Wayne, and in 1798 was appointed senior surgeon of the United States Navy. He retired to private practice in 1804, remaining in Norfolk until his death on August 28, 1830. He is buried beside his parents in the churchyard of St. John's, Hampton.

VHS Mss7:1 B1975:1; *Occasional Bulletin*, no. 17 (1968): 1–5 (both portraits reproduced); *Virginia Historical Register and Literary Note Book* 3 (1850): 18–23; *VMHB* 77 (1969): 239; *Antiques* 95 (1969): 646 (both portraits reproduced) and 116 (1979): 1132 (both portraits reproduced).

Portrait I. James Balfour, with his son, George
See Plate 3

By MATTHEW PRATT. 1773

Oil on canvas: 49 x 40 in. (124.5 x 101.6 cm.)

Received in 1968 as a bequest of Emma (Collier) Akin (Mrs. Allen T. Akin) of Vicksburg, Mississippi. Por968.2

James Balfour holds a letter addressed "To Mr. Balfour, Little England, Virginia. Per The Hanbury, Capt. Esten."

Portrait II. Mary Jemima Balfour   *See* Plate 4

By MATTHEW PRATT. 1773

Oil on canvas: 49 x 39½ in. (124.5 x 100.3 cm.)

Received in 1968 as a bequest of Emma (Collier) Akin (Mrs. Allen T. Akin) of Vicksburg, Mississippi. Por968.3

Matthew Pratt, "lately from England and Ireland, but last from New York," advertised in the *Virginia Gazette* of March 18, 1773, that he "will continue some Time in this Colony, if any Gentlemen or Ladies are desirous to employ him, and will please to leave a Line for him at the Post Office in *Williamsburg*, with their Directions, he will endeavour to wait on them in his Way down from the Place where he is at present employed, near *Richmond*, as he intends to spend the Summer Months at *Hampton*." It was in all likelihood during his sojourn in Hampton in the summer of 1773 that he painted the portraits of James and Mary Jemima Balfour.

Thomas Ball, 1836–1917

Born in Northumberland County on December 10, 1836, the eldest son of Thomas and Mary Louisa (Hurst) Ball, he attended the College of William and

4. Mary Jemima Balfour

3. James Balfour with his son, George

Mary 1854–56, studied law, and was admitted to the bar in 1858. He served in the Confederate army as a lieutenant in the 47th Virginia Infantry and later as captain of a battery of heavy artillery. Captured, he escaped after eight months' imprisonment. In 1869 he removed to Texas, where he practiced law and served in the Texas Senate 1874–76. On February 27, 1878, in Galveston, Texas, he married Lalla Gresham, daughter of the Reverend Edward Gresham and Isabella (Mann) Gresham of King and Queen County, Virginia; the couple became the parents of six children. Ball was appointed assistant attorney general of Texas in 1879; on the expiration of his term in 1881 he returned to Northumberland County, Virginia, bought a farm, and continued his legal practice. His death occurred in Los Angeles, California, on May 11, 1917.

Biographic Catalogue (Addenda); *Virginia Genealogies*, pp. 70–71.

By HERMAN M. LINDING. Signed. Dated 1926

Oil on canvas: 30 x 25¼ in. (76.2 x 64.1 cm.)

Presented to the R. E. Lee Camp, Confederate Veterans, in 1926; acquired by the Virginia Historical Society in 1946 through merger with the Confederate Memorial Association. Por946.53

John Strode Barbour, 1790–1855
See The Convention of 1829–30

Philip Pendleton Barbour, 1783–1841
See The Convention of 1829–30

George Ainsley Barksdale, 1835–1910

Youngest child of William Jones Barksdale and Marianna Elizabeth (Tabb) Barksdale of Clay Hill, Amelia County, the subject was born on January 3, 1835. During the Civil War he served as a captain in the Army of the Confederacy. Thereafter he was treasurer of the Gallego Mills and resided at 509 East Grace Street, Richmond. He was a member and vestryman of St. Paul's Episcopal Church and for many years was vice-consul in Richmond of the Argentine Republic, Brazil, and Uruguay. Barksdale was twice married: first, on January 18, 1860, to Elise Florence Warwick, daughter of Abraham and Sally Magee (Chevallié) Warwick, who died in 1880; his second wife was Edmonia Powers. By his first wife he had a son and a daughter. Barksdale became

a member of the Virginia Historical Society in 1858 and was elected recording secretary in 1872 and a member of the executive committee in 1875. He died in Albemarle County on November 19, 1910, and is buried in Hollywood Cemetery, Richmond.

John Augustus Barksdale, *Barksdale Family History* (Richmond, 1940), pp. 187–92; Richmond directories; VHS Mss file Sept. 1940, Mss5:7 B2473, and Mss4 C7a2; *VMHB* 56 (1948): 238.

By MARY TRAVIS BURWELL. Signed

Oil on canvas: 30 x 25 in. (76.2 x 63.5 cm.)

Presented in 1947 by Elise Warwick (Barksdale) Wickham (Mrs. Henry Taylor Wickham), the subject's daughter. Por947.24

Judith Frances Carter Bassett, 1836–1907   (later Mrs. Charles Tunis Mitchell)

Born at Lansdowne, Spotsylvania County, on December 19, 1836, the subject, known as "Fanny" within the family circle, was the daughter of George Washington Bassett and Betty Burnet (Lewis) Bassett. She grew up at Clover Lea, Hanover County, and there married, on December 1, 1863, Charles Tunis Mitchell (1816–1893). Her husband, son of James and Margaret Sutherland (Seylor) Mitchell of Charleston, South Carolina, and twenty years his wife's senior, was a cotton broker and rice planter; in the 1870s he was active in the rehabilitation of the Charleston and Savannah Railroad. The family later removed to Jefferson County, West Virginia, where they resided at Mordington, near Charles Town. Mrs. Mitchell is said to have had "an unusually bright and retentive mind and was many years ahead of her time in her political, educational and social views." She died in Jefferson County, West Virginia, on August 20, 1907. Mr. and Mrs. Mitchell had seven children.

Merrow Egerton Sorley, *Lewis of Warner Hall: The History of a Family* (Columbia, Mo., 1937), pp. 241–42; *Hanover County Historical Society Bulletin*, no. 8 (1973): 6–7; *Magazine of the Jefferson County Historical Society* 6 (1940): 27–28; VHS Mss6:4 B2946:1; *W. & M. Quart.*, 1st ser., 5 (1896–97): 37; *Portraiture*, pp. 118–19.

By DAVID ENGLISH HENDERSON. 1863

Miniature on ivory: 2½ x 1¾ in. (6.4 x 4.5 cm.) (oval). Inscribed on the back: "Judith Frances Carter Bassett. Painted from Memory by David Henderson of Jeff. Co. W. Va. in 1863. Presented to J.F.C.B. on her marriage to Charles Tunis Mitchell of Charleston, South Carolina Dec. 1st 1863. Clover Lea, Hanover Co. Va. Judith Frances Carter Bassett."

Presented in 1943 by the subject's children, Virginia and Laura Landon Mitchell of Charles Town, West Virginia, and Lucy Neville (Mitchell) Smith (Mrs. S. Fahs Smith) of York, Pennsylvania. Por943.13

Fleming Bates, 1778–1831
See The Convention of 1829–30

Sarah Battaile, b. 1731
See Henry Fitzhugh, 1723–1783

John Baxter
See The Convention of 1829–30

John Baylor, 1705–1772

Son of John and Lucy (Todd) O'Brien Baylor, the subject was born at Walkerton, King and Queen County, on May 12, 1705. He received his early education at the Putney Grammar School in England. First elected to the House of Burgesses in 1742, he represented Caroline County in that body almost continuously for the next twenty-three years; he also became colonel of the county militia. On January 2, 1744, at Yorktown he married Frances Walker, daughter of Jacob Walker; she bore her husband eight children. In addition to his seat at Newmarket in Caroline County, Baylor owned extensive acreage in Orange County, spent summers there, and in 1752 became county lieutenant of Orange. He was one of the chief importers and breeders of thoroughbred horses in colonial America; at the time of his death, which occurred on April 16, 1772, the Newmarket stud comprised no less than "fifty choice blooded horses." His lavish mode of living and the dishonesty of some of his agents brought about the encumbering of his estates. Consequently his son and namesake inherited a considerably reduced property, a circumstance which did not, however, deter him from embarking on the construction at Newmarket of a vast, never-to-be-completed Palladian mansion.

VMHB 6 (1898–99): 198–99, 25 (1917): 314 (portrait reproduced), 35 (1927): 355 (portrait reproduced), and 86 (1978): 239–40; Fairfax Harrison, *The Equine F.F.Vs.* (Richmond, 1928), pp. 104–5 (portrait reproduced); *Occasional Bulletin*, no. 36 (1978): 2–5 (portrait reproduced).

ARTIST UNIDENTIFIED. Ca. 1720

Oil on canvas: 48 3/4 x 40 1/4 in. (123.8 x 102.2 cm.)

Presented in 1977 by Pelham Blackford, Jr., of Richmond. Por977.16

John Baylor

Thomas M. Bayley, 1775–1834
See The Convention of 1829–30

Pierre Gustave Toutant Beauregard, 1818–1893

Son of Jacques and Hélène Judith (de Reggio) Beauregard, the subject was born in the parish of St. Bernard, near New Orleans, on May 28, 1818. He graduated from West Point in 1838. During the Mexican War he served on the staff of General Winfield Scott (q.v.) and was twice wounded and twice brevetted. In February 1861 he resigned his commission and was shortly thereafter appointed brigadier general in the provisional army of the Confederate States. As commander of the forces around Charleston, South Carolina, he ordered the bombardment of Fort Sumter. Beauregard was promoted to full general on July 21, 1861. In April of the following year he assumed command of the Army of Tennessee; illness forced him to relinquish the command two months later; on his recovery he was put in charge of the defenses of the South Carolina and Georgia coast. In May 1864 he provided support to Lee's forces in Virginia, and during the last months of the war he was second in command to Joseph E. Johnston in the Carolinas. After the surrender he returned to New Orleans where he was employed variously as president of the New Orleans, Jackson and Mississippi Railway, manager of the Louisiana lottery, and commissioner

Pierre Gustave Toutant Beauregard (Portrait I)

of public works. He was the author of several books and numerous articles on Civil War subjects and served for many years as adjutant general of Louisiana. He died on February 20, 1893, and is buried in Metairie Cemetery, New Orleans. General Beauregard was twice married: first, in 1841, to Marie Laure Villieré, who bore him two sons and a daughter; and second, in 1860, to Caroline Deslonde.

DAB; *Generals in Gray*; *Biographic Catalogue*.

Portrait I

ARTIST UNIDENTIFIED

Oil on panel: 21¹/₂ x 18¹/₄ in. (54.6 x 46.4 cm.)

Presented to the R. E. Lee Camp, Confederate Veterans, in 1910; acquired by the Virginia Historical Society in 1946 through merger with the Confederate Memorial Association. Por946.50

The panel bears on its back what appears to be a cutting from an auction or art dealer's catalogue: "[Am]erican Portrait (In Oils). A very fine painting in oils of [Ge]neral Beauregard (in uniform) General in the American Con[federa]te Army 1860–64. Size of painting 17¹/₂ x 21 inches on a panel, in a broad [fr]ame, size 26¹/₂ x 30 inches. Circa 1862. [A] fine portrait presented by General Beauregard to the late Captain D. Bullock [i.e., James Dunwody Bulloch, 1823–1901] who was [the re]presentative of the Confederate States in Europe during the war and author of the [Secret] Service of the Confederate States in Europe, 2 vols. The painting came direct

from [the] effects of Capt. Bullock." The panel bears a stencil: "Muller. Paris."

Portrait II

See The Battle Abbey Murals. The Summer Mural

Barnard Elliott Bee, 1824–1861

Born on February 8, 1824, at Charleston, South Carolina, he was the son of Barnard Elliott Bee the elder, who removed in 1835 to Texas. He graduated from West Point in the class of 1845, saw action in the Mexican War, and was there twice brevetted for gallantry. Resigning his captain's commission in the spring of 1861, he was commissioned a major in the Confederate States Army and on June 17, 1861, was appointed brigadier general. At First Manassas his brigade suffered heavy losses, and he himself fell, mortally wounded. He died the following day, July 22, 1861. His remains are buried in Pendleton, South Carolina. General Bee is credited with having first applied the sobriquet "Stonewall" to General Thomas Jonathan Jackson.

DAB; *Generals in Gray*; *Biographic Catalogue*.

BY MARION PATTERSON RIDGEWAY. Signed

Oil on canvas: 50 x 39 in. (127 x 99.1 cm.)

Presented to the R. E. Lee Camp, Confederate Veterans, in 1926; acquired by the Virginia Historical Society in 1946 through merger with the Confederate Memorial Association. Por946.211

Andrew Beirne, 1771–1845
See The Convention of 1829–30

Samuel Merrifield Bemiss, 1894–1966

Son of Eli Lockert Bemiss and Cyane Dandridge (Williams) Bemiss, the subject was born on February 21, 1894. He received his formal education at McGuire's University School, Woodberry Forest School, and the University of Virginia. During World War I he was a first lieutenant in the American Expeditionary Forces. He was vice-president of the Richmond Trust Company 1920–25, vice-president and executive director of FitzGerald and Company, and president of Virginia Sky-Line Company and was closely associated with various other corporations. Appointed to numerous legislative study commissions, he served as special assistant to the governor for civil defense 1949–62 and in 1956 received the Distinguished Public Service Award of the Virginia State Chamber of Commerce. His civic interests included the Richmond Memorial Hospital, the Jamestown Foundation, the Medical College of Virginia, the Virginia State Library, and the Children's Home Society. He contributed numerous monographs to historical journals, many of which were later collected and published in *Ancient Adventurers* (1959) and *Causeries* (1962). Bemiss was president of the Virginia Historical Society 1952–59 and a member of its executive committee from 1944 until his death, which occurred on August 7, 1966. He was survived by his wife, Doreen (FitzGerald) Bemiss, whom he married in 1921, and by a son and a daughter.

Richard Lee Morton, *Virginia Lives* (Hopkinsville, Ky., 1964), p. 67; *VMHB* 73 (1965): 244.

Samuel Merrifield Bemiss

By GEORGE VICTOR AUGUSTA. Signed. Dated 1964

Oil on canvas: 36 x 30 in. (91.4 x 76.2 cm.)

Acquired in 1964 with funds contributed for the purpose by friends of the subject. Por964.40

An earlier portrait, noted in the *Virginia Magazine of History and Biography* 70 (1962): 237, was relinquished to the subject's family when the Augusta portrait was received.

Judah Philip Benjamin, 1811–1884

Born on the island of St. Croix in the West Indies, on August 6, 1811, the son of Philip and Rebecca

(deMendes) Benjamin, he moved with his parents to Charleston, South Carolina, at an early age. He entered Yale University at fourteen, left without taking a degree, and found employment with a commercial house in New Orleans. At the same time he prepared for a legal career and worked as a tutor; in both undertakings he was successful, being admitted to the bar in 1832 and marrying one of his pupils, Natalie St. Martin, in 1833. His ability led him to rapid prominence in his profession and to his election to the United States Senate in 1853 where he represented the state of Louisiana until his resignation to become attorney general in the provisional government of the Confederate States. In August 1861 he became secretary of war of the Confederate States, a post he held until his appointment the following February as secretary of state, in which capacity he served the Confederate States until the war's end. He moved to Great Britain in 1865, was admitted to the bar in London the following year, and built up a successful practice, being appointed queen's counsel in 1872. Following his retirement in 1883 he established himself, with his wife and daughter, in Paris, where he died on May 8, 1884.

DAB; *Biographical Directory*; *Biographic Catalogue*.

By JOHN P. WALKER. Signed. Dated 1902

Oil on canvas: 60 x 40 in. (152.4 x 101.6 cm.)

Presented to the R. E. Lee Camp, Confederate Veterans, in 1902; acquired by the Virginia Historical Society in 1946 through merger with the Confederate Memorial Association. Por946.222

Norborne Berkeley, Baron de Botetourt, 1717–1770

Colonial governor of Virginia, Norborne Berkeley was born in December 1717, son of John Symes Berkeley and Elizabeth (Norborne) Berkeley of Gloucestershire, England. On his coming of age in 1738 he inherited his late father's considerable estates, and in 1741 he won a seat in the House of Commons. He became colonel of the South Gloucestershire militia in 1758, lord lieutenant of the county in 1762, and the same year colonel of the North Gloucestershire militia. In 1764 he claimed and won the long-dormant family title Baron de Botetourt; three years later he obtained a post at court as lord of the bedchamber, and an appointment as constable of the Tower of London. Financial reverses, however, made it expedient for him to accept an overseas assignment; on August 12, 1768, he was named governor of Virginia. On his arrival in Virginia he was received by James Balfour (q.v.) of Little England, then proceeded in state to Williamsburg. Lord Botetourt was governor of Virginia from October 26,

1768, until his death in office on October 15, 1770. It is indicative of his character that despite worsening relations between colony and crown during his administration, he himself was regarded with such favor that a county was named for him in 1769, and his statue was erected at public expense in Williamsburg shortly after his death. Lord Botetourt, a bachelor, was buried in the chapel of the College of William and Mary.

DAB; *VMHB* 63 (1955): 379–409 (original portrait reproduced) and 71 (1963): 240; *Virginia Historical Portraiture*, pp. 192–95 (original portrait reproduced); *Occasional Bulletin*, no. 4 (1962): 10–11 (portrait reproduced).

COPIED BY STANLEY TARDREW HEADLEY. 1961

Oil on canvas: 30 x 25 in. (76.2 x 63.5 cm.)

Acquired in 1962 with funds contributed for the purpose by Norborne Berkeley of Bethlehem, Pennsylvania. Por962.1

The original portrait, painted by an unidentified artist, is owned by the duke of Beaufort.

George Munford Betts, 1838–1863

Eldest child of William Spencer Betts and Mary (Faulkner) Betts of Halifax County, Major Betts was born on August 23, 1838. He attended school at Meadsville. A member of the 3d Virginia Cavalry, he was killed in action at Kelly's Ford, on March 17, 1863. His remains were taken to Snow Hill, Halifax County, for burial.

Biographic Catalogue; CMA Archives, folio Z1n; Landon Covington Bell, *The Old Free State* (Richmond, 1927), 2: 149–54.

BY ALEXANDER VON JOST. Signed. Dated 1926

Oil on canvas: 30 x 25 in. (76.2 x 63.5 cm.)

Presented to the R. E. Lee Camp, Confederate Veterans, in 1926; acquired by the Virginia Historical Society in 1946 through merger with the Confederate Memorial Association. Por946.64

Susannah Beverley, ca. 1692–1768
See Sir John Randolph, 1693–1737

Elizabeth Iris Southall (Clarke) Gordon Biddle, 1871–1958
See Douglas Huntly Gordon, 1866–1918

Joseph Virginius Bidgood, 1841–1921

Born on April 28, 1841, in Portsmouth, the subject attended the College of William and Mary until the outbreak of the Civil War whereupon he enlisted as a private in the Williamsburg Junior Guards, which later became Company C, 32d Virginia Infantry. He saw action in the Seven Days battles, Sharpsburg (where he was commissioned adjutant of the regiment), Petersburg, Five Forks, and Sayler's Creek, where he was wounded and taken prisoner. On his release from Point Lookout prison in July 1865, he joined his brother George L. Bidgood in the establishment of a publishing house in Richmond; he later joined the publishing firm of J. W. Randolph and Company. He was one of the charter members of the 1st Virginia Regiment of state troops, rising in rank from lieutenant to lieutenant colonel; in 1890 he was commissioned colonel of the 1st Virginia Cavalry. Colonel Bidgood was a commander of the R. E. Lee Camp, a member of the George E. Pickett Camp, and adjutant general of the Grand Camp of Confederate Veterans of Virginia. His death occurred on September 11, 1921, with burial in Hollywood Cemetery, Richmond. Colonel Bidgood was twice married: his first wife, Sarah Miller (Maupin) Bidgood, from Williamsburg, by whom he had five children, died in 1883; his second wife, Anne Winifred (Maupin) Bidgood, survived him. Colonel Bidgood became a member of the Virginia Historical Society in 1899.

Richmond Times-Dispatch, Sept. 12, 1921, pp. 1, 10; *Confederate Military History* 3: 724; *Confederate Veteran* 6 (1898): 528; *Biographic Catalogue*; CMA Archives, folio Z1n.

BY JOHN P. WALKER. Signed. Dated 1924

Oil on canvas: 30 x 25 in. (76.2 x 63.5 cm.)

Presented to the R. E. Lee Camp, Confederate Veterans, in 1924 by the subject's widow; acquired by the Virginia Historical Society in 1946 through merger with the Confederate Memorial Association. Por946.60

Black Hawk, 1767–1838

Ma-ka-tai-me-she-kia-kiak (Black Sparrow Hawk), Sauk war chief, was born in Illinois near the confluence of the Rock River and the Mississippi River in 1767. His long-standing hatred of the Americans compelled him in 1804 to dispute the legality of William Henry Harrison's treaty whereby the Sauk and Fox nations agreed, under the influence of alcohol, to cede to the United States the whole of their territory east of the Mississippi. On the outbreak of the War of 1812 he joined the British under Tecumseh, fighting at Frenchtown, Fort Meigs, and Fort Stephenson; later he attempted to enlist the support of the British in Canada for a great Indian uprising against the Americans. In April 1832 Black Hawk led an attack across the Mississippi River, but the apathy of his allies, both British and Indian, and the military opposition of General Henry Atkinson led to the collapse of the revolt; hostilities resumed when a flag of truce dispatched by the Indian chief was violated by a body of Illinois volunteers. The Black Hawk War ended on August 2, 1832, with the capture of the chief, his two sons, and the prophet White Cloud. In 1833 he was taken east, received widespread attention, met President Andrew Jackson, and became something of a popular hero. After a short confinement at Fortress Monroe, he was returned to his lands in Iowa; here he dictated his autobiography, published in 1833, and here he died, shortly after a second visit to the east, on October 3, 1838.

DAB.

Black Hawk

By Robert Matthew Sully. 1833

Oil on canvas: 36 x 29 in. (91.4 x 73.7 cm.)

Presented by the artist in 1852. Por852.1

In 1833 Black Hawk, his son Loud Thunder, and the prophet White Cloud were incarcerated at Fortress Monroe. During their enforced stay Robert Matthew Sully visited them and painted their portraits. Almost twenty years later, in 1852, the artist gave the Virginia Historical Society the three portraits[1] (not, as has been stated, a single canvas bearing likenesses of all three).[2] Shortly thereafter he agreed to paint copies of the three portraits for the Wisconsin Historical Society. It appears, however, that he copied only one, Black Hawk, and that he prevailed

on the officers of the Virginia Historical Society to relinquish the original portraits of the other two. Thus it is reported in the first annual report (1855) of the State Historical Society of Wisconsin that "as this page is going through the press, the noble portraits of Black Hawk, his Son, and the Prophet, painted by Robert M. Sully, have safely arrived, and been placed in the rooms of the State Historical Society. Those of . . . Loud Thunder . . . [and] the Prophet, are originals, taken from life, in May 1833, at Fortress Monroe, Old Point Comfort, Va.; and that of Mak-ka-tai-meh-shi-ka-ka, or Black Hawk, is a copy from the original taken at the same time—the copy being deemed, in tone and execution, superior to the original."[3] The disappearance of the portraits of Loud Thunder and the prophet from the Society's collection, long a matter of speculation, is explained, but the motivation behind their removal and by whose authority it was permitted remains unclear. In 1895 it was reported in the pages of the *Virginia Magazine of History and Biography* that Charles M. Wallace had offered to lend the Society a collection of paintings that included a portrait of "Black Hawk and son, by Ford."[4] It is not known if this portrait was ever exhibited in the Society's rooms, but it has added to the confusion that has surrounded the Society's portrait and is perhaps responsible for the R. M. Sully portrait's being twice attributed in print to James W. Ford.[5] It should be noted that there are in Richmond two portraits of Black Hawk that are in fact by Ford: one, which represents Black Hawk and the prophet, is in the collection of the Valentine Museum; the other, representing Black Hawk, his son, and the prophet, is owned by the Commonwealth of Virginia.

1. *Virginia Historical Register* 6 (1853): 50, 52.   2. *Portraiture*, p. 21.   3. *Collections of the State Historical Society of Wisconsin* 1 (1903): 12, 72.   4. *VMHB* 3 (1895–96): viii.   5. *VMHB* 35 (1927): 67 and 39 (1931): 304.

James Blair, 1655–1743

Commissary, acting governor of Virginia, founder and first president of the College of William and Mary, James Blair was born in Scotland in 1655, son of Robert Blair, minister of the parish of Alvah, Banffshire. Following his graduation from the University of Edinburgh in 1673, he was ordained in the Church of Scotland and became rector of Cranston Parish. Urged by Henry Compton, bishop of London, to enter the mission field, he came to Virginia in 1685 and became rector of Varina Parish. On June 2, 1687, he married Sarah Harrison, daughter of Benjamin and Hannah Harrison of Wakefield, Surry County. On December 15, 1689, Bishop Compton appointed him commissary, or deputy, with authority to supervise the Virginia clergy, but without the power of ordination or confirmation. As commissary he urged the establishment of a college and in 1691 went to England to petition for this undertaking. The charter of the College of William and Mary, granted on February 8, 1693, named Blair president for life. On his return to Virginia he became rector of Jamestown Church where he remained until he took charge of Bruton Parish Church, Williamsburg, in 1710. In the spring of 1694 he was appointed to the colonial Council, a post he retained for the rest of his life. Contentious by nature, Blair never hesitated to do battle, even with the highest authority in the colonies; he was instrumental in the removal of three of Virginia's royal governors, Andros, Nicholson, and Spotswood. From December 1740 to July 1741, in his capacity as president of the Council, Blair served as acting governor of the colony. He died on April 18, 1743.

DAB; Parke Rouse, Jr., *James Blair of Virginia* (Chapel Hill, N.C., 1971); *VMHB* 18 (1910): x, 31 (1923): 83 (portrait reproduced), and 84 (1976): 21 (portrait reproduced); *Antiques* 116 (1979): 1137 (portrait reproduced).

ARTIST UNIDENTIFIED

Miniature on ivory: 1 1/2 x 1 1/4 in. (3.8 x 3.2 cm.) (oval)

Received in 1909 as a bequest of Sally Cary Peachey of Portland, Maine, and as a gift from her sister, Mary (Peachey) Rogers (Mrs. Francis Y. Rogers), of the same place, great-great-great-nieces of the subject. Por909.3

John Durburrow Blair, 1759–1823

"Parson" Blair was born on October 15, 1759, at Fagg's Manor, Pennsylvania, the son of the Reverend John Blair and Elizabeth (Durburrow) Blair. He graduated from the College of New Jersey (now Princeton University) in 1775 at sixteen years of age. In 1780 he came to Virginia to teach at Washington-Henry Academy in Hanover County. Turning to the study of theology, he was licensed to preach by Hanover Presbytery in 1784 and for several years combined his teaching duties with preaching at nearby Pole Green Church. On March 4, 1785, he married Mary Winston, second daughter of Geddes and Mary (Jordan) Winston of Laurel Grove, Hanover County; they became the parents of eight children, two of whom died young. Blair moved to Richmond around 1792. Because the Presbyterians had no building, Blair began in 1799 to hold services in the state Capitol, alternating services with his close friend the Reverend John Buchanan (q.v.), minister to the Episcopal congregation. When Monumental Church, a memorial to the victims of the Richmond Theatre fire of December 26, 1811, was conveyed by a single vote to the Episcopal congregation, Parson Blair devoted himself to establishing a building for his own congregation; the Presbyterian Church on Shockoe Hill, as it was called, was completed a few months before his death. Concurrent with his pastoral duties, Parson Blair taught school in a building behind his residence on the northwest corner of Seventh and Leigh streets. Later he was principal of a female

James Blair

John Durburrow Blair

seminary and president of the Richmond Hill Academy in a building near St. John's Church. In 1796 he declined an invitation to become president of Hampden-Sydney College. Parson Blair died at his residence in Richmond on January 10, 1823; he is buried in Shockoe Cemetery.

Richmond Portraits, pp. 18–19 (portrait reproduced); *Historic Virginia Portraiture*, pp. 282–83 (portrait reproduced); Louisa Coleman Gordon Blair, *Blairs of Richmond, Virginia: The Descendants of Reverend John Durburrow Blair and Mary Winston Blair, His Wife* (Richmond, 1933), pp. 87–93 (portrait reproduced).

BY CEPHAS THOMPSON. 1810

Oil on canvas: 27½ x 22½ in. (69.9 x 57.2 cm.) (framed as an oval)

Presented in 1930 by Louisa Wills (Claiborne) Frick (Mrs. George Arnold Frick) of Baltimore. Por930.14

It is known from newspaper advertisements that Cephas Thompson spent the winter of 1809–10 in Richmond.[1] His sitter's book, an invaluable record of his productive sojourn in Virginia, includes a "List of names of those who engage there Portraits in Richmond"; Blair's name is one of the 139 entries.[2] Other versions of the portrait, either copies or replicas, exist, as does a later watercolor sketch and a small portrait in oils now at the Virginia State Library.[3] An engraving of Thompson's portrait, made by John Blennerhassett Martin, was used as the frontispiece in *Sermons Collected from the Manuscripts of the Late Rev. John D. Blair* (Richmond, 1825). The engraving bears the notation: "Painted by Thompson. 1810. Engrav'd by J. B. Martin, Richmd." The original engraving plate is in the Society's possession.

1. *Richmond Portraits*, pp. 233–34. 2. VHS Mss7:1 T3723:1. 3. *Historic Virginia Portraiture*, pp. 282–83 (portrait and engraving reproduced); Louisa Coleman Gordon Blair, *Blairs of Richmond, Virginia: The Descendants of Reverend John Durburrow Blair and Mary Winston Blair, His Wife* (Richmond, 1933), p. 95; *Portraits and Statuary*, p. 9.

Wyndham Bolling Blanton, 1890–1960

Physician, medical historian, and president of the Virginia Historical Society, Wyndham Bolling Blanton, a native of Richmond, was born on June 3, 1890, the son of Dr. Charles Armistead Blanton and Elizabeth (Wallace) Blanton. After graduating from Hampden-Sydney College in 1910 and receiving his master's degree from the University of Virginia in 1912 and his medical degree from the College of Physicians and Surgeons in New York in 1916, he did postgraduate work in New York, Berlin, and Edinburgh and served as a captain in the Army Medical Corps during World War I. He married Natalie Friend McFaden, daughter of the Reverend

Frank T. McFaden and Mary Minge (Friend) McFaden, on January 1, 1918; they became the parents of four children. In 1920 Dr. Blanton began the practice of internal medicine in Richmond; at the Medical College of Virginia he was appointed associate professor of medicine in 1930, professor of the history of medicine in 1933, and professor of clinical medicine in 1939. From 1936 until 1954 he was director of the Immunology Clinic at the Medical College. A prolific writer on medical and historical subjects, he was a frequent contributor to professional journals; his three-volume history of *Medicine in Virginia* (1930–33) remains the standard work on the subject; he edited the *Virginia Medical Monthly* 1932–42 and served on the editorial boards of the *Journal of the History of Medicine*, the *Annals of Medical History*, and the *Bulletin of the History of Medicine*. He was a member and elder of the Second Presbyterian Church, Richmond, wrote its history, *The Making of a Downtown Church* (1945), and was chairman of the board of trustees of the Union Theological Seminary, Richmond. He became a member of the Virginia Historical Society in 1927, was elected to its executive committee in 1945, and at the time of his death had completed two terms as the Society's president. His death occurred on January 6, 1960.

Who Was Who in America 4 (1968): 93; *Bulletin of the History of Medicine* 38 (1964): 80–81; *Men of Mark in Virginia*, 2d ser., 1: 37–39; *Occasional Bulletin*, no. 3 (1961): 4–5 (portrait reproduced); *VMHB* 70 (1962): 236–37.

Wyndham Bolling Blanton

By Winslow Williams. Signed. Dated 1961

Oil on canvas: 36 x 28 in. (91.4 x 71.1 cm.)

Presented in 1961 by the subject's widow. Por961.9

George Washington Bolling, 1808–1875

Son of Robert and Anne Dade (Stith) Bolling of Centre Hill, Petersburg, the subject was born on November 20, 1808. He graduated from Princeton University in the class of 1826. He married Martha S. Nicholls, daughter of William N. Nicholls and Margaret Nicholls of Georgetown, D.C.; the couple had three children, one of whom, Mary Tabb Bolling, married William Henry Fitzhugh Lee (q.v.) and is represented in the Society's portrait collection. Bolling, an attorney, resided in 1860 on the northwest corner of Liberty and Sycamore streets, Petersburg, and had his office in the Merchants Exchange. He represented Sussex, Prince George, and Dinwiddie counties in the Virginia state Senate 1865–66, 1866–67. He died on July 10, 1875, and is buried in Blandford Cemetery, Petersburg.

VMHB 4 (1896–97): 331–32; "Blandford Cemetery Epitaphs" (typescript at VHS), p. 6; Petersburg directories.

By Louis Mathieu Didier Guillaume

Oil on canvas: 30 x 25 in. (76.2 x 63.5 cm.)

Received in 1949 from the heirs of Dr. George Bolling Lee. Por949.38

Mary Tabb Bolling, 1848–1924
See William Henry Fitzhugh Lee, 1837–1891

Rebecca Bonum, d. 1715
See George Eskridge, d. 1735

Ann Mary (Wetzel) Aulick Booker, 1759–1834
See Ann Mary (Wetzel) Aulick, 1759–1834

Hannah Ann Bosher, 1839–1923
See Hannah Ann (Bosher) Lyon, 1839–1923

John Henry Bosher, 1816–1895
Emily (Dill) Bosher, 1819–1857
(Mrs. John Henry Bosher)

The eldest son of James and Ann (Hopkins) Bosher, John Henry Bosher was born in Richmond on April 12, 1816. He married, first, on May 3, 1838, Emily Dill, daughter of Adolph Dill of Richmond; she died in childbirth and was buried in Shockoe Cemetery, Richmond, on September 4, 1857. Shortly before the Civil War he resigned his position as secretary of the Richmond Fire Association, an insurance company of which his father was president, and removed to Missouri, where he remained throughout the hostilities. After a brief sojourn in Detroit, he spent sixteen years in Buffalo, New York. During that time he became a friend and staunch political supporter of Grover Cleveland. Soon after Cleveland's election to the presidency, Bosher was offered a post in the Internal Revenue Service, but failing health prevented him from accepting it. He resided in Richmond for several years before his death, which occurred on February 20, 1895. His second wife, Mary A. (Ball) Bosher, predeceased him by about a year. A portrait of the subjects' daughter, Hannah Ann (Bosher) Lyon (q.v.), is also in the Society's collection.

Men of Mark in Virginia, 2: 769–71; Richmond *Times*, Feb. 21, 1895, p. 2; Mary Wingfield Scott, *Houses of Old Richmond* (Richmond, 1941), p. 172; Richmond directories, 1852, 1856, 1859; *VMHB* 80 (1972): 238.

Portrait I. John Henry Bosher

Artist unidentified

Oil on canvas: 30¼ x 25 in. (76.8 x 63.5 cm.)

Received in 1971 as a bequest of Cornelia (Lyon) Wailes (Mrs. Edward T. Wailes) of Washington, D.C. Por971.8

Portrait II. Emily (Dill) Bosher

Artist unidentified

Oil on canvas: 30¼ x 25 in. (76.8 x 63.5 cm.)

Received in 1971 as a bequest of Cornelia (Lyon) Wailes (Mrs. Edward T. Wailes) of Washington, D.C. Por971.7

Robert Semple Bosher, 1843–1904

Born in Richmond on May 17, 1843, the subject was the son of Robert H. Bosher and Elizabeth B. (Eubank) Bosher. His business career began at the early age of fifteen in the offices of James Thomas, a Richmond tobacco merchant. Three years later he joined the 2d Company of the Richmond Howitzers, serving with this unit throughout the Civil War. After the surrender he returned to his former employer, who had become a partner with T. C. Williams and Company, tobacco manufacturers, and remained with that firm for the rest of his professional life. Bosher became president of the firm on the death in 1889 of Williams and continued in that capacity until his retirement. He was an active member of the First Baptist Church and served for fifteen years on the board of the YMCA. He died in New York City on January 13, 1904, about a year after his retirement, leaving a widow, Mattie E. (Cox) Bosher, and five children. He is buried in Hollywood Cemetery, Richmond. He was elected to membership in the Virginia Historical Society in 1889.

Richmond *Times-Dispatch*, Jan. 14, 1904, pp. 1, 3; *Virginia and Virginians*, 2: 771; *Confederate Military History*, 3: 742–44; *Biographic Catalogue*.

By JOHN P. WALKER. Signed. Dated 1905

Oil on canvas: 30 x 25 in. (76.2 x 63.5 cm.)

Presented to the R. E. Lee Camp, Confederate Veterans, in 1905; acquired by the Virginia Historical Society in 1946 through merger with the Confederate Memorial Association. Por946.128

Reuben Beverley Boston, 1834–1865

Born at Red Hill, Fluvanna County, April 21, 1834, the subject was the son of Reuben H. Boston and Margaret (Ragland) Boston. He entered the University of Virginia in 1855 as a student of law but left without taking a degree to gain practical experience in the Charlottesville law office of William J. Robertson; thereafter he removed to Memphis, Tennessee, to pursue his career. The failing health of his parents, however, compelled him to return to Fluvanna County in 1859. On the outbreak of the Civil War he enlisted as a scout, later raising a company which subsequently became Company I, 5th Virginia Cavalry. He led the company in the battles of Seven Pines, Second Manassas, Chancellorsville, and Spotsylvania; at the cavalry engagement at Aldie in June 1863 he and his brother were captured and held prisoner for nine months. Released and again captured, at Trevilians in the summer of 1864, he escaped; he returned to see action at Kelly's Ford, Winchester, and the Valley campaign. Colonel Boston was killed in action on April 6, 1865, at High Bridge. His body, recovered from a battlefield grave, was reinterred at Red Hill.

The University Memorial, pp. 740–43; *Biographic Catalogue*.

By JOHN P. WALKER. Signed. Dated 1910

Oil on canvas: 30 x 25 in. (76.2 x 63.5 cm.)

Presented to the R. E. Lee Camp, Confederate Veterans, in 1910; acquired by the Virginia Historical Society in 1946 through merger with the Confederate Memorial Association. Por946.118

Norborne Berkeley, Baron de *Botetourt*, 1717–1770

See Norborne *Berkeley*, Baron de Botetourt, 1717–1770

Jane Bowles, born ca. 1726

See Ralph Wormeley, 1715–1790

Elisha Boyd, 1767–1841

See The Convention of 1829–30

James Read Branch, 1828–1869

The second son of Thomas Branch and Sarah Pride (Read) Branch, the subject was born at New Market, Prince George County, on July 28, 1828. Graduating with honors from Randolph-Macon College in 1847, he and his younger brother John Patteson Branch joined their father in founding the banking firm of Thomas Branch and Sons in 1853. On December 3, 1856, he married his second cousin, Martha Louise Patteson, daughter of Dr. William Anderson Patteson, who bore him three daughters and a son. On the outbreak of the Civil War, Branch raised a company of infantry known as the Lee Guard which was later transferred to the artillery and designated the Branch Field Artillery. He saw action at Malvern Hill, Fredericksburg, and the siege of Plymouth, North Carolina, rising in due course to the rank of lieutenant colonel. At the last-named engagement, however, he was so severely wounded as to necessitate his retirement from active service; he rejoined his family, which had removed in 1863 from Petersburg to Richmond. After the war he entered politics as a candidate for the state Senate. Colonel Branch died at a political picnic, killed by the falling of a footbridge on Vauxhall Island, in the James River, on July 2, 1869.

Biographic Catalogue; James Branch Cabell, *Branchiana* (Richmond, 1907), pp. 61–69.

ARTIST UNIDENTIFIED

Oil on canvas: 30 x 25 in. (76.2 x 63.5 cm.)

Presented to the R. E. Lee Camp, Confederate Veterans, in 1912; acquired by the Virginia Historical Society in 1946 through merger with the Confederate Memorial Association. Por946.131

Samuel Branch, d. 1847

See The Convention of 1829–30

Thomas Alexander Brander, 1839–1900

A native and lifelong resident of Richmond, Thomas Alexander Brander was born on December 12, 1839, the son of Alexander Carter Brander and Louisiana (Harris) Adkins Brander. At the time of the John Brown affair he abandoned his mercantile pursuits in Richmond, volunteered as a private in the 1st Virginia Regiment, and served at Harpers Ferry and Charles Town. Promoted to second lieutenant in the 20th Regiment of Virginia Volunteers, he participated in the campaign in West Virginia until called on to help organize the Letcher Artillery, with which unit he served throughout the war, attaining the rank of major and seeing action at Mechanicsville, Malvern Hill, Chancellorsville, Gettysburg, Spotsylvania Court House, and the siege of Petersburg. On January 10, 1865, Major Brander married Elizabeth Louisa Walke, daughter of the Reverend Lewis Walke of Richmond; they were the parents of seven children. At the conclusion of the Civil War he entered the insurance business. Active in Confederate organizations, he served at various times as commander of the R. E. Lee Camp of Confederate Veterans, commander of the Grand Camp of the Confederate Veterans, and vice-president of the Soldiers' Home. Major Brander died on January 28, 1900, and is buried in Hollywood Cemetery.

Confederate Military History, 3: 749–50; *Confederate Veteran* 8 (1900): 82; Return Jonathan Meigs, *A Record of the Descendants of James Brander* (Westfield, N.J., 1937), p. 8; *Biographic Catalogue*.

BY WILLIAM LUDWELL SHEPPARD. Signed. Dated 1900

Oil on canvas: 30 x 25 in. (76.2 x 63.5 cm.). Inscribed on the back: "Major Thomas A. Brander, C.S.A. from photo, 1864–5. Painted by Wm. L. Sheppard."

Presented to the R. E. Lee Camp, Confederate Veterans, in 1900; acquired by the Virginia Historical Society in 1946 through merger with the Confederate Memorial Association. Por946.147

Judith (Robinson) Braxton, 1736–1757   (Mrs. Carter Braxton)

Born on June 2, 1736, daughter of Christopher and Mary (Berkeley) Robinson of Hewick, Middlesex County, the subject married on July 16, 1755, Carter Braxton, one of the Virginia signers of the Declaration of Independence. The couple lived at Elsing Green, King William County. She died in childbirth, aged twenty-one, on December 30, 1757. Two daughters were born of the union.

Alonzo Thomas Dill, *Carter Braxton, Last Virginia Signer* (Richmond, 1976); *VMHB* 17 (1909): 93–94; *W. & M. Quart.*, 1st ser., 4 (1895–96): 119 and 18 (1909–10): 182.

COPIED BY JULIA STANARD WOOLDRIDGE

Watercolor on cardboard: 14 x 10 in. (35.6 x 25.4 cm.). Inscribed on the back: "Judith Robinson (1736–1757) wife of Carter Braxton. Copied by Julia S. Wooldridge from portrait in possession of Mrs. Mary Newton Pole of Hot Springs, 1903/4."

Presented in 1929 by William Glover Stanard in memory of his wife, Mary Mann Page (Newton) Stanard. Por929.5

Anne Butler Brayne
See Alexander Spotswood, 1676–1740

Cary Breckinridge, 1839–1918

The fourth child of Cary and Emma Walker (Gilmer) Breckinridge, the subject was born on October 5, 1839, in Botetourt County. He was a member of the class of 1860 at the Virginia Military Institute, enlisted as a private at the outbreak of the Civil War, and rose rapidly to the rank of colonel of the 2d Virginia Cavalry. He served throughout the conflict, was three times wounded, and reputedly had five horses shot from under him. In the final days of the struggle he was promoted to brigadier general, but never having borne the rank on the field of battle, he never claimed it. He was married on June 2, 1866, at Brierfield, West Virginia, to Virginia Caldwell, who bore him seven children. Breckinridge represented Botetourt County in the Virginia House of Delegates 1869–71 and was appointed superintendent of Botetourt County schools in 1886. He died at his home in Fincastle on May 11, 1918.

Seldens of Virginia, 1: 105; *Confederate Veteran* 26 (1918): 452; *Biographic Catalogue*.

ARTIST UNIDENTIFIED

Oil on canvas: 30 x 25 in. (76.2 x 63.5 cm.)

Acquired in 1946 through merger with the Confederate Memorial Association. Por946.179

John Cabell Breckinridge, 1821–1875

The only son of Joseph Cabell Breckinridge and Mary Clay (Smith) Breckinridge, the subject was born in Lexington, Kentucky, on January 16, 1821. He was educated in Kentucky, at Pisgah Academy and Centre College, pursued legal studies at Transylvania Institute, and was admitted to the bar in 1840. After a brief sojourn in Iowa he returned in

1845 to practice his profession in Lexington, Kentucky. Responding to a call for troops to serve in the Mexican War, he accepted a major's commission in the 3d Kentucky Volunteers. On his release from active service he entered politics, first as a member of the Kentucky legislature 1849–51, then as a representative in the United States Congress 1851–55. The following year Breckinridge was elected vice-president of the United States on Buchanan's Democratic ticket, being the youngest vice-president who had ever held that office. Defeated as a candidate for president in 1860 by Abraham Lincoln, Breckinridge took his seat in the United States Senate but withdrew in 1861 to accept a commission as brigadier general in the Confederate army. He commanded the Reserve Corps at Shiloh, distinguished himself at Vicksburg, Murfreesboro, and Chickamauga, and on February 4, 1865, became secretary of war in the cabinet of the Confederate States, a post he held till the war's end. He resided in England and Canada until given permission by the federal government in 1869 to return to Kentucky, where he received a cordial welcome. Disclaiming political ambitions, he resumed the practice of law in Lexington, and became vice-president of the Elizabethtown, Lexington and Big Sandy Railroad. He died in Lexington on May 17, 1875, survived by his wife, Mary Cyrene (Burch) Breckinridge, whom he had married in 1843, and by whom he had six children.

DAB; Biographical Directory; Generals in Gray; Biographic Catalogue; The Cabells and Their Kin, pp. 538–40.

By NICOLA MARSCHALL. Signed. Dated 1904

Oil on canvas: 30 x 25 in. (76.2 x 63.5 cm.)

Presented to the R. E. Lee Camp, Confederate Veterans, in 1905; acquired by the Virginia Historical Society in 1946 through merger with the Confederate Memorial Association. Por946.138

—— Briggs
See The Convention of 1829–30

Charles William Penn Brock, 1836–1916

Son of Ansalem and Elizabeth Beverley (Buckner) Brock, the subject was born in the Valley of Virginia on June 1, 1836. After attending private schools and the University of Virginia, he obtained his professional training at the Medical College of Virginia, graduating from that institution in 1859. Dr. Brock served in the Confederate army throughout the Civil War, first as a private soldier, then as surgeon in the 46th Virginia Infantry, and afterwards as chief surgeon on the staff of Major General James L. Kemper (q.v.). At the war's end he practiced his profession in Richmond. He became surgeon of the Police Department of the city of Richmond in 1865, chief surgeon of the Chesapeake and Ohio Railway in 1882, president of the National Association of Railway Surgeons in 1892, and president of the Medical Society of Virginia in 1898. He was an active worker in Masonic circles and a past master of Richmond lodge no. 10. His wife, Elizabeth (Tyler) Brock, daughter of John H. Tyler of Richmond, whom he married on October 1, 1863, bore him four children. Dr. Brock died on October 19, 1916.

Biographic Catalogue; Men of Mark in Virginia, 1:181–82; *The Beverley Family of Virginia*, pp. 743–44; *Richmond Times-Dispatch*, Oct. 20, 1916, p. 1.

By JOHN P. WALKER. 1911

Oil on canvas: 30 x 25 in. (76.2 x 63.5 cm.). Inscribed on the back: "J. P. Walker, 1911."

Acquired in 1946 through merger with the Confederate Memorial Association. Por946.129

William H. Brodnax, 1786–1834
See The Convention of 1829–30

Francis Taliaferro Brooke, 1763–1851

Judge Brooke was born on August 27, 1763, at Smithfield, four miles below Fredericksburg on the Rappahannock, the son of Richard and Elizabeth (Taliaferro) Brooke. At sixteen he joined the Revolutionary army as first lieutenant in General Harrison's regiment of artillery, serving in Virginia during the campaign of 1781. After the Revolution he studied law with his brother Robert, was licensed to practice in 1788, and removed to Morgantown, (West) Virginia, where he was appointed Commonwealth's attorney for the district. In two years he was back in eastern Virginia, settling in Tappahannock, and marrying on October 3, 1791, Mary Randolph Spotswood, daughter of General Alexander Spotswood and Elizabeth (Washington) Spotswood. Elected to the Virginia legislature in 1794, he represented Essex County for two terms; in 1800 he was elected to the state Senate, serving that body until 1804 when, as Speaker of the Senate, he was elected judge of the General Court. In 1811 he was elected judge of the Supreme Court of Appeals, serving that court forty years, six of them as its president. Judge Brooke's first wife died in 1803, having borne him four children; he married second, in 1804, Mary Champe Carter, daughter of Edward and Sarah (Champe) Carter of

Blenheim, Albemarle County, by whom he had two children. Respecting his marriages he wrote candidly, "though I have married into two families that had been among the wealthiest in Va., it did not profit me very much." Judge Brooke rose to the rank of brigadier general in the state militia, was a member of the Society of the Cincinnati in the State of Virginia, and in 1833 was elected to membership in the Virginia Historical Society. For more than fifty years he carried on a lively correspondence with Henry Clay, and in 1849 he published his memoirs, *A Narrative of My Life*. He died at St. Julien, his home in Spotsylvania County, on March 3, 1851.

DAB; Virginia State Bar Association, *Proceedings* 40 (1928): 407–21; Francis Taliaferro Brooke, *A Narrative of My Life, for My Family* (Richmond, 1849); *Occasional Bulletin*, no. 34 (1977): 1–4 (portrait reproduced); George Wesley Rogers, *Officers of the Senate of Virginia, 1776–1956* (Richmond, 1959), pp. 25–27.

Francis Taliaferro Brooke

ATTRIBUTED TO GEORGE COOKE

Oil on canvas: 38¼ x 31 in. (97.2 x 78.7 cm.)

Received in 1977 as a bequest of the Reverend Robert Semple Bosher of Richmond. Por977.1

In addition to the Society's portrait, several other portraits purporting to represent Judge Brooke are recorded. The likeness reproduced in *The Carters of Blenheim* presents some difficulties. It depicts a young man perhaps in his thirties, in feature not unlike the Judge Brooke of the Society's portrait; his costume, however, is not the costume of 1800 (when Judge Brooke would have been that age) but of a period some forty years later. Another likeness, of which two versions apparently exist, depicts the judge in old age. One version, reproduced as the frontispiece to the Virginia State Bar Association *Proceedings* 40 (1928), hung at that time in the Virginia Supreme Court of Appeals building in Richmond; it has now been replaced by a copy executed in 1963. A second version of the portrait, reproduced in Edgar Erskine Hume's *Sesquicentennial History and Roster of the Society of the Cincinnati in the State of Virginia* (Richmond, 1934), p. 131, was at that time the property of Mrs. Anne Carter Ossman of Richmond. Although the published reproductions of the two portraits are far from satisfactory and suggest that both canvases had been heavily overpainted, the subject in both is clearly past threescore years and ten. It is possible that this is the portrait of Judge Brooke, aged eighty-three, that the young artist William Garl Brown noted in an advertisement published in the Richmond *Whig* on November 19, 1846.

George Selden Wallace, *The Carters of Blenheim: A Genealogy of Edward and Sarah Champe Carter of "Blenheim," Albemarle County, Virginia* (Richmond, 1955), p. 98; *Portraits and Statuary*, p. 12; *Richmond Portraits*, p. 216 (cites advertisement in Richmond *Whig*, Nov. 19, 1846).

David Andrew Brown, 1846–1918

Born on April 29, 1846, son of David Arnold Brown and Margaret (Forloine) Brown of Richmond, the subject was on the point of accepting an appointment to West Point when the Civil War began. Although under military age, he enlisted in the 20th Virginia Infantry with his older brother John Thompson Brown (q.v.), and the two later served together in Parker's Battery. Second Manassas, Sharpsburg, Fredericksburg, Gettysburg, Chickamauga, Knoxville, the Wilderness, Spotsylvania, and Second Cold Harbor are but some of the sixteen engagements in which he saw action. Wounded at Sharpsburg and taken prisoner at Sayler's Creek, he was kept in prison for some months after the close of the war. Returning to Richmond, David Brown joined and later took over his father's saddle and harness business, operating under the firm name D. A. Brown's Son. On October 19, 1871, he married Mary Etta Ellett, who bore him three sons; the family later resided at 2207 Monument Avenue. Brown was greatly involved in Confederate organizations, serving at various times as adjutant, R. E. Lee Camp of Confederate Veterans, quartermaster general of the Virginia Division of the United Confederate Veterans, and member of the board of governors of the Soldiers' Home. David Brown died at his home on October 7, 1918, and is buried in Hollywood Cemetery.

Robert K. Krick, *Parker's Virginia Battery, C.S.A.* (Berryville, Va., 1975), p. 312; *Confederate Veteran* 28 (1920): 68–69; *Richmond Times-Dispatch*, Oct. 8, 1918; *Biographic Catalogue*.

By JOHN P. WALKER. Signed. Dated 1909 (or 1919)

Oil on canvas: 30 x 25 in. (76.2 x 63.5 cm.)

Acquired in 1946 through merger with the Confederate Memorial Association. Por946.153

John Thompson Brown, 1840–1921

Not to be confused with Colonel John Thompson Brown (1835–1864) also a member of the Confederate artillery, a Virginian, but no kin, Lieutenant John Thompson Brown, the son of David Arnold Brown and Margaret (Forloine) Brown, was born in Richmond on May 4, 1840. He graduated from Randolph-Macon College, Boydton, in 1861 and immediately thereafter enlisted in Company A, 20th Virginia Infantry, as first sergeant. When the company was disbanded he was instrumental in forming Parker's Virginia Battery, with which unit he saw action at Fredericksburg, Gettysburg, Chickamauga, the Wilderness, Spotsylvania, and Sayler's Creek. Following the war Brown was employed in his father's saddle and harness business in Richmond; later, in 1872, he established his own real estate and auctioneering house. Entering the political arena in 1871, Brown was elected to the Virginia legislature on the mechanics ticket, serving in the House of Delegates until 1873. As president of the Richmond Union Passenger Railway Company, Brown introduced an electric trolley system to Richmond streets in 1887, claimed to be the first of its kind in America. Active in Confederate organizations, he was commander of the Grand Camp of Confederate Veterans and commander of the Virginia Division of the United Confederate Veterans. He became a member of the Virginia Historical Society in 1882. John Thompson Brown died on April 23, 1921, and is buried in Hollywood Cemetery. He was predeceased by his wife, Elizabeth Holloway (Harrison) Brown, whom he married in Mecklenburg County on February 6, 1863, and by seven of his eleven children.

Biographic Catalogue; Robert K. Krick, *Parker's Virginia Battery, C.S.A.* (Berryville, Va., 1975), pp. 353–56; *Virginia Cavalcade* 8, no. 2 (1958): 21–31.

By JOHN P. WALKER. Signed. Dated 1922

Oil on canvas: 30 x 25 in. (76.2 x 63.5 cm.)

Acquired in 1946 through merger with the Confederate Memorial Association. Por946.180

Charles Bruce, 1826–1896
Sarah Alexander (Seddon) Bruce, 1829–1907 (Mrs. Charles Bruce)

Youngest of the three children of James Bruce (q.v.) by his second wife, Elvira (Cabell) Henry Bruce, Charles Bruce was born on August 7, 1826. He graduated from the University of North Carolina and studied law at Harvard University. On September 19, 1848, he married Sarah Alexander Seddon, daughter of Thomas and Susan Pearson (Alexander) Seddon of Fredericksburg and sister of James A. Seddon, later Confederate secretary of war. The couple resided at Staunton Hill, Charlotte County, and became the parents of ten children, one of whom, Philip Alexander Bruce (q.v.), became corresponding secretary of the Virginia Historical Society. Charles Bruce was a member of the Virginia state Senate 1857–65. At his own expense he raised and equipped the Staunton Hill Artillery, and as its captain saw active duty in the Army of the Confederate States. After the war he declined public office to devote himself to the cultivation of the Staunton Hill estate. He died on October 4, 1896; his wife died in 1907.

The Cabells and Their Kin, pp. 365–66; *Occasional Bulletin*, no. 34 (1977): 14–15 (Portraits I and II reproduced); *VMHB* 12 (1904–5): 93–94 and 85 (1977): 239.

Portrait I. Charles Bruce

By GEORGE LETHBRIDGE SAUNDERS. 1845

Miniature on ivory: 5½ x 4¼ in. (14 x 10.8 cm.) (oval)

Presented in 1976 by David Kirkpatrick Este Bruce of Washington, D.C., a grandson of the subject. Por976.18

According to a notice in the Richmond *Times and Compiler*, George Lethbridge Saunders was painting miniatures in Richmond in May 1845. A letter written from Richmond by William C. Carrington on May 11, 1845, confirms the date and indicates that other members of the Bruce family were painted by Saunders at the same time. "We have as our next door neighbour Mr. Saunders, a celebrated English miniature painter. His reputation is so great that he charges $160 for one likeness. Miss Sally Bruce has had the likeness of Mrs. Morson, her Mother, and Miss Ann Eliza Ritchie taken by him; and they are all said to be excellent. He has had about a dozen applications already in Richmond. His great charm to the ladies is that he makes their pictures much prettier than they are themselves." Sally Bruce and Ellen Carter (Bruce) Morson (q.v.) were sisters of Charles Bruce. Their mother, Elvira (Cabell) Henry

Bruce, also painted by Saunders according to the letter, was the second wife of James Bruce (q.v.) of Halifax County. Ann Eliza Ritchie, a daughter of Thomas and Isabella (Foushee) Ritchie, married William B. Cross.

Richmond *Times and Compiler*, May 26, 1845; VHS Mss1 C2358g 197.

Sarah Alexander (Seddon) Bruce (Portrait II)

Portrait II. Sarah Alexander (Seddon) Bruce

By GEORGE LETHBRIDGE SAUNDERS

Miniature on ivory: 5¼ x 4½ in. (14 x 10.8 cm.)

Presented in 1976 by David Kirkpatrick Este Bruce of Washington, D.C., a grandson of the subject. Por976.19

Portrait III. Sarah Alexander (Seddon) Bruce

By ALEXANDER GALT. Signed. Dated 1856

Pencil on paper: 7 x 5¼ in. (17.8 x 13.3 cm.). Inscribed: "Sketch by Mr. Galt of Mrs. Charles Bruce. A. Galt. June 26th 1856."

Received with the Bruce family papers in 1974. Por974.47

This sketch appears to be a preliminary study for Galt's marble bust of the subject.

David Kirkpatrick Este Bruce, 1898–1977

Diplomat and statesman, David K. E. Bruce was born in Baltimore on February 12, 1898, son of William Cabell Bruce and Louise Este (Fisher) Bruce. His college career at Princeton was interrupted in 1917 by military service overseas in the 29th Division. After his discharge from the army he studied law at the University of Virginia, was admitted to the bar, and practiced law in Baltimore 1921–25. He was a member of the Maryland House of Delegates 1924–26. Bruce was vice-consul at Rome 1926–28 but resigned from the foreign service to manage extensive business interests and his farming operations at Staunton Hill, his estate in Charlotte County. He represented Charlotte County in the Virginia legislature 1939–42. During World War II he was chief of the European Office of Strategic Services; thereafter he was assistant secretary of commerce 1947–48, chief of the Economic Cooperation Administration mission to France 1948–49; ambassador to France 1949–52, and undersecretary of state 1952–53. Bruce was American ambassador to the Federal Republic of Germany 1957–59, ambassador to Great Britain 1961–69, and American representative to the Vietnam peace talks in Paris 1970–71. In 1972 he was appointed liaison officer with the People's Republic of China, Peking, a post he left in 1974 to become ambassador to

David Kirkpatrick Este Bruce (Portrait II)

NATO in Brussels. He died in Washington on December 5, 1977. Bruce was twice married: first to Ailsa Mellon, second to Evangeline Bell; he had one child by his first marriage and three children by his second. Elected to membership in the Virginia Historical Society in 1938, he was a vice-president of the Society from 1939 until he became one of its honorary vice-presidents in 1954, an office he held until his death. On January 19, 1957, he delivered the Society's annual address in celebration of the 350th anniversary of the settlement of Virginia, and over the years he contributed substantially to the Society's work.

Who's Who in America (Chicago, 1978), 1: 442; *Virginia and the Virginia County* 6, no. 7 (July 1952): 6–7, 41.

Portrait I

By H. Starr Herman. Signed. Dated 1950

Oil on canvas: 24 x 18 in. (61 x 45.7 cm.)

Presented in 1978 by David S. Bruce of Staunton Hill, a son of the subject. Por978.17

Portrait II

By Robert Lutyens. Signed

Oil on canvas: 36 x 28 in. (91.4 x 71.1 cm.)

Presented in 1979 by the subject's widow. Por979.4

Ellen Carter Bruce, 1820–1862

See Ellen Carter (Bruce) Morson, 1820–1862

James Bruce, 1763–1837

Born on March 20, 1763, the eldest son of Charles and Diana (Banks) Bruce of Soldier's Rest, Orange County, the subject developed an early taste for mercantile pursuits that eventually brought him great wealth. At the age of sixteen he found employment in Petersburg with a Mr. Colquhoun who conducted a profitable business buying tobacco and selling English manufactured goods. Bruce was soon entrusted with establishing a branch of this business in Amelia County; he prospered, became a partner in the business, and then established another branch in Halifax County. Here he remained for the rest of his life, conducting an extensive mercantile business and investing heavily in tobacco and lands. On August 1, 1799, he married Sarah Coles, daughter of Walter and Mildred (Lightfoot) Coles of Halifax County; she died on May 21, 1806, having borne him three children, two of whom died in infancy. He married, second, on April 20, 1819, Elvira (Cabell) Henry, daughter of William and Anne (Carrington) Cabell and widow of Patrick Henry, Jr. The couple resided at Woodburn, Bruce's estate in Halifax

County; they became the parents of four children, two of whom, Charles Bruce and Ellen Carter (Bruce) Morson (qq.v.), are represented in the Society's portrait collection. Bruce died in Philadelphia on May 12, 1837, and was buried there in St. Andrew's churchyard; he was at that time reputedly the richest man in Virginia. Elvira Bruce, who survived her husband by more than twenty years, spent the years of her widowhood in Richmond. James Bruce was a founding member (1831) of the Virginia Historical Society.

The Cabells and Their Kin, pp. 353–56; William Bedford Coles, *The Coles Family of Virginia* (New York, 1931), pp. 81–84; *VMHB* 11 (1903–4): 329–31 and 54 (1946): 172 (subject misidentified as John Y. Mason); *Virginia Historical Portraiture*, pp. 368–70 (original portrait reproduced).

Copied by Rudolf V. Smutny. 1947

Oil on canvas: 30 x 25 in. (76.2 x 63.5 cm.). Inscribed on the back: "Copy by R. V. Smutny 4015—72nd St. Jackson Heights, New York. After the original by John Neagle of James Bruce, Esquire."

Presented in 1947 by David Kirkpatrick Este Bruce of Washington, D.C., a great-grandson of the subject. Por947.25

Philip Alexander Bruce, 1856–1933

Historian and first editor of the *Virginia Magazine of History and Biography*, Philip Alexander Bruce was the grandson of James Bruce (q.v.) and the sixth child of Charles and Sarah Alexander (Seddon) Bruce (qq.v.) of Staunton Hill, Charlotte County. He was born there on March 7, 1856, graduated from the University of Virginia in 1876, and studied law at Harvard University. He remained but a short time in the legal profession. Turning to the study and writing of history, he published his first book, *The Plantation Negro as a Freeman*, in 1889. Thereafter he served two years on the editorial staff of the Richmond *Times* and in 1892 became corresponding secretary of the Virginia Historical Society and founding editor of the *Virginia Magazine of History and Biography*, posts he held until 1898 when he resigned to devote himself to research and writing. His three monumental studies of seventeenth-century Virginia remain classics in their field: *Economic History of Virginia in the Seventeenth Century* (1895), *Social Life of Virginia in the Seventeenth Century* (1907), and *Institutional History of Virginia in the Seventeenth Century* (1910). In 1916 he removed to Charlottesville to write the centennial history of the University; the five-volume *History of the University of Virginia* was published between 1920 and 1922. In 1929 he published *The Virginia Plutarch*, a two-volume compilation of Virginia biography. Bruce died at his residence in Charlottesville on August 16, 1933. His wife, whom he married on October 19, 1896, was Elizabeth Tunstall (Taylor) Newton, of Norfolk, by whom he had one child, a daughter.

DAB (Supplement 1); *Occasional Bulletin*, no. 1 (1960): 14–15 (portrait reproduced); *VMHB* 69 (1961): 239.

COPIED BY HELEN SCHUYLER SMITH HULL BAILEY. 1960

Oil on canvas: 36 x 28 in. (91.4 x 71.1 cm.). Inscribed on the back: "Philip Alexander Bruce (1856–1933) copied in 1960 by Helen Schuyler (Smith) Hull (1920–) From the original portrait by Pierre Troubetzkoy (1864–1936)."

Purchased from the artist in 1960 with funds contributed by David Kirkpatrick Este Bruce of Washington, D.C., a nephew of the subject. Por960.72

The original portrait, painted by Pierre Troubetzkoy, is owned by the University of Virginia.

Joseph Bryan, 1845–1908

The eighth child of John Randolph Bryan and Elizabeth Tucker (Coalter) Bryan of Eagle Point, Gloucester County, Joseph Bryan was born on August 13, 1845. He attended the Episcopal High School in Alexandria and in July 1863 interrupted his studies at the University of Virginia to join the Confederate army. A broken arm, however, delayed his assignment to active duty and necessitated his accepting a post at the government niter and mining bureau in Pulaski County. Later, as a member of the 2d Company of the Richmond Howitzers, he participated in the battle of Spotsylvania Court House in May 1864 and saw action and received wounds in Mountjoy's company of Mosby's command. At the war's end, Bryan, not yet twenty, resumed his studies, turning his attention to the legal profession. He was admitted to the bar in 1868 and two years later established himself in Richmond where for the rest of his life he played a major role in the city's financial, cultural, and social life. In 1871 Bryan married Isobel Lamont Stewart, daughter of John and Mary Amanda (Williamson) Stewart of Brook Hill; they became the parents of five sons. Business gradually superseded law as Bryan's chief interest; he was closely connected with coal and iron works and railroad and rapid transit companies and was a director of the Southern Railway Company and the New York Equitable Life Assurance Association. In 1889 he became owner and editor of the Richmond *Times*, consolidating it in 1903 with the *Richmond Dispatch* to form the Richmond *Times-Dispatch*. He was a trustee of the Episcopal High School and the University of Virginia, delegate to the General Convention of the Episcopal Church from 1866 to the end of his life,

director of the Jamestown Exposition of 1907, and benefactor of the Association for the Preservation of Virginia Antiquities. It was largely through Bryan's influence that the Virginia Historical Society was granted occupancy of the Lee House at 707 East Franklin Street; it remained the Society's headquarters from 1892 to 1957. A staunch friend and benefactor to the Society, he served as its seventh (1892) and ninth (1906) president. Joseph Bryan died at his home, Laburnum, on November 29, 1908.

Confederate Veteran 17 (1909): 606–7 and 18 (1910): 164, 166; Robert Camillus Glass, *Virginia Democracy* (Springfield, Ill., 1937), 2: 30–33; John Stewart Bryan, *Joseph Bryan: His Times, His Family, His Friends* (Richmond, 1935); *VMHB* 17 (1909): iii–xxix; *Biographic Catalogue*.

Joseph Bryan (Portrait I)

Portrait I

COPIED BY DUNCAN SMITH. 1913

Oil on canvas: 56 x 35¼ in. (142.2 x 89.5 cm.). Inscribed on the back: "Virginia Historical Society. Portrait of Joseph Bryan, Esq. After W. Funk. [Monogram] 1913."

Presented in 1915 by the sons of the subject. Por915.1

Portrait II

By John P. Walker. 1909

Oil on canvas: 30 x 25 in. (76.2 x 63.5 cm.). Inscribed on the back: "Joseph Bryan, 1845–1908. Painted by J. P. Walker, 1909. No. 2."

Presented to the R. E. Lee Camp, Confederate Veterans, in 1909; acquired by the Virginia Historical Society in 1946 through merger with the Confederate Memorial Association. Por946.57

Clarence Archibald Bryce, 1849–1928

Son of Benjamin Franklin Bryce and Mildred (Chewning) Bryce of Hanover County, the subject was born on January 9, 1849. He received his formal education at the Morris Academy in Hanover, at Richmond College, and the Medical College of Virginia, graduating from the latter institution in 1871. The following year he began the practice of his profession in Richmond. In 1878 Dr. Bryce founded the *Southern Clinic*, of which he was owner and editor for forty years; he was also a contributor to other professional journals and wrote and published medical works and several books in a lighter vein such as *"Ups and Downs" of a Virginia Doctor* (1904), *Kitty Dixon* (1907), and *The Gentleman's Dog* (1909). Dr. Bryce was particularly noted for his work in electrotherapeutics. He died in Richmond on September 21, 1928, survived by his wife, Virginia (Keane) Bryce, daughter of Hugh Payne Keane (q.v.) and Annette (Naret) Keane, whom he married on September 19, 1885. Five children were born of the union, four of whom survived their father.

Richmond Times-Dispatch, Sept. 22, 1928, p. 3; Marie Keane Dabney, *Mrs. T.N.T.*, (Richmond, 1949), p. 33; VHS Mss6:1 B8435:1; *VMHB* 83 (1975): 237.

By Virginia Keane Bryce. Signed. Dated 1888

Oil on canvas: 20 x 24 in. (50.8 x 61 cm.)

Presented in 1974 by the subject's daughter, Virginia Bryce of Richmond. Por974.30

The portrait, entitled *The Charity Patient*, depicts the subject ministering to an elderly black woman. It is the work of the subject's wife.

John Buchanan, 1743–1822

Born in Scotland in 1743, Parson Buchanan studied law after graduating from the University of Edinburgh, but finding the legal profession not to his taste, came to Virginia to join his brother James who was a successful merchant in Richmond. Mercantile pursuits were likewise uncongenial, so Buchanan returned to Scotland to study for the ministry; he came back to Virginia in 1775 as an ordained clergyman. After some years in Lexington Parish, Amherst County, he was called to St. John's, Henrico Parish, as assistant to the rector. A few weeks later, on June 7, 1785, he was named rector of the parish; he retained this charge until his death thirty-seven years later, becoming during that time one of Richmond's best-known and beloved citizens. On the death of his brother James in 1787 Parson Buchanan inherited a large estate which enabled him over the years to contribute generously to worthy individuals, charities, and undertakings. He accepted a doctorate of divinity from the College of William and Mary in 1794, was the founder and first president (1819) of the Bible Society of Virginia, and for twenty-nine years was treasurer of the Diocese of Virginia. In addition to his duties as rector of St. John's, Buchanan for many years conducted divine service in the state Capitol, alternating weeks with his great friend and Presbyterian counterpart, Parson James Durburrow Blair (q.v.); he likewise volunteered to serve as assistant to Bishop Moore when Monumental Church opened its doors in 1814. Parson Buchanan died, unmarried, on December 19, 1822, and is buried at St. John's. A charming account of Buchanan and Blair, their friendship and ministry in Richmond, can be found in G. W. Munford's *The Two Parsons* (Richmond, 1884).

Richmond Portraits, pp. 24–26; *Virginia Historical Portraiture*, pp. 280–81 (portrait reproduced).

John Buchanan

By John Blennerhassett Martin

Oil on canvas: 27 x 21 3/4 in. (68.6 x 55.3 cm.)

Acquired by the Society before 1911; source unknown. Por910.1

Samuel D. Buck, 1841–1920

The subject was born at Buckton, Warren County, March 2, 1841, the son of John Gill Buck and Eliza (McKay) Buck. At the outbreak of the Civil War he left the employment of J. P. Heironimus and Company, in Winchester, to join the 13th Virginia Infantry. He served in this regiment throughout the war, seeing action at First and Second Manassas, Sharpsburg, Fredericksburg, Chancellorsville, Brandy Station, and numerous other engagements, rising from the rank of sergeant to captain. His account of his wartime experiences was published posthumously in 1925 under the title *With the Old Confeds*. Baltimore became Buck's residence after the war where for thirty years he engaged in the wholesale shoe business. In 1905 he became secretary and general manager of the Baltimore Credit Men's Association, remaining with the association until 1919 when ill health caused him to resign from active work. He was survived on his death, June 29, 1920, by his wife, Alice (Parkins) Buck, and one son.

Confederate Veteran 28 (1920): 429; Samuel D. Buck, *With the Old Confeds.: Actual Experiences of a Captain in the Line* (Baltimore, 1925).

By J. Bennett. Signed

Oil on canvas: 30 x 25 in. (76.2 x 63.5 cm.)

Acquired in 1946 through merger with the Confederate Memorial Association. Por946.122

The daguerreotype from which the Society's portrait was taken is reproduced as the frontispiece to Buck's autobiography.

Benjamin Burton, 1784–1860
Eliza (Shipp) Burton, 1804–1862 (Mrs. Benjamin Burton)

Born on June 22, 1784, Benjamin Burton was the son of May and Sarah (Head) Burton of Orange County. He removed to Madison County at an undetermined date and acquired Rock Hill, the estate of his maternal grandfather, Captain Benjamin Head. On September 20, 1820, he married Eliza Shipp; the couple became the parents of two sons, Dr. John May Burton (q.v.) and Benjamin Burton, Jr. Benjamin Burton died in 1860; his wife died two years later.

Vee Dove, *Madison County Homes* (Madison, Va., 1975), p. 43; John Frederick Dorman, *Virginia Revolutionary Pension Applications* (Washington, D.C., 1958–), 13: 54–57; *Occasional Bulletin*, no. 24 (1972): 2–4 (Portrait II reproduced); *VMHB* 80 (1972): 238 and 83 (1975): 236; *Antiques* 116 (1979): 1137 (Portrait II reproduced).

Portrait I. Benjamin Burton

By John Toole. 1841

Oil on canvas: 30 x 25 in. (76.2 x 63.5 cm.)

Presented in 1971 by Mrs. Erastus E. Deane and her daughter Mrs. Sterling Gibson, both of Ruckersville. Por971.34

Portrait II. Eliza (Shipp) Burton

By John Toole. 1841

Oil on canvas: 30 x 25 in. (76.2 x 63.5 cm.)

Presented in 1971 by Mrs. Erastus E. Deane and her daughter Mrs. Sterling Gibson, both of Ruckersville. Por971.29

Unsigned, the portraits of Benjamin Burton, his wife, and their son John May Burton (q.v.) are attributed to John Toole on the basis of their style and confirming documentary evidence provided in a letter from the artist to his wife, dated Orange Courthouse, July 18, 1841: "Dear Jane, I got down safely, and finished my work at Mr. Ships', collected what was due me in that neighbourhood, and have engaged some more work, which will detain me from home longer than I at first expected. Mr. Ship's Brother in law (Mr. Burton) wishes 3 portraits painted."

William Bainter O'Neal, *Primitive into Painter: Life and Letters of John Toole* (Charlottesville, Va., 1960), pp. 75, 85.

Elizabeth R. Burton
See Elizabeth R. (Burton) Royster

John May Burton, 1823–1893

Born at Rock Hill, Madison County, on June 1, 1823, the subject was the son of Benjamin and Eliza (Shipp) Burton (qq.v.) He attended the University of Virginia in 1842 and graduated in medicine from the University of Pennsylvania in 1844. He married, first, on December 7, 1847, Juliette Theresa Szymanski, daughter of Dr. Adrian J. Szymanski (q.v.) and Louisa (Waller) Szymanski of Spotsylvania County; the couple had four children, all of whom died in childhood. Dr. Burton married, second, on December 27, 1875, his first wife's niece, Louisa (Szymanski) Beverley of Whig Hill, Spotsylvania County; there were three children by this marriage. Dr. Burton practiced his profession in Greene and Madison counties and resided at Chatsworth, a short distance from the place of his birth. He died on March 1, 1893.

Vee Dove, *Madison County Homes* (Madison, Va., 1975), p. 43; *The Beverley Family*, pp. 607–8; *Occasional Bulletin*, no. 24 (1972): 2–4; *VMHB* 80 (1972): 238 and 83 (1975): 236.

John May Burton

BY JOHN TOOLE. 1841

Oil on canvas: 30 x 25 in. (76.2 x 63.5 cm.)

Presented in 1971 by Mrs. Erastus E. Deane and her daughter Mrs. Sterling Gibson, both of Ruckersville. Por971.31

See portrait note under Benjamin Burton and Eliza (Shipp) Burton.

Lucy (Randolph) Burwell, ca. 1744–1802 (Mrs. Lewis Burwell)

Daughter of William and Anne (Harrison) Randolph (qq.v.) of Wilton, the subject was born about 1744. In 1764 she married Lewis Burwell, son of Lewis and Frances (Thacker) Bray Burwell of Kingsmill, James City County. Her husband, who was educated in England, an anglophile, and a tory during the American Revolution, was known as "English Lewis." Lucy died without issue in 1802; her husband later removed to Rustic Lodge, Botetourt County, and became the guardian of the children of his deceased brother, Nathaniel Burwell.

The Randolphs of Virginia, p. 27, no. 138; *W. & M. Quart.*, 1st ser., 7 (1898–99): 195–96; VHS Mss 32-7-5 and Mss6:1

B9582:1–2; Linda Grant DePauw and Conover Hunt, *Remember the Ladies: Women in America, 1750–1815* (New York, 1976), p. 113 (portrait reproduced); *Occasional Bulletin*, no. 8 (1964): 13–15 (portrait reproduced); *Antiques* 116 (1979): 1131 (portrait reproduced). See chart on Randolph Portraits for relationships.

ATTRIBUTED TO JOHN DURAND   *See* Plate 5

Oil on canvas: 36 x 29 in. (91.4 x 73.7 cm.)

Received in 1951 as a bequest of Kate Brander (Harris) Mayo Skipwith Williams (Mrs. Berkeley Williams; previously Mrs. Grey Skipwith, and prior to that Mrs. Edward Carrington Mayo). Por951.35

Thomas N. Burwell, ca. 1788–1869

Son of Nathaniel and Martha (Digges) Burwell, the subject was born about 1788 and spent most of his life in Botetourt County. He was a justice of the county in 1815, a delegate to the Virginia legislature 1820–25, and one of the trustees of the Botetourt Seminary. An active churchman, he was an early mover for the establishment of an Episcopal church in Fincastle and represented Botetourt Parish at the annual council of the diocese 1834–62. Colonel Burwell removed to Richmond during the Civil War, became affiliated with St. James's Church, and served on its vestry from December 2, 1862, until his death, which occurred on January 7, 1869. By his wife, Elizabeth (Nicholson) Burwell, he had issue.

Stella Pickett Hardy, *Colonial Families of the Southern States of America* (New York, 1911), p. 102; Robert Douthat Stoner, *A Seed-bed of the Republic* (Roanoake, Va. 1962); Charles Francis Cocke, *St. Mark's Episcopal Church, Fincastle, Virginia* (Roanoke, Va. 1969); *Daily Richmond Enquirer*, Jan. 9, 1869, p. 1, col. 6.

ARTIST UNIDENTIFIED

Charcoal on paper: 11 1/2 x 9 in. (29.2 x 22.9 cm.)

Provenance unknown. PorX320

Matthew Calbraith Butler, 1836–1909

Born on March 8, 1836, in Greenville, South Carolina, Matthew Calbraith Butler was the son of Dr. William Butler, a naval surgeon, and Jane (Perry) Butler, a sister of Commodore Oliver Hazard Perry. After attending the local academy and South Carolina College in Columbia, he studied law and was admitted to the bar in 1857. The following year he married Maria Pickens, daughter of Governor Francis W. Pickens. Elected to the state legislature in 1860, he resigned on the outbreak of the Civil War to accept a commission in the Hampton Legion. Butler served throughout the war, attaining the rank of

5. Lucy (Randolph) Burwell

major general, and seeing action at First Manassas, Williamsburg, Brandy Station, Trevilian Station, and other engagements. At the war's end he resumed his political career, first as a representative in the South Carolina legislature, later as unsuccessful candidate for lieutenant governor, and finally as senator in the United States Congress 1877–95. During the Spanish-American War he was appointed major general of the United States Volunteers and a member of the commission for the Spanish evacuation of Cuba. General Butler died on April 14, 1909, and is buried in Edgefield, South Carolina.

DAB; *Generals in Gray*; *Biographical Directory*; *Biographic Catalogue*.

By CORNELIUS HANKINS. Signed. Dated 1897

Oil on canvas: 30 x 25 in. (76.2 x 63.5 cm.)

Presented to the R. E. Lee Camp, Confederate Veterans, in 1897; acquired by the Virginia Historical Society in 1946 through merger with the Confederate Memorial Association. Por946.70

William Byars, 1776–1856
See The Convention of 1829–30

William Byrd, 1674–1744

William Byrd II, of Westover, son of William and Mary (Horsmanden) Byrd, was born in Virginia on March 28, 1674. He received his formal education in England but returned to Virginia in 1692, in which year he was elected to the House of Burgesses. He was again in England 1697–1704, serving in the defense of Sir Edmund Andros (q.v.) and as agent for the colony. On the death of his father in 1704, Byrd fell heir to large estates; he took up residence in Virginia, succeeding his father as receiver general of the colony and in 1709 taking his seat in the Council of State. With the arrival of Governor Spotswood in 1710 there began a decade of strife between governor and Council in which Byrd played an active part. Spotswood's attempt to have Byrd removed from the Council in 1718 was unsuccessful; it was the governor who was in fact removed from office four years later. Byrd was one of the commissioners appointed to run the dividing line between Virginia and North Carolina in 1728, and in 1736 he surveyed the boundaries of the Northern Neck of Virginia. At Westover, his estate in Charles City County, he built about 1730 the splendid residence that still stands; here he assembled the largest private library in the colony, maintained a lively correspondence, and composed "The History of the Dividing Line," "A Journey to the Land of Eden," the "Progress to the

Mines," and other graceful pieces that were collected and posthumously published under the title *The Westover Manuscripts*. His diaries for the years 1709–12, 1717–21, and 1739–41 and his letters also have been published. Byrd was a Fellow of the Royal Society and a close friend of Charles Boyle, earl of Orrery. In 1743 he became president of the Council. He died on August 26, 1744, and is buried in the garden at Westover. Colonel Byrd was twice married: first, in 1706, to Lucy Parke, daughter of Daniel Parke, by whom he had four children, only two of whom survived infancy; second, in 1724, to Maria Taylor, daughter of Thomas Taylor of Kensington, England, by whom he had four children.

DAB.

Portrait I

COPIED BY WILLIAM LUDWELL SHEPPARD

Oil on canvas: 49 x 39 in. (124.5 x 99.1 cm.). Inscribed on the back: "Colonel William Byrd II of Westover. Painted by William Sheppard after the portrait at Brandon."

Presented in 1963 by Mary M. W. Taylor of Louisa County. Por963.18

The portrait, purchased by the donor and her sister shortly after the artist's death in 1912, is a copy of the so-called Brandon portrait of Byrd. The Brandon portrait, which hung originally at Westover, came into the possession of the Harrison family when Evelyn Taylor Byrd, a granddaughter of the subject, married Benjamin Harrison (1743–1807) of Brandon. It has been attributed variously to Sir Godfrey Kneller and to Charles Bridges. William Ludwell Sheppard also painted a full-length portrait of Byrd based on the Brandon portrait which hung for many years in the Richmond City Hall.

Richmond Portraits, p. 28; *VMHB* 60 (1952): 26 and 72 (1964): 241.

Portrait II   *See* Frontispiece

ATTRIBUTED TO SIR GODFREY KNELLER. Ca. 1704

Oil on canvas: 50 x 41 in. (127 x 104.1 cm.). Inscribed on the back: "The picture of Wm. Byrd Esqr. of Virginia Given by him to Charles Earl of Orrery. Anno 1725."

Presented in 1973 by William Byrd of Princeton, New Jersey. Por973.6

The provenance of the portrait was traced by the father of the donor: "The portrait . . . was painted by Sir Godfrey Kneller in 1704 and hung in Colonel Byrd's house in London until 1725. In that year it was given by Colonel Byrd to his friend Charles Boyle, fourth Earl of Orrery. On the original canvas back of the portrait there was a notation to this effect in the handwriting of the Earl of Orrery. The portrait was bequeathed by the Earl of Orrery to Sarah Otway, daughter of Colonel Francis Otway of the Horse Guards and Anne Taylor, his wife. Anne Taylor was a younger sister of Maria Taylor, Colonel Byrd's second wife. They were daughters and co-heiresses of Thomas Taylor of Kensington. Sarah Otway was also Colonel Byrd's goddaughter. The portrait descended in the Otway family until it came into the ownership of Major Otway Mayne of 'Walton Lodge,' Aylesbury, Buckinghamshire, from whom it was purchased by the present owner."

Virginia Historical Portraiture, pp. 156–60 (includes quote; portrait reproduced); *VMHB* 82 (1974): 238; *Occasional Bulletin*, no. 27 (1973): 5–7 (portrait reproduced); *Antiques* 116 (1979): 1130 (portrait reproduced).

Benjamin William Sheridan Cabell, 1793–1862

See The Convention of 1829–30

Henry Coalter Cabell, 1820–1889

A member of the executive committee of the Virginia Historical Society from 1856 until his death, the subject was born on February 14, 1820, youngest child of Governor William H. Cabell and his second wife, Agnes Sarah Bell (Gamble) Cabell. He graduated from the University of Virginia in 1839 and from its law school in 1842, forming a partnership in Richmond shortly thereafter with Sydney S. Baxter, attorney general of Virginia. On May 1, 1850, he married Jane C. Alston, only child of James and Catherine (Hamilton) Alston of South Carolina; they became the parents of six children. On the outbreak of the Civil War, Cabell was commissioned captain in the Fayette Artillery, then colonel of the 1st Virginia Regiment of Artillery. In July 1862 he was appointed chief of artillery, McLaws's Division, Army of Northern Virginia, in which post he served until the end of the war, seeing action at Seven Pines, Sharpsburg, Fredericksburg, Chancellorsville, Gettysburg, the Wilderness, Spotsylvania Court House, Cold Harbor, and Petersburg. Although he was promoted to brigadier general, his commission did not reach him till after the surrender, so he did not assume the rank. Returning to legal practice after the war, he formed a partnership with his brother-in-law, Judge William Daniel. At various times during his life he was director of the Central Railroad, the Chesapeake and Ohio Railway, and the James River and Kanawha Canal Company. He died in Richmond on January 31, 1889, and is buried in Hollywood Cemetery.

42

Biographic Catalogue; *The Cabells and Their Kin*, p. 639.

Oil on canvas: 30 x 25 in. (76.2 x 63.5 cm.)

Presented to the R. E. Lee Camp, Confederate Veterans, in 1907; acquired by the Virginia Historical Society in 1946 through merger with the Confederate Memorial Association. Por946.59

James Branch Cabell, 1879–1958

The eldest son of Robert Gamble Cabell and Anne Harris (Branch) Cabell, the subject was born in Richmond on April 14, 1879. After graduating from the College of William and Mary in 1898, he ventured briefly into journalism, coal mining, and genealogical research, the last interest resulting in three printed works, *Branchiana* (1907), *Branch of Abingdon* (1911), and *The Majors and Their Marriages* (1915). His first novel, *The Eagle's Shadow* (1904), was followed by *The Line of Love* (1905), *Gallantry* (1907), *The Cords of Vanity* (1909), and others in rapid succession. The alleged immorality of *Jurgen* (1919) brought him enormous publicity, assuring the success of such subsequent novels as *Figures of Earth* (1921), *The Silver Stallion* (1926), and *Something about Eve* (1927) and placing him in the ranks of bestselling authors throughout the decade. Although his popularity as

James Branch Cabell

an author waned during the latter part of his life, his output continued undiminished; his books continue to be admired by a faithful coterie. By the time of his death, which took place in Richmond on May 5,

1958, Cabell had written fifty-two volumes, an average of almost one a year during the course of his productive career. He was twice married: first, on November 8, 1913, to Priscilla Bradley Shepherd, by whom he had one son; second, on June 15, 1950, to Margaret Waller Freeman.

Who Was Who in America 3 (1960): 130; James Branch Cabell, *Branchiana* (Richmond, 1907), p. 71; Welford Dunaway Taylor, *Virginia Authors Past and Present* (Richmond, 1972), pp. 20–21; *VMHB* 70 (1962): 237.

BY DAVID SILVETTE. Signed. Dated 1934

Oil on canvas: 40 x 35 in. (101.6 x 88.9 cm.)

Presented in 1961 by the subject's widow, Margaret Waller (Freeman) Cabell (Mrs. James Branch Cabell) of Richmond. Por961.27

Helen Calvert, 1750–1833
See Helen (Calvert) Maxwell Read, 1750–1833

Louis Antoine Jean Baptiste, Chevalier de Cambray-Digny, 1751–1822

Born in Florence, Italy, on June 7, 1751, the subject became a cadet in the French Royal Artillery in 1770. He came to America with recommendations from Benjamin Franklin and the duc de la Rochefoucauld and joined Washington's army on September 10, 1777. Less than a year later he was commissioned a lieutenant colonel in the engineers; he took part in the battle of Monmouth and in 1778 was dispatched to the Ohio where he oversaw the construction of Fort MacIntosh. Ordered to the Southern Department, he proceeded by way of Baltimore and Edenton, North Carolina, to Savannah and later to Charleston, taking part in the sieges of both these cities. Captured at Charleston, on May 12, 1780, he was exchanged on November 26, 1782. Before his departure for France in the spring of 1783, he was promoted to colonel by special resolution of the United States Congress dated May 2, 1783. On his return to France he became a major in the provincial troops. He died in 1822 at his home, the château de Villers-aux-Erables, Somme. The chevalier de Cambray-Digny was an original member of the Society of the Cincinnati.

Portraits and Miniatures, pp. 47–48, 304 (original portrait reproduced); Ludovic Guy Marie du Bessey de Contenson, *La Société des Cincinnati de France et la guerre d'Amérique, 1778–1783* (Paris, 1934), p. 150; André Lasseray, *Les Français sous les treize étoiles* (Mâcon, 1935), pp. 139–40, 622, 648.

BY CHARLES WILLSON PEALE

Oil on canvas: 25½ x 21 in. (64.8 x 53.3 cm.)

Presented about 1854 by Catherine Power (Lyons) Chevallié (Mrs. Jean Auguste Marie Chevallié) of Richmond. Por857.5

This portrait, together with the portrait of the chevalier de la Luzerne (q.v.), was misidentified in the Society's 1894 list of portraits and again in Weddell's *Portraiture* (1945). Both sources identify the subject as Major General Henry Knox (1750–1806). The portrait is in fact a likeness of the chevalier de Cambray-Digny, a replica of the Charles Willson Peale portrait in the Independence Hall collection, Philadelphia. It is one of four Peale portraits (the others being the portraits of the chevalier de la Luzerne, Conrad Alexandre Gérard, and Martha Washington) presented to the Society by Mrs. J. A. M. Chevallié of Richmond and later, in 1858, authenticated by the artist's son Rembrandt Peale on his visit to Richmond as "having been in his father's collection."

A List of the Portraits, Engravings, &c., in the Library of the Virginia Historical Society (Richmond, 1894); *Portraiture*, pp. 54–55; VHS Mss1 R5685b 812.

Louis Antoine Jean Baptiste, chevalier de Cambray-Digny

Alexander Campbell, 1786–1866
See The Convention of 1829–30

Edward Campbell, born ca. 1785

See The Convention of 1829–30

William Campbell

See The Convention of 1829–30

Theodore Myers Carson, 1834–1902

Born on April 30, 1834, son of Judge Joseph F. Carson of Winchester, the subject graduated from Dickinson College, Carlisle, Pennsylvania, in 1852, and three years later received his master's degree from the same institution. Shortly after his graduation he entered the ministry of the Methodist Episcopal church, serving during the next years churches in Alexandria, Washington, and Baltimore. In 1860 he married Victoria Ellen Allison, daughter of William and Ann (Waters) Allison of Richmond, by whom he had two children. On the outbreak of the Civil War, Carson entered the Confederate army as chaplain of the 7th Virginia Regiment, remaining with the unit for three years. At the battle of Sayler's Creek he was made prisoner and placed in confinement in the old Capitol prison in Washington on the afternoon of the night Lincoln was assassinated. He was later transferred to Johnson's Island and shortly thereafter released. Entering the ministry of the Episcopal church, he served first in the Valley of Virginia and second at Orange Courthouse, whence on January 1, 1870, he was called to St. Paul's Church in Lynchburg, where he remained until his death more than thirty years later. His ministry was a distinguished one; he was president of the Standing Committee of the Diocese of Southern Virginia and dean of the Convocation of Southwest Virginia, and in 1897 Washington and Lee University conferred on him the honorary degree of Doctor of Divinity. He died, after two years of declining health, on September 23, 1902.

Biographic Catalogue; *Men of Mark in Virginia*, 4: 59–60; Rosa Faulkner Yancey, *Lynchburg and Its Neighbors* (Richmond, 1935), p. 284; *Southern Churchman* 67, no. 39 (Sept. 27, 1902): 6; Don Peters Halsey, *Historic and Heroic Lynchburg* (Lynchburg, Va., 1935), pp. 55–57.

By KATE MONTAGUE CARSON. Signed. Dated 1923

Oil on canvas: 48 x 36 in. (121.9 x 91.4 cm.)

Presented to the R. E. Lee Camp, Confederate Veterans, in 1923; acquired by the Virginia Historical Society in 1946 through merger with the Confederate Memorial Association. Por946.207

44

Robert ("King") Carter, 1663–1732

Called "King" Carter by reason of his enormous wealth and influence, the subject, son of John and Sarah (Ludlow) Carter, was born in 1663 at Corotoman, Lancaster County. He sat in the House of Burgesses 1691–92 and 1695–99, being twice chosen Speaker. Carter became a member of the colonial Council in 1699, retaining his seat until his death thirty-three years later, and serving as president of that body during the last six years of his life. He was treasurer of the colony 1699–1705, and for more than a year, from the death of Governor Drysdale until the arrival of Governor Gooch in 1727, he was acting governor. As agent for the proprietors of the Northern Neck 1702–11, and 1722–32, he was in a favorable position to increase his already considerable landholdings. He was rector and a member of the board of visitors of the College of William and Mary and builder of Christ Church, Lancaster County, where he and his wives are buried. On his death, which took place on August 4, 1732, he left over three hundred thousand acres of land and a thousand slaves. Carter was twice married: first, in 1688, to Judith Armistead (1665–1699); second, in 1701, to Elizabeth (Landon) Willis (1684–1719). By his two consorts Robert Carter had twelve children.

DAB; *Virginia Historical Portraiture*, p. 166; *Occasional Bulletin*, no. 28 (1974): 5; Louise Pecquet du Bellet, *Some Promi-*

Robert ("King") Carter

6. Robert Carter, 1728–1804

nent *Virginia Families* (Lynchburg, Va., 1907), 2: 198 (original? portrait reproduced); *VMHB* 82 (1974): 238.

COPIED BY MARIETTA MINNIGERODE ANDREWS. Ca.1900

Oil on canvas: 60 x 44 in. (152.4 x 111.8 cm.)

Received in 1973 as a bequest of Louise (Anderson) Patten (Mrs. Clarence Wesley Patten) of Winchester. Por973.15

The Society's portrait was copied from the portrait, now unlocated, that formerly hung at Oatlands, Loudoun County.

Robert Carter, 1728–1804

Robert Carter the Councillor was born in February 1728, son of Robert and Priscilla (Churchill) Carter and grandson of Robert ("King") Carter (q.v.). He attended the College of William and Mary, spent 1749–51 in England, and on his return married, on April 5, 1754, Frances Tasker, youngest daughter of Benjamin Tasker of Maryland. The couple resided at Nomini Hall, Westmoreland County; details of their domestic life are recorded in the journal of Philip Fithian, a young tutor who spent a year in the Carter household. In March 1758 he was appointed to the colonial Council, and three years later he took up residence in Williamsburg. With the waning influence of the Tidewater aristocracy and the Council that they controlled, Carter began to find public life less congenial; in 1771 he returned to Nomini Hall and thereafter rarely attended meetings of the Council. Opposed to separation from England, he nonetheless supported the American cause once independence was declared. After the Revolution, Carter devoted himself to his large estates, to the manufacture of iron and textiles, and to philosophical inquiry. Much given to religious speculation, he embraced successively Anglicanism, deism, the Baptist faith, Arminianism, and Swedenborgianism; opposed in principle to slavery, he freed over the years a large number of his slaves. Carter spent the final ten years of his life in Baltimore; he died in March 1804 and is buried in that city. His wife, who died in 1787, bore him twelve children.

Louis Morton, *Robert Carter of Nomini Hall* (Williamsburg, Va., 1941) (portrait reproduced as frontispiece); *Occasional Bulletin*, no. 28 (1974): 3 (portrait reproduced); *Encyclopedia of Virginia Biography*, 1: 160; *VMHB* 82 (1974): 238; *Antiques* 116 (1979): 1133 (portrait reproduced).

ATTRIBUTED TO THOMAS HUDSON. Ca.1750
See Plate 6

Oil on canvas: 50 x 40 in. (127 x 101.6 cm.)

Received in 1973 as a bequest of Louise (Anderson) Patten (Mrs. Clarence Wesley Patten) of Winchester. Por973.17

Thomas Henry Carter, 1831–1908

Born on June 13, 1831, at Pampatike, King William County, home of his parents Thomas Nelson Carter and Juliet (Gaines) Carter, the subject graduated from the Virginia Military Institute in 1849 and in preparation for a medical career attended the University of Virginia and the University of Pennsylvania. Graduating from the latter institution in 1852 with the degree of Doctor of Medicine, he spent a year in Blockley Hospital, Philadelphia, but gave up his profession to take charge of the Pampatike plantation. On November 7, 1855, he married Susan Elizabeth Roy, a daughter of William H. Roy and Anne (Seddon) Roy of Mathews County; of this marriage were born six children, two of whom died in infancy. At the beginning of the Civil War, Carter was made commander of the King William Artillery; rising from the rank of captain to colonel, he was placed in command of General Early's artillery in the Valley of Virginia. He took part in the battles of Seven Pines, the Seven Days, Sharpsburg, Fredericksburg, Chancellorsville, Gettysburg, and the Wilderness. Colonel Carter surrendered with Lee at Appomattox. From his farm in King William County he was called to become the first railroad commissioner of Virginia; thereafter he served the Southern Railway and Steamship Association both as arbitrator and commissioner for a period of sixteen years. In 1897 he was elected proctor of the University of Virginia, an office he held for eight years. He died at Romancoke, King William County, home of his son-in-law Captain Robert E. Lee (q.v.), on June 2, 1908.

Men of Mark in Virginia, 4: 61–62; Clarke County Historical Association, *Proceedings* 3 (1943): 40–42 (William Garl Brown portrait reproduced); *Biographic Catalogue*.

BY CORNELIUS HANKINS. Signed

Oil on canvas: 30 x 25 in. (76.2 x 63.5 cm.)

Presented to the R. E. Lee Camp, Confederate Veterans, in 1899 by the subject's son; acquired by the Virginia Historical Society in 1946 through merger with the Confederate Memorial Association. Por946.224

Although the Society's portrait depicts the subject in uniform, the facial likeness was probably taken from a portrait of the subject in civilian clothes painted by William Garl Brown.

Constance Cary, 1843–1920
See Burton Norvell Harrison, 1838–1904

Hetty Cary, 1871–1943
See Fairfax Harrison, 1869–1938

John Baytop Cary, 1819–1898

Colonel Cary was born in Hampton on October 18, 1819, eldest child of Gill Armistead Cary and Sally Elizabeth Smith (Baytop) Cary. After graduating from the College of William and Mary, a member of the class of 1839, he became principal of the Syms-Eaton School in Hampton, relinquishing the post in 1852 to establish Hampton Military Academy, where he served as headmaster until the beginning of the Civil War. Cary was appointed major of the Virginia Volunteers; for gallantry at the battle of Bethel he was promoted to lieutenant colonel of the 32d Virginia Regiment and afterwards was appointed assistant adjutant and inspector general of the Army of the Peninsula on the staff of General Magruder. Disabled, he was transferred to the pay department, where he served until Lee's surrender. Settling in Richmond after the war, he engaged in business as a general commission merchant and later as general agent of various life insurance companies. Colonel Cary was treasurer and superintendent of the Democratic City Committee and in 1886 was appointed superintendent of the city schools. In the latter position he was instrumental in securing for the Confederate Memorial Literary Society the former residence of Jefferson Davis, then used by the city as a public school. Other Confederate organizations in which he took an active interest were the Confederate Memorial Association, the Jefferson Davis Monument Association, and the Confederate reunion of 1896. He became a member of the Virginia Historical Society in 1896. Colonel Cary's death occurred on January 13, 1898; he was survived by his wife, Columbia H. (Hudgins) Cary, daughter of Thomas Hudgins of Gwynn's Island, Mathews County, by whom he had six children.

Biographic Catalogue; Confederate Military History, 3: 789–90; *Virginia and Virginians*, 2: 774–75; Fairfax Harrison, *The Virginia Carys: An Essay in Genealogy* (New York, 1919), pp. 73–75.

BY CORNELIUS HANKINS. Signed. Dated 1898

Oil on canvas: 30 x 25 in. (76.2 x 63.5 cm.)

Presented to the R. E. Lee Camp, Confederate Veterans, in 1898; acquired by the Virginia Historical Society in 1946 through merger with the Confederate Memorial Association. Por946.169

Virginia (Randolph) Cary, 1786–1852   (Mrs. Wilson Jefferson Cary)

Born on January 30, 1786, the subject was the youngest of thirteen children born to Thomas Mann Randolph of Tuckahoe, Goochland County, and his first wife, Anne (Cary) Randolph. After the death of her father in 1793 she resided at Edgehill, Albemarle County, the residence of her elder brother Thomas Mann Randolph II and Martha (Jefferson) Randolph, a daughter of President Thomas Jefferson. She married at Monticello, Albemarle County, on August 28, 1805, Wilson Jefferson Cary (1784–1823), son of Wilson and Jean Barbara (Carr) Cary. Cary studied law in Richmond, bore arms in the War of 1812, and in 1817 inherited Carysbrook, Fluvanna County, from his grandfather. He represented Fluvanna County in the Virginia House of Delegates 1821–23. After the death of her husband in 1823, Mrs. Cary turned to writing; her books, which enjoyed some success at the time, include *Letters on Female Character* (1828), *Christian Parent's Assistant* (1829), and two novels published anonymously, *Mutius* (1829) and *Ruth Churchill* (1851). She died in Alexandria on May 2, 1852. Of the nine children she bore her husband, two died in infancy; their son Archibald was the father of Constance (Cary) Harrison (q.v.).

Fairfax Harrison, *The Virginia Carys: An Essay in Genealogy* (New York, 1919), pp. 112–13; Jonathan Daniels, *The Randolphs of Virginia* (Garden City, N.Y., 1972), p. 214; Washington, D.C., *National Intelligencer* (tri-weekly), May 8, 1852; VHS Mss6:4 C2595:1; *VMHB* 45 (1937): 72 and 57 (1949): 206.

BY CHARLES CROMWELL INGHAM

Oil on canvas: 21 1/2 x 17 in. (54.6 x 43.2 cm.)

Presented in 1948 by Ursula (Harrison) Baird (Mrs. Charles Baird) of Markham, Virginia. Por948.4

Virginia (Randolph) Cary

George M. Cayce, d. 1886

Probably a native of Cumberland County, George M. Cayce joined the Confederate army in 1862 as a private; he was later promoted to captain in command of the Purcell Battery of Light Artillery. Captured at Petersburg on April 2, 1865, he was imprisoned at Johnson's Island and released the following July. He returned to Cumberland County. In 1881 he moved to Richmond where he became the manager of J. N. Boyd and Company, a firm dealing in leaf tobacco. He died in 1886. Two brothers, Milton Cayce and E. M. Cayce, also served in the Army of Northern Virginia.

Biographic Catalogue; Confederate Military History, 3: 798; Lee Alphonzo Wallace, *A Guide to Virginia Military Organizations, 1861–1865* (Richmond, 1964), p. 29; Hester Elizabeth Garrett, *A Book of Garretts, 1600 to 1960* (Lansing, Mich., 1963), pp. 340–53; Confederate Service Records, National Archives, microfilm roll 276; Richmond directories, 1881, 1882–83.

BY JOHN P. WALKER. Signed. Dated 1897

Oil on canvas: 30 x 25 in. (76.2 x 63.5 cm.)

Presented to the R. E. Lee Camp, Confederate Veterans, in 1897; acquired by the Virginia Historical Society in 1946 through merger with the Confederate Memorial Association. Por946.155

Edward R. Chambers, 1795–1872

Son of Edward and Martha (Cousins) Chambers of Flat Rock, Lunenburg County, the subject was born on May 23, 1795. He married on February 11, 1824, Lucy Goode Tucker, daughter of John and Agnes (Goode) Tucker of Brunswick County. The couple had twelve children; portraits of three of them are in the Society's collection: Henrietta Lucy Chambers, Rosa (Chambers) Goode, and Martha Eppes (Chambers) Laird (qq.v.). The family resided at Flat Rock until financial difficulties obliged them to leave the estate in 1829; they removed to Boydton where Chambers practiced law. In 1842, when Randolph-Macon College (then located in Boydton) opened a school of law, Chambers was appointed to the faculty. He was for many years Commonwealth's attorney for Mecklenburg County; he served as the county's representative in the State Constitutional Convention of 1850 and in the Secession Convention of 1861. In September 1865 he became judge of the circuit court, a post he held until March 1869, when he retired to resume the practice of law in partnership with his son-in-law Thomas Francis Goode. He died on March 20, 1872.

Rose Chambers Goode McCullough, *Yesterday When It Is Past* (Richmond, 1957), pp. 163–88, 201 (miniature reproduced opposite p. 166); George Brown Goode, *Virginia Cousins: A Study of the Ancestry and Posterity of John Goode of Whitby* (Richmond, 1887), p. 124; *VMHB* 83 (1975): 237.

ATTRIBUTED TO EDWARD SAMUEL DODGE

Miniature on ivory: 2¼ x 1¾ in. (5.7 x 4.5 cm.) (oval)

Presented in 1974 by Philip Briscoe Bateson of Dallas, Texas. Por974.14

Henrietta Lucy Chambers, 1826–1845

Eldest child of Edward R. Chambers (q.v.) and Lucy Goode (Tucker) Chambers of Flat Rock, Lunenburg County, the subject was born on January 18, 1826. She died, unmarried, nineteen years old, on August 27, 1845.

Rose Chambers Goode McCullough, *Yesterday When It Is Past* (Richmond, 1957), pp. 6–17 (cropped miniature reproduced opposite p. 5); *VMHB* 84 (1976): 239.

ATTRIBUTED TO EDWARD SAMUEL DODGE

Miniature on ivory: 2½ x 2 in. (6.4 x 5.1 cm.) (oval)

Presented in 1975 by Houston (Trippe) Bateson (Mrs. Philip Briscoe Bateson) of Dallas, Texas. Por975.26

Martha Eppes Chambers, 1830–1878
See Martha Eppes (Chambers) Laird, 1830–1878

Rosa Chambers, 1842–1921
See Rosa (Chambers) Goode, 1842–1921

John Randolph Chambliss, 1833–1864

Born at Hicksford (now Emporia), Greensville County, on January 23, 1833, eldest son of John Randolph Chambliss and Sarah (Blow) Chambliss, the subject graduated from West Point in 1853. As brevet second lieutenant he was on duty at the cavalry school in Carlisle, Pennsylvania, until he resigned from the army on March 4, 1854, to engage in agricultural pursuits in Greensville County. From 1856 to 1860 he was aide-de-camp on the staff of Governor Henry A. Wise (q.v.). At the outbreak of the Civil War, Chambliss was commissioned colonel of the 41st Virginia Infantry and stationed at Sewall's Point, where he remained until the evacuation of Norfolk. In August 1862 he assumed command of the 13th Virginia Cavalry with the rank of colonel; later he was commissioned brigadier general to rank from December 19, 1863. He served in the battles of Chancellorsville, Gettysburg, Spotsylvania, and Cold Harbor. On August 16, 1864, he was killed while leading a cavalry charge in the action at Deep Bottom, Virginia. He is buried in the family cemetery in Hicksford. His wife, whom he married on September 19, 1853, was Emaline Ann (Turner) Chambliss, daughter of Joseph A. Turner and Mary Peyton (Mason) Turner.

Generals in Gray; *Biographic Catalogue*; George Washington Cullum, *Biographical Register of the Officers and Graduates of the U.S. Military Academy at West Point, N.Y.* (New York, 1868), 2: 354; *National Cyclopedia*, 12: 274; Douglas Summers Brown, *Historical and Biographical Sketches of Greensville County, Virginia, 1650–1967* (Richmond, 1968), pp. 116–17.

BY JOHN P. WALKER. Signed. Dated 1899

Oil on canvas: 30 x 25 in. (76.2 x 63.5 cm.)

Presented to the R. E. Lee Camp, Confederate Veterans, in 1899 by the subject's widow and children and by the Chambliss-Barham Camp, Confederate Veterans; acquired by the Virginia Historical Society in 1946 through merger with the Confederate Memorial Association. Por946.143

Amélie Louise (Rives) Chanler, 1863–1945

See Amélie Louise (Rives) Chanler Troubetzkoy, 1863–1945

Henley Chapman, 1779–1864

See The Convention of 1829–30

Elisha Chase, 1790–1844

Born in Swansea, Massachusetts, on March 13, 1790, Elisha Chase was the son of Royal and Patience (Luther) Chase. He removed as a young man to Ocracoke, North Carolina. He married Theresa Howard, and in partnership with his father-in-law, William Howard, operated a shipping line under the firm name Howard and Chase. Elisha Chase died in Portland, Missouri, on July 3, 1844. The subject was the great-grandfather of the Society's friend and benefactor Virginia (Chase) Steedman Weddell (Mrs. Alexander Wilbourne Weddell) (q.v.).

VHS Mss, Mrs. J. A. Johnston Papers.

ARTIST UNIDENTIFIED

Miniature on ivory: 2¾ x 2¼ in. (7 x 5.7 cm.) (oval)

Received in 1948 as a bequest of Mr. and Mrs. Alexander Wilbourne Weddell of Richmond. Por948.30

Virginia Chase, 1874–1948

See Alexander Wilbourne Weddell, 1876–1948

Roger Preston Chew, 1843–1921

This brilliant Confederate artillery officer was born in Loudoun County on April 9, 1843, son of Roger and Sara West (Aldridge) Chew. Three years later the family removed to Jefferson County, now West Virginia, where they made their home at Hermitage Farm near Charles Town. Chew attended the Charles Town Academy, graduated from the Virginia Military Institute in 1861, and in September of that year raised a company of artillery which was attached first to Ashby's Brigade and later to Stuart's Horse Artillery. In 1864 he was assigned to General Hampton and served until the close of the war as chief of horse artillery with the rank of lieutenant colonel. After the war Colonel Chew returned to his farm. He married on August 5, 1871, Louisa Fontaine Washington, daughter of Colonel John Augustine Washington and Eleanor (Selden) Washington; they became the parents of six children. Elected to represent Jefferson County in the West Virginia legislature in 1883, he was three times reelected. Later he engaged in the real estate business, and under his guidance the Charles Town Mining, Manufacturing and Improvement Company developed what later became the town of Ranson. Colonel Chew played an active part in community affairs and in Confederate organizations until his death, which occurred on March 15, 1921.

Biographic Catalogue; *Confederate Veteran* 30 (1922): 149; J. E. Norris, *History of the Lower Shenandoah Valley Counties of Frederick, Berkeley, Jefferson, and Clarke* (Chicago, 1890), pp. 657–58; Millard Kessler Bushong, *Historic Jefferson County* (Boyce, Va., 1972), pp. 408–9; James Morton Callahan, *History of West Virginia Old and New* (Chicago, 1923), 2: 321–22.

BY JOHN P. WALKER. Signed. Dated 1926

Oil on canvas: 30 x 25 in. (76.2 x 63.5 cm.)

Presented to the R. E. Lee Camp, Confederate Veterans, in 1927; acquired by the Virginia Historical Society in 1946 through merger with the Confederate Memorial Association. Por946.166

Julia (Sully) Chichester, ca.1833–1863

See Julia Sully, ca.1833–1863

Catherine Mildred (Lee) Childe, 1811–1856   (Mrs. Edward Vernon Childe)

Daughter of Henry ("Light-Horse Harry") Lee and his second wife, Anne Hill (Carter) Lee, and sister of General Robert Edward Lee, C.S.A. (q.v.), Catherine Mildred Lee was born in Alexandria on February 27, 1811. She married in 1831 Edward Vernon Childe, a writer and political observer; the couple became the parents of four children. She spent the last fifteen years of her life with her family in Paris and died there in 1856.

Lee of Virginia, pp. 342–43; VHS Mss1 L51b 65. See chart on Lee Portraits for relationships.

ARTIST UNIDENTIFIED

Pastel on paper: 36 x 30 in. (91.4 x 76.2 cm.) (oval)

Received in 1949 from the heirs of Dr. George Bolling Lee. Por949.39

Elizabeth (Randolph) Chiswell, 1715–1776   (Mrs. John Chiswell)

Daughter of William Randolph II and Elizabeth (Beverley) Randolph (qq.v.), the subject was born on October 24, 1715. She married on May 19, 1736, John Chiswell, son of Charles and Esther Chiswell of Scotchtown, Hanover County. Chiswell represented Hanover County in the House of Burgesses 1742–55 and was a burgess from Williamsburg 1756–58. In 1766 Chiswell killed Robert Rutledge in a quarrel; while awaiting trial for the crime he committed suicide in Williamsburg on October 15, 1766. Mrs. Chiswell, by whom he had four daughters, died in 1776 at the residence of her son-in-law in Caroline County.

The Beverley Family, pp. 118–19; Virginia Genealogical Society, *Bulletin* 7 (1969): 77–83; Massachusetts Historical Society, *Proceedings* 76 (1964): 3–29; *VMHB* 25 (1917): 403; *The Randolphs* (portrait reproduced opposite p. 36). See chart on Randolph Portraits for relationships.

BY JOHN WOLLASTON

Oil on canvas: 36 x 29 in. (91.4 x 73.7 cm.)

Presented in 1927 by Kate Brander (Harris) Mayo Skipwith (Mrs. Grey Skipwith; formerly Mrs. Edward Carrington Mayo; subsequently Mrs. Berkeley Williams). Por927.15

George Llewellyn Christian, 1841–1924

Born at Balfours, Charles City County, on April 13, 1841, son of Edmund Thomas Christian and Tabitha Rebecca (Graves) Christian, the subject enlisted in the Richmond Howitzers at the beginning of the Civil War, taking part in all the engagements of that command until disabled by wounds. Rising to the rank of sergeant, Christian saw action at Yorktown, Seven Pines, Fredericksburg, Chancellorsville, Gettysburg, the Wilderness, and Spotsylvania; the loss of a foot in May 1864 rendered him unfit for further active duty. He enrolled in the University of Virginia law school, was admitted to the bar in 1867, and began a successful practice in Richmond. From 1878 until 1883 he served as judge of the Richmond Hustings Court, returning thereafter to private practice. He was active in the city's political and commercial life, serving as president of the city council 1876–78 and president of the Chamber of Commerce 1892–95; he was elected president of the National Bank of Virginia in 1893 and president of the Virginia State Insurance Company in 1902. Keenly interested in preserving the records of the Confederacy, Judge Christian was chairman of the history committee of the Grand Camp of Confederate Veterans and a member of the history committee of the United Confederate Veterans; he published a number of historical and biographical monographs; for nearly twenty years he was treasurer of the Confederate Memorial Association; and he was elected to membership in the Virginia Historical Society in 1893. Judge Christian was twice married; he married, first, on April 21, 1869, Ida Morris; he married, second, on November 23, 1881, his cousin Emma Christian, a

George Llewellyn Christian

49

daughter of William H. Christian of Richmond. On his death on July 26, 1924, he was survived by his wife and by four sons.

Biographic Catalogue; Men of Mark in Virginia, 5: 67–68; *Confederate Military History*, 3: 803–4; Virginia State Bar Association, *Proceedings* 36 (1924): 88–91.

BY EDITH LEESON EVERETT

Oil on canvas: 34 x 30 in. (86.4 x 76.2 cm.)

Presented to the R. E. Lee Camp, Confederate Veterans, in 1925; acquired by the Virginia Historical Society in 1946 through merger with the Confederate Memorial Association. Por946.223

Augustine Claiborne

See The Convention of 1829–30

Dorothea Claiborne, 1765–1844

See Dorothea (Claiborne) Tatum, 1765–1844

William Claiborne, ca. 1600–ca. 1677

Progenitor of the Claiborne family in Virginia, William Claiborne, councillor, secretary, and treasurer of the Virginia colony, was born around 1600, second son of Thomas and Sarah (Smith) James Claiborne of Crayford, Kent, England. On June 13, 1621, he was appointed surveyor of the colony by the Virginia Company of London; he arrived at Jamestown in October 1621, and one of his early tasks was laying out the area of Jamestown Island known as New Towne. He was appointed to the colonial Council in 1623; he was secretary of the colony 1625–37, 1652–60 and treasurer of the colony 1642–60. In recognition of his services against the Indians he received large land grants and a license to trade with the Indians along the shores of the Chesapeake; in 1631 he established his principal trading post on Kent Island, near the present city of Annapolis, Maryland. The following year the part of Virginia lying north of the Potomac River was granted to Lord Baltimore; thereafter, for six years, Claiborne and Baltimore struggled for control of the island; it was awarded to Baltimore by the Commissioners of Plantations in 1638. As a supporter of the Puritan Protectorate in England, Claiborne was appointed in 1652 to a commission to secure the allegiance of Virginia and Maryland to the new regime. After the restoration of the Stuarts in 1660, he devoted himself increasingly to agricultural pursuits, having previously removed from Elizabeth City County to Romancoke, King William County. During Bacon's Rebellion in 1676 he sided with the government; he

died shortly afterward, probably about 1677. His wife, whom he married about 1635, was Elizabeth (Butler) Claiborne, daughter of John and Jane (Elliott) Butler; the couple had five children.

DAB; Encyclopedia of Virginia Biography, 1: 96–97; Nathaniel Claiborne Hale, *Virginia Venturer: A Historical Biography of William Claiborne, 1600–1677* (Richmond, 1951); John Herbert Claiborne, *William Claiborne of Virginia, with Some Account of His Pedigree* (New York, 1917); Annie Lash Jester, *Adventurers of Purse and Person, 1607–1625* (Princeton, N.J., 1956), pp. 131–33; *Portraits and Statuary*, p. 24.

COPIED BY MARY R. GILMER

Pastel on canvas: 20 x 16 in. (50.8 x 40.6 cm.)

Presented by the artist before 1945. Por945.18

Mary Gilmer also painted a full-length portrait of Claiborne which is owned by the Commonwealth of Virginia. The Society's portrait appears to be based on a painting reproduced as the frontispiece to John Herbert Claiborne's *William Claiborne of Virginia*.

Elijah Lewis Clarke, 1836–1916

Born on May 15, 1836, at Charlotte Courthouse, the subject attended Randolph-Macon College. On July 18, 1861, he enlisted as a private in the Charlotte Greys, later designated Company I, 56th Virginia Infantry. He subsequently fought with the Goochland Light Artillery and was captured at Fort Harrison on September 30, 1864. After some months of imprisonment at Point Lookout, Maryland, he was exchanged. After the war he taught in various public and private schools in Virginia. In his last years he served as an elder in the Franklin Street Presbyterian Church in Danville. He died in Danville during the winter of 1916. Clarke's wife, Patty (Cook) Clarke, daughter of John Cook, bore him two sons and three daughters.

Biographic Catalogue; CMA Archives, folio Z1n.

BY CARL DAME CLARKE. Signed

Oil on canvas: 30 x 24 in. (76.2 x 61 cm.)

Presented to the R. E. Lee Camp, Confederate Veterans, in 1925; acquired by the Virginia Historical Society in 1946 through merger with the Confederate Memorial Association. Por946.193

The artist was a grandson of the subject.

Elizabeth Iris Southall Clarke, 1871–1958

See Douglas Huntly Gordon, 1866–1918

Henry Clay, 1777–1852

A native of Virginia, Henry Clay was born in Hanover County on April 12, 1777, son of John and Elizabeth (Hudson) Clay. After keeping store for a year in Richmond he became clerk of Virginia's High Court of Chancery, amanuensis to Chancellor George Wythe (q.v.), and in 1796 began the study of law in the office of Attorney General Robert Brooke. He removed to Kentucky in 1797 and thereafter was closely associated with that state. He sat in the United States Congress both as a representative and as a senator in numerous sessions from 1806 until the time of his death, serving on various occasions as Speaker of the House. Clay was one of the "war hawks" who led the country into the War of 1812 and one of the commissioners who negotiated the treaty of peace with Great Britain in 1814. He succeeded in making the Missouri Compromise effective in 1821, was secretary of state under John Quincy Adams 1825–29, advocated rechartering the Second United States Bank, led the anti-Jacksonians, resolved the nullification controversy in 1833, and secured the Compromise of 1850 in an attempt to avert secession by the southern states and to save the Union. He was an unsuccessful candidate in the presidential elections of 1824, 1832, and 1844. Clay, the "Great Compromiser," who with Webster and Calhoun dominated the American legislature during the period, died in Washington on June 29, 1852. His wife, whom he married in 1799, was Lucretia (Hart) Clay, by whom he had eleven children; all six of his daughters and one of his sons predeceased him. He was elected to honorary membership in the Virginia Historical Society in 1847.

DAB; Biographical Directory; Richmond Portraits.

By C. Younglove Haynes. 1850

"Promatheotype" bas-relief: 28 x 23 in. (71.1 x 58.4 cm.)

Source unknown. Por958.26

In a cartouche below the portrait: "Designed and promatheotyped by C. Younglove Haynes of Philada. from a spirited daguerreotype taken expressly for the work, by England & Gunn, sanctioned by the signature of its great prototype, the venerated sage of Ashland, Hon. Henry Clay. Design Patented Nov: 12th, 1850." The entry for Haynes in the *Dictionary of Artists in America* refers to the bas-relief portrait of Clay.

George C. Groce and David H. Wallace, *The New-York Historical Society's Dictionary of Artists in America, 1564–1860* (New Haven, 1957), p. 302.

Samuel Claytor

See The Convention of 1829–30

John Bacon Clopton, 1789–1860

See The Convention of 1829–30

Gordon Cloyd, 1771–1833

See The Convention of 1829–30

John Coalter, 1769–1838

See The Convention of 1829–30

Sallie Browne Cocke, 1840–1909

See Sallie Browne (Cocke) Wilson, 1840–1909

Samuel Coffman

See The Convention of 1829–30

Frances Fielding (Lewis) Taylor Coke, ca.1802–ca.1846

See Frances Fielding (Lewis) Taylor, ca.1802–ca.1846

Sarah Coles, 1789–1848

See Andrew Stevenson, 1784–1857

Elizabeth Collins, 1768?–1858

See Richard Bland Lee, 1761–1827

Elizabeth (Marshall) Colston, 1756–1842   (Mrs. Rawleigh Colston)

Eldest daughter of Colonel Thomas Marshall and Mary Randolph (Keith) Marshall and sister of Chief Justice John Marshall (q.v.), the subject was born near Germantown, Fauquier County, in 1756. She received her education from her father, and she in turn became the teacher of her younger brothers and sisters. On October 15, 1785, she married Rawleigh Colston (1747–1823), son of Travers and Susanna (Opie) Kenner Colston. Her husband, who had received legal training under George Wythe and had been a commercial agent in Santo Domingo during the Revolution, took his bride to Frederick County, where for some years he engaged in agricultural pursuits; in 1801 the family removed to Honeywood, Berkeley County, (West) Virginia. After the death of her husband in 1823, Mrs. Colston remained at Honeywood until her death in 1842. She bore her husband seven children.

William McClung Paxton, *The Marshall Family* (Cincinnati, 1885), pp. 45–46; *VMHB* 25 (1917): 281 and 78 (1970): 239.

Elizabeth (Marshall) Colston

ARTIST UNIDENTIFIED

Oil on canvas: 29 x 24¼ in. (73.7 x 62.2 cm.)

Presented in 1969 by Sally (Colston) Mitchell (Mrs. Mark L. Mitchell) of Cincinnati. Por969.17

The portrait was presented to the Society as a likeness of Sarah Jane (Brockenbrough) Colston b.1804 (Mrs. Edward Colston) and was so designated in the Society's annual report for 1970. Shortly thereafter, its similarity to a portrait firmly identified as Sarah Jane's mother-in-law, Elizabeth (Marshall) Colston (1756–1842) (Mrs. Rawleigh Colston), owned by the Association for the Preservation of Virginia Antiquities, John Marshall House collection, was noted. This led in due course to its reidentification. The triangular corner of a red chair is visible on the right; a similar detail is found in the Society's portrait of Reade Macon Washington (q.v.)

James Conner, 1829–1883

Son of Henry Workman Conner and Juliana (Courtney) Conner, the subject was born in Charleston, South Carolina, on September 1, 1829. He attended South Carolina College, graduating in 1849, and, having chosen to enter the legal profession, was admitted to the bar in 1851. As United States district attorney, to which office he was appointed in 1856, he prosecuted the celebrated case of the slave ship *Echo*; he resigned the office in December 1860. Entering the Confederate service as captain in the Washington Light Infantry, later part of Hampton's Legion, Conner was present at First Manassas. Soon afterwards he was promoted to major and then became colonel of the 22d North Carolina Infantry, which command he kept until his promotion to brigadier general on June 1, 1864. In August 1864 he assumed command of Kershaw's Brigade, but the loss of a leg at Cedar Creek two months later terminated his active service. Returning to South Carolina after the war, he resumed the practice of law, became solicitor for the South Carolina Railroad, receiver for the Greenville and Columbia Railroad Company, and, on a more domestic note, took to himself a wife in 1866, Sallie Enders. General Conner was elected attorney general of South Carolina in 1876, his principal assignment being to establish the legality of the election of General Wade Hampton (q.v.) as governor of the state. This accomplished, and his health failing, he resigned in December 1877. General Conner died in Richmond on June 26, 1883, and is buried in Charleston, South Carolina.

DAB; *Generals in Gray*; *Biographic Catalogue.*

BY WILLIAM HASKELL COFFIN. Signed

Oil on canvas: 30 x 25 in. (76.2 x 63.5 cm.)

Acquired in 1946 through merger with the Confederate Memorial Association. Por946.69

Daniel Conrad, 1771–1806
Rebecca (Holmes) Conrad, 1779–1835   (Mrs. Daniel Conrad)

Dr. Daniel Conrad, son of Frederick and Marie Clara (Ley) Conrad of Winchester, was born on October 6, 1771. He reputedly studied medicine in Edinburgh. He established himself in Winchester as a physician and surgeon but died there "at an early period in his professional career" on September 14, 1806. His wife, Rebecca (Holmes) Conrad, daughter of Joseph and Rebecca (Hunter) Holmes, bore him four children, but only two, David Holmes Conrad and Robert Young Conrad (qq.v.), lived to maturity.

History of Virginia, 5: 95; J. E. Norris, *History of the Lower Shenandoah Valley* (Chicago, 1890), pp. 571–72; *Alexandria Advertiser*, Oct. 4, 1806; Winchester–Frederick County Historical Society, *Publications* 1 (1931): 195, 203–4, and 5 (1960): 54.

ARTIST UNIDENTIFIED

Hollow-cut silhouette: 3¼ in. (8.3 cm.) in height, on paper 5½ x 6½ in. (14 x 16.5 cm.)

Received in 1945 in a collection of Conrad family papers presented by Augusta Forman Conrad and Carter Bryan Conrad, both of Winchester, and Bryan Conrad of Richmond. Por945.19

This double silhouette is thought to be a modern copy. The silhouettes of the subjects' sons, David Holmes Conrad and Robert Young Conrad (qq.v.), received at the same time and apparently the work of the same copyist, are on paper bearing a "Hammermill Bond" watermark.

David Holmes Conrad, 1800–1877

Born on January 15, 1800, David Holmes Conrad was the son of Daniel and Rebecca (Holmes) Conrad (qq.v.) of Winchester and the brother of Robert Young Conrad (q.v.). He attended Winchester Academy, studied law, and was admitted to the bar. In 1821 he removed to Martinsburg, (West) Virginia, where he practiced his profession, took a prominent part in the affairs of the Episcopal church, and wrote a *Memoir of Rev. James Chisholm* (1856). His wife was Nancy Addison (Carr) Conrad, daughter of Judge Dabney Carr of the Virginia Supreme Court of Appeals. The couple had children; two sons were killed almost simultaneously at the first battle of Manassas. David Holmes Conrad died in 1877.

J. E. Norris, *History of the Lower Shenandoah Valley* (Chicago, 1890), pp. 571–72; Winchester–Frederick County Historical Society, *Publications* 1 (1931): 169–232; *VMHB* 2 (1894–5): 224.

Portrait note: *see* Robert Young Conrad, 1805–1875 (Portrait II)

Robert Young Conrad, 1805–1875

Son of Daniel and Rebecca (Holmes) Conrad (qq.v.) of Winchester and brother of David Holmes Conrad (q.v.), the subject was born on December 5, 1805. He attended but did not graduate from the United States Military Academy, studied law, and began the practice of his profession in Winchester. Active in the affairs of the Whig party, he was a member of the Virginia state Senate 1840–44 and in 1861 was elected to the Secession Convention. Although he voted against secession, he later signed the ordinance.

He remained in Winchester throughout the Civil War. In 1865 he was elected to the United States House of Representataives but was denied admission. Thereafter he continued the practice of law in Winchester until his death, which occurred on May 5, 1875. By his wife, Elizabeth Whiting (Powell) Conrad, daughter of Burr and Catharine (Brooke) Powell of Loudoun County, he had nine children.

History of Virginia, 5: 95–96; J. E. Norris, *History of the Lower Shenandoah Valley* (Chicago, 1890), pp. 571–72; William Harris Gaines, *Biographical Register of Members, Virginia State Convention of 1861* (Richmond, 1969), pp. 28–29; Silas Emmett Lucas, *The Powell Families of Virginia and the South* (Vidalia, Va., 1969), p. 326.

Portrait I

ARTIST UNIDENTIFIED

Hollow-cut silhouette: 8½ in. (21.6 cm.) in height, on paper 10½ x 5½ in. (26.7 x 14 cm.)

Received in 1945 in a collection of Conrad family papers presented by Augusta Forman Conrad and Carter Bryan Conrad, both of Winchester, and Bryan Conrad of Richmond. Por945.20

Portrait II. Robert Young Conrad and David Holmes Conrad

ARTIST UNIDENTIFIED

Hollow-cut silhouette: 3 in. (7.6 cm.) in height, on paper 5½ x 6½ in. (14 x 16.5 cm.). Details in pencil.

Received in 1945 in a collection of Conrad family papers presented by Augusta Forman Conrad and Carter Bryan Conrad, both of Winchester, and Bryan Conrad of Richmond. Por945.21

Portrait I is a full-length silhouette; Portrait II is a bust-length silhouette. Robert Young Conrad is the right-hand figure in this double portrait (the other likeness being that of the subject's brother, David Holmes Conrad). On the basis of the watermarked paper, both portraits are thought to be modern copies of early silhouettes.

Elizabeth (Fitzhugh) Conway, 1754–1823   (Mrs. Francis Conway)

Born in Stafford County on October 10, 1754, the fifth child of John and Alice (Thornton) Fitzhugh of Bellair, Stafford County, the subject married, first, on March 20, 1770, Francis Conway of Mount Sion, Caroline County, by whom she had ten children. Her husband, a member of the King George County Committee of Safety 1774–76, served in the Continental Line during the Revolutionary War; in 1784 he established the town of Port Conway in King George County. After Conway's death in 1794 his widow married James Taylor, son of James and

Alice (Thornton) Taylor of Orange County. Elizabeth (Fitzhugh) Conway Taylor died on February 21, 1823.

Overwharton Parish, p. 230; *Virginia Genealogies*, pp. 263–64; *Occasional Bulletin*, no. 10 (1965): 10–12 (portrait reproduced); *VMHB* 7 (1899–1900): 426–27 and 63 (1955): 229. See chart on Fitzhugh, Knox, and Gordon Portraits for relationships.

Elizabeth (Fitzhugh) Conway

By John Hesselius. Ca.1770

Oil on canvas: 30¼ x 25¼ in. (76.8 x 64.1 cm.)

Received in 1954 as a bequest of Mrs. Elizabeth C. Lewis of Louisville, Kentucky. Por954.1

Hayden's *Virginia Genealogies* (p. 264) states that "a full length portrait of Mrs. C. at the age of 18, and a miniature in old age, is owned by Mrs. F. S. Conway, Smithfield, Va." The Society's portrait is thought to have been painted about the time of the subject's first marriage.

Giles Buckner Cooke, 1838–1937

Born in Portsmouth on May 13, 1838, son of John Kearns Cooke and Fannie Bracken (New) Cooke, the subject graduated from the Virginia Military Institute in 1859 and began the study of law in Petersburg under the tutelage of Roger Pryor. On the day Virginia seceded from the Union, Cooke enlisted in the state forces at Norfolk; the next day he took part in the capture of ammunition at the Norfolk Navy Yard, conveyed it to Richmond, and then

was appointed first lieutenant and aide-de-camp to General Philip St. George Cocke. In January 1862 he was transferred to General Beauregard's staff, serving until October 8, 1864, when he became assistant adjutant and inspector general on Robert E. Lee's staff, with the rank of major; in this capacity he served to the end of the war. After Appomattox, Cooke repaired to Petersburg where he and Dr. Thomas Hume opened a preparatory school; after several years he left this school and, being concerned for the educational needs of the newly emancipated blacks, opened a Negro day school. Throughout his years of school teaching Major Cooke studied for the ministry; he was ordained deacon in the Protestant Episcopal church in 1871 and priest in 1874 and was called to be rector of St. Stephen's Church, Petersburg, in 1873. About this time he added a theological department to his day school. Known as the Bishop Payne Divinity School, it was during the years of its existence the only theological school for blacks in the Protestant Episcopal church. Retiring from parochial work in 1917, he removed to Mathews Courthouse where he resided until his death, which occurred on February 4, 1937, little more than three months short of his ninety-ninth birthday. Major Cooke was twice married; first, on October 19, 1870, to Martha Frances (Mallory) Southall, daughter of Francis Mallory of Hampton; second, on April 27, 1893, to Sarah Katharine Grosh, daughter of Warren Rinehart Grosh of Cecil County, Maryland, by whom he had three children.

Tyler's Quart. 19 (1937–38): 1–6; CMA Archives, folio Z1n; *Biographic Catalogue.*

By Cherry Ford White

Oil on canvas: 40 x 30 in. (101.6 x 76.2 cm.)

Presented to the R. E. Lee Camp, Confederate Veterans, in 1924; acquired by the Virginia Historical Society in 1946 through merger with the Confederate Memorial Association. Por946.195

John Rogers Cooke, 1788–1854
Maria (Pendleton) Cooke, d.1850 (Mrs. John Rogers Cooke)

Born in Bermuda on June 17, 1788, the third child of Dr. Stephen Cooke and Catherine (Esten) Cooke, John Rogers Cooke accompanied his parents in 1791 to Alexandria, and later to Leesburg. During the Chesapeake Affair in 1807 he held a commission in the Frederick Troop, and in 1812 he participated in the defense of the coast. After studying law he was admitted to the bar and began the practice of his profession at Martinsburg, (West) Virginia. Here he married on November 18, 1813, Maria Pendleton,

8. Maria (Pendleton) Cooke

7. John Rogers Cooke, 1788–1854

daughter of Philip and Agnes (Patterson) Pendleton and great-niece of Edmund Pendleton (q.v.). The couple removed to Winchester where they remained for twenty-five years, and Cooke became one of the most prominent lawyers in the region. Although he had previously served only one term, 1814–15, in the Virginia legislature, he was elected to represent Frederick and Jefferson counties in the Virginia Constitutional Convention of 1829; as one of the chief spokesmen of the western party, he distinguished himself for his oratory and served with John Marshall and James Madison on a select committee of seven to draw up a compromise constitution. His part in the convention enhanced his already excellent reputation in legal circles. In 1840 he removed to Richmond where for the remainder of his life he practiced his profession, chiefly before the superior and appellate courts. He died on December 15, 1854; his wife had died on March 12, 1850. The couple had thirteen children, one of whom was the novelist John Esten Cooke and another of whom, Sallie Dandridge (Cooke) DuVal (q.v.), is represented in the Society's portrait collection.

DAB; *Seldens of Virginia*, 2: 267; *VMHB* 40 (1932): 386 and 57 (1949): 207; VHS Mss5:1 C7754:1 (this manuscript, Cooke's diary, bears on the back a notation indicating that Cooke was born on June 17, 1786; other sources give 1788 as the correct date); *Antiques* 116 (1979): 1135 (Portrait I and Portrait II reproduced).

Portrait I. John Rogers Cooke   *See* Plate 7

By CEPHAS THOMPSON. Ca. 1810

Oil on canvas: 27 $^3/_4$ x 22$^3/_4$ in. (70.5 x 57.8 cm.)

Presented in 1948 by Edmund Pendleton Randolph Duval of Norman, Oklahoma, a grandson of the subject. Por948.18a

Portrait II. Maria (Pendleton) Cooke   *See* Plate 8

By CEPHAS THOMPSON. Ca. 1810

Oil on canvas: 27$^3/_4$ x 22$^3/_4$ in. (70.5 x 57.8 cm.)

Presented in 1948 by Edmund Pendleton Randolph Duval of Norman, Oklahoma, a grandson of the subject. Por948.18b

"John Cooke Esqr" appears in Cephas Thompson's sitter's book under "A List of names of those who engage there Portraits in Richmond." Mrs. Cooke's name does not appear. Although the scenic background in Mrs. Cooke's portrait is not characteristic of Thompson's Virginia portraits, there is little doubt that it is Thompson's work.

VHS Mss7:1 T3723:1 (typescript).

Portrait III. John Rogers Cooke
See The Convention of 1829–30

John Rogers Cooke, 1833–1891

John Rogers Cooke was born to a soldier's heritage at Jefferson Barracks, Missouri, June 9, 1833, the son of General Philip St. George Cooke of Virginia and Rachel (Hertzog) Cooke. He was educated at Harvard University for the profession of civil engineer, then entered the United States Army as a second lieutenant in 1855. When Virginia seceded, Cooke and his brother-in-law, J. E. B. Stuart (q.v.), offered their services to the South; his father remained loyal to the Union. Assigned to General Holmes's staff, Cooke participated in the first battle of Manassas, raised a company of light artillery, and saw action in the campaigns in Pennsylvania, Virginia, and Maryland. In April 1862 he became colonel of the 27th North Carolina Infantry; the following November, after the battle of Sharpsburg, he was promoted to brigadier general, with which rank he served until the surrender. Struck by a bullet just over the left eye at the battle of Fredericksburg, he sustained what Heros von Borcke described as "the most beautiful wound I ever saw"; on no less than six other occasions he was wounded in action. General Cooke married on January 5, 1864, Nannie Gordon Patton, daughter of Dr. William Fairlie Patton of Norfolk. After the war he settled in Richmond, engaging in various mercantile endeavors and devoting himself to such organizations as the R. E. Lee Camp of Confederate Veterans, the Soldiers' Home, and the Southern Historical Society. Survived by his wife and eight children, General Cooke died on April 10, 1891; he is buried in Hollywood Cemetery.

Generals in Gray (which cites, p. 370, family authority for June 9 birth date); *SHS Papers* 18 (1890): 322–27 (which gives June 10 as Cooke's birth date); *Virginia and Virginians*, 2: 777–78; *Biographic Catalogue*.

By JOHN P. WALKER. Signed. Dated 1891

Oil on canvas: 48 x 36 in. (121.9 x 91.4 cm.)

Acquired in 1946 through merger with the Confederate Memorial Association. Por946.209

Sallie Dandridge Cooke, 1828–1887
See Robert Randolph DuVal, 1817–1875

William Wilson Corcoran, 1798–1888

Banker, philanthropist, and officer of the Virginia Historical Society, Corcoran was born on December 27, 1798, the son of Thomas and Hannah (Lemmon) Corcoran of Baltimore. After attending private schools and one year of college, he entered the dry goods business in Georgetown, D.C.; the business failed in 1823. From 1828 to 1836 he was associated with the Bank of the United States and the Bank of Columbia; in 1837 he opened a brokerage business and three years later formed Corcoran and Riggs, a banking firm which became enormously successful. He retired from active business in 1854, devoting himself thereafter to educational and philanthropic interests, which included the Corcoran Gallery of Art, the University of Virginia, the College of William and Mary, the Virginia Military Institute, Washington and Lee University, the Virginia Historical Society, the Episcopal Theological Seminary in Virginia, the Southern Historical Society, the Protestant Orphan Asylum in Washington, and the Louise Home for elderly women. His sympathy with the Confederate cause, reflected in his numerous southern benefactions, obliged him to reside in Europe during the Civil War. At the time of his death, which occurred on February 24, 1888, it was estimated that he had contributed more than five million dollars to charitable causes. His wife, whom he married in 1835, was Louise Amory (Morris) Corcoran; the couple had one daughter. Corcoran became a member of the Virginia Historical Society in 1870 and a vice-president of the Society in 1881.

DAB; Corcoran Gallery of Art, *Corcoran* (Washington, D.C., 1976).

ARTIST UNIDENTIFIED

Oil on canvas: 30 x 25 in. (76.2 x 63.5 cm.) (framed as an oval)

Received in 1946. Por946.32

Montgomery Dent Corse, 1816–1895

A lifelong resident of Alexandria, the subject was the son of John Corse, editor of the *Alexandria Herald*, and Julia (Granville) Corse. Born on March 14, 1816, he attended military school, took part in the Mexican War as captain of the 1st Regiment of Virginia Volunteers, joined the great emigration to California in 1849, and remained there seven years during which time he worked variously as a miner, merchant, steamboat agent, customs officer, and hotel proprietor. Banking claimed his attention on his return to Alexandria in 1856. In 1860 he organized a volunteer rifle company, the Old Dominion Rifles, which became, on the outbreak of hostilities the next year, a part of the 17th Virginia Infantry. As colonel of the unit, Corse took part in the battles of First Manassas, Yorktown, Williamsburg, Seven Pines, and the Seven Days. Promoted to brigadier general on November 1, 1862, he took command of a brigade in Pickett's Division, serving in Tennessee, North Carolina, and the sieges of Petersburg and Richmond. Taken pris-

oner at Sayler's Creek, April 6, 1865, General Corse was held at Fort Warren in Boston harbor until August, then returned to his family in Alexandria and again became associated with the banking interests of the city. Failing eyesight and eventual blindness afflicted his latter years. He died on February 11, 1895, just a few weeks after the death of his wife, Elizabeth (Beverley) Corse, daughter of James Bradshaw Beverley and Jane (Peter) Beverley, whom he married in Alexandria on November 22, 1862, and by whom he had four children.

Generals in Gray; *The Beverley Family*, pp. 552–53, 565–66; *Eminent and Representative Men*, pp. 429–31; *Biographic Catalogue*.

BY JOHN P. WALKER. Signed. Dated 1899

Oil on canvas: 30 x 25 in. (76.2 x 63.5 cm.)

Presented to the R. E. Lee Camp, Confederate Veterans, in 1899; acquired by the Virginia Historical Society in 1946 through merger with the Confederate Memorial Association. Por946.97

Edwin Cox, 1902–1977

Chemist, soldier, and president of the Virginia Historical Society, Edwin Cox was born in Richmond on September 20, 1902, son of Judge Edwin Piper Cox and Sallie Bland (Clarke) Cox. He graduated from the Virginia Military Institute, receiving degrees in chemistry and chemical engineering. On May 19, 1927, he married Virginia Bagby DeMott of Lynchburg, daughter of Charles Leonard DeMott and Kate Jeter (Hatcher) DeMott; they became the parents of one son. He was associated with the Virginia-Carolina Chemical Corporation, 1920–57, part of the time as its vice-president; he was also president of the Commonwealth Laboratory and of the Tobacco By-Products Chemical Corporation. Long active in the Virginia National Guard, he served with distinction throughout the Second World War, commanded the 176th Infantry Regiment, and in 1944 was assigned to the War Department General Staff, on the Joint Chiefs of Staff secretariat. Later he was assigned to the General Staff of SHAEF in France and Germany; he retired with the rank of brigadier general. General Cox belonged to numerous professional organizations and hereditary societies and was active in the work of the Protestant Episcopal church and in the Democratic party; he was personal aide to five governors of Virginia 1926–50. Keenly interested in state and local history, he sat on the boards of the Valentine Museum, the Virginia State Library, and the Association for the Preservation of Virginia Antiquities; he was elected to the executive committee of the Virginia Historical Society in 1964 and became the Society's twenty-second president in 1972. He resided at Holly Hill, near Aylett. General Cox died on February 22, 1977.

Richard Lee Morton, *Virginia Lives* (Hopkinsville, Ky., 1964), pp. 217–18.

Edwin Cox

By CARROLL N. JONES

Oil on canvas: 30 x 36 in. (76.2 x 91.4 cm.)

Purchased in 1977 with funds contributed by friends of the subject. Por977.17

William Ruffin Cox, 1832–1919

General William Ruffin Cox, Confederate general and politician, was born at Scotland Neck, North Carolina, on March 11, 1832, the son of Thomas and Olivia (Norfleet) Cox. On the death of his father, he and his mother moved to Nashville, Tennessee, where he pursued his academic and legal education, graduating from Franklin College in 1851 and Lebanon College law school two years later. After practicing his profession in Nashville, he returned to North Carolina in 1857, married Penelope Battle of Edgecombe County, and turned his attention to agriculture. Early in the Civil War he joined the Confederate army as major of the 2d North Carolina Infantry, serving with the Army of Northern Virginia for the next four years. Promoted to brigadier general after his outstanding conduct at Spotsylvania Court House, Cox led his brigade through the campaigns of the Shenandoah Valley and Petersburg, finally being paroled with his troops at Appomattox. At the war's end General Cox resumed his legal career and embarked on a political one. He became solicitor of the sixth district in 1866, delegate to the Democratic National Convention in 1868, judge of the superior court for the sixth district in 1877, and chairman of the Democratic State Committee in 1875. Elected to the United States Congress, he served 1881–87, be-

coming in 1893 secretary of the Senate, an office he held until 1900. His withdrawal from political life enabled him to devote himself more fully to other interests: the councils of the Protestant Episcopal church, the North Carolina State Agricultural Society, the Masonic order, and the University of the South at Sewanee. In 1883 he married Fannie Augusta Lyman, who bore him two sons, and in 1905 he married Catherine Hamilton (Cabell) Claiborne of Richmond. He died in Richmond on December 26, 1919, and is buried in Oakwood Cemetery, Raleigh, North Carolina.

DAB; *Generals in Gray*; *Biographic Catalogue*; *Biographical Directory*.

ARTIST UNIDENTIFIED

Oil on canvas: 57 x 38½ in. (144.8 x 97.8 cm.)

Acquired in 1946 through merger with the Confederate Memorial Association. Por946.220

Hannah Crane, 1757–1830
See Hannah (Crane) Gifford, 1757–1830

Joshua Skinner Creecy, 1788–1817

A resident of Chowan County, North Carolina, the subject was born there in 1788, the son of Lemuel and Penelope (Skinner) Creecy. He married on October 3, 1807, Mary Benbury, daughter of Richard and Penelope (Creecy) Benbury of Benbury Hall, near Edenton, North Carolina; two sons and two daughters were born to the couple. Their daughter Penelope Margaret (Creecy) Wright (Mrs. David Minton Wright) (q.v.) is represented in the Society's portrait collection. Joshua Skinner Creecy died on February 21, 1817, aged twenty-nine.

Virginia Armistead Garber, *The Armistead Family, 1635–1910* (Richmond, 1910), p. 249; VHS Mss, Mrs. J. A. Johnston Papers.

ARTIST UNIDENTIFIED

Miniature on ivory: 2¼ x 1¾ in. (5.7 x 4.5 cm.) (oval)

Received in 1948 as a bequest of Mr. and Mrs. Alexander Wilbourne Weddell of Richmond. Por948.29

Penelope Margaret Creecy, 1816–1889
See David Minton Wright, 1809–1863

Sarah Ann Cruft, 1771–1849

See John William Ware Godbold, 1760–1842

John Jeter Crutchfield, 1844–1920

Justice John, as he was known in his native Richmond and elsewhere, was born on September 20, 1844, son of George Knox Crutchfield and Ann (Clark) Crutchfield. As a private in the 4th Virginia Cavalry he served with the Army of Northern Virginia throughout the war and participated in the majority of its engagements. After the war he embarked on a business career as deputy clerk and weighmaster of the Second Market. In 1870 he was appointed a justice of the peace for Monroe ward and two years later became senior justice, which office he held until July 1, 1880, when poor health obliged him to relinquish it. After a year devoted to the recovery of his health he accepted a position with the Chesapeake and Ohio Railway. On July 4, 1888, Crutchfield was appointed justice of the Richmond Police Court, a position he held for the next thirty-two years, during which time his forceful personality and colorful pronouncements from the bench made him a local celebrity. Active in Masonic affairs, he was at the time of his death one of the oldest past masters in Richmond and a member of St. John's Lodge no. 36. Mr. Justice Crutchfield died on November 21, 1920, survived by five children; his wife of more than fifty years, Alice (Brown) Crutchfield, whom he married on October 13, 1868, died about a year before him.

John Hastings Gwathmey, *Justice John: Tales from the Courtroom of the Virginia Judge* (Richmond, 1934); *Richmond Times-Dispatch*, Nov. 22, 1920; CMA Archives, folio Z1n; VHS Mss5:7 C8895:2; *Biographic Catalogue*.

By George Bagby Matthews. Signed

Oil on canvas: 30 x 25 in. (76.2 x 63.5 cm.)

Presented to the R. E. Lee Camp, Confederate Veterans, in 1924 by the subject's daughter, Ella (Crutchfield) Goddin (Mrs. Aylett Trueheart Goddin); acquired by the Virginia Historical Society in 1946 through merger with the Confederate Memorial Association. Por946.80

"Stapleton Crutchfield"

Identified by the donor simply as "Stapleton Crutchfield," the subject could be one of several persons of that name who resided in Spotsylvania, Caroline, and Goochland counties at the end of the eighteenth and the beginning of the nineteenth centuries. One likely candidate is Stapleton Crutchfield (1775–1818) of Spring Forest, Spotsylvania County, who

married on April 2, 1799, Elizabeth Lewis Minor (1773–1839), daughter of Colonel Garret Minor and Mary Overton (Terrell) Minor of Sunning Hill, Louisa County. During the War of 1812 he commanded a Virginia militia unit. He represented Spotsylvania County in the House of Delegates 1807–11 and was reelected for the 1817–18 session, but he died on January 14, 1818, before the completion of his term of office. His wife "and eight tender children" survived him; one of the children, Oscar Minor Crutchfield (1800–1861), was Speaker of the Virginia House of Delegates 1852–61.

John Barbie Minor, *The Minor Family of Virginia* (Lynchburg, Va., 1923), pp. 12, 32–33; Edward Griffith Dodson, *Speakers and Clerks of the Virginia House of Delegates, 1776–1955* (Richmond, 1956), p. 77.

Artist unidentified

Oil on canvas: 27 1/2 x 22 1/2 in. (69.9 x 57.2 cm.)

Received in 1976 as a bequest of John Crutchfield Goddin of Richmond. Por976.11

Thomas Culpeper, second Baron Culpeper of Thoresway, 1635–1689

Margaret (Van Hesse) Culpeper, 1635–1710 (Lady Culpeper of Thoresway)

The eldest surviving son of John Colepeper, first Baron Colepeper of Thoresway and his wife Judith, Thomas Culpeper was born in 1635. He went abroad in 1651 and remained on the Continent with the exiled Stuarts until the Restoration. On August 3, 1659, he married at The Hague, Margaret Van Hesse, daughter of Jan Van Hesse, a noble lady of the House of Orange who brought him a handsome fortune. The following year Culpeper and his father returned to England with the restored Charles II; a few months later, on his father's death, he inherited the title and family seat, Leeds Castle in Kent. In recognition of the family's loyalty to the crown during the interregnum, he and Lord Arlington were granted in 1673 proprietary rights for thirty-one years to all of Virginia lying south of the Rappahannock River; on July 8, 1675, he received a commission from the crown promising him the governorship of Virginia for life, effective on the death or removal of the incumbent, Sir William Berkeley. Shortly after Berkeley's death in 1677, Culpeper became governor of Virginia. Although he resided in Virginia for just a few months, from May to August 1680, and again from December 1682 to May 1683, he held office for six years. During this period the administrative duties of the post were in the hands of his deputies, Colonel Herbert Jeffreys and Sir Henry Chicheley, while Culpeper devoted himself almost exclusively to extracting as much revenue as possible out of the young colony. Removed from office in 1683 for having twice quit the colony without permission, Culpeper returned to London. In the political confusion leading up to James II's flight and abdication in 1688, Culpeper secured a perpetual charter to the more than five million acres of land lying between the Potomac and Rappahannock rivers known as the Northern Neck of Virginia. Culpeper's proprietorship, however, was of short duration; he died in London on January 27, 1689. His widow, long neglected by her husband, served for some years as proprietress of the Northern Neck; in 1690 their only daughter, Catherine, married Thomas Fairfax, fifth Baron Fairfax of Cameron; Fairfax thereupon became proprietor of the Northern Neck of Virginia in his wife's right. Margaret, Lady Culpeper, died in 1710.

DNB; *Virginia Historical Portraiture*, pp. 105–7 (Portrait I reproduced); *Portraiture*, pp. 24–25; Fairfax Harrison, *The Proprietors of the Northern Neck: Chapters of Culpeper Genealogy* (Richmond, 1926), pp. 73–88, 115–20 (original of Portrait I reproduced as frontispiece); *VMHB* 85 (1977): 239.

Portrait I. Thomas Culpeper, second Baron Culpeper of Thoresway

COPIED BY C. LIDDELL. 1853

Oil on canvas: 32 x 26 in. (81.3 x 66 cm.)

Presented in 1854 by Charles Wykeham-Martin of Leeds Castle, Kent, England. Por854.3

Margaret, Lady Culpeper of Thoresway

The portrait is a copy of the original portrait by an unidentified artist which hung at one time in Leeds Castle.

Portrait II. Margaret (Van Hesse) Culpeper, Lady Culpeper of Thoresway

ARTIST UNIDENTIFIED. 1653

Oil on canvas: 32 x 24½ in. (81.3 x 62.2 cm.). Inscribed: "The Lady Culpeper. 1653."

Acquired by purchase in 1976. Por976.13

Edward Cunningham, 1771–1836
Ariana (Gunn) McCartney Cunningham, 1770–1838
(Mrs. Edward Cunningham)

Edward Cunningham was born in 1771, son of Richard and Elizabeth (Hoope) Cunningham of Church Hill, County Down, Ireland. He came to Virginia in 1784 with his brother John to establish a mercantile business; in 1790 he became a naturalized citizen in Petersburg, and two years later he was residing in Cumberland County. On August 18, 1796, he married Ariana (Gunn) McCartney, born in 1770, the widow of Robert McCartney; she bore him six children. Although Cunningham had business interests in Richmond as early as 1803, he did not move to the city until 1811, the same year he acquired Rutherfoord's flour mills. Thereafter he became involved in numerous commercial enterprises, cotton mills, a chain of stores that extended as far as the borders of the Ohio River, and an iron manufactory known as the Richmond Mills which merged the year after his death with the Virginia Foundry Company to become the Tredegar Iron Company. Cunningham was a director of the Mutual Assurance Society and the Bank of Virginia, a subscriber to Warrell and Lorton's Virginia Museum, and a sometime member of the Richmond Common Council. In 1825 he sold his Richmond house, a handsome residence on the northeast corner of Sixth and Franklin streets designed by Robert Mills, and withdrew to Howard's Neck, his country house in Goochland County. He died there on March 14, 1836; Mrs. Cunningham died two years later; both are buried at Howard's Neck.

Portraiture, pp. 25–26; *Richmond Portraits*, pp. 54–55; Mary Wingfield Scott, *Houses of Old Richmond* (Richmond, 1941), p. 118–21.

Portrait I. Edward Cunningham

BY JOHN BLENNERHASSETT MARTIN

Oil on canvas: 30¼ x 25½ in. (76.8 x 64.8 cm.)

Presented in 1944 by Mr. and Mrs. Alexander Wilbourne Weddell of Richmond. Por944.32

Portrait II. Ariana (Gunn) McCartney Cunningham

By John Blennerhassett Martin

Oil on canvas: 30¼ x 25 in. (76.8 x 63.5 cm.)

Presented in 1944 by Mr. and Mrs. Alexander Wilbourne Weddell of Richmond. Por944.33

Jabez Lamar Monroe Curry, 1825–1903

A zealous advocate of improved education in the South, Curry was born in Lincoln County, Georgia, on June 5, 1825, the second son of William and Susan (Winn) Curry. He attended Franklin College (later the University of Georgia) and Harvard University, where he took his law degree in 1845. Coming under the influence of Horace Mann, the great exponent of public schooling, Curry became a lifelong advocate of universal education. During the Mexican War he was a private in the Texas Rangers; he sat in the Alabama legislature 1847, 1853–55 and in the United States Congress 1857–61. On the secession of his state he was at once elected to the Provisional Confederate Congress; he served in the Confederate legislature until 1863 when he became an aide on the staffs of Generals Joseph E. Johnston and Joseph Wheeler with the rank of lieutenant colonel of cavalry. After the war Curry studied theology and became a Baptist preacher. He was called to the presidency of Howard College, Birmingham, Alabama, in 1865 and three years later came to Richmond as professor of English at Richmond College (later the University of Richmond), a post he held until 1881. As agent of the George Peabody Fund and later of the John F. Slater Fund, Curry devoted himself unstintingly to the improvement of public education in the southern states, duties which occupied him for the remaining years of his life, except for the years 1885–88 when he represented the United States as minister to Spain under President Cleveland. He died in Asheville, North Carolina, on February 12, 1903; his funeral was held at the University of Richmond, with burial in Hollywood Cemetery. Curry was twice married: first, on March 4, 1847, to Anne Bowie, who bore him four children, two of whom died in infancy, and second, on June 25, 1867, to Mary Wortham Thomas of Richmond, who died three months after her husband. Curry was elected to the executive committee of the Virginia Historical Society in 1870; he was elected vice-president of the Society in 1884 and again in 1894.

DAB; *Biographical Directory*; Ezra J. Warner, *Biographical Register of the Confederate Congress* (Baton Rouge, La., 1975); *Portraiture*, pp. 26–27; *VMHB* 53 (1945): 149.

Artist unidentified

Oil on canvas: 30 x 23 in. (76.2 x 58.4 cm.). Inscribed on the back: "Otto Moeller—restorer—Oct.—1944."

Presented in 1944 by Mary Lamar Turpin of Barnstead, New Hampshire, a granddaughter of the subject. Por944.8

Jonathan Peter Cushing, 1793–1835

President of Hampden-Sydney College and a founding member of the Virginia Historical Society, Jonathan Peter Cushing was born in Rochester, New Hampshire, on March 12, 1793, son of Peter and Hannah (Hanson) Cushing. He attended Phillips Academy, Exeter, and graduated from Dartmouth College in 1817. Immediately thereafter, on his way to Charleston, South Carolina, where he hoped to practice law, he met Dr. John Holt Rice of Richmond, who induced him to accept a teaching position at Hampden-Sydney College. So great were his abilities that he advanced rapidly to the professorship of chemistry and natural philosophy. On the death of Moses Hoge, president of the college, in 1820, Cushing was asked to fill the vacancy on a

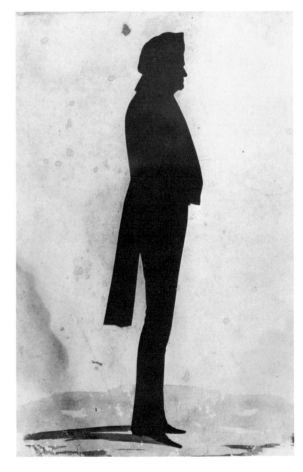

Jonathan Peter Cushing

temporary basis; the following year he was elected president, being the first man to fill that office who was neither a Presbyterian nor a clergyman. During his administration he raised the academic standards of the college, increased its endowment, erected buildings, enlarged the library, and introduced new courses of study. His health, never strong, deteriorated after he received a severe electric shock while performing an experiment in the college laboratory; advised to travel to the West Indies to recover his strength, he got only as far as Raleigh, North Carolina, where he died on April 25, 1835. Cushing was a founding member (1831) and vice-president of the Virginia Historical Society; in 1833 he delivered the first annual address to the Society. His wife, whom he married in 1827, was Lucy (Page) Cushing, daughter of Carter and Lucy (Nelson) Page of Cumberland County; the couple had two daughters.

National Cyclopaedia, 2: 23–24; *The Page Family*, p. 109; *VMHB* 39 (1931): 289–91 (silhouette reproduced) and 71 (1963): 240.

ARTIST UNIDENTIFIED

Silhouette: 10¼ in. (26 cm.) in height, mounted on paper 11¾ x 8 in. (29.9 x 20.3 cm.)

Presented in 1962 by the Reverend George MacLaren Brydon of Richmond, a great-grandson of the subject. Por962.3

John Cussons, 1838–1912

An adventurous spirit led the youthful John Cussons, child of John and Elizabeth (Jackson) Cussons, to quit his native England for America, where from 1855 to 1859 he lived in the wilds of the Northwest with the Sioux Indians. In 1859 he went to Selma, Alabama, engaged in newspaper work, and became half owner of the *Selma Reporter*; on the secession of the state he abandoned his journalistic duties for military ones. As a member of the Governor's Guard, he was assigned to the 4th Alabama Infantry and transferred to Virginia. Cussons served as a scout assigned to outpost, flank, rearguard, and detached duty, performing valuable service at Fort Stribling, Thoroughfare Gap, and other engagements. On the third day of the struggle at Gettysburg he was captured; he was confined for eight months and exchanged. Reassigned to his old division, he spent the remainder of the war in the West, serving at the end with Forrest's Cavalry Corps. After the war Captain Cussons settled in Virginia, devoting himself to a printing business and to the improvement of Forest Lodge, his estate in Glen Allen which he tried unsuccessfully to develop into a summer resort. He published autobiographical and historical articles, led a crusade against history text-

books written with a Yankee bias, and was active in the affairs of Confederate organizations. In 1864 he married Sue Annie (Sheppard) Allen, daughter of Mosby Sheppard and widow of Benjamin Allen. Captain Cussons died on January 4, 1912.

Men of Mark in Virginia, 3: 102–8; *Confederate Military History*, 3: 824–25; *Biographic Catalogue*.

BY JOHN P. WALKER

Oil on canvas: 30 x 25 in. (76.2 x 63.5 cm.)

Presented to the R. E. Lee Camp, Confederate Veterans, in 1923; acquired by the Virginia Historical Society in 1946 through merger with the Confederate Memorial Association. Por946.160

Elizabeth Parke Custis, 1776–1832   (later Mrs. Thomas Law)

Granddaughter of Martha (Dandridge) Custis Washington (q.v.) and daughter of John Parke Custis and Eleanor (Calvert) Custis, the subject was born on August 21, 1776, at her parents' residence, Abingdon, Fairfax County. Because her father died when she was only five years old, she spent much time as a member of the Mount Vernon household. She married on March 20, 1796, an English barrister more than twice her age, Thomas Law of Georgetown, D.C., son of the Right Reverend Edmund Law, bishop of Carlisle. Among the earliest residents of Washington, Mr. and Mrs. Law lived together in considerable style for several years; they separated in 1804, and were divorced in 1811. Mrs. Law's later years were spent unhappily. She died on January 1, 1832, and is buried at Mount Vernon. A portrait of her brother, George Washington Parke Custis (q.v.), is also in the Society's collection.

Fillmore Norfleet, *Saint-Mémin in Virginia: Portraits and Biographies* (Richmond, 1942), pp. 181–82; *The Diaries of George Washington* (Charlottesville, Va., 1976–79), 4: 129–30 (portraits of the four Custis children reproduced).

ARTIST UNIDENTIFIED

Oil on canvas: 19¾ x 16 in. (50.2 x 40.6 cm.)

Received in 1949 from the heirs of Dr. George Bolling Lee. Por949.27

Robert Edge Pine painted Mrs. Washington's four grandchildren during his visit to Mount Vernon in 1785. The portraits of Martha Parke Custis and Eleanor Parke Custis are at Mount Vernon; Washington and Lee University owns the portraits of George Washington Parke Custis and Elizabeth Parke Custis. Elizabeth, the eldest child, was nine years old when the portraits were painted, but she looks considerably older. The Society's portrait of

Elizabeth, which is virtually identical to the portrait at Washington and Lee, has been thought to be a replica of the original. However, Robert G. Stewart in his study of Pine's American portraits states that the Society's portrait "is a copy by an unidentified artist," adding that "possibly the artist was Ernest Fisher in Baltimore, who made other copies for the Lee family."

Robert G. Stewart, *Robert Edge Pine, a British Portrait Painter in America, 1784–1788* (Washington, D.C., 1979), pp. 50–55, 104.

George Washington Parke Custis, 1781–1857

Son of John Parke Custis (George Washington's stepson) and Eleanor (Calvert) Custis, the subject was born on April 30, 1781. Because of the early death of his father he was raised by George and Martha Washington at Mount Vernon, remaining there until Mrs. Washington's death in 1802, at which time he removed to Arlington and began construction of the neoclassical house that still stands on the property. In 1804 he married Mary Lee Fitzhugh, daughter of William and Anne (Randolph) Fitzhugh; the only one of their four children to survive childhood was Mary Ann Randolph Custis, who married Robert Edward Lee (q.v.). Custis applied the latest methods of cultivation to his plantation, inaugurated an annual agricultural fair at Arlington, and bred sheep. During the War of 1812 he served as a volunteer in the defense of the capital. Custis did much to perpetuate the memory of George Washington: he assembled family portraits and heirlooms at Arlington, wrote *Recollections and Private Memoirs of Washington*, and painted very large pictures of Revolutionary scenes in which the general figured prominently. He also wrote plays, several of which, including *The Indian Prophecy* (1827) and *Pocahontas* (1830), were performed in Philadelphia. Custis

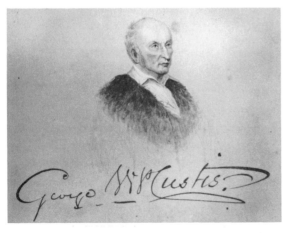

George Washington Parke Custis (Portrait I)

never fully recovered from the death of his wife in 1852; he died on October 10, 1857, and is buried at her side at Arlington. He was elected to honorary membership in the Virginia Historical Society in 1852. A portrait of his sister Elizabeth Parke Custis (q.v.) is also in the Society's collection.

DAB; Murray Homer Nelligan, *Lee Mansion National Memorial* (Washington, D.C., 1950); *VMHB* 69 (1961): 240.

Portrait I

By BENSON JOHN LOSSING. Signed. 1853

Watercolor on cardboard: 2¼ in. (5.7 cm.) in height, on a card 7¾ x 6 in. (19.7 x 15.2 cm.). Inscribed: "From life by B. Lossing."

Acquired by purchase in 1960. Por960.78

Benson Lossing visited Arlington in 1853 to sketch portraits and heirlooms to illustrate his article "Arlington House" published in *Harper's New Monthly Magazine*.[1] At the time of Lossing's visit Custis was more than seventy years old, and in Brady's photograph of him taken at about the same time, he presented a very old and battered figure.[2] Although Lossing's sketch of Custis bears the pencil notation "From life by B. Lossing," it seems highly unlikely that the portrait is a life portrait of the elderly Custis. The inscription should probably be interpreted "Copied directly from the original portrait." For there was in fact a portrait of Custis at Arlington, and Lossing's sketch clearly derives from it. The portrait, reproduced as an engraving, was used as the frontispiece to Custis's *Recollections and Private Memoirs of Washington* (New York, 1860), and bears the inscriptions "Painted by G. Stuart" and "Engraved by J. C. Buttre." If the original was, in fact, the work of Gilbert Stuart, its present whereabouts are not now known.[3] A copy of the lost Stuart portrait by Junius Brutus Stearns (1810–1885) is at Washington and Lee University.[4]

1. *Harper's New Monthly Magazine* 7 (1853): 433–54. 2. *American Heritage* 17, no. 2 (Feb. 1966): 21. 3. Lawrence Park, *Gilbert Stuart: An Illustrated Descriptive List of His Works* (New York, 1926), 1: 248. 4. International Exhibitions Foundation, *Washington-Custis-Lee Family Portraits from the Collection of Washington & Lee University, Lexington, Virginia* (Washington, D.C., 1974), plate 11 (Stearns portrait reproduced).

Portrait II

By ROBERT FIELD. Signed: "R.F." Dated 1804

Miniature on ivory: 3 x 2½ in. (7.6 x 6.4 cm.) (oval)

Received from the heirs of Dr. George Bolling Lee. Por977.26

Martha (Dandridge) Custis, 1732–1802

See George Washington, 1732–1799

Custis Children

By MATTHEW PRATT. Ca.1773

Oil on canvas: 30 x 24½ in. (76.2 x 62.2 cm.)

Received in 1949 from the heirs of Dr. George Bolling Lee. Por949.35

Although the identity of the children depicted in Pratt's portrait is not known, the portrait's provenance substantiates the tradition that they are members of the Custis family. It has been suggested that they are John Parke Custis (1755–1781) and his sister, Martha Parke Custis (1757–1773), Martha (Dandridge) Custis Washington's children by her first marriage. This identification, however, is not possible if the portrait was painted during Pratt's visit to Virginia in 1773—unless, as has also been suggested, the portrait was painted as a memorial piece shortly after the death of Martha Parke Custis and derives from earlier likenesses. The supposed date of the portrait and the fact that the boy is clearly the elder child likewise eliminates the possibility that the subjects are one of Martha (Dandridge) Custis Washington's three granddaughters and their younger brother, George Washington Parke Custis (1781–1857).

Custis children

William Sawitzky, *Matthew Pratt, 1734–1805* (New York, 1942), pp. 76–77 (portrait reproduced, plate 17); VHS Mss7:1 P8895:1.

Wilfred Emory Cutshaw, 1838–1907

Son of George W. Cutshaw and Martha (Moxley) Cutshaw, the subject was born on January 25, 1838, at Harpers Ferry, (West) Virginia. He graduated from the Virginia Military Institute in 1858, then taught at Hampton Military Institute until he resigned to enter the service of the Confederate army, rising during the course of the war from lieutenant to lieutenant colonel. Cutshaw participated in the Peninsular campaigns of 1861 and in Jackson's campaigns in the Valley of Virginia in the spring of 1862. Wounded and captured at the battle of Winchester, he spent a year in prison before being exchanged. Pronounced unfit for further active duty, he was assigned to the Virginia Military Institute as acting commander of cadets, a post he held until September 1863 when he was readmitted to active duty despite his unhealed wound. As inspector general of artillery in the 2d Corps, Army of Northern Virginia, he participated in the battles of Bristoe Station, Rappahannock Station, the Wilderness, Spotsylvania, and Cold Harbor. Promoted to lieutenant colonel in February 1865, he commanded an artillery battalion until he was again severely wounded, losing his right leg, at the battle of Sayler's Creek, just three days before the surrender. Colonel Cutshaw returned to the faculty of the Virginia Military Institute in 1866. In 1873 he came to Richmond as city engineer, an office he ably filled for the next thirty-four years, his most notable achievement being Richmond's City Hall which was constructed under his supervision. Colonel Cutshaw was a member of the Southern Historical Society and president of the Society of the Alumni of the Virginia Military Institute; he was elected to membership in the Virginia Historical Society in 1890. He was twice married: first, in December 1876, to Mrs. E. S. Norfleet, who died two months later; second, in January 1890, to Miss M. W. Morton, who died in December the same year. Colonel Cutshaw died in Richmond without issue on December 19, 1907.

Confederate Veteran 16 (1908): 83–84; *Confederate Military History*, 3: 825–26; *Eminent and Representative Men*, pp. 423–33; *Biographic Catalogue*.

By JOHN P. WALKER. Signed (initials). Dated 1907

Oil on canvas: 30 x 24¾ in. (76.2 x 62.9 cm.)

Presented to the R. E. Lee Camp, Confederate Veterans, in 1908; acquired by the Virginia Historical Society in 1946 through merger with the Confederate Memorial Association. Por946.161

James Madison Cutts, 1805–1863
Ellen Elizabeth (O'Neale) Cutts, ca. 1811–1897 (Mrs. James Madison Cutts)

James Madison Cutts, eldest child of Richard and Anna (Payne) Cutts (qq.v.), was born on July 29, 1805. Around 1822, during his father's tenure as second comptroller of the United States Treasury, he became a clerk in the second comptroller's office. He remained in this section of the Treasury Department all his life, becoming second comptroller under President Buchanan. He died on May 11, 1863. Cutts married, on December 17, 1833, Ellen Elizabeth O'Neale, daughter of John O'Neale of Montgomery County, Maryland, who bore him two children, one of whom, Rose Adèle (Cutts) Douglas (q.v.), is represented in the Society's portrait collection. Ellen Elizabeth (O'Neale) Cutts died in February 1897.

Cecil Hampton Cutts Howard, *Genealogy of the Cutts Family in America* (Albany, N.Y., 1892), p. 167; *Portraiture*, pp. 29–30.

Portrait I. James Madison Cutts

By GEORGE PETER ALEXANDER HEALY. Signed. Dated 1857

Oil on canvas: 30 x 25 in. (76.2 x 63.5 cm.)

Presented in 1944 by Mildred (Williams) Farwell (Mrs. Walter Farwell) of Syosset, Long Island, New York, a granddaughter of the subject. Por944.17

Portrait II. James Madison Cutts

By GEORGE PETER ALEXANDER HEALY

Oil on canvas: 30¼ x 25 in. (76.8 x 63.5 cm.)

Presented in 1944 by Mildred (Williams) Farwell (Mrs. Walter Farwell) of Syosset, Long Island, New York, a granddaughter of the subject. Por944.18

Portrait III. Ellen Elizabeth (O'Neale) Cutts

By GEORGE PETER ALEXANDER HEALY

Oil on canvas: 30¼ x 25 in. (76.8 x 63.5 cm.)

Presented in 1944 by Mildred (Williams) Farwell (Mrs. Walter Farwell) of Syosset, Long Island, New York, a granddaughter of the subject. Por944.19

Richard Cutts, 1771–1845
Anna (Payne) Cutts, d. 1832 (Mrs. Richard Cutts)

Richard Cutts, son of Thomas and Elizabeth (Scammon) Cutts, was born on Cutts Island, Saco, Massachusetts (now Maine), on June 28, 1771. He graduated from Harvard University in 1790, studied law, and engaged in navigation and commercial pursuits. After serving in the state legislature in 1799 and 1800, he was elected to the Seventh United States Congress and to the five succeeding congresses, representing his district 1801–13. On March 31, 1804, he married Anna Payne, daughter of John and Mary (Coles) Payne and sister of Dolley (Payne) Todd

James Madison Cutts (Portrait II)

Richard Cutts

Madison (q.v.), wife of President James Madison (q.v.), who bore him five sons and two daughters. On June 3, 1813, Cutts was appointed superintendent general of military supplies; since the post was created to meet the needs of the War of 1812 and the months immediately after, it was abolished in 1817; Cutts thereupon became second comptroller of the Treasury. He resigned in 1829 and spent his remaining years as a private citizen in Washington, D.C. Richard Cutts died on April 7, 1845; Anna (Payne) Cutts died on August 4, 1832. The subjects' son, James Madison Cutts, his wife, and the subjects' granddaughter, Rose Adèle (Cutts) Douglas (qq.v.), are also represented in the Society's portrait collection.

Biographical Directory; New England Historical and Genealogical Register 2 (1848): 277–78; Cecil Hampton Cutts Howard, *Genealogy of the Cutts Family in America* (Albany, N.Y., 1892), pp. 44, 86, 167; *Portraiture*, pp. 27–28.

Portrait I. Richard Cutts

BY GILBERT STUART. 1804

Oil on canvas: 29 x 24¼ in. (73.7 x 61.6 cm.)

Presented in 1944 by Mildred (Williams) Farwell (Mrs. Walter Farwell) of Syosset, Long Island, New York. Por944.15

Portrait II. Anna (Payne) Cutts

COPIED BY CHARLES BIRD KING

Oil on canvas: 30 x 25 in. (76.2 x 63.5 cm.)

Presented in 1944 by Mildred (Williams) Farwell (Mrs. Walter Farwell) of Syosset, Long Island, New York. Por944.16

The portrait of Mrs. Cutts is a copy of Gilbert Stuart's original portrait. The following anecdote from Anne Hollingsworth Wharton's *Social Life in the Early Republic* (pp. 143–44) relates to the painting of the original in 1804 and to the "profile" drapery in the background. "Gilbert Stuart was in Georgetown while Mr. Madison was Secretary of State, and at this time painted a portrait of Mrs. Madison and a companion picture of her husband. Among numerous other portraits executed by Stuart were those of Colonel and Mrs. John Tayloe of the Octagon, and of Mr. and Mrs. Richard D. Cutts. In the background of this latter portrait, for which Mrs. Cutts sat a short time before her marriage, is to be found an exaggerated outline of the artist's own features. The story runs, that while Anna Payne's portrait was being painted that lively young woman entered into an animated discussion with the artist as to which feature of the face is the most expressive. Mr. Stuart gave his verdict in favor of the nose, while Miss Payne contended for the superior claims of the eyes and mouth. Stuart, who greatly relished a joke, even at his own expense, presented to his sitter the next morning a canvas upon which *his own* profile, the long nose somewhat exaggerated, occupied the place of the usual drapery in the background, inquiring, with a triumphant smile, whether he had not proved to her satisfaction that the nose was the most expressive feature of the face. Although the laugh was against her, Miss Payne was so much pleased to have secured a profile of her old friend, that she insisted that the very odd background should remain a part of the portrait."

Anne Hollingsworth Wharton, *Social Life in the Early Republic* (Philadelphia, 1902); Andrew J. Cosentino, *The Paintings of Charles Bird King* (Washington, D.C., 1977), p. 131 (Portrait II reproduced); Lawrence Park, *Gilbert Stuart* (New York, 1926), 1: 248–50, 3: 121–22 (Portrait I and original of Portrait II reproduced).

Rose Adèle Cutts, 1835–1899

See Rose Adèle (Cutts) Douglas, 1835–1899

Robert Lewis Dabney, 1820–1898

Presbyterian theologian and teacher, Dabney was born in Louisa County on March 5, 1820, son of Charles and Elizabeth R. (Price) Dabney. He attended both Hampden-Sydney College and the University of Virginia, graduating from the latter institution in 1842. Thereafter he studied at the Union Theological Seminary of Virginia, was licensed to preach in 1846, and became pastor of Tinkling Spring Church, Augusta County, the following year. In 1853 he was appointed to the faculty of the Union Theological Seminary; he remained there for thirty years, at the same time achieving widespread recognition for his contributions to church publications and as the author of such works as *Sacred Rhetoric* (1870), *Syllabus and Notes of the Course of Systematic and Polemic Theology* (1871), and *Parental Obligation* (1880). On the outbreak of the Civil War he became a chaplain in the Confederate army; in 1862 he was appointed to Stonewall Jackson's staff, serving in that capacity until Jackson's death. His most popular book, *Life and Campaigns of Lieut.-Gen. Thomas J. Jackson* (1866), draws on his own close association with Jackson during the war years. Dabney remained at the Union Theological Seminary until 1883; in that year he removed for reasons of health to Texas, where he occupied the chair of moral philosophy at the University of Texas until 1894 and was instrumental in founding the Austin School of Theology. Although infirm and totally blind during the last eight years of his life, he remained active as a writer, teacher, and lecturer. He died in Texas on January 3, 1898; his body was taken for burial to Hampden-Sydney, Virginia. Dabney's wife, whom he married on March 28, 1848, was Lavinia (Morrison) Dabney, daughter of the Reverend James Morrison of Rockbridge County; she survived her husband, as did their three sons.

DAB; Thomas Cary Johnson, *The Life and Letters of Robert Lewis Dabney* (Richmond, 1903); *Biographic Catalogue* (Addenda).

By EMMA MOREHEAD WHITFIELD. Signed. Dated 1926

Oil on canvas: 30 x 25 in. (76.2 x 63.5 cm.). Inscribed on the back: "Major Robert L. Dabney. Painted by E. M. Whitfield. 1926."

Presented to the R. E. Lee Camp, Confederate Veterans, in 1926; acquired by the Virginia Historical Society in 1946 through merger with the Confederate Memorial Association. Por946.175

John Dandridge, 1700–1756

John Dandridge, the father of Martha Washington (q.v.), was born in England on July 14, 1700, son of John Dandridge of London, master of the Painter-Stainers Company, and Ann Dandridge. In 1715 the youth accompanied his elder brother William Dandridge (q.v.) to Virginia. After living some years in Elizabeth City County, the brothers settled on opposite sides of the Pamunkey River, John in New Kent County, and William at Elsing Green, King William County. On July 22, 1730, John Dandridge married Frances Jones, daughter of Orlando and Martha (Macon) Jones; they became the parents of eight children, of whom Martha, later the wife of General Washington, was the eldest. Dandridge was a vestryman and churchwarden of St. Peter's, New Kent, and in 1747 was clerk of the county. He died on August 31, 1756; his tombstone is in St. George's churchyard, Fredericksburg.

Encyclopedia of Virginia Biography, 1: 220; *W. & M. Quart.*, 1st ser., 5 (1896–97): 30–34; *Portraiture*, p. 31; *Genealogists' Magazine* 15 (1965–68): 608–13; *Seldens of Virginia*, 2: 13–14.

ARTIST UNIDENTIFIED

Oil on canvas: 22 x 18 in. (55.9 x 45.7 cm.)

Acquired by purchase in 1895. Por893.2

This portrait of George Washington's father-in-law is one of the few portraits purchased for the collection. In 1895 the Library Committee was authorized to secure the picture if it could be done "at a cost not exceeding twenty-five dollars." The portrait has been twice restored, first by John Elder and then by William L. Sheppard.

VHS Archives, liber A6, pp. 88, 90.

John Dandridge

Martha Dandridge, 1732–1802
See George Washington, 1732–1799

William Dandridge, 1689–1743

Born in England on December 29, 1689, son of John Dandridge of London, master of the Painter-Stainers Company, and Ann Dandridge, the subject came to Virginia in 1715 with his younger brother, John Dandridge (q.v.). In 1717 he was residing in Elizabeth City County, a merchant and shipowner with a house and wharf in Hampton. Dandridge married, first, Euphan (Wallace) Roscow, daughter of the Reverend James Wallace and widow of William Roscow; she died April 22, 1717, at twenty years of age. Two years later he removed to King William County, to Elsing Green, an estate he acquired on his marriage to Unity West, only child of Colonel Nathaniel West; his brother John settled on the other side of the Pamunkey River in New Kent County. In 1727 he became a member of the colonial Council, and on December 14 of that year he was appointed with Colonel William Byrd (q.v.) one of the commissioners to run the dividing line between Virginia and North Carolina. In 1737 he was on active duty with the Royal Navy, commanding the twelve-gun sloop *Wolf* on the Virginia station; in November 1741 he was transferred to the command of the forty-gun vessel *South Sea*, which took part in the attack on St. Augustine and the siege of Cartagena; he subsequently commanded the man-of-war

William Dandridge

Ludlow Castle. Colonel Dandridge died in 1743 while on a visit to his estates in Hanover County; he left four children.

Encyclopedia of Virginia Biography, 1: 154; *Seldens of Virginia*, 2: 13–17; *W. & M. Quart.*, 1st ser., 5 (1896–97): 30–35; *Portraiture*, p. 30; *Genealogists' Magazine* 15 (1965–68): 608–13; *VMHB* 13 (1905–6): viii and 32 (1924): 237–38 (portrait reproduced).

ARTIST UNIDENTIFIED

Oil on canvas on panel: 36 x 28 in. (91.4 x 71.1 cm.)

Received in 1905 from Mrs. Frank W. Chamberlayne of Richmond. Por905.9

The portrait, which appears to have been extensively restored and overpainted, has previously been attributed to John Hesselius. Either the attribution is in error or the subject has been wrongly identified, for Hesselius did not begin painting portraits in Virginia until about 1751, some eight years after William Dandridge's death.

John Warwick Daniel, 1842–1910

The only son of William and Sarah Anne (Warwick) Daniel, the subject was born in Lynchburg on September 5, 1842. He joined the Confederate army as a private on the outbreak of the Civil War, rising to lieutenant and drill master in the Stonewall Brigade and subsequently to major on the staff of General Early. A severe wound inflicted in May 1864 at the

battle of the Wilderness ended his active service and put him on crutches for the rest of his life. After a year at the University of Virginia he was admitted to the bar and began the practice of law with his father in Lynchburg. In 1869 he married Julia Elizabeth Murrell, daughter of Dr. Edward H. Murrell and Elmira (Halsey) Murrell of Lynchburg; they became the parents of five children. Daniel served in the Virginia House of Delegates 1869–72 and the state Senate 1875–81, was an unsuccessful candidate for governor, and in 1884 was elected to the Congress of the United States. The following year he was elected to the United States Senate, serving continuously thereafter until his death more than twenty years later. As an author of historical monographs and legal treatises, his work won wide acclaim; as an orator, his style was "copious, ornate, solemn, touched always with emotion, appealing at once to the head and to the heart." Daniel became a member of the Virginia Historical Society in 1870. He died in Lynchburg on June 29, 1910, and is buried in Spring Hill Cemetery.

DAB; *Biographical Directory*; *Men of Mark in Virginia*, 1: 224–33; *Virginia Genealogies*, pp. 319–20; *Encyclopedia of Virginia Biography*, 3: 103–5; *Biographic Catalogue.*

BY JOHN P. WALKER. Signed. Dated 1911

Oil on canvas: 40 x 30 in. (101.6 x 76.2 cm.)

Acquired in 1946 through merger with the Confederate Memorial Association. Por946.194

Nathaniel Darby, 1754–1811

Son of Benjamin and Rachel (Bell) Darby of Oak Grove, Northampton County, the subject was born on June 15, 1754. He was commissioned an ensign in the 9th Virginia Regiment on August 14, 1776, serving with that unit until his capture at Germantown in October 1777; he was evidently exchanged and promoted, for he is listed as lieutenant of a company of the 5th Virginia Regiment from January to April 1782. Darby was then assigned to the 8th Virginia Regiment, and from December 1, 1782, to May 1, 1783, his name appears on the muster roll of Captain Alexander Parker's Battalion. He received land warrants for a total of seven years and ten months of military service. After the Revolution "his time and talents were usefully employed in various offices for the publick good" in Northampton County; he represented the county in the Virginia House of Delegates in 1793 and 1798–1802. He died, presumably unmarried, on November 13, 1811. Darby was an original member of the Society of the Cincinnati.

Occasional Bulletin, no. 2 (1961): 7 (portrait reproduced); Louis Alexander Burgess, *Virginia Soldiers of 1776* (Richmond, 1927–29), 3: 1097; Edgar Erskine Hume, *Sesquicen-*

tennial History and Roster of the Society of the Cincinnati in the State of Virginia, 1783–1933 (Richmond, 1934), p. 278; Ralph Thomas Whitelaw, *Virginia's Eastern Shore: A History of Northampton and Accomack Counties* (Richmond, 1951), 1: 556; information supplied by Miss Marianna Higgins.

Nathaniel Darby

ATTRIBUTED TO LAWRENCE SULLY

Miniature on ivory: 2 x 1³/₄ in. (5.1 x 4.5 cm.) (oval)

Received in 1961 as a bequest of Harriet Burleigh Higgins of Chicago. Por961.2

Harriet Jane Davies, 1820–1896
See Harriet Jane (Davies) Early, 1820–1896

Jefferson Davis, 1808–1889

Jefferson Davis, president of the Confederate States of America, was born in Christian (now Todd) County, Kentucky, on June 3, 1808, the tenth child of Samuel and Jane (Cook) Davis. The family moved to Mississippi where Jefferson Davis attended country schools before enrolling in St. Thomas's College, a Roman Catholic secondary school in Kentucky. He entered Transylvania University in 1821 but left without a degree upon securing an appointment to the United States Military Academy. Graduating from West Point in 1828, the young lieutenant spent nearly seven years in Wisconsin and Illinois, served in the Black Hawk Indian War, and in 1835 resigned his commission to marry, against the wishes of her

father, Sarah Knox Taylor, daughter of Colonel Zachary Taylor (q.v.) and Margaret (Smith) Taylor. Three months later his wife was dead of malarial fever. Davis spent the next ten years farming his cotton plantation in Mississippi. On February 26, 1845, Varina Anne Howell, daughter of William Burr Howell and Margaret Louisa (Kempe) Howell, became his second wife; the next month he began his first term as a United States congressman. Resigning in June 1846 to assume command of the 1st Regiment of Mississippi Riflemen, he distinguished himself at the siege of Monterrey and the battle of Buena Vista. Appointed thereafter to the United States Senate to fill an unexpired term, he was subsequently elected in his own right, serving from 1847 to 1851. Following an unsuccessful campaign for governor of Mississippi, he was appointed secretary of war by President Pierce, holding the office 1853–57, when again he took his place in the United States Senate. On January 21, 1861, he announced to the Senate the secession of Mississippi from the Union and his own official resignation. Chosen president of the Confederate States by the Provisional Congress and inaugurated in Montgomery, Alabama, on February 18, 1861, he was officially inaugurated president of the Confederacy in Richmond on February 22, 1862. Davis was made prisoner at Irwinville, Georgia, on May 10, 1865; he was for two years incarcerated in Fortress Monroe, then released on bond. After living abroad for several years he returned to Mississippi; he sought to repair his fortunes through a series of business ventures, none of which succeeded. From 1878 to 1881 he devoted himself to writing *The Rise and Fall of the Confederate Government*. He died at New Orleans, on December 6, 1889, survived by his wife and two of his six children. He was buried in Metairie Cemetery, New Orleans, but was reinterred on May 31, 1893, in Hollywood Cemetery, Richmond.

DAB; *Biographical Directory*; *The South in the Building of the Nation* (Richmond, 1909–13), 11: 260–65; *Biographic Catalogue*.

Portrait I

By JOHN P. WALKER. Signed. Dated 1902

Oil on canvas: 60 x 40 in. (152.4 x 101.6 cm.)

Presented to the R. E. Lee Camp, Confederate Veterans, in 1902; acquired by the Virginia Historical Society in 1946 through merger with the Confederate Memorial Association. Por946.37

The minutes of the December 19, 1902, meeting of the R. E. Lee Camp Portrait Committee record that a three-quarter-length portrait of Davis had been received and that "the old portrait of President Davis was by order of the camp sent to the Soldiers' Home."

Portrait II

Bronze bust: 12 in. (30.5 cm.) in height, including base

Presented in 1896 by Mercer Slaughter. Por895.4

The base of the bust is inscribed "Davis." Cast into the back is the inscription "Copyrighted 1894. All rights reserved. By J. E. Miller, Atlanta, Ga. O. Frazee Sc."

VHS Archives, liber A6, pp. 107, 133, and liber B1, p. 44.

Varina Anne Jefferson Davis, 1864–1898

Known affectionately as Winnie and The Daughter of the Confederacy, Varina Anne Jefferson Davis was the youngest child of Jefferson Davis (q.v.) and Varina Anne (Howell) Davis. She was born in Richmond on June 27, 1864. In 1877 she was enrolled in school in Karlsruhe, Germany, where she remained five years. On her return to the United States she resided with her parents in Mississippi and turned her attention to writing. During her father's lifetime she was his close companion both at home and on his travels through the South. On her father's death in 1889 she accompanied her mother to New York where both mother and daughter wrote articles for periodicals as a means of support. In addition to short pieces and poems, Winnie Davis wrote two novels, *The Veiled Doctor* (1895) and *A Romance of Summer Seas* (1898). She died, unmarried, at Narragansett Pier, Rhode Island, on September 18, 1898.

The South in the Building of the Nation (Richmond, 1909–13), 11: 269–70.

By John P. Walker. Signed. Dated 1899

Oil on canvas: 68 x 42 in. (172.7 x 106.7 cm.)

Presented to the R. E. Lee Camp, Confederate Veterans, in 1899; acquired by the Virginia Historical Society in 1946 through merger with the Confederate Memorial Association. Por946.219

James Dearing, 1840–1865

The last Confederate general officer to die of wounds received in action, General Dearing was the son of Colonel James Griffin Dearing and Mary Anna (Lynch) Dearing. He was born at Otterburne, Campbell County, on April 25, 1840, attended Hanover Academy, and received an appointment to West Point in 1858. Resigning on the outbreak of the Civil War, he entered the Confederate army as a lieutenant in the Washington Artillery. At the battle of Gettysburg with the rank of major he commanded a battalion of artillery; he was then transferred to the cavalry and promoted to colonel. For gallantry at the battle of Plymouth, North Carolina, he was promoted, on April 29, 1864, to brigadier general; his brigade thereafter participated in all the principal engagements of the Army of Northern Virginia, distinguishing itself particularly during the Petersburg campaign and the retreat from Richmond. On April 6, 1865, General Dearing was mortally wounded at High Bridge in a pistol duel with General Theodore Read of the Union forces, whom he killed. He was taken to Lynchburg and died in the hospital there on April 23, 1865, two weeks after Lee's surrender and two days before his twenty-fifth birthday. By his wife, Roxana (Birchett) Dearing, whom he married in 1864, he had one daughter.

Generals in Gray; *History of Virginia*, 5: 351–52, 6: 69–70; *National Cyclopedia*, 11: 511; *Biographic Catalogue*.

By Flavius J. Fisher. Signed. Dated 1899

Oil on canvas: 27 x 22 in. (68.6 x 55.9 cm.)

Presented to the R. E. Lee Camp, Confederate Veterans, in 1900; acquired by the Virginia Historical Society in 1946 through merger with the Confederate Memorial Association. Por946.159

Joseph Coleman Dickerson, 1839–1913

Born in Richmond on June 26, 1839, the subject established a saddle and harness business there in 1858. On the outbreak of the Civil War he enlisted as a private in Company A, 1st Virginia Infantry; he was later transferred to Company G, 12th Virginia Infantry, serving in all that unit's engagements from Norfolk to Gettysburg. Wounded, taken prisoner, and exchanged, he was again captured at the battle of Sayler's Creek. On his return to Richmond after the war he resumed his business at 1512 East Franklin Street, remaining at that location until his removal in 1899 to more commodious quarters at 1412 East Franklin Street, where he maintained a factory and salesroom for all manner of horse and stable goods. Dickerson was active in community affairs, serving sixteen consecutive years on the board of aldermen of the city of Richmond, six years of which he was its president; for twenty years he was connected with the city public schools, serving part of that time on the city school board. He was commander of the R. E. Lee Camp, United Confederate Veterans, 1901–2. He was married, had a son who assisted him in his business, and died on September 1, 1913.

Biographic Catalogue; *Richmond the Pride of Virginia, an Historical City* (Philadelphia, 1900), p. 155; CMA Archives, folio Z1n.

By JOHN P. WALKER. Signed. Dated 1926

Oil on canvas: 30 x 25 in. (76.2 x 63.5 cm.)

Presented to the R. E. Lee Camp, Confederate Veterans, in 1926; acquired by the Virginia Historical Society in 1946 through merger with the Confederate Memorial Association. Por946.95

Sir Dudley Digges, 1583–1639

Sir Dudley Digges, diplomat, traveler, author, member of Parliament, and friend of the Virginia enterprise, was born in 1583, son of Thomas and Agnes (St. Leger) Digges of Digges Court, Barham, Kent. He took his degree at University College, Oxford, in 1601, was knighted in 1607, and was elected to various parliaments between 1610 and 1628, his independence and outspoken criticism of highly placed persons resulting in brief imprisonment on at least two occasions. Digges was one of a parlimentary deputation that was instrumental in securing the Petition of Right. Much interested in exploration, particularly in the Northwest Passage project, he wrote a tract on the subject and was active in the affairs of the East India Company and the Muscovy Company. In 1618 he represented the former company in a diplomatic mission to Russia, and two years later he undertook a similar mission to Holland. Digges was an early member of the Virginia Company of London and a member of the royal Council for Virginia in 1609 and ten years later sat on the committee to codify the laws of the colony. The same year he served on a committee to establish a college in Virginia. Digges's Hundred was established on the James River about 1611; in 1622 he and his associates were assigned land in Virginia to further a proposal to transport "great multitudes of people and cattle to Virginia." Sir Dudley became Master of the Rolls in 1636 but died three years later, on March 18, 1639. By his wife, Mary (Kempe) Digges, daughter of Sir Thomas Kempe of Ollantigh, near Wye, Kent, he had eight sons and three daughters. One of his sons, Edward Digges, settled in Virginia and was a member of the colonial Council and governor of the colony in 1656.

DNB; Alexander Brown, *The Genesis of the United States* (Boston, 1890), 2: 878–79; Annie Lash Jester, *Adventurers of Purse and Person, 1607–1625* (Princeton, N.J., 1956), pp. 154–55; *Encyclopedia of Virginia Biography*, 1: 28; *Occasional Bulletin*, no. 4 (1962): 2–3 (portrait reproduced); *VMHB* 71 (1963): 239; *Antiques* 116 (1979): 1129 (portrait reproduced).

By CORNELIUS JANSSEN. Signed. Dated 1636

See Plate 9

Oil on canvas: 29¼ x 24 in. (74.3 x 61 cm.). Inscribed on the face of the canvas: "Sir Dudley Diggs. Corns Jansen 1636." Inscribed on the back: "Sir Dudley Diggs   C. Janson 1636."

Acquired by purchase in 1962. Por962.2

Emily Dill, 1819–1857
See John Henry Bosher, 1816–1895

Philip Doddridge, 1773–1832
See The Convention of 1829–30

William Donaldson
See The Convention of 1829–30

Henry Thompson Douglas, 1838–1926

Born at Cherry Hall, James City County, on September 15, 1838, the son of William Robert Christian Douglas and Lucy Ann (Hankins) Douglas, the subject attended private schools in New Kent County, did field work as a civil engineer, and at the beginning of the Civil War joined the Confederate army as a lieutenant in the engineer corps. He served on General Magruder's staff and later became chief engineer of General A. P. Hill's division. Among the engineering projects he carried to completion were the construction of the intermediate line of defenses around Richmond and the defenses of Chaffin's Bluff on the north side of the James River. During the latter part of the war he was promoted to colonel and assigned to the Trans-Mississippi Department as chief engineer. After the war Douglas turned his attention to railroad construction; in this capacity he worked for the Chesapeake and Ohio, the Richmond and Danville, and the York River lines; he was at one time chief engineer of the Baltimore and Ohio. Douglas volunteered his services at the beginning of the Spanish-American War, was commissioned brigadier general, and served on the staff of General Fitzhugh Lee. From 1900 till his retirement in 1918 he was principal assistant engineer of the Rapid Transit Subway Construction Company, which was engaged in the construction of the New York subway system. General Douglas retired to Kaimes, his residence near Providence Forge, where he died on July 20, 1926. He was survived by his widow, Minnie (Robbins) Douglas, whom he married in 1868.

Biographic Catalogue; *Richmond Times-Dispatch*, July 21, 1926; VHS Mss7:1 D7463:1.

By JOHN P. WALKER. Signed. Dated 1922

Oil on canvas: 30 x 25 in. (76.2 x 63,5 cm.)

9. Sir Dudley Digges

Acquired in 1946 through merger with the Confederate Memorial Association. Por946.135

Rose Adèle (Cutts) Douglas, 1835–1899 (Mrs. Stephen Arnold Douglas)

Daughter of James Madison Cutts and Ellen Elizabeth (O'Neale) Cutts (qq.v.) and granddaughter of Richard and Anna (Payne) Cutts (qq.v.), the subject was born on December 27, 1835. As a young woman she was an extremely popular figure in Washington society; it was therefore something of a surprise when she married on November 20, 1856, Senator Stephen Arnold Douglas, of Illinois, unromantic, untidy, and more than twenty years her senior. The marriage, apparently a happy one, was of short duration; Douglas died on June 3, 1861. The couple's only child had died in infancy just a year before. She married, second, in January 1866, Brigadier General Robert Williams (1829–1901), a native Virginian who fought for the North during the Civil War and later became adjutant general of the United States Army. The couple were the parents of six children. Rose Adèle (Cutts) Douglas Williams died in 1899 and is buried in Arlington Cemetery.

Cecil Hampton Cutts Howard, *Genealogy of the Cutts Family in America* (Albany, N.Y., 1892), p. 293; *Portraiture*, pp.

107–8; *Catholic Historical Review* 31 (1945–46): 180–91; Marie de Mare, *G. P. A. Healy, American Artist* (New York, 1954) (Portrait II reproduced, plate 15); *Antiques* 116 (1979): 1136 (Portrait II reproduced).

Portrait I

ARTIST UNIDENTIFIED

Oil on canvas: 24½ x 19 in. (62.2 x 48.3 cm.) (oval)

Presented in 1944 by Mildred (Williams) Farwell (Mrs. Walter Farwell) of Syosset, Long Island, New York, a daughter of the subject. Por944.20

Portrait II

BY GEORGE PETER ALEXANDER HEALY. Signed. Dated Chicago 1857

Oil on canvas: 62 x 47 in. (157.5 x 119.4 cm.)

Presented in 1944 by Mildred (Williams) Farwell (Mrs. Walter Farwell) of Syosset, Long Island, New York, a daughter of the subject. Por944.21

Portrait III

BY GEORGE PETER ALEXANDER HEALY. Signed. Dated 1857

Oil on canvas: 30 x 25½ in. (76.2 x 64.8 cm.)

Presented in 1944 by Mildred (Williams) Farwell (Mrs. Walter Farwell) of Syosset, Long Island, New York, a daughter of the subject. Por944.22

Sir Francis Drake, ca. 1540–1596

Sir Francis Drake, circumnavigator and admiral, was born about 1540, probably in Devon, to a family of yeoman stock. In 1566 he shipped to the Spanish West Indies as a seaman; he was later given command of a ship in Captain John Hawkins's fleet. Between 1570 and 1572 he led raiding parties against the Spanish in the West Indies and Panama; on the third such expedition he bore off enough bullion to win unofficial approbation and a reputation for courage and daring. On his voyage of circumnavigation Drake set out from Plymouth on December 13, 1577, with five ships; he returned on September 26, 1580, with only one ship, the *Golden Hind*, "very richly fraught with gold, silver, silk, pearls, and precious stones." In recognition of his achievement—Magellan's was the only previous circumnavigation, and Magellan had not lived to complete it—Queen Elizabeth I knighted Drake aboard the *Golden Hind* on April 4, 1581. In the ensuing war with Spain, incited in no small part by Drake's raids on Spanish shipping, Drake with a fleet of some twenty ships captured Santo Domingo and Cartegena, destroyed the Spanish fort at St. Augustine, and on his homeward voyage relieved the Roanoke Colony, bringing back to England not only the disgruntled settlers

Rose Adèle (Cutts) Douglas (Portrait II)

but, it is thought, two hitherto unknown plants: tobacco and potatoes. His fleet inflicted heavy damage at Cadiz in 1587, and the following year he served ably as vice admiral of the fleet that destroyed the Spanish Armada in the English Channel. Drake's subsequent voyages were largely unsuccessful. He died on January 28, 1596, in the course of yet another expedition against the Spanish West Indies; he was buried at sea. Sir Francis was twice married: first, on July 4, 1569, to Mary Newman; second, to Elizabeth Sydenham; he had no issue, and on his death his considerable estate passed to his youngest and only surviving brother, Thomas Drake, the companion of most of his voyages.

DNB; *Encyclopedia Americana*; *Virginia House*, p. 46.

Sir Francis Drake

ARTIST UNIDENTIFIED

Oil on canvas: 20½ x 18½ in. (52.1 x 47 cm.)

Received in 1948 as a bequest of Mr. and Mrs. Alexander Wilbourne Weddell of Richmond. Por948.66

Martha Bickerton Drew, 1818–1892
See Hancock Lee, 1797–1860, and Family

George Coke Dromgoole, 1797–1847
See The Convention of 1829–30

Richard Thomas Walker Duke, 1822–1898

A Virginia congressman and prominent member of the bar, Richard Thomas Walker Duke was a native of Albemarle County, born June 6, 1822, son of Richard and Maria (Walker) Duke of Milbrook. He attended private schools, graduated from the Virginia Military Institute in 1845, and taught school at the Richmond Academy. On July 26, 1846, he married Elizabeth Scott Eskridge, daughter of William S. Eskridge and Margaret (Brown) Eskridge of Lexington; they became the parents of five children, two of whom died in infancy. Duke was principal of a school in Lewisburg, (West) Virginia, until 1849, during which time he studied law; on the death of his father he returned to Albemarle County, continued his legal studies, and graduated from the University of Virginia law school in 1850. Elected Commonwealth's attorney for the county of Albemarle in 1858, he held that office until 1869. At the time of the John Brown raid Duke organized the Albemarle Rifles, later part of the 19th Virginia Regiment, and served at Harpers Ferry and First Manassas. He became thereafter colonel of the 46th Virginia Infantry and colonel of the 2d Battalion of Reserves. Captured at Sayler's Creek, he was imprisoned at the Old Capitol prison in Washington, then at Johnson's Island. On his return to Virginia in the summer of 1865 he resumed his legal practice and entered politics. Elected as a Conservative to the United States Congress, Colonel Duke served in Washington 1870–73; he was elected to one term in the Virginia House of Delegates in 1879. Duke died at his home, Sunnyside, near Charlottesville, on July 2, 1898.

Biographical Directory; *History of Virginia*, 5: 6–7; *Eminent and Representative Men*, pp. 435–37; CMA Archives, folio Z1n.

ARTIST UNIDENTIFIED

Oil on canvas: 27¼ x 22 in. (69.2 x 55.9 cm.)

Presented to the R. E. Lee Camp, Confederate Veterans, in 1926; acquired by the Virginia Historical Society in 1946 through merger with the Confederate Memorial Association. Por946.203

Edwin Steele Duncan, 1789–1858
See The Convention of 1829–30

Samuel Scott Dunlap, b. 1830

Born in Jasper County, Georgia, on July 31, 1830, the subject was the son of David and Hetty (Wingate) Dunlap. He came to Macon, Georgia, in November 1849, became a clerk in a grocery store, and within three years had saved enough to start a business of his own, which prospered. On the outbreak of the Civil War he joined a cavalry company as a first lieutenant; after six months he resigned to organize the Bibb Cavalry, in which he served as a captain. The unit participated in the battles of Second Manassas, Harpers Ferry, Sharpsburg, and Gettysburg. Wounded at Gettysburg, Dunlap spent several months in a Richmond hospital. After the war he returned to Macon where he opened a hardware business; under his direction it developed into one of the largest such enterprises in the South. He subsequently became president of the Macon Agricultural Works, president of the Macon Fire Insurance Company, director of several banks, and a substantial stockholder in the Southwestern Railroad. His wife, Mary (Birgh) Dunlap, whom he married on May 15, 1855, was a daughter of J. L. Birgh of Bibb County, Georgia; she bore him seven children.

Memoirs of Georgia, Containing Historical Accounts of the State's Civil, Military, Industrial, and Professional Interests, and Personal Sketches of Many of Its People (Atlanta, 1895), 1: 331–32.

BY ADELE WILLIAMS. Signed. Dated 1902?

Oil on canvas: 30 x 25 in. (76.2 x 63.5 cm.)

Presented to the R. E. Lee Camp, Confederate Veterans, by the subject's daughter, Florine (Dunlap) Starke (Mrs. Ashton Starke); acquired by the Virginia Historical Society in 1946 through merger with the Confederate Memorial Association. Por946.111

John Murray, fourth Earl of *Dunmore*, 1732–1809

See John *Murray*, fourth Earl of Dunmore, 1732–1809

William Logan Dunn, 1839–1922

Dr. William Logan Dunn, "a country doctor of high standing," was born at Glade Spring, Washington County, on September 15, 1839, son of Dr. Samuel Dunn. He attended Emory and Henry College and was studying medicine at the Jefferson Medical College in Philadelphia when the Civil War began. He enlisted in Company D, 1st Virginia Cavalry, was later transferred to the medical staff, continued his training at the Richmond Medical College, and spent the remaining war years as assistant surgeon and later as surgeon in the field with Mosby's cavalry. After the war Dr. Dunn returned to Glade Spring to practice medicine. He was twice married: in 1868 to Fannie Beattie, daughter of Absolom and Eliza (Davis) Beattie; in 1889 to Lou Reid. He was brother-

in-law to General William Edmondson ("Grumble") Jones (q.v.). In 1895 Dr. Dunn was appointed local surgeon for the Norfolk and Western Railway. He was a member of the Medical Society of Virginia and the American Medical Association, a Freemason, and surgeon to the W. E. Jones Camp and Mosby Camp, United Confederate Veterans. He died in 1922 and is buried in Glade Spring Cemetery.

Men of Mark in Virginia, 3: 117–18; *Confederate Military History*, 3: 845–47; *Virginia and Virginians*, 2: 717–18; *Biographic Catalogue.*

BY JACKSON. Signed

Oil on canvas: 30 x 25 in. (76.2 x 63.5 cm.)

Acquired in 1946 through merger with the Confederate Memorial Association. Por946.104

Maria Beverley (Randolph) DuVal, 1794–1845 (Mrs. Philip DuVal)

Born on April 4, 1794, at Blandfield, Essex County, the subject was the daughter of Richard and Maria (Beverley) Randolph of Curles, Henrico County. She married Philip DuVal (1789–1847), son of Benjamin and Elizabeth (Warrock) DuVal, who owned a well-known pharmacy in Richmond. She bore her husband five children, one of whom, Robert Randolph DuVal (q.v.), also became a pharmacist in Richmond and is represented in the Society's portrait collection. Mrs. DuVal died in Richmond on June 10, 1845; her husband died on December 3, 1847; both are buried in Shockoe Cemetery, Richmond.

The Beverley Family, p. 536; *Richmond Portraits*, p. 61.

ARTIST UNIDENTIFIED

Oil on wood panel: 22 x 18 in. (55.9 x 45.7 cm.)

Presented in 1948 by Edmund Pendleton Randolph Duval of Norman, Oklahoma, a grandson of the subject. Por948.18c

Robert Randolph DuVal, 1817–1875
Sallie Dandridge (Cooke) DuVal, 1828–1887 (Mrs. Robert Randolph DuVal)

Robert Randolph DuVal was born in 1817, the second of five children born to Philip and Maria Beverley (Randolph) DuVal (q.v.) of Richmond. Following in his father's footsteps, he became a pharmacist in Richmond, conducting his business in various locations in the city from before 1845 until about 1871, when he retired to his country residence, Oropax, in New Kent County. Here he died on May 25,

1875. His wife, whom he married on June 6, 1849, was Sallie Dandridge (Cooke) DuVal, daughter of John Rogers Cooke and Mary (Pendleton) Cooke (qq.v.) and a sister of the novelist John Esten Cooke; she was born on March 18, 1828, bore her husband eight children, and died on December 14, 1887. Mr. and Mrs. DuVal are buried in Hollywood Cemetery, Richmond.

The Beverley Family, p. 539; *Richmond Portraits*, p. 61 (Portrait I reproduced); *VMHB* 56 (1948): 238.

Portrait I. Robert Randolph DuVal

ATTRIBUTED TO WILLIAM JAMES HUBARD

Oil on canvas: 30 x 25 in. (76.2 x 63.5 cm.)

Received in 1947 as a bequest of Florence Beverley Duval of Lexington, Virginia, a daughter of the subject. Por947.26

Portrait II. Sallie Dandridge (Cooke) DuVal

ATTRIBUTED TO WILLIAM JAMES HUBARD

Oil on canvas: 30 x 25 in. (76.2 x 63.5 cm.)

Received in 1947 as a bequest of Florence Beverley Duval of Lexington, Virginia, a daughter of the subject. Por947.28

"James Edmund Dyer"

The portrait came to the Society as a bequest of Dr. Bernard Samuels of New York City, who identified the subject as "Judge James Edmund Dyer of Virginia and Iowa." Efforts to identify the sitter further have been to no avail.

ARTIST UNIDENTIFIED

Oil on canvas: 30 x 26 in. (76.2 x 66 cm.)

Received in 1960 as a bequest of Dr. Bernard Samuels of New York City. Por960.50

Elias Earle, 1762–1823

A native of Frederick County, the subject was born on June 19, 1762, son of Samuel and Elizabeth (Holbrook) Earle. He married on September 17, 1782, Frances Wilton Robinson; five years later they removed to Greenville County, South Carolina. One of the earliest ironmasters of the South, he prospected in the iron region of Georgia, then turned to politics. After serving in the South Carolina House of Representatives 1794–98 and the South Carolina Senate 1798–1804, he was elected to the United States Congress, where he represented his district 1805–7, 1811–15, and 1817–21. He died at Anderson, South Carolina, on May 19, 1823, and is buried in the family burying ground at Greenville.

Biographical Directory; Emily Bellinger Reynolds, *Biographical Directory of the Senate of the State of South Carolina, 1776–1964* (Columbia, S.C. 1964).

ARTIST UNIDENTIFIED

Bas-relief in wax: 3³⁄₄ in. (9.5 cm.) in height

Presented in 1903 by Mrs. M. L. Eubank of Warm Springs. Por903.6

Annie (Fielding) Early (Mrs. Charles Early)

Daughter of Michael B. Fielding of New York City and his wife (q.v.), the subject married Charles Early, the youngest son of Dr. Robert Early and Harriet Jane (Davies) Early (q.v.) of Lynchburg. The couple resided in Lynchburg and Washington, D.C.

Tyler's Quart. 8 (1926–27): 141; *W. & M. Quart.*, 1st ser., 18 (1909–10): 284; George S. Jack, *History of Roanoke County* (Roanoke, 1912), pp. 189–90.

BY PAUL HALLWIG. Signed. Dated Baltimore 1924

Oil on canvas: 60 x 40 in. (152.4 x 101.6 cm.)

Presented in 1963 by Annie Ridge (Early) Fairfax (Mrs. Ronald Randolph Fairfax) of Roanoke, the subject's daughter. Por963.28

Clifford Cabell Early, 1883–1967
Harriet (Harman) Early (Mrs. Clifford Cabell Early)

Clifford Cabell Early, son of John Cabell Early and Mary Washington (Cabell) Early of Bedford County, was born on April 9, 1883. He graduated from the United States Military Academy in 1905 and became a career officer in the United States Army. He was on duty in San Francisco after the great earthquake, served in the Philippines, on the Mexican border, and at Tientsin, China. He was attached to the office of the Chief of Staff in Washington during World War I. Between 1925 and 1930 he was professor of military science and tactics at North Carolina State University; he was then attached to the history section of the Army War College. During World War II Colonel Early was commanding officer of Fort McPherson. He retired in 1944, thereafter making his home in Atlanta, Georgia, where he died on April 11, 1967. His wife, whom he married in 1921, was Harriet (Harman) Early. Likenesses of Colonel Early's grandfather, Samuel Henry Early (q.v.), and his sister, Evelyn Russell Early (q.v.), are also in the Society's collection.

Family of Early, p. 113; United States Military Academy, Register of Graduates (West Point, N.Y., 1966); ibid., 1976.

Portrait I. Clifford Cabell Early

By "Van Court." Signed. Dated 1937

Silhouette: 6½ in. (16.5 cm.) in height, on paper 9½ x 6½ in. (24.1 x 16.5 cm.)

Acquired in a collection of Early family papers purchased in 1975. Por975.34

Portrait II. Clifford Cabell Early

Artist unidentified. Dated 1931

Silhouette: 4 in. (10.2 cm.) in height, on paper 5½ x 3¾ in. (14 x 9.8 cm.). Inscribed: "Clifford Cabell Early. Feb. 25, 1931."

Acquired in a collection of Early family papers purchased in 1975. Por975.35

Portrait III. Harriet (Harman) Early

Artist unidentified. Dated 1931

Silhouette: 3¾ in. (9.5 cm.) in height, on paper 5½ x 3¾ in. (14 x 9.8 cm.). Inscribed: "Harriet (Harman) Early. February 24, 1931."

Acquired in a collection of Early family papers purchased in 1975. Por975.36

Evelyn Russell Early, 1877–1940

The subject was the daughter of John Cabell Early and Mary Washington (Cabell) Early of Bedford County, the granddaughter of Samuel Henry Early (q.v.), and the sister of Clifford Cabell Early (q.v.). Born in 1877, she grew up in Lynchburg but later moved to Washington, D.C., where she spent much of her life. During World War I she was active in the Red Cross; she was a member of the Colonial Dames and the United Daughters of the Confederacy. Miss Early died in Washington, D.C., on February 21, 1940; burial took place in Spring Hill Cemetery, Lynchburg.

Family of Early, p. 112; VHS Mss1 Ea765b 336.

By Robert Knight Ryland. Signed. Dated 1901

Pen and ink on cardboard: 12 x 9¼ in. (30.5 x 23.5 cm.)

Acquired in a collection of Early family papers purchased in 1975. Por975.38

Harriet Jane (Davies) Early, 1820–1896   (Mrs. Robert Early)

Born on September 11, 1820, daughter of Dr. Howell Davies and his first wife, Harriet (Godfrey) Davies,

of Campbell and Bedford counties, the subject married Dr. Robert Early, a native of Philadelphia and a graduate of the Philadelphia Medical College. The couple established themselves in Lynchburg, where for more than forty years Dr. Early practiced dentistry. Two of their sons, Robert Davies Early and William Early (qq.v.), were killed in the Civil War; another son, Charles, married Annie Fielding (q.v., Annie [Fielding] Early), whose portrait is in the Society's collection. Dr. Robert Early died in Lynchburg on December 29, 1883; his wife died on February 27, 1896.

Ruth Hairston Early, Campbell Chronicles and Family Sketches Embracing the History of Campbell County, Virginia, 1782–1926 (Lynchburg, Va., 1927), p. 396; Tyler's Quart. 8 (1926–27): 141; Mary Denham Ackerly and Lula Eastman Jeter Parker, Our Kin: The Genealogies of Some of the Early Families Who Made History in the Founding and Development of Bedford County, Virginia (Lynchburg, Va., 1930), p. 349; Lynchburg Virginian, Dec. 31, 1883, p. 3, col. 1; Mr. Raymond Booth, Superintendent, Presbyterian Cemetery, Lynchburg; Mr. Eric Frank, Jones Memorial Library, Lynchburg.

Artist unidentified

Oil on canvas: 23¾ x 20 in. (60.3 x 50.8 cm.)

Received in 1965 as a bequest of Annie Ridge (Early) Fairfax (Mrs. Ronald Randolph Fairfax) of Roanoke, a granddaughter of the subject. Por965.7

John Early, 1786–1873

John Early, bishop of the Methodist Episcopal Church, South, was born in Bedford County on January 1, 1786, the thirteenth child of Joshua and Mary (Leftwich) Early. Although his parents were Baptists, he joined the Methodist Episcopal church in 1804. Licensed to preach two years later, he was admitted to the Virginia Conference in 1807 and in 1813 became presiding elder of the Meherrin District. His early pastoral work with Thomas Jefferson's slaves at Poplar Forest, Bedford County, led to an abiding interest in the welfare of the black race; in 1825 he became president of the Colonization Society. In addition to carrying out his ministerial duties, he applied himself energetically to the civic improvement of Lynchburg. He was an early proponent of free public education, worked for many years to establish a railroad from Lynchburg through the southwestern part of the state, assisted in the development of a municipal water supply, and was president of the Spring Hill Cemetery Association. Although Early was repeatedly nominated for Congress, was offered the governorships of the territories of Illinois and Arkansas, and was asked by President Tyler to become the comptroller of the Treasury, he steadfastly declined all political posts. One of the founders of Randolph-Macon College in 1830, he was for forty years president of its board of trustees. He took an active part in the 1844 General Conference of the Methodist Episcopal church which led to the formation of the Methodist Episcopal Church, South. In 1854 he became one of the church's bishops, serving in that capacity until 1866 when poor health necessitated his retirement. He died in Lynchburg after a long illness on November 5, 1873. He was twice married: first, to Anne Jones, who died without issue; second, in 1822, to Elizabeth Browne Rives; he had seven children by his second marriage. Bishop Early became a member of the Virginia Historical Society in 1833.

DAB; *Family of Early*, pp. 188–91; *VMHB* 63 (1955): 230.

John Early

ARTIST UNIDENTIFIED

Oil on canvas: 30 x 24³/₄ in. (76.2 x 62.9 cm.)

Presented in 1954 by Annie Ridge (Early) Fairfax (Mrs. Ronald Randolph Fairfax) of Roanoke. Por954.16

The plate in Ruth Hairston Early's genealogy of the family (opposite p. 188) reproduces an engraving of a portrait depicting the bishop as a slightly younger man. The same source (p. 190) states that "a fine portrait of Bishop John Early is owned by his family, and hung for many years in Court Street Methodist Church, at Lynchburg, but was taken down when the old church building was razed." It is not known whether the portrait referred to is the Society's portrait, the portrait reproduced as an engraving, or yet another likeness.

Jubal Anderson Early, 1816–1894

Jubal Anderson Early was born in Franklin County on November 3, 1816, the son of Joab and Ruth (Hairston) Early. He graduated from West Point in 1837, saw service in Florida against the Seminoles, then resigned to study law. Admitted to the bar in 1840, he practiced in Rocky Mount. He represented his native county in the Virginia legislature 1841–42, being at the time the youngest member of the House; he served with the 1st Virginia Regiment in the Mexican War, during which he saw no action, but narrowly avoided death when the steamboat on which he was traveling home on sick leave blew up. Early voted against secession at the State Convention of 1861, to which he was a delegate, but entered the Confederate army immediately thereafter as colonel of the 24th Virginia Infantry. He was promoted to brigadier general on July 21, 1861, and took part in all the subsequent engagements of the Army of Northern Virginia from 1862 to 1864, rising in due course to the rank of lieutenant general. In June 1864 his corps was ordered into the Shenandoah Valley; at Winchester and Fisher's Hill it suffered heavily, and in March 1865 what remained of his command was dispersed at Waynesboro. After the surrender, Early escaped to Mexico, spent some time in Canada, where he wrote his memoirs, and in 1869 returned to Virginia, making his home in Lynchburg. In his latter years he became one of the supervisors, with General Beauregard, of the Louisiana state lottery; his salary from this work he donated to charity. Keenly interested in the history of the Confederacy, General Early became the first president of the Southern Historical Society and contributed articles to its publication. General Early died, unmarried, at Lynchburg, on March 2, 1894; he was buried with military honors at Spring Hill Cemetery.

DAB; *Generals in Gray*; *Family of Early*, p. 116 (Portrait II reproduced); *Biographic Catalogue*; *VMHB* 83 (1975): 237.

Portrait I

BY JOHN P. WALKER. Signed. Dated 1898

Oil on canvas: 48 x 39 in. (147.3 x 99.1 cm.)

Acquired in 1946 through merger with the Confederate Memorial Association. Por946.216

Portrait II

BY JOHN WYCLIFFE LOWES FORSTER. Signed. 1912   *See* Plate 10

Oil on canvas: 42 x 30 in. (106.7 x 76.2 cm.). Inscribed on the back: "Lieut. General Jubal A. Early. Painted from photographs taken of him in 1865. By J. W. L. Forster. Lynchburg, 1912."

Received in 1974 as a bequest of Henrianne Cabell Early of Washington, D.C. Por974.25

10. Jubal Anderson Early (Portrait II)

Robert Davies Early, 1841–1864 and His Brother William Early, 1843–1865

The subjects of this double portrait are the two eldest sons of Dr. Robert Early of Lynchburg and Harriet Jane (Davies) Early (q.v.). Both were killed in action in the Civil War: Robert, born on September 23, 1841, was killed at the battle of the Wilderness on May 5, 1864; William, born on March 13, 1843, was killed at Five Forks on April 1, 1865.

Information received with the portrait; information received from the superintendent of the Presbyterian Cemetery, Lynchburg.

William and Robert Davies Early

ARTIST UNIDENTIFIED

Oil on canvas: 30¼ x 24 in. (76.8 x 61 cm.)

Presented in 1954 by Annie Ridge (Early) Fairfax (Mrs. Ronald Randolph Fairfax) of Roanoke, a niece of the subjects. Por954.10

In a letter from the donor the subjects are identified: "Robert is the one in the plain velvet, my uncle Willie [is] the one in the scotch plaid woolen kilt."

VHS correspondence file, 1954.

Samuel Henry Early, 1813–1874

Samuel Henry Early was born in 1813, eldest child of Joab and Ruth (Hairston) Early of Franklin County and brother of Jubal Anderson Early (q.v.). He received his formal education at Patrick Henry Academy and the College of William and Mary, graduating from the latter institution in 1832. After studying law in Fredericksburg, he began the practice of law in Franklin but did not continue. For a time he served as postmaster at Cooper's in Franklin County. On April 29, 1846, he married Henrian Cabell, daughter of John Jordan Cabell and Henri-anne (Davies) Cabell; the couple had seven children, three of whom died in childhood. After a short sojourn in Kanawha County, where he was engaged in the manufacture of salt, he removed to Lynchburg to devote himself to farming operations in Bedford County. At the commencement of the Civil War, Early enlisted in the Wise Troop of 2d Virginia Cavalry; he later became an aide-de-camp on the staff of his brother, General Jubal A. Early (q.v.), seeing action at Antietam, Second Manassas, Seven Pines, and Malvern Hill. Wounded at Gettysburg and incapacitated for further service in the field, he was appointed assistant conscripting officer at Lynchburg. After the war he resumed farming in Bedford County and in Kanawha County, West Virginia; he also contracted to supply large quantities of railroad ties from his West Virginia properties for the use of the Chesapeake and Ohio Railway Company. He died in Charleston, West Virginia, in March 1874; his body was brought to Lynchburg for burial in Spring Hill Cemetery.

Family of Early, pp. 108–11; *The Cabells and Their Kin*, pp. 598–99.

ARTIST UNIDENTIFIED

Silhouette: 10½ in. (26.7 cm.) in height, mounted on cardboard 12¼ x 8½ in. (31.1 x 21.6 cm.). Inscribed: "Silhouette of Samuel Henry Early Sr. as a student at William & Mary."

Acquired in a collection of Early family papers purchased in 1975. Por975.3

The silhouette is a modern copy of an original which was owned in 1938 by Evelyn and Henrian Early of Washington, D.C., nieces of the subject. Another copy of the original was apparently presented to the College of William and Mary in 1938 by the Misses Early. According to a newspaper clipping datelined "Williamsburg, Jan. 29, 1938" and received with the Society's silhouette, the likeness "was made when Early was 17 years old and showed the style of dress worn by students of that day." A portrait of Samuel Henry Early in Confederate uniform was painted by John Wycliffe Lowes Forster of Toronto, a companion piece, perhaps, to the Society's portrait of Jubal Anderson Early (q.v., Portrait II) by the same artist.

William Early, 1843–1865

See Robert Davies Early, 1841–1864

Francis Howard, fifth Baron Howard of *Effingham*, 1643–1695

See Francis Howard, fifth Baron *Howard of Effingham*, 1643–1695

John Echols, 1823–1896

Confederate general, lawyer, and businessman, John Echols was born in Lynchburg on March 20, 1823. His parents were Joseph and Elizabeth F. (Lambeth) Echols. He graduated from Washington College (now Washington and Lee University) in 1840, did graduate work at the Virginia Military Institute, and studied law at Harvard. Admitted to the bar of Rockbridge County in 1843, he practiced briefly at Staunton, then removed to Monroe County (now West Virginia) where he became Commonwealth's attorney and represented the county at the Convention of 1861. After the adoption of the Ordinance of Secession he returned to Monroe County, organized a company which was assigned to the 27th Regiment, and led the company at First Manassas and later at Kernstown where he was severely wounded. Commissioned brigadier general April 16, 1862, he later served largely in the western part of the state as commander of the Department of Southwestern Virginia. General Echols escorted Jefferson Davis from Greensboro to Charlotte, North Carolina, after Appomattox and was later paroled. After the war he became senior partner of the law firm of Echols, Bell and Catlett in Staunton; he became president of the National Valley Bank of Staunton in 1872, retaining the office until his death; and he was for twenty years a director of the Chesapeake and Ohio Railway and its associated lines, attention to its affairs compelling him to reside for the last ten years of his life in Louisville, Kentucky. General Echols was a member of the board of visitors of the Virginia Military Institute and a trustee of Washington and Lee University; he became a member of the Virginia Historical Society in 1884. He married, first, Mary Jane Caperton and, second, Mrs. Mary Cochran Reid of New York City. Two sons and a daughter, both by his first wife, survived childhood. General Echols died in Staunton on May 24, 1896, and is buried in Thornrose Cemetery.

DAB; Generals in Gray; Men of Mark in Virginia, 5: 124–28; *Biographic Catalogue.*

By JOHN P. WALKER. Signed. Dated 1902

Oil on canvas: 30 x 25 in. (76.2 x 63.5 cm.)

Presented to the R. E. Lee Camp, Confederate Veterans, in 1902; acquired by the Virginia Historical Society in 1946 through merger with the Confederate Memorial Association. Por946.58

Joseph Dupuy Eggleston, 1867–1953

Son of Joseph Dupuy Eggleston and Anne Carrington (Booker) Eggleston, the subject was born at Marble Hill, Prince Edward County, on November 13, 1867. After graduating from Hampden-Sydney College in 1886, he taught school in Virginia, Georgia, and North Carolina; in 1891 he was invited to become superintendent of public schools in Asheville, North Carolina, a post he held until 1900. Returning to Virginia, he did editorial work for the B. F. Johnson Publishing Company in Richmond and for the Southern Education Board and for three years was superintendent of schools for Prince Edward County. In 1905 he was elected state superintendent of public instruction, serving in that capacity until 1913; he was president of Virginia Polytechnic Institute 1913–19 and president of Hampden-Sydney College from 1919 until his retirement in 1939, whereupon he was named president emeritus. Eggleston was the author of monographs dealing with the history and families of Prince Edward and surrounding counties; he also contributed numerous articles to daily and weekly newspapers and was in demand as a speaker on educational and historical topics. He died on March 13, 1953. Eggleston married, on December 18, 1895, Julia Jane Johnson, daughter of William and Elizabeth Cabell (Carrington) Johnson; the couple had two children, a daughter and a son. Eggleston was elected to membership in the Virginia Historical Society in 1903 and was the Society's president 1938–43.

Who Was Who in America 3 (1960): 253; *History of Virginia*, 6: 6–7; *Virginia and the Virginia County* 4, no. 2 (Feb. 1950): 6; *VMHB* 56 (1948): 237; Hampden-Sydney College, *The Record* 55, no. 1 (1978): 5.

By MARCIA SILVETTE. Signed

Oil on canvas: 30 x 25 in. (76.2 x 63.5 cm.)

Presented in 1947 by friends of the subject. Por947.34

Thomas Harding Ellis, 1814–1898

Son of Charles and Margaret Keeling (Nimmo) Ellis, the subject was born on September 6, 1814. He received his formal education in private schools in Richmond and at the University of Virginia, from which institution he graduated in 1832. After his graduation he spent several years in Mexico as pri-

Thomas Harding Ellis

Richmond Dispatch, April 12, 1898, p. 9; *Occasional Bulletin*, no. 31 (1975): 11–13 (portrait reproduced); Thomas Harding Ellis, *Family Register* (n.p., n.d.).

ARTIST UNIDENTIFIED. 1836

Miniature on ivory: 2½ x 2 in. (6.4 x 5.1 cm.) (oval). Engraved on the back of the case: "T. H. E. 1836."

Presented in 1975 by Armistead Churchill Young, Jr., of Richmond, a great-great-nephew of the subject. Por975.14

James Taylor Ellyson, 1847–1919

Prominent in the political life of Virginia for forty years, James Taylor Ellyson was born in Richmond on May 20, 1847, son of Henry K. Ellyson and Elizabeth P. (Barnes) Ellyson. He attended private schools in Richmond, then entered Hampden-Sydney College, but left after only a few months to enter the Confederate army. As a private in the 2d Company of the Richmond Howitzers, he participated in the principal battles of the Army of Northern Virginia until he surrendered with his company at Appomattox. After the war he attended both Richmond College and the University of Virginia, graduating from the latter in 1869. Embarking on a business career, he founded with Henry Taylor of Baltimore the firm of Ellyson and Taylor, booksellers and stationers; he also turned to the newspaper business, being associated at various times with the *Richmond Dispatch* and the *Religious Herald*. He was president of the Alleghany Coal Company and director of several railroad companies. Ellyson began a long career of public service with his election to the Richmond City Council in 1878; he was three times reelected; he represented Richmond and Henrico County in the state Senate 1885–88; and he was mayor of Richmond 1888–94. He was three times lieutenant governor of Virginia and for twenty-five years chairman of the Democratic State Committee. Ellyson's numerous civic and cultural interests included the Richmond school board, of which he was president for sixteen years, Richmond College, the Southern Baptist Convention, the Baptist General Association, and the association's Board of Education. He was a member of the R. E. Lee Camp, United Confederate Veterans, and played an important role in the campaign to raise funds for the construction of Battle Abbey; he was elected to membership in the Virginia Historical Society in 1892. On December 2, 1869, he married in Albemarle County Lora E. Hotchkiss, daughter of Nelson H. Hotchkiss and Harriet (Russell) Hotchkiss of New York; the Ellysons had one daughter, Nannie Moore Ellyson. James Taylor Ellyson died in Richmond on March 18, 1919.

vate secretary to the American ambassador, his uncle, Judge Powhatan Ellis, of Mississippi. Returning to Richmond in 1841, Ellis reorganized the family tobacco business and directed it until the firm closed in 1852; thereupon he succeeded John Young Mason (q.v.) as president of the James River and Kanawha Canal Company, a post he held at the request of Governor Letcher throughout the Civil War years. In 1868, in partnership with Matthew Fontaine Maury (q.v.), he formed a real estate firm; two years later he removed to Chicago where in time he became president of the Bank of Chicago. For the last thirteen years of his life he was employed in the Auditor's Office of the Treasury Department in Washington, D.C. Ellis was one of the founders of the University of Virginia Alumni Association, a colonel in the Richmond Fayette Artillery, first president of the Hollywood Cemetery Association, and a vestryman at St. Paul's Episcopal Church 1846–70. He was elected to membership in the Virginia Historical Society in 1837, became a member of its executive committee ten years later, and in 1868 succeeded Dr. George W. Bagby (q.v.) as its corresponding secretary. Ellis died in Richmond on April 11, 1898, and is buried in Hollywood Cemetery. His wife, Euphania Claiborne (Taylor) Harrison Ellis, daughter of Thomas Taylor and widow of Archibald Harrison, whom he married in Richmond on April 27, 1848, died just a few months before her husband, on July 10, 1897; the couple had no children.

Men of Mark in Virginia, 1: 183–85; *Virginia and Virginians*, 2: 781; George Wesley Rogers, *Officers of the Senate of Virginia, 1776–1956* (Richmond, 1959), pp. 67–68; *Biographic Catalogue*.

By George Bagby Matthews. Signed

Oil on canvas: 46 x 35³/₄ in. (116.8 x 90.8 cm.)

Acquired in 1946 through merger with the Confederate Memorial Association. Por946.221

George Eskridge, d.1735
Rebecca (Bonum) Eskridge, d.1715 (Mrs. George Eskridge)

George Eskridge came to Virginia at an undetermined date late in the seventeenth century; he established himself in Westmoreland County and became an extensive landholder, lawyer, and political figure. He represented his county in the House of Burgesses almost without interruption from 1705 until his death thirty years later. He married, first, around 1680, Rebecca Bonum, daughter of Samuel and Margaret (Philpot) Bonum of Westmoreland County; she bore him four sons and three daughters; her death occurred in 1715. Colonel Eskridge married, second, around 1717, Elizabeth (Vaulx) Craddock Porten, a daughter of Robert and Mary (Foxall) Vaulx. She had previously been twice married, first to Richard Craddock and second to Daniel Porten; one daughter was born of her union with Colonel Eskridge. He appears to have established his residence at Sandy Point, Westmoreland County, about five years after his second marriage. Eskridge became legal guardian of Mary Ball in 1720, serving in this capacity until her marriage in 1731 to Augustine Washington; her firstborn, George Washington (q.v.), was named for her former guardian. George Eskridge died in 1735.

Northern Neck of Virginia Historical Magazine 3 (1953): 233–36 and 16 (1966): 1451–67; *Virginia Tidewater Genealogy* 9 (1978): 7–15; *VMHB* 22 (1914): 307–9.

Portrait I. George Eskridge

Artist unidentified

Oil on canvas: 26 x 21 in. (66 x 53.3 cm.)

Received in 1914 as a bequest of Peter C. Rust of New York City. Por914.6

Portrait II. Rebecca (Bonum) Eskridge

Artist unidentified

Oil on canvas: 26 x 21 in. (66 x 53.3 cm.)

Received in 1914 as a bequest of Peter C. Rust of New York City. Por914.7

Heretofore there was uncertainty as to whether Mrs. Eskridge's portrait represented the first or second Mrs. Eskridge. The question is resolved by an entry in the inventory of Colonel Eskridge's goods and chattels taken shortly after his death. The list of furnishings "In the Hall" includes "2 Pictures of Col. Eskridge and former wife." Since Elizabeth Eskridge, the second wife, was alive at the time the

George Eskridge   Rebecca (Bonum) Eskridge

inventory was made—she survived her husband by nine years—the inventory reference establishes that the portrait is a likeness of Rebecca (Bonum) Eskridge.

Portraiture, pp. 31–32; *Northern Neck of Virginia Historical Magazine* 14 (1964): 1311–15.

"The Earl of Essex"

The minutes of a meeting of the Society's executive committee held on December 15, 1859, record that "the Corresponding Secretary exhibited to the Committee a portrait, supposed to be authentic, of the Earl of Essex, presented by Mr. Augustus A. Hughes of Richmond to the Society, which the Committee accepted with suitable acknowledgements to Mr. Hughes." The portrait, known as "The Earl of Essex" from that time, depicts a young man in the costume of about 1630. When it is recalled that Robert Devereux (1591–1646), holder of the title in 1630, was at that time a man of almost forty, the identification becomes doubtful. Furthermore, the features of the man depicted in the Society's portrait are quite unlike those in the authentic portrait at Welbeck Abbey.

VHS Archives, liber A3, p. 87; *Portraiture*, p. 33.

ARTIST UNIDENTIFIED

Oil on canvas: 25½ x 21 in. (64.8 x 53.3 cm.)

Presented in 1858 by Augustus A. Hughes of Richmond. Por858.4

William McKendree Evans, 1847–1939

Born in Richmond on February 1, 1847, only child of William and Margaret (Patrick) Evans, the subject was left an orphan in 1861. The following March, although only fifteen years of age, he offered his services to the Confederacy as a private in Parker's Battery, taking part in virtually all the battles in which that unit was engaged and acting as courier to Generals Stephen D. Lee and Edward P. Alexander. In June 1862 he was wounded at Malvern Hill, but thereafter he fought at Sharpsburg, Fredericksburg, Chancellorsville, Gettysburg, and the Wilderness. Captured at Sayler's Creek, he contracted typhoid fever during his imprisonment at Point Lookout and nearly died. After his release and recovery, he entered the mercantile trade in Petersburg, remaining there until October 1876, when he returned to Richmond to join the jobbing house of Milhiser and Company. Evans remained with the company until 1900, then established his own accounting firm, se-

curing from the state of Virginia certificate no. 1 as a certified public accountant. Evans was long a member of the Richmond Light Infantry Blues, rising in rank to major and assistant adjutant general; he was active in Masonic and veterans affairs; in 1928 he became commander, Virginia division, United Confederate Veterans, and in 1933 commander, Department of the Army of Northern Virginia, United Confederate Veterans. He died in Richmond on October 23, 1939, and is buried in Mount Calvary Cemetery. Evans was married three times: first, in 1868, to Mary L. Covington; second, in 1877, to Mattie F. Taylor; third, in 1880, to Lelia Louise Pizzini. He had children by each of his wives.

History of Virginia, 4: 243–44; *Confederate Military History*, 3: 863–64; Robert K. Krick, *Parker's Virginia Battery, C.S.A.* (Berryville, Va., 1975), p. 319.

BY MARCIA SILVETTE. Signed. Dated 1935

Oil on canvas: 40 x 32¼ in. (101.6 x 81.9 cm.)

Acquired in 1946 through merger with the Confederate Memorial Association. Por946.186

Susannah Everard

See David Meade, 1710–1757

Richard Stoddert Ewell, 1817–1872

Born in Georgetown, D.C. on February 8, 1817, son of Dr. Thomas Ewell and Elizabeth (Stoddert) Ewell, the subject graduated from West Point in 1840 and spent the years before the Civil War in the Southwest, fighting in the Mexican War and winning commendation for action against the Apaches in New Mexico. At the beginning of the Civil War he resigned his commission and was appointed brigadier general in the Confederate army; in time he rose to the rank of lieutenant general, succeeding Stonewall Jackson as commander of the 2d Corps. Ewell saw action at First Manassas, the Valley campaign of 1862, the Seven Days, and Cedar Mountain. At Groveton he lost a leg; thereafter, equipped with a wooden one, he rode strapped to the saddle. After Gettysburg, where his military judgment has been the subject of criticism, he continued to command his corps until a heavy fall from his horse at Spotsylvania Court House incapacitated him from further active duty. Given command of the Department of Henrico, Ewell was put in charge of the defenses of Richmond. He was captured at Sayler's Creek on April 6, 1865, and imprisoned for almost four months at Fort Warren. He settled after the war on a farm near Spring Hill, Maury County, Tennessee, where he died January 25, 1872, two days after the death of his wife, Leczinska (Campbell) Brown, whom he had married on May 24, 1863.

DAB; *Generals in Gray*; *Biographic Catalogue*.

Portrait I

BY JOHN P. WALKER. Signed. Dated 1899

Oil on canvas: 60 x 40 in. (152.4 x 101.6 cm.)

Presented to the R. E. Lee Camp, Confederate Veterans, by Dr. Hunter Holmes McGuire in 1899; acquired by the Virginia Historical Society in 1946 through merger with the Confederate Memorial Association. Por946.43

Portrait II

See The Battle Abbey Murals. The Summer Mural

Ferdinando Fairfax, 1769–1820

Third son of Bryan Fairfax, eighth Baron Fairfax of Cameron, and Elizabeth (Cary) Fairfax, the subject was born in 1769; at his baptism his godparents were George and Martha Washington (qq.v.). On the death of a childless uncle, George William Fairfax, in 1787, the youth inherited an enormous estate; he devoted the rest of his life to its disposition. He lived lavishly, entertained liberally, and delighted in giving splendid gifts. On February 18, 1796, he married at Ceelys, near Hampton, Elizabeth Blair Cary, daughter of Wilson Miles Cary and Sarah (Blair) Cary, who bore her husband sixteen children, one of whom, Octavius Fairfax (q.v.), is represented in the

Ferdinando Fairfax

Society's portrait collection. He resided at Shannon Hill, Jefferson County, (West) Virginia, and at Mount Eagle, Fairfax County. A Freemason, he became a member of the Alexandria-Washington Lodge no. 22 in 1792. He died at Mount Eagle on September 24, 1820. His widow died at Shannon Hill on January 19, 1822.

Franklin Longdon Brockett, *The Lodge of Washington: A History of the Alexandria Washington Lodge, No. 22, A.F. and A.M. of Alexandria, Va., 1783–1876* (Alexandria, Va., 1876), pp. 118–20; Alexandria Association, *Our Town, 1749–1865: Likenesses of This Place & Its People Taken from Life, by Artists Known and Unknown* (Alexandria, Va., 1956), p. 20; Kenton Kilmer, *The Fairfax Family in Fairfax County* (Fairfax, Va., 1975), p. 50 (portrait reproduced, p. 49); Fairfax Harrison, *The Virginia Carys* (New York, 1919), pp. 108–10.

ARTIST UNIDENTIFIED

Oil on canvas: 18 x 14¾ in. (45.7 x 37.5 cm.)

Received in 1963 as a bequest of Martha Maury (Robinson) Upshur (Mrs. Francis Whittle Upshur) of Richmond. Por963.7

Octavius Thornton Fairfax, 1810–1837

Son of Ferdinando Fairfax (q.v.) and Elizabeth Blair (Cary) Fairfax, the subject was born at Shannon Hill, Jefferson County, (West) Virginia, on December 1, 1810. He joined the United States Navy as a midshipman on January 1, 1828, and died at Pensacola, Florida, on January 4, 1837.

"Fairfax Genealogy" (VHS CS71 F167 1896), p. 608; Edward William Callahan, *List of Officers of the Navy* (New York, 1901); Virginia State Library, Samuel Bassett French Papers.

BY WILLIAM HENRY FAIRFAX

Oil on panel: 6½ x 5 in. (16.5 x 12.7 cm.). Inscribed on paper attached to the frame: "Octavius Fairfax. By Wm. Henry [paper torn] supposed 1st sitting."

Received in 1963 as a bequest of Martha Maury (Robinson) Upshur (Mrs. Francis Whittle Upshur) of Richmond. Por963.8

The portrait was painted by the subject's elder brother.

Edwin Farrar, b. 1806

Born on September 4, 1806, Edwin Farrar was a son of Peter Field Farrar and Susanna (Tompkins) Farrar of Chesterfield County. He was a ship broker and commission merchant in Richmond and resided on Grace Street at Twenty-eighth. His wife was Martha Ann (Lewis) Farrar. He died without issue, probably between 1856 and 1859.

Elizabeth Hawes Ryland, "Brief Sketches of the Farrar, Tompkins and Fleet Families of Virginia" (typescript at Virginia State Library), pp. 16–17; *VMHB* 10 (1902–3): 309 and 66 (1958): 237.

ARTIST UNIDENTIFIED

Oil on canvas: 38 x 29¼ in. (96.5 x 74.3 cm.)
Received in 1957 as a bequest of Lilian (Farrar) Thompson (Mrs. Drewry P. Thompson) of Richmond. Por957.1

The subject was the twin brother of the donor's grandfather.

John Charles Featherston, 1837–1917

Born at Athens, Alabama, on August 14, 1837, the son of Howell C. Featherston and Dulaney (Odom) Featherston, both natives of North Carolina, the subject graduated from the Kentucky Military Institute, then entered the Confederate army in April 1861 as lieutenant of Company F, 9th Alabama Infantry. He accompanied the unit to Virginia and took part in the battles of First Manassas, Yorktown, and the Seven Days. Promoted to captain, he remained with his company throughout the war, seeing action at Fredericksburg, Chancellorsville, Gettysburg, where he was severely wounded, the defense of Petersburg, and the battle of the Crater. His military career ended with his parole at Decatur, Alabama, in May 1865. Having married on January 19, 1864, Letitia Preston Floyd, daughter of Nathaniel Wilson Floyd and Eliza W. (Anderson) Floyd of Lynchburg, Captain Featherston made his home on a farm near that city. He was at one time agricultural statistician for the state of Virginia, and he represented Campbell County in the Virginia legislature 1897–1904. Survived by his wife and two sons, Captain Featherston died in Lynchburg on October 31, 1917.

Biographic Catalogue; Confederate Military History, 3: 867–68; *Richmond Times-Dispatch*, Nov. 1, 1917, p. 4; Rosa Faulkner Yancey, *Lynchburg and Its Neighbors* (Richmond, 1935), pp. 305–6.

BY JOHN P. WALKER. Signed. Dated 1924

Oil on canvas: 30 x 25 in. (76.2 x 63.5 cm.)

Presented to the R. E. Lee Camp, Confederate Veterans, in 1924; acquired by the Virginia Historical Society in 1946 through merger with the Confederate Memorial Association. Por946.103

Annie Fielding
See Annie (Fielding) Early

Mrs. Michael B. Fielding

The subject was the wife of Michael B. Fielding (d. 1903). Her husband, a native of Scotland, came to this country, settled in New York City, and was twice president of the New York Cotton Exchange. Their daughter Annie (Fielding) Early (q.v.) was the wife of Charles Early of Lynchburg.

VHS Mss4 N4202 a1; information received with the portrait; New-York Historical Society.

ARTIST UNIDENTIFIED

Oil on canvas: 30 x 25 in. (76.2 x 63.5 cm.)

Received in 1965 as a bequest of Annie Ridge (Early) Fairfax (Mrs. Ronald Randolph Fairfax) of Roanoke, a granddaughter of the subject. Por965.6

Fitzhugh, Knox, and Gordon Portraits

This chart shows the relationship of members of the Fitzhugh, Knox, and Gordon families depicted in portraits owned by the Virginia Historical Society. Subjects of the Society's portraits are indicated in italics.

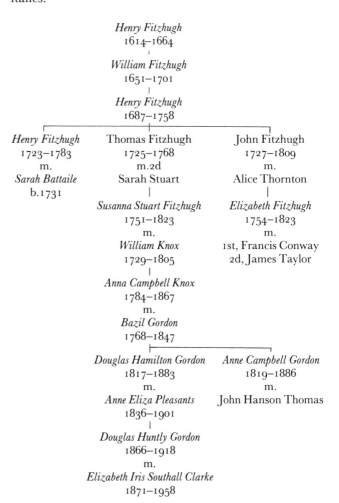

Henry Fitzhugh
1614–1664

William Fitzhugh
1651–1701

Henry Fitzhugh
1687–1758

Henry Fitzhugh
1723–1783
m.
Sarah Battaile
b.1731

Thomas Fitzhugh
1725–1768
m.2d
Sarah Stuart

Susanna Stuart Fitzhugh
1751–1823
m.
William Knox
1729–1805

Anna Campbell Knox
1784–1867
m.
Bazil Gordon
1768–1847

John Fitzhugh
1727–1809
m.
Alice Thornton

Elizabeth Fitzhugh
1754–1823
m.
1st, Francis Conway
2d, James Taylor

Douglas Hamilton Gordon
1817–1883
m.
Anne Eliza Pleasants
1836–1901

Douglas Huntly Gordon
1866–1918
m.
Elizabeth Iris Southall Clarke
1871–1958

Anne Campbell Gordon
1819–1886
m.
John Hanson Thomas

Elizabeth Fitzhugh, 1754–1823

See Elizabeth (Fitzhugh) Conway, 1754–1823

Henry Fitzhugh, 1614–1664

Henry Fitzhugh, a woolen draper of Bedford, England, progenitor of the Fitzhugh family in Virginia, was born in 1614, son of William Fitzhugh (d.1636). He married Mary King, daughter of Giles King of Tempsford, Bedfordshire. They were the parents of Colonel William Fitzhugh (1651–1701) (q.v.), who emigrated to Virginia around 1673. Henry Fitzhugh died in Ireland in 1664.

William Fitzhugh, *William Fitzhugh and His Chesapeake World, 1676–1701* (Chapel Hill, N.C., 1963), pp. 7–8 (portrait reproduced opposite p. 112); *VMHB* 7 (1899–1900): 197–98 (portrait reproduced), 75 (1967): 168 (portrait reproduced), and 81 (1973): 237. See chart on Fitzhugh, Knox, and Gordon Portraits for relationships.

COPIED BY JOHN HESSELIUS. 1751

Oil on canvas: 30¼ x 25 in. (76.8 x 63.5 cm.)

Received in 1972 as a bequest of Alice-Lee (Thomas) Stevenson (Mrs. Robert H. Stevenson) of Boston. Por972.19

This portrait and that of William Fitzhugh (1651–1701) the immigrant (q.v.), were copied by Hesselius in 1751 from originals now lost. The portrait has been relined. The back of the original canvas was inscribed: "Henry Fitzhugh Son of Willm Fitzhugh of Bedford Aetatis 20 1634 Copd by John Hesselius 1751."

Henry Fitzhugh, 1687–1758

The subject was the second son of Colonel William Fitzhugh (1651–1701) (q.v.), the immigrant to Virginia, and Sarah (Tucker) Fitzhugh. He was born on January 15, 1687, and received at least a part of his education in England. On the death of his father in 1701 he inherited a large estate, including half of the large Ravensworth tract. He became sheriff of Stafford County in 1715 and a captain in the county militia. On February 24, 1718, he married Susanna Cooke (1693–1749), daughter of Mordecai and Frances (Ironmonger) Cooke of Gloucester County; the couple resided at Bedford, Stafford County, and became the parents of nine children, one of whom, Henry Fitzhugh (1723–1783) (q.v.), is represented in the Society's portrait collection. The portrait suggests that the subject, who was known as "Blind Harry," did in fact inherit the weak eyes that were considered a Fitzhugh family trait. He died on December 12, 1758. He and his wife are buried in the family cemetery at Bedford.

William Fitzhugh, *William Fitzhugh and His Chesapeake World, 1676–1701* (Chapel Hill, N.C., 1963), pp. 194–95 (portrait reproduced opposite p. 144); *Overwharton Parish*, p. 225; *VMHB* 7 (1899–1900): 318 (portrait reproduced), 75 (1967): 168–69 (Rennolds portrait reproduced), and 81 (1973): 237. See chart on Fitzhugh, Knox, and Gordon Portraits for relationships.

Henry Fitzhugh, 1687–1758

BY JOHN HESSELIUS. 1752

Oil on canvas: 30 x 25 in. (76.2 x 63.5 cm.)

Received in 1972 as a bequest of Alice-Lee (Thomas) Stevenson (Mrs. Robert H. Stevenson) of Boston. Por972.21

The portrait bore on the back of the original canvas the inscription: "Cap Henry Fitzhugh 1687 1758 son of Col William Fitzhugh aetatis 65 1651–1701." Although the portrait has been relined, a photograph of the inscription has been preserved. A closely similar portrait, owned by Mrs. E. Addison Rennolds of Richmond, is inscribed: "Cap. Henry Fitzhugh son of Coll. Will Fitzhugh aetat 70 1756 J. Hesselius Pinx."

Henry Fitzhugh, 1723–1783
Sarah (Battaile) Fitzhugh, b.1731
(Mrs. Henry Fitzhugh)

Henry, eldest son of Henry Fitzhugh (1687–1758) (q.v.) and Susanna (Cooke) Fitzhugh, was born on September 10, 1723. On October 23, 1746, he mar-

84

ried Sarah Battaile, daughter of John and Sarah (Taliaferro) Battaile of Caroline County; the couple became the parents of fourteen children. In 1752 he became a colonel in the Stafford County militia, and on the death of his father in 1758 he inherited Bedford, Stafford County. He died in 1783; the date of his wife's death has not been found.

Overwharton Parish, p. 225; *VMHB* 7 (1899–1900): 425, 63 (1955): 229, and 75 (1967): 169 (both portraits reproduced). See chart on Fitzhugh, Knox, and Gordon Portraits for relationships.

Portrait I. Henry Fitzhugh

BY JOHN HESSELIUS

Oil on canvas: 30 x 25½ in. (76.2 x 64.8 cm.)

Presented in 1954 by Francis Carter Fitzhugh, Jr., of Cape Charles, and Horace Ashton Fitzhugh of King George County. Por954.2

Portrait II. Sarah (Battaile) Fitzhugh

BY JOHN HESSELIUS

Oil on canvas: 30¼ x 25 in. (76.8 x 63.5 cm.)

Presented in 1954 by Francis Carter Fitzhugh, Jr., of Cape Charles, and Horace Ashton Fitzhugh of King George County. Por954.3

Susanna Stuart Fitzhugh, 1751–1823
See William Knox, 1729–1805

William Fitzhugh, 1651–1701

Colonel William Fitzhugh, the immigrant to Virginia, was born in 1651, the youngest son of Henry Fitzhugh (1614–1664) (q.v.) and Mary (King) Fitzhugh of Bedford, England. He came to Virginia around 1673. On May 1, 1674, he married Sarah Tucker, daughter of John and Rose Tucker of Westmoreland County; the couple resided at Bedford, Stafford County. In addition to managing an extensive tobacco plantation, Fitzhugh, who had probably read law in England, conducted a successful legal practice and was widely sought for his counsel. He represented Stafford County in various sessions of the House of Burgesses between 1677 and 1693, sat on the Committee on Grievances and Propositions, and became a person of considerable political influence. In 1684 he was named justice of the peace of Stafford County and deputy commander of the Stafford militia. From 1693 to the end of his life he served, with George Brent, as resident agent for the proprietors of the Northern Neck. A collection of his extant letters was published by the Virginia Historical Society in 1963 under the title *William Fitzhugh and His Chesapeake World*. Fitzhugh died on October

21, 1701, leaving in his estate some 54,000 acres of land. His wife, who survived him, bore him six children, five sons and a daughter, one of whom, Captain Henry Fitzhugh (1687–1758), is represented in the Society's portrait collection.

William Fitzhugh

William Fitzhugh, *William Fitzhugh and His Chesapeake World, 1676–1701* (Chapel Hill, N.C., 1963), pp. 3–55 (portrait reproduced as frontispiece); *Occasional Bulletin*, no. 28 (1974): 14–15 (portrait reproduced); *Overwharton Parish*, pp. 224–25; *VMHB* 75 (1967): 168 (portrait reproduced) and 81 (1973): 237. See chart on Fitzhugh, Knox, and Gordon Portraits for relationships.

COPIED BY JOHN HESSELIUS. 1751

Oil on canvas: 30 x 25 in. (76.2 x 63.5 cm.)

Received in 1972 as a bequest of Alice-Lee (Thomas) Stevenson (Mrs. Robert H. Stevenson) of Boston. Por972.20

This portrait and that of the subject's father, Henry Fitzhugh (1614–1664) (q.v.), were copied by Hesselius in 1751 from originals now lost. Relined, the portrait bore on its original canvas the inscription: "Col. William Fitzhugh, 1651–1701, son of Henry Fitzhugh (aetatis 46) born 1614. Cop by John Hesselius 1751." A photograph of the original inscription has been preserved.

William Henry Fitzhugh, 1792–1830
See The Convention of 1829–30

Nathan Bedford Forrest, 1821–1877

Considered by some the most brilliant cavalry commander in American military history, Nathan Bedford Forrest had little formal education but an unerring tactical instinct. Born in Bedford County, Tennessee, on July 13, 1821, son of William Forrest and Mariam (Beck) Forrest, he devoted the years before the Civil War to agricultural pursuits, gradually accumulating sufficient capital to purchase property in Mississippi and Arkansas. After 1849 he lived in Memphis, Tennessee, and was for some time a city alderman. In June 1861 he enlisted in the Confederate army as a private but was soon appointed lieutenant colonel of a battalion that he raised and equipped at his own expense. At Fort Donelson he opposed the decision to surrender, leading his command through the encircling enemy forces to safety; he was elected colonel of the 3d Tennessee Cavalry just before the battle of Shiloh. In July 1862 he was appointed brigadier general and began the audacious cavalry raids deep within Union lines that won him fame. He took part in the Chattanooga campaign, but a quarrel with General Bragg led to his being reassigned to an independent command. In April 1864 he captured Fort Pillow; in June he defeated superior forces at Brices Cross Roads; and in July he fought General A. J. Smith to a standstill at Tupelo, sustaining wounds and leading his cavalry in a buggy until he could ride once more. Promoted to lieutenant general in February 1865, he was finally overwhelmed by superior forces at Selma, Alabama, in April 1865. At the war's end he returned to his cotton plantation in Tennessee and later became president of the Selma, Marion and Memphis Railroad, a venture that proved less than profitable. He died in Memphis on October 29, 1877. General Forrest married, on September 25, 1845, Mary Ann Montgomery.

DAB; *Generals in Gray*; *Biographic Catalogue*.

By CORNELIUS HANKINS. Signed. Dated 1897

Oil on canvas: 30 x 25¼ in. (76.2 x 64.1 cm.)

Presented to the R. E. Lee Camp, Confederate Veterans, in 1899; acquired by the Virginia Historical Society in 1946 through merger with the Confederate Memorial Association. Por946.200

Peter Francisco, 1760–1831

Although the antecedents of Peter Francisco, Virginia's "Hercules of the Revolution," are unclear, it is thought that he was born in the Azores on July 9, 1760. Kidnapped and brought to Virginia in 1765, he was found as a small child abandoned at City Point harbor. The lad was raised, and later adopted, by Judge Anthony Winston of Hunting Towers, Buckingham County. At the outbreak of the Revolution he enlisted in the 10th Virginia Regiment of Continental troops; although only sixteen years of age, he stood six and a half feet tall, weighed 260 pounds, and soon proved himself a formidable fighter. He participated in the battles of Brandywine, Germantown, Monmouth, Stony Point, and Camden, receiving severe wounds and achieving an almost legendary reputation by virtue of his fearlessness and feats of strength. He was left for dead at Guilford Courthouse after dispatching eleven British soldiers but subsequently recovered to fight again. After the Revolution he operated a business and a tavern at New Store, Buckingham County, and re-

Peter Francisco

sided at Locust Grove. He was three times married: first, to Susannah Anderson of Cumberland County, by whom he had one son; second to Catherine Fauntleroy Brooke, who bore him four children; and third to Mary Beverley (Grymes) West. During the last six years of his life Francisco served as sergeant at arms of the Virginia House of Delegates. On his death, on January 16, 1831, the Virginia legislature and the Richmond City Council adjourned to attend his funeral. He was buried in Shockoe Cemetery. Peter Francisco has numerous descendants in Virginia and elsewhere.

Charles Henry Hamilton, *Peter Francisco, Soldier Extraordinary* (Richmond, 1976); *Virginia Cavalcade* 1, no. 2 (1951): 36–39; *Occasional Bulletin*, no. 17 (1968): 11–12 (portrait reproduced); *The Beverley Family*, p. 499; *VMHB* 77 (1969): 239.

ARTIST UNIDENTIFIED

Miniature on ivory: 3 x 2¼ in. (7.6 x 5.7 cm.) (oval)

Presented in 1968 by Martha Dunlop Spotswood of Petersburg. Por968.6

Benjamin Franklin, 1706–1790

Philosopher, diplomat, scientist, author, and in Thomas Jefferson's view "the greatest man and ornament of the age and country in which he lived," Benjamin Franklin was born in Boston on January 17, 1706, the youngest child of Josiah and Abiah

Benjamin Franklin (Portrait I)

(Folger) Franklin. After a brief apprenticeship in his brother's printing shop and a year and a half in England, he established his own press in Philadelphia in 1726. Here, over the years, he published the *Pennsylvania Gazette*, wrote and published *Poor Richard's Almanac*, and became public printer of the province and postmaster of the city; he was instrumental in founding a circulating library (1731), a fire company (1736), the American Philosophical Society (1743), a voluntary militia company (1747), a college, later to become the University of Pennsylvania (1749), and a city hospital (1751). His pioneering studies into the nature of electricity led to the development of a unified theory of electricity and to at least one practical application of the theory—the

lightning rod. Franklin was elected to the Pennsylvania Assembly in 1751; in 1757 he was appointed its agent in England, a post he retained, with a single interruption, until 1775, laboring during this time for a greater measure of self-government for the colonies. Between April 1775, when he returned to America, and October 1776, when he left for France, Franklin served in the second Continental Congress, was elected postmaster general, and helped draft the Declaration of Independence. In France, working with Silas Deane and Arthur Lee (q.v.), he secured in 1778 the vital support of the French, and thereafter, as minister to the court of Versailles, he exercised his immense influence to expedite the flow of ships, troops, arms, supplies, and cash to North America. After the British surrender at Yorktown, Franklin, with John Adams and John Jay, negotiated the Peace of Paris, signing the document that guaranteed American independence on September 3, 1783. Returning home in 1785, he was chosen president of the Executive Council of Pennsylvania, serving in that capacity for three years until he was elected to the Constitutional Convention of 1787. Although disagreeing with many of the Constitution's provisions, he urged its ratification. His last public act was to sign a memorial to Congress for the abolition of slavery. Franklin died on April 17, 1790, at the age of eighty-four. His wife, whom he married on September 1, 1730, was Deborah (Read) Franklin, who bore him a son who died as a child and a daughter; he also had two illegitimate children.

DAB.

Portrait I

COPIED BY LOUIS MATHIEU DIDIER GUILLAUME. Ca. 1852

Pastel on paper on panel: 29 x 24 in. (73.7 x 61 cm.) (oval)

Presented in 1853 by William Cabell Rives of Albemarle County. Por853.1

The portrait came to the Society in 1853 as a gift of William Cabell Rives, the American minister to France and third president of the Virginia Historical Society. It is a copy by Guillaume of an original life portrait that has been attributed in print to Jean Baptiste Greuze. The original is now thought to be the work of Charles Philippe Amedée Vanloo (1719–1795), and since 1948 has been in the collection of the American Philosophical Society, Philadelphia.

Portraiture, pp. 34–35; *VMHB* 40 (1932): 77–78 and 58 (1950): 290 (Portrait II); *Virginia Historical Reporter* 1 (1854): 12–14; Richmond *Daily Dispatch*, July 28, 1857; Charles Coleman Sellers, *Benjamin Franklin in Portraiture* (New Haven, 1962), pp. 394–96; VHS Archives, folio D1, letter from Rives dated Nov. 14, 1853.

Portrait II

Bronze bust: 12 in. (30.5 cm.) in height, including base

Presented in 1949 by Martha Dunlop Spotswood of Petersburg. Por949.46

Douglas Southall Freeman, 1886–1953

Historian and newspaperman, Douglas Southall Freeman was born in Lynchburg on May 16, 1886, son of Walker Burford Freeman and Bettie Allen (Hamner) Freeman. He graduated from Richmond College in 1904 and received his doctorate from Johns Hopkins University in 1908. After brief employment on the staff of the Richmond *Times-Dispatch* and with the Virginia Tax Commission, he joined the editorial staff of the Richmond *News-Leader* in 1913; two years later he became editor, a post he held until 1949. Best known of his historical works are his four-volume *R. E. Lee* (1934–35), for which he won a Pulitzer Prize, *Lee's Lieutenants* (1942–44) in three volumes, and the six-volume *George Washington* (1948–54). His scholarship earned him honorary degrees from more than a score of universities, including Harvard, Yale, Princeton, and Columbia; he was rector and president of the board of trustees of the University of Richmond 1934–49, last president of the Southern Historical Society, a member of the American Philosophical Society and the American Antiquarian Society, and an honorary member of the executive committee of the Virginia Historical Society. By virtue of remarkable self-discipline, Freeman was able to undertake, in addition to his editorial and historical work, a wide range of other activities; he was a member of the planning committee of the Library of Congress, a trustee of the Rockefeller Fund and of the Carnegie Endowment for International Peace, a member of the national councils of the Boy Scouts and the Girl Scouts, a director of the Equitable Life Assurance Society and of the Southern Railway, and a member of the council and honorary lay canon of Washington Cathedral. Freeman died on June 13, 1953; he was survived by his wife, Inez Virginia (Goddin) Freeman, whom he married on February 5, 1914, and by three children.

Who Was Who in America 3 (1960): 301; American Antiquarian Society, *Proceedings* 63 (1953): 288–90; *VMHB* 62 (1954): 240.

BY MELVIN M. NICHOLS. Signed. 1953

Oil on canvasboard: 23¹/₂ x 19¹/₂ in. (59.7 x 49.5 cm.)

Presented in 1953 by Melvin J. Nichols of Summit, New Jersey, a nephew of the artist. Por953.1

Oliver Funsten, ca. 1780–1826

The progenitor of the Funsten family in America, the subject was born near Belfast, Ireland, around 1780, came first to Philadelphia, then settled at White Post, Frederick County. "He was a very prosperous merchant, and enjoyed pre-eminently the confidence of all who knew him, for his integrity, sound judgment and the firm maintenance of his convictions." His wife, Margaret (McKay) Funsten (1779–1843), was a daughter of Andrew and Jane (Ridgway) McKay of Frederick County; the couple had ten children. Funsten built a brick residence in White Post which later burned (1870); on its site the Meade Memorial Church was built, constructed from brick salvaged from the earlier structure. He died at White Post in September 1826.

Hortense Funsten Durand, *The Ancestors and Descendants of Colonel David Funsten* (New York, 1926), pp. 3–5; J. E. Norris, *History of the Lower Shenandoah Valley* (Chicago, 1890), p. 625; *VMHB* 79 (1971): 241.

Watercolor on paper: 3³/₄ x 2¹/₄ in. (9.5 x 5.7 cm.)

Received in 1970 from the estate of Maude Littlepage (Kennerly) Blackwell of White Post, Virginia, a great-great-granddaughter of the subject. Por970.14

In Durand's genealogy it is stated that "no portrait of him [Oliver Funsten] is in existence, but a silhouette, in the possession of one of his descendants, was thought by his children to be an excellent profile likeness" (pp. 4–5). The Society's somewhat primitive watercolor profile is thought to be the "silhouette" referred to.

Christopher Gale, 1680–1734

Chief justice of North Carolina, Christopher Gale was born in Yorkshire, England, in 1680, the son of Miles and Margaret (Stones) Gale. He came to North Carolina about 1700 and three years later was appointed to the General Court of the colony; he likewise served on the Council as a deputy for one of the Lords Proprietors. During the Indian war he was dispatched to Charleston for aid; on his way back he was captured by the French; on his release some months later he became colonel of the Bath County militia. Gale was appointed chief justice in 1712. In 1717 and again in 1725 he visited England, the latter visit to prefer charges against Governor George Burrington, who had laid siege to Gale's house and threatened to blow it up with gunpowder. He was successful in the removal of the governor and in his own reinstatement as chief justice, an office Burrington maintained he had forfeited. Gale presided over the General Court until Burrington's return in 1731. In 1729 he was appointed one of the commissioners to run the boundary between Virginia and North Carolina, an expedition vividly chronicled by William Byrd (q.v.) of Westover. On Burrington's return to North Carolina, Gale relinquished the office of chief justice; thereafter he continued as collector of customs at Edenton until his death in the spring of 1734. Gale's wife was Sarah Catherine (Laker) Harvey Gale, daughter of Benjamin Laker, a judge of the General Court, and widow of Governor Harvey; the couple had issue.

Virginia House, pp. 37–38; William L. Saunders, ed., *The Colonial Records of North Carolina* (Raleigh, N.C., 1886–1910), 2: 561–62, 3: 342–43; Samuel A. Ashe, ed., *Biographical History of North Carolina* (Greensboro, N.C., 1905–17), 1: 292–93.

Copied by Charles X. Harris. 1929

Oil on canvas: 30 x 25 in. (76.2 x 63.5 cm.). Inscribed on the back: "Christopher Gale 1680–1734 Chief Justice of North Carolina, Judge of Admiralty of North Carolina 1712 Copy after an 18th Century Original by Chas. X. Harris 1929."

Received in 1948 as a bequest of Mr. and Mrs. Alexander Wilbourne Weddell of Richmond. Por948.75

The portrait is a copy of an original in the Supreme Court of North Carolina, Raleigh.

Joseph Gallego, 1758–1818

Born in Málaga, Spain, in 1758, the subject came to America by way of Portugal and was in Richmond by 1788, operating a ship chandlery at Rocketts. About 1798 he established the Gallego Mills, which continued in operation for more than a hundred years and became one of the largest flour mills in the world. Gallego married Mary Magee (1761–1811), daughter of Alexander and Mary Magee of Philadelphia; the couple had no children. They resided after 1804 in a house on the southwest corner of Fifth and Main streets, Richmond. He became an American citizen, a staunch Republican, and served from time to time as a grand juror in both the hustings and circuit courts. "Though very rich," we are told, "he was unassuming and unostentatious in his manners. He was warm towards his friends, kind to the needy, unaffected in his intercourse with others." During the Chesapeake Affair in 1807 he joined the Silver Grays, a military company formed for the defense of Richmond. Mrs. Gallego and her niece Sally Conyers

died in the Richmond Theatre fire on December 26, 1811, a loss from which Gallego never fully recovered. He was an early and substantial subscriber to the Monumental Church which was erected on the theater site. Joseph Gallego died in Richmond on July 2, 1818, leaving a large estate; his principal beneficiary was his wife's nephew, Peter Chevallié, who was also the son of his close friend and business partner J. A. M. Chevallié.

Richmond Portraits, pp. 71–73 (portrait reproduced); *Occasional Bulletin*, no. 35 (1977): 6–8 (portrait reproduced).

Artist unidentified

Oil on canvas: 30 x 25 in. (76.2 x 63.5 cm.)

Presented in 1977 by India Watson Thomas of Richmond. Por977.2

The printed label of James Evans, carver and gilder, of Richmond, that was affixed to the back of the frame in 1949 when the portrait was exhibited in the Valentine Museum's Exhibition of Makers of Richmond was not present when the portrait was received by the Society. The portrait note in *Richmond Portraits*, the exhibition catalogue, states that Thomas Sully's register for 1803 lists a portrait of Gallego copied from one by Robert Field, size 12 x 10 inches. The Society's portrait was inherited by the donor from her mother, Ella (Chevallié) Thomas, a great-granddaughter of Gallego's business partner.

Samuel Garland, 1830–1862

General Garland, a young Virginian who died in the Civil War, was a native of Lynchburg. Born on December 16, 1830, only child of Maurice H. Garland and Caroline M. (Garland) Garland, he graduated from the Virginia Military Institute in 1849 and from the law school of the University of Virginia in 1851. He then practiced law in Lynchburg, lectured at the newly established Lynchburg College, and organized the Lynchburg Home Guard which in 1861 was mustered into Confederate service as Company G, 11th Virginia Infantry. Garland was commissioned colonel of the regiment; he saw action at First Manassas, Dranesville, and Williamsburg. Promoted brigadier general on May 23, 1862, he was given command of four North Carolina regiments which served at Seven Pines, Gaines's Mill, and Second Manassas and was the first to cross the river in the campaign into Maryland. While holding the pass near Boonsboro, just before the battle of Sharpsburg, General Garland was mortally wounded, dying on the field on September 14, 1862. His remains were taken to Lynchburg for burial. His wife, whom he married in 1856, and who predeceased him, was Eliza Campbell (Meem) Garland, youngest daughter of John Gaw Meem of Lynchburg.

Generals in Gray; The University Memorial, pp. 263–71; Rosa Faulkner Yancey, *Lynchburg and Its Neighbors* (Richmond, 1935), pp. 96–98; *History of Virginia*, 6: 131; *Biographic Catalogue*; Don Peters Halsey, *Historic and Heroic Lynchburg* (Lynchburg, Va., 1935), pp. 41–43.

By John P. Walker. Signed. Dated 1921

Oil on canvas: 30 x 25 in. (76.2 x 63.5 cm.)

Presented to the R. E. Lee Camp, Confederate Veterans, in 1922; acquired by the Virginia Historical Society in 1946 through merger with the Confederate Memorial Association. Por946.55

James Mercer Garnett, 1770–1843
See The Convention of 1829–30

Robert Selden Garnett, 1789–1840

Born at Mount Pleasant, Essex County, on April 26, 1789, the subject was the youngest son of Muscoe and Grace Fenton (Mercer) Garnett. He attended Princeton University, studied law, and started practice at Lloyds in Essex County. Turning to politics, he was elected to the 1816–17 session of the Virginia House of Delegates and served in the United States House of Representatives 1817–27. He was a personal friend and supporter of Andrew Jackson. Garnett was not a candidate for renomination in 1826; he withdrew from public life, resumed his legal practice at Lloyds, and resided for the rest of his life at

Robert Selden Garnett

Champlain, his estate in Essex County. Here he died on August 15, 1840. His wife, whom he married in Philadelphia on December 30, 1812, was Olympe Charlotte (de Gouges) Garnett, daughter of General Jean Pierre de Gouges of the French army and sister of the governor of the French West Indies; she bore her husband four children. Mr. and Mrs. Garnett were buried in the family cemetery at Champlain.

Biographical Directory; VMHB 42 (1934): 363 and 65 (1957): 253.

By John Wesley Jarvis

Miniature on ivory: 2³/4 x 2¹/4 in. (7 x 5.7 cm.) (oval)

Received in 1956 as a bequest of Kennedy Porter Garnett through the estate of William Garnett Chisholm of Leesburg. Por956.11

Edward S. Gay, 1846–1916

Son of Edward S. Gay of the Virginia Public Guard, the subject was born in Richmond on December 5, 1846. Although very young at the time of the outbreak of the Civil War, he organized a company of boys which became Company G of the 3d Regiment for local defense; as captain of the unit he took part in the defense of Richmond against the Federal raid led by Colonel Dahlgren in March 1864. The regiment left the city with the army when Richmond was evacuated the following year and fought at Sayler's Creek, where many were made prisoner. Captain Gay spent the last twenty years of his life in Atlanta, Georgia, where he died on November 16, 1916.

Biographic Catalogue; Richmond *Times-Dispatch*, Nov. 17, 1916; CMA Archives, folio Z1n.

By John P. Walker. Signed. Dated 1924

Oil on canvas: 30 x 25 in. (76.2 x 63.5 cm.)

Presented to the R. E. Lee Camp, Confederate Veterans, in 1924; acquired by the Virginia Historical Society in 1946 through merger with the Confederate Memorial Association. Por946.189

John B. George, 1795?–1854
See The Convention of 1829–30

Conrad Alexandre Gérard, 1729–1790

Born in Alsace on December 12, 1729, eldest son of Claude and Françoise (Wetzel) Gérard, the subject graduated from the University of Strasbourg in 1749 and shortly thereafter entered the French diplomatic service. After assignments in Mannheim, Sweden, and Vienna, he was recalled to Versailles in 1766 to become secretary of the Council of State. He married on November 16, 1768, Marie Nicole Grossart de Virly, daughter of Hector and Ann (DuBois) Grossart de Virly; the couple had one daughter, born in 1771. Gérard was appointed one of the French commissioners for the reception in 1770 of the dauphin's fiancée, Marie Antoinette, and after the dauphin's accession to the throne as Louis XVI in 1774, Gérard received appointments of increasing importance in the Foreign Office. He became commissioner of boundaries in 1776; two years later, in recognition of his services to the crown, he was ennobled; in March 1778 he was named minister plenipotentiary to the United States. The first diplomatic representative to be accredited to the new country, he arrived in Philadelphia on July 12, 1778. His mission, although of brief duration, was an arduous one; he assumed responsibility for the financing and provisioning of the armed forces, for maintaining peace with Canada, Spain, and the Indians, and for maintaining Franco-American harmony, no easy assignment, particularly since many of his compatriots felt that their rank and military expertise were underrated by the Americans. His own services, however, were recognized and appreciated by the United States Congress; when poor health obliged him to request relief from his duties, Congress ordered a full-length portrait of him to be painted and hung in its assembly hall. Gérard left North America on October 18, 1779; on his return he was honored with the post of *conseiller d'etat*, and spent his final years in Alsace. He died on April 16, 1790. Gérard was an original member of the Society of the Cincinnati.

Portraits and Miniatures, pp. 86, 297 (full-length portrait reproduced); Charles Coleman Sellers, *Charles Willson Peale with Patron and Populace* (Philadelphia, 1969), pp. 63–64 (corrects previous error in the subject's given names); John Joseph Meng, *Despatches and Instructions of Conrad Alexandre Gérard* (Baltimore, 1939), pp. 35–122; *Portraiture*, pp. 35–36 (portrait reproduced).

BY CHARLES WILLSON PEALE

Oil on canvas: 26 x 21¾ in. (66 x 55.3 cm.)

Presented about 1854 by Catherine Power (Lyons) Chevallié (Mrs. Jean Auguste Marie Chevallié) of Richmond. Por858.1

Peale's bust-length portrait of Gérard is derived from his full-length portrait in the Independence Hall collection, Philadelphia.

James Gibbon, 1758–1835

Born in Philadelphia on June 8, 1758, son of James and Mary (Miller) Gibbon, the subject took part in the American Revolution, serving in the Pennsylvania Line; in July 1779 he was brevetted captain for distinguished conduct at the battle of Stony Point. After the war he returned to Philadelphia where in 1782 he married Anne Phyle, daughter of Frederick and Elizabeth Phyle of Philadelphia; she bore him two daughters and two sons, one of whom died in the Richmond Theatre fire endeavoring to save his fiancée Sally Conyers. At some time after his marriage Gibbon and his wife removed to Petersburg where he engaged in business. In 1800 President John Adams

Conrad Alexandre Gérard   James Gibbon

appointed him first customs collector for the port of Richmond, a post he held until his death thirty-five years later. He and his family resided on the northeast corner of Main and Fifth streets in a house built by him in 1809 and later occupied by the Reverend Moses D. Hoge (q.v.). During the War of 1812 Major Gibbon was a member of Richmond's Committee of Vigilance. He was an original member of the Society of the Cincinnati. He died in Richmond on July 1, 1835, and is buried in Shockoe Cemetery.

Richmond Portraits, p. 78 (portrait reproduced); *Portraiture*, pp. 36–38 (portrait reproduced).

BY JOHN BLENNERHASSETT MARTIN

Oil on canvas: 30¼ x 24¾ in. (76.8 x 62.9 cm.)

Presented in 1884 by the Reverend S. Taylor Martin, a son of the artist. Por884.3

Hannah (Crane) Gifford, 1757–1830 (Mrs. John Gifford)

Born in New Jersey in 1757, Hannah Crane was the daughter of Joseph and Patience Crane. She married Captain John Gifford, son of Archer and Catherine (Waldron) Gifford of Newark, New Jersey. Captain Gifford "obtained a position in a court in Newark, afterwards became sheriff of the county, and held this office eleven years"; he died of paralysis on June 28, 1821, aged sixty-eight years. Mrs. Gifford died on February 6, 1830. The couple had eight children; the eldest, Catherine Waldron Gifford, married Dr. Ennion W. Skelton and removed in 1802 to Powhatan County, Virginia; their descendants in Virginia are legion.

Patrick Hamilton Baskerville, *The Skeltons of Paxton, Powhatan County, Virginia, and Their Connections* (Richmond, 1922), pp. 86–87 (a similar portrait is reproduced opposite p. 85).

ARTIST UNIDENTIFIED

Pastel on cardboard: 9 x 7 in. (22.9 x 17.8 cm.) (oval)

Provenance unknown. PorX321

Elizabeth Peyton Giles, died ca. 1916
See Elizabeth Peyton (Giles) Robinson

William Branch Giles, 1762–1830

Governor of Virginia and United States senator and representative, William Branch Giles was born in Amelia County on August 12, 1762, the youngest child of William and Ann (Branch) Giles. He attended Hampden-Sydney College and Princeton University, graduating from the latter institution in 1781. After studying law with George Wythe (q.v.) at the College of William and Mary, he was admitted to the bar in 1786 and began practicing his profession in Petersburg. Elected to the First United States Congress to fill the vacancy caused by the death of Theodorick Bland and reelected to the four succeeding Congresses, he served from 1790 until his resignation in 1798. As an Anti-Federalist, he introduced resolutions condemning Hamilton's management of the Treasury, opposed Jay's Treaty, and used his debating skills to forward Jeffersonian policies. He was a member of the Virginia House of Delegates 1798–1800, was again in the United States House of Representatives 1801–3, then was appointed to the United States Senate to fill the vacancy caused by the resignation of Abraham B. Venable, representing Virginia in the Senate from 1804 to 1815. Returned to the Virginia House of Delegates for the sessions of 1816–17, and 1826–27, he was elected governor in 1827, serving as Virginia's chief executive from March 4, 1827, to March 4, 1830. Although opposed to calling the Virginia Constitutional Convention of 1829–30, he was a member of it, upholding the conservative position. He died at his home, Wigwam, in Amelia County on December 4, 1830. Governor Giles was twice married: first, in 1797 to Martha Peyton Tabb, daughter of John and Frances (Peyton) Tabb, who died in 1808, leaving three children; second, in 1810 to Frances Ann Gwynn, by whom he had two daughters and a son.

William Branch Giles (Portrait I)

DAB; *Biographical Directory*; *Virginia Historical Portraiture*, pp. 384–86 (Portrait I reproduced), also a half-length portrait that may be Portrait II); *VMHB* 83 (1975): 236.

Portrait I

By CHESTER HARDING. 1829

Oil on canvas: 71 1/4 x 51 3/4 in. (181 x 131.5 cm.)

Presented in 1853 by Thomas Harding Ellis. Por853.2

Portrait II

By BASS OTIS

Oil on canvas: 30 x 25 in. (76.2 x 63.5 cm.)

Presented in 1974 by Peyton (Hawes) Dunn of Washington, D.C. Por974.10

Portrait III

By BASS OTIS

Oil on canvas: 30 x 25 in. (76.2 x 63.5 cm.)

Presented by Lelia (Morgan) Wardwell (Mrs. Edward Rogers Wardwell) of New York City. Por959.19

Portrait IV
See The Convention of 1829–30

The Bass Otis portraits of William Branch Giles (Portraits II and III) differ only in their backgrounds. The drapery that forms the backgrounds of both portraits is pulled back to reveal, in Portrait II, an open window, in Portrait III, the base of a column on a wall, with the sky beyond. It is likely that one of the two is the original portrait painted by Otis for Joseph Delaplaine in 1816, the other a replica. Delaplaine, a Philadelphia publisher, intended to bring out a multivolume biographical work, *Delaplaine's Repository of the Lives and Portraits of Distinguished American Characters*, and commissioned Otis to paint twenty-four portraits with a view to having them engraved for use as illustrations. Only three volumes were, in fact, published, and only one of Otis's portraits (Thomas Jefferson) appeared in engraved form as an illustration.[1] Much of the confusion that surrounds the portraiture of William Branch Giles stems from the fact that the Bass Otis likenesses of 1816 so closely resemble the Chester Harding portrait painted thirteen years later at the Virginia Convention of 1829. Although the Harding is a full-length portrait and the Otis portraits are bust length, the heads are virtually identical. Hugh Blair Grigsby, that faithful observer of persons and events, was present at the Convention of 1829 and described William Branch Giles, then in the last year of his life: "In all things but in the vigor of his intellect, he was but the shadow of his former self. He could neither move nor stand without the aid of his crutches, and,

when on the conclusion of his able speech on the basis question, the members pressed their congratulations upon him, he seemed to belong rather to the dead than to the living. His face was the face of a corpse."[2] Although the crutch is faithfully represented in Harding's portrait, the face of the subject is certainly not the face of a corpse. A hypothesis here suggested as a way of reconciling apparently contrary facts is that Harding, commissioned to paint a dying man, was importuned by the subject or by the subject's family to base his likeness on the ruddy, vigorous features of the Otis portrait painted thirteen years earlier. A version of the Otis portrait (the original according to its owner) hung at that time in Giles's residence, Wigwam, and could with little trouble have been transported to Harding's studio in Richmond for copying.[3] The provenance of the Harding portrait before its acquisition by the Society in 1853 is somewhat confused. The donor, Thomas Harding Ellis, wrote in his letter of transmittal, dated December 14, 1853: "The accompanying portrait is one of the late governor William B. Giles of this state—and I believe was painted by Hardin [*sic*] during the Convention of 1829–30. I am not sure to whom it belongs. For some years it was in the law office of Mr. Henry L. Brooke—who permitted Col. Walter Gwynn to take it: and he left it in the office I now occupy as president of the James river and Kanawha company. I have heard that Dr. Mayo of Washington city probably has the best right to it. Not doubting but that you would be pleased to receive it for the Virginia Historical Society, I beg to place it with you on deposite, until it shall be called for by its rightful owner."[4] Although the hypothesis noted above may perhaps explain the similarities of the Bass Otis portraits of 1816 and the Chester Harding one of 1829, it by no means answers all questions surrounding the portraiture of Governor Giles. Where, for example, is the 1813 miniature to which he refers in a letter to his wife?[5] Clearly the miniature that is claimed to be this likeness is far too early: its youthful features are not those of a man of fifty-one. And where is the portrait by Ford, to which Grigsby refers both in "The Virginia Convention of 1829–30" and in his diary for October 27, 1829?[6]

1. Historical Society of Delaware, *Bass Otis, Portraitist, and Engraver* (Wilmington, Del., 1976), pp. 14–17 (Portrait III reproduced). 2. *Virginia Historical Reporter* 1, pt. 1 (1854): 35. 3. Clarence Winthrop Bowen, *The History of the Centennial Celebration of the Inauguration of George Washington* (New York, 1892), pp. 464–66 (portraits reproduced opposite p. 112). 4. VHS Archives, folio G1–1853. 5. Dice Robins Anderson, *William Branch Giles* (Menasha, Wis., 1914), pp. 238–39 (miniature reproduced as frontispiece, Portrait I reproduced opposite p. 207). 6. *Virginia Historical Reporter* 1, pt. 1 (1854): 35; VHS Mss1 G8782b 72, p. 155 (the diary entry is quoted in the note appended to the entry for Charles Stephen Morgan).

Robert Hobson Gilliam, 1838–1923

The subject was born in Prince Edward County on September 25, 1838, son of Charles W. Gilliam and Caroline S. (Gilliam) Gilliam. The family removed to Richmond in 1853. At the beginning of the Civil War, Gilliam, who was employed in the tobacco factory of his uncle George W. Gilliam, enlisted in Company F, 21st Virginia Infantry; he served with this unit in Jackson's Valley campaign and was wounded at Cedar Mountain on August 9, 1862. Commissioned lieutenant in August 1863, he was captured at Sayler's Creek on April 6, 1865. After his release from Johnson's Island prison he returned to Richmond and devoted himself to the real estate and auctioneering businesses, first with the R. B. Chaffin Company and later, around 1895, establishing his own firm under the name Robert H. Gilliam and Company. Gilliam died on August 14, 1923, and is buried in Hollywood Cemetery. On January 18, 1865, he married Nannie M. Gay, the daughter of Peter F. and Ann M. (Christian) Gay of Charles City County; the couple had nine children.

Richmond the Pride of Virginia, an Historical City (Philadelphia, 1900), p. 59; *Hardesty's Historical and Geographical Encyclopedia*, Virginia edition with Richmond and Henrico Supplement (New York, 1885), p. 415; *Richmond Times-Dispatch*, Aug. 15, 1923; CMA Archives, folio Z1n; *Biographic Catalogue*.

By JOHN P. WALKER. Signed. Dated 1924

Oil on canvas: 30 x 25 in. (76.2 x 63.5 cm.)

Presented to the R. E. Lee Camp, Confederate Veterans, in 1924 by the subject's daughter, Carrie (Gilliam) Fisher; acquired by the Virginia Historical Society in 1946 through merger with the Confederate Memorial Association. Por946.114

Lucinda Gillies, d. 1814
See John Mutter, d. 1820

Lewis Ginter, 1824–1897

A native of New York City, the subject was born on April 4, 1824, son of John and Elizabeth Ginter. He came to Richmond at eighteen years of age and established a profitable dry goods business. Here he remained until the outset of the Civil War, whereupon he enlisted in the Confederate army. He was first a quartermaster under General Joseph R. Anderson, then commissary of General Thomas's brigade, seeing action at Cedar Run, Gettysburg, and Second Manassas. After Appomattox, Major Ginter returned to New York, devoting himself to business until 1869, in which year the great panic led to the

failure of many brokerage firms, his included. He again came to Richmond where in 1872 he established, with John F. Allen as partner, a firm later known as Allen and Ginter for the manufacture and sale of tobacco and cigars. In 1875 the firm introduced a new product—cigarettes—and the novelty rapidly became a worldwide addiction. Allen and Ginter's displays at the Centennial Exposition in Philadelphia, together with attractive packaging and marketing techniques, contributed to the early success of the business. In 1890 when Allen and Ginter became a part of the American Tobacco Company, Major Ginter realized a fortune in the transaction. He continued to serve on the board of directors until shortly before his death. Major Ginter devoted a large part of his wealth to civic improvements and benefactions; he developed a residential suburb north of Richmond and built the Jefferson Hotel, first opened in 1895, so that Richmond could enjoy the distinction of having the finest hotel in the South. In declining health for several years, he died on October 2, 1897, at Westbrook, his estate north of Richmond, and was buried in Hollywood Cemetery. Major Ginter never married. He became a member of the Virginia Historical Society in 1875.

DAB; *Men of Mark in Virginia*, 5: 154–63; *Biographic Catalogue*.

By JOHN P. WALKER. Signed. Dated 1898

Oil on canvas: 30 x 25 in. (76.2 x 63.5 cm.)

Presented to the R. E. Lee Camp, Confederate Veterans, in 1898; acquired by the Virginia Historical Society in 1946 through merger with the Confederate Memorial Association. Por946.101

Arthur Graham Glasgow, 1865–1955

Son of Francis Thomas Glasgow and Anne Jane (Gholson) Glasgow, the subject was born in Buchanan on May 30, 1865. After graduating from Stevens Institute of Technology in Hoboken, N.J., in 1885, he joined the United Gas Improvement Company in Philadelphia and in 1891 became engineer and general manager of the Standard Gas-Light Company of New York. The following year he founded the firm of Humphreys and Glasgow of London, England, contracting engineers, later becoming the firm's chairman of the board. He was also the president and chairman of the Building Supplies Corporation of Norfolk. During World War I he served as vice-chairman of the American Red Cross Commission to Rumania, served with the United States War Department in Washington, France and England, and in 1919 was the fixed-nitrogen administrator of the War Department. Glasgow was president of the Alumni Association of Stevens Institute, belonged to numerous professional and social clubs both in England and in this country, and maintained residences in Richmond, Palm Beach, and London. He died on October 28, 1955, and is buried in Hollywood Cemetery, Richmond. His wife, whom he married on October 1, 1901, was Margaret Elizabeth (Branch) Glasgow, daughter of John Patteson Branch and Mary Louise Merritt (Kerr) Branch; the couple had one child, a daughter. Glasgow became a member of the Virginia Historical Society in 1921. A portrait of his sister, the novelist Ellen Anderson Gholson Glasgow (q.v.), is also in the Society's collection.

Who Was Who in America 3 (1960): 328; James Mallory Black, Families and Descendants in America of Golsan (Salt Lake City, 1959), pp. 112–13; James Branch Cabell, Branchiana (Richmond, 1907), pp. 77–82.

Arthur Graham Glasgow

By CHANNING HARE. Signed. Dated 1946

Oil on canvas: 39³/4 x 34 in. (101 x 86.4 cm.)

Presented by the subject in 1946. Por946.29

Ellen Anderson Gholson Glasgow, 1873–1945

Ellen Glasgow, Virginia novelist, was born in Richmond on April 22, 1873, the ninth of ten children born to Francis Thomas Glasgow and Anne Jane (Gholson) Glasgow. She received little formal education but resolved at an early age to become an author. Her first novel, The Descendant (1897), was published anonymously; her second, Phases of an In-

ferior Planet, appeared the following year under her own name. After sojourns in Europe and New York, she returned to her residence at One West Main Street, Richmond, and decided to embark on a series of novels illustrative of the social history of Virginia; included in the series were The Voice of the People (1900), The Battle-Ground (1902), The Deliverance (1904), The Wheel of Life (1906), The Ancient Law (1908), and Virginia (1913). On a trip abroad in 1914 she was cordially received by members of England's literary establishment; the outbreak of the World War immediately thereafter, together with a crisis in her personal life, brought on a profound depression, and the two novels she wrote during this period were not successful. With the publication of Barren Ground in 1925 she reclaimed her following and achieved widespread recognition as an author of importance; this success was followed by two comedies of manners, The Romantic Comedians (1926) and They Stooped to Folly (1929), and a highly successful tragicomedy, The Sheltered Life (1932). Her last novels were Vein of Iron (1935), an austere work set in the mountains of Virginia, and In This Our Life (1941), for which she was awarded a Pulitzer Prize. The Woman Within (1954), a remarkably frank autobiographical study, was published posthumously. Ellen Glasgow suffered a heart attack in 1939 and a second one the following year; her activities thereafter were restricted. She died in Richmond on November 21, 1945, and is buried in Hollywood Cemetery, Richmond. She became a member of the Virginia Historical Society in 1921.

DAB (Supplement 3).

Portrait I

By I. CARREGI. Signed

Miniature on ivory: 3³/4 x 3 in. (9.5 x 7.6 cm.) (oval)

Received in 1946 as a bequest of the subject. Por946.2

The miniature, which depicts the subject in her twenties, is taken from a photograph which is reproduced in Glasgow's The Woman Within (New York, 1954), opposite p. 68.

Portrait II   See Plate 11

By RAYMOND PERRY RODGERS NEILSON. Signed

Oil on canvas: 30 x 25 in. (76.2 x 63.5 cm.)

Presented in 1946 by Arthur Graham Glasgow of London, England, the subject's brother. Por946.30

The portrait is derived from a 1938 photograph which is reproduced in Glasgow's The Woman Within (New York, 1954), opposite p. 69.

95

John William Ware Godbold, 1760–1842

Sarah Ann (Cruft) Godbold, 1771–1849 (Mrs. John William Ware Godbold)

Born in Boston, Massachusetts, in 1760, John William Ware Godbold was the son of John and Mary (Marshall) Godbold. He married in 1800 Sarah Ann Cruft of Boston, who bore him five children. John Godbold died in 1842; his wife died seven years later.

Information received with the portraits.

Portrait I. John William Ware Godbold

ARTIST UNIDENTIFIED

Silhouette in India ink: 2³/4 in. (7 cm.) in height, on paper 3¹/4 x 2³/4 in. (8.3 x 7 cm.)

Presented in 1974 by the Reverend George Julius Cleaveland of Richmond, a great-great-grandson of the subject. Por974.46.a

Portrait II. Sarah Ann (Cruft) Godbold

ARTIST UNIDENTIFIED

Silhouette in India ink: 2¹/2 in. (6.4 cm.) in height, on paper 3¹/4 x 2³/4 in. (8.3 x 7 cm.)

Presented in 1974 by the Reverend George Julius Cleaveland of Richmond, a great-great-grandson of the subject. Por974.46.b

The silhouettes of this New England couple appear to have been made in the present century, copies perhaps of early originals. They have been mounted on a single piece of paper inscribed with the names and life dates of the subjects.

India Charlotte Goddin, 1838–1900
See Joshua C. Hallowell, ca.1831–1863

Gooch Family, Unidentified Member

ARTIST UNIDENTIFIED

Miniature on ivory: 2¹/2 x 2 in. (6.4 x 5.1 cm.) (oval)

Presented in 1969 by Claiborne Watts Gooch III of Potomac, Maryland. Por969.6

Rosa (Chambers) Goode, 1842–1921 (Mrs. Thomas Francis Goode)

Born on February 6, 1842, the subject was a daugh-

ter of Edward R. Chambers and Lucy Goode (Tucker) Chambers (qq.v.) of Boydton, formerly of Flat Rock, Lunenburg County. She married on November 27, 1860, Thomas Francis Goode (1825–1905) of Boydton, son of Thomas and Mary Ann (Knox) Goode. Her husband was a lawyer and a member of the Secession Convention of 1861 and served as an officer in the 3d Virginia Cavalry under General J. E. B. Stuart until poor health necessitated his retirement from active service; he represented Mecklenburg County in the Virginia House of Delegates in the session of 1863–64. After the Civil War, Goode resumed his law practice but discontinued it in 1875 to become proprietor of the Buffalo Lithia Springs in Mecklenburg County. Colonel Goode died on January 6, 1905; his wife died on January 20, 1921. The couple had five children.

Rose Chambers Goode McCullough, *Yesterday When It Is Past* (Richmond, 1957), pp. 201, 363–72; George Brown Goode, *Virginia Cousins: A Study of the Ancestry and Posterity of John Goode of Whitby* (Richmond, 1887), p. 238; *Encyclopedia of Virginia Biography*, 3: 370; William Harris Gaines, *Biographical Register of Members, Virginia State Convention of 1861, First Session* (Richmond, 1969), pp. 37–38; *VMHB* 84 (1976): 239.

ARTIST UNIDENTIFIED

Miniature on ivory: 3¹/4 x 2¹/2 in. (8.3 x 6.4 cm.) (oval)

Presented in 1975 by Houston (Trippe) Bateson (Mrs. Philip Briscoe Bateson) of Dallas, Texas. Por975.27

William Osborne Goode, 1798–1859
See The Convention of 1829–30

Anne Campbell Gordon, 1819–1886
See Anne Campbell (Gordon) Thomas, 1819–1886

Armistead Churchill Gordon, 1855–1931

Armistead Churchill Gordon was born at Edgeworth, Albemarle County, on December 20, 1855, son of George Loyall Gordon and Mary Long (Daniel) Gordon. He attended the University of Virginia, and after four years of teaching in Charlottesville he began the study of law. In 1879 he removed to Staunton where he practiced law from 1883 to 1891 in partnership with Meade F. White and later with William Patrick. Gordon was mayor of Staunton 1884–86, Commonwealth's attorney of Staunton 1890–92, for ten years city attorney of Staunton, and Commonwealth's attorney of Augusta County 1898–

11. Ellen Anderson Gholson Glasgow (Portrait II)

1900. He was a member of the board of visitors of the University of Virginia, serving part of the time as rector; chairman of the State Library Board 1903–19; a member of the Royal Charter Board of the College of William and Mary 1897–1906; and a member of the executive committee of the Virginia Historical Society. A speaker much in demand, a poet, and a versatile writer, he was a contributor to such periodicals as *Scribner's*, the *Century Magazine*, *Harper's*, and the *Atlantic Monthly*; his published books include *Congressional Currency* (1895), *Envion and Other Tales of Old and New Virginia* (1899), *The Gift of the Morning Star* (1905), *J. L. M. Curry, a Biography* (1911), *Maje, a Love Story* (1914), *Ommirandy, Plantation Life at Kingsmill* (1917), *Jefferson Davis* (1918), *Gordons in Virginia* (1918), and *In the Picturesque Shenandoah Valley* (1930). He died on October 21, 1931. His wife, whom he married on October 17, 1883, was Maria Breckinridge (Catlett) Gordon, daughter of Nathaniel Pendleton Catlett and Elizabeth (Breckinridge) Catlett; the couple had five children.

Men of Mark in Virginia, 1: 120–29; *History of Virginia*, 4: 3–4; *Who Was Who in America* 1 (1943): 470.

By C. Alonzo? Signed. Dated 1928

Silhouette: 4¹⁄₂ in. (11.4 cm.) in height, on cardboard 5¹⁄₄ x 3 ³⁄₄ in. (13.3 x 9.5 cm.)

Presented in 1978 by the children and grandchildren of the subject. Por978.18

Bazil Gordon, 1768–1847
Anna Campbell (Knox) Gordon, 1784–1867 (Mrs. Bazil Gordon)

Born on May 15, 1768, at Lochdougan, Scotland, Bazil Gordon was the sixth child of Samuel and Nicola (Brown) Gordon. In 1783 he followed his elder brother, Samuel to Virginia. Settling in Falmouth, he established a highly successful mercantile business. In 1814 he married Anna Campbell Knox, daughter of William and Susannah (Fitzhugh) Knox (qq.v.) of Stafford County; the couple had seven children, two of whom, Douglas Hamilton Gordon and Anne Campbell (Gordon) Thomas (qq.v.), are represented in the Society's portrait collection. On his death in Falmouth on April 20, 1847, "he left to his heirs one of the largest fortunes in the state, accumulated by indefatigable industry and the strictest integrity. He was a man of enlarged benevolence and great mercantile sagacity, but with the simplicity and purity of a child." Mrs. Gordon died on October 8, 1867. A monument to the couple's memory was erected in the Masonic burying ground in Fredericksburg.

Armistead Churchill Gordon, *Gordons in Virginia* (Hackensack, N.J., 1918), pp. 106, 122; George Adolphus Hanson, *Old Kent, the Eastern Shore of Maryland* (Baltimore, 1876), pp. 134–35; Dora Chinn Jett, *Minor Sketches of Major Folk and Where They Sleep* (Richmond, 1928), pp. 45–47; *VMHB* 79 (1971): 241 and 83 (1975): 237. See chart on Fitzhugh, Knox, and Gordon Portraits for relationships.

Portrait I. Bazil Gordon

COPIED BY AN UNIDENTIFIED ARTIST

Oil on canvas: 30 x 25 in. (76.2 x 63.5 cm.)

Presented in 1974 by Douglas Huntly Gordon of Baltimore. Por974.2

The Society's portrait is a copy of an original portrait by William Edward West.

Portrait II. Anna Campbell (Knox) Gordon

COPIED BY AN UNIDENTIFIED ARTIST

Oil on canvas: 30 x 25 in. (76.2 x 63.5 cm.)

Presented in 1974 by Douglas Huntly Gordon of Baltimore. Por974.3

The Society's portrait is a copy of an original portrait by William Edward West.

Portrait III. Anna Campbell (Knox) Gordon

BY GEORGE LINEN

Oil on canvas: 11¹⁄₄ x 9¹⁄₂ in. (28.6 x 24.1 cm.) (oval)

Presented in 1970 by Douglas Huntly Gordon of Baltimore. Por970.5

Douglas Hamilton Gordon, 1817–1883
Anne Eliza (Pleasants) Gordon, 1836–1901 (Mrs. Douglas Hamilton Gordon)

Douglas Hamilton Gordon was born in Falmouth on October 17, 1817, son of Bazil and Anna Campbell

Anne Eliza (Pleasants) Gordon

(Knox) Gordon (qq.v.). He read law at the University of Virginia in 1836 but never practiced. He married, first, in 1845, Mary Ellen Clark, daughter of Major Colin Clark of Gloucester County; the couple resided in Fredericksburg; he married second, in 1857, Anne Eliza Pleasants, daughter of John Hampden Pleasants and Mary (Massie) Pleasants of Richmond. During the Civil War, Gordon represented Spotsylvania County in the Virginia House of Delegates. At the war's end he removed with his family to Baltimore, Maryland. Although he remained a resident of Baltimore for the rest of his life, he maintained close ties with Virginia, spending his summers at Wakefield Manor near Chester Gap in the Blue Ridge Mountains. He died in Baltimore on January 20, 1883, survived by his widow, two sons, and four daughters (one, the child of his first marriage). Portraits of his son, Douglas Huntly Gordon, and of his sister, Anne Campbell (Gordon) Thomas (qq.v.), are also in the Society's collection. Mrs. Gordon died in Atlantic City, New Jersey, on June 27, 1901.

Armistead Churchill Gordon, *Gordons in Virginia* (Hackensack, N.J., 1918), pp. 107, 155; Dora Chinn Jett, *Minor Sketches of Major Folk and Where They Sleep* (Richmond, 1928), pp. 47–48; VHS Mss1 G6596c 3483–3489; Maryland Historical Society, obituary file; Andrew Oliver, *Auguste Edouart's Silhouettes of Eminent Americans, 1839–1844* (Charlottesville, Va., 1977), p. 524; *VMHB* 79 (1971): 241, 84 (1976): 239, and 86 (1978): 240. See chart on Fitzhugh, Knox, and Gordon Portraits for relationships.

Portrait I. Douglas Hamilton Gordon

BY AUGUSTE EDOUART. 1844

Silhouette: 9¼ in. (23.5 cm.) in height, on paper 11 x 4½ in. (27.9 x 11.4 cm.). Inscribed on paper mounted with the silhouette: "6 ft. 3½. D. H. Gordon, Virga. Saratoga. 15 July 1844."

Presented in 1970 by Douglas Huntly Gordon of Baltimore. Por970.10

Portrait II. Douglas Hamilton Gordon

ARTIST UNIDENTIFIED

Cameo profile: 1¾ x 1¼ in. (4.5 x 3.2 cm.) (oval)

Presented in 1975 by Douglas Huntly Gordon of Baltimore. Por975.23

Portrait III. Anne Eliza (Pleasants) Gordon

BY PHILIPPE BOILEAU. Signed. Dated 1900

Oil on canvas: 29½ x 37½ in. (74.9 x 95.3 cm.)

Presented in 1977 by Douglas Huntly Gordon of Baltimore. Por977.9

Douglas Huntly Gordon, 1866–1918
Elizabeth Iris Southall (Clarke) Gordon, 1871–1958 (Mrs. Douglas Huntly Gordon)

Douglas Huntly Gordon was born on October 5, 1866, son of Douglas Hamilton Gordon and Anne Eliza (Pleasants) Gordon (qq.v.) of Baltimore. In 1897 he married Elizabeth Iris Southall Clarke, born

Douglas Hamilton Gordon (Portrait I)

on August 26, 1871, the daughter of John Eldridge Clarke and Anastasia (Southall) Clarke of Henderson, North Carolina. Gordon was one of the founders of the International Trust Company; he served the company as its president until it merged with the Baltimore Trust and Guaranty Company. He thereupon became first vice-president of the Baltimore Trust and in 1912 was elected its president. A substantial investor in numerous southern businesses, his interests included the Alabama Consolidated Coal and Iron Company and the *Baltimore News*. Poor health compelled him to retire in 1916. He died in Baltimore on April 8, 1918, survived by his widow, one son, and four daughters. Mrs. Gordon married, second, J. Wilmer Biddle of Philadelphia; they resided in Philadelphia until Biddle's death in 1927. She married, third, in 1933, Alexander Gordon of Baltimore, a cousin of her first husband; the marriage ended in divorce two years later. Mrs. Gordon, active in the social life of Baltimore, was president of the Society of the Colonial Dames and a regent of the Kenmore Association. She died on December 1, 1958.

Baltimore News, April 8, 1918; *Baltimore Sun*, Dec. 3, 1958; Maryland Historical Society, obituary file; *VMHB* 79 (1971): 241 and 85 (1977): 239. See chart on Fitzhugh, Knox, and Gordon Portraits for relationships.

Portrait I. Douglas Huntly Gordon

By C. Bernard Pereira. Signed

Miniature on ivory: 3½ x 2½ in. (8.9 x 6.4 cm.). The subject's name and life dates are engraved on the back of the frame.

Presented in 1970 by Douglas Huntly Gordon of Baltimore, the subject's son. Por970.11

Portrait II. Douglas Huntly Gordon

By Louis P. Dieterich. Signed. Date obscured by spandrel

Pastel on paper: 16½ x 13½ in. (41.9 x 34.3 cm.) (oval)

Presented in 1976 by Douglas Huntly Gordon of Baltimore, the subject's son. Por976.5

Portrait III. Elizabeth Iris Southall (Clarke) Gordon

By Hugh Nicholson. Signed. Dated 1905

Miniature on ivory: 4¼ x 3¼ in. (10.8 x 8.3 cm.). The subject's name and life dates are engraved on the back of the frame.

Presented in 1970 by Douglas Huntly Gordon of Baltimore, the subject's son. Por970.12

Elizabeth Iris Southall (Clarke) Gordon
(Portrait IV)

Portrait IV. Elizabeth Iris Southall (Clarke) Gordon

By Philippe Boileau

Oil on canvas: 35½ x 22 in. (90.2 x 55.9 cm.)

Presented in 1978 by Elizabeth (Gordon) Bingley. Por978.9

James Gordon, ca. 1714–1768

The subject was the eldest son of James and Sarah (Greenway) Gordon of Sheepbridge, County Down, Ireland, and a brother of John Gordon (q.v.) of Middlesex and Richmond counties, Virginia. Born in Ireland around 1714, he came to Lancaster County before 1738 and resided at Merry Point on the Corotoman River. Colonel Gordon was a tobacco planter and exporter, operating ships for transporting the leaf to Whitehaven, England; he also maintained two stores in Lancaster for the sale of English goods brought home in his ships; he amassed through these various enterprises a tidy fortune. A devout Presbyterian, he built the local meetinghouse and offered hospitality to visiting clergy, notably to the great evangelist George Whitefield. Details of his domestic and business life are recorded in his journal, covering the years 1758–63, published in the *William and Mary Quarterly*, 1st ser., 11 (1902–3) and 12 (1903–4). He died in Lancaster County on January 2, 1768. Colonel Gordon was twice married: first, on March 28, 1742, to Milicent Conway, daughter of Edwin Conway of Lancaster County, who bore him four children, three of whom died in infancy; second, on November 12, 1748, to Mary Harrison, daughter of Nathaniel Harrison of Surry County, who bore him four sons and five daughters.

Armistead Churchill Gordon, *Gordons in Virginia* (Hackensack, N.J., 1918), pp. 43–44; Armistead Churchill Gordon, *Colonel James Gordon of Lancaster* (Staunton, Va., 1913), pp. 6–11; *Portraiture*, pp. 39–40.

COPIED BY HARRY M. WEGNER. 1921

Oil on canvas: 30 x 25 in. (76.2 x 63.5 cm.). Inscribed in upper right corner: "Colonel James Gordon of Lancaster, 1714–1768. After the portrait by Hesselius."

Received in 1932 from the estate of Armistead Churchill Gordon of Staunton. Por932.4

The Society's portrait is a bust-length copy of John Hesselius's original three-quarter-length portrait. The original, painted in 1750, is reproduced in the *Virginia Magazine of History and Biography* 31 (1923): 380. The donor apparently had another, earlier, copy made, for his monograph *Colonel James Gordon of Lancaster* was "read at the presentation by his descendants to the County of Lancaster, Virginia, of a portrait of Col. James Gordon, July 21, 1913."

John Gordon, ca. 1720–1780

Third son of James and Sarah (Greenway) Gordon, and younger brother of James Gordon (q.v.) of Lancaster County, the subject was born at the family home in Sheepbridge, County Down, Ireland, probably around 1720. He emigrated to Virginia before 1756, settling in Urbanna, where he became a merchant and was engaged in the tobacco trade; he also owned land in Middlesex County. On December 15, 1756, he married Lucy Churchill, daughter of Armistead and Hannah (Harrison) Churchill of Bushy Park, Middlesex County; she bore him a son and a daughter. In 1762 Gordon sold his property in Middlesex County and removed with his family to Richmond County where he served for a time as justice of the peace. He died in 1780.

Armistead Churchill Gordon, *Gordons in Virginia* (Hackensack, N.J., 1918), pp. 61–62; *Portraiture*, p. 40.

COPIED BY HARRY M. WEGNER. Signed. Dated 1914

Oil on canvas: 30 x 25 in. (76.2 x 63.5 cm.). Inscribed in upper left corner: "John Gordon, Painted by Hesselius 1751. Copied by H. M. Wegner, 1914."

Received in 1932 from the estate of Armistead Churchill Gordon of Staunton. Por932.5

John Brown Gordon, 1832–1904

Considered the most important military figure in the history of Georgia, General Gordon was at the beginning of the Civil War totally without military training or experience. He was born in Upson County, Georgia, on February 6, 1832, son of the Reverend Zachariah Herndon Gordon and Melinda (Cox) Gordon, attended the University of Georgia but did not graduate, and was admitted to the bar after a period of private study. The outbreak of the Civil War found him developing coal mines in northwest Georgia. Elected captain of a company of mountaineers calling themselves the "Raccoon Roughs," he was shortly in the front line in Virginia; he ended the war as lieutenant general in command of the 2d Army Corps, having fought in nearly every engagement in which the Army of Northern Virginia participated. After Appomattox, where he led the last charge, General Gordon returned to Atlanta and entered politics, struggling to secure home rule for the state. He was elected to the United States Senate in 1873, serving until 1880 when he resigned to promote the building of the Georgia Pacific Railroad. He was governor of Georgia 1886–90 and was once again a United States senator 1891–97. General Gordon published his *Reminiscences of the Civil War* in 1903 and served as commander-in-chief of the United Confederate Veterans from its founding in 1890 until his death, which occurred in Miami, Florida, on January 9, 1904. He married in September 1854 Fanny Haralson of La Grange, Georgia.

DAB; *Generals in Gray*; *Biographical Directory*; *Biographic Catalogue*.

Portrait I

BY CORNELIUS HANKINS. Signed. Dated 1895

Oil on canvas: 60 x 40 in. (152.4 x 101.6 cm.)

Presented to the R. E. Lee Camp, Confederate Veterans, in 1898; acquired by the Virginia Historical Society in 1946 through merger with the Confederate Memorial Association. Por946.217

Portrait II

See The Battle Abbey Murals. The Summer Mural

John Wotton Gordon, 1847–1928

Son of George Bradford Gordon and Elizabeth Ann (Jones) Gordon, the subject was born on March 25, 1847, at Hertford, North Carolina. He attended the military academy at Hillsboro, North Carolina, and in January 1863, at fifteen years of age, enlisted as private in Company C, 2d North Carolina Cavalry. At Brandy Station he was wounded and taken prisoner; ten weeks later he was exchanged and returned to active duty. Promoted to corporal, to sergeant, and finally to lieutenant, Gordon became aide-de-camp to General W. P. Roberts. He saw action with his regiment at Suffolk, Yellow Tavern, Salem Church, Malvern Hill, Reams's Station, and other engagements. The eighteen-year-old veteran found his family penniless at the end of the war and for the next several years devoted himself to their support. In 1871, after trying his hand at schoolteaching, he entered the fire insurance business in Wilmington, North Carolina, continuing in that field of employment for the rest of his life. Eight years later he removed to Richmond to become general agent for Virginia and North Carolina; in time he added other areas and other companies to his agency and developed a highly successful business. Colonel Gordon was commander of R. E. Lee Camp, Confederate Veterans, general chairman of the Confederate reunion of 1907, a member of the board of the Soldiers' Home, a Freemason, and a member of the Virginia Historical Society. He died on January 5, 1928, survived by his wife, Annie Laurie (Pender) Gordon, whom he married on April 4, 1877, daughter of Robert Pender of Tarboro, North Carolina, and by three of his five children.

Confederate Veteran 36 (1928): 65; *Confederate Military History*, 3: 899–900; *History of Virginia*, 4: 43–45; CMA Archives, folio Z11; *Biographic Catalogue*.

By EMMA MOREHEAD WHITFIELD. Signed. Dated 1924

Oil on canvas: 23 x 19¼ in. (58.4 x 48.9 cm.). Inscribed on the back: "Painted by E. M. Whitfield. 1924."

Presented to the R. E. Lee Camp, Confederate Veterans, in 1924 by the subject's wife; acquired by the Virginia Historical Society in 1946 through merger with the Confederate Memorial Association. Por946.61

William Fitzhugh Gordon, 1787–1858
See The Convention of 1829–30

Archibald Gracie, 1832–1864

Born in New York City on December 1, 1832, General Gracie was the son of Archibald and Elizabeth Davidson (Bethune) Gracie and the grandson of Archibald Gracie, first of the name, who emigrated from Scotland to Petersburg, Virginia, and became a prominent businessman both in Petersburg and in New York. The subject received his education in Heidelberg, Germany, and at the Military Academy at West Point, from which he graduated in the class of 1854. Following duty with the army in the Far West, he resigned his commission in 1856 to join his father who was in business in Mobile, Alabama. On November 19, 1856, he married Josephine Mayo, daughter of Edward C. Mayo, of Richmond. As captain of the Washington Light Infantry Company of Mobile (later a part of the 3d Alabama Infantry) he came to Virginia at the beginning of the Civil War; on July 12, 1861, he was promoted to major of the 11th Alabama Infantry, and the following spring he raised a regiment of his own, the 43d Alabama Infantry, which he commanded, as colonel, in eastern Tennessee. Gracie led the expedition against Fort Cliff, took part in the Kentucky campaign, and was in command of Lexington, Kentucky, during its occupation. Promoted to brigadier general on November 4, 1862, he led his command at Chickamauga, was severely wounded at Bean's Station, and thereafter served at Petersburg, where he was killed on December 2, 1864. General Gracie is buried in Woodlawn Cemetery in New York City. A portrait of his son Archibald Gracie (1858–1912) (q.v.) is also in the Society's collection.

DAB; *Generals in Gray*.

ARTIST UNIDENTIFIED

Oil on canvas: 37½ x 30 in. (95.3 x 76.2 cm.)

Presented in 1937 by Constance Elise (Schack) Gracie (Mrs. Archibald Gracie) of New York City, the subject's daughter-in-law. Por937.11

An early note attached to the back of the frame states that the portrait was "Painted on the Battlefield by one of his [the subject's] Adoring Artist Soldiers."

Archibald Gracie, 1858–1912
Constance Elise (Schack) Gracie, ca. 1852–1937 (Mrs. Archibald Gracie)

Son of General Archibald Gracie (q.v.) and Josephine (Mayo) Gracie, the subject was born in Mobile, Alabama, in 1858. In 1890 he married Constance Elise Schack, daughter of a former minister from Denmark to the United States, Count Otto Wilhelm Christian Schack, and Elizabeth Innes (McCarty) Schack. The Gracies were active in the social life of New York City and Washington and maintained residences in both places. Gracie, one of the survivors of the *Titanic*, died on December 4, 1912, less than a year after the tragedy in which he played a heroic part. His account of the sinking, *The Truth about the Titanic* (1913), was published posthumously; he had earlier written *The Truth about Chickamauga* (1911). Gracie's widow, a native of New York City, married, second, in 1924, Humberto Aquirre de Urbina; the marriage was later annulled, and she resumed her first husband's name. She died in Washington on December 12, 1937, at about eighty-five years of age; the four children she bore Archibald Gracie all predeceased her.

Portraiture, pp. 42–43; *New York Times*, Dec. 5, 1912, p. 1, and Dec. 13, 1937, p. 27.

Portrait I. Archibald Gracie

BY JOHN WYCLIFFE LOWES FORSTER. Signed. Ca.1890

Oil on canvas: 30 x 25 in. (76.2 x 63.5 cm.)

Presented in 1937 by the subject's widow. Por937.12

Portrait II. Constance Elise (Schack) Gracie

BY BARIN DELLA NOCE. Signed. Ca.1890

Oil on canvas: 28 x 19 in. (71.1 x 48.3 cm.)

Presented in 1937 by the subject. Por937.10

John Granbery, 1759–1815
Susanna Butterfield (Stowe) Granbery, 1772–1852 (Mrs. John Granbery)
Two Unidentified Granbery Daughters

John Granbery was born on October 7, 1759, the eldest son of Josiah and Christian (Gregory) Granbery, Virginians who were living at the time in Sunbury, North Carolina. About 1768 the family moved to Suffolk, Virginia. He received his formal education in Scotland, then returned to Virginia during the Revolutionary War. Although his father had left him a handsome inheritance, "the effects of the war . . . considerably injured his fortunes, and he commenced Merchant." His ships operated between Norfolk, Bermuda, and Charleston, South Carolina. On September 23, 1789, he married Susanna Butterfield Stowe, daughter of Joseph and Betsey (Holladay) Stowe of Spanish Point, Bermuda, who bore

her husband eleven children, four of whom died in childhood; the family resided at No. 4 Boush Street, Norfolk. John Granbery was a member of the Norfolk Borough Council in 1802, first vice-president of the Chamber of Commerce in 1806, and president of the Marine Insurance Company. On August 20, 1815, he embarked on the schooner, *Martha and Eliza*, together with his brother-in-law Willis R. Stowe and his son George Granbery (a promising young artist); the ship, bound for Bermuda, went down in a storm a week later, and all were lost. Mrs. Granbery, who survived her husband more than thirty-five years, died on June 23, 1852, and is buried in Cedar Grove Cemetery, Norfolk. Five of John and Susanna Granbery's daughters lived to maturity; it is not known which two are depicted in the silhouettes in the Society's collection.

Julian Hastings Granbery, *John Granbery, Virginia* (New York, 1964), pp. 25–35.

Portrait I. John Granbery

BY GEORGE GRANBERY

Hollow-cut silhouette: 3 in. (7.6 cm.) in height, on paper 4¼ x 3½ in. (10.8 x 8.9 cm.) (oval). Mounted on black bakelite.

Presented in 1944 by Julian Hastings Granbery of Richmond. Por944.6.0.1

Portrait II. Susanna Butterfield (Stowe) Granbery

BY GEORGE GRANBERY

Hollow-cut silhouette: 3 in. (7.6 cm.) in height, on paper 4¼ x 3¼ in. (10.8 x 8.3 cm.) (oval). Mounted on black bakelite.

Presented in 1944 by Julian Hastings Granbery of Richmond. Por944.6.0.2

Portrait III. Miss Granbery

BY GEORGE GRANBERY

Hollow-cut silhouette: 3 in. (7.6 cm.) in height, on paper 4¼ x 3¼ in. (10.8 x 8.3 cm.). Mounted on black bakelite.

Presented in 1944 by Julian Hastings Granbery of Richmond. Por944.6.0.3

Portrait IV. Miss Granbery

BY GEORGE GRANBERY

Hollow-cut silhouette: 3 in. (7.6 cm.) in height, on paper 4¼ x 3½ in. (10.8 x 8.9 cm.). Mounted on black bakelite.

Presented in 1944 by Julian Hastings Granbery of Richmond. Por944.6.0.4

These four open-cut silhouettes were cut by George Granbery, who was lost at sea in 1815, a few days before his twenty-first birthday. They depict the young artist's parents and two of his sisters. A note on the back of one states that they were mounted on black bakelite in 1928 by the donor. They are mentioned on page 32 of Julian Hastings Granbery's *John Granbery, Virginia.*

Prudence (Nimmo) Granbery, 1807–1903 (Mrs. Henry Augustus Thaddeus Granbery)

Born on December 28, 1807, the subject was the daughter of Gershom and Elizabeth Jacomine (Boush) Smith Nimmo of Princess Anne County and Norfolk. On October 19, 1828, she married Henry Augustus Thaddeus Granbery (1808–1904), third son of John and Susanna Butterfield (Stowe) Granbery (qq.v.) of Norfolk. The couple resided on the estate in Norfolk County that she inherited from her father in 1817; they also had a residence in the borough of Norfolk. Her husband, who operated a tobacco business, removed with his family to New York City in 1841. He eventually sold his property in Virginia and, continuing in the wholesale tobacco business, remained in New York City until his death, which occurred on February 14, 1904. Prudence (Nimmo) Granbery bore her husband nine children. She died on December 8, 1903. Mr. and Mrs. Granbery are buried in the family plot in Cedar Grove Cemetery, Norfolk.

Julian Hastings Granbery, *John Granbery, Virginia* (New York, 1964), pp. 57–58; VHS Mss6:4 G7627:1–2; *VMHB* 59 (1951): 266.

BY VIRGINIA GRANBERY. Signed. "V.G."

Miniature on ivory: 4 x 3 in. (10.2 x 7.6 cm.) (oval)

Presented in 1950 by Julian Hastings Granbery of Richmond. Por950.1

The miniature was painted by the subject's daughter from a photograph taken in 1887.

François Joseph Paul, Marquis de Grasse-Tilly, 1722–1788

Admiral de Grasse was born near Grasse, France, on September 13, 1722. He entered the French navy in 1738 and served during the War of the Austrian Succession, 1740–48, and the Seven Years War, 1756–63. With France's entrance into the American Revolution, he took part in the indecisive battle of Ushant in July 1778, then was dispatched to the West Indies, where he commanded a squadron under Admiral d'Estaing in the battle off Grenada. In 1781 he was named commander in chief of the Atlantic fleet; he defeated Admiral Hood and took the island of Tobago. Responding to Washington's call for naval support for the Yorktown campaign, de Grasse arrived in the lower Chesapeake; reinforced by the ships of the comte de Barras, he outmaneuvered the British fleet under Admiral Thomas Graves on September 15, 1781, forcing it to withdraw. This naval success was instrumental in the American victory at Yorktown and the subsequent surrender of General Cornwallis. The following year de Grasse captured the island of St. Kitts, but in April he was defeated by Admiral Rodney of the British navy, and taken prisoner. On his release in 1783 he returned to France to face charges of incompetence; although acquitted by a court-martial the following year, he was banished from the royal court and spent the remaining four years of his life in seclusion at the château de Tilly. He died in Paris on January 14, 1788. De Grasse was three times married; on the outbreak of the French Revolution his four daughters escaped to America; they joined their brother in Charleston, South Carolina, around 1795.

Encyclopedia Americana; Encyclopaedia Britannica; Virginia Historical Portraiture, pp. 254–57 (original portrait reproduced); *New-York Historical Society Quarterly* 61 (1977): 19 (portrait reproduced).

COPIED BY CHARLES X. HARRIS. 1929

Oil on canvas: 31 x 26 in. (78.7 x 66 cm.). Inscribed on the back: "Admiral De Grasse, 1723–1788. After Jean Baptiste Mauzaisse, Musee de Versailles."

Presented in 1946 by Mr. and Mrs. Alexander Wilbourne Weddell of Richmond. Por946.25

Another copy of the original, which hangs at Versailles, was painted by Albert Rosenthal and is in the Independence Hall collection, Philadelphia.

Anne Elizabeth Greaner, 1820–1862

See Anne Elizabeth (Greaner) Higgins, 1820–1862

William Greaner, 1793–1868

William Greaner was born in Baltimore in 1793. He enlisted as a volunteer soldier in 1812 and served at North Point, near Baltimore, during the hostilities with the British. Trained to the tobacco trade, he came to Richmond in 1815 where he remained for the rest of his life, becoming a successful tobacco manufacturer. In 1839 he bought the house at 1920 East Broad Street that had formerly been the residence of John Holt Rice; he lived there until his death almost thirty years later. His tobacco manufactory occupied the building that later became the Civil War prison Castle Thunder. The summer before his death he visited his native city; his reminiscences were published at that time in the *Baltimore Sun*. He died on December 31, 1868, and is buried in Hollywood Cemetery. In his obituary it was noted that "the deceased commenced life poor, but by his untiring energy, sagacity and probity he succeeded in amassing a handsome property, which, however, became somewhat impaired during the rebellion."

Mary Wingfield Scott, *Houses of Old Richmond* (Richmond, 1941), p. 144; *Richmond Whig and Advertiser* (semiweekly), Jan. 1, 1869, p. 1, col. 6; *Richmond Enquirer*, Jan. 2, 1869; *VMHB* 87 (1979): 241.

ARTIST UNIDENTIFIED

Miniature on ivory: 2 in. (5.1 cm.) in diameter (circular)

Received in 1978 as a bequest of Frances (Nolting) Hoare-Smith (Mrs. Gerald W. Hoare-Smith) of Baltimore, a great-great-granddaughter of the subject. Por978.5

Berryman Green, 1754–1825

Born in Westmoreland County in 1754, the subject was the son of Thomas and Anna (Berryman) Green. Although lame from youth, he enlisted as a private in the 4th Troop of Light Horse at the outbreak of the Revolution. He was among the Virginians who spent the wretched winter of 1777–78 at Valley Forge. Shortly afterward, General Henry Lee selected Green to help organize the commisary and alleviate the shortages of food and supplies that were undermining the strength and morale of the American army. At first reluctant to accept for fear of jeopardizing his chances for advancement in the regular army, Captain Green at length accepted a post on the quartermaster general's staff. It was while he was at Valley Forge that he met his future wife, Ann Pritchard, daughter of Anthony Pritchard, a Quaker and a loyalist; they were married on May 25, 1778, and she returned to Westmoreland County with him at the war's end. She bore him five children who were still young when their mother died. After her death Green removed to Halifax County where he married, second, on January 6, 1789, Nancy Terry, daughter of Colonel Nathaniel and Sarah (Royal) Terry, who also bore her husband five children. He resided with his family on a farm about two miles from the county seat of Halifax County; here he constructed a house known as Green's Folly because of its size where he intended the county court to sit; it did in fact convene at his residence until the courthouse was constructed. Green was for some years deputy clerk of Halifax County. He died on September 13, 1825.

Tyler's Quart. 7 (1925–26): 201; William Breckenridge Barbour, *Halifacts* (Danville, Va., 1941), pp. 160–63; *Occasional Bulletin*, no. 25 (1972): 10–12 (portrait reproduced); Wirt Johnson Turner Carrington, *A History of Halifax County* (Richmond, 1924), pp. 184–190; *Richmond Standard*, Jan. 18, 1879, p. 4, col. 2.

Berryman Green

ARTIST UNIDENTIFIED

Miniature on ivory: 2³/4 x 2 in. (7 x 5.1 cm.) (oval)

Presented in 1972 by Martha Jefferson (Taylor) Stedman (Mrs. Edgar Stedman) of Frederick, Maryland, a great-great-great-granddaughter of the subject. Por972.11

John Williams Green, 1781–1834
See The Convention of 1829–30

Mary Browne Green, 1779–1860
See Mary Browne (Green) Rives, 1779–1860

William Green, 1806–1880

Born on November 10, 1806, son of Colonel John Williams Green and Mary (Brown) Green of Fredericksburg, the subject attended the local school, then studied law with his father. It was said that when he began studying he did not speak a word to anyone for as much as six months at a time; that "his habit was to put on his dressing-gown, put a kitten in each pocket, and walk the floor with his book in his hand studying all day and until late in the night." He was admitted to the bar in 1827, before he was twenty-one years of age, and removed to Culpeper County, where he developed a large practice in Culpeper and the surrounding counties. The success of his appellate practice led him to move to Richmond, where he remained for the rest of his life, achieving prominence at the Virginia bar. Green was retained by John Brown after his conviction for treason in 1859. During the Civil War he served the Confederate government in the Department of the Treasury, and later he officiated as judge for the court of conciliation for the city of Richmond. Judge Green was for a short time professor of law at Richmond College, but the pressure of his practice compelled him to resign. In his youth he contributed articles on various subjects to the *Culpeper Gazette* and the *Southern Literary Messenger*; subsequently he was a frequent contributor to legal journals; a bibliophile, he collected a large library which he annotated copiously. He married on April 6, 1837, Columbia E. Slaughter, daughter of Samuel and Virginia (Stanard) Slaughter of Culpeper County; two children were born of the union. He died in Richmond on July 29, 1880, and is buried in Hollywood Cemetery. Judge Green became a vice-president of the Virginia Historical Society in 1870.

DAB; *Virginia Law Register* 14 (1909): 670–71; Philip Slaughter, *A History of St. Mark's Parish, Culpeper County, Virginia* (Baltimore, 1877), p. 160; Armistead Churchill Gordon, *Virginian Portraits* (Staunton, Va., 1924), pp. 43–74.

COPIED BY WILLIS PEPOON. 1910

Oil on canvas: 30 x 25 in. (76.2 x 63.5 cm.). Inscribed on the back: "Portrait of Judge William Green done by Willis Pepoon 1910   No 229."

Presented in 1946 by William Green Hayes of Richmond. Por946.27

Martha Bickerton Greenhow, 1820–1909
See Robert Henry Maury, 1816–1886

Roger Gregory, ca. 1685–ca. 1730

Born about 1685, Roger Gregory was a resident of Stratton Major Parish, King and Queen County, as early as 1711, in which year he received a land patent for 300 acres. Between 1714 and 1718 he married Mildred Washington (1696–1747), only daughter of Lawrence and Mildred (Warner) Washington. In May 1726 Roger and Mildred Gregory sold and conveyed to Mildred's brother, Augustine Washington, 2,500 acres on Hunting Creek, Stafford (now Fairfax) County, a tract of land that became the nucleus of the Mount Vernon estate. The couple had

three daughters; the youngest, Elizabeth, married, as her fourth husband, Dr. Thomas Walker of Castle Hill, Albemarle County. Roger Gregory died between October 1730 and May 1731. His widow on April 5, 1732, stood sponsor in baptism for her nephew George Washington, the future president. Mrs. Gregory married, second, on January 5, 1734, Henry Willis of Fredericksburg; she bore him a son and died on September 5, 1747.

Charles Arthur Hoppin, *The Washington Ancestry* (Greenfield, Ohio, 1932), 1: 163; Beverley Fleet, *Virginia Colonial Abstracts: King and Queen County* (Richmond, 1938–48), 3: 48, 8: 8; George Washington, *The Diaries of George Washington* (Charlottesville, Va., 1976–79), 2: 30; *VMHB* 56 (1948): 42–52, 238.

ARTIST UNIDENTIFIED

Oil on canvas: 29 x 24½ in. (73.7 x 62.2 cm.) (oval)

Presented in 1947 by the Rives estate through Sarah Landon Rives of Albemarle County. Por947.35

John Summerfield Griffith, 1829–1901

The son of Michael Berry Griffith, the subject was born in Montgomery County, Maryland, on June 17, 1829. As a child he moved with his parents to Missouri and later to San Augustine, Texas. In December 1851 he married at Nacogdoches, Texas, Sarah Emily Simpson, daughter of John J. Simpson and Jane Simpson; eight years later they removed to Kaufman County, Texas. With the coming of the Civil War he organized a company of cavalry at Rockville, Texas; when the company became a part of the 6th Texas Cavalry, Griffith was elected lieutenant colonel. He saw action with the regiment and distinguished himself at the raid on Holly Springs, Mississippi, a move that has been credited with delaying the fall of Vicksburg for some months. Failing health led to his resignation from the army; he returned to Texas in June 1863, was appointed brigadier general of state troops on March 1, 1864, and won a seat in the legislature, serving as chairman of the Committee on Military Affairs. At the war's end although in poor health, he devoted himself to business; he moved his residence to Terrell, Texas, in 1874, and two years later was again elected to the state legislature, where he played a part in putting the new state constitution into successful operation. He died at his home in Terrell, Texas, on August 6, 1901.

Confederate Veteran 13 (1905): 136.

COPIED BY ISABELLE BRANSON CARTWRIGHT

Oil on canvas: 30 x 25 in. (76.2 x 63.5 cm.). Inscribed on the back: "Copy of portrait by Miriam Fort Gill."

Presented to the Confederate Memorial Association in 1939 by the subject's grandson, Summerfield G. Roberts of Dallas, Texas; acquired by the Virginia Historical Society in 1946 through merger with the Confederate Memorial Association. Por946.87

Richard Griffith, 1814–1862

A native Pennsylvanian, General Griffith was born on January 11, 1814. He graduated from Ohio University in Athens, Ohio, in 1837 and removed to Vicksburg, Mississippi, where he taught school until enlisting in the 1st Mississippi Rifles for service in the Mexican War. On his return from Mexico he turned his attention to finance, first as a banker in Jackson, Mississippi, later as state treasurer, an office he held for two terms. On the secession of Mississippi he became colonel of the 12th Mississippi Regiment, and on November 12, 1861, he was commissioned brigadier general in command of four Mississippi regiments in Virginia. As a part of Magruder's Division, Griffith's troops took part in the battles of the Seven Days; General Griffith was wounded at the battle of Savage's Station on June 29, 1862, and died the same day in Richmond; he is buried in Jackson, Mississippi. By his wife, Sarah E. (Whitfield) Griffith, he had issue.

Generals in Gray; Biographic Catalogue.

BY EMMA MOREHEAD WHITFIELD. Signed. Dated 1905

Oil on canvas: 30 x 25 in. (76.2 x 63.5 cm.)

Presented to the R. E. Lee Camp, Confederate Veterans, by the artist in 1905; acquired by the Virginia Historical Society in 1946 through merger with the Confederate Memorial Association. Por946.78

Thomas Griggs, 1780–1860
See The Convention of 1829–30

Hugh Blair Grigsby, 1806–1881

Historian and fourth president of the Virginia Historical Society, Hugh Blair Grigsby, a native of Norfolk, was born on November 22, 1806, son of the Reverend Benjamin Porter Grigsby and Elizabeth (McPherson) Grigsby. Following two years at Yale University he studied law and was admitted to the bar in Norfolk, but he never practiced owing to his delicate constitution and increasing deafness. He strove to improve his health through a regimen of boxing and pedestrian exercise, on one occasion making a trip to Canada and back on foot. Turning to politics, he represented Norfolk in the Virginia

House of Delegates 1828–30 and served as a member of the Virginia Constitutional Convention of 1829–30. In 1834 Grigsby bought an interest in the Norfolk newspaper the *American Beacon*; four years later he became its owner and editor, but he sold the paper in 1840 because of his health. After his marriage on November 19, 1840, to Mary Venable Carrington, daughter of Clement Carrington of Charlotte County, he resided at Edgehill, Charlotte County, and devoted himself to scholarly pursuits. His chief works are *The Virginia Convention of 1829–30* (1854), *The Virginia Convention of 1776* (1855), and *The History of the Virginia Federal Convention of 1788* (1890–91). Grigsby became a member of the Virginia Historical Society's executive committee in 1834; he became its corresponding secretary in 1857 and its president in 1870, holding that office for the last eleven years of his life. He served on the board of visitors of the College of William and Mary and was elected chancellor of the college in 1871; he was a voluminous correspondent, poet, book collector, and patron of the arts. He died at Edgehill on April 28, 1881, and is buried in Elmwood Cemetery, Norfolk. A son and a daughter survived him.

DAB; VMHB 62 (1954): 240 (where artist is identified as *Thomas* Swain); *Portraiture*, pp. 43–44.

Hugh Blair Grigsby (Portrait I)

Portrait I

BY WILLIAM SWAIN

Oil on canvas: 30 x 25 in. (76.2 x 63.5 cm.)

Received in 1953 as a bequest of Hugh Blair Grigsby Galt of Norfolk. Por953.3

In his diary entry for April 14, 1828, Grigsby noted that "young Swain the portrait painter spent the evening with me—lent him two vols. of my Encyclopaedia." Grigsby at the time was twenty-one years of age; "young Swain" was twenty-four. No record has been found in Grigsby's diary of his sitting for the portrait. Swain visited Norfolk at various times during his life and died there on February 18, 1847.

VHS Mss1 G8782b 70, p. 53.

Portrait II

By W. Irving Taylor. Signed. 1881

Chalk and charcoal on paper: 30 x 25 in. (76.2 x 63.5 cm.)

Received in 1935 from Hugh Blair Grigsby Galt, William Richard Galt, Mary Carrington (Galt) Vance (Mrs. Deane Harold Vance), and Susan Duane (Galt) Zimermann (Mrs. Alfred Zimermann). Por935.8

This is one of two likenesses of Grigsby drawn shortly before his death by W. Irving Taylor. In a letter to Grigsby's son, Hugh Carrington Grigsby, dated June 10, 1881, Taylor stated: "I have a fine life size portrait, in crayon, of your father, the late Hon. H. B. Grigsby. I have just finished some changes after suggestions received from him, when last in my studio; it is a work similar to the one I made for Mr. Whitehead and universally considered a striking likeness. I am only a sojourner in Norfolk, and am now about to close out my studio and leave here. The work is one of my best efforts in Norfolk. I want if possible to sell the picture and Mr. Whitehead has kindly referred me to you." Grigsby *fils*, it appears from another letter, purchased the crayon portrait at the asking price of fifty dollars.

VHS Mss1 G8782b 5414–5415.

Portrait III

See The Convention of 1829–30

Bryan Grimes, 1828–1880

Bryan Grimes, a major general in the Army of the Confederate States, was born on November 2, 1828, in Pitt County, North Carolina, at Grimesland, the plantation of his parents, Bryan and Nancy Grimes. He graduated from the University of North Carolina in 1848, and on April 9, 1851, married Elizabeth Hilliard Davis, who died six years later. He traveled to Europe in 1860 and the following year was elected to the North Carolina Secession Convention. A few days after the secession of the state Grimes accepted an appointment as major of the 4th North Carolina Regiment and led his troops to Virginia. Grimes saw action with the Army of Northern Virginia in most of

its principal engagements: Seven Pines, Mechanicsville, Sharpsburg, Fredericksburg, Chancellorsville, Gettysburg, and Spotsylvania Court House, rising to the rank of major general. At Cedar Creek, Petersburg, Sayler's Creek, and finally at Appomattox, where he commanded one of the last attacks, General Grimes proved himself an able and courageous leader. After the war he returned to his plantation in Pitt County, North Carolina, where he resided until his death on August 14, 1880, at the hands of an assassin hired by persons whom Grimes was attempting to expel from the area as undesirable citizens. He was survived by his second wife, whom he married on September 5, 1863, Charlotte Emily (Bryan) Grimes, daughter of John H. Bryan of Raleigh, North Carolina, by whom he had four daughters and four sons.

Generals in Gray; *Biographic Catalogue*; Henry Armand London, *Memorial Address on the Life and Services of Bryan Grimes, Major-General in the Provisional Army of the Confederate States* (Raleigh, N.C., 1886).

By William George Randall. 1898

Oil on canvas: 30 x 25 in. (76.2 x 63.5 cm.). Inscribed on the back: "W. G. Randall '98. Painted from a photograph and a portrait by Wm. Garl Brown."

Presented to the R. E. Lee Camp, Confederate Veterans, in 1898; acquired by the Virginia Historical Society in 1946 through merger with the Confederate Memorial Association. Por946.199

Charles Grymes, b. 1748
See Grymes Children

Elizabeth (Randolph) Grymes, born ca. 1742
See Elizabeth Randolph, born ca. 1742

John Randolph Grymes, 1747–1796
See Grymes Children

Lucy Grymes, 1743–1830
See Grymes Children

Philip Ludwell Grymes, 1746–1805
See Grymes Children

Grymes Children

The children depicted in this charming portrait are the four eldest children of Philip Grymes (1721–

1762) and Mary (Randolph) Grymes of Brandon, Middlesex County. Philip Grymes, son of John and Lucy (Ludwell) Grymes, was a burgess, receiver general of the colony 1749–54, and a member of the colonial Council from 1751 until his death in 1762. His wife, whom he married on December 8, 1742, was a daughter of Sir John and Lady Randolph (qq.v.); she bore her husband ten children, four of whom are here depicted (left to right).

1. Lucy Grymes (1743–1830) married on July 29, 1762, Thomas Nelson (1738–1789) (q.v.), signer of the Declaration of Independence and governor of Virginia.

2. John Randolph Grymes (1747–1796), still in skirts at the time the portrait was painted, received his formal education in England, was a loyalist during the American Revolution, and served under Simcoe in the Queen's Rangers. After living for a time in England, he returned to Virginia where he prospered as a planter in Orange County. On May 20, 1779, he married in London his first cousin Susannah Randolph, daughter of John Randolph, former attorney general of Virginia; the couple had four children.

3. Philip Ludwell Grymes (1746–1805), the eldest son, was educated in England, inherited Brandon on the death of his father, represented Middlesex County in the House of Burgesses 1769–70, and was sheriff of the county. He later became a member of the House of Delegates and the Council of State. He married, first, Elizabeth Randolph (q.v.), daughter of William and Anne (Harrison) Randolph (qq.v.), and, second, Judith Wormeley, daughter of Ralph Wormeley (1745–1806) (q.v.) and Eleanor (Tayloe) Wormeley of Rosegill, Middlesex County; he had children by his second wife.

4. Charles Grymes (b.1748) of whom little is known. It was probably he who married in 1773 Ann Lightfoot of York County.

VMHB 28 (1920): 90–96, 189, 283–85 (portrait reproduced, p. 93); National Gallery of Art, *The Eye of Thomas Jefferson* (Washington, D.C., 1976), p. 10 (portrait reproduced); *The Beverley Family*, pp. 392–93, 494, 498, 515; VHS Mss1 J4105a 19–21 and Mss6:4 G9294:1; *W. & M. Quart.*, 2d ser., 21 (1941): 175; *Portraiture*, pp. 44–46; *Antiques* 116 (1979): 1130 (portrait reproduced).

ATTRIBUTED TO JOHN HESSELIUS   *See* Plate 12

Oil on canvas: 56 x 66¼ in. (142.2 x 168.3 cm.)

Received in 1893 as a bequest of Nora Crena (Braxton) Macon (Mrs. William Hartwell Macon) of Hanover County. Por893.3

Francis North, first Earl of *Guilford*, 1704–1790

See Francis *North*, first Earl of Guilford, 1704–1790

Ariana Gunn, 1770–1838

See Edward Cunningham, 1771–1836

Maria Carter Hall

See Warner Lewis Wormeley, 1785–1814

Martha Minor Hall, 1827–1883

See Martha Minor (Hall) Scott, 1827–1883

Joshua C. Hallowell, ca.1831–1863
India Charlotte (Goddin) Hallowell, 1838–1900   (Mrs. Joshua C. Hallowell)

Born in Richmond about 1831, Joshua C. Hallowell became as a young man a clerk in the offices of the Mutual Assurance Society. On December 20, 1854, he married India Charlotte Goddin, born July 16, 1838, daughter of Wellington and Eliza Povall (Winston) Goddin of Richmond. In 1862 he enlisted in Parker's Battery, Virginia Light Artillery. According to one comrade-in-arms, Sergeant Hallowell was "the best gunner in Parker's Battery." He was mortally wounded at Gettysburg and died on July 20, 1863; on November 22, 1865, his remains were reinterred in Hollywood Cemetery in Richmond. His widow, who devoted the rest of her life to teaching, became assistant principal of the Richmond Female Institute and later principal of the Richmond Seminary. She died on April 30, 1900, leaving one child.

Robert K. Krick, *Parker's Virginia Battery, C.S.A.* (Berryville, Va., 1975), p. 323; Confederate Service Records, National Archives, microfilm roll 326; *Tyler's Quart.* 1 (1919–20): 172–73; *Richmond Dispatch*, May 1, 1900, p. 1; *VMHB* 81 (1973): 238.

Portrait I. Joshua C. Hallowell

ATTRIBUTED TO WILLIAM JAMES HUBARD

Oil on canvas: 29¾ x 25 in. (75.6 x 63.5 cm.)

Received in 1972 as a bequest of Lizette Wellington (Winston) McGeorge. Por972.14

Portrait II. India Charlotte (Goddin) Hallowell

ATTRIBUTED TO WILLIAM JAMES HUBARD

Oil on canvas: 29¾ x 25 in. (75.6 x 63.5 cm.)

Received in 1972 as a bequest of Lizette Wellington (Winston) McGeorge. Por972.15

12. Grymes children

Don Peters Halsey, 1836–1883

Born in Lynchburg on September 15, 1836, son of Seth and Julia D. B. (Peters) Halsey, the subject graduated from Emory and Henry College in 1855 and then pursued his studies at the University of Virginia and in Germany. Returning from abroad at the time of Virginia's secession from the Union, Halsey entered the Confederate army as second lieutenant in Company G, 2d Virginia Cavalry; in the spring of 1862 when the company was reorganized he was transferred to General Garland's staff as aide-de-camp with the rank of captain; later he served on the staffs of Generals Iverson and R. D. Johnston. Halsey participated in the battles of the Peninsula, Seven Pines, where he lost the sight of his right eye, Sharpsburg, Chancellorsville, Gettysburg, the Valley campaign of 1864, and Waynesboro where he was taken prisoner on March 2, 1865. On his release at the end of the war he began the practice of law in Lynchburg in partnership with Judge William Daniel and his son John Warwick Daniel (q.v.). On March 7, 1866, he married Judge Daniel's daughter, Sarah Ann Warwick Daniel, who bore him six children. In 1874 Captain Halsey removed to Richmond where he developed a successful law practice, being especially popular with the large German element of that city because of his fluency in their language. Poor health compelled him to retire from his profession in 1880; he spent the remainder of his life at his farm, Fern Moss, in Nelson County, where he died on January 1, 1883.

History of Virginia, 4: 367–68; *SHS Papers* 31 (1903): 193–207; CMA Archives, folio Z1n; *Biographic Catalogue*.

By John P. Walker. Signed. Dated 1924

Oil on canvas: 30 x 25 in. (76.2 x 63.5 cm.)

Presented to the R. E. Lee Camp, Confederate Veterans, in 1924; acquired by the Virginia Historical Society in 1946 through merger with the Confederate Memorial Association. Por946.183

Wade Hampton, 1818–1902

Confederate soldier, governor of South Carolina, and United States senator, Wade Hampton was born in Charleston, South Carolina, on March 28, 1818, eldest child of Wade and Ann (FitzSimons) Hampton. He graduated from South Carolina College in 1836, oversaw his extensive plantation holdings, and served in the South Carolina legislature 1852–61. Although without military experience or training, he organized and equipped at his own expense the Hampton Legion which he led to Virginia on the outbreak of the Civil War, arriving in time to participate in the battle of First Manassas. Rising in rank from colonel to lieutenant general, Hampton served in J. E. B. Stuart's Cavalry Corps until Stuart's death, whereupon he succeeded to the command of the corps. In this post he participated in most of the principal engagements of the Army of Northern Virginia. In January 1865 he was ordered to join General J. E. Johnston in the Carolinas, where he served until the surrender. During the years immediately after the war Hampton, finding himself at odds with the Republican regime in South Carolina, devoted himself to his plantations. In 1876, however, he was elected governor of the state; two years later he became United States senator, serving from 1879 to 1891. Defeated in his bid for a third term in the Senate, he accepted an appointment as commissioner of Pacific railways which he held from 1893 to 1897. He died at Columbia, South Carolina, on April 11, 1902, and is buried there. General Hampton was twice married: first, in 1838, to Margaret Preston, a daughter of Francis and Sarah (Campbell) Preston; second, in 1858, to Mary Singleton McDuffie, daughter of Governor George McDuffie of South Carolina; he had children by both marriages.

DAB; *Generals in Gray*; *Biographical Directory*; *Biographic Catalogue*.

Wade Hampton (Portrait I)

Portrait I

By CLARA BARRETT STRAIT. Signed. Dated 1922

Oil on canvas: 60 x 40 in. (152.4 x 101.6 cm.)

Acquired in 1946 through merger with the Confederate Memorial Association. Por946.215

Portrait II

See The Battle Abbey Murals. The Summer Mural

Harriet Harman
See Clifford Cabell Early, 1883–1967

Nathaniel Harrison Harris, 1834–1900

The son of William Mercer Harris and Caroline (Harrison) Harris, the subject was born at Natchez, Mississippi, on August 22, 1834. He studied law at the University of Louisiana and after graduating practiced his profession in Vicksburg until the outbreak of the Civil War. On June 1, 1861, the Warren Rifles, which he organized, was mustered into the Confederate army as Company C, 19th Mississippi Infantry. As colonel of this regiment, Harris took part in the Maryland campaign, Chancellorsville, and Gettysburg. Promoted to brigadier general on January 20, 1864, he was assigned a brigade in Mahone's division of the 3d Corps and fought at Spotsylvania, the siege of Petersburg, Richmond, and Appomattox. After the surrender, General Harris returned to his law practice in Vicksburg; later he became president of the Mississippi Valley and Ship Island Railroad. In 1885 he was appointed register of the United States Land Office at Aberdeen, South Dakota, and five years later removed to San Francisco. General Harris, a bachelor, died in Malvern, England, on August 23, 1900.

DAB; *Generals in Gray*; *Biographic Catalogue*.

By BESSIE A. CATLIN. Signed (initials). Dated 1898

Oil on canvas: 30 x 25 in. (76.2 x 63.5 cm.)

Acquired in 1946 through merger with the Confederate Memorial Association. Por946.84

Anne Harrison, died post-1769
See William Randolph, d.1761

Anne (Randolph) Harrison, ca.1740–1767
See Anne Randolph, ca.1740–1767

110

Benjamin Harrison, 1726–1791

Signer of the Declaration of Independence and governor of Virginia, Benjamin Harrison was born in 1726 at Berkeley, Charles City County, son of Benjamin and Anne (Carter) Harrison. He attended the College of William and Mary and in 1745 inherited his father's estate. In 1749 he was elected to the Virginia House of Burgesses; he held the seat until 1775. Harrison was one of a committee to protest the imposition of the Stamp Act in 1764; he was a member of the Committee of Correspondence, took part in planning Virginia's resistance to the crown, and was a member of the Revolutionary Conventions of 1775 and 1776. Elected to the Continental Congress, he was one of the signers of the Declaration of Independence and later was instrumental in the establishment of the State Department, the War Department, and the Navy Department. After his retirement from the Continental Congress in 1777, he represented Charles City County in the Virginia House of Delegates until he took office in 1781 as governor of Virginia. On the expiration of his term in 1784 Harrison again became a member of the House of Delegates and for the third time was chosen to preside over that body. As a delegate to the Virginia Convention of 1788, convened to ratify the federal Constitution, he opposed approving a constitution without first approving a bill of rights. Harrison died at Berkeley on April 24, 1791. His wife, whom he married about 1750, was Elizabeth Bassett, daughter of William and Elizabeth (Churchill) Bassett of Eltham, New Kent County; she bore her husband

Benjamin Harrison

seven children, one of whom was President William Henry Harrison.

DAB; *Occasional Bulletin*, no. 18 (1969): 3–6 (portrait reproduced); Edward Griffith Dodson, *Speakers and Clerks of the Virginia House of Delegates, 1776–1955* (Richmond, 1956), p. 15; *VMHB* 32 (1924): (portrait reproduced opposite p. 298) and 77 (1969): 239; *Antiques* 116 (1979): 1137 (portrait reproduced).

ARTIST UNIDENTIFIED

Miniature on ivory: 1½ x 1¼ in. (3.8 x 3.2 cm.) (oval)

Presented in 1968 by Merritt H. Taylor of Bryn Mawr, Pennsylvania. Por968.28

At one time attributed to Henry Benbridge, the miniature is noted in *Henry Benbridge (1743–1812), American Portrait Painter*, a catalogue published in 1971 by the National Portrait Gallery, Washington, D.C., in connection with its exhibition of Benbridge's works. There it is stated of the Harrison miniature that "the work is not characteristic of Henry Benbridge" (p. 79, item 131).

Betty Harrison, ca. 1724–1783

See Peyton Randolph, ca. 1721–1775

Burton Norvell Harrison, 1838–1904
Constance (Cary) Harrison, 1843–1920   (Mrs. Burton Norvell Harrison)

Burton Norvell Harrison was born in New Orleans on July 7, 1838, the son of Jesse Burton Harrison and Frances Anne (Brand) Harrison. He attended Yale University, taught at Oxford College in Mississippi, and during the Civil War was private secretary to President Jefferson Davis. It was during the war years that he first met, in Richmond, Constance Cary, born in Fairfax County on April 25, 1843, daughter of Archibald and Monimia (Fairfax) Cary, who had come to Richmond with her widowed mother after their home, Vaucluse, near Alexandria had been destroyed and had become an active participant in the social life of the Confederate capital. After the war Constance Cary went with her mother to Europe to study music and French; the visit was a brief one, for on November 26, 1867, she and Burton Harrison were married at Morrisania, New York. The couple resided in New York City, where Burton Harrison practiced law and Constance (Cary) Harrison pursued her musical interests and began to write short stories. Encouraged by the popularity of such early efforts as "A Little Centennial Lady," published in the July 1876 issue of *Scribner's Monthly*,

she continued for more than thirty years to write stories, articles, and novels, among them *Flower de Hundred* (1890), *A Daughter of the South* (1892), *Sweet Bells Out of Tune* (1893), *An Errant Wooing* (1895), and *The Carlyles* (1905); her best-known volume, *Recollections Grave and Gay* (1911), is an autobiographical work. Burton Harrison died in Washington, D.C., on March 22, 1904; thereafter his widow spent much time in Europe but lived the last years of her life in Washington, D.C. She died there on November 21, 1920. The Harrisons had three sons; a portrait of the eldest, Fairfax Harrison (q.v.), is in the Society's collection. Burton Norvell Harrison was elected to membership in the Virginia Historical Society in 1874.

DAB; Francis Burton Harrison, *Burton Chronicles of Colonial Virginia* (Darmstadt, Ger., 1933), pp. 322–23; *VMHB* 68 (1960): 242.

Portrait I. Burton Norvell Harrison

BY MARIETTA MINNIGERODE ANDREWS. Signed. Dated 1914

Oil on canvas: 26 x 20 in. (66 x 50.8 cm.) (oval)

Acquired in 1946 through merger with the Confederate Memorial Association. Por946.232

Portrait II. Constance (Cary) Harrison

BY ALICE PIKE BARNEY. Signed

Oil on canvas: 27¼ x 22¼ in. (69.2 x 56.5 cm.)

Presented in 1959 by Ursula (Harrison) Baird (Mrs. Charles Baird) of Dunnsville, a granddaughter of the subject. Por959.32

Constance (Cary) Harrison

Elizabeth (Page) Harrison, born ca.1751

See Elizabeth Page, born ca.1751

Fairfax Harrison, 1869–1938
Hetty (Cary) Harrison, 1871–1943 (Mrs. Fairfax Harrison)

Fairfax Harrison was born in New York City on March 13, 1869, the eldest son of Burton Norvell Harrison and Constance (Cary) Harrison (qq.v.). He graduated from Yale University in 1890, studied law at Columbia University, and was admitted to the New York bar in 1892. After working for several years on legal questions posed by the creation of the Southern Railway, he was appointed solicitor for the railroad in 1896 and removed to Washington, D.C. In 1903 he became assistant to the president of the Southern Railway, three years later he became vice-president in charge of financial affairs, and from 1910 to 1913 he served his presidential apprentice-ship as chief executive of the Chicago, Indianapolis and Louisville Railway. He was elected president of the Southern Railway in 1913, holding that office until October 1937 and bringing the company through the First World War and the Great Depression. In addition to the administrative skill he displayed as a railroad executive, Harrison was a prolific writer on historical subjects; the range of his interests is reflected in the titles of such books as *Cato's Farm Management* (1910), *The Devon Carys* (1920), *Landmarks of Old Prince William* (1924), *Virginia Land Grants* (1925), *The Proprietors of the Northern Neck* (1926), and *Early American Turf Stock* (1934); he was also a frequent contributor of historical articles to the *Virginia Magazine of History and Biography*. Harrison became a member of the Virginia Historical Society in 1911 and subsequently was a member of its executive committee and a vice-president. He established his residence at Belvoir, Fauquier County, in 1907; here he resided with his wife, Hetty (Cary) Harrison, daughter of John Brune Cary and Frances (Daniel) Cary of Baltimore, whom he married on June 6, 1894. The couple had four children. Fairfax Harrison died in Baltimore on February 2, 1938, and is buried at Ivy Hill Cemetery, Alexandria; Mrs. Harrison died in 1943.

DAB (Supplement 2); *Portraiture*, pp. 46–47; *VMHB* 46 (1938): 153–57 and 82 (1974): 239; *W. & M. Quart.*, 1st ser., 18 (1910): 286.

Portrait I. Fairfax Harrison

By Eugen Weisz. 1939

Oil on canvas: 44 x 36 in. (111.8 x 91.4 cm.). Inscribed on the back: "Fairfax Harrison, 1869–1938

Fairfax Harrison

Hetty (Cary) Harrison (Portrait II)

Presented to Mrs. Fairfax Harrison by the Officers of the Southern Railway Co. Painted by Eugen Weisz, 1939."

Presented in 1944 by the subject's daughter, Ursula (Harrison) Baird (Mrs. Charles Baird) of Dunnsville. Por944.12

Portrait II. Hetty (Cary) Harrison

BY CHARLES DANA GIBSON. Signed

Pencil on paper: 11 1/2 x 7 in. (29.2 x 17.8 cm.)

Presented in 1973 by the subject's daughter, Ursula (Harrison) Baird (Mrs. Charles Baird) of Dunnsville. Por973.19

Portrait III. Hetty (Cary) Harrison

BY CHARLES DANA GIBSON. Signed

Pencil on paper: 11 x 7 1/4 in. (27.9 x 18.4 cm.)

Presented in 1973 by the subject's daughter, Ursula (Harrison) Baird (Mrs. Charles Baird) of Dunnsville. Por973.20

Lucy Harrison, ca. 1757–1809
See Peyton Randolph, ca. 1738–1784

Peachy Harrison, 1777–1848
See The Convention of 1829–30

Samuel Horace Hawes, 1838–1922

Son of Samuel Pierce Hawes and Judith Anna (Smith) Hawes, the subject was born in Powhatan County on June 5, 1838. Later the family removed to Richmond where in 1848 his father established a coal business that remained in the family for three generations. In April 1861 Hawes became a private in the Richmond Howitzers, and he took part with that command in the campaign of the Peninsula. Promoted to second lieutenant, he served in the Williamsburg Battery and in the Orange County Battery until he was taken prisoner, May 12, 1864, at the Bloody Angle at Spotsylvania Court House. For fourteen months he was held prisoner at Fort Delaware and Morris Island. At the war's end Hawes returned to Richmond and the family's coal yards, becoming on his father's death in 1866 president of the company, an office he retained for the rest of his life. On October 3, 1867, he married Martha C. Heath, who died in 1897, and by whom he had issue. Hawes was several times elected president of the Richmond Chamber of Commerce; he was a member of the Police Benevolent Association and an elder in the Second Presbyterian Church. He died on Feb-

ruary 10, 1922, survived by his second wife, Mary Mayo (Blair) Fitts Hawes, by a son, a daughter, and by his sister, the novelist Mary Virginia (Hawes) Terhune, better known by her pseudonym, Marion Harland.

Confederate Military History, 3: 927; *Richmond Times-Dispatch*, Feb. 11, 1922; VHS Mss1 H3112a; *Biographic Catalogue*.

BY LLOYD FREEMAN. Signed. Dated 1899

Oil on canvas: 27 x 22 in. (68.6 x 55.9 cm.)

Acquired in 1946 through merger with the Confederate Memorial Association. Por946.151

Gertrude P. (Moore) Hawkins (Mrs. George Hawkins)

The subject was the daughter of Richard Channing Moore (q.v.), Episcopal bishop of Virginia, and his second wife, Sarah (Mersereau) Moore. She married in Richmond, on July 4, 1816, George Hawkins, a merchant from Philadelphia. The couple had no children.

David Moore Hall, *Six Centuries of the Moores of Fawley, Berkshire, England* (Richmond, 1904), p. 42; Virginia Historical Society marriage and obituary file; information received with the portrait.

ARTIST UNIDENTIFIED

Oil on canvas: 29 x 23 3/4 in. (73.7 x 60.3 cm.)

Received in 1966 as a bequest of Sarah Landon Rives of Albemarle County. Por966.22

James Ewell Heath, 1792–1862

James Ewell Heath was born on July 8, 1792, son of John Heath, first president of the Phi Beta Kappa society, and Sarah (Ewell) Heath. He was elected to the Virginia General Assembly at the age of twenty-two and represented Prince William County 1814–17. During his third term he became a member of the Council, and in 1819 he became state auditor, an office he held for the next thirty years. Referred to by Edgar Allan Poe as "almost the only person of any literary distinction residing in Richmond," Heath was the author of *Edge-Hill* (1828), a two-volume romance of plantation life in Virginia, and *Whigs and Democrats* (1839), a political satire in three acts, both works published anonymously; he was also editorial adviser to the *Southern Literary Messenger* during its first year and at intervals thereafter. Heath was a founding member (1831) of the Virginia Historical Society and its first recording secretary. During President Fillmore's administration he was appointed commissioner of pensions. He died on June 28, 1862. Heath was twice married: first, to Fannie Weems, daughter of Mason Locke ("Parson") Weems; second, in 1820, to Elizabeth Ann Macon, daughter of William Hartwell Macon and Hannah (Selden) Macon of New Kent County; he had a son and a daughter by his second marriage.

DAB; *Richmond Portraits*, p. 87 (which reproduces a portrait of the subject painted at a younger age); *Virginia Genealogies*, pp. 340–41; *VMHB* 82 (1974): 239.

James Ewell Heath

ARTIST UNIDENTIFIED

Oil on canvas: 30 x 25 in. (76.2 x 63.5 cm.)

Presented in 1973 by Virginius Dabney of Richmond, a great-grandson of the subject. Por973.4

Richard H. Henderson, 1781–1841
See The Convention of 1829–30

Patrick Henry, 1736–1799

Orator and leader of the American Revolution and first governor of the Commonwealth of Virginia, Patrick Henry was born in Hanover County on May 29, 1736, son of John and Sarah (Winston) Syme Henry. As a young man he was unsuccessful both at farming and at storekeeping; he turned to law, was licensed in 1760, and quickly developed a successful practice. His reputation became more than local with his success in the celebrated "Parson's Cause," argued before the Hanover County court in November 1763. Henry was elected to the House of Burgesses in 1765, where he opposed the efforts of Vir-

ginia's elder statesmen to cover up the financial irregularities of John Robinson (q.v.), treasurer of the colony; with the adoption on May 30, 1765, of his resolutions opposing the Stamp Act, he became the most influential political figure in Virginia. He was a delegate to the first Continental Congress in 1774, and at the Revolutionary Convention held in St.

Patrick Henry (Portrait I)

John's church in Richmond on March 23, 1775, he moved that the colony adopt a posture of military preparedness, supporting the motion with the speech ending with the words "Give me liberty, or give me death." Active in organizing militia units, he led the Hanover troops to Williamsburg to demand the return of the colony's powder seized by the governor, Lord Dunmore (q.v.). On June 29, 1776, Henry was elected first governor of the Commonwealth of Virginia, serving as chief executive until 1779, and again, after the Revolution, from 1784 to 1786. He was a member of the Virginia state legislature 1786–90 and of the 1788 convention to ratify the United States Constitution, which he opposed on the grounds that its protection of the rights of the states was inadequate. Henry retired in 1794 to his farm, Red Hill, in Charlotte County where he died on June 6, 1799. He was twice married: first, in 1754, to Sarah Shelton, daughter of John Shelton of Hanover County, who bore him six children; second, in 1777, to Dorothea Dandridge, a daughter of Nathaniel West Dandridge, who bore him ten children.

DAB; *VMHB* 63 (1955): 230 and 71 (1963): 168–84 (Portrait I reproduced).

13. Patrick Henry Arguing the "Parson's Cause"

Portrait I

By Thomas Sully. 1851

Oil on canvas: 30 x 24 3/4 in. (76.2 x 62.9 cm.)

Presented by the artist in 1851. Por851.1

At the fourth annual meeting of the Society, held on December 12, 1850, William Maxwell, the corresponding secretary, announced that "Mr. Thomas Sully, the well-known artist, formerly of this city, but more recently of Philadelphia, had very handsomely offered and engaged to paint a copy of his own celebrated portrait of Patrick Henry, (now in the possession of John Henry, Esq. of Red-Hill, Charlotte) as a complimentary contribution to the generous cause in which the Society is engaged." A year later, in the published report of the fifth annual meeting, "a portrait of Patrick Henry, painted for the Society by Thomas Sully, Esq., of Philadelphia," is included in the list of donations received during the year. The painting, begun June 6, 1851, and finished June 28, appears as item 771 in Sully's portrait register.

Virginia Historical Register 4 (1851): 1–2 and 5 (1852): 55; Edward Biddle and Mantle Fielding, *The Life and Works of Thomas Sully* (Philadelphia, 1921), p. 173.

Portrait II. Plaque bearing likenesses of Washington, Henry, and Jefferson

See George Washington, 1732–1799 (Portrait VII)

Portrait III

Copied by an unidentified artist

Oil on canvas: 12 3/4 x 11 in. (32.4 x 27.9 cm.)

Presented in 1954 by D. Tennant Bryan of Richmond. Por954.11

The portrait is a reduced copy of the Sully portrait.

Portrait IV

By Nan Lemmon Lightfoot

Silhouette: India ink on paper 3 1/4 x 2 3/4 in. (8.3 x 7 cm.)

Presented in 1963 by Mary Lightfoot Garland of Richmond. Por963.38

Portrait V. Patrick Henry Arguing the "Parson's Cause"   *See* Plate 13

Attributed to George Cooke. Ca.1830

Oil on canvas: 28 x 36 in. (71.1 x 91.4 cm.)

Acquired by purchase in 1965. Pic965.2

Patrick Henry first achieved widespread recognition on December 1, 1763, when he unleashed a blaze of oratory at Hanover Courthouse on behalf of the defendants in the "Parson's Cause." His daring defense challenged the crown's right to nullify laws desired by the people and launched the young orator not only as a political leader but as a popular hero. The Society's canvas, painted well after the event, possibly in the 1830s, is thought to be the work of George Cooke. The wealth of detail strongly suggests an artist who was acquainted with the setting and dramatis personae. Visible through the open doors is a glimpse of Hanover Tavern, and depicted in the crowded courtroom are Henry's father, John Henry, the presiding officer, and William Winston, frontiersman and patriarch, who stands at the right of the picture in backwoodsman's dress.

Occasional Bulletin, no. 10 (1965): 2–4 (painting reproduced); *VMHB* 74 (1966): 243; *Antiques* 102 (1972): 448–54 (painting reproduced, p. 452).

William Wirt Henry, 1831–1900

Grandson of Patrick Henry (q.v.), historian, lawyer, and sixth president of the Virginia Historical Society, the subject was born on February 14, 1831, at Red Hill, Charlotte County, son of John and Elvira Henry (McClelland) Henry. He received a Master of Arts degree from the University of Virginia in 1850 and after studying law began practice in 1853; he was for some years Commonwealth's attorney of Charlotte County. Although opposed to secession he served during the Civil War in a local artillery company. In 1873 he removed to Richmond where he achieved prominence in the bar and embarked on a brief political career, representing Richmond in the Virginia House of Delegates 1877–79, and sitting in the state Senate 1879–80. Much in demand as a speaker at historical and patriotic gatherings, he was likewise a prolific writer of monographs and historical articles; his principal work was a three-volume biography of his grandfather, *Patrick Henry: Life, Correspondence, and Speeches* (1891). Henry became a member of the Virginia Historical Society in 1870, a vice-president in 1877, and in 1891 the Society's sixth president; he was also a member of the Massachusetts Historical Society, the Long Island Historical Society, the American Antiquarian Society, and the American Historical Association, serving the last-named organization as president 1890–91. The honors conferred on him by his own profession included the presidency of the Richmond City Bar Association and of the Virginia State Bar Association and the vice-presidency of the American Bar Association. Both the College of William and Mary and Washington and Lee recognized his academic accomplishments with honorary doctorates, and the Virginia Historical Society conferred honorary membership on him in 1900. Henry died on December 5, 1900, survived by his wife, Lucy Gray (Marshall) Henry, whom he married on November 8, 1854, and by four children.

DAB; *Portraiture*, pp. 47–48; *The Cabells and Their Kin*, pp. 373–76; *VMHB* 8 (1900–1901): xiii–xvi.

By Cornelius Hankins. Signed

Oil on panel: 15½ x 18 in. (39.4 x 45.7 cm.)

Presented in 1923 by the subject's son, William Wirt Henry, Jr., of Markham, Virginia. Por923.1

Henry Heth, 1825–1899

Reputedly the only officer in the Army of Northern Virginia whom General Lee addressed by his given name, Henry Heth was born on December 16, 1825, at Black Heath, Chesterfield County, the son of John and Margaret (Pickett) Heth. Following his graduation from West Point in 1847, he served in the Mexican War and at various posts in the West. Resigning from the United States Army on April 25, 1861, he offered his services to the Confederacy, serving first in western Virginia under General Floyd and later as a brigadier general commanding a military district in the vicinity of Lewisburg, (West) Virginia. Transferred in January 1863 to the Army of Northern Virginia, Heth was assigned a brigade in A. P. Hill's Division; at Chancellorsville when Hill was wounded he took command of the division. He was promoted to major general on Lee's personal recommendation on May 24, 1863. The conflict at Gettysburg was precipitated by Heth's outposts, who unexpectedly engaged a superior Union force; in the subsequent battle his division lost more than a third of its men. Although severely wounded at Gettysburg, Heth participated in all subsequent engagements of the army until Lee's surrender. After the war General Heth was employed in the insurance business in Richmond. He served the government from 1880 to 1884 as a civil engineer, later as an agent for the Office of Indian Affairs, and finally as a commissioner for marking the graves of the Confederate dead at Antietam battlefield. General Heth died in Washington on September 27, 1899, survived by his wife, Harriet (Selden) Heth, daughter of Miles Cary Selden and Harriet (Heth) Selden; the couple had three children.

DAB; *Generals in Gray*; *Biographic Catalogue*.

By John P. Walker. Signed. Dated 1910

Oil on canvas: 30 x 25 in. (76.2 x 63.5 cm.)

Presented to the R. E. Lee Camp, Confederate Veterans, in 1910 by the Harry Heth Camp, United Confederate Veterans, of Washington, D.C.; acquired by the Virginia Historical Society in 1946 through merger with the Confederate Memorial Association. Por946.126

Anne Elizabeth (Greaner) Higgins, 1820–1862 (Mrs. Robert J. Higgins)

The subject was born in 1820, the daughter of William Greaner (q.v.) of Richmond. She married Robert J. Higgins, who is listed in the 1850 Richmond directory as the manager of W. Greaner and Son, tobacco manufacturers; the census taken the same year indicates that the couple had at that time a daughter, Catherine, five years of age, and a son, William, two years old. Anne Elizabeth Higgins died on July 21, 1862; her funeral took place from St. John's Church, with burial in Hollywood Cemetery. Her husband died at the age of seventy-six at Springfield, New Kent County, and was buried at Hollywood Cemetery on June 21, 1893.

Daily Richmond Examiner, July 22, 1862; *Richmond Dispatch*, June 22, 1893, p. 3.

Artist unidentified

Oil on canvas: 30 x 25 in. (76.2 x 63.5 cm.)

Received in 1978 as a bequest of Frances (Nolting) Hoare-Smith (Mrs. Gerald W. Hoare-Smith) of Baltimore, a great-granddaughter of the subject. Por978.4

Ambrose Powell Hill, 1825–1865

Better known by his initials than by his given names, the subject was a native Virginian, born in Culpeper on November 9, 1825, son of Thomas and Fannie Russell (Baptist) Hill. He graduated from West Point in 1847 and, after serving in Mexico and against the Seminoles, resigned from the United States Army to join the Army of the Confederate States. Following a year's service as colonel of the 13th Virginia Infantry, he was promoted to brigadier general and major general, distinguishing himself at Williamsburg, the Peninsular campaign, the Seven Days, Cedar Mountain, and Chancellorsville. In the reorganization of the Confederate army that followed the death of Stonewall Jackson, Hill, promoted to lieutenant general on May 23, 1863, was put in command of the 3d Corps. In this capacity he fought at Gettysburg, the Wilderness campaign, and the defense of Petersburg. He was killed at Petersburg on April 2, 1865, and is buried in Richmond under a monument erected to his memory. General Hill married in May 1859 Kitty Grosh Morgan, daughter of Calvin Cogswell Morgan and Henrietta (Hunt) Morgan and sister of John Hunt Morgan (q.v.); they had four children.

DAB; *Generals in Gray*; *Biographic Catalogue*.

Ambrose Powell Hill (Portrait I)

Portrait I

BY WILLIAM LUDWELL SHEPPARD. Signed.
Dated 1898

Oil on canvas: 56 x 38 in. (142.2 x 96.5 cm.)

Presented to the R. E. Lee Camp, Confederate Veterans, in 1898; acquired by the Virginia Historical Society in 1946 through merger with the Confederate Memorial Association. Por946.39

Portrait II

See The Battle Abbey Murals. The Summer Mural

Daniel Harvey Hill, 1821–1889

A native of York District, South Carolina, the son of Solomon and Nancy (Cabeen) Hill, General Hill was born on July 12, 1821. Graduating from West Point in the class of 1842, he served with distinction in the Mexican War, then resigned from the army in 1849 to become professor of mathematics at Washington College (now Washington and Lee University); later he taught for five years at Davidson College and in 1859 was appointed superintendent of the North Carolina Military Institute at Charlotte. At the beginning of the Civil War he became

colonel of the 1st North Carolina Infantry. Promoted to brigadier general in the summer of 1861 and to major general the following spring, he distinguished himself at Big Bethel, the Seven Days, Second Manassas, and Sharpsburg. After service in North Carolina he was assigned to the defense of Richmond. On July 11, 1863, he was promoted to lieutenant general and transferred to General Bragg's Army of Tennessee; he commanded a corps at Chickamauga and the Chattanooga campaign. His criticism of Bragg, however, led to his removal from command and his failure to receive congressional confirmation of his rank. Except for brief service at Petersburg and Bentonville, General Hill saw little further active duty. Settling in Charlotte, North Carolina, at the war's end, he established in 1866 a monthly magazine, *The Land We Love*, and three years later a weekly, *The Southern Home*. Resuming his academic career, he was president of the University of Arkansas 1877–84 and of the Middle Georgia Military and Agricultural College 1886–89. His death occurred in Charlotte on September 24, 1889. General Hill married on November 2, 1852, Isabella Morrison, daughter of Robert Hall Morrison and Mary (Graham) Morrison; he was a brother-in-law to Generals Stonewall Jackson and Rufus Barringer.

DAB; *Generals in Gray*; *Biographic Catalogue*.

COPIED BY HARRY M. WEGNER. Signed. Dated 1923

Oil on canvas: 30 x 25 in. (76.2 x 63.5 cm.). Inscribed on the upper left corner of the painting: "Copy by H. M. Wegner. Pinxt. 1923."

Presented to the R. E. Lee Camp, Confederate Veterans, in 1923; acquired by the Virginia Historical Society in 1946 through merger with the Confederate Memorial Association. Por946.198

James Christian Hill, 1831–1896

Born in Charles City County on May 29, 1831, son of John T. Hill and Tabitha (Christian) Hill, the subject removed with his parents at an early age to New Kent County where he received his education; he then spent eight years in Richmond as a clerk, leaving in 1860 to make his home and conduct his business in Albemarle County. At the commencement of the Civil War, Hill enlisted as a private in Company E, 45th Virginia Infantry, rising in due course to major of the same command. His military record includes participation in the Seven Days battles, the operations around Charleston, South Carolina, and the engagements around Richmond and Petersburg in 1864. The loss of an arm at Petersburg on June 17, 1864, disqualified him from further active duty. After the war Major Hill returned to Albemarle County and engaged in the transportation business. In 1869 he was elected to the Virginia state legislature, serving as a delegate from Albemarle until 1873. In 1877 he became sergeant at arms of the House of Delegates, an office he held for ten years. Major Hill was elected railroad commissioner of Virginia in 1877 and was five times reelected. He died on September 21, 1896. Twice married, his first wife was Harriet N. (Ragland) Hill, who died in 1863; on May 3, 1866, he took as his second wife Mary E. Lamb of Charles City County; he had issue by both wives.

Virginia and Virginians, 2: 789–90; *Confederate Military History*, 3: 932–33; *Biographic Catalogue*.

BY ELLIS MEYER SILVETTE. Signed. 1936

Oil on canvas: 30 x 25 in. (76.2 x 63.5 cm.). Inscribed on the back: "Maj. James C. Hill. Painted by Ellis M. Silvette, 1936."

Acquired in 1946 through merger with the Confederate Memorial Association. Por946.105

Thomas Carmichael Hindman, 1828–1868

A native of Knoxville, Tennessee, General Hindman was born on January 28, 1828, son of Thomas Carmichael Hindman and Sallie (Holt) Hindman. He removed with his parents first to Alabama, then to Mississippi; he received his education in New Jersey. After participating with distinction in the Mexican War, he studied law, was admitted to the bar in 1851, and entered the political arena. In 1854 he was elected to the Mississippi legislature; two years later he moved to Helena, Arkansas, where on November 11, 1856, he married Mary Watkins Biscoe, daughter of Henry L. Biscoe. Elected as a Democrat to the Thirty-sixth United States Congress in 1858, he served one term but refused, although reelected, to take his seat in the succeeding Congress. On the secession of Arkansas, Hindman entered the Confederate army as colonel of the 2d Arkansas Infantry; promoted to brigadier general on September 28, 1861, and to major general the following April, he commanded the Trans-Mississippi Department, then took to the field, leading his command in the battles of Prairie Grove, Shiloh, Chickamauga, Chattanooga, and Atlanta. A severe wound in the eye disabled him from further military service. After the war he resided briefly in Mexico but in 1867 returned to Arkansas where he again turned to law and politics. On September 28, 1868, he was killed by an unknown assailant who fired through the window of his home in Helena.

DAB; *Generals in Gray*; *Biographical Directory*; *Biographic Catalogue* (Addenda).

BY CORNELIUS HANKINS. Signed

Oil on canvas: 30 x 25 in. (76.2 x 63.5 cm.)

Presented to the Confederate Memorial Association in 1930 by the subject's son, Biscoe Hindman, of Chicago; acquired by the Virginia Historical Society in 1946 through merger with the Confederate Memorial Association. Por946.167

Moses Drury Hoge, 1818–1899

A Presbyterian leader of international repute, Moses Drury Hoge was born at Hampden-Sydney on September 17, 1818, son of the Reverend Samuel Davies Hoge and Elizabeth Rice (Lacy) Hoge. A graduate of Hampden-Sydney College in 1839 and of Virginia's Union Theological Seminary, he became in 1843 assistant to William S. Plumer, pastor of the First Presbyterian Church in Richmond. Two years later he was installed as first pastor of the Second Presbyterian Church, Richmond, which became in time the church with the largest membership in the synod of Virginia. Despite many calls to other congregations, Hoge remained at the Second Church the rest of his life, serving his charge for more than fifty years. During the Civil War he volunteered his services as chaplain at the Camp of Instruction in Richmond, was appointed honorary chaplain to the Confederate Congress, and in 1862 ran the blockade from Charleston, South Carolina, to England to procure Bibles and religious books for the troops. After the war he sought to improve education in the South; to this end he founded the *Richmond Eclectic*, edited church newspapers, worked with the black community, and founded missions. As a speaker he was in great demand; he took part in innumerable councils and conferences and crossed the Atlantic sixteen times on church business. Both Hampden-Sydney and Washington and Lee conferred honorary doctorates on him, and in 1895 he was honored at a public reception marking the fiftieth anniversary of his pastorate at the Second Church. Hoge died on January 6, 1899. By his wife, Susan Morton (Wood) Hoge, whom he married in 1844, and who predeceased him, he had five children, two of whom left descendants.

DAB; *Richmond Portraits*, pp. 92–93; *SHS Papers* 26 (1898): 255–91.

Portrait I

BY JOHN BLENNERHASSETT MARTIN

Oil on canvas: 30 x 24³/₄ in. (76.2 x 62.9 cm.)

In the Society's possession in 1882. Source unknown. Por882.15

John Blennerhassett Martin, the artist, was one of those who accompanied Hoge when he left Richmond's First Presbyterian Church in 1845 to establish the Second Presbyterian Church. He was elected to the new church's first session, became its first Sunday school superintendent, and was a close friend of Hoge, who considered him one of the most thorough Bible scholars he had ever met, outside those trained in theological schools. "It was his custom while working at his art—he was a portrait-painter and wood-engraver—to keep a Bible open beside him, and to take up a verse at a time for meditation, turning it over in his mind, looking at what came before and after, assimilating it to his previous knowledge, and never leaving it until he had arrived at some interpretation that satisfied him." Other recorded portraits of Hoge include a second portrait by Martin, a full-length likeness by William Garl Brown—he is said to have painted Hoge several times—owned by the Second Presbyterian Church, and a portrait by James W. Ford. In connection with the latter, the sculptor Edward Virginius Valentine noted that when Ford was painting Hoge he "let his palate come down into his lap and said, 'You've the most diabolical expression I ever saw.' Dr. Hoge replied, 'I am not surprised. My ancestor was a pirate.'"

Peyton Harrison Hoge, *Moses Drury Hoge: Life and Letters* (Richmond, 1899), p. 85; *Richmond Portraits*, pp. 92–93 (another portrait by Martin reproduced); Wyndham Bolling Blanton, *The Making of a Downtown Church: The History of the Second Presbyterian Church, Richmond, Virginia, 1845–1945* (Richmond, 1945), pp. 91, 152.

Moses Drury Hoge (Portrait I)

Portrait II

BY WILLIAM EDWARD TRAHERN. Signed. Dated 1900

Oil on canvas: 60 x 40 in. (152.4 x 101.6 cm.)

Presented to the R. E. Lee Camp, Confederate Veterans, in 1900; acquired by the Virginia Historical Society in 1946 through merger with the Confederate Memorial Association. Por946.208

The portrait was offered to the R. E. Lee Camp Portrait Gallery by the Sons of Confederate Veterans. Before accepting it, the portrait committee requested the subject's children to approve it; this they declined to do. The artist made various changes and the would-be donors secured an affidavit signed by three of the subject's former associates affirming that the portrait was indeed a good likeness. The portrait was accepted by the R. E. Lee Camp Portrait Committee on April 9, 1900, but was not formally presented until the following December.

VHS Mss, R. E. Lee Camp Portrait Committee, Minute book, pp. 71, 76, 83, 85.

Waller Holladay, 1776–1860
See The Convention of 1829–30

Rebecca Holmes, 1779–1835
See Daniel Conrad, 1771–1806

John Bell Hood, 1831–1879

The fifth child of Dr. John W. Hood and Theodocia (French) Hood, the subject was born at Owingsville, Bath County, Kentucky, June 1, 1831. He graduated from West Point in the class of 1853, served with the army in California and Texas, and resigned his commission April 17, 1861, to join the Army of the Confederacy. Rising in rank to full general (temporary) during the course of the war, Hood fought through the Peninsular campaign, the Maryland campaign, Gettysburg, where he was wounded, and Chickamauga, where his leg was so badly damaged as to necessitate its amputation. Although crippled, he was assigned a corps in Georgia under General Joseph Eggleston Johnston; later, when Johnston was removed from command, Hood took command with the temporary rank of full general. Repulsed by Sherman, he withdrew into Tennessee, where again he suffered defeats at Franklin and Nashville; in January 1865 he was relieved of command at his own request. Assigned to the Trans-Mississippi Department, he was on his way to his new command when he received word of

119

John Bell Hood (Portrait I)

the capitulation of the last Confederate army; he surrendered at Natchez, Mississippi, on May 31, 1865. After the war General Hood became a commission merchant in New Orleans, but owing to business reverses he spent his last years in poverty. His wife, Anna Marie (Hennen) Hood, whom he married in 1868, died of yellow fever on August 24, 1879; on August 30, 1879, General Hood and his eldest daughter died of the same disease. Ten orphans survived, including three-week-old twins. General Hood is buried in Metairie Cemetery, New Orleans.

DAB; *Generals in Gray*.

Portrait I

ARTIST UNIDENTIFIED

Oil on cardboard: 22 x 18 in. (55.9 x 45.7 cm.)

Acquired in 1946 through merger with the Confederate Memorial Association. Por946.40

Portrait II

See The Battle Abbey Murals. The Summer Mural

Bernard Hooe, 1791–1869

Born on January 20, 1791, the subject was the son of Bernard and Mary Symes (Chichester) Hooe of Prince William County. He married on March 5, 1811, Eleanor Buchanan Briscoe, daughter of John Hanson Briscoe and Mary Elizabeth Attaway

(Bond) Briscoe of Maryland, who bore him eight children. He was a justice of the peace for Prince William County in 1816 and represented the county in the Virginia House of Delegates 1819–22. He afterwards removed to Alexandria and was mayor of the city 1833–35, 1837–39. He died on February 4, 1869.

Virginia Genealogies, p. 718; Virginia State Library, Samuel Bassett French Papers; VHS Mss6:4 H7612:1; George Adolphus Hanson, *Old Kent: The Eastern Shore of Maryland* (Baltimore, 1876), p. 121; *VMHB* 84 (1976): 239.

ARTIST UNIDENTIFIED

Oil on canvas on panel: 34 1/2 x 27 1/2 in. (87.6 x 69.9 cm.)

Presented in 1975 by Ellice Throckmorton DeForest Enyart (Mrs. Byron K. Enyart) of Arlington. Por975.12

Harriet Hopkins, born ca. 1855

The subject was the daughter of William Evelyn Hopkins (1821–1894) and Louise (Kimball) Hopkins and niece of John Page Hopkins (q.v.). The portrait was painted in Rome, Italy, in 1867 by Emilie Rouillon from a photograph supplied by the subject's father who was then commanding the U.S.S. *Shamrock* in the European Squadron.

Information received with the portrait; VHS Mss6:2 B9588:2.

BY EMILIE ROUILLON. 1867

Oil on canvas on panel: 21 1/2 x 17 in. (54.6 x 43.2 cm.)

Received in 1973 as a bequest of Louise (Anderson) Patten (Mrs. Clarence Wesley Patten) of Winchester. Por973.14

Mounted on the back of the portrait are two pieces of canvas which were probably preserved when the portrait was cut down and relined. One, cut from the face of the canvas, bears the artist's signature and date: "Emilie Rouillon Rome 1867." The second is apparently from the back of the original canvas: "Peint par Madame Emilie Rouillon Rome. Via Banchi Ruovi No. 19. 1867."

John Page Hopkins, ca. 1825–1857

Born about 1825, son of John and Abby Byrd Nelson (Page) Hopkins of Page Brook, Clarke County, and Winchester, the subject graduated in medicine from the Medical College at Philadelphia. He was commissioned assistant surgeon in the United States Navy on September 30, 1850, and was assigned to the sloop-of-war *Marion*, on which his brother William Evelyn Hopkins also served. He resigned from the navy in 1857; the same year he was appointed United States consul in Tabasco, Mexico, where he died a short time after. His remains were returned to Virginia and interred at the Old Chapel, Clarke County. Dr. Hopkins was unmarried.

Walter Lee Hopkins, *Hopkins of Virginia and Related Families* (Richmond, 1931), p. 216; *The Page Family*, p. 143; information received with the portrait; VHS Mss6:2 B9588:2; *Occasional Bulletin*, no. 28 (1974): 5.

ARTIST UNIDENTIFIED

Oil on canvas on panel: 31 1/2 x 26 in. (80 x 66 cm.)

Received in 1973 as a bequest of Louise (Anderson) Patten (Mrs. Clarence Wesley Patten) of Winchester, Por973.18

Painted in Hopkins's youth by an unidentified artist, the portrait was given by the subject's niece, Maria Byrd (Hopkins) Wright, to Maria (Carter) Anderson, and from her passed to Louise (Anderson) Patten.

John Page Hopkins

Francis Howard, fifth Baron Howard of Effingham, 1643–1695

Philadelphia (Pelham) Howard, 1654–1685 (Lady Howard of Effingham)

Francis, Lord Howard of Effingham, governor of Virginia, was born in 1643, son of Sir Charles Howard of Eastwick, Surrey, England, and Frances (Courthope) Howard, daughter of Sir George Courthope. He succeeded his father in 1673, and on July 8 of the same year he married Philadelphia Pelham, daughter of Sir Thomas Pelham. In 1681 his cousin the earl of Nottingham died without direct heirs; the earldom became extinct, but the barony of Howard of Effingham, also held by the cousin, passed to Sir Francis. Since little or no estate came with the title, he was prepared to accept in 1683 the governorship of Virginia, succeeding the grasping Lord Culpeper (q.v.) in the office. Instructed to restore order to the colony, recently torn by unrest and rebellion, and to place it on a profitable footing, Howard of Effingham arrived at Jamestown in February 1684 and for the next five years engaged in a struggle with the General Assembly. His wife, to whom by all accounts he was devoted, arrived in Virginia a few months after the governor, but her health, never robust, deteriorated, and she died on August 13, 1685. Howard of Effingham remained in Virginia until February 1689, whereupon he embarked for England to rebut charges made against him by Philip Ludwell and to

justify the course of his administration. Although he never returned to Virginia, he retained the governorship until 1692. He took part in the coronation of William and Mary on April 11, 1689, and married as his second wife on January 20, 1690, Susan (Felton) Harbord, a daughter of Sir Henry Felton and widow of Philip Harbord. He died on March 30, 1695, and was succeeded by his second, but eldest surviving, son.

Sir Bernard Burke, *Burke's Genealogical and Heraldic History of the Peerage, Baronetage, and Knightage* (London, 1938), p. 911; *Library of Congress Quarterly Journal* 10 (1952–53): 63–71; *Virginia Historical Portraiture*, pp. 113–15 (Portraits II and III reproduced); *Occasional Bulletin*, no. 2 (1961): 10–11 (Portrait III reproduced); *VMHB* 75 (1967): 387 (Portrait I reproduced); *Antiques* 116 (1979): 1129 (Portrait III reproduced).

Portrait I. Francis, Lord Howard of Effingham

ATTRIBUTED TO THE SCHOOL OF SIR GODFREY KNELLER

Oil on canvas: 91 x 55 in. (231.1 x 139.7 cm.)

Acquired in 1960 from Mowbray Henry Gordon Howard, sixth earl of Effingham, with funds contributed by Samuel Merrifield Bemiss of Richmond. Por960.15

Portrait II. Francis, Lord Howard of Effingham

ATTRIBUTED TO THE SCHOOL OF SIR GODFREY KNELLER

Oil on canvas: 28 1/2 x 23 1/2 in. (72.4 x 59.7 cm.) (oval)

Francis, Lord Howard of Effingham (Portrait I)

Acquired in 1960 from Mowbray Henry Gordon Howard, sixth earl of Effingham, with funds contributed by the Thomas F. Jeffress Memorial. Por960.16

Portrait III. Philadelphia, Lady Howard of Effingham *See* Plate 14

BY MARY BEALE

Oil on canvas: 30 x 25¼ in. (76.2 x 64.1 cm.)

Acquired in 1960 from Mowbray Henry Gordon Howard, sixth earl of Effingham, with funds contributed by Samuel Merrifield Bemiss of Richmond. Por960.17

Robert Mercer Taliaferro Hunter, 1809–1887

United States congressman and senator and Confederate secretary of state, the subject was born at Mount Pleasant, Essex County, on April 21, 1809, son of James and Maria (Garnett) Hunter. He grad-

Robert Mercer Taliaferro Hunter

uated from the University of Virginia in 1828, read law, and after being admitted to the bar in 1830 commenced practice at Lloyds. After three terms in the Virginia House of Delegates representing his native county, he was in the United States Congress 1837–43 and 1845–47, serving part of the time as Speaker. Elected to the United States Senate, he held his seat from 1847 until his resignation on March 28, 1861. As chairman of the Senate Committee on Finance he was instrumental in drawing up the tariff bill of 1857, and in 1860 he was a candidate for the presidential nomination. Hunter was twice offered and twice declined the secretaryship of state. During the Civil War he served the Confederate States as secretary of state from July 25, 1861, to February 18, 1862, and thereafter was a member of the Confederate Senate; he was one of the commissioners sent to the peace conference at Hampton Roads in February 1865. Following the war Hunter helped organize the local Conservative party and for six years was treasurer of the state of Virginia. We are told that "in personal appearance Mr. Hunter was short and thick-set, and when his face was in repose his underjaw dropped in a manner that was not at all prepossessing and suggested indolence. But when aroused and interested he was the embodiment of sturdy resistance and intellectual force." He died at his residence, Fonthill, Essex County, on July 18, 1887. His wife, whom he married on October 4, 1836, was Mary Evelina (Dandridge) Hunter, daughter of Adam Stephen Dandridge and Sarah (Pendleton) Dandridge of Jefferson County, (West) Virginia; the couple had nine

14. Philadelphia, Lady Howard of Effingham

children. Hunter was elected to membership in the Virginia Historical Society in 1836.

DAB; *Biographical Directory*; *Seldens of Virginia*, 2: 153–57; *VMHB* 58 (1950): 290 and 81 (1973): 387 (portrait reproduced); *Virginia Cavalcade* 25 (1975–76): 133 (portrait reproduced, detail).

BY GEORGE PETER ALEXANDER HEALY

Oil on canvas on panel: 27 x 23 in. (68.6 x 58.4 cm.)

Presented in 1949 by an anonymous donor. Por949.3

Eppa Hunton, 1822–1908

Born on September 22, 1822, son of Eppa and Elizabeth Marye (Brent) Hunton of Fauquier County, the subject studied at New Baltimore Academy, taught school for three years, studied law, and was admitted to the bar in 1843. Settling in Prince William County, he became in 1849 Commonwealth's attorney and successively colonel and brigadier general of the Virginia militia. As a member of the Convention of 1861 he advocated prompt secession; as colonel of the 8th Virginia Infantry he was at Manassas three days before the battle and contributed significantly to its outcome. In command of his regiment he participated in most of the campaigns of the Army of Northern Virginia, being wounded at Gettysburg, promoted to brigadier general on August 9, 1863, and finally taken prisoner at Sayler's Creek. After his release from Fort Warren he returned to his native county and to the practice of law in Warrenton. He was elected to the United States House of Representatives three times, serving 1873–81, and was a member of the Electoral Commission created by Congress to decide the contests in various states in the presidential election of 1876. Not a candidate for renomination, General Hunton practiced law in Washington until his return to public life as a United States senator 1892–95. He died in Richmond on October 11, 1908, and is buried in Hollywood Cemetery. By his wife, Lucy Caroline (Weir) Hunton, of Prince William County, whom he married in 1848, he had one son.

DAB; *Generals in Gray*; *Men of Mark in Virginia*, 1: 300–304; *Biographic Catalogue*; *Biographical Directory*.

COPIED BY JOHN P. WALKER. Signed. Dated 1902

Oil on canvas: 30 x 25 in. (76.2 x 63.5 cm.). Inscribed in the upper left corner of the painting: "Painted by J. P. Walker, 1902 from portrait by Uhl."

Presented to the R. E. Lee Camp, Confederate Veterans, in 1902; acquired by the Virginia Historical Society in 1946 through merger with the Confederate Memorial Association. Por946.48

Eppa Hunton, 1904–1976

Born in Richmond on July 31, 1904, son of Eppa Hunton, Jr., and Virginia Semmes (Payne) Hunton and grandson of Eppa Hunton (1822–1908) (q.v.), the subject attended the Chamberlayne School and the Episcopal High School before going to the University of Virginia, where he received a Bachelor of Arts degree in 1925 and a degree in law in 1927. He thereupon became associated with Hunton, Williams, Anderson and Gay, the Richmond law firm established by his father; he became a partner on June 1, 1934, and continued with the firm for the rest of his life. From 1932 until his death he was a director of the First and Merchants National Bank. He was on the board of the Medical College of Virginia 1932–51, 1960–63 and was president of the Medical College of Virginia Foundation. During World War II he was adjutant of the 45th General Hospital which was staffed by Medical College of Virginia personnel; his active duty took him to North Africa and Italy, and he was awarded the Bronze Star for distinguished service. Hunton was a member of the commission that studied the merger of the Medical College of Virginia and Richmond Professional Institute; he became a member of the board of visitors of the Virginia Commonwealth University, created by the merger, and rector of the new university in 1969. A lifelong Episcopalian, he was a vestryman and sometime senior warden of St. Paul's Church, Richmond. In 1946 Hunton was elected to the executive committee of the Virginia Historical Society;

Eppa Hunton, 1904–1976 (Portrait II)

he was the Society's president 1966–69. His wife, whom he married on September 28, 1936, was Caroline Homassel (Marye) Hunton. On Hunton's death on November 23, 1976, he was survived by a son and two daughters.

Who's Who in America, 40th ed. (Chicago, 1978); *Richmond News Leader*, Nov. 24, 1976; Thomas Benjamin Gay, *The Hunton Williams Firm and Its Predecessors* (Richmond, 1971), 1: 380; *VMHB* 86 (1978): 240–41.

Portrait I

BY HUGO STEVENS. Signed

Pastel on paper: 22¼ x 18¼ in. (56.5 x 46.4 cm.)

Received in 1977 from the estate of the subject. Por977.10

Portrait II

BY HUGO STEVENS. Signed

Oil on canvas: 30 x 25 in. (76.2 x 63.5 cm.)

Presented in 1978 by the subject's children, Caroline (Hunton) High (Mrs. John H. High) of Rocky Mount, North Carolina, and Virginia (Hunton) Totten (Mrs. Randolph Totten) and Eppa Hunton, both of Richmond. Por978.6

Isabella, Queen of Castile, 1451–1504

Queen of Castile and patroness of Christopher Columbus, Isabella was born at Madrigal on April 22, 1451, the daughter of John II of Castile and Isabella, his second wife. In 1468 she was named lawful heir to her brother, Henry IV of Castile, and the following year she married Ferdinand of Aragon. On the death of her brother in 1474 she was proclaimed queen of Castile and León. Intelligent, resolute, and pious, Isabella reformed her court, encouraged learning, and attempted to consolidate royal power. An intense religious conviction led Isabella *la Católica*, as she was known, to reestablish the Inquisition in Castile, to press for the expulsion of the Spanish Jews, and to confront the Muslims in Granada. In 1491 she conferred her patronage on Christopher Columbus and financed his westward voyage of discovery. Her last years were darkened by the death of three children and the insanity of her daughter Juana. She died at Medina del Campo on November 26, 1504.

Encyclopedia Americana; *Encyclopaedia Britannica*.

ARTIST UNIDENTIFIED

Oil on canvas: 25 x 16 in. (63.5 x 40.6 cm.). Inscribed: "Ysabel la Catolica."

Received in 1948 as a bequest of Mr. and Mrs. Alexander Wilbourne Weddell of Richmond. Por948.79

124

Mary Isham, d. 1735

See William Randolph, ca. 1651–1711

Thomas Jonathan Jackson, 1824–1863

Best known as "Stonewall" Jackson, the subject was born on January 21, 1824, in Clarksburg, (West) Virginia, son of Jonathan and Julia Beckwith (Neale) Jackson. A member of the West Point class of 1846, he fought in the Mexican War but resigned in 1852 to become a member of the faculty of the Virginia Military Institute. On the outbreak of the Civil War he was commissioned colonel of Virginia militia and dispatched to Harpers Ferry; shortly thereafter he was made brigadier general, distinguished himself at First Manassas, and was promoted to major general. In the Shenandoah Valley campaign of 1862 Jackson displayed consummate skill in military strategy; he did likewise at the Seven Days, Second Manassas, Harpers Ferry, and Sharpsburg. With the reorganization of the Army of Northern Virginia, Jackson, promoted to lieutenant general, was made commander of the 2d Corps. In December 1862 he commanded the right wing in the victory at Fredericksburg. The following May at Chancellorsville he was severely wounded, and he died at Guiney's Station, south of Fredericksburg, on May 10, 1863. His body was carried to Richmond where it lay in state before being taken to Lexington for burial. Jackson was twice married; his first wife, Eleanor (Junkin) Jackson, died in 1854 fourteen months after their marriage; his second wife, whom he married on July 16, 1857, was Mary Anna (Morrison) Jackson, daughter of Robert Hall Morrison and Mary (Graham) Morrison, by whom he had one daughter.

DAB; *Generals in Gray*; *Virginia Cavalcade* 12, no. 2 (1962): 4–12; *Biographic Catalogue*.

Portrait I   *See* Plate 15

BY WILLIAM GARL BROWN

Oil on canvas: 36 x 30 in. (91.4 x 76.2 cm.)

Acquired in 1946 through merger with the Confederate Memorial Association. Por946.41

Information on the provenance of this portrait is found in a memorandum dated April 6, 1949, prepared by Clayton Torrence, then director of the Virginia Historical Society. "Relative to the portraits [*sic*] of General Thomas J. (Stonewall) Jackson, C.S.A., in entry hall to west wing of Battle Abbey, Richmond, Virginia. Dr. Douglas S. Freeman today informed me that this portrait was acquired, by purchase, from Jackson Christian (grandson of General Jackson), with funds contributed for that pur-

15. Thomas Jonathan Jackson (Portrait I)

pose; and that Jackson Christian said that his mother (Mrs. Julia Jackson Christian) told him that her mother (Mrs. Thomas J. Jackson) had said that this was her favorite picture of General Jackson; that the portrait was painted from a photograph of General Jackson, with suggestions to the artist by Mrs. Jackson. The artist's name is now unknown. Clayton Torrence." The question of attribution is clarified in a letter in the Society's manuscript collection (Mss2 P9264a1) from the subject's granddaughter, Julia Jackson (Christian) Preston (Mrs. Randolph Preston), dated January 8, 1951. "In answer to your note received today about the painter who painted my grandfather's (General Jackson) portrait, which now hangs in Battle Abbey, my grandmother always told me that it was painted by Mr. Garl Brown of New York. . . . The painting is copied from a small photograph taken in Lexington during the war. . . . My grandmother always thought that this was the finest likeness of my grandfather. At the same time that this portrait was painted Garl Brown did one of my mother who was about three, she was only six months old when her father was killed—this painting is exquisite and is done from a little picture circulated all over the South in the 'Land We Love.'"

Portrait II

BY JOHN P. WALKER. Signed. Dated 1900

Oil on canvas: 60 x 40 in. (152.4 x 101.6 cm.)

Presented to the R. E. Lee Camp, Confederate Veterans, in 1900 by the artist; acquired by the Virginia Historical Society in 1946 through merger with the Confederate Memorial Association. Por946.213

Portrait III

BY WILLIAM FREDERICK SIEVERS. Signed. Dated 1916

Plaster model: 22 in. (55.9 cm.) in height

Acquired in 1946 through merger with the Confederate Memorial Association. Por946.238

Sievers's heroic equestrian statue of Jackson that commands the intersection of Monument Avenue and the Boulevard in Richmond was commissioned in 1910 and unveiled on October 11, 1919. This plaster study for the work was presented by the sculptor to Mrs. G. T. W. Kern of Richmond, who in turn presented it to the Confederate Memorial Association on December 13, 1928.

Portrait IV

ARTIST UNKNOWN

Cameo: 3/4 x 1/2 in. (1.9 x 1.3 cm.)

Presented in 1957 by C. S. Sherwood, Jr., of Portsmouth. Por957.23

The donor, long engaged in the retail jewelry business, stated in a letter dated January 31, 1957, that the cameo of Jackson and the matching cameo of George Washington (q.v., Portrait VII) came into his possession in 1919, on the death of his father, among whose personal effects they were found.

Portrait V

BY WILLIAM G. WILLIAMSON

Pencil on paper: 3³/4 x 3 in. (9.5 x 7.6 cm.)

Acquired in 1946 through merger with the Confederate Memorial Association. VHS Mss2 J1385 b1

Portraits V, VI, and VII are field sketches hastily drawn by unskilled hands. Each is mounted on a larger sheet of paper, and each mounting sheet bears annotations by Jedediah Hotchkiss. The inscription below Portrait V identifies the figure as "'Stonewall' Jackson in an attitude that he often took when standing alone apparently lost in thought. It strikingly recalls one of his *awkward* appearances. Sketched by Lt. Wm. G. Williamson at the Moss Neck winter quarters of 1862–3. Jed. Hotchkiss."

Portrait VI

BY WILLIAM G. WILLIAMSON

Wash on cardboard: 4¹/2 x 3¹/4 in. (11.4 x 8.3 cm.)

Acquired in 1946 through merger with the Confederate Memorial Association. VHS Mss2 J1385 b2

This sketch, one of three (Portraits V, VI, and VII) made of Jackson in the field, bears the following note by Jedediah Hotchkiss: "The above is a sketch of 'Stonewall' Jackson seated on a pine log, in the rain, at the ford of the Shenandoah at Alma, Page County, Va., after the battle of Sharpsburg, awaiting the crossing of the army on its way across the Blue Ridge at Milam's Gap to Fredericksburg. It was made on the spot by Lt. Wm. G. Williamson. Jed. Hotchkiss."

Portrait VII

BY ALEXANDER ROBINSON BOTELER

Pencil on paper: 4¹/4 x 3¹/4 in. (10.8 x 8.3 cm.)

Acquired in 1946 through merger with the Confederate Memorial Association. VHS Mss2 J1385 b3

This sketch, together with the two preceding sketches (Portraits V and VI), provides an informal glimpse of the commander as recorded by an untrained observer. Jedediah Hotchkiss's caption states: "The above is a sketch of 'Stonewall' Jackson leaning against a plank seat fastened between two trees, at the church at Mechanicsville some 6 miles from Gordonsville [sic], considering a dispatch that he had just received. It was made in my note book at the time by Col. Alex. R. Boteler a volunteer aid on his staff . . . Jed. Hotchkiss." A closely similar sketch is inserted in a copy of John Esten Cooke's *The Life of Stonewall Jackson* (Richmond, 1863) in the Tracy W. McGregor Library, University of Virginia. The sketch bears the notation: "Gen. T. J. Jackson considering dispatches—at the Old Church near Mechanicsville, Louisa Co. Va—Tuesday July 29th 1862 Drawn by Hon. A. R. Boteler." The McGregor Library sketch illustrates (opposite p. 16) Richard H. Harwell's edition of Cooke's *Stonewall Jackson and the Old Stonewall Brigade* (Charlottesville, Va., 1954) and is described on page 66 of that work. Alexander Robinson Boteler (1815–1892), of Shepherdstown, (West) Virginia, was a brother of the artist Henry Boteler and a great-grandson of Charles Willson Peale. He did not, however, make painting his profession. A member of the United States Congress 1859–61, he later served on General Jackson's staff and represented Virginia in the Confederate Congress. After the war he was variously a member of the Tariff Commission and pardon clerk in the Department of Justice. The New-York Historical Society owns Boteler's sketch of George Edward Pickett.

Portrait VIII

See The Battle Abbey Murals. The Spring Mural

Portrait IX

See The Battle Abbey Murals. The Summer Mural

James I, King of England, Scotland, and Ireland, 1566–1625

The first member of the House of Stuart to reign in England, James was born in Edinburgh Castle on June 19, 1566, son of Mary, Queen of Scots, and Lord Darnley. Thirteen months after his birth he succeeded to the throne as James VI of Scotland. He married Princess Anne of Denmark on November 24, 1589. Through both his parents James was heir to the throne of England; on the death of Queen Elizabeth I on March 24, 1603, he was proclaimed King James I of England and was crowned at Westminster the following July. At the outset of his reign he attempted to establish peace abroad and religious tolerance at home; however, his absolutist convictions, his disregard for Parliament, and his misplaced reliance on favorites at court prevented to a large degree the realization of these laudable objectives. James I granted the first charter to the Virginia Company on April 10, 1606; the following November he issued his Articles, Instructions, and Orders for the Government of Virginia; the second and the third charters were granted by the king in 1609 and 1612 respectively. Contemptuous of Virginia's only exportable product, in *A Counterblast to Tobacco* (1616)

the king inveighed against the "filthy novelty" as a "custom loathsome to the eye, hateful to the nose, harmful to the brain, [and] dangerous to the lungs." Virginia came under the direct protection of the crown after the revocation of the company's charter in 1624. James I, sponsor of the first permanent English settlement in the New World and sovereign whom Jamestown and the James River honor through their names, died on March 27, 1625, and was succeeded by his son Charles I.

Encyclopedia Americana; Alexander Brown, *The Genesis of the United States* (Boston, 1890), 2: 1026–27; *Portraiture*, p. 49; *Virginia Historical Portraiture*, pp. 38–40.

Copied by Charles X. Harris

Oil on canvas: 42 x 36 in. (106.7 x 91.4 cm.)

Presented in 1944 by Mr. and Mrs. Alexander Wilbourne Weddell of Richmond. Por944.14

The portrait is a copy of an original by Frans Pourbus which hung at Virginia House during the exhibition of historical Virginia portraiture in 1929, and which was owned at that time by Lucius Wilmerding of New York City.

Edward Wilson James, 1848–1906

Edward Wilson James was born in Norfolk in 1848, son of John and Mary Moseley (Hunter) James. He attended Roanoke College from 1866 to 1869. A lifelong resident of Norfolk, and one with ample means, he devoted himself to the study of local history; he was a frequent contributor to the *Virginia Magazine of History and Biography* and the *William and Mary College Quarterly*. *The Lower Norfolk County Virginia Antiquary*, of which he was founder, editor, and proprietor, began publication in 1895 and continued to appear until his death in 1906; it remains a valuable source for the study of Norfolk and the adjacent areas. James was a director of the Norfolk Public Library and held membership in the American Historical Association, the American Geographic Society, and the Phi Beta Kappa society. He became a member of the Virginia Historical Society in 1891 and was elected to its executive committee in 1896. On his death, which occurred in Norfolk on October 11, 1906, he left a welcome legacy to the Society. James, who never married, is buried in Cedar Grove Cemetery, Norfolk.

Portraiture, pp. 50–52; *Encyclopedia of Virginia Biography*, 3: 375; *VMHB* 15 (1907–8): 229–32; *W. & M. Quart.*, 1st ser., 15 (1906–7): 214.

By Harry M. Wegner. Signed. Dated 1909

Oil on canvas: 30 x 25 in. (76.2 x 63.5 cm.)

Purchased from the artist in 1909. Por909.4

Thomas Jefferson, 1743–1826

Third president of the United States, author of the Declaration of Independence, and founder of the University of Virginia, Thomas Jefferson was born at Shadwell, Albemarle County, on April 13, 1743, son of Peter and Jane (Randolph) Jefferson. After graduating from the College of William and Mary in 1762, he studied law under George Wythe (q.v.) and was admitted to the bar in 1767. Two years later he was elected to the House of Burgesses, retaining his seat until 1774 and becoming a vocal spokesman for the Revolutionary movement. Elected to the Continental Congress in 1775, he was the principal author of the Declaration of Independence, submitted it to Congress, and was one of its signers. Jefferson succeeded Patrick Henry (q.v.) as governor of Virginia on June 2, 1779, serving until June 3, 1781; he wrote the Statute for Religious Freedom, which was presented during his administration and was later passed by the General Assembly. After sitting again in the Continental Congress he was appointed minister to France in 1784; during his sojourn abroad he first published his *Notes on the State of Virginia*. On the establishment of the new American government, Washington appointed him secretary of state; he remained in the cabinet from 1789 to 1793. Following three years of retirement at Monticello, his estate in Albemarle County, he returned to public life, serving as vice-president of the United States 1797–1801. Twice elected to the presidency, Jefferson's term of office extended from March 4, 1801, to March 3,

1809. He then retired to Monticello, where he devoted himself to his scientific, architectural, bibliographical, and educational interests and, during his last years, sought to avert financial ruin. He established the University of Virginia, designed its buildings, and in 1819 secured its charter. Jefferson died at Monticello on the fiftieth anniversary of the signing of the Declaration of Independence, July 4, 1826. His wife, Martha (Wayles) Skelton Jefferson, whom he married on January 1, 1772, was a daughter of John and Martha (Eppes) Wayles and widow of Bathurst Skelton. In the ten years of their marriage she bore six children, only two of whom reached maturity.

DAB; *Biographical Directory*; *Portraiture*, pp. 52–53.

Portrait I

COPIED BY LOUIS MATHIEU DIDIER GUILLAUME

Oil on canvas: 26³/4 x 22 in. (68 x 55.9 cm.)

Presented in 1858 by Thomas Jefferson Randolph and George W. Randolph of Richmond. Por858.3

The portrait, a copy of an original by Gilbert Stuart painted in 1805, was accompanied by the following letter, dated Richmond, February 17, 1858, addressed to Conway Robinson, chairman of the executive committee: "Dear Sir. We beg leave to present through you to the Historical Society of Va. a copy by L. M. D. Guillaume of an original portrait of Thomas Jefferson by Gilbert Stuart. The original portrait now in the possession of Mr. Jefferson's family is considered by them as the best likeness extant, and the painting presented to your Society is an admirable copy. With our best wishes for the success of the Society in its praiseworthy efforts to form a gallery of the portraits of eminent Virginians, we remain, very respectfully, your obt. servants Thomas J. Randolph [and] Geo. W. Randolph."

VHS Archives, liber A3, p. 65, and folio C4a–1858 (Randolph).

Portrait II. Plaque bearing likenesses of Washington, Henry, and Jefferson

See George Washington, 1732–1799 (Portrait VII)

Portrait III

BY THEODORE KALIDE

Bronze statuette: 15 in. (38.1 cm.) in height, exclusive of base

Acquired by purchase in 1976. Por976.1

Portrait IV

BY B. E. L. PRICE

Thomas Jefferson (Portrait I)

Silhouette: 6¹/₄ in. (15.9 cm.) in height, mounted on paper 9 x 4¹/₂ in. (22.9 x 11.4 cm.). Inscribed on the back: "Thomas Jefferson, by B.E.L.P."

Provenance unknown. PorX319

This full-length silhouette is inexpertly executed and probably dates from the present century.

Thomas Jefferson (Portrait V)

Portrait V

ATTRIBUTED TO JOHN TRUMBULL

Watercolor on paper: 2³/₄ x 2¹/₂ in. (7 x 6.4 cm.). Bears inscription on the back: "Portrait of Mr. Jefferson."

Presented in 1978 by Dr. Frederick D. Gillespie of Parkersburg, West Virginia. Por978.22

This miniature watercolor portrait is similar in pose to the miniatures in oil given by Trumbull in 1788 to Maria Cosway, Angelica (Schuyler) Church, and to Jefferson's daughter Martha. All are derived from Trumbull's life portrait of Jefferson in the original version of the *Declaration of Independence*.

National Gallery of Art, *The Eye of Thomas Jefferson* (Washington, D.C., 1976), pp. 103, 196; *W. & M. Quart.*, 3d ser., 9 (1952): 152–55.

Charles Edmund Jenings

The subject was the only surviving son of Edmund Jenings (1731–1819) (q.v.) and Elizabeth Jenings of Kensington, London, England. He was an attorney and conveyancer and after the death of his father in 1819 became the head of the family. His life dates have not been determined, nor the name of his wife. He was alive, however, as late as 1837, and had at least one child.

VHS Mss1 J4105a 17–18.

ARTIST UNIDENTIFIED

Miniature on ivory: 3¹/₂ x 2¹/₂ in. (8.9 x 6.4 cm.) (oval)

Received in 1949 as a bequest of Alexander Wilbourne Weddell of Richmond, who received it as a legacy from Mrs. Eleanor Louise Jenings of London, England. Por949.14

Edmund Jenings, 1731–1819

Born in Annapolis, Maryland, in August 1731, son of Edmund Jenings (1703–1756) and Ariana (van der Heyden) Frisby Bordley Randolph Jenings, the subject was sent to England at an early age for his education, attending Eton and Trinity Hall, Cambridge. He studied law and was admitted to the bar, but being possessed of independent means, he was not obliged to practice his profession. Jenings befriended the young American artist Charles Willson Peale during Peale's sojourn in London, 1767–69. On the outbreak of the Revolution he espoused the cause of the colonists and is said to have resided for a time in Brussels as a secret agent for the Americans, during which time he corresponded with Franklin, the Lees, and John Adams. After his return to London he resided in the vicinity of Kensington Square and "was accustomed until lately to repair to the Westminster library daily." He died on July 27, 1819, in his eighty-eighth year, having "preserved a certain agility about him that enabled him to take more exercise than a person of 50. Mr. Jenings was a man of sound understanding and when he chose to exert himself of very agreeable manners." He was survived by his widow, Elizabeth Jenings, and a son, Charles Edmund Jenings (q.v.), his two elder sons, Jonathan and William, having predeceased him.

Encyclopedia of Virginia Biography, 1: 264; Beatrice Mackey Doughtie, *Documented Notes on Jennings and Allied Families* (Decatur, Ga., 1961), pp. 18–20; VHS Mss1 J4105a 17–21; *VMHB* 58 (1950): 290.

Portrait I

ARTIST UNIDENTIFIED

Oil on canvas: 30 x 25 in. (76.2 x 63.5 cm.)

Presented in 1949 by the heirs of Walter Jennings of Farmington, Connecticut. Por949.9

Portrait II

ARTIST UNIDENTIFIED

Miniature on ivory: 1¹/₂ x 1 in. (3.8 x 2.5 cm.) (oval)

Received in 1949 as a bequest of Alexander Wilbourne Weddell of Richmond, who received it as a legacy from Mrs. Eleanor Louise Jenings of London, England. Por949.13

Edmund Jenings (Portrait I)

"Sarah Jenings"

The subject of this English miniature was identified by the donor as Sarah Jenings, possibly Sarah (Jennings) Churchill, first duchess of Marlborough (1660–1744). The Marlborough possibility, long thought to be wishful thinking, has recently been rejected on excellent authority. The lady, therefore, remains unidentified save for her name.

VMHB 58 (1950): 290.

ARTIST UNIDENTIFIED

Miniature on ivory: 2 x 1³/₄ in. (5.1 x 4.5 cm.) (oval)

Received in 1949 as a bequest of Alexander Wilbourne Weddell of Richmond, who received it as a legacy from Mrs. Eleanor Louise Jenings of London. Por949.15

John Melville Jennings, 1916–

John Melville Jennings, for twenty-five years director of the Virginia Historical Society, was born in James City County on October 22, 1916, the son of John Melville Jennings and Grace Armistead (Davis) Jennings. After completing his undergraduate study at the College of William and Mary in 1938 he became curator of rare books and manuscripts at the college library, remaining there until the outbreak of World War II when he accepted a commission in the United States Navy. At the end of the war he returned to his former position where he continued until 1947. The following year, having earned his Master of Arts degree at American University in Washington, he became the librarian of the Virginia Historical Society. Military commitments again interrupted his work in 1951. After completing his service in the Korean conflict he returned to Richmond in 1953 as the Society's newly designated director. From that time until his retirement in December 1978, he guided the Society into the most productive period of its history. Under his direction its financial position improved substantially, Battle Abbey was enlarged and refurbished to become the Society's new headquarters, and the research collections grew enormously and at the same time were brought under control through detailed cataloguing. He expanded the Society's book publication program to include the Documents series and established the twice-yearly *Occasional Bulletin*, writing with characteristic wit and charm virtually all the articles in the first thirty-seven numbers. In recognition of his services to scholarship and the Commonwealth of Virginia, the College of William and Mary conferred an honorary degree of Doctor of Laws on him in 1968. Jennings was a founder-member of the Virginia Colonial Records Project and of the Virginia Historic Landmarks Commission; he has served on the advisory boards of the Papers of James Madison, the Papers of John Marshall, and the Virginia Independence Bicentennial Commission. He is a fellow of the Society of American Archivists, a member of the Bibliographical Society of America, the Massachusetts Historical Society, and the American Antiquarian Society, and a past president of the Alpha of Virginia chapter, Phi Beta Kappa.

Richard Lee Morton, *Virginia Lives* (Hopkinsville, Ky., 1964), p. 509; *Who's Who in America*, 40th ed. (Chicago, 1978).

BY CARROLL N. JONES. Signed. Dated 1977
See Plate 1

Oil on canvas: 30 x 36 in. (76.2 x 91.4 cm.)

Purchased from the artist in 1977 with funds contributed for the purpose by friends of the subject. Por977.15

Frances Augusta Jessup, 1832–1905
See William Allen, 1815–1875

Bradley Tyler Johnson, 1829–1903

General Johnson was born in Frederick, Maryland, on September 29, 1829, son of Charles Worthington Johnson and Eleanor Murdock (Tyler) Johnson. He graduated with honors from Princeton University in 1849, studied law, and was admitted to the bar in 1851. The same year he married Jane Claudia Saunders of North Carolina. Embarking on a political career, he became state's attorney, Democratic candidate for comptroller, state chairman of the Democratic Committe, and a delegate to the conventions of 1860 at Charleston and Baltimore. At the beginning of the Civil War he helped recruit the 1st Maryland Regiment for the Confederate army, serving with it as major and later as colonel at First Manassas, Front Royal, Winchester, Harrisonburg, Malvern Hill, and Gettysburg. Promoted to brigadier general on June 28, 1864, he was given command of a cavalry brigade which under General Early's orders burned the town of Chambersburg, Pennsylvania. Johnson spent the final months of the war in North Carolina as commander of prisoners at Salisbury. With the return of peace, Johnson established himself in Richmond where he practiced law and represented railroad interests before the legislature. He was elected to the legislature in 1875, serving three terms in the Virginia state Senate before removing to Baltimore in 1879 where he engaged in the practice of his profession until 1890. The final years of his life were spent in Amelia, Virginia, where he died on October 5, 1903. General Johnson was elected to membership in the Virginia Historical Society in 1875.

DAB; Generals in Gray; Biographic Catalogue.

By Cornelius Hankins. Signed. Dated 1898

Oil on canvas: 30 x 25 in. (76.2 x 63.5 cm.)

Presented to the R. E. Lee Camp, Confederate Veterans, in 1899; acquired by the Virginia Historical Society in 1946 through merger with the Confederate Memorial Association. Por946.56

Chapman Johnson, 1779–1849
See The Convention of 1829–30

Edward Johnson, 1816–1873

Born on April 16, 1816, at Salisbury, Chesterfield County, the subject was the son of Dr. Edward Johnson and Caroline (Turpin) Johnson. Removing at an early age to Kentucky with his parents, he received his early education there, accepted an appointment to West Point, and graduated with the class of 1838.

Johnson saw active duty in the Seminole War and the Mexican War, being twice brevetted for gallantry. On June 10, 1861, he resigned from the United States Army, entered Confederate service as a colonel, but was soon promoted to brigadier general. He participated in the Shenandoah Valley campaign of 1862, was wounded at McDowell, and took part with Early's Corps in the engagement at Winchester and the occupation of Carlisle, Pennsylvania. Promoted to major general, he led Stonewall Jackson's old division at Gettysburg and the Wilderness; at Spotsylvania he was taken prisoner at the Bloody Angle on May 12, 1864. Subsequently exchanged, he commanded a division in the invasion of Tennessee and at Nashville was again captured; he was held at the Old Capitol prison in Washington until the war's end. General Johnson, a bachelor, spent his last years farming at his old home in Chesterfield County; he died in Richmond on March 2, 1873, and is buried in Hollywood Cemetery.

DAB; Generals in Gray; Biographic Catalogue.

By John P. Walker. 1909

Oil on canvas: 30 x 25 in. (76.2 x 63.5 cm.). Inscribed on the back: "J. P. Walker. 1909."

Acquired in 1946 through merger with the Confederate Memorial Association. Por946.62

Albert Sidney Johnston, 1803–1862

The youngest son of Dr. John Johnston and Abigail (Harris) Johnston, the subject was born at Washington, Kentucky, on February 2, 1803. He received his formal education at Transylvania University and at West Point. Graduating with the class of 1826, he fought in the Black Hawk War and in 1836 resigned his commission to enlist in the Army of Texas. He became in due course adjutant general, senior brigadier general, commander of the army, and secretary of war of the Republic of Texas 1838–40. In the Mexican War he was commissioned colonel of the 1st Texas Rifle Volunteers; he commanded the Department of Texas 1856–58, the Department of Utah 1858–60, and the Department of the Pacific from 1860 until his resignation the following year when Texas seceded from the Union. Appointed general in the Army of the Confederacy, Johnston was assigned to command the Western Department. He was fatally wounded at the battle of Shiloh, bleeding to death on the battlefield on April 6, 1862. General Johnston was twice married: on January 20, 1829, to Henrietta Preston, daughter of William and Caroline (Hancock) Preston; on October 3, 1843, to Eliza Griffin; there were children by both marriages.

DAB; Generals in Gray; Biographic Catalogue.

By JOHN P. WALKER. Signed. Dated 1922

Oil on canvas: 60 x 40 in. (152.4 x 101.6 cm.)

Acquired in 1946 through merger with the Confederate Memorial Association. Por946.212

Joseph Eggleston Johnston, 1807–1891

A native Virginian, Joseph Eggleston Johnston was born February 3, 1807, at Longwood, Prince Edward County, the residence of his parents, Peter and Mary (Wood) Johnston. He received his schooling at Abingdon Academy, then became a cadet at West Point, graduating in 1829. In the Seminole and Mexican wars he saw action, was wounded, and was brevetted for distinguished service. In 1855 he was promoted to lieutenant colonel, 1st Cavalry, and in 1860 to brigadier general. When Virginia seceded from the Union, Johnston resigned his commission and in May 1861 became brigadier general in the Confederate army, assigned to Harpers Ferry. His conduct at First Manassas led to his promotion to full general and to the command of the Army of Northern Virginia. Johnston led the Confederate troops in the Peninsular campaign until he was wounded at Seven Pines and was obliged to relinquish command to General R. E. Lee. On his return to active duty in November 1863 he was assigned to the Department of the West, commanding at Vicksburg and at Chattanooga until relieved of his command on July 17, 1864. Reassigned to oppose Sherman's march north, he fought in North Carolina until his surrender to Sherman on April 26, 1865. For ten years after the war General Johnston engaged in the insurance business in Savannah, Georgia. He removed to Richmond in 1877 and was elected in 1879 to one term in the United States Senate. Thereafter he remained in Washington, D.C., serving as United States commissioner of railroads from 1885 until his death on March 21, 1891, the result of his presence, bareheaded, at the funeral of General Sherman. General Johnston's wife, whom he married on July 10, 1845, was Lydia (McLane) Johnston, daughter of Louis and Catherine (Milligan) McLane of Maryland; they had no children.

DAB; Generals in Gray; Biographical Directory; Biographic Catalogue.

Portrait I

By S. T. SHUMAN. Signed. Dated 1891

Oil on canvas: 24 x 20 in. (61 x 50.8 cm.)

Acquired in 1946 through merger with the Confederate Memorial Association. Por946.51

Portrait II

See The Battle Abbey Murals. The Summer Mural

Robert Daniel Johnston, 1837–1919

Born at Mount Welcome, Lincoln County, North Carolina, on March 19, 1837, son of Dr. William Johnston, the subject graduated from the University of North Carolina and in 1860 from the University of Virginia law school. He joined the Confederate army as a private, later became captain of Company K, 23d North Carolina Infantry, and took part in the Peninsular campaign. As lieutenant colonel he was wounded in the battle of Seven Pines, took part in the battles of South Mountain and Sharpsburg, and for distinguished conduct at Chancellorsville and Gettysburg was promoted to brigadier general. After sustaining wounds at Spotsylvania, he again led his brigade in Early's Valley campaign of 1864 and the siege of Petersburg. After the war General Johnston practiced law for twenty years in Charlotte, North Carolina. In 1887 he removed to Birmingham, Alabama, to become president of the Birmingham National Bank; he was also for many years register in the United States Land Office in Birmingham. He retired to a farm in Clarke County, Virginia, in 1909, and there he died on February 1, 1919. In 1871 he married Lizzie Johnston Evans of Greensboro, North Carolina, who survived him, along with four sons and four daughters.

Generals in Gray; Confederate Veteran 28 (1920): 110; *Richmond Times-Dispatch*, Feb. 2, 1919, p. 1; CMA Archives, folio Z1n; *Biographic Catalogue.*

Joseph Eggleston Johnston (Portrait I)

Signed. Dated 1925

Oil on canvas: 30 x 25 in. (76.2 x 63.5 cm.). Inscribed, front and back: "Copy by E. M. Whitfield. 1925."

Presented to the R. E. Lee Camp, Confederate Veterans, in 1925; acquired by the Virginia Historical Society in 1946 through merger with the Confederate Memorial Association. Por946.192

John Marshall Jones, 1820–1864

Born in Charlottesville on July 26, 1820, the son of Colonel John Russell Jones, the subject graduated from the United States Military Academy at West Point in 1841. After serving on frontier duty he returned to West Point as assistant instructor of infantry tactics 1845–52. Commissioned captain in 1855, he was garrisoned at various forts, participated in the Utah Expedition of 1859–60, and resigned his commission on the outbreak of the Civil War to join the Confederate army. After serving as assistant adjutant general and adjutant and inspector general under Generals Magruder, Ewell, and Early, he was promoted to brigadier general in 1863 and put in command of a brigade in General Edward Johnson's division of the 2d Corps. He was severely wounded at Gettysburg and again at the action at Payne's Farm and was killed in action on May 4, 1864, at the Wilderness. General Jones is buried in Maplewood Cemetery, Charlottesville.

Generals in Gray; National Cyclopaedia, 13: 443; *Encyclopedia of Virginia Biography*, 3: 62; *Magazine of Albemarle County History* 22 (1963–64): 196–97.

Artist unidentified

Oil on canvas: 29³/₄ x 24 in. (75.6 x 61 cm.)

Acquired in 1946 through merger with the Confederate Memorial Association. Por946.130

John William Jones, 1836–1909

The Reverend John William Jones, a native of Louisa County, was born on September 25, 1836, the son of Francis William Jones and Ann Pendleton (Ashby) Jones. He attended the University of Virginia and the Southern Baptist Theological Seminary. Ordained in June 1860, he was appointed a missionary to China, but when Virginia seceded from the Union and called for soldiers, he enlisted in Company D, 13th Virginia Infantry, where he served for one year as a private before being made chaplain of the regiment. In November 1863 he was appointed missionary chaplain to A. P. Hill's corps. As soldier and as chaplain he participated with his unit in all the principal engagements of the Army of Northern Virginia. After Appomattox he was for several years pastor at Lexington, serving at the same time as chaplain to the students at Washington College (later Washington and Lee University) and the Virginia Military Institute. He was agent of the Southern Baptist Theological Seminary, general superintendent of the Virginia Baptist Sunday School, and assistant secretary of the home board of the Southern Baptist Convention. As a lecturer and writer on Civil War subjects he was highly regarded, contributing numerous articles to periodicals and serving as secretary of the Southern Historical Society 1876–86 and as editor of its *Papers*. The best known of his published works are *Personal Reminiscences, Anecdotes, and Letters of General Robert E. Lee* (1874), *Army of Northern Virginia Memorial Volume* (1880), and *Christ in the Camp* (1887). In 1890 he was made chaplain general of the United Confederate Veterans, and in 1893 he became chaplain to the students at the University of Virginia. He died on March 17, 1909. His wife, whom he married on December 20, 1860, was Judith Page (Helm) Jones; they had ten children, of whom four became clergymen. The Reverend Mr. Jones was a member of the Virginia Historical Society.

Men of Mark in Virginia, 1: 250–53; *Confederate Military History*, 3: 970–71; *Confederate Veteran* 17 (1909): 239; *Biographic Catalogue*.

By John P. Walker. Signed. Dated 1915

Oil on canvas: 30 x 25 in. (76.2 x 63.5 cm.)

John William Jones

Acquired in 1946 through merger with the Confederate Memorial Association. Por946.144

John Winston Jones, 1791–1848

See The Convention of 1829–30

Lorraine Farquhar Jones, 1837–1920

Son of the Reverend Alexander Jones and Ann Northey (Churchill) Jones, the subject was born in Charles Town, (West) Virginia, on November 9, 1837. In the Civil War he was captain of the 2d Company, Richmond Howitzers, serving throughout the war and distinguishing himself at the Bloody Angle near Spotsylvania Court House. After the war Captain Jones went to St. Louis where he entered the employ of George R. Robinson, a commission and bagging merchant; shortly thereafter he went into a similar business for himself. On November 9, 1870, he married Matilda Fontaine Berkeley, daughter of the Reverend E. F. Berkeley, founder of St. Peter's Episcopal Church, St. Louis. Captain Jones was one of the founders of the American Manufacturing Company, manufacturers of bagging and cordage, and served as its treasurer; in 1906 he became president of the State National Bank of St. Louis; he was director of various businesses, among them the St. Louis Union Trust Company. He retired from active life in 1908 and died at his home, Ivy Lodge, Kirkwood, Missouri, on October 19, 1920, survived by his wife, three sons, and four daughters. Two brothers of Captain Jones, Dr. George W. Jones and William M. Jones, were residents of Richmond.

Confederate Veteran 28 (1920): 466–67; *Biographic Catalogue* (Addenda).

BY TAKUMA KAJIWARA

Oil on canvas: 17 x 14 in. (43.2 x 35.6 cm.)

Acquired in 1946 through merger with the Confederate Memorial Association. Por946.191

William Jones, 1782–1846

Born in Hanover County on January 21, 1782, William Jones was commissioned a captain in the 8th Infantry Regiment on July 6, 1812. He served throughout the War of 1812 and received an honorable discharge on June 15, 1815. At an undetermined time he removed to Georgia where he died on September 9, 1846. By his wife, Elizabeth (Talbot) Jones, daughter of Thomas and Elizabeth (Cresswell) Talbot, he had issue.

Portraiture, p. 54; Francis B. Heitman, *Historical Register and Dictionary of the United States Army* (Washington, D.C., 1903), 1: 582; *Historical Collections of the Joseph Habersham Chapter, Daughters American Revolution* (Atlanta, 1902–10), 2: 229–30.

COPIED BY EMMA C. WILKINS. Signed.
Dated 1910

Oil on canvas: 30 x 25 in. (76.2 x 63.5 cm.). Inscribed on the back: "Col. William Jones, born Hanover Co. Va. Jan. 21, 1782. Capt. 8th Infantry U. S. A. Served through War of 1812. Copy 1910 by E. C. Wilkins from old portrait painted 1811."

Presented in 1917 by Mrs. Elizabeth Talbot Belt of Millen, Georgia. Por917.2

William Edmondson Jones, 1824–1864

Often referred to as "Grumble" Jones, General William Edmondson Jones was born on the middle fork of the Holston River, Washington County, on May 9, 1824, son of Robert Jones. He attended Emory and Henry College and graduated from West Point in 1848; thereafter he spent three years in Oregon as a second lieutenant in the Mounted Rifles. On January 13, 1852, while on furlough, he married Eliza M. Dunn, daughter of Dr. Samuel Dunn of Washington County; she drowned two months later when the ship that the young couple was taking to a new post in the West was wrecked at Pass Cavallo, Texas. In 1857 he resigned his commission, visited Europe, and returned to plant extensive vineyards on his estate near Glade Spring, Washington County. On the secession of Virginia he organized the Washington Mounted Rifles which as captain he led at First Manassas. Promoted to colonel, he commanded the 1st and then the 7th Virginia Cavalry before becoming brigadier general on September 19, 1862. At Brandy Station, on June 3, 1863, he rendered conspicuous service. A serious disagreement between Jones and J. E. B. Stuart led to Jones's reassignment to the Department of Southwest Virginia and East Tennessee, where he rendered excellent service at Rogersville, the siege of Knoxville, and Cloyd's Mountain. General Jones was killed at the battle of Piedmont, on June 5, 1864; he is buried in Old Glade Spring churchyard, Washington County.

Generals in Gray; Confederate Veteran 11 (1903): 266–67; Lewis Preston Summers, *History of Southwest Virginia, 1746–1786* (Richmond, 1903), pp. 753–54; *Biographic Catalogue.*

BY JOHN P. WALKER. Signed. Dated 1901

Oil on canvas: 30 x 25 in. (76.2 x 63.5 cm.)

Presented to the R. E. Lee Camp, Confederate Veterans, in 1901 by the subject's family and friends;

acquired by the Virginia Historical Society in 1946 through merger with the Confederate Memorial Association. Por946.109

Thomas Robinson Joynes, 1789–1858
See The Convention of 1829–30

Hugh Payne Keane, 1807–1891

Born in England on February 27, 1807, the subject was the son of Hugh Perry Keane and Susan (Payne) Keane. He attended Harrow School, spent some years of his childhood and youth on the island of St. Vincent, British West Indies, and traveled in Sicily, Italy, and elsewhere in Europe. He married a Frenchwoman, Annette Naret; the couple traveled extensively. Their child Marie (later Mrs. Thomas Todd Dabney) was born in Virginia when he was sixty years old; another child, Virginia, married Dr. Clarence Archibald Bryce (q.v.). After residing in Paris and England for some years, he returned to Virginia around 1879 where he spent the rest of his life.

Information received with the portraits; Marie Keane Dabney, *Mrs. T.N.T.* (Richmond, 1949); VHS Mss6:4 K1995:1.

Portrait I. The subject with his brother and sisters

By SAMUEL DRUMMOND. 1810

Oil on canvas: 72 x 60 in. (182.9 x 152.4 cm.)

Presented in 1974 by the subject's granddaughter, Virginia Bryce of Richmond. Por974.28

The Keane children in Drummond's portrait are, left to right: Susan Keane (b.1798); the subject; Lionel Richard Keane (1808–1850); and Marianna Keane (b. 1799), later Mrs. Henry Palmer of Clifton, Bedfordshire. The diary of the children's mother, Susan (Payne) Keane, which is preserved in the Society's manuscript collection (VHS Mss5:1 K1993:1), records that the children sat for the portrait during the spring of 1810 and that it cost £26 5s.

Portrait II

By VIRGINIA KEANE BRYCE

Oil on canvas: 21½ x 17½ in. (54.6 x 44.5 cm.) (oval)

Presented in 1974 by the subject's granddaughter, Virginia Bryce of Richmond. Por974.29

The portrait, which is the work of his daughter, depicts the subject in old age.

Lionel Richard Keane, 1808–1850
See Hugh Payne Keane, 1807–1891

Marianna Keane, b.1799
See Hugh Payne Keane, 1807–1891

Susan Keane, b. 1798
See Hugh Payne Keane, 1807–1891

James Lawson Kemper, 1823–1895

James Lawson Kemper, Confederate general and governor of Virginia, was born in Madison County on June 11, 1823, son of William and Maria Elizabeth (Allison) Kemper. He graduated from Washington College (now Washington and Lee University) in 1842, studied law, and started practice in Madison. After brief, uneventful service in the Mexican War, he turned to politics; he was elected to the Virginia legislature in 1853 and was returned four times, serving variously as chairman of the Committee on Military Affairs, president of the board of visitors of the Virginia Military Institute, and Speaker of the House of Delegates 1861–63. Volunteering for service in the Confederate army, he was commissioned colonel of the 7th Virginia Infantry on May 2, 1861, leading this regiment from First Manassas to Williamsburg; promoted to brigadier general, he was given a brigade in Pickett's Division which he led until he was severely wounded and captured at Gettysburg. Subsequently exchanged, he was promoted to major general, but being unfit for active service, he was put in charge of the Conscript Bureau. At the war's end he returned to the practice of law in Madison, reentered the political arena, and was elected governor of Virginia, serving as Virginia's chief executive from 1874 to 1878. On his return to private life he again devoted himself to the practice of law. He died on April 7, 1895, in Orange County. General Kemper married on July 4, 1853, Cremora Conway Cave, daughter of Belfield and Cremora (Jones) Cave of Madison County; they had six children. He was elected to membership in the Virginia Historical Society in 1875.

DAB; Generals in Gray; Virginia and Virginians, 1: 242–48; *SHS Papers* 30 (1902): 360–68; *Biographic Catalogue.*

By JOHN P. WALKER. Signed. Dated 1902

Oil on canvas: 30 x 25 in. (76.2 x 63.5 cm.)

Presented to the R. E. Lee Camp, Confederate Veterans, in 1902; acquired by the Virginia Historical Society in 1946 through merger with the Confederate Memorial Association. Por946.177

Gordon Cloyd Kent, 1806–1869
Jane Logan (McKee) Kent, 1812–1883 (Mrs. Gordon Cloyd Kent)

Gordon Cloyd Kent, son of Colonel Joseph Kent and Margaret (McGavock) Kent of Wythe County, was born on June 29, 1806. He was three times married: first, on March 14, 1832, to Margaret Cloyd, who died fourteen months later; second, to Lucinda Cloyd, who died without issue on December 18, 1843; third, on April 9, 1850, to Jane Logan McKee. The last-named was the daughter of George and Elizabeth (McElwee) McKee, natives of Ireland; she was born in Fannettsburg, Pennsylvania, on October 10, 1812. Gordon Cloyd Kent had two sons, one by his first wife and one by his third wife. He died at his homestead on Reed Creek, Wythe County, on September 18, 1869; his wife died on December 25, 1883.

Robert Gray, *The McGavock Family: A Genealogical History of James McGavock and His Descendants from 1760 to 1903* (Richmond, 1903), p. 38; VHS Mss6:4 K4195:1; *VMHB* 80 (1972): 238.

Portrait I. Gordon Cloyd Kent

ARTIST UNIDENTIFIED

Oil on canvas: 24 x 20 in. (61 x 50.8 cm.)

Presented in 1971 by Arthur Meaux Kent of Wytheville. Por971.1

Portrait II. Jane Logan (McKee) Kent

ARTIST UNIDENTIFIED

Oil on canvas: 24 x 20 in. (61 x 50.8 cm.). Stencil on the back: "G. Rowney & Co. Manufacturers. 51 Rathbone Place London."

Presented in 1971 by Arthur Meaux Kent of Wytheville. Por971.2

Joseph Brevard Kershaw, 1822–1894

Born at Camden, South Carolina, on January 5, 1822, the son of John and Harriette (DuBose) Kershaw, the subject studied law and was admitted to the bar in 1843. The following year he married Lucretia Douglas, by whom he had one son and four daughters. As a lieutenant in the Palmetto Regiment he saw action during the Mexican War but was compelled by illness to resign from the army and resume the practice of law. Entering politics, he was elected to the South Carolina legislature in 1852 and again in 1854; he was a member of the state's Secession Convention. At the beginning of hostilities in 1861 he recruited the 2d South Carolina Volunteers and as its colonel was present during the bombardment of Fort Sumter and later at First Manassas.

Promoted to brigadier general, his command, known as Kershaw's Brigade, took part in the Peninsular campaign, South Mountain, Sharpsburg, Fredericksburg, Chancellorsville, and Gettysburg; later the brigade was active at Chickamauga and in the Tennessee campaign. On May 18, 1864, Kershaw was promoted to major general; he commanded a division of Longstreet's Corps at the Wilderness, Spotsylvania, Cold Harbor, and Petersburg. At Sayler's Creek he was made prisoner and confined for several months at Fort Warren, Boston. General Kershaw returned to law and politics after the war. He was elected to the South Carolina Senate in 1865; in 1870 he was a member of the Union Reform party convention that prepared resolutions recognizing the Reconstruction acts; in 1877 he was elected judge of the fifth circuit court of South Carolina, holding that office for sixteen years. Poor health necessitated his resignation in 1893; thereafter he was postmaster at Camden until his death on April 13, 1894. He was buried in the Quaker cemetery in Camden.

DAB; *Generals in Gray*; *Biographic Catalogue*; CMA Archives, folio Z11.

BY W. P. HIX. Signed. Dated 1873

Oil on canvas: 55 x 42 in. (139.7 x 106.7 cm.)

Received by the Confederate Memorial Association in 1924 as a bequest of the subject's widow, Lucretia (Douglas) Kershaw; acquired by the Virginia Historical Society in 1946 through merger with the Confederate Memorial Association. Por946.204

Ella Louise (Rives) King, 1851–1925 (Mrs. David King)
See Ella Rives, 1834–1892

Anna Campbell Knox, 1784–1867
See Bazil Gordon, 1768–1847

William Knox, 1729–1805
Susanna Stuart (Fitzhugh) Knox, 1751–1823 (Mrs. William Knox)

William Knox, born in 1729, was the son of William and Janet (Somerville) Knox of Renfrew, Scotland. He emigrated to Virginia with his three brothers, settling at Falmouth where he became a prosperous merchant. He married, around 1766, Susanna Stuart Fitzhugh, daughter of Thomas and Sarah (Stuart) Fitzhugh of Boscobel, Stafford County, and granddaughter of Henry Fitzhugh (1687–1758) (q.v.) of Bedford, Stafford County; they had ten children, one of whom, Anna Campbell (Knox) Gordon (q.v.), is represented, as is her husband Bazil Gordon (q.v.), in the Society's portrait collection. William Knox died in 1805; thereafter Mrs. Knox resided with their son, Dr. Thomas Fitzhugh Knox, at Belmont, near Falmouth, until her own death which occurred in 1823.

Emily Woolsey Dix, *Reminiscences of the Knox and Soutter Families of Virginia* (New York, 1895), pp. 6, 16 (original portraits reproduced); Fitzhugh Knox, *Genealogy of the Fitzhugh, Knox . . . Families* (Atlanta, 1932), pp. 7–8 (original portraits reproduced); *Overwharton Parish*, pp. 221–22; *VMHB* 7 (1899–1900): 426 (original portrait of Mrs. Knox reproduced) and 82 (1974): 239. See chart on Fitzhugh, Knox, and Gordon Portraits for relationships.

Portrait I. William Knox

COPIED BY AN UNIDENTIFIED ARTIST

Oil on canvas: 30 x 25 in. (76.2 x 63.5 cm.)

Presented in 1973 by Douglas Huntly Gordon of Baltimore. Por973.7

Portrait II. Susanna Stuart (Fitzhugh) Knox

COPIED BY AN UNIDENTIFIED ARTIST

Oil on canvas: 30 x 25 in. (76.2 x 63.5 cm.)

Presented in 1973 by Douglas Huntly Gordon of Baltimore. Por973.8

The Society's portraits are copies of originals painted by John Hesselius.

Marie Joseph Paul Yves Roch Gilbert du Motier, Marquis de Lafayette, 1757–1834

The marquis de Lafayette was born in the château of Chavaniac in Auvergne, France, on September 6, 1757, the son of Gilbert, marquis de Lafayette, and his wife, née Marie Louise Julie de la Rivière. He entered the army in 1771, but military reforms and economies forced him out five years later. Having inherited great wealth on the death of his grandfather and gained great influence through his marriage in 1774 to Marie Adrienne Françoise de Noailles, he determined to offer assistance to the American colonists, whose republican ideals he greatly admired. Defying the wishes of the king, he sailed to America in his own ship. Landing in North Carolina on June 13, 1777, he was commissioned major general by the Continental Congress and took part in the battles of Brandywine, Barren Hill, and Monmouth Court House. In 1778 he departed for France to enlist further aid for the Americans; he was promptly arrested but made peace with the king. Returning to the United States in April 1780, he was entrusted by Washington with the defense of Virginia. His evasive tactics proved successful, eventually leading to the encirclement of the British army at Yorktown and Cornwallis's surrender on October 19, 1781. For some years after the war he enjoyed immense popularity in France; during the early years of the French Revolution, however, his popularity waned, for he was a supporter of constitutional monarchy and opposed the Jacobins. He spent 1792–97 in prison, from which the United States sought in vain to effect his release. Liberated at length, Lafayette and his family settled at La Grange, about forty miles from Paris, where in greatly reduced circumstances he engaged in agricultural pursuits. In 1824 Lafayette was invited to visit the United States as the guest of the nation; he arrived in New York City on July 12, 1824, and embarked on a fifteen-month triumphal tour. He returned to France in 1825, thereafter emerging from retirement to take part in the July Revolution of 1830. He died on May 20, 1834, and is buried in Picpus Cemetery, Paris.

DAB; *Virginia Historical Portraiture*, pp. 249–50 (portrait reproduced); *Portraiture*, pp. 55–56.

BY CHARLES WILLSON PEALE. Signed. Dated 1777 *See* Plate 16

Oil on canvas: 47 x 40 in. (119.4 x 101.6 cm.)

Presented in 1848 by Thomas Harding Ellis of Richmond. Por848.1

This was the first portrait to come into the Society's possession. The donor, Thomas Harding Ellis, subsequently a member of the executive committee and corresponding secretary, recalled more than thirty years later that he "had the pleasure of presenting an original of General Lafayette, painted by the elder Peale, which I bought from an auction house in Richmond, and which in the estimation of many is a particularly fine painting." His letter of transmittal, dated November 10, 1848, is in the Society's archives. The subject's identity is questioned in Sellers's *Portraits and Miniatures*.

Richmond Standard, Sept. 24, 1881; *Virginia Historical Portraiture*, p. 250; *Portraits and Miniatures*, pp. 119, 295 (portrait reproduced); *Antiques* 116 (1979): 1134 (portrait reproduced).

John Laidley, 1781–1863
See The Convention of 1829–30

Martha Eppes (Chambers) Laird, 1830–1878 (Mrs. Thomas Harvey Laird)

Born on November 21, 1830, the subject, nicknamed "Pink," was a daughter of Edward R. Chambers and

16. The Marquis de Lafayette

Lucy Goode (Tucker) Chambers (qq.v.) of Boydton, formerly of Flat Rock, Lunenburg County. On January 17, 1849, she married Dr. Thomas Harvey Laird, a physician who had studied at the Jefferson Medical College in Philadelphia. After ten years of marriage Dr. Laird died; the couple had no children. Thereafter she looked after her father until his death in 1872. Martha Eppes (Chambers) Laird died on September 7, 1878.

Rose Chambers Goode McCullough, *Yesterday When It Is Past* (Richmond, 1957), pp. 159, 189–201 (cropped reproduction opposite p. 200); *VMHB* 83 (1975): 237.

Attributed to Edward Samuel Dodge

Miniature on ivory: 3½ x 2½ in. (8.9 x 6.4 cm.)

Presented in 1974 by Philip Briscoe Bateson of Dallas, Texas. Por974.13

John Lamb, 1840–1924

John Lamb, for sixteen years a United States congressman from the Third District, was born in Sussex County on June 12, 1840, son of Lycurgus A. Lamb and Ann Elizabeth (Christian) Lamb. Five years later the family returned to their original home in Charles City County. On the early death of his father, John Lamb, though only fifteen years of age, went to work to support the family. In 1859 he joined the Charles City Troop which was mustered into service as Company D, 3d Virginia Cavalry, at the beginning of the Civil War. As first sergeant, and later as lieutenant and captain, he served with this regiment throughout the war, seeing action at the Seven Days, Sharpsburg, Chancellorsville, Gettysburg, the Wilderness, Spotsylvania, Yellow Tavern, and Appomattox. After the war he returned to his farm in Charles City County; he was elected sheriff of the county, and subsequently treasurer and surveyor; he was also chairman of the Democratic Central Committee. Elected as a Democrat to the Fifty-fifth Congress and to the seven succeeding United States Congresses, he represented his district 1897–1913. Captain Lamb, an author of monographs on Civil War subjects and a popular speaker, spent the latter years of his life in Richmond, where he was active in the R. E. Lee Camp, Confederate Veterans, and in the work of the Confederate Memorial Association, acting for many years as superintendent of Battle Abbey. He died in Richmond on November 21, 1924, and is buried in Hollywood Cemetery. Captain Lamb married on November 20, 1869, Mattie R. Wade, daughter of the rector of Westover Parish, the Reverend Anderson Wade, and Mary Waller (Clarke) Wade; the couple had nine children.

Men of Mark in Virginia, 3: 201–2; *Confederate Military History*, 3: 988–89; *Biographical Directory*; *Biographic Catalogue*.

John Lamb

Copied by James F. Banks. 1939

Oil on canvas: 30 x 25 in. (76.2 x 63.5 cm.). Inscribed on the back: "Copy of C. Hoffbauer by Jas. F. Banks. 1939."

Acquired in 1946 through merger with the Confederate Memorial Association. Por946.106

Robert Alexander Lancaster, 1863–1940

Historian and corresponding secretary of the Virginia Historical Society, the subject was born in Richmond on August 16, 1863, son of Robert Alexander Lancaster and Mary (Ely) Lancaster. After completing his studies at McGuire's University School and the Norwood School, he entered the banking and investment house of Lancaster and Lucke as a bookkeeper. In 1893 he turned to real estate appraisal and financing, in which business he continued for forty years. Lancaster was on the board of directors of the Family Service Society, the Richmond School of Social Service and Public Health, and the Guarantee Trust Company; he was also a member of numerous patriotic and lineage societies. In 1902 he was elected to membership in the Virginia Historical Society; five years later he took on the duties of treasurer of the Society, an office he held for the rest of his life. In 1933 he succeeded William Glover Stanard (q.v.) as corresponding secretary and librarian of the Virginia

Historical Society and editor of the *Virginia Magazine of History and Biography*. An able historian, he was the author of *Historic Virginia Homes and Churches* (1915) and assembled an extensive photographic collection of Virginia's historical and architectural landmarks; he served on the advisory boards of the Association for the Preservation of Virginia Antiquities and the Robert E. Lee Memorial Foundation. He died, unmarried, in Richmond on August 26, 1940.

VMHB 49 (1941): 29–32; *Men of Mark in Virginia*, 2d ser., 1: 179–81; *New England Historical and Genealogical Register* 95 (1941): 82.

By HELEN SCHUYLER SMITH HULL BAILEY. 1972

Oil on canvas: 30 x 25 in. (76.2 x 63.5 cm.). Inscribed on the back: "Robert Alexander Lancaster, Jr. Virginia Historical Society 1933–1940 Corresponding Secretary, Editor, Librarian. By Helen Schuyler Bailey 1972 From Black and White photograph."

Presented in 1972 by Katherine (Lancaster) Guy (Mrs. John H. Guy) of Richmond, Dabney Stewart Lancaster of Millboro Springs, and Robert Bolling Lancaster of Ashland. Por972.22

John Landstreet, 1818–1891

Born in Baltimore, Maryland, on April 23, 1818, son of John and Anne Verlinda (Orme) Landstreet, the subject entered the ministry of the Methodist Episcopal Church, South, on September 24, 1847. For the next forty-four years, until his death, he devoted himself to the calling of an itinerant minister. At the beginning of the Civil War he enlisted as a private in the 1st Virginia Cavalry, took part in the battle of First Manassas, and the following year was made chaplain of the regiment, serving in that capacity until the war's end. Twice captured and imprisoned in the Old Capitol prison in Washington, D.C., Chaplain Landstreet was twice released through the influence of his brother, a colonel in the Union army, and returned to active duty with his regiment. After the war he resumed his ministry. He was pastor of the Methodist church in Martinsburg, West Virginia, 1881–84. He died in Martinsburg on November 21, 1891, and was buried there; at least one son survived him.

CMA Archives, folio Z1n; *Biographic Catalogue*.

By JOHN P. WALKER. Signed. Dated 1924

Oil on canvas: 30 x 25 in. (76.2 x 63.5 cm.)

Presented to the R. E. Lee Camp, Confederate Veterans, in 1925 by the subject's son; acquired by the Virginia Historical Society in 1946 through merger with the Confederate Memorial Association. Por946.146

James Henry Lane, 1833–1907

Son of Walter Gardner Lane and Mary Ann Henry (Barkwell) Lane, the subject was born at Mathews, Virginia, on July 28, 1833. He graduated from the Virginia Military Institute in 1854, then spent a year at the University of Virginia. Thereafter he taught at the Virginia Military Institute and at other schools; when the Civil War began he was teaching military tactics at the North Carolina Military Institute. As major of the 1st Regiment of North Carolina Volunteers he took part in the battle of Bethel. He was later made colonel of the 28th North Carolina Regiment, and on November 1, 1862, was promoted to brigadier general. General Lane served with the Army of Northern Virginia throughout the war, participating in all its principal engagements; his conduct was particularly distinguished during the retreat from Sharpsburg, in Pickett's charge at Gettysburg, and as commander of the rear guard during Lee's withdrawal into Virginia. After Appomattox he resumed his academic career; he taught at private schools in Virginia and North Carolina 1865–72; he was professor of natural philosophy and commandant of the Virginia Polytechnic Institute in Blacksburg 1872–80; and for the last twenty-five years of his life he was professor of civil engineering at the Alabama Polytechnic Institute. He died at Auburn, Alabama, on September 21, 1907. General Lane married in 1869 Charlotte Randolph Meade, daughter of Benjamin and Jane (Hardaway) Meade; they had four children.

DAB; *Generals in Gray*; *Biographic Catalogue*.

By JOHN P. WALKER. Signed. Dated 1908

Oil on canvas: 29½ x 25 in. (75.6 x 63.5 cm.)

Presented to the R. E. Lee Camp, Confederate Veterans, in 1908 by the subject's daughters; acquired by the Virginia Historical Society in 1946 through merger with the Confederate Memorial Association. Por946.196

Elizabeth Dabney Langhorne, 1851–1946
See Elizabeth Dabney (Langhorne) Lewis, 1851–1946

Nancy Witcher Langhorne, 1879–1964
See Nancy Witcher (Langhorne) Shaw Astor, Viscountess Astor, 1879–1964

John E. Laughton, 1844–1913

Born in Richmond on March 30, 1844, the subject

served in the Army of Northern Virginia as captain of Company D, 12th Virginia Infantry. Seven times wounded, he lost an arm at the battle of the Crater, June 30, 1864; he later rejoined his command and was with it at Appomattox. Returning to Richmond after the war, he was employed as an auctioneer. Captain Laughton was at one time commander of the R. E. Lee Camp, Confederate Veterans, and was instrumental in the formation of the portrait collection. He spent the last years of his life in Washington, D.C., where he died on April 5, 1913, survived by his wife, Emma (Bailey) Laughton, and three sons. His remains were brought to Richmond for burial in Shockoe Cemetery.

Biographic Catalogue; Richmond *Times-Dispatch*, April 6, 1913, and Dec. 15, 1920, p. 12.

By JOHN P. WALKER. Signed. Dated 1907

Oil on canvas: 30 x 25 in. (76.2 x 63.5 cm.)

Acquired in 1946 through merger with the Confederate Memorial Association. Por946.76

Elizabeth Parke (Custis) Law, 1776–1832

See Elizabeth Parke Custis, 1776–1832

Josiah Jordan Leake, 1870–1945

Son of William Josiah Leake and Sarah Rebecca (Jordan) Leake, the subject was born in Ashland on February 13, 1870; he attended Norwood's University School in Richmond, graduated from Randolph-Macon College in 1890, and took his law degree at the University of Richmond in 1893. Immediately thereafter he established an office in Richmond for the general practice of law; in 1894 he entered into a partnership with William C. Preston which continued until Preston's death in 1901; in 1908 he formed a partnership with A. S. Buford, Jr., and under the firm name of Leake and Buford continued until the subject's death more than thirty-five years later. Leake was a director and general counsel for the State-Planters Bank and Trust Company and the Mutual Assurance Society; in a like capacity he served the Virginia Fire and Marine Insurance Company and the German-American Building and Loan Corporation. He was a vestryman and senior warden of Holy Trinity Episcopal Church, a Freemason, and in 1913 served as president of the Richmond Bar Association. Leake became a member of the Virginia Historical Society in 1909; he was elected to the Society's executive committee in 1920 and later became one of the Society's vice-presidents. His wife, whom he married on December 7, 1904, was Lisa Foulke (Beirne) Leake, daughter of Richard F. Beirne

and Clara Haxall (Grundy) Beirne. Leake died on February 23, 1945.

Virginia State Bar Association, *Proceedings* 57 (1946): 211–14; *History of Virginia*, 4: 193; *VMHB* 55 (1947): 202.

By DAVID SILVETTE. Signed. Dated 1946

Oil on canvas: 30 x 25 in. (76.2 x 63.5 cm.)

Presented in 1946 by the subject's widow. Por946.28

Lee Portraits

This chart shows the relationship of members of the Lee family depicted in portraits owned by the Virginia Historical Society. Subjects of the Society's portraits are indicated in italics.

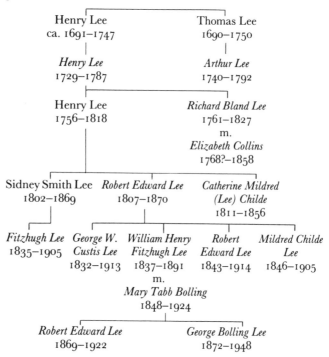

Arthur Lee, 1740–1792

Born at Stratford, Westmoreland County, on December 21, 1740, Arthur Lee was the eleventh child of Thomas and Hannah (Ludwell) Lee. He received his formal education abroad, at Eton College, and at the University of Edinburgh, where he received a degree in medicine in 1764. After traveling in Europe he returned to Virginia, practiced his profession a short time in Williamsburg, but abandoned it for law and politics; he returned to England in 1766 to study at Lincoln's Inn and the Middle Temple. During his residence in London he gained a reputation for his political pamphlets but was disappointed in his hope of becoming a member of Parliament. In 1770 Lee was commissioned by Massachusetts as its agent in

London; in 1775 he was appointed the London correspondent of the Continental Congress, and the following year, after the outbreak of armed hostilities between Britain and the colonies, he became one of the three commissioners (together with Benjamin Franklin and Silas Deane) appointed to negotiate a treaty with France. Despite the jealousy that existed between the commissioners and the resultant intrigue and squabbles, a treaty was in time drawn up and signed on February 6, 1778. Lee's charges, however, brought about Deane's recall to America; Deane's countercharges, in turn, brought about Lee's recall. Arthur Lee returned to America in September 1780; the following year he was elected to the Virginia House of Delegates and shortly thereafter to the Continental Congress, where he sat from 1781 to 1784. In 1785 Congress appointed him to the Treasury board, a post he held until 1789. He then retired to Lansdowne, his residence in Middlesex County; there he died on December 12, 1792. Arthur Lee never married.

DAB; *Biographical Directory*; *Portraiture*, pp. 61–62 (portrait reproduced); *Virginia Historical Portraiture*, pp. 236–38 (portrait reproduced); *Portraits and Miniatures*, pp. 124, 308. See chart on Lee Portraits for relationships.

Arthur Lee

BY CHARLES WILLSON PEALE

Oil on canvas: 30 x 25 in. (76.2 x 63.5 cm.)

Presented in 1854 by Charles Carter Lee of Powhatan County. Por854.1

140

The Society's portrait is probably a replica of the 1785 portrait in the Independence Hall collection, Philadelphia.

Catherine Mildred Lee, 1811–1856
See Catherine Mildred (Lee) Childe, 1811–1856

Charlotte Lee, 1836–1908
See Hancock Lee, 1797–1860, and Family

Elizabeth Collins Lee, ca. 1875–1927

Great-granddaughter of Richard Bland Lee (q.v.) of Virginia and daughter of Richard Henry Lee and Isabella (Wilson) Lee of Baltimore, the subject was born in Baltimore around 1875. She studied nursing and graduated as a trained nurse from the Maryland University Hospital. During the First World War she volunteered for service overseas and was sent abroad with the 42d Division. In France she was assigned to Base Hospital 43 at Blois, Base Hospital 15 at Chaumont, and Evacuation Hospital 4; she was twice mentioned in dispatches during the Meuse-Argonne drive for heroic conduct under fire. In 1919 when her own health broke down from overwork, Miss Lee was demobilized and returned to this country. Despite her failing health she resumed her nursing duties but was shortly obliged to retire. She spent the remaining years of her life in Towson, Maryland. She was one of the organizers of the Society of the Lees of Virginia and at the time of her death was on its board of managers. She died in Baltimore on May 16, 1927, and is buried in Arlington National Cemetery.

Magazine of the Society of the Lees of Virginia 5 (1927): 56–57; *Portraiture*, pp. 63–64.

BY ALICE MATILDA READING

Oil on canvas: 20 x 16 in. (50.8 x 40.6 cm.)

Presented in 1934 by Mr. and Mrs. J. Collins Lee of Hartford, Connecticut, brother and sister-in-law of the subject. Por934.25

Fitzhugh Lee, 1835–1905

"Fitz" Lee, soldier and governor of Virginia, was the eldest son of Sidney Smith Lee and Anna Maria (Mason) Lee; he was born at Clermont, Fairfax County, on November 19, 1835. His father, the second son of Henry ("Light-Horse Harry") Lee, was an elder brother to General Robert E. Lee. Graduating from West Point in 1856, he served in Texas, then returned to West Point as an assistant instructor of tactics. Resigning his commission in May 1861, he entered Confederate service as staff officer to Richard Stoddert Ewell and Joseph Eggleston Johnston in the Manassas campaign. Promoted to brigadier general on July 24, 1862, for distinguished service during the Peninsular campaign and to major general a year later, following the invasion of Pennsylvania, he took part in all the cavalry operations of the Army of Northern Virginia, rendering conspicuous service at Kelly's Ford, Chancellorsville, and Spotsylvania. Seriously wounded at Winchester, he became in January 1865 senior cavalry commander of the Army of Northern Virginia, serving in that capacity until the surrender. After the war General Lee farmed in Stafford County, then embarked on a political career, being elected governor of Virginia in 1885. His term of office ending in 1890, he campaigned unsuccessfully for nomination to the United States Senate. In 1896 he became consul general to Havana; with the outbreak of the Spanish-American War he was commissioned major general and was charged with reestablishing order in Havana. Keenly interested in matters historical, he traveled extensively in 1882 and 1883 to promote the Southern Historical Society; he wrote a biography of his uncle Robert E. Lee, *General Lee* (1894); and he became a member of the Virginia Historical Society in 1881. On his retirement in 1901, General Lee worked on plans for the Jamestown Exposition of 1907 but did not live to see the fruits of his labors. He died in Washington, D.C., on April 28, 1905, survived by his wife, Ellen Bernard (Fowle) Lee, whom he married on April 19, 1871, and by five children.

DAB; *Generals in Gray*; *Virginia and Virginians*, 2: 546–49; *Men of Mark in Virginia*, 5: 258–63; *Biographic Catalogue*. See chart on Lee Portraits for relationships.

Portrait I

By CORNELIUS HANKINS. Signed. Dated 1898

Oil on canvas: 30 x 25 in. (76.2 x 63.5 cm.)

Acquired in 1946 through merger with the Confederate Memorial Association. Por946.65

Portrait II

By CORNELIUS HANKINS. Signed. Dated 1898

Oil on canvas: 30 x 25 in. (76.2 x 63.5 cm.)

Acquired in 1946 through merger with the Confederate Memorial Association. Por946.83

Portrait III

See The Battle Abbey Murals. The Summer Mural

George Bolling Lee, 1872–1948

Son of William Henry Fitzhugh Lee and Mary Tabb (Bolling) Lee (qq.v.), the subject was born in Lex-

ington, Virginia, on August 21, 1872. He graduated from Washington and Lee University in 1893, and after taking a degree as Doctor of Medicine at the College of Physicians and Surgeons (Columbia University) and completing his internship at Bellevue Hospital 1896–99, he began the practice of his profession in New York City, where he remained all his life. He was an associate surgeon at the Women's Hospital 1900–1914, professor of gynecology and obstetrics at the Polyclinic Medical School and Hospital, and during World War I served as a captain in the Medical Officers Reserve Corps. Dr. Lee married Helen Keeney of San Francisco on April 21, 1920; the couple had one son and one daughter. He was a member of numerous professional and lineage societies and became a member of the Virginia Historical Society in 1925. Dr. Lee died on July 13, 1948.

Who Was Who in America 2 (1950): 317; *Burke's Presidential Families of the United States of America* (London, 1975), p. 47. See chart on Lee Portraits for relationships.

By "CHARLES J. FOX" (i.e., Irving Resnikoff)

Miniature on ivory: 4^{1}/4 x 3^{1}/4 in. (11 x 8.3 cm.)

Received from the heirs of Dr. George Bolling Lee. Por977.31

The miniature, depicting the subject as an infant with his black nurse, is derived from a photograph by Michael Miley.

George Washington Custis Lee, 1832–1913

The eldest son of Robert Edward Lee (q.v.) and Mary Anna Randolph (Custis) Lee, the subject was born at Fortress Monroe, September 16, 1832. Following his graduation from West Point, at the head of the class of 1854, he served at various posts as an officer in the Corps of Engineers. At the commencement of the Civil War, Lee offered his services to the Confederacy. As captain of engineers he worked on the fortification of Richmond until his appointment on August 31, 1861, to President Davis's staff with the rank of colonel. Much against his will Lee remained on the president's staff for all but the closing days of the war, rising to the rank of major general. It was not until the final retreat from Petersburg that Lee was at last given command of a brigade, one composed of clerks and mechanics, but which performed with great gallantry under his leadership. General Lee and most of his command were captured at Sayler's Creek on April 6, 1865. At the war's end he became professor of military and civil engineering at the Virginia Military Institute, remaining there until his father's death, whereupon he was invited to succeed him as president of Washington

College, soon to be renamed Washington and Lee University. Lee served in this capacity from February 1, 1871, until July 1, 1897, when he retired to Ravensworth in Fairfax County. He died, unmarried, on February 18, 1913, and is buried in Lexington. General Lee was elected to membership in the Virginia Historical Society in 1875.

DAB; *Generals in Gray*; CMA Archives, folio Z1n; *Biographic Catalogue*. See chart on Lee Portraits for relationships.

Portrait I

By JOHN P. WALKER. Signed. Dated 1924

Oil on canvas: 30 x 25 in. (76.2 x 63.5 cm.)

Presented to the R. E. Lee Camp, Confederate Veterans, in 1925 by Dr. George Bolling Lee and the daughters of Captain Robert Edward Lee; acquired by the Virginia Historical Society in 1946 through merger with the Confederate Memorial Association. Por946.68

A pastel portrait of the subject is listed in the R. E. Lee Camp's 1905 portrait inventory and in the 1913 catalogue. What became of it is not clear; perhaps it was returned to the family in 1925 when Walker's oil portrait was acquired.

Portrait II

By "CHARLES J. FOX" (i.e., Irving Resnikoff)

Miniature on ivory: 4¼ x 3¼ in. (11 x 8.3 cm.) (oval)

Received from the heirs of Dr. George Bolling Lee. Por977.29

The likeness was taken from a photograph.

Hancock Lee, 1797–1860, and Family

Born on July 26, 1797, probably in Goochland County, fourth son of Kendall and Judith Burton (Payne) Lee, the subject was employed as a teller in the Farmers' Bank of Virginia; he resided in Richmond on the north side of Grace Street between Fifth and Sixth streets. Lee's first wife, whom he married on July 8, 1824, was Mary Henderson, daughter of James and Mary (Ogleby) Henderson of Manchester, by whom he had ten children, only three of whom lived to maturity; she died on March 29, 1844. His second wife, whom he married on August 12, 1847, was Martha Bickerton Drew, daughter of Carter Henry Drew and Juliet (Shore) Drew of Richmond, who bore him four children. Lee was a member and an elder of the First Presbyterian Church. He died in Richmond on November 5, 1860, and is buried in Shockoe Cemetery.

Lee of Virginia, pp. 546, 550–51; *Portraiture*, pp. 122–24; VHS Mss6:4 L5167: 2; *VMHB* 46 (1938): 159.

Hancock Lee and family

ARTIST UNIDENTIFIED

Silhouettes on paper: 14 x 16½ in. (35.6 x 41.9 cm.)

Received in 1937 from the estate of Juliet Lee of Richmond. Por937.9a

Depicted in this family group are, from left to right, James Kendall Lee (1829–1861), who died of wounds received at First Manassas; Hancock Lee, father of the family; Martha Bickerton (Drew) Lee (1818–1892), second wife of Hancock Lee; Juliet Lee (1853–1937), seated on her mother's lap; Margaret Henderson Lee (1838–1915); and Charlotte Lee (1836–1908).

Henry Lee, ca. 1729–1787

Third son of Henry and Mary (Bland) Lee, the subject was born around 1729, probably at Lee Hall, Westmoreland County. He removed at an unknown date to family lands in Prince William County; here he built Leesylvania, where he resided for the rest of his life. On December 1, 1753, he married Lucy Grymes, daughter of Charles and Frances (Jenings) Grymes of Morattico, Lancaster County; she bore him eight children, three of whom, Charles (attorney general of the United States), Henry ("Light-Horse Harry"), and Richard Bland Lee (q.v.), attained national prominence. Henry Lee, the subject, represented Prince William County in the House of Burgesses 1758–75, was a member of the Conventions of 1774, 1775, and 1776, and was a state senator from 1776 until his death, which occurred on August 15, 1787.

Lee of Virginia, pp. 291–99; *Portraiture*, p. 59; Ethel Armes, *Stratford Hall, the Great House of the Lees* (Richmond, 1936), p. 93 (portrait reproduced). See chart on Lee Portraits for relationships.

COPIED BY ALICE MATILDA READING

Oil on canvas: 30 x 25 in. (76.2 x 63.5 cm.)

Presented in 1934 by Mr. and Mrs. J. Collins Lee of Hartford, Connecticut. Por934.26

An inscription on the back of the frame states that the portrait was copied from a miniature.

James Kendall Lee, 1829–1861

See Hancock Lee, 1797–1860, and Family

Juliet Lee, 1853–1937

See Hancock Lee, 1797–1860, and Family

Lettice Lee, d. 1776

See Lettice (Lee) Wardrop, d. 1776

Margaret Henderson Lee, 1838–1915

See Hancock Lee, 1797–1860, and Family

Mildred Childe Lee, 1846–1905

The youngest child of General Robert Edward Lee (q.v.) and Mary Anna Randolph (Custis) Lee, the subject was born at Arlington on February 10, 1846. At the outbreak of the Civil War she was in school in Winchester. As a young woman she devoted much time to the care of her invalid mother. After the death of her parents she continued to reside in Lexington, though she traveled frequently both in this country and abroad. Miss Lee, who never married, was active in the work of Confederate associations; she attended reunions, was president of the Home for Confederate Women in Richmond, worked closely with the United Daughters of the Confederacy, and was Virginia regent for the Confederate Memorial Literary Society. She died near New Orleans on March 27, 1905, while on a visit to Mrs. William Preston Johnston, and is buried in the Lee Chapel in Lexington.

Burke's Presidential Families of the United States of America (London, 1975), p. 48; Richmond *Times-Dispatch*, March 28, 29, 1905. See chart of Lee Portraits for relationships.

ARTIST UNIDENTIFIED

Miniature on ivory: $3^1/2$ x $2^1/4$ in. (8.9 x 5.7 cm.) (oval)

Received from the heirs of Dr. George Bolling Lee. Por977.33

Richard Bland Lee, 1761–1827
Elizabeth (Collins) Lee, 1768?–1858 (Mrs. Richard Bland Lee)

Richard Bland Lee, son of Henry Lee (q.v.) and Lucy (Grymes) Lee and brother of Henry ("Light-Horse Harry") Lee, was born on January 20, 1761, at Leesylvania, Prince William County. He attended the College of William and Mary in 1780. As a young man he removed to Sully, an estate in Loudoun County (later Fairfax County) which in 1787 he inherited from his father. He represented Loudoun County in the Virginia House of Delegates 1784–88, sat in the First United States Congress and the two subsequent Congresses 1789–95, and was thereafter returned to the state legislature 1796, 1799–1800. Lee moved to Washington, D.C., in 1815; the next year he was appointed by President James Madison to the commission to settle claims for property destroyed during the War of 1812. In 1819 President Monroe appointed him judge of the Orphan's Court of the District of Columbia, an office he held until his death in Washington, D.C., on March 12, 1827. Lee's wife, whom he married on June 19, 1794, was Elizabeth (Collins) Lee, daughter of Stephen and Mary (Parish) Collins of Philadelphia; she bore him six children, two of whom died in infancy; she survived her husband by more than thirty years, dying on June 25, 1858, in her ninety-first year.

DAB; *Biographical Directory*; *Lee of Virginia*, pp. 370–72; *Virginia Cavalcade* 20, no. 2 (1970): 26–33 (both portraits reproduced, p. 27). See chart on Lee Portraits for relationships.

Portrait I. Richard Bland Lee

COPIED BY ALICE MATILDA READING

Oil on canvas: $30^1/4$ x 25 in. (76.8 x 63.5 cm.)

Presented in 1934 by Mr. and Mrs. J. Collins Lee of Hartford, Connecticut. Por934.23

Portrait II. Elizabeth (Collins) Lee

COPIED BY ALICE MATILDA READING

Oil on canvas: $9^1/2$ x $7^1/2$ in. (24.1 x 19.1 cm.) (oval)

Presented in 1934 by Mr. and Mrs. J. Collins Lee of Hartford, Connecticut. Por934.24

Robert Edward Lee, 1807–1870

Robert Edward Lee, a commanding figure in the nation's history and the South's most revered son, was born at Stratford, Westmoreland County, January 19, 1807, the fifth child of Henry ("Light-Horse Harry") Lee and Ann Hill (Carter) Lee. He graduated from West Point in 1829 and as a career army officer spent the next seventeen years in routine duty at Fort Pulaski, Fortress Monroe, and Fort Hamilton and in St. Louis. In 1846 he participated in General Winfield Scott's Veracruz expedition, winning for his conduct in Mexico three brevets and promotion to the rank of colonel. On his return to the United States he supervised the construction of Fort Carroll in Baltimore; in 1852, greatly against his wishes, he was appointed superintendent of the Military Academy at West Point. Reassigned to line duty at his own request, Lee was on the West Texas frontier 1857–61. On the secession of Virginia he resigned his commission and was made general in the Army of the Confederate States. Much of the first year of the war he spent as military adviser to President Davis, but with the wounding of General Joseph E. Johnston at the battle of Seven Pines, on May 31, 1862, he was transferred to the command of the Army of Northern Virginia where he remained until the war's end. Initially successful at such engagements as the Seven Days battles and Second Manassas, Lee was obliged, after reverses in the Maryland and Pennsylvania campaigns, to adopt a largely defensive posture. From the Wilderness to Petersburg he fought what was essentially a rearguard action; dislodged at Petersburg, his depleted forces were surrounded by Grant's larger forces at Appomattox; he surrendered on April 6, 1865. General Lee spent the months immediately after the war at his house in Richmond and later at Derwent, his farm in Powhatan County. Accepting the presidency of Washington College (later Washington and Lee University), he removed with his family to Lexington in the autumn of 1865. An example to all former Confederates, he devoted the remaining five years of his life to education and to the healing of old animosities. He died, universally mourned, on October 12, 1870, and is buried in Lexington. General Lee married on June 30, 1831, Mary Anna Randolph Custis, only daughter of George Washington Parke Custis (q.v.) and Mary Lee (Fitzhugh) Custis; she bore him seven children, only two of whom left issue.

DAB; *Generals in Gray*; *Biographic Catalogue*. See chart on Lee Portraits for relationships.

Portrait I   *See* Plate 17

BY EDWARD CALEDON BRUCE

Oil on canvas: 21 x 17 in. (53.3 x 43.2 cm.). Inscribed on the back: "Gen. R. E. Lee by E. C. Bruce, after his study from life."

Received in 1906 as a bequest of Dr. James Brown McCaw of Richmond. Por906.1

This likeness is thought to be a study for Bruce's full-length portrait painted in Richmond in the fall of 1864. The full-length portrait was exhibited in the state Capitol the following February. There Warren

Akin, a representative from Georgia to the Confederate Congress, saw it and described it in a letter to his wife, adding, "The picture does not come up to my expectation, but it is a good picture." In 1898 it became the property of Charles Broadway Rouss (q.v.) of New York City. In a lengthy autobiographical letter the artist recalled that during his residence in Richmond during the Civil War "I executed, in such leisure moments as I could get, 8 or 10 portraits besides that of General Lee, among them the family of Dr. McCaw" (*Portraiture*, pp. 143–44). It will be observed that the Society's canvas came as a bequest of the same Dr. McCaw. Two other Lee portraits which closely resemble the Society's portrait are owned by the National Portrait Gallery, Washington, D.C., and the Pennsylvania Academy of the Fine Arts. Still another wartime life portrait of Lee is supposed to have been painted by J. W. King (see portrait note under William Edwin Starke); its present whereabouts are not known.

Louise Pecquet du Bellet, *Some Prominent Virginia Families* (Lynchburg, Va., 1907), 2: 222 (full-length portrait reproduced); Warren Akin, *Letters of Warren Akin, Confederate Congressman*, ed. Bell Irvin Wiley (Athens, Ga., 1959), p. 107; *Portraiture*, pp. 62–63, 143–44; Roy Meredith, *The Face of Robert E. Lee in Life and Legend* (New York, 1947), pp. 70–71 (portrait reproduced); *Virginia Cavalcade* 19, no. 1 (1969): 45 (portrait reproduced); *VMHB* 14 (1906–7): vii.

Portrait II

BY MARIETTA MINNIGERODE ANDREWS and ELIPHALET FRAZER ANDREWS. 1907

Oil on canvas: 48 x 38 in. (121.9 x 96.5 cm.). Inscribed on the back: "Gen. Robert E. Lee. Painted by E. F. Andrews and M. M. Andrews. Jan. 19, 1907."

Presented by Marietta Minnigerode Andrews in 1907. Por907.2

In a letter to the president of the Virginia Historical Society dated January 15, 1907, Marietta Minnigerode Andrews made the following observations about the portrait: "We—my husband and I—for without his assistance and advice I had been unable to accomplish this work—have based this portrait upon a photograph taken by Brady, of Washington, on the porch of this very house, now the home of your Society, at the time when General Lee resided in it. We have also used a death-mask by Clarke [*sic*] Mills, numerous other photographs, and been greatly assisted by the criticisms of many persons whose memory of Gen'l. Lee is still vivid. Our aim has been to emphasise the resolution, vigor and intellect of this remarkable man, with his calm, dignified and unostentatious bearing. If the portrait seems at first unfamiliar and unusual to you, we feel that in time it will grow upon you and win for itself a place in your esteem."

17. Robert Edward Lee, 1807–1870 (Portrait I)

Portrait III

BY ALEXANDER DOYLE. Signed. Dated 1884

Statuette in bronze: 20³/4 in. (52.7 cm.) in height, exclusive of base

Presented in 1937 by William A. Willingham of Richmond. Por937.13

Portraiture, p. 129.

Portrait IV

BY JOHN P. WALKER. Signed. Dated 1896

Oil on canvas: 81 x 48 in. (205.7 x 121.9 cm.)

Acquired in 1946 through merger with the Confederate Memorial Association. Por946.233

Roy Meredith, *The Face of Robert E. Lee in Life and Legend* (New York, 1947), p. 118 (portrait reproduced).

Portrait V

BY MOSES JACOB EZEKIEL. Signed

Bronze bust: 7 in. (17.8 cm.) in height, including base

Presented in 1948 by an anonymous donor. Por948.2

At some time in the 1880s Ezekiel was approached by a committee that planned to place a statue of the youthful Robert E. Lee at Stratford, Lee's birthplace in Westmoreland County. To help raise money for the proposed monument, Ezekiel modeled a seven-inch bust of Lee and sent a "boxfull" of the small bronze casts to the committee to sell. And that, according to the sculptor, was the last he ever heard of either the monument or the box full of small bronzes. Several of the latter are now in institutional collections: at Washington and Lee University, Virginia Military Institute, the Corcoran Gallery, the Confederate Museum, and the Virginia Historical Society.

Joseph Gutmann and Stanley F. Chyet, eds., *Moses Jacob Ezekiel: Memoirs from the Baths of Diocletian* (Detroit, 1975), p. 33, 68 (bust reproduced p. 34); *VMHB* 57 (1949): 206, 220; VHS Archives, liber A11, p. 60.

Portrait VI

ATTRIBUTED TO W. B. COX

Oil on canvas: 21¹/2 x 17¹/2 in. (54.6 x 44.5 cm.)

Presented in 1957 by Sally (Wellford) Hamilton of Charlottesville and the estate of Roberta Wellford. Por957.29

Formerly the property of Major Philip Alexander Wellford, C.S.A., the portrait came to the Society from his daughters as a memorial to their father. Information received with the portrait states that the subject's daughter, Mildred Lee, was especially fond of the portrait and considered it one of the best likenesses of her father she had ever seen. The painting appears to be derived from two photographs of Lee taken at the Richmond studio of J. Vannerson early in 1864, the body from a full-length pose depicting Lee wearing his military sash and dress sword, the head from a three-quarter view taken on the same occasion. Although the Society's portrait is not signed, it may well be the work of the Missouri artist W. B. Cox, for a second portrait exists which is strikingly similar to the Society's portrait and which bears Cox's name on the face of the canvas, and on the back "By W. B. Cox, Richmond, Virginia. 1865." Cox's likeness of Lee, presumably the signed portrait, was the subject of the following notice in the *Richmond Times* of August 2, 1865: "Portrait Painting . . . We notice a full length portrait of General Lee in the window of Mr. E. O. Townsend's bookstore. It has deservedly attracted much attention. . . . The artistic performance, the blending of light and shade, the almost tangible distinctness of the various articles of dress and uniform, are the work of the most unusual talent. The artist is Mr. W. B. Cox, a young Missourian, who, since the war, has located himself in this city on Marshall St., between 9th and 10th." Despite minor differences in the uniform and quite different backgrounds (the Society's portrait depicts Lee against a mountain landscape, while the signed portrait shows him standing outside his tent, his war-horse and an orderly in the background), it is

Robert Edward Lee, 1807–1870 (Portrait VI)

not unlikely that the two portraits are by the same hand.

Roy Meredith, *The Face of Robert E. Lee in Life and Legend* (New York, 1947), pp. 47, 49; VHS correspondence files, 1957, letters of Sally Wellford Hamilton; *VMHB* 66 (1958): 237; *Virginia Cavalcade* 11, no. 4 (1962): 4 (portrait reproduced); photographs of the Cox portrait filed in the Society's collection of prints and photographs.

Portrait VII

See The Battle Abbey Murals. The Summer Mural

Robert Edward Lee, 1843–1914

The youngest son of Robert Edward Lee (1807–1870) (q.v.) and Mary Anna Randolph (Custis) Lee, the subject was born at Arlington on October 27, 1843. He entered the University of Virginia in the autumn of 1860 but interrupted his academic career a few months later to take up arms, first in the Southern Guard, one of the university companies, and later as a private in the Rockbridge Artillery. With this command he participated in the Valley campaign, the Seven Days, Cedar Mountain, Second Manassas, and Sharpsburg. In October 1862 he was appointed to the staff of his brother General William Henry Fitzhugh Lee (q.v.) and in that capacity served till the end of the war, rising to the rank of captain. After Appomattox he turned to farming, first at White House in New Kent County, a year later at his own estate, Romancoke, in King William County. He remained at Romancoke for the rest of his life with the exception of a period of five or six years in the 1890s when he was engaged in the real estate business in Washington, D.C. On November 16, 1871, he married Charlotte Taylor Haxall, daughter of Richard Barton Haxall and Octavia (Robinson) Haxall of Richmond; she died without issue less than a year later. After spending more than twenty years as a widower, he married second, on March 8, 1894, Juliet Carter, daughter of Thomas Henry Carter (q.v.) and Susan (Roy) Carter of Pampatike, King William County. Captain Lee was the author of *Recollections and Letters of General Robert E. Lee* (1904). He died at Nordley, his summer home in Fauquier County, on October 19, 1914, survived by his wife and two daughters. He became a member of the Virginia Historical Society in 1881.

Biographic Catalogue; *VMHB* 23 (1915): xxxvi–li; *Lee of Virginia*, pp. 507–8. See chart on Lee Portraits for relationships.

By JOHN P. WALKER. Signed. Dated 1924

Oil on canvas: 30 x 25 in. (76.2 x 63.5 cm.)

Presented to the R. E. Lee Camp, Confederate Veterans, in 1925 by the daughters of the subject; acquired by the Virginia Historical Society in 1946

through merger with the Confederate Memorial Association. Por946.66

Robert Edward Lee, 1869–1922

Eldest son of William Henry Fitzhugh Lee and Mary Tabb (Bolling) Lee (qq.v.) and grandson of General Robert Edward Lee, C.S.A. (q.v.), the subject was born in Petersburg on February 11, 1869. He attended the Episcopal High School in Alexandria 1880–86 and in 1892 graduated from the law school of Washington and Lee University. After practicing his profession for several years, he retired because of frail health. He represented Fairfax County in the Virginia House of Delegates 1901–2, 1904–6 and served for some time as aide-de-camp to Governor Andrew Jackson Montague. On July 2, 1919, he married Mary Wilkinson (Middleton) Pinckney of Charleston, S.C., daughter of Ralph Izard Middleton and widow of Gustavus Memminger Pinckney; the couple resided at Ravensworth, Lee's Fairfax County estate, until his death, which occurred on September 7, 1922. They had no children. Lee was a member of the Virginia Historical Society.

History of Virginia, 5: 46–47; *Burke's Presidential Families of the United States of America* (London, 1975), p. 47. See chart on Lee Portraits for relationships.

By "CHARLES J. FOX" (i.e., Irving Reskinoff). Signed

Miniature on ivory: 3¾ x 3 in. (9.5 x 7.6 cm.)

Received from the heirs of Dr. George Bolling Lee. Por977.30

The subject is depicted as an infant.

Stephen Dill Lee, 1833–1908

The youngest lieutenant general in the Confederate army, General Lee was born at Charleston, South Carolina, on September 22, 1833, son of Thomas and Caroline (Allison) Lee. He graduated from West Point in 1854, performed frontier duty in Texas, and took part in the Seminole War. At the beginning of hostilities he entered Confederate service as aide-de-camp to General Beauregard; later, as major of artillery, he took part in the engagements at Seven Pines, Malvern Hill, Second Manassas, and Sharpsburg. Promoted to brigadier general on November 6, 1862, he was sent to Vicksburg, remaining there until its capitulation. Rising successively to major general and lieutenant general, Lee commanded all cavalry west of Alabama, then led General Hood's old corps through the Tennessee campaign and the final days of the war. Thereafter for twelve years General Lee resided on his farm in Mississippi; in 1878 he was elected to the state Senate. In 1880 he became first president of the Mississippi Agricultural and Mechanical College, holding that office until appointed in 1899 to the Vicksburg Military Park Commission. General Lee published numerous articles on Civil War subjects; he was president of the Mississippi Historical Society and one of the organizers of the State Department of Archives and History. He was commander in chief of the United Confederate Veterans from 1904 until his death in Vicksburg on May 28, 1908. His wife, Regina (Harrison) Lee, whom he married on February 9, 1865, was a daughter of James Thomas Harrison and Regina (Blewett) Harrison of Columbus, Mississippi.

DAB; Generals in Gray; Biographic Catalogue.

ARTIST UNIDENTIFIED

Oil on canvas: 60 x 39½ in. (152.4 x 100.3 cm.)

Presented to the R. E. Lee Camp, Confederate Veterans, in 1907; acquired by the Virginia Historical Society in 1946 through merger with the Confederate Memorial Association. Por946.218

William Henry Fitzhugh Lee, 1837–1891
Mary Tabb (Bolling) Lee, 1848–1924 (Mrs. William Henry Fitzhugh Lee)

"Rooney," as he was known alike to family and friends, was the second son of Robert Edward Lee (1807–1870) (q.v.) and Mary Anna Randolph (Custis) Lee; he was born at Arlington on May 31, 1837. After studying at Harvard, he spent two years in the United States Army then resigned his commission in 1859 to devote himself to farming at White House, his plantation in New Kent County. When Virginia seceded from the Union he offered his services to the Confederacy; he organized a cavalry company, and later, under the command of J. E. B. Stuart, he participated with the 9th Virginia Cavalry in nearly all the cavalry operations of the Army of Northern Virginia. In November 1862 he was promoted to brigadier general, commanding his brigade at Chancellorsville, Fredericksburg, and Gettysburg. He was captured in June 1863 and not exchanged until the following March, whereupon he was promoted to major general and for the remaining months of the war distinguished himself in such engagements as Globe Tavern, Five Forks, and Appomattox. After the war Lee returned to farming, removing in 1874 to Ravensworth in Fairfax County; he was at one time president of the Virginia Agricultural Society. Entering politics, he was elected to one term in the

Virginia state Senate 1875–78 and to three terms in the United States Congress, serving from 1887 until his death at Ravensworth on October 15, 1891. General Lee was twice married: first in 1859 to Charlotte Wickham; second, on November 28, 1867, to Mary Tabb Bolling, a daughter of George Washington Bolling (q.v.) and Martha S. (Nicholls) Bolling of Petersburg. Mary Tabb (Bolling) Lee, who was born on August 27, 1848, and died in Richmond on May 24, 1924, bore her husband two sons, Robert Edward Lee and George Bolling Lee (qq.v.); the children of Lee's first marriage died in infancy.

DAB; Generals in Gray; Biographical Directory; CMA Archives, folio Z1n; *Biographic Catalogue.* See chart on Lee Portraits for relationships.

Portrait I. William Henry Fitzhugh Lee

BY JOHN P. WALKER. Signed. Dated 1924

Oil on canvas: 30 x 25 in. (76.2 x 63.5 cm.)

Presented to the R. E. Lee Camp, Confederate Veterans, in 1925 by the subject's son, Dr. George Bolling Lee; acquired by the Virginia Historical Society in 1946 through merger with the Confederate Memorial Association. Por946.171

Portrait II. William Henry Fitzhugh Lee

BY WILLIAM GARL BROWN. Signed

Oil on canvas: 30¼ x 25¼ in. (76.8 x 64.1 cm.)

Received in 1949 from the heirs of Dr. George Bolling Lee. Por949.19

Portrait III. William Henry Fitzhugh Lee

ARTIST UNIDENTIFIED

Miniature on ivory: 1 in. (2.5 cm.) in diameter (round)

Received from the heirs of Dr. George Bolling Lee. Por977.32

Portrait IV. Mary Tabb (Bolling) Lee

ARTIST UNIDENTIFIED

Oil on canvas: 31¼ x 26¼ in. (79.4 x 66.7 cm.)

Received in 1949 from the heirs of Dr. George Bolling Lee. Por949.20

Portrait V. Mary Tabb (Bolling) Lee

BY "CHARLES J. FOX" (i.e., Irving Resnikoff). Signed. Ca. 1930

Miniature on ivory: 3¼ x 2½ in. (8.3 x 6.4 cm.) (oval)

Received from the heirs of Dr. George Bolling Lee. Por977.27

The likeness was taken from a photograph by Michael Miley.

Portrait VI. Mary Tabb (Bolling) Lee

By "CHARLES J. FOX" (i.e., Irving Resnikoff)

Miniature on ivory: 4¼ x 3¼ in. (11 x 8.3 cm.) (oval)

Received from the heirs of Dr. George Bolling Lee. Por977.28

Benjamin Watkins Leigh, 1781–1849

Born in Chesterfield County on June 18, 1781, the subject was the son of the Reverend William Leigh and Elizabeth (Watkins) Leigh. He attended the College of William and Mary, studied law, and began practicing in Petersburg in 1802. After representing Dinwiddie County in the Virginia House of Delegates 1811–13, he removed to Richmond where he rose rapidly in his chosen profession. He prepared the revised Code of Virginia in 1819 and in 1822 represented Virginia in the controversy with Kentucky concerning Revolutionary bounty lands. He was a delegate to the Virginia Convention of 1829–30, a reporter of the Virginia Court of Appeals 1829–41, and was again elected to the Virginia legislature, representing Henrico County in the session of 1830–31. Leigh was elected as a Whig to the United States Senate to fill the vacancy caused by the resignation of William Cabell Rives (q.v.); he was reelected in 1835 and served from February 26, 1834, until his resignation on July 4, 1836. Thereafter he resumed the practice of law in Richmond. He died there on February 2, 1849, and is buried in Shockoe Cemetery. Leigh was married three times: on December 24, 1802, to Mary Selden Watkins; on November 30, 1813, to Susan Colston; on November 24, 1821, to Julia Wickham; he left numerous descendants. Benjamin Watkins Leigh was a founding member (1831) of the Virginia Historical Society and first chairman of its standing committee.

DAB; *Biographical Directory*; *Portraiture*, pp. 64–65 (Portrait II reproduced); *Richmond Portraits*, p. 107 (Portrait I reproduced); *VMHB* 29 (1921): 156 (Portrait III reproduced) and 67 (1959): 353 (Portrait II reproduced).

Portrait I

BY JAMES BARTON LONGACRE. 1835

Watercolor on cardboard: 7 x 5 in. (17.8 x 12.7 cm.) (oval). Inscribed on the back: "B. W. Leigh 1835 Painted by Mr. Longacre of Philadelphia."

Provenance unknown. PorXi

In 1928 the Society received from Miss Agnes C. Robinson of Washington, D.C., a daughter of Conway Robinson and a granddaughter of Benjamin Watkins Leigh, what is described in the Society's accession records as an "engraved portrait of Benjamin Watkins Leigh by Longacre, 1835." Inasmuch as the Society owns a watercolor portrait of Leigh with Longacre's name and the date 1835 inscribed on the back, and inasmuch as there is no information in the Society's records as to how the watercolor came into its possession, and inasmuch as there is no engraving of Leigh in the Society's collection, it is not unreasonable to suppose that the watercolor was, in fact, the likeness presented by Miss Robinson, and that the accession record erred in stating that it was an engraved portrait. It is known that Longacre painted another likeness of Leigh in 1856, some seven years after Leigh's death, a copy from "an early portrait." For this copy, executed for Mrs. Conway Robinson, the artist received the sum of $3.

Robert G. Stewart, *A Nineteenth-Century Gallery of Distinguished Americans* (Washington, D.C., 1969), p. 2; VHS Archives, liber B6, p. 169; *Portraiture*, p. 65; *Richmond Portraits*, p. 107 (Portrait I reproduced).

Portrait II

ARTIST UNIDENTIFIED

Oil on canvas: 30¼ x 25 in. (76.8 x 63.5 cm.) (oval)

Presented in 1936 by Benjamin Watkins Leigh of Vineyard Haven, Massachusetts, and Ellen Carter Leigh, grandchildren of the subject. Por936.6

Portrait III

COPIED BY —— ANDERSON. Signed: "Anderson, 785 B'way, New York."

Watercolor on paper: 14½ x 11½ in. (36.8 x 29.2 cm.)

Benjamin Watkins Leigh (Portrait II)

Provenance unknown. PorX323

Portrait III is a copy of Portrait II.

Portrait IV
See The Convention of 1829–30

William Leigh, 1773–1871
See The Convention of 1829–30

Elizabeth Dabney (Langhorne) Lewis, 1851–1946 (Mrs. John Henry Lewis)

Born in Botetourt County on December 9, 1851, daughter of John Scaisbrooke Langhorne and Sarah Elizabeth (Dabney) Langhorne, the subject later moved with her parents to Lynchburg, where she was educated by tutors and in private schools. On August 13, 1873, she married John Henry Lewis (1841–1907), a Lynchburg attorney, son of Henry Harrison Lewis and Lucy (Schoolfield) Lewis; the couple had three children. Well known for her quick wit and intense interest in politics, she was active in the women's suffrage movement, in promoting legislation for improving working conditions for women in industry, and in the League of Nations Association, the American Red Cross, the Unitarian church, and the League of Women Voters. She remained

Elizabeth Dabney (Langhorne) Lewis

active and an independent thinker through the whole of her long life; "she voted Socialist at eighty," according to one member of her family, "because she said she was tired of both Republicans and Democrats." Invited to preside over a reception in Lynchburg honoring her niece, Nancy, Lady Astor (q.v.), she was taken sick on the day of the event and died on January 30, 1946.

Occasional Bulletin, no. 32 (1976): 3–5 (portrait reproduced); Virginia State Bar Association, *Proceedings* 20 (1907): 64–66; Lynchburg *Daily Advance*, Jan. 31, 1946; *VMHB* 85 (1977): 240.

By Scaisbrooke Langhorne Abbot. Signed. Dated 1929

Oil on canvas: 49 x 40 in. (124.5 x 101.6 cm.)

Presented in 1976 by Elizabeth (Otey) Watson (Mrs. William C. Watson) of Lynchburg, a granddaughter of the subject. Por976.2

Frances Fielding Lewis, ca. 1802 – ca. 1846
See Frances Fielding (Lewis) Taylor, ca. 1802 – ca. 1846

Ellen Bankhead Lightfoot, 1818–1887
See Ellen Bankhead (Lightfoot) Wormeley, 1818–1887

Reuben Lindsay, 1747–1831

Son of James and Sarah (Daniel) Lindsay, the subject was born on January 15, 1747. He removed to Albemarle County about 1776, making his home on the east side of the Southwest Mountains on an estate of seven hundred and fifty acres; during the next twenty years he acquired a further two thousand acres. He served during the Revolution as a colonel of the Albemarle County militia; he was also a county magistrate. He was twice married: first, on October 20, 1774, to Sarah Walker, daughter of Dr. Thomas and Mildred (Thornton) Walker of Castle Hill, Albemarle County; second, to Hannah Tidwell. He had children by both marriages. Lindsay was a member of the Virginia General Assembly for the session 1807–8. He died in Albemarle County in 1831.

Fillmore Norfleet, *Saint-Mémin in Virginia: Portraits and Biographies* (Richmond, 1942), p. 186; Edgar Woods, *Albemarle County in Virginia* (Bridgewater, Va., 1932), p. 257; *VMHB* 10 (1902–3): 97, 203, and 72 (1964): 241.

Copied by an unidentified artist

Oil on canvas: 30 x 25 in. (76.2 x 63.5 cm.) (oval)

Received in 1963 as a bequest of Marie-Louise B. Pryor (Mrs. Morris McKim Pryor) of New York City. Por963.19

The portrait is an adaptation in oils of a profile likeness made in 1808 by Charles B. J. Fevret de Saint-Mémin.

Richard Logan, 1789?–1869

See The Convention of 1829–30

Thomas Muldrup Logan, 1840–1914

The tenth child of Judge George William Logan and Anna D'Oyley (Glover) Logan, the subject was born in Charleston, South Carolina, on November 3, 1840. He graduated from South Carolina College in 1860, took part as a private in the Washington Light Infantry in the bombardment of Fort Sumter, and was elected first lieutenant of Company A, Hampton Legion. Seeing action at First and Second Manassas, he was wounded at Gaines's Mill and promoted to major for bravery at Sharpsburg. He became on February 15, 1865, the youngest brigadier general then in the Confederate army; transferred to Johnston's army, he commanded a cavalry brigade during the closing operations against Sherman. On May 25, 1865, Logan married Kate Virginia Cox, daughter of Judge James H. Cox and Martha Reid (Law) Cox of Chesterfield County; they became the parents of eleven children. Establishing himself in Richmond, he practiced law, then embarked on what was to become a highly successful career in railroads. In 1878 he formed a new corporation, the Richmond and West Point Terminal Company, which gained control of the Richmond & Danville Railroad and various other southern lines, becoming in time the Southern Railway system. In 1890 Logan acquired the Seattle, Lake Shore and Eastern Railroad, which he later sold at a substantial profit to the Northern Pacific. During the latter years of his life he invested heavily in the development of communications equipment. General Logan was chairman of the Virginia Democratic Executive Committee in 1879 and of the Virginia Gold Democratic Party in 1896. He became a member of the Virginia Historical Society in 1881. He died in New York City on August 11, 1914, and is buried in Hollywood Cemetery, Richmond.

DAB; *Generals in Gray*; *Men of Mark in Virginia*, 4: 257–61; *Biographic Catalogue*.

ARTIST UNIDENTIFIED

Oil on canvas: 44 x 27 in. (111.8 x 68.6 cm.)

Presented to the R. E. Lee Camp, Confederate Vet-

150

erans, by the subject prior to 1903; acquired by the Virginia Historical Society in 1946 through merger with the Confederate Memorial Association. Por946.210

John Tayloe Lomax, 1781–1862

Judge Lomax was born on January 19, 1781, at Portobago, Caroline County, son of Thomas and Anne Corbin (Tayloe) Lomax. He graduated from St. John's College, Annapolis, studied law, and in 1805 was admitted to the bar. From 1810 to 1818 he practiced his profession in Richmond County, serving during the War of 1812 as an officer in the militia for the defense of the area. Thereafter he returned to Fredericksburg, where he attained eminence at the bar; in 1826 he was invited to Charlottesville as first professor of law at the University of Virginia; the following year he became chairman of the faculty. His sojourn at the university was of brief duration, for in 1830 the General Assembly elected him associate judge of the circuit superior court of law and chancery; assigned to the fifth judicial circuit, he returned to Fredericksburg, where he resided for the rest of his life. In addition to his judicial duties, Judge Lomax conducted a private law school in Fredericksburg and wrote a three-volume *Digest of the Laws Respecting Real Property* (1839) and a two-volume *Treatise on the Law of Executors and Administrators* (1841). After twenty-seven years of faithful service on the bench, he resigned his judgeship in 1857. Deeply shocked by the developing hostility between North and South, Judge Lomax is said to have burst into tears as he cast his ballot in favor of the Ordinance of Secession and to have exclaimed, "To think that I have survived the nation!" He did not long survive; he died a few weeks before the defeat of Burnside at Fredericksburg, on October 1, 1862. Judge Lomax's wife, whom he married on July 25, 1805, was Charlotte Belson (Thornton) Lomax, daughter of Presley and Elizabeth (Thornton) Thornton of Northumberland County; the couple had two sons.

DAB; *Occasional Bulletin*, no. 12 (1966): 2–5 (portrait reproduced); [Edward Lloyd Lomax], *Genealogy of the Virginia Family of Lomax* (Chicago, 1913), pp. 29–33, 38 (portrait reproduced, p. 30).

BY WALTER GOULD. Signed. Dated: 18[ ]

Oil on canvas: 34 1/4 x 25 in. (87 x 63.5 cm.)

A bequest of Edward Lloyd Lomax of Fredericksburg. Received in 1966 from his son, Edward Lloyd Lomax of Redwood City, California. Por966.2

The Fredericksburg *Weekly Advertiser* of August 1, 1857, announced that Judge Lomax had consented to sit for a full-length portrait by John Adams Elder.

VMHB 75 (1967): 240; *Occasional Bulletin*, no. 12 (1966): 2–5; *Appletons' Cyclopaedia of American Biography* (New York, 1887), 2: 696; Nicholas B. Wainwright, *Paintings and Miniatures at the Historical Society of Pennsylvania* (Philadelphia, 1974), p. 320; *Portraits and Statuary*, p. 68.

John Tayloe Lomax

The December 19 issue stated that the finished portrait was on display and that lithographic copies of it were available to subscribers. On the basis of these notices the Society's portrait, although not full length, has heretofore been attributed to Elder. It is now reattributed to Walter Gould (1829–1893) on the evidence of a partial signature, "W. Go[   ] 18[   ]" barely visible in the lower right corner of the painting. Flaking paint where the canvas is attached to the stretcher accounts for the loss. A native Philadelphian and one of Thomas Sully's pupils, Gould first exhibited at the Artists' Fund Society in 1843. He worked thereafter in Philadelphia and in Fredericksburg "where he painted a large number of portraits, nearly all of which were destroyed during the Civil War." In 1849 he went to Florence, Italy; he never returned to the United States. It will be noted that Gould's removal to Florence took place when he was twenty years old. Thus the American career of this prodigy extended from his fourteenth to his twentieth year! The Society's portrait of Judge Lomax is an appealing and sensitive likeness; it is the more remarkable as the work of an artist not yet out of his teens. A painting thought to be a replica or a copy of the Society's canvas belongs to the Commonwealth of Virginia. The Commonwealth owns a second portrait of Lomax: a three-quarter-length, unattributed portrait that may possibly be the likeness painted by Elder in 1857.

Armistead Lindsay Long, 1825–1891

General Long, born on September 3, 1825, was a native of Campbell County, the son of Armistead and Calista (Cralle) Long. After graduating from West Point in the class of 1850, he served with the regular army in the Indian Territory, Kansas, and Nebraska. In 1860 he married Mary Heron Sumner, daughter of General Edwin Vose Sumner, United States Army. He was appointed aide-de-camp to his father-in-law on May 20, 1861, but resigned his commission three weeks later to join the Army of the Confederacy as a major in the artillery. After brief service in western Virginia, he was assigned to General Robert E. Lee in Charleston, South Carolina; when General Lee became commander of the Army of Northern Virginia he appointed Long to his staff as military secretary with the rank of colonel. Although Long was a valuable member of Lee's headquarters, his tactical abilities were later needed in the field; in September 1863 he was assigned to command the artillery of the 2d Corps, with the rank of brigadier general. He continued in this capacity until Appomattox. After the war General Long became chief engineer of the James River and Kanawha Canal Company, but blindness led to his retirement in 1870. Thereafter he devoted himself to writing, contributing articles to various periodicals and publishing in 1886 his major work, *Memoirs of Robert E. Lee*. General Long died on April 29, 1891, in Charlottesville, where his wife had been for some years employed as postmistress.

DAB; *Generals in Gray*.

ARTIST UNIDENTIFIED

Oil on canvas: 30 x 25 in. (76.2 x 63.5 cm.)

Acquired in 1946 through merger with the Confederate Memorial Association. Por946.142

James Longstreet, 1821–1904
See The Battle Abbey Murals. The Summer Mural

George Loyall, 1797–1868
See The Convention of 1829–30

Anne César, Chevalier de la Luzerne, 1741–1791

Born in Paris in 1741, la Luzerne embarked as a mere lad on a military career, rising rapidly to the rank of major general of the cavalry. Abandoning the military life for that of a diplomat, he was sent as envoy to the elector of Bavaria in 1777; he conducted himself with distinction, successfully concluding a delicate assignment in July 1778. Appointed minister to the United States on November 17, 1779, to replace Conrad Alexandre Gérard (q.v.), who had requested to be relieved because of poor health, la Luzerne arrived in Philadelphia on September 21, 1779, and for four years carried out the duties of his post with consummate tact and skill. Like his predecessor he devoted himself to financing and provisioning the army, exceeding his diplomatic powers to this end and exerting himself tirelessly to enlist congressional support for these objectives. La Luzerne was the first person in Philadelphia to receive news of the victory at Yorktown; to prevent profiteering and speculation that might well have followed the haphazard spread of the news, he dispatched thirty announcements that made the information known virtually simultaneously in various parts of the city. La Luzerne visited Williamsburg in March 1782; he left the United States in 1783, an honored and respected figure. In poor health, he remained for five years with his family; he was made a marquis in 1785, and in January 1788 was appointed ambassador to Great Britain; he died in England on September 14, 1791. La Luzerne was an original member of the Society of the Cincinnati.

Portraits and Miniatures, p. 133; *Michaud's Biographie universelle* (Paris, 1843); Ludovic Guy Marie du Bessey de Contenson, *La Société des Cincinnati de France et la guerre d'Amérique, 1778–1783* (Paris, 1934), p. 201.

By CHARLES WILLSON PEALE

Oil on canvas: 25½ x 21 in. (64.8 x 53.3 cm.)

Presented about 1854 by Catherine Power (Lyons) Chevallié (Mrs. Jean Auguste Marie Chevallié) of Richmond. Por857.4

The subject was misidentified as far back as 1894 when the portrait appeared in the Society's published list as "Duc de Lauzun, bust. Participated in battle of Yorktown as commander of a legion under Rochambeau." The error was not corrected in Weddell's *Portraiture* (1945). The similarity between the names "Luzerne" and "Lauzun" and the fact that both Frenchmen played a significant part in the American War for Independence perhaps account for the confusion and its longevity. The Society's portrait of la Luzerne is a replica of the Charles Willson Peale portrait long displayed in Indepen-

Anne César, chevalier de la Luzerne

dence Hall, Philadelphia. It came into the Society's possession about 1854, together with portraits of the chevalier de Cambray-Digny, Conrad Alexandre Gérard, and Martha Washington. On Rembrandt Peale's visit to Richmond in 1858 he was shown the portraits and "recognized them at once as having been in his father's collection. One of the Frenchmen was the Chevalier De Luzerne, the first [actually the second] French ambassador to the U.S."

A List of the Portraits, Engravings, &c., in the Library of the Virginia Historical Society (Richmond, 1894); *Portraiture*, pp. 56–57; *Portraits and Miniatures*, p. 133; VHS Mss1 R5685b 812.

Hannah Ann (Bosher) Lyon, 1839–1923   (Mrs. Daniel Lyon)

Daughter of John Henry Bosher and Emily (Dill) Bosher (qq.v.) of Richmond, the subject was born in 1839. She married Daniel Lyon, a Richmond tobacco manufacturer who was associated first with the tobacco manufactory of Joseph G. Dill and in the last years of his life with the J. B. Pace Tobacco Company. On his death on May 29, 1905, he was survived by his wife, a son, and two daughters. Mrs. Lyon remained in Richmond after her husband's death. She died in February 1923; she and her husband are buried in Hollywood Cemetery.

Information received with the portrait; Richmond *Times-Dispatch*, May 30, 1905, p. 3, col. 1; *VMHB* 80 (1972): 238; Richmond directories.

ARTIST UNIDENTIFIED

Oil on canvas on panel: 15³/4 x 13 in. (40 x 33 cm.)
(oval)

Received in 1971 as a bequest of Cornelia (Lyon)
Wailes (Mrs. Edward T. Wailes) of Washington,
D.C., a granddaughter of the subject. Por971.9

William Gordon McCabe, 1841–1920

William Gordon McCabe was born in Richmond on
August 4, 1841. He was the son of the Reverend John
Collins McCabe and Sophia Gordon (Taylor) Mc-
Cabe. He grew up in Smithfield and in Hampton;
after his graduation from Hampton Academy he was
tutor to the children of the Selden family at Westover,
then enrolled in the University of Virginia in the
autumn of 1860. The following spring he withdrew
to enlist as a private in the Confederate army. He
served as a private through the Peninsular campaign,
was commissioned first lieutenant of artillery in 1862,
and saw action in the Seven Days and Chancellorsville. After duty in Charleston, South Carolina, and
a brief period on the staff of General Stevens, he
became adjutant of Pegram's Battalion with the
rank of captain, participating with this command in
all its battles from the Wilderness to Appomattox.
Immediately after the war, McCabe opened a school
for boys in Petersburg known as McCabe's University School, or simply McCabe's. He was its headmaster for the thirty years it remained in that city
and for the six years, 1895–1901, it operated in Richmond. The breadth of his scholarship is manifest in
the historical monographs he contributed to various
periodicals and in his biographical studies, classical
textbooks, and literary and poetical works. Elected
to membership in the Virginia Historical Society in
1871, McCabe became the Society's eighth president
in 1903 and its tenth president in 1909. Honorary
degrees were conferred on him by the College of
William and Mary, Williams College, and Yale University. He was a member of the Society of the Cincinnati in Virginia, its twelfth president, and a member of the standing committee of the General Society.
Captain McCabe was twice married: first, on April
9, 1867, to Jane Pleasants Harrison Osborne, who
died in 1912; second, on March 16, 1915, to Gillie
Armistead Cary. Captain McCabe died on June 1,
1920, survived by his second wife and by the children
of his first marriage.

VMHB 28 (1920): 193–205; *Men of Mark in Virginia*, 3:
233–40; *Biographic Catalogue*.

Portrait I

By ELLIS MEYER SILVETTE

Oil on canvas: 30¹/4 x 25 in. (76.8 x 63.5 cm.)

Presented in 1926 by McCabe's University School
Alumni Association. Por926.9

Portrait II

By ELLIS MEYER SILVETTE. Signed. Dated 1927

Oil on canvas: 30 x 24 in. (76.2 x 61 cm.)

Acquired in 1946 through merger with the Confederate Memorial Association. Por946.112

Edward Stephens McCarthy, 1837–1864

The subject was born in Richmond in 1837, the son
of Florence and Julia Anne (Humes) McCarthy. In
1859 he was a salesman for Spotts, Harvey and
Company, wholesale grocers and commission merchants in Richmond. At the outbreak of the Civil
War he became a first lieutenant in the 1st Company
of Richmond Howitzers. He served with this company until his death, rising in rank to captain, and
fighting at First Manassas, the Peninsular campaign,
Fredericksburg, Chancellorsville, Gettysburg, the
Wilderness, and Spotsylvania. He was killed in action
at Cold Harbor on June 4, 1864. His younger brother, Carlton McCarthy, was mayor of Richmond
1904–8.

Carlton McCarthy, ed., *Contributions to a History of the Rich-
mond Howitzer Battalion* (Richmond, 1883–86), 4: 35; *Men of
Mark in Virginia*, 2: 261–63; VHS Mss1 M1275a; CMA
Archives, folio Z1n; Richmond directory, 1859; *Biographic
Catalogue*.

ARTIST UNIDENTIFIED

Oil on canvas: 30 x 25 in. (76.2 x 63.5 cm.)

Presented to the R. E. Lee Camp, Confederate Veterans, in 1898 by the Richmond Howitzer Association; acquired by the Virginia Historical Society in
1946 through merger with the Confederate Memorial Association. Por946.157

Ariana (Gunn) McCartney, 1770–1838
See Edward Cunningham, 1771–1836

John McCausland, 1836–1927

Born on September 13, 1836, shortly after his parents,
John and Harriet (Kyle) McCausland, had moved
to St. Louis, Missouri, from Lynchburg, Virginia,
the subject returned to Virginia for his higher education. Graduating from the Virginia Military Insti-

tute in 1857, he studied one year at the University of Virginia before returning to the Institute as assistant professor of mathematics. At the head of a detachment of cadets he witnessed the execution of John Brown at Charles Town in 1859. On the secession of Virginia he was commissioned colonel of the 36th Virginia Infantry and dispatched to western Virginia and then to Kentucky; he distinguished himself at Fort Donelson and protected the Virginia and Tennessee railroad and the saltpeter works at Saltville from enemy attack. Promoted to brigadier general in May 1864, he was responsible for the defense of Lynchburg and for the Confederate success at Monocacy. On General Early's orders McCausland's men burned Chambersburg, Pennsylvania, on July 30, 1864; subsequently they fought in the Valley, at Petersburg, Five Forks, and Appomattox. Paroled at Charleston, West Virginia, he wandered for two years through Europe and Mexico, then returned to West Virginia where he spent the rest of his years on the large estate he purchased in the Kanawha Valley near Point Pleasant. He married on October 3, 1878, Emma Charlotte Hannah, by whom he had four children. General McCausland died at his home on January 23, 1927.

DAB; Generals in Gray; West Virginia History 4 (1942–43): 239–93; *Biographic Catalogue.*

BY JOHN P. WALKER. Signed. Dated 1926

Oil on canvas: 30 x 25 in. (76.2 x 63.5 cm.)

Presented to the R. E. Lee Camp, Confederate Veterans, in 1926; acquired by the Virginia Historical Society in 1946 through merger with the Confederate Memorial Association. Por946.89

William McComb, 1828–1918

Born on November 21, 1828, in Mercer County, Pennsylvania, McComb removed in 1854 to Clarksville, Tennessee, where he engaged in various commercial enterprises, including the construction of a flour mill on the Cumberland River. When the Civil War began he enlisted as a private in the 14th Tennessee Infantry, rising in rank during the course of the war to brigadier general. He saw action at Cedar Mountain, Second Manassas, and all the battles of the Army of Northern Virginia from the Seven Days to Appomattox. The severe wounds he received at Sharpsburg and Chancellorsville prevented his taking part in the battle of Gettysburg, but he participated in the Overland campaign of 1864 and in the siege of Petersburg. He was made brigadier general to rank from January 20, 1865. After the surrender General McComb spent several years in Alabama and Mississippi, then established himself on a farm in Louisa County, Virginia, where he resided for

more than fifty years. Annie L. Quarles of Louisa became his wife in 1868 and predeceased him by twenty-three years to the day. General McComb died in Gordonsville at the home of his daughter on July 21, 1918, survived by three daughters and a son.

Generals in Gray; Richmond Times-Dispatch, July 22, 1918; *Biographic Catalogue.*

BY JOHN P. WALKER. Signed. Dated 1922

Oil on canvas: 30 x 25 in. (76.2 x 63.5 cm.)

Acquired in 1946 through merger with the Confederate Memorial Association. Por946.162

William McCoy, d. 1864
See The Convention of 1829–30

Hunter Holmes McGuire, 1835–1900

Hunter Holmes McGuire, physician and surgeon, was born in Winchester on October 11, 1835, the son of Dr. Hugh Holmes McGuire and Ann Eliza (Moss) McGuire. He studied at Winchester Academy and graduated from the Winchester Medical College in 1855. Withdrawing from the University of Pennsylvania and the Jefferson Medical College in Philadelphia at the time of the John Brown raid, he resumed his studies in Richmond, then taught briefly at the medical college of the University of Louisiana. With Virginia's secession from the Union he joined the army as a private; he was shortly commissioned and appointed medical director of the Army of the Shenandoah, serving under Stonewall Jackson's command until Jackson's death in 1863. Thereafter Dr. McGuire was surgeon of the 2d Army Corps and successively medical director of the Army of Northern Virginia and of the Army of the Valley. Settling in Richmond at the end of the war, Dr. McGuire was elected to the chair of surgery in the Medical College of Virginia, a position he retained until 1878. In 1883 he founded St. Luke's Home for the Sick (later St. Luke's Hospital) together with a nurse's training school; he was one of the founders in 1893 of the University College of Medicine. His many honors included election to the presidency of the Richmond Academy of Medicine in 1869, the Medical Society of Virginia in 1880, the Southern Surgical and Gynecological Association in 1889, and the American Medical Association in 1896. Dr. McGuire was a contributor to medical and surgical publications; he also contributed monographs on historical subjects, among them an account of the wounding and death of Stonewall Jackson. His death occurred on September 19, 1900. His wife, whom he married in 1866, was Mary (Stuart) McGuire, daughter of Alexander Hugh Holmes Stuart and Frances (Baldwin) Stuart; they had nine children. Dr. McGuire was elected to membership in the Virginia Historical Society in 1875.

DAB; Men of Mark in Virginia, 5: 279–81; *Virginia and Virginians*, 2: 792–93; *Biographic Catalogue*.

Portrait I

BY CORNELIUS HANKINS. Signed. Dated 1897

Oil on canvas: 30 x 25 in. (76.2 x 63.5 cm.)

Presented to the R. E. Lee Camp, Confederate Veterans, in 1897; acquired by the Virginia Historical Society in 1946 through merger with the Confederate Memorial Association. Por946.110

Portrait II

BY JOHN BRODNAX. Signed

Bronze bust: 35¼ in. (89.5 cm.) in height, including base. Base bears inscription: "Hunter Holmes McGuire, 1835–1900, Medical Director Stonewall Jackson's Corps, Army of Northern Virginia."

Presented to the R. E. Lee Camp, Confederate Veterans, in 1924; acquired by the Virginia Historical Society in 1946 through merger with the Confederate Memorial Association. Por946.231

David Gregg McIntosh, 1836–1916

David Gregg McIntosh, son of James H. McIntosh and Martha J. (Gregg) McIntosh of Society Hill, South Carolina, was born there on March 16, 1836. After receiving his formal education at St. David's Academy and South Carolina College in Columbia, he studied law and was admitted to the bar in 1858. When his native state called for troops, he enlisted on January 2, 1861, thereafter serving in the Army of the Confederacy, principally in the artillery, for four years, and rising in rank to colonel. After Appomattox he spent three years in Virginia and South Carolina before removing to Towson, Maryland, where he remained for the rest of his life. Having formed a law partnership with Richard J. Gittings and Arthur W. Machen, he shortly became recognized as one of the leaders of the Maryland bar. In 1879 he was elected by the Democrats as state's attorney for Baltimore County, Maryland. He was a member of the Episcopal church and for many years a member of the vestry of Trinity Church, Towson. His death occurred on October 6, 1916; his remains were taken to Richmond for burial in Hollywood Cemetery. Colonel McIntosh's wife, whom he married on November 8, 1865, was Virginia Johnson (Pegram) McIntosh, a daughter of General James West Pegram and Virginia (Johnson) Pegram and a sister of Wil-

liam Ransom Johnson Pegram (q.v.); the couple had three children, two of whom survived him.

Biographic Catalogue; VHS Mss1 P3496a 440–453; *Virginia Genealogies*, p. 314; Philip Slaughter, *A History of Bristol Parish, with Genealogies of Families Connected Therewith, and Historical Illustrations* (Richmond, 1879), p. 209.

BY THOMAS CROMWELL CORNER. Signed

Oil on canvas: 30 x 25 in. (76.2 x 63.5 cm.)

Acquired in 1946 through merger with the Confederate Memorial Association. Por946.226

Jane Logan McKee, 1812–1883
See Gordon Cloyd Kent, 1806–1869

Joseph Benjamin McKenney, ca. 1842–1898

Born around 1842, the subject enlisted in the Otey Battery, 13th Virginia Battalion, Army of Northern Virginia, on March 27, 1862, and served with the battery until the surrender. He settled in Richmond where he established a dyeing establishment on Marshall Street near Fifth. Active in veterans' affairs, he was one of the founders of the R. E. Lee Camp no. 1 and in 1885 was elected a member of the board of visitors of the Soldiers' Home. On his death, which occurred on April 16, 1898, he was survived by his wife, Sarah Frances McKenney, and eight children; his funeral was from Grace Street Baptist Church, with interment in Shockoe Cemetery.

Biographic Catalogue; Richmond Dispatch, April 17, 1898, p. 14; Richmond *Evening Leader*, April 18, 1898, p. 6; *Richmond Times-Dispatch*, May 28, 1923, p. 9; CMA Archives, folio Z1n.

ARTIST UNIDENTIFIED

Oil on canvas: 30¼ x 25¼ in. (76.8 x 64.1 cm.)

Acquired in 1946 through merger with the Confederate Memorial Association. Por946.117

Lafayette McLaws, 1821–1897

The subject was born in Augusta, Georgia, on January 15, 1821; his parents were James and Elizabeth (Huguenin) McLaws. Following a year at the University of Virginia he entered West Point as a member of the class of 1842. After his graduation he was assigned to various posts in the Indian Territory, Mississippi, Louisiana, and Florida; during the Mexican War he took part in the capture of Monterrey and Veracruz. McLaws resigned from the United States Army on March 23, 1861, and entered Confederate service as colonel of the 10th Georgia Infantry; promoted to brigadier general on September 25, 1861, he earned by his distinguished conduct in the Yorktown campaign a promotion to major general the following May. During 1862 and 1863 his division saw action in the principal engagements of the Army of Northern Virginia, including the capture of Harpers Ferry, Sharpsburg, Fredericksburg, Chancellorsville, and Gettysburg. Charged with failure to prepare adequately for the assault on Knoxville, Tennessee, he was removed from command by Longstreet; subsequently exonerated, he was transferred to the district of Georgia and surrendered with Joseph E. Johnston at Greensboro, North Carolina. After the war General McLaws was employed in the insurance business in Augusta, Georgia. He died in Savannah, Georgia, July 24, 1897, and is buried there. General McLaws married Emily Allison Taylor, a niece of President Zachary Taylor (q.v.).

DAB; *Generals in Gray*.

By Mary McPherson Wickliffe. Signed. Dated 1930

Oil on canvas: 30¼ x 25 in. (76.8 x 63.5 cm.)

Acquired in 1946 through merger with the Confederate Memorial Association. Por946.141

Andrew McMillan
See The Convention of 1829–30

Sarah Catherine Macmurdo, 1833–1909
See Sarah Catherine (Macmurdo) Rives, 1833–1909

John Macrae, 1791–1830
See The Convention of 1829–30

George William Madison

The donor, a great-great-great-nephew of the subject, stated that Madison was a civil engineer for the Richmond, Fredericksburg and Potomac Railroad, responsible for the construction of many of the railroad's bridges. Efforts to identify the sitter further have been unsuccessful.

Artist unidentified

Watercolor on paper mounted on cardboard: 7½ x 6 in. (19.1 x 15.2 cm.) (oval)

Presented in 1977 by Robert W. Corstaphney of Dallas, Texas. Por977.25

James Madison, 1749–1812

The Right Reverend James Madison, first bishop of the Protestant Episcopal Church in Virginia, president of the College of William and Mary, and cousin of the fourth president of the United States, was born on August 27, 1749, near Staunton, the son of John and Agatha (Strother) Madison. He graduated from the College of William and Mary in 1771, studied law, and was admitted to the bar; instead of entering the legal profession, however, he returned to the college in 1773 as professor of natural philosophy and mathematics. Two years later he went to England to study theology; he was ordained, returned to Virginia, and in 1777, although only twenty-eight years of age, was elected president of the College of William and Mary, an office he held for the rest of his life. During the Revolutionary War he served as chaplain to the House of Delegates and as captain of a company of militia recruited from the college. At the end of hostilities he reorganized the college, which had been severely disrupted by the war, its buildings occupied by troops; under his leadership it became once again an effective institution of higher learning. He was appointed in 1779 one of the commissioners to establish the boundary between Virginia and Pennsylvania; he also was responsible for surveys used as a basis for *A Map of Virginia* (1807), commonly known as Madison's Map. Active in revitalizing the Episcopal church in the years after the Revolution, he presided over the first convention of the church in 1785, was elected bishop of Virginia five years after, and on September 19, 1790, was consecrated by the archbishop of Canterbury. Thereafter he devoted himself unstintingly to both ecclesiastical and academic responsibilities, his principal episcopal duty being to organize Virginia's weak, disestablished parishes into a unified diocese. Bishop Madison died on March 6, 1812, and is buried in the college chapel. He married on April 28, 1779, Sarah Tate of Williamsburg; she bore him two children, a son and a daughter.

DAB; *Portraiture*, pp. 69–70; *Virginia Historical Portraiture*, pp. 284–85 (portrait reproduced); *VMHB* 29 (1921): 140–41 (portrait reproduced).

Artist unidentified

Oil on canvas: 64 x 48 in. (162.6 x 122 cm.)

Received in 1901 from Emily Hall and Edwin Hall, great-great-grandchildren of the subject. Por901.1

James Madison, 1751–1836

Dolley (Payne) Todd Madison, 1768–1849 (Mrs. James Madison)

Fourth president of the United States and father of the Constitution, James Madison was born at Port Conway, King George County, on March 16, 1751, eldest child of James and Eleanor (Conway) Madison of Orange County. He graduated from Princeton University in 1771, studied law, and was admitted to the bar. In 1774 he became a member of the Orange County Committee of Safety, and two years later he went to Williamsburg as a delegate to Virginia's Revolutionary Convention. He was elected to the Virginia General Assembly in 1776, to the Executive Council in 1778, and to the Continental Congress in 1780; at the Constitutional Convention held in Philadelphia in 1787 Madison played a dominant part in drafting the federal Constitution. He urged the adoption of the Constitution by the state of Virginia, contributed to the *Federalist Papers*, and was a vocal proponent of the Bill of Rights. Madison sat in the United States House of Representatives 1789–97; while in Congress he supported Jeffersonian policies and collaborated with Jefferson in drafting the Kentucky and Virginia Resolves; he was Jefferson's secretary of state 1801–9. On September 15, 1794, Madison married Dolley (Payne) Todd, daughter of John and Mary (Coles) Payne and widow of John Todd; since Jefferson was a widower, it was Dolley Madison who, as wife of the secretary of state, presided as acting first lady; afterwards she served as first lady in her own right; thus the formidable Dolley held sway over Washington's social scene for more than sixteen years. Madison's two presidential terms extended from March 4, 1809, to March 3, 1817, a period dominated by the War of 1812, its preliminaries and aftermath. In 1817 he retired to Montpelier, his estate in Orange County. Thereafter he dispensed liberal hospitality to innumerable guests, served as rector of the University of Virginia, visitor to the College of William and Mary, and in 1829 emerged from retirement to attend the Virginia Constitutional Convention. He died at Montpelier on June 28, 1836; Dolley Madison died in Washington on July 12, 1849; the couple had no children.

DAB; *Biographical Directory*; *W. & M. Quart.*, 3d ser., 8 (1951): 25–47.

Portrait I. James Madison

COPIED BY THOMAS SULLY

Oil on canvas: 30 x 25 in. (76.2 x 63.5 cm.)

Presented in 1856 by Jaquelin Plummer Taylor of Richmond. Por856.2

Thomas Sully began work on this portrait, a copy of

an original by Gilbert Stuart, on June 6, 1856. He finished it on July 3, 1856.

Edward Biddle and Mantle Fielding, *The Life and Works of Thomas Sully* (Philadelphia, 1921), p. 223; *Portraiture*, pp. 66–69.

James Madison, 1751–1836 (Portrait II)

Portrait II. James Madison

BY PETER CARDELLI. 1819

Plaster bust: 19 in. (48.3 cm.) in height. Inscribed: "Madison."

Presented by John Willis of Orange in 1875. Por875.4

The bust, formerly attributed to John Henry Isaac Browere, has recently been reattributed to Peter Cardelli.

Conover Hunt-Jones, *Dolley and the "Great Little Madison"* (Washington, D.C., 1977), p. 82; *Portraiture*, p. 130; Gaillard Hunt, *The Life of James Madison* (New York, 1902), portrait reproduced as frontispiece; *VMHB* 39 (1931): 324.

Portrait III. James Madison   *See* Plate 18

BY JOSEPH WOOD. Signed. Dated 1817

Oil on wood panel: 9 x 7 in. (22.9 x 17.8 cm.)

Deeded to the Society in 1962 by Katherine W. Davidge (Mrs. John Washington Davidge) of Washington, D.C., and received by the Society in 1967. Por967.13

This life portrait and the companion piece of Dolley Madison (Portrait V) were presented by the subjects in 1817 to their close friends Mr. and Mrs. Richard Bland Lee (qq.v.); they remained in the possession of Lee descendants until their acquisition by the Society. Photographs of the two portraits, tinted by Alice Reading, were given to the Society in 1934; they have heretofore been thought to be paintings.

Occasional Bulletin, no. 15 (1967): 2–6 (Portraits III and V reproduced); Conover Hunt-Jones, *Dolley and the "Great Little Madison"* (Washington, D.C., 1977), pp. 56–57 (Portraits III and V reproduced); *The Papers of James Madison* (Chicago, 1962–), 1: xiii (Portrait III reproduced as frontispiece); *Portraiture*, p. 69 (Reading photographs); *VMHB* 43 (1935): 183 (Reading photographs) and 76 (1968): 242.

Portrait IV. Dolley (Payne) Todd Madison

Artist unidentified

Hollow-cut silhouette: 3 in. (7.6 cm.) in height, on paper $4^{1}/2$ x $3^{3}/4$ in. (11.4 x 9.5 cm.)

Presented in 1950 by Edmund Putzel Waller of Martinsville. Por950.22

Portrait V. Dolley (Payne) Todd Madison
See Plate 19

By Joseph Wood. Signed. Dated 1817

Oil on wood panel: 9 x 7 in. (22.9 x 17.8 cm.)

Deeded to the Society in 1962 by Katherine W. Davidge (Mrs. John Washington Davidge) of Washington, D.C., and received by the Society in 1967. Por967.14

This life portrait is a companion piece to Portrait III.

Portrait VI. James Madison
See The Convention of 1829–30

John Bankhead Magruder, 1807–1871

Born at Port Royal, Virginia, on May 1, 1807, son of Thomas and Elizabeth (Bankhead) Magruder, the subject enrolled in the University of Virginia in 1825 but withdrew after two years to enter West Point. Graduating with the class of 1830, he became an officer in the United States Army. He took part in the occupation of Texas and the Seminole War; in the war with Mexico he commanded the light artillery of Pillow's Division. Resigning his commission on the outbreak of the Civil War, Magruder was appointed colonel in the Confederate army and put in charge of the troops on the Virginia peninsula. Rising in rank

to major general, his initial success on the peninsula was followed by reverses during the Seven Days, for which General Lee held him personally responsible. On October 10, 1862, he was transferred to the command of the District of Texas, which was later enlarged to embrace New Mexico and Arizona. Here he embarked on the fortification of the Texas coast, captured the city of Galveston, and dispersed the blockading fleet. After the war General Magruder refused to seek parole; he went to Mexico where he became a major general in the service of Maximilian. With the downfall of the emperor he settled in Houston, Texas, remaining there until his death, which occurred on February 18, 1871. Although most published sources state that General Magruder never married, one contends that he married Henrietta Von Kapff of Baltimore in 1831, and that at least three children were born of the marriage.

DAB; *Generals in Gray*; *Biographic Catalogue*.

By John P. Walker

Oil on canvas: $30^{1}/4$ x 25 in. (76.8 x 63.5 cm.)

Presented to the R. E. Lee Camp, Confederate Veterans, in 1897; acquired by the Virginia Historical Society in 1946 through merger with the Confederate Memorial Association. Por946.42

John Bowie Magruder, 1839–1863

Born at Scottsville, Virginia, on November 24, 1839, the son of Benjamin Henry Magruder and Maria (Minor) Magruder, the subject removed with his family at an early age to Glenmore, about seven miles from Charlottesville. He attended private schools and the Albemarle Military Academy before enrolling in the University of Virginia in 1856. Graduating with the degree of Master of Arts in June 1860, he taught briefly at Nelson's Academy in Culpeper County until the outbreak of the Civil War, whereupon he left for Lexington for a two-month course of military instruction at the Virginia Military Institute. Thereafter he organized the Rivanna Guards, which became a part of the 57th Virginia Infantry. As captain of Company H, he took part in the battles of Malvern Hill, Cedar Mountain, Thoroughfare Gap, Harpers Ferry, Sharpsburg, and Fredericksburg. Promoted to lieutenant colonel on July 31, 1862, and to colonel the following January, Magruder was posted to Suffolk, then to Gettysburg, where he fell mortally wounded; he died in hospital on July 5, 1863, at twenty-three years of age. His remains were transported to Virginia and interred at Glenmore, Albemarle County.

Biographic Catalogue; *SHS Papers* 27 (1899): 205–10; CMA Archives, folio Z1n.

19. Dolley (Payne) Todd Madison (Portrait V)

18. James Madison, 1751–1836 (Portrait III)

By JOHN P. WALKER. Signed. Dated 1922

Oil on canvas: 30 x 25 in. (76.2 x 63.5 cm.)

Presented to the R. E. Lee Camp, Confederate Veterans, in 1924; acquired by the Virginia Historical Society in 1946 through merger with the Confederate Memorial Association. Por945.145

William Mahone, 1826–1895

Politician, senator, and Confederate general, William Mahone was born on December 1, 1826, in Southampton County, son of Fielding Jordan Mahone and Martha (Drew) Mahone. He graduated from the Virginia Military Institute in 1847, taught at the Rappahannock Military Academy, and became engineer of several Virginia railroads. In 1855 he married Ortelia Butler; they became the parents of three children. By the time of the secession crisis he had become president, chief engineer, and superintendent of the Norfolk and Petersburg Railroad. Offering his services to the Confederacy, he was appointed colonel of the 6th Virginia Infantry, took part in the capture of the Norfolk Navy Yard, and commanded the Norfolk district until its evacuation. Thereafter Mahone remained with the Army of Northern Virginia from Seven Pines to Appomattox, rising in rank to brigadier general on November 16, 1861, and, for gallantry at the battle of the Crater, to major general on July 10, 1864. At the war's end he turned again to railroads, merging several lines into

William Mahone

a system that later became the Norfolk and Western. Having served in the Senate of Virginia 1863–65, he sought further political involvement but was unsuccessful in his bid for the Conservative gubernatorial nomination in 1877. Undaunted, he organized the Readjusters, a party dedicated to renegotiating the state's enormous public debt. The popularity of this movement in the state brought about his election to the United States Senate. Serving in Washington 1881–87, he created a political machine that dominated the Republican party of Virginia and brought him great personal power. Mahone died in Washington on October 8, 1895; he is buried in Petersburg, in Blandford Cemetery.

DAB; Generals in Gray; Biographic Catalogue.

By CORNELIUS HANKINS. Signed. Dated 1897

Oil on canvas: 30 x 25 in. (76.2 x 63.5 cm.)

Presented to the R. E. Lee Camp, Confederate Veterans, in 1898; acquired by the Virginia Historical Society in 1946 through merger with the Confederate Memorial Association. Por946.201

Charles Marshall, 1830–1902

Son of Alexander J. Marshall and Maria Rosalie (Taylor) Marshall, the subject was born on October 3, 1830, in Warrenton. He graduated from the University of Virginia in 1848, taught mathematics briefly at Indiana University, and in 1853 settled in Baltimore where he practiced law. At the outbreak of the Civil War he joined the Army of the Confederacy; appointed aide-de-camp and military secretary to General Robert E. Lee, he remained with Lee throughout the war and was the only Confederate officer to accompany Lee to the surrender formalities at Appomattox. Colonel Marshall's wartime papers, edited by General Sir Frederick Maurice, were published in 1927 under the title *An Aide-de-Camp of Lee*. After the war Marshall returned to his practice in Baltimore, remaining in that city until his death on April 19, 1902. Colonel Marshall was twice married: first on December 18, 1856, to Emily Rosalie Andrews; second, on December 12, 1866, to Sarah R. Snowden. He was elected to membership in the Virginia Historical Society in 1881.

Encyclopedia of Virginia Biography, 5: 1037; William McClung Paxton, The Marshall Family, or A Genealogical Chart of the Descendants of John Marshall and Elizabeth Markham (Cincinnati, 1885), p. 260; Biographic Catalogue.

By JOHN P. WALKER. Signed. Dated 1899

Oil on canvas: 30 x 25 in. (76.2 x 63.5 cm.)

Presented to the R. E. Lee Camp, Confederate Veterans, in 1899; acquired by the Virginia Historical

Society in 1946 through merger with the Confederate Memorial Association. Por946.150

Elizabeth Marshall, 1756–1842

See Elizabeth (Marshall) Colston, 1756–1842

John Marshall, 1755–1835

Chief justice of the United States and founder of the American system of constitutional law, John Marshall was born on September 24, 1755, in Prince William (now Fauquier) County, the eldest child of Thomas and Mary Randolph (Keith) Marshall. He saw active military duty during the Revolutionary War at Brandywine, Germantown, and Monmouth. On being mustered out of service in 1780 he studied law for a short time under George Wythe (q.v.) and was admitted to the bar in Fauquier County on August 28, 1780. He married on January 3, 1783, Mary Willis Ambler, daughter of Jaquelin and Rebecca (Burwell) Ambler; the couple had six children. Marshall established himself in Richmond, the newly designated capital of the Commonwealth, where he soon became an acknowledged leader in his profession. He was a member of the Executive Council of Virginia 1782–95, served several terms in the House of Delegates, and was a delegate to the 1788 convention for the ratification of the federal Constitution. Financial problems compelled him to refuse Washington's request that he serve as attorney general of the United States in 1795, and the following year he declined the ambassadorship to France for the same reason. In 1797, however, he agreed to go to France as one of the envoys to negotiate the XYZ claims. In 1798 he declined an appointment to the Supreme Court; he was elected to the Sixth United States Congress, but served little more than a year, March 4, 1799, to June 7, 1800, when he resigned to become secretary of state in John Adams's cabinet. On January 20, 1801, he was appointed chief justice of the United States Supreme Court. Of the opinions handed down by the Marshall court, *Marbury* v. *Madison* was the most far-reaching, establishing, as it did, the right of federal courts to pass on the validity of congressional legislation. Subsequent rulings during the almost thirty-five years he presided over the Supreme Court "were all in favor of the national power as opposed to that of the states, and in the extension of the judicial function at the expense of the executive and legislative branches of the federal government." Marshall maintained throughout his life a simple, direct manner; he was often seen carrying a shopping basket to market or enjoying a game of quoits at the Barbecue Club; his residence at the corner of Ninth and Marshall streets in Richmond still stands. The chief justice died in Philadelphia on July 6, 1835; he is buried at Shockoe Cemetery, Richmond. Marshall was the first president of the Virginia Historical Society.

DAB; *Biographical Directory*; *Encyclopedia Americana*; *Portraiture*, pp. 71–72.

John Marshall (Portrait I)

Portrait I

COPIED BY WILLIAM BARKSDALE MYERS. 1857

Oil on canvas: 37 x 30 in. (94 x 76.2 cm.)

Presented by the artist in 1857. Por857.1

Copied by William Barksdale Myers from Henry Inman's original, the Society's portrait came into the collection in 1857 as a gift from the seventeen-year-old artist. Accompanying it was the following letter, dated Richmond, January 11, 1857, addressed to Conway Robinson, president of the Virginia Historical Society: "Dear Sir. Desirous as far as is in my power to contribute to the gallery of portraits so happily commenced by the Historical Society, permit me, through the Committee over which you preside, to ask its acceptance of a copy I have just completed of Inman's likeness of the late Chief Justice Marshall; a name endeared to Virginia by the recollection of his private virtues, and a source of pride and admiration to his countrymen for his great and eminent ability as a Jurisconsult. I am, with great respect, your obt. Ser. Wm. B. Myers." The minutes of the executive committee meeting of January 15, 1857, state that after reading the letter "the members of the committee inspected the original portrait and the copy; several remarked that it was difficult to tell which was the original and which the copy; and there was a general expression of satisfaction at the admirable manner in which the youthful artist had done his work, and of thanks for his handsome present. It being intimated that Mr. W. B. Myers desires to copy Mr. Thomas Sully's portrait of Pocahontas, *Resolved unanimously*, that leave be given him to withdraw the same from the library room, for such time as he may require to make the copy."

Andrew Oliver, *The Portraits of John Marshall* (Charlottesville, Va., 1977), pp. 147–48 (portrait reproduced); *Portraiture*, pp. 71–72; *VMHB* 67 (1959): 3 (portrait reproduced); VHS Archives, liber A3, pp. 49–50, and folio C4a–1857 (Myers).

Portrait II. John Marshall and Richard Channing Moore

By William Henry Brown

Silhouette: 9³/4 in. (24.8 cm.) in height, mounted on cardboard 11¹/4 x 13 in. (28.6 x 33 cm.); Moore silhouette 8¹/2 in. (21.6 cm.) in height.

Presented in 1882 by Alexander Hugh Holmes Stuart of Staunton. Por882.17

Andrew Oliver, *The Portraits of John Marshall* (Charlottesville, Va., 1977), pp. 125–27 (portrait reproduced); *Portraiture*, p. 122; VHS Archives, liber A4, p. 48.

Portrait III

By William Henry Brown. 1830

Silhouette: 10 in. (25.4 cm.) in height, mounted on cardboard 13¹/4 x 10¹/2 in. (33.7 x 26.7 cm.)

Presented in 1882 by Robert Alonzo Brock of Richmond. Por882.23

The subject's name is inscribed below the silhouette, together with the notation "[Silhou]ette from life by [   ] Brown, cut in 1830—the original in the possession of James Evans Esqr. Richmond, Va."

Andrew Oliver, *The Portraits of John Marshall* (Charlottesville, Va., 1977), pp. 125–28 (portrait reproduced); *The Green Bag: An Entertaining Magazine for Lawyers* 13 (1901): 181 (portrait reproduced); *Portraiture*, p. 122.

Portrait IV

By Beverley Waugh

Wax bas-relief: 4 in. (10.2 cm.) in height, mounted on backing 5³/4 x 4 in. (14.6 x 10.2 cm.) (oval)

Presented in 1881 by the Reverend Horace Edwin Hayden of Wilkes-Barre, Pennsylvania. Por882.16

The *Richmond Standard* of August 6, 1881, printed the following announcement of the receipt by the Society of this likeness of Marshall: "There has just been

presented to the Virginia Historical Society by the Rev. Horace Edwin Hayden, Wilkesbarre, Pennsylvania, an interesting memorial of Chief-Justice John Marshall—a wax figure of him in basso-relievo which Mr. Hayden states 'was executed by the artist

John Marshall (Portrait IV)

Beverley Waugh some forty or more years ago. My father, Edwin P. Hayden, Esq., a lawyer of Howard County, Maryland, was a great admirer of the Chief-Justice. When I was a boy I remember that this figure, handsomely framed, hung in my father's office. Before he died, which was in 1850, he presented me with the figure, which was then "full length," giving the Chief-Justice's style of dress as I have read it described in print. In my frequent removals since then the lower part of the figure has been broken into so many fragments that I was obliged to cut it off at the waist. It represented the Chief-Justice in the attitude of one delivering a speech, and I judge the likeness is very accurate.' The execution of the figure exhibits delicacy of treatment and artistic excellence, and is unmistakeably a delineation from life. The present length of the figure is four inches and the color of the material white. The hair is arranged in a cue, the style of the last century, in which style it was worn, with the accompanying dress of the flapped waistcoat and knee breeches, by the Chief-Justice during life." Through Andrew Oliver's indefatigable researches it is known that a second, virtually identical wax portrait survives unbroken; it provides a means of knowing what the Society's likeness must have looked like before the lower half was lost.

Andrew Oliver, *The Portraits of John Marshall* (Charlottesville, Va., 1977), pp. 93–96 (portrait reproduced); *Portraiture*, pp. 130–31; VHS Archives, liber A4, p. 46.

Portrait V

ARTIST UNIDENTIFIED

Plaster mask: 5¹/₂ in. (14 cm.) in height, on plaque 11 x 7³/₄ in. (27.9 x 19.7 cm.)

Presented in 1882 by Innes Randolph of Baltimore. Por882.20

The Society's mask is an early reproduction of the original mask (all that remains of a terra-cotta bust) that was long thought to be the work of Jean Antoine Houdon. Although the attribution is no longer accepted as correct, the original likeness, exhibited since 1948 in the John Marshall House in Richmond, is a valuable portrait of Marshall and has been several times reproduced. The Society's portrait, a plaster copy, is the same size as the original, but the crack which runs diagonally across the face of the original has been eliminated. The Society also owns (Portrait VI) a later version of this likeness which has been modified by the addition of neck and shoulders, properly attired, to form a bust-length bas-relief. The framed plaster plaque, which has been painted to resemble bronze, has a printed information sheet affixed to the back.

Andrew Oliver, *The Portraits of John Marshall* (Charlottesville, Va., 1977) pp. 9–13 (portrait reproduced); *Portraiture*, pp. 130–31 (portrait reproduced as frontispiece).

Portrait VI

ARTIST UNIDENTIFIED

Plaster bas-relief: 8¹/₄ in. (21 cm.) in height, on plaque 10³/₄ x 7³/₄ in. (27.3 x 19.7 cm.). Inscribed on the plaque: "John Marshall. 3rd Chief Justice of U.S."

Presented in 1917 by Douglas H. Thomas of Baltimore, a great-great-nephew of the subject. Por917.3

See note under Portrait V.

Portrait VII

ARTIST UNIDENTIFIED

Oil on canvas: 29 x 24¹/₂ in. (73.7 x 62.2 cm.)

Presented in 1969 by Sally (Colston) Mitchell (Mrs. Mark L. Mitchell) of Cincinnati. Por969.18

Originally owned by the subject's nephew Edward Colston, this portrait may perhaps be an early, inexpert copy of the Edward F. Peticolas portrait now at Lafayette College, Easton, Pennsylvania.

Andrew Oliver, *The Portraits of John Marshall* (Charlottes-

ville, Va., 1977), pp. 180–81 (portrait reproduced); *VMHB* 78 (1970): 239.

Portrait VIII

See The Convention of 1829–30

Credit is due Andrew Oliver for his exhaustive study of Marshall portraiture; virtually all the information here presented on the subject is derived from his work. It should be noted, however, that the Society does not, in fact, have a portrait of Marshall by William James Hubard as stated on pp. 169–70 of Oliver's *The Portraits of John Marshall*. The portrait depicted there is an early photograph made by Michael Miley (1841–1918) of an unidentified portrait. The Society owns the photograph but unfortunately not the painting.

Joseph Martin, 1785–1850
See The Convention of 1829–30

Rawley White Martin, 1835–1912

Rawley White Martin, physician and soldier, was born in Pittsylvania County on September 30, 1835, son of Chesley and Rebecca (White) Martin. He received his education at the University of Virginia and his professional training at the Medical Department of the University of New York, graduating as Doctor of Medicine in 1858. Hardly had he commenced practice in Chatham, Virginia, than he withdrew to enlist in the Confederate army. As a member of the 53d Virginia Infantry, he rose from private to lieutenant colonel, seeing action at Seven Pines, the Seven Days, Second Manassas, Sharpsburg, Harpers Ferry, and Fredericksburg. Wounded and taken prisoner in Pickett's charge at Gettysburg, Martin was not exchanged until July 1864. Unfit for further active duty, he was sent to South Carolina to select a site for a military prison and thereafter commanded a detachment of reserves until paroled at Bowling Green in June 1865. After the war Dr. Martin returned to Chatham to resume his professional career. He married on November 7, 1867, Ellen Johnson, daughter of James Johnson; they became the parents of four sons and two daughters. In 1895 he removed to Lynchburg. His numerous professional appointments included the presidency of the Board of Medical Examiners of Virginia, the State Board of Health, and the State Medical Society. He also served on the board of visitors of both the University of Virginia and the Virginia Military Institute. Dr. Martin died on April 20, 1912, and is buried at Chatham.

Confederate Military History, 3: 1034–35; *University of Virginia*, 1: 524–25; CMA Archives, folio Z1n; *Biographic Catalogue*.

By GEORGE T. BREWSTER. Signed. Dated 1913

Bronze bust: 32 1/2 in. (82.6 cm.) in height, including base. Base bears inscription: "Rawley White Martin, M.D., Lieut. Col. 53d Va. Infantry, C.S.A., 1835–1912." Lower base bears further inscription.

Presented to the R. E. Lee Camp, Confederate Veterans, in 1924, by the Rawley W. Martin Memorial Association; acquired by the Virginia Historical Society in 1946 through merger with the Confederate Memorial Association. Por946.225

George Mason, 1725–1792

Statesman, constitutionalist, and author of the Virginia Declaration of Rights, Mason was born in 1725, son of George and Ann (Thomson) Mason. In 1752 he became a member of the Ohio Company, later serving as its treasurer; he was a trustee of the newly established town of Alexandria from 1754 until its incorporation in 1779; in 1759 he was elected a member of the House of Burgesses but withdrew at the end of his first term with no favorable opinion of that body. His position behind the scenes, however, became increasingly important. It was he who drafted the Nonimportation Resolutions that the Virginia legislature adopted in 1769; he it was who set forth in the Fairfax Resolves of 1774 a statement of the colony's constitutional rights that was successively adopted by the Fairfax County court, the Virginia Convention, and the Continental Congress; it was he who drafted, while a member of the State Constitutional Convention of 1776, Virginia's first constitution and the Virginia Declaration of Rights (later the basis for the federal Bill of Rights). Mason was a member of the Virginia House of Delegates 1776–81, 1786–88; he helped to develop a plan, adopted in 1780, for the cession to the federal government of Virginia's western land claims. Although he played a significant part in drafting the federal Constitution, he refused to sign it, opposing its ratification by Virginia on the grounds that it perpetuated slavery, an institution "disgraceful to mankind," and that it provided no bill of rights, an omission later (1791) corrected in the first ten amendments. Refusing to serve as a United States senator from Virginia, Mason retired to Gunston Hall, his home in Fairfax County; here he died on October 7, 1792. Mason was twice married: first, on April 4, 1750, to Anne Eilbeck of Charles County, Maryland, who bore him five sons and four daughters; second, on April 11, 1780, to Sarah Brent, daughter of George and Catherine (Trimmingham) Brent of Stafford County.

DAB; *Encyclopedia Americana*; *Virginia Cavalcade*, 1, no. 1 (1951): 4–8 (portrait reproduced, p. 4).

George Mason

COPIED BY LOUIS MATHIEU DIDIER GUILLAUME. 1857

Oil on canvas on panel: 30 x 25 in. (76.2 x 63.5 cm.)

Presented in 1858 by Thomas Tabb Giles of Richmond. Por858.2

The original portrait of Mason, together with a companion piece of his wife, was painted by John Hesselius in 1750. In 1811 John Mason, a son of the subject, commissioned Dominic W. Boudet to paint three sets of copies of the Hesselius originals. Sometime after the completion of the copies, the originals were lost in a fire. The Society's portrait, painted in 1857 by Louis M. D. Guillaume, is a copy of the Boudet portrait that was at that time in the possession of James Murray Mason, a grandson of the subject. It is probable that Guillaume's copy was painted specifically for the Virginia Historical Society; it entered the collection, the gift of Thomas Tabb Giles, a year after it was painted.

Portraiture, pp. 72–74; Hugh Blair Grigsby, *Virginia Convention of 1776* (Richmond, 1855), p. 155; VHS Archives, folio C4a– 1858 (Giles).

John Young Mason, 1799–1859

United States congressman, cabinet member, and diplomat, John Young Mason was born on April 18, 1799, in Greensville County, son of Edmunds and Frances Ann (Young) Mason. He graduated from the University of North Carolina in 1816, studied law, was admitted to the bar in 1819, and began practice in his native county. After his removal to Southampton County in 1822, he served in the Virginia legislature 1823–31, at the same time sitting as a delegate in the Constitutional Convention of 1829. Elected as a Democrat to the Twenty-second United States Congress and to the two succeeding congresses, Mason represented his district from 1831 until his resignation in 1837. He served the eastern district of Virginia as a federal judge 1837–44, resigning to accept an appointment to President Tyler's cabinet as secretary of the navy 1844–45. In President Polk's administration he was attorney general 1845–46 and secretary of the navy 1846–49, during which time he supervised the naval operations of the Mexican War. After his retirement from national affairs he resumed the practice of law in Richmond, became president of the James River and Kanawha Company, and was a delegate to the Constitutional Convention of 1850. On January 22, 1854, Mason was named United States minister plenipotentiary to France, an appointment he held until his death in Paris on October 3, 1859. His remains were conveyed to the United States and interred in Hollywood Cemetery, Richmond. Ma-

son's wife, whom he married August 9, 1821, was Mary Anne (Fort) Mason; the couple were the parents of eight children. He was elected to the vice-presidency of the Virginia Historical Society in 1850.

DAB; *Biographical Directory*; *Portraiture*, pp. 131–32; *VMHB* 38 (1930): xxii, 53 (1945): 149, 54 (1946): 172, and 75 (1967): 305–30.

Portrait I
By EUGENE WARBURG. Signed. Dated 1855

Marble bust: 23 in. (58.4 cm.) in height

Presented in 1927 by Mrs. Fanny Mason Cooke of Emporia, Virginia, a granddaughter of the subject. Por927.21

The bust, executed in Paris in 1855, was presented to Mason by a group of his compatriots. The letter of presentation, dated Paris, September 1, 1855, is in the Society's manuscript collection: "Dr Sir We have the pleasure of transmitting to you herewith the names of some of your fellow citizens who are now or have been recently in Paris, and at whose instance a marble bust of yourself has been executed by Mr. Eugene Warburg of Louisiana, and placed at your disposal in the department of the Beaux Arts of the Universal Exposition. In requesting your acceptance of this testimonial of the respect due to you, we congratulate you on your restoration to health, and tender you our sincerely expressed wishes for your welfare in all respects. We are very respectfully yours Jas. Swaim [etc.]." Attached is a list of the sixty-one subscribers. Mason's rough draft of his letter of thanks is also present.

VHS Mss 2 M3814c.

Portrait II
COPIED BY ANNE FLETCHER

Oil on canvas: 24 x 20 in. (61 x 50.8 cm.)

Presented in 1945 by Mary Mason (Anderson) Williams (Mrs. Francis Deane Williams) of Richmond, a granddaughter of the subject. Por945.15

The Society's portrait is a copy of an original by Thomas Sully.

Portrait III
ARTIST UNIDENTIFIED

Miniature on ivory: 3 1/4 x 2 1/2 in. (8.3 x 6.4 cm.)

Presented in 1966 by Frances Leigh Williams of Delray Beach, Florida, a great-granddaughter of the subject. Por966.34

Portrait IV
See The Convention of 1829–30

John Young Mason (Portrait I)

Thomas Massie, 1783–1864

See The Convention of 1829–30

John P. Mathews

See The Convention of 1829–30

Allen Maury, 1854–1907

See Robert Henry Maury, 1816–1886 (Portrait IV)

Ann Hoomes Maury, 1852–1920

See Robert Henry Maury, 1816–1886 (Portrait IV)

Dabney Herndon Maury, 1822–1900

Born in Fredericksburg on May 21, 1822, the subject was the son of John Minor Maury and Eliza (Maury) Maury. He graduated from the University of Virginia in 1842 and, after studying law briefly, secured an appointment to West Point. Graduating with the class of 1846, he performed with gallantry in Mexico, taught at West Point for two years, then served on the Texas frontier. With the secession of Virginia he resigned his commission and became captain in the Confederate cavalry. Early in 1862 Maury was promoted to colonel and made chief of staff to General Van Dorn, commander of the Trans-Mississippi Department. His conduct at Pea Ridge in March 1862 was highly praised by his commander and earned him promotion to brigadier general. Later, with the Army of the West he fought at Iuka, Corinth, and Hatchie Bridge before being again promoted and transferred to Mobile as commander of the District of the Gulf. Here he remained, ably defending the city of Mobile until overwhelmed in the final days of the war. After brief sojourns in Fredericksburg and Louisiana, General Maury settled in Richmond where he lived in straitened circumstances. In 1868 he organized the Southern Historical Society, serving as chairman of it executive committee until 1886 and contributing numerous articles to its *Papers*; he also published *Recollections of a Virginian* (1894) and *Young People's History of Virginia* (1896). He was United States minister to Columbia 1885–89, and he served the National Guard Association as a member of its executive committee until 1890. General Maury died at the home of his son in Peoria, Illinois, on January 11, 1900. In 1852 he married Nannie Mason of King George County, daughter of Wiley Roy Mason and Susan (Smith) Mason; the couple had six children. He became a member of the Virginia Historical Society in 1875.

DAB; *Generals in Gray*; *SHS Papers* 27 (1899): 335–49; *Biographic Catalogue*.

BY CORNELIUS HANKINS. Signed. Dated 1897

Oil on canvas: 30 x 25 in. (76.2 x 63.5 cm.)

Presented to the R. E. Lee Camp, Confederate Veterans, in 1897 by the Westmoreland Club of Richmond; acquired by the Virginia Historical Society in 1946 through merger with the Confederate Memorial Association. Por946.115

George Greenhow Maury, 1850–1853

See Robert Henry Maury, 1816–1886 (Portrait IV)

Isabel Maury, 1842–1934

See Robert Henry Maury, 1816–1886 (Portrait III)

James Maury, 1746–1840

James Maury, "The Old Consul," was born in King William County on February 3, 1746, son of the Reverend James Maury and Mary (Walker) Maury. He attended his father's school in Albemarle County, then conducted a business in Fredericksburg. He is said to have been on board de Grasse's flagship at the time of the Yorktown surrender. Financially ruined by the Revolution, he determined to open a commission house in England to ship manufactured goods to Virginia in return for consignments of tobacco. Through the influence of his friends George Washington and Thomas Jefferson he also received an appointment as American consul in Liverpool. Maury arrived in Liverpool on August 31, 1786, and remained there for more than forty years as president of the firm of Maury and Latham and as official representative of the United States government. A victim of the spoils system, he was relieved of his consulship by Andrew Jackson on August 31, 1829. Maury was twice married: first, on June 15, 1782, to Catherine Armistead, who died without issue on May 22, 1794; second, on August 16, 1796, to Margaret Rutson, an Englishwoman, who bore him five children. After the loss of his consulship in 1829 and the death of his wife the following year, Maury returned to the United States, where he remained until his death, which occurred on March 23, 1840.

Anne Fontaine Maury, *Intimate Virginiana, a Century of Maury Travels by Land and Sea* (Richmond, 1941), pp. 1–21; Sue Crabtree West, *The Maury Family Tree* (Birmingham, Ala., 1971), p. 98; VHS Mss6:4 M4485:1; *Portraiture*, pp. 133–34.

ARTIST UNIDENTIFIED

Plaster bust: 24 in. (61 cm.) in height

Received in 1921 as a bequest of the Reverend Mytton Maury, a grandson of the subject. Por921.1.c

Matthew Fontaine Maury, 1806–1873

Known as the pathfinder of the seas for his pioneering work in oceanography, Matthew Fontaine Maury was a native of Spotsylvania County. He was born on January 14, 1806, the fourth son of Richard and Diana (Minor) Maury. In 1825 he became a midshipman in the United States Navy, and during the next nine years he traveled to Europe, around the world, and to the west coast of South America. After marrying on July 15, 1834, Ann Hull Herndon, he settled in Fredericksburg to write *A New Theoretical and Practical Treatise on Navigation* (1836) which was favorably received; several years later he wrote a series of pseudonymous articles for the *Richmond Whig* (1838) and the *Southern Literary Messenger* (1840–41) sharply critical of the navy's leadership. In 1842 Maury was appointed superintendent of the Navy Department's Depot of Charts and Instruments, at the same time taking charge of the United States

Matthew Fontaine Maury

Naval Observatory. During his tenure he issued *Wind and Current Chart of the North Atlantic* (1847), which together with his supporting publications won him international acclaim; following the Brussels congress of 1853 his office became the center for oceanographic research based on data supplied from all parts of the world. In 1855 he published *The Physical Geography of the Sea*, the first textbook of modern oceanography. Three days after the secession of Virginia, Maury resigned from the United States Navy; commissioned commander in the Confederate navy, he experimented with electric mines as a means of harbor defense, then went to England in the autumn of 1862 to secure ships for the Confederacy. At the war's end he resided briefly in Mexico, then returned to England where he prepared a series of popular geography books for school use. In 1868 he accepted the invitation of the Virginia Military Institute to become professor of meteorology, a post he held for the last four years of his life. His *Physical Survey of Virginia* was published in 1868. He died in Lexington on February 1, 1873, and is buried in Hollywood Cemetery, Richmond. By his wife, Ann Hull (Herndon) Maury, he had five daughters and three sons.

DAB; *History of Virginia*, 4:450–51; *Biographic Catalogue*.

BY JOHN P. WALKER. Signed. Dated 1902

Oil on canvas: 60 x 40 in. (152.4 x 101.6 cm.)

Presented to the R. E. Lee Camp, Confederate Veterans, in 1902 by John L. Williams; acquired by the Virginia Historical Society in 1946 through merger with the Confederate Memorial Association. Por946.49

Richard Wortham Maury, 1843–1916
See Robert Henry Maury, 1816–1886 (Portrait III)

Robert Henry Maury, 1816–1886
Martha Bickerton (Greenhow) Maury, 1820–1909 (Mrs. Robert Henry Maury)
His Children by Both Marriages

Robert Henry Maury, born on October 28, 1816, was the son of William Grymes Maury and Anne Hoomes (Woolfolk) Maury of the Old Mansion, Bowling Green. He married first, on December 17, 1840, Sarah Ann Wortham (1817–1846), daughter of R. C. Wortham and Mary Woolfolk (Coleman)

Wortham; the children of this union are noted below. He married second, on December 19, 1848, Martha Bickerton Greenhow, born on September 3, 1820, daughter of George and Elizabeth Ambler (Lewis) Greenhow; the six children born of this marriage also are listed below. Maury, a banker and broker, was president of the Richmond Stock Exchange in the 1870s. The family resided at 1105 East Clay Street. Robert Henry Maury died on October 10, 1886; his wife died on March 25, 1909. Robert Henry Maury and his first wife, Sarah Ann (Wortham) Maury, had the following children: (1) Isabel Maury, born on January 16, 1842, house regent at the Confederate Museum for over twenty years, died, unmarried, on July 2, 1934; (2) Richard Wortham Maury, born on October 3, 1843, died, unmarried, on February 19, 1916; (3) Sarah Ann Maury, born on July 19, 1846, died, unmarried, on September 16, 1909. Robert Henry Maury and his second wife, Martha Bickerton (Greenhow) Maury, had the following children: (4) George Greenhow Maury, born on November 25, 1850, died on July 2, 1853: (5) Ann Hoomes Maury, born on August 26, 1852, married on January 31, 1878, Poitiaux Robinson, had three children, Robert, Jourdan, and Martha Maury (who married Dr. Francis Whittle Upshur), died on October 22, 1920; (6) Allen Maury, born on January 17, 1854, married May Brawles on April 7, 1885, died without issue on December 11, 1907; (7) Robert Walker Maury, born on March 25, 1855, died without issue on January 26, 1903; (8) Jourdan Woolfolk

Maury, born on October 8, 1856, died without issue on November 24, 1886; (9) Alice Maury, died without issue.

Sue Crabtree West, *The Maury Family Tree* (Birmingham, Ala., 1971), pp. 154–55; *Richmond Portraits*, p. 122 (Portrait III reproduced); *VMHB* 72 (1964): 241.

Portrait I. Robert Henry Maury

By George Linen. Ca. 1856

Oil on canvas: 11 x 8½ in. (28 x 21.6 cm.)

Received in 1963 as a bequest of Martha Maury (Robinson) Upshur (Mrs. Francis Whittle Upshur) of Richmond, a granddaughter of the subject. Por969.9

Portrait II. Martha Bickerton (Greenhow) Maury

By George Linen. Ca. 1856

Oil on canvas: 11 x 8½ in. (28 x 21.6 cm.)

Received in 1963 as a bequest of Martha Maury (Robinson) Upshur (Mrs. Francis Whittle Upshur) of Richmond. Por963.10

Portrait III. Robert Henry Maury with the children of his first marriage, left to right: Richard Wortham Maury, Sarah Ann Maury, Isabel Maury

By George Linen. Ca. 1856

Oil on canvas: 19 x 15½ in. (48.3 x 39.4 cm.)

Received in 1963 as a bequest of Martha Maury (Robinson) Upshur (Mrs. Francis Whittle Upshur) of Richmond. Por963.11

Portrait IV. Three of Robert Henry Maury's children by his second marriage, left to right: Allen Maury, George Greenhow Maury, Ann Hoomes Maury

By George Linen. Ca. 1856

Oil on canvas: 16 x 13 in. (40.6 x 33 cm.)

Received in 1963 as a bequest of Martha Maury (Robinson) Upshur (Mrs. Francis Whittle Upshur) of Richmond. Por963.12

A note received with the portraits states that "at the time Linen painted this portrait George G. Maury had died. His face was copied from a photograph. A cousin of the same age, John Skelton Williams, posed for Linen to complete the portrait."

Portrait V. Sarah Ann Maury and Robert Walker Maury

By George Linen. Ca. 1856

Oil on canvas: 8 x 7 in. (20.3 x 17.8 cm.)

Received in 1963 as a bequest of Martha Maury (Robinson) Upshur (Mrs. Francis Whittle Upshur) of Richmond. Por963.13

Robert Henry Maury with his three oldest children
(Portrait III)

Robert Walker Maury, 1855–1903

See Robert Henry Maury, 1816–1886 (Portrait V)

Sarah Ann Maury, 1846–1909

See Robert Henry Maury, 1816–1886 (Portrait III and Portrait V)

Helen (Calvert) Maxwell, 1750–1833

See Helen (Calvert) Maxwell Read, 1750–1833

William Maxwell, 1784–1857

Born in Norfolk on February 27, 1784, the son of James and Helen (Calvert) Maxwell (q.v., Helen [Calvert] Maxwell Read), the subject graduated from Yale University in 1802, studied law in Richmond, and was admitted to the bar in 1808, soon achieving, through a combination of intellect, oratory, and wit, a prominent position in his profession. He represented Norfolk in the Virginia legislature 1830–38. Maxwell was called to the presidency of Hampden-Sydney College in 1838, held the post until 1844, and thereafter devoted himself to the practice of law in Richmond. He labored throughout his life for the improvement of education and religion in Virginia; he was a trustee of Hampden-Sydney College, a member of the Virginia Colonization Society, a ruling elder of the Presbyterian church, and a member of the Virginia Bible Society. Of his own writings, which included poetry and church and secular history, the most ambitious work is *A Memoir of Rev. John H. Rice* (1835); he edited the *New York Journal of Commerce*, 1827–28, and the *Virginia Historical Register*, 1848–53, a publication of the Virginia Historical Society. Maxwell became a member of the Society in 1832, just a few months after its founding; three years later he was elected vice-president, and in 1847 he was active in revitalizing the Society after a period of dormancy, serving thereafter as its corresponding secretary. He died near Williamsburg on January 10, 1857, and is buried in Hollywood Cemetery, Richmond. His wife, whom he married on May 31, 1839, was Mary Frances (Robertson) Maxwell.

DAB; *Lower Norfolk County Virginia Antiquary* 3 (1899–1901): 24; *Old Dominion Magazine* 4 (1870): 179–89; *Richmond Portraits*, p. 123 (portrait reproduced); *Portraiture*, pp. 74–75; *VMHB* 68 (1960): 96 (portrait reproduced); *Antiques* 116 (1979): 1135 (portrait reproduced).

By Cephas Thompson. 1811

Oil on canvas: 30 x 25 in. (76.2 x 63.5 cm.)

Received in 1899 from the estate of Mary Frances (Robertson) Maxwell (Mrs. William Maxwell), the subject's widow. Por899.5

Cephas Thompson was painting portraits in Norfolk during the winter of 1811–12. His sitter's book records the names of 102 Norfolk sitters; William Maxwell's is ninth on the list.

VHS Mss7:1 T3723:1.

Meade Portraits

This chart shows the relationship of members of the Meade family depicted in portraits owned by the Virginia Historical Society. Subjects of the Society's portraits are indicated in italics.

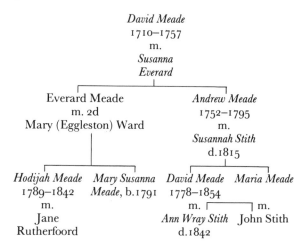

Andrew Meade, 1752–1795
Susannah (Stith) Meade, d. 1815 (Mrs. Andrew Meade)

Andrew Meade, son of David and Susanna (Everard) Meade (qq.v.) of Mount Pleasant, Nansemond County, was born on April 15, 1752. He married on September 18, 1772, Susannah Stith, daughter of Buckner Stith of Brunswick County. The couple resided at Octagon, Brunswick County, and Andrew Meade represented the county in the Virginia House of Delegates 1783–84, 1787–88. On his death in May 1795 he was survived by his widow, two sons, and three daughters. Mrs. Meade died at Octagon on July 1, 1815.

Encyclopedia of Virginia Biography, 1: 288; *W. & M. Quart.*, 1st ser., 13 (1904–5): 101 and 21 (1912–13): 190–91; Landon Covington Bell, *The Old Free State* (Richmond, 1927), 2: 109; William Armstrong Crozier, *The Buckners of Virginia* (New York, 1907), p. 207; *Occasional Bulletin*, no. 23 (1971): 1–4 (Portrait II reproduced); *VMHB* 75 (1967): 240. See chart on Meade Portraits for relationships.

Portrait I. Andrew Meade

Copied by Anna Mercer Dunlop

Oil on canvas: 30 x 25 in. (76.2 x 63.5 cm.)

Susannah (Stith) Meade

David Meade, 1710–1757

Presented in 1966 by Flora (Allen) Penick (Mrs. Charles A. Penick) of South Boston, Virginia. Por966.11

The portrait, according to information that accompanied it, is a copy by Anna Dunlop of Petersburg of an original by John Durand. After the copy was completed the original was destroyed because it was in poor condition!

Portrait II. Susannah (Stith) Meade

BY JOHN DURAND

Oil on canvas: 29³/4 x 25 in. (75.6 x 63.5 cm.)

Presented in 1966 by Flora (Allen) Penick (Mrs. Charles A. Penick) of South Boston, Virginia. Por966.12

David Meade, 1710–1757
Susanna (Everard) Meade
(Mrs. David Meade)

David Meade was the son of Andrew Meade, the immigrant, and Mary (Latham) Meade. He was born in 1710 in Nansemond County. As a young man he became enamoured of Susanna Everard, the eldest daughter of the governor of North Carolina, Sir Richard Everard, and Susanna (Kidder) Everard, Lady Everard. Not everyone, however, found the Everard offspring to their liking; in 1728 the North Carolina colonial Council, in a petition to the

king, described them as "a pack of rude children who give offence every day." Relieved of his governorship, Everard and his family visited the Meades on their way home in 1730. David Meade, eager to pursue his suit of Susanna, decided to accompany them to England; his father, loath to lose his only son, proposed an immediate marriage to which all assented. According to the memoirs of their eldest son, "No pair ever enjoyed more happiness in the hymeneal state than they did. They were both of them very young . . . and with very little experience in mankind." They became the parents of seven children, one of whom, Andrew Meade (q.v.), is represented, together with his wife, in the Society's portrait collection. In 1745 David Meade inherited his father's estate near Suffolk and took his father's place as a vestryman in the Upper Parish of Suffolk in Nansemond County. He lived, according to his son, "a monotonous and tranquil life" and died in the year 1757. Mrs. Meade's life dates have not been ascertained.

Patrick Hamilton Baskervill, *Andrew Meade of Ireland and Virginia: His Ancestors and Some of His Descendants and Their Connections* (Richmond, 1921), pp. 23–30 (similar portraits reproduced); *Occasional Bulletin*, no. 14 (1967): 8–10 (Portrait I reproduced); *VMHB* 32 (1924): 140–42 (similar portraits reproduced); 75 (1967): 240; *W. & M. Quart.*, 1st ser., 13 (1904–5): 37–41; *The Colonial Records of North Carolina* (Raleigh, N.C., 1886–90), 3: 3. See chart on Meade Portraits for relationships.

Portrait I. David Meade

By John Wollaston

Oil on canvas: 36 x 28¹/₂ in. (91.4 x 72.4 cm.)

Presented in 1966 by Flora (Allen) Penick (Mrs. Charles A. Penick) of South Boston. Por966.9

Susanna (Everard) Meade

Portrait II. Susanna (Everard) Meade

By John Wollaston

Oil on canvas: 36 x 28¹/₂ in. (91.4 x 72.4 cm.)

Presented in 1966 by Flora (Allen) Penick (Mrs. Charles A. Penick) of South Boston. Por966.10

David Meade, 1778–1854
Ann Wray (Stith) Meade, d.1842
(Mrs. David Meade)

David Meade, the eldest son of Andrew and Susannah (Stith) Meade (qq.v.) of Octagon, Brunswick County, and grandson of David and Susanna (Everard) Meade (qq.v.), was born on December 22, 1778. He married on February 13, 1798, Ann ("Nancy") Wray Stith, daughter of Robert and Mary Townshend (Washington) Stith; she bore her husband three children. Mrs. Meade died on January 12, 1842; Meade died on October 29, 1854. A portrait of David Meade's sister, Maria (Meade) Stith (q.v.), is also in the Society's collection; she married Mrs. Meade's brother.

Landon Covington Bell, *The Old Free State* (Richmond, 1927), 2: 109; VHS Mss6:4 M4613:3; *W. & M. Quart.*, 1st ser., 21 (1912–13): 270; information received with the portraits; *Occasional Bulletin*, no. 14 (1967): 10; *VMHB* 75 (1967): 240 and 83 (1975): 236. See chart on Meade Portraits for relationships.

David Meade, 1778–1854 (Portrait I)

Portrait I. David Meade

Attributed to David Boudon

Miniature on ivory: 2 x 1¹/₂ in. (5.1 x 3.8 cm.) (oval)

Presented in 1966 by Flora (Allen) Penick (Mrs. Charles A. Penick) of South Boston, Virginia. Por966.7

The miniature is attributed to David Boudon in the Virginia Museum of Fine Arts, *An Exhibition of Virginia Miniatures* (Richmond, 1941), where it appears as item 15. It is not, however, included in the checklist of Boudon's works that is appended to Nancy E. Richards's monograph on the artist published in the *Winterthur Portfolio* 9 (1974): 77–101.

Portrait II. David Meade

Artist unidentified. 1836

Oil on canvas: 30 x 25 in. (76.2 x 63.5 cm.). Inscribed on the back: "Aged 58."

Presented in 1966 by Flora (Allen) Penick (Mrs. Charles A. Penick) of South Boston, Virginia. Por966.13

Portrait III. Ann Wray (Stith) Meade

Artist unidentified. 1836

Oil on canvas: 30 x 25 in. (76.2 x 63.5 cm.)

Presented in 1966 by Flora (Allen) Penick (Mrs. Charles A. Penick) of South Boston, Virginia. Por966.14

Portraits II and III are companion pieces. On the evidence of the inscription on the back of David Meade's portrait, both are thought to have been painted in 1836.

Hodijah Meade, 1789–1842 with His Sister Mary Susanna Meade, b.1791

The subjects of this portrait are thought to be Hodijah and Mary Susanna Meade, children of Everard Meade by his second wife, Mary (Eggleston) Ward Meade, and grandchildren of David and Susanna (Everard) Meade (qq.v.). Hodijah married on January 11, 1815, Jane Rutherfoord, daughter of Thomas Rutherfoord (q.v.) and Sally (Winston) Rutherfoord of Richmond; they resided at The Hermitage, Amelia County, where they raised a family of eleven children. Mrs. Meade died on October 2, 1839; her husband died on January 1, 1842. Mary Susanna Meade, younger sister of Hodijah Meade, was born on October 1, 1791. It is thought that she died young, for no further references to her have been found.

Hodijah and Mary Susanna Meade

VHS Mss6:4 M4613:1 and Mss6:2 R9337:1; Louise Fontaine Cadot Catterall, "Comments on a Portrait of Meade Children," typescript filed with portrait. See chart on Meade Portraits for relationships.

ARTIST UNIDENTIFIED

Oil on canvas: 23 x 19 in. (58.4 x 48.3 cm.)

Presented in 1962 by Mrs. William Everard Meade of Danville. Por962.7

Maria Meade
See Maria (Meade) Stith

Mary Susanna Meade, b.1791
See Hodijah Meade, 1789–1842

Unidentified Member of the Meade Family

ARTIST UNIDENTIFIED

Miniature on paper: 2 1/2 x 2 1/4 in. (6.4 x 5.7 cm.) (oval)

Received in 1967 from the estate of Flora (Allen) Penick (Mrs. Charles A. Penick) of South Boston, Virginia. Por967.12

Charles Fenton Mercer, 1778–1858
See The Convention of 1829–30

Louis Mertens, b.1750

Louis Mertens, of Bordeaux, France, was born in 1750. He was the father of John Louis Mertens, who settled in Petersburg and married on August 22, 1810, Susanna B. Wills.

Information received with the miniature; Thomas Proctor Hughes, *Petersburg, Virginia, Hustings Court Marriage Bonds, Marriage Register, and Ministers' Returns, 1784–1854* (Memphis, Tenn., 1971), p. 88.

ARTIST UNIDENTIFIED

Miniature on ivory: 2 1/2 x 2 in. (6.4 x 5.1 cm.) (oval)

Received in 1967 from the estate of Flora (Allen) Penick (Mrs. Charles A. Penick) of South Boston, Virginia. Por967.11

Fleming Bowyer Miller, 1793–1874
See The Convention of 1829–30

Edmund Christian Minor, 1845–1903

The son of Dr. George Gilmer Minor and Caroline (Christian) Minor, the subject was born at Creighton, Henrico County, on February 20, 1845. When the Civil War began he left his private school in Albemarle County to enlist in the New Kent Cavalry, later Company F, 3d Virginia Cavalry. He was captured near Fredericksburg in 1863, imprisoned for eight months at Point Lookout, then exchanged. Shortly after returning to his company he sustained a severe wound at Milford, near Harrisonburg, which resulted in the amputation of his right arm. At the end of the war he studied law at the University of Virginia, graduated in 1867, and commenced the practice of his profession in Richmond. Soon afterward he was elected judge of the county court of Henrico; he was at the time the youngest judge in the Commonwealth. This office he held, with one brief interval, until 1894, at which time he became judge of the newly created law and equity court. He was reelected to the office without opposition and was in the middle of his second term when he died, on September 9, 1903, at Norwich, Connecticut, where he had gone to recover from an illness. Judge Minor married in April 1877 Kate Pleasants, daughter of Adair Pleasants of Richmond, by whom he had six children, three of whom survived him.

Virginia State Bar Association, *Proceedings* 17 (1904): 61–63; Richmond *Times-Dispatch*, Sept. 10, 1903; *Biographic Catalogue*.

BY ADELE WILLIAMS. Signed

Oil on canvas: 32 x 25 in. (81.3 x 63.5 cm.)

Acquired in 1946 through merger with the Confederate Memorial Association. Por946.174

Judith Frances Carter (Bassett) Mitchell, 1836–1907
See Judith Frances Carter Bassett, 1836–1907

Maggie Lena Mitchell, 1867–1934
See Maggie Lena (Mitchell) Walker, 1867–1934

James Monroe, 1758–1831

The fifth president of the United States, James Monroe was born on April 28, 1758, in Westmoreland County, son of Spence and Elizabeth (Jones) Monroe. He interrupted his education at the College of William and Mary to join the army of the Revolution, seeing action at Trenton, Brandywine, Germantown, and Monmouth. He studied law under the tutelage of Thomas Jefferson, who encouraged him to pursue a political career, which began in 1782 with his election to the Virginia legislature and continued with his membership in the Continental Congress 1783–86 and the United States Senate 1790–94. During Washington's administration he was minister to France 1794–96, and after serving a term as governor of Virginia, 1799–1802, he returned to France to help negotiate the Louisiana Purchase; thereafter he was appointed by Jefferson minister plenipotentiary to England, remaining abroad 1803–7. On his return home, after brief attendance in the Virginia legislature, he was again elected governor of the Commonwealth; he resigned on April 3, 1811, after only three months to become secretary of state in Madison's cabinet, an office he held from 1811 to 1817. Twice elected president of the United States, Monroe was the nation's chief executive from March 4, 1817, to March 3, 1825. After the expiration of his term of office he resided at Oak Hill, his estate in Loudoun County, emerging from retirement in 1829 to preside over the Virginia Constitutional Convention. He died in New York City on July 4, 1831, and was buried in Marble Cemetery on Second Street; his remains were reinterred in Hollywood Cemetery, Richmond, on July 4, 1858. Monroe's wife, whom he married on February 18, 1786, was Eliza (Kortright) Monroe, daughter of Lawrence Kortright of New York; the couple had two daughters.

DAB; *Biographical Directory*; *Portraiture*, pp. 75–76.

Portrait I

COPIED BY JAMES BOGLE

Oil on canvas: 40 x 33 in. (101.6 x 83.8 cm.)

Presented about 1880 by Norman Stewart Walker of Richmond. Por880.1

At the regular meeting of the Society's executive committee held on December 1, 1859, "The Chairman laid before the Committee a letter of the 23rd of February 1858, to Mrs. Robert Stanard, referring to a portrait of Mr. Monroe in her possession, and suggesting that it should be placed in the Society's library room; and Mr. Macfarland was desired to speak to her on the subject."[1] Mrs. Stanard, it appears, resisted Macfarland's blandishments, and the portrait, painted by John Paradise (1783–1833), remained in the family's possession.[2] It was not until about 1880 that the Society received a portrait of the fifth president. A copy by Bogle of the original Gilbert Stuart portrait (owned at that time by Andrew Lowe of New York), it was given to the Society by Norman Stewart Walker.[3] In 1881 the Society's portrait was copied by Virginia Keane (later Mrs. Clarence Archibald Bryce) for the Commonwealth of Virginia; the portrait hangs in the Virginia state Capitol.[4]

1. VHS Archives, liber A3, p. 85.   2. Clarence Winthrop Bowen, *The History of the Centennial Celebration of the Inauguration of George Washington* (New York, 1892), opp. p. 108, pp. 509–12.   3. VHS Archives, liber B2, p. 673.   4. *Virginia Record* 77, no. 1 (Jan. 1955): 18–19, 60; *Portraits and Statuary*, p. 83.

Portrait II

See The Convention of 1829–30

William Lewis Moody, 1828–1920

A native of Essex County, Virginia, this prominent Texas businessman was born on May 19, 1828, the eighth child of Jameson and Mary Susan (Lankford) Moody. The family removed to Chesterfield County when Moody was only two years of age; at fifteen he was left an orphan. He graduated from the University of Virginia in 1850 and set out for the West, settling in Fairfield, Texas, where he engaged in the practice of law, then entered the mercantile business in partnership with his brothers who had followed him from Virginia. On January 19, 1860, Moody married Pherabe Elizabeth Bradley, daughter of Francis Meriwether Bradley and Zillah Pherabe (Goldsby) Bradley; they became the parents of six children, of whom three lived to maturity. At the beginning of the Civil War he entered the service of the Confederacy as captain of Company G, 7th Texas Infantry. Captured at Fort Donelson, he was imprisoned, exchanged, and returned to his old regiment. Promoted to lieutenant colonel, he fought with his regiment in Mississippi until he was so severely wounded at the battle of Jackson, July 10, 1863, that he was forced from active duty and served the final years of the war as colonel on garrison duty in Austin, Texas. At the war's end Colonel Moody moved to Galveston where he became a highly successful cotton merchant. He was a founder and director of the Gulf, Colorado and Santa Fe Railroad Company, founder and for many years president of the Galveston Cotton Exchange, and president of the National Bank of Texas and the W. L. Moody Bank. By the time of his death, on July 17, 1920, he was one of Galveston's most successful businessmen. He was buried in Chesterfield County in the family burying ground.

University of Virginia, 1: 508–9; CMA Archives, folio Z1n; W. L. Moody & Co., *Three Quarters of a Century of Progress: W. L. Moody and Company, Bankers* (Galveston, Tex., 1941); *Biographic Catalogue*; VHS Mss9:1 M7765:1.

By JOHN P. WALKER. Signed. Dated 1924

Oil on canvas: 30 x 25 in. (76.2 x 63.5 cm.)

Presented to the R. E. Lee Camp, Confederate Veterans, in 1924 by the subject's son, William Lewis Moody, Jr.; acquired by the Virginia Historical Society in 1946 through merger with the Confederate Memorial Association. Por946.154

Young Marshall Moody, 1822–1866

Born in Chesterfield County on June 23, 1822, General Moody was the son of Carter and Sarah (Pankey) Moody. At the age of twenty he left Virginia, settling in Marengo County, Alabama, where he taught school, engaged in mercantile enterprises, and was clerk of the circuit court. On Alabama's secession from the Union he entered the Confederate army as a captain in the 11th Alabama Infantry. After serving with the regiment for a year he returned to Alabama to organize the 43d Alabama Infantry; as lieutenant colonel he saw action with the regiment in the Tennessee and Kentucky campaigns, and at Chickamauga he led it with the rank of colonel. He was present at the seige of Knoxville, Petersburg, and Drewry's Bluff, where he was wounded. On the death of General Archibald Gracie (q.v.) in December 1864 he took charge of the brigade, being promoted to brigadier general on March 4, 1865. He was captured just one day before the surrender at Appomattox. On his return to civilian life General Moody became a commission merchant in Mobile, Alabama. While in New Orleans to establish a branch of his business he contracted yellow fever and died on September 18, 1866. His wife was Frances Annette (Floyd) Moody; the couple had one child, a son.

Generals in Gray; *Confederate Military History*, 7: 426–27; George Edward Pankey, *John Pankey of Manakin Town, Virginia, and His Descendants* (Ruston, La., 1969–72), 1: 77, 139–40; *Biographic Catalogue*.

By CORNELIUS HANKINS. Signed. Dated 1897

Oil on canvas: 30 x 25 in. (76.2 x 63.5 cm.)

Presented to the R. E. Lee Camp, Confederate Veterans, by the subject's sister; acquired by the Virginia Historical Society in 1946 through merger with the Confederate Memorial Association. Por946.172

Gertrude P. Moore
See Gertrude P. (Moore) Hawkins

Richard Channing Moore, 1762–1841

The second bishop of the Protestant Episcopal Diocese of Virginia, Richard Channing Moore was born in New York City on August 21, 1762, son of Thomas and Elizabeth (Channing) Moore. After a classical education and a brief exposure to seafaring life, he studied medicine and for a short period practiced this profession in New York City and eastern Long Island. Shortly thereafter, resolving to enter the church, he studied theology under Bishop Provoost; in July 1787 he was ordained deacon, and the following September he entered the priesthood. Following two years at Grace Church, Rye, New York, he was called to St. Andrew's Parish, Staten Island, where for more than twenty years he served as rector, at the same time conducting school and continuing the practice of medicine. In 1809 he became rector of St. Stephen's Church, New York City, and in 1814 he became bishop of Virginia and rector of Monumental Church, Richmond; his consecration took place in Philadelphia on May 18, 1814. For twenty-seven years he directed the affairs of the diocese with devotion, piety, and zeal. Under his tactful guidance the diocese flourished; churches were reestablished, the number of clergy increased, and the Virginia Theological Seminary was founded. Even in old age he was described as "full of vivacity and cheerfulness, abounding in anecdote and sprightly conversation . . . the chief attraction of every circle." Bishop Moore was twice married: first to Christian Jones of New York, who died in 1796, leaving him with three children; second, in 1797, to Sarah Mersereau, who bore him six children. Bishop Moore died in Lynchburg, on November 11, 1841, and is buried in Shockoe Cemetery, Richmond.

DAB; *Richmond Portraits*, pp. 136–37; *Antiques* 116 (1979): 1137 (Portrait IV reproduced).

Richard Channing Moore (Portrait IV)

Portrait I. Richard Channing Moore and John Marshall

See John Marshall (Portrait II)

Portrait II

BY MARTHA ANN HONEYWELL

Silhouette: 8³/4 in. (22.2 cm.) in height, mounted on paper 10 x 7¹/2 in. (25.4 x 19.1 cm.). Inscribed: "Bishop Moore taken by Miss Honeywell."

Presented in 1902 by William P. Craighill of Charles Town, West Virginia. Por902.6

Portrait III

COPIED BY WILLIAM VER BRYCK

Oil on canvas: 34 x 27 in. (86.4 x 68.6 cm.)

Presented in 1947 by the Rives estate through Sarah Landon Rives of Albemarle County. Por947.29

The portrait is a copy of an original by Henry Inman.

Portrait IV

ARTIST UNIDENTIFIED

Miniature on ivory: 2³/4 x 2¹/4 in. (7 x 5.7 cm.) (oval)

Presented in 1951 by Sarah Landon Rives of Albemarle County. Por951.1

Portrait V

See The Convention of 1829–30

Samuel McDowell Moore, 1796–1875

See The Convention of 1829–30

Charles Stephen Morgan, 1799–1859

Born near Morgantown, (West) Virginia, on June 4, 1799, the subject was the son of Stephen and Sarah (Somerville) Morgan. At twenty-one years of age he took his seat in the Virginia House of Delegates representing Monongalia County, (West) Virginia, 1821–24; he was then elected to the higher branch of the legislature and served as state senator 1824–32. Morgan represented his district at the Convention of 1829, distinguishing himself before that body by the brilliance of his oratory and the soundness of his judgment. Declining to pursue a career in national politics or in diplomacy, for which many thought him admirably suited, Morgan abandoned politics altogether to devote himself to the cause of prison reform. On March 23, 1832, two days after relinquishing his place in the state Senate, he became superintendent of the Virginia State Penitentiary. For the next twenty-seven years he labored to improve sanitary conditions in the prison, to rehabilitate the inmates, and to provide them with religious instruction; he encouraged prisoners to develop manual skills, and to this end established a shoe manufactory inside the walls. Colonel Morgan, whose rank was one of the perquisites of his office, enabling him to call out state troops in the event of disorder in the prison, was keenly interested in the history of Virginia. He sought support for the preservation of such sites as Jamestown Island and for the proper observance of the two hundred and fiftieth anniversary of the landing of the colonists. He was elected to membership in the Virginia Historical Society in 1832. Colonel Morgan, a notable humanitarian, died on February 15, 1859, and is buried in Hollywood Cemetery, Richmond. His wife, Alcinda G. (Moss) Morgan, bore her husband two sons and two daughters.

Encyclopedia of Virginia Biography, 4: 452–54; Bernard Lee Butcher, *Genealogical and Personal History of the Upper Monongahela Valley* (New York, 1912), 3: 956–58; *VMHB* 49 (1941): 97.

Portrait I

By James Westhall Ford. 1829

Oil on canvas: 25 3/4 x 20 in. (65.4 x 50.8 cm.). Inscribed on the back: "Charles S. Morgan, Born June 4th 1799. Painted by J. W. Ford March 1st 1829 Richmond. Copy from original back by Otto Moeller, Restorer. Oct. 30, 1942."

Presented in 1940 by Morgan Poitiaux Robinson

Charles Stephen Morgan (Portrait I)

and John Enders Robinson of Richmond, grandsons of the subject. Por940.14

James W. Ford, together with such other artists as Chester Harding, Robert Matthew Sully, and George Catlin, took advantage of the opportunity afforded by the Virginia Convention of 1829–1830 to paint likenesses of the delegates, some of whom—Marshall, Madison, Monroe, Randolph of Roanoke—ranked among the nation's elder statesmen. Charles S. Morgan, a young delegate, sat for Ford on March 1. An even younger delegate, Hugh Blair Grigsby, noted in his diary a visit to the artist's studio on October 27: "In the afternoon visited the room of Mr. Forde the painter, and examined several very strong likenesses of my acquaintances; among which were those of Mr. Tazewell, Mr. Giles, Mr. Reynolds, Peter Francisco, Dr. Brockenbrough, and others."

VHS Mss1 G8782b 72, p. 155.

Portrait II

See The Convention of 1829–30

Daniel Morgan, 1736–1802

Born in 1736, probably in Hunterdon County, New Jersey, the son of James and Eleanor Morgan, the subject left home as a youth and found employment in 1754 as a farm laborer and wagoner in the Shenandoah Valley. He was a member of Braddock's ill-starred expedition, a lieutenant in Pontiac's War, and took part in Dunmore's expedition to western Pennsylvania in 1774. On June 22, 1775, he was commissioned captain of a Virginia rifle company; he was ordered first to Boston, later to Quebec, where he joined Arnold in the assault on the city; when Arnold was wounded, Morgan took command and fought until overcome by superior forces. After a period of imprisonment he joined Washington in the spring of 1777 with a corps of sharpshooters and saw action in New Jersey and in the Saratoga campaign. After Burgoyne's surrender Morgan fought in the campaigns around Philadelphia during the winter of 1777–78. Poor health and disagreements with Congress led to his resignation from the army in the summer of 1779; he withdrew to Virginia where he devoted himself to the construction of Saratoga, his residence in Clarke County. Recalled to duty in 1780 with the rank of brigadier general, Morgan commanded the troops in western North Carolina; on January 17, 1781, he achieved one of the most decisive victories of the war, at Cowpens, South Carolina. He again withdrew from active service, and except for a brief association with Lafayette in Virginia, he took no further part in the war. Retiring to

Saratoga, he devoted himself to the acquisition of western lands, eventually coming into possession of more than a quarter of a million acres on the Ohio and Monongahela rivers. After a brief return to the colors during the Whiskey Insurrection in 1794, he turned to politics, as an unsuccessful candidate for election to the Fourth United States Congress and as the successful candidate for election to the Fifth Congress, 1797–99. General Morgan died in Winchester on July 6, 1802. By his marriage to Abigail Baily he was the father of two daughters.

DAB; *Biographical Directory*; North Callahan, *Daniel Morgan, Ranger of the Revolution* (New York, 1961); Charles Coleman Sellers, *Charles Willson Peale with Patron and Populace* (Philadelphia, 1969), pp. 72–73, 130 (portrait reproduced); *Occasional Bulletin*, no. 1 (1960): 12–14 (portrait reproduced); *VMHB* 68 (1960): 242–43.

Daniel Morgan

BY CHARLES WILLSON PEALE

Oil on canvas: 26 x 20½ in. (66 x 52.1 cm.)

Presented in 1959 by Percy Robert Blythe of San Francisco. Por960.1

John Hunt Morgan, 1825–1864

John Hunt Morgan, Confederate raider, was born at Huntsville, Alabama, on June 1, 1825, son of Calvin Cogswell Morgan, a Virginian, and Henrietta (Hunt) Morgan. About five years after his birth the family removed to his mother's home near Lexing-

ton, Kentucky. After service in the Mexican War, during which he saw action at Buena Vista, Morgan entered business in Lexington and in 1857 organized the Lexington Rifles. He entered Confederate service as a scout in September 1861 and early in 1862 began his celebrated raids which were to win him fame and a vote of thanks from the Confederate Congress. He was promoted to colonel on April 4, 1862, took part in the Shiloh campaign, then led raids into Tennessee and Kentucky; for his bold move at Hartsville, Tennessee, resulting in the capture of over 1,700 prisoners, he was promoted to brigadier general and given a cavalry division. In June 1863 he led a raid through Indiana and Ohio, but pursued by superior forces his command was dispersed and he himself was taken prisoner. Four months later Morgan escaped from the Ohio State Penitentiary and made his way south; in April 1864 he was assigned to command the Department of Southwest Virginia. While on the way to attack federal forces near Knoxville, he was surprised by a detachment of Union cavalry and was killed in Greenville, Tennessee, on September 4, 1864. General Morgan's wife was Rebecca Gratz (Bruce) Morgan, daughter of John and Margaret Bruce of Lexington, Kentucky, who became an invalid shortly after their marriage; their only child died soon after birth.

DAB; *Generals in Gray*; *Biographic Catalogue*.

BY FLORENCE BARLOW. Signed. Dated 1912

Oil on canvas: 60 x 44 in. (152.4 x 111.8 cm.)

Acquired in 1946 through merger with the Confederate Memorial Association. Por946.214

William Augustine Morgan, 1831–1899

The subject was born near Mount Vernon, Fairfax County, on March 30, 1831, the son of Jacob and Mary (Smith) Morgan. When a child he moved with his family to Jefferson County, (West) Virginia, and remained in that county the rest of his life, the war years excepted. On the outbreak of the Civil War the Shepherdstown Troop, of which Morgan was captain, was incorporated into the 1st Virginia Cavalry as Company F. Participating with this unit in more than three hundred battles and skirmishes, Morgan rose to the rank of colonel and was in command of Payne's Brigade at Appomattox. After the war Colonel Morgan resided on his farm in Jefferson County. He was deputy sheriff from 1872 until the time of his death and was a member of the Convention of 1872 that framed the West Virginia state constitution. He died at his home on February 14, 1899. Colonel

Morgan married in Winchester, Virginia, on December 20, 1854, Anna J. Smith, daughter of Augustine Charles Smith and Elizabeth (Magill) Smith; the couple became the parents of eight children.

Confederate Veteran 7 (1899): 179, 562–63; Millard Kessler Bushong, *Historic Jefferson County* (Boyce, Va., 1972), pp. 432–33; H. H. Hardesty, *Historical Hand Atlas, Illustrated*, with special history of the Virginias, and Berkeley and Jefferson County supplement (Chicago, 1883), p. 27; *Biographic Catalogue.*

BY JOHN P. WALKER. Signed. Dated 1909

Oil on canvas: 30 x 25 in. (76.2 x 63.5 cm.)

Acquired in 1946 through merger with the Confederate Memorial Association. Por946.120

John Morris

Born around 1800, son of William and Ann (Watson) Morris of Louisa County, the subject studied medicine at the University of Maryland Medical School, receiving his degree in 1826. He returned to Virginia and on February 21, 1828, married Susannah Pleasants (1802–1887), daughter of Governor James Pleasants. The couple resided at Appenwall and became the parents of children. Dr. Morris remained in Goochland County, practicing his profession until his death.

Virginia Genealogist 11 (1967): 114; *Portraiture*, p. 77–78.

ARTIST UNIDENTIFIED

Oil on canvas: 30¼ x 25¼ in. (76.8 x 64.1 cm.)

Provenance unknown. PorX.4

Richard Morris, 1778–1833
See The Convention of 1829–30

Ellen Carter (Bruce) Morson, 1820–1862   (Mrs. James Marion Morson)

Eldest of the three children of James Bruce (q.v.) by his second wife, Elvira (Cabell) Henry Bruce, the subject was born on August 15, 1820. On September 13, 1843, she married James Marion Morson (1817–1868) of Fredericksburg, son of Alexander and Anne Casson (Alexander) Morson. The couple bought from Dr. John Brockenbrough in 1844 the house at 1201 East Clay Street, Richmond, later known as the White House of the Confederacy. They remained there only a year before removing to Dover, in Goochland County, where they raised a family of eight children. In 1853 Morson built the three houses, still standing on Governor Street in Richmond, known as

Morson Row. On the outbreak of the Civil War the subject moved to Wilton, her husband's sugar plantation in St. James's Parish, Louisiana; here she died in February 1862; here, too, her husband died on December 30, 1868.

The Cabells and Their Kin, p. 361; Mary Wingfield Scott, *Houses of Old Richmond* (Richmond, 1941), pp. 148, 291–93; *VMHB* 11 (1903–4): 442 and 79 (1971): 241; VHS Mss1 G1875a 219–229; *Occasional Bulletin*, no. 21 (1970): 10–12 (Portrait I reproduced).

Portrait I

BY ALEXANDER GALT. Signed (monogram)

Marble bust: 22 in. (55.9 cm.) in height

Presented in 1970 by members of the Garnett family,

Ellen Carter (Bruce) Morson (Portrait I)

through Alexander Yelverton Peyton Garnett of Greenwich, Connecticut, and James Harper Poor Garnett of Northeast Harbor, Maine. Por970.17

Portrait II

BY ALEXANDER GALT. Signed (monogram)

Marble bust: 27½ in. (69.9 cm.) in height

Presented in 1974 by David Kirkpatrick Este Bruce of Washington, D.C. Por974.4

A letter from the artist to Charles Bruce, dated Florence, September 25, 1857, states: "I have only one regret in sending the bust [the bust of Mrs. Charles

Bruce, q.v.] that it no longer ornaments my studio—the reason why I did not send it before was that I was desirous of sending at the same time the bust of Mrs. Morson, but it will not be finished for over a month and not sent for about two months."

VHS Mss1 B8306b 252.

John Singleton Mosby, 1833–1916

The celebrated Confederate ranger was born in Powhatan County on December 6, 1833, the son of Alfred D. Mosby and Virginia (McLaurine)Mosby. The family moved to a farm near Charlottesville in 1838; Mosby attended the University of Virginia, studied law, and was admitted to the bar at Bristol in 1855. Pauline Clarke, daughter of Beverly J. Clarke of Franklin, Kentucky, became his wife on December 30, 1857. With the outbreak of hostilities Mosby enlisted in the Confederate cavalry, participated at First Manassas, and rode with J. E. B. Stuart in the peninsula and at Sharpsburg. In January 1863 he began operating as a ranger; his raids on Fairfax Court House and Chantilly earned him promotions to captain and major respectively. The following year Mosby and a growing force of rangers continued harassing Federal detachments, appropriating military supplies, miscellaneous plunder, and, in the so-called greenback raid, more than $150,000 in cash. Rising in rank to colonel, he operated in the Shenandoah Valley, was severely wounded, and after Lee's surrender disbanded his men at Salem, Virginia. Mosby settled in Warrenton, where he practiced law. His reputation in the South suffered in the years after the war because of his Republican sympathies and his friendship with Ulysses S. Grant. He was United States consul in Hong Kong 1878–85; a land agent in Colorado 1901–4, and an assistant attorney in the Department of Justice 1904–10. Mosby published a number of brief monographs and two volumes: *Mosby's War Reminiscences* (1887) and *Stuart's Cavalry in the Gettysburg Campaign* (1908). He died in Washington, D.C., on May 30, 1916, survived by three daughters and a son.

DAB; *Biographic Catalogue.*

Portrait I

By LOUIS MATHIEU DIDIER GUILLAUME. Signed

Oil on canvas: 22 x 18 in. (55.9 x 45.7 cm.) (oval)

Presented to the R. E. Lee Camp, Confederate Veterans, before 1905; acquired by the Virginia Historical Society in 1946 through merger with the Confederate Memorial Association. Por946.54

Portrait II

See The Battle Abbey Murals. Flanking Panels

Thomas Taylor Munford, 1831–1919

Born in Richmond on March 29, 1831, son of George Wythe Munford and Lucy Singleton (Taylor) Munford, the subject graduated from the Virginia Military Institute in 1852. The following year he married Elizabeth Henrietta Tayloe, daughter of George Plater Tayloe of Roanoke County; she died in 1863. He was engaged in farming when the Civil War began. Assigned to the 30th Virginia Mounted Infantry, he participated in the battle of First Manassas; when the unit was reorganized as the 2d Virginia Cavalry he was commissioned its colonel. Munford fought at Cross Keys, Second Manassas, where he was wounded, Sharpsburg, Chancellorsville, and Gettysburg and was with General Early in the Valley campaign of 1864. In November 1864 he was promoted to brigadier general and given command of Fitzhugh Lee's division, which he led at Five Forks and Appomattox. After the war he returned to his farm in Bedford County. His second wife, whom he married in 1866, was Emma Tayloe, daughter of William Henry Tayloe and Henrietta (Ogle) Tayloe. In 1873 General Munford moved from Bedford to Lynchburg, where he engaged in the manufacture of iron and built the first iron bridge in Lynchburg. He later removed to Alabama to oversee cotton plantations in Hale and Perry counties. He died there on April 16, 1919. Munford had children by both marriages.

History of Virginia, 5: 565; *Virginia and Virginians*, 2: 579; *The South in the Building of the Nation* (Richmond, 1909–13), 12: 220–21; *Biographic Catalogue.*

BY BERNHARD GUTMANN. Signed. Dated 1898

Oil on canvas: 29 x 23 in. (73.7 x 58.4 cm.)

Presented to the R. E. Lee Camp, Confederate Veterans, in 1899; acquired by the Virginia Historical Society in 1946 through merger with the Confederate Memorial Association. Por946.94

John Murray, fourth Earl of Dunmore, 1732–1809

Virginia's last royal governor, the subject was the eldest son of William Murray, third earl of Dunmore, and Catherine (Nairne) Murray, Lady Dunmore. He was born in 1732 and succeeded to the title on the death of his father in 1756. Between 1761 and 1769 he sat in the House of Lords as a representative peer of Scotland. He was appointed governor of New York in 1770, arriving in the colony with his family on October 19, 1770. Less than a year later he accepted the governorship of Virginia. His initial popularity was quickly eroded by confrontations with the burgesses that led more than once to the dissolution of the lower house. In 1773 he visited the northwestern frontier and to defend the area from an increased Indian threat established Fort Dunmore at the present site of Pittsburgh; at the battle of Point Pleasant on October 10, 1774, the Virginia militia commanded by Colonel Andrew Lewis defeated the Shawnees, and the governor signed a treaty with them at Camp Charlotte. As revolutionary fervor increased, Dunmore's position in Virginia became precarious. His clandestine removal of gunpowder from the magazine in Williamsburg led to rioting and threats to his person, whereupon on June 1, 1775, he retired to the warship *Fowey* lying off Yorktown. During the next twelve months he attempted unsuccessfully to restore order; he declared martial law, suffered a defeat of his troops at Great Bridge on December 9, 1775, burned Norfolk, and after a final skirmish at Gwynne's Island, withdrew to England. He resumed his seat in the House of Lords and later was governor of the Bahamas 1787–96. Dunmore died in Ramsgate, England, on March 5, 1809. He married on February 21, 1759, Lady Charlotte Stewart, daughter of Alexander Stewart, sixth earl of Galloway; she bore her husband five sons and four daughters.

DAB; *DNB*; *Virginia Historical Portraiture*, pp. 197–98 (original portrait reproduced); *Virginia House*, pp. 37, 42.

COPIED BY CHARLES X. HARRIS. 1929

Oil on canvas: 94 x 58 in. (238.8 x 147.3 cm.)

Received in 1948 as a bequest of Mr. and Mrs. Alexander Wilbourne Weddell of Richmond. Por948.76

This copy was made from the original portrait by Sir Joshua Reynolds when it was in this country for the exhibition of Virginia historical portraiture held at Virginia House in 1929.

John Mutter, d. 1820
Lucinda (Gillies) Mutter, d. 1814 (Mrs. John Mutter)

John Mutter is listed in the 1819 Richmond city directory as a merchant whose firm, John Mutter and Company, was located on Cary Street between Twelfth and Thirteenth streets. He and his wife resided "near Bellville," on the site of the present Commonwealth Club. Mrs. Mutter died in Baltimore on October 18, 1814; her husband died in Richmond in 1820. Their son, Dr. Thomas Dent Mutter, born in 1811, became a professor of surgery at Jefferson Medical College, Philadelphia.

Richmond Portraits, p. 141 (both portraits reproduced); *Encyclopedia of Virginia Biography*, 3: 294; *VMHB* 57 (1949): 207.

Portrait I. John Mutter

COPIED BY AN UNIDENTIFIED ARTIST

Oil on canvas: 27 x 22 in. (68.6 x 55.9 cm.) (framed as an oval)

Presented in 1948 by Aimée (Leffingwell) McKenzie (Mrs. Kenneth McKenzie) and the Misses Leffingwell of New Haven, Connecticut. Por948.15a

Portrait II. Lucinda (Gillies) Mutter

COPIED BY AN UNIDENTIFIED ARTIST

Oil on canvas: 27 x 22 in. (68.6 x 55.9 cm.) (framed as an oval)

Presented in 1948 by Aimée (Leffingwell) McKenzie (Mrs. Kenneth McKenzie) and the Misses Leffingwell of New Haven, Connecticut. Por948.15b

The portraits are copies of originals by Cephas Thompson.

Gustavus Adolphus Myers, 1801–1869

Described by Myron Berman as "the most promi-

John Murray, Lord Dunmore

nent of all Jewish citizens of Richmond in the ante-bellum period," Gustavus Adolphus Myers, born on August 9, 1801, was the son of Samuel and Judith (Hays) Myers. Trained for a legal career, Myers built one of the largest practices in Richmond and acted as legal adviser to various out-of-state firms. He was president of the Richmond Publishing Company, which owned and published the *Enquirer* and the *Examiner*, and a director of the Richmond, Fredericksburg and Potomac Railroad and of the Mutual Assurance Society. Active in politics for most of his adult life, Myers first served on the Richmond City Council in 1827, was reelected to that body twenty-six times, and served as its president 1843–55. He was a member of the board of Beth Shalome synagogue and was active in Richmond's Masonic affairs. When hardly out of his teens Myers translated Duport's one-act play *Nature and Philosophy* and published it anonymously in Richmond (1821); it was performed both in Richmond and New York and remained popular for many seasons. He was a founding member (1831) of the Virginia Historical Society and for many years its recording secretary. Myers married Anne Augusta (Giles) Conway, daughter of Governor William Branch Giles (q.v.) and the widow of Dr. James Conway; the couple had one child, William Barksdale Myers, who achieved a reputation as an artist. Gustavus Adolphus Myers died on August 20, 1869, and is buried in Hollywood Cemetery.

Richmond Portraits. pp. 142–43 (Portrait I reproduced);

Herbert T. Ezekiel and Gaston Lichtenstein, *The History of the Jews of Richmond from 1769 to 1917* (Richmond, 1917), pp. 60–62; Myron Berman, *Richmond's Jewry, 1769–1976: Shabbat in Shockoe* (Charlottesville, Va., 1979), pp. 127–30; Malcolm H. Stern, *Americans of Jewish Descent: A Compendium of Genealogy* (Cincinnati, 1960), p. 156.

Portrait I

By THOMAS SULLY

Oil on canvas: 24 x 20 in. (61 x 50.8 cm.)

Presented by Lelia (Morgan) Wardwell (Mrs. Edward Rogers Wardwell) of New York City, a great-granddaughter of the subject. Por959.17

Portrait II

By WILLIAM BARKSDALE MYERS. Signed (initials). Dated 1868

Oil on composition board: 36½ x 29½ in. (92.7 x 74.9 cm.). Inscribed on the back: "Gustavus A. Myers 1801–1869   By Wm B. Myers 1839–1873."

Presented by Lelia (Morgan) Wardwell (Mrs. Edward Rogers Wardwell) of New York City, a great-granddaughter of the subject. Por959.18

Portrait III

By WILLIAM BARKSDALE MYERS. Signed (initials). Dated 1873

Oil on canvas: 30 x 25 in. (76.2 x 63.5 cm.). Inscribed on the back: "G. A. Myers by W. B. Myers."

Presented by Lelia (Morgan) Wardwell (Mrs. Edward Rogers Wardwell) of New York City, a great-granddaughter of the subject. Por959.34

Gustavus Adolphus Myers (Portrait I)

Gustavus Adolphus Myers (Portrait II)

William Nash and Two Ladies of His Family

William Nash of North Carolina was the father of Eliza (Nash) Meaux (Mrs. Thomas Oliver Meaux) and grandfather of Tarmesia (Meaux) Randolph (Mrs. Edmund Randolph). The accompanying silhouettes probably represent Nash's wife and daughter.

Information received with the silhouettes; VHS Mss6:4 M4645:1; *W. & M. Quart.*, 1st ser., 16 (1907–8): 71; *The Randolphs of Virginia*, p. 199.

Portrait I. William Nash

ARTIST UNIDENTIFIED

Hollow-cut silhouette: 3 in. (7.6 cm.) in height, on paper 5 x 4 in. (12.7 x 10.2 cm.). Inscribed: "Wm. Nash."

Presented in 1971 by Arthur Meaux Kent of Wytheville. Por971.56.a

Portrait II. William Nash

ARTIST UNIDENTIFIED

Hollow-cut silhouette: 3 in. (7.6 cm.) in height, on paper 5 x 4 in. (12.7 x 10.2 cm.)

Presented in 1971 by Arthur Meaux Kent of Wytheville. Por971.56.b

This is a duplicate cutting of Portrait I.

Portrait III. Lady of the Nash family

ARTIST UNIDENTIFIED

Hollow-cut silhouette: 2¼ in. (5.7 cm.) in height, on paper 4½ x 3¾ in. (11.4 x 9.5 cm.). Hair painted in ink.

Presented in 1971 by Arthur Meaux Kent of Wytheville. Por971.57

Portrait IV. Lady of the Nash family

ARTIST UNIDENTIFIED

Hollow-cut silhouette: 2¼ in. (5.7 cm.) in height, on paper 3¼ x 2½ in. (8.3 x 6.4 cm.)

Presented in 1971 by Arthur Meaux Kent of Wytheville. Por971.58

William Naylor, b. 1769

See The Convention of 1829–30

Augustine Neale, 1777–1852

See The Convention of 1829–30

Hugh Nelson, 1768–1836

Virginia congressman and diplomat, Hugh Nelson was born in York County on September 30, 1768, son of Thomas Nelson, Revolutionary governor of Virginia, and Lucy (Grymes) Nelson (qq.v.). He graduated from the College of William and Mary in 1790 and shortly thereafter removed to Albemarle County. On April 28, 1799, he married Eliza Kinloch, only child of Francis and Mildred (Walker) Kinloch; the couple resided at Belvoir, Albemarle County, and there raised a large family, nine of whom lived to adulthood. Nelson practiced law and sat in the Virginia state Senate 1797–1800 and in the House of Delegates 1805–9; he also served as judge of the General Court of Virginia. Elected to the United States Congress, Nelson represented his district from March 4, 1811, to January 14, 1823, when he resigned to accept an appointment as minister plenipotentiary to the court of Spain. He held this diplomatic post during Monroe's administration, resigning on November 23, 1824. He then returned to Albemarle County, where for the rest of his life, with the exception of one further term in the House of Delegates, 1828–29, he devoted himself to his family, his estate, and the affairs of the Episcopal church, of which he was an active member. He died on March 18, 1836.

DAB; *Biographical Directory*; Edward Griffith Dodson, *Speakers and Clerks of the Virginia House of Delegates, 1776–1955* (Richmond, 1956), p. 47; VHS Archives, folio C4a—1881 (Nelson).

ARTIST UNIDENTIFIED

Oil on panel: 8¾ x 6¾ in. (22.2 x 17.2 cm.)

Presented in 1881 by Virginia (Massie) Ligon (Mrs. Joseph Ligon) of Massie's Mill, Virginia. Por882.22

Jane Byrd Nelson, 1775–1808 (later Mrs. Francis Walker)

Eldest child of Hugh and Judith (Page) Nelson, the subject was born at Yorktown in May 1775. She married in 1798 Francis Walker (1764–1806) of Castle Hill, Albemarle County, youngest son of Dr. Thomas Walker and Mildred (Thornton) Walker. Francis Walker represented Albemarle County in the Virginia House of Delegates 1788–91, 1797–1801; he was a representative in the Third United States Congress 1793–95. He died at Castle Hill in 1806. Jane Byrd (Nelson) Walker died February 6, 1808. The couple had three children, one of whom, Judith, married William Cabell Rives (q.v.).

The Page Family, pp. 173, 215, 223, 231 (a cut based on the miniature is reproduced on p. 230).

Jane Byrd Nelson

ATTRIBUTED TO LOUIS CHEFDEBIEN. Ca.1779

Miniature on ivory: 1½ x 1¼ in. (3.8 x 3.2 cm.) (oval)

Presented in 1977 by Anne Page Brydon of Charlottesville. Por977.18

This appealing miniature, depicting the subject as a child no more than four years old, was painted, on the evidence of the subject's age, around 1778–79. It was included in the exhibition of Virginia miniatures at the Virginia Museum of Fine Arts in 1941–42 where it was attributed to John Singleton Copley. This attribution and another assigning the work to Charles Willson Peale are untenable as neither artist is known to have been in Virginia at the time. It has recently been attributed to Louis Chefdebien, an itinerant miniature artist known to have been in Virginia in 1779.

Virginia Museum of Fine Arts, *An Exhibition of Virginia Miniatures* (Richmond, 1941), p. 17, item 33; *Occasional Bulletin*, no. 37 (1978): 13–16 (portrait reproduced).

Lucy (Grymes) Nelson, 1743–1830
See Grymes Children

Thomas Nelson, 1738–1789

Signer of the Declaration of Independence and governor of Virginia, Thomas Nelson was born on December 26, 1738, son of William and Elizabeth (Burwell) Nelson of Yorktown. He was educated in England at Hackney School in London and Christ's College, Cambridge. While on his way home from England in 1761 he was elected to the Virginia House of Burgesses; he remained a member of that body until the outbreak of the Revolution. Elected to Virginia's Revolutionary Conventions and to the Continental Congress, he supported Patrick Henry's militant position and urged Virginia to prepare itself for war. It was he who introduced to the Virginia Convention the resolutions calling on Congress to declare the American colonies free and independent, and after the resolutions had been adopted by the convention, it was he who carried them to Philadelphia. When the Declaration of Independence was finally approved, Nelson was one of the signers. Poor health, however, obliged him to withdraw from Congress in 1777; he returned to Virginia, was appointed commander of the armed forces, and raised a company of troops at his own expense. In 1779 he resumed his seat in Congress, but his health again forced him to return home, where he helped organize the state militia and extended personal credit to maintain the Virginia regiments. In 1781 Nelson succeeded Jefferson as governor of Virginia; in September of that year he brought three thousand Virginia militiamen to Washington's aid at Yorktown and did not hesitate to bombard his own residence, which was being used by Cornwallis as a headquarters; he stood with Washington to receive the surrender of the British on October 19, 1781. Shortly thereafter his health obliged him to give up public office. Having exhausted his fortune for the Revolutionary cause, he retired to Offley, a modest house in Hanover County where he spent the last years of his life. He died on January 4, 1789, and was buried in Yorktown. His wife, whom he married on July 29, 1762, was Lucy (Grymes) Nelson, daughter of Philip and Mary (Randolph) Grymes (q.v., Grymes Children); she bore her husband eleven children and survived him by more than forty years.

DAB; National Gallery of Art, *The Eye of Thomas Jefferson* (Washington, D.C., 1976), p. 11 (original portrait reproduced); *The Page Family*, p. 170; *Virginia Historical Portraiture*, p. 264 (original portrait reproduced); *Portraiture*, pp. 78–79.

COPIED BY DUNCAN SMITH. 1925

Oil on canvas: 30 x 25 in. (76.2 x 63.5 cm.). Inscribed on the back: "Th. Nelson copy after Chamberlayne 1925 by Duncan Smith."

Presented in 1926 by John Stewart Bryan of Richmond and Dr. John Randolph Page of New York City. Por926.10

The Society's portrait is a copy of an original now in the collection of the Virginia Museum of Fine Arts. According to family tradition the original was painted by Mason Chamberlin (d.1787) while Nelson was in England for his schooling.

Philip Norborne Nicholas, 1776–1849

See The Convention of 1829–30

Wilson Cary Nicholas, 1761–1820

Governor of Virginia and United States senator and congressman, Wilson Cary Nicholas was born in Williamsburg on January 31, 1761, son of Robert Carter Nicholas and Anne (Cary) Nicholas. He withdrew from the College of William and Mary in 1779 to enlist in the Revolutionary army, serving in Washington's Life Guard throughout the conflict. He married Margaret Smith, daughter of John Smith of Baltimore; the couple resided at Warren, Albemarle County, and became the parents of nine children. He represented his county in the Virginia General Assembly 1784–89, 1794–99; he was also a delegate to the state Constitutional Convention of 1788 which ratified the federal Constitution. Nicholas was a member of the United States Senate 1799–1804 and became a leader of the Jeffersonians. Returning to private life, he was collector of the port of Norfolk 1804–7. Again elected to Congress, this time to the lower house, he represented his district from March 4, 1807, until poor health necessitated his resignation on November 27, 1809. Nicholas became governor of Virginia on December 11, 1814, and continued in office until December 11, 1816; during his administration he devoted himself to the problems of internal improvement and assisted Jefferson in the establishment of the University of Virginia. After a brief term as president of the Richmond branch of the Bank of the United States, he was again forced into retirement by reason of poor health. He died on October 10, 1820, at the home of his son-in-law Thomas Jefferson Randolph and is buried in the Jefferson family burying ground at Monticello.

DAB; *Biographical Directory*; Edgar Woods, *Albemarle County in Virginia* (Charlottesville, Va., 1901), p. 291; *VMHB* 79 (1971): 241.

COPIED BY AN UNIDENTIFIED ARTIST

Oil on canvas: 30 x 25 in. (76.2 x 63.5 cm.)

Received in 1970 as a bequest of Anna Deane (Carr) Davids (Mrs. H. G. Davids) of Washington, D.C., a great-granddaughter of the subject. Por970.22

The portrait is a copy of an original by Gilbert Stuart.

Andrew Nicolson, 1763–1810

Son of Robert and Mary (Waters) Nicolson of Williamsburg, Andrew Nicolson was born on April 29, 1763. He removed to Richmond in 1782 where his

Andrew Nicolson

brothers George and Thomas already resided and became a successful businessman, later moving across the river to Manchester. He was a partner with Henry Heth, Beverley Randolph, and Edward D. Digges in the development of the Midlothian coal mines in Chesterfield County, operating under the firm name of Nicolson, Heth and Company. He married on October 20, 1798, Judith Wormeley Digges, daughter of Dudley and Elizabeth (Wormeley) Digges of Williamsburg; the couple became the parents of six children. Andrew Nicolson died on August 22, 1810; his wife survived him by almost forty years.

Fillmore Norfleet, *Saint-Mémin in Virginia: Portraits and Biographies* (Richmond, 1942), p. 197 (portrait reproduced p. 83); Janice Nicolson Holmes, *The Nicolson Family of Virginia, 1655–1975* (Fort Worth, Tex., 1976), pp. 23–26; VHS Mss file Nov. 1937, W; *W. & M. Quart.*, 1st ser., 14 (1905–6): 45, and 2d ser., 12 (1932): 59–60; *VMHB* 38 (1930): xv.

BY CHARLES BALTHAZAR JULIEN FÉVRET DE SAINT-MÉMIN

Charcoal on paper: 20 x 14 in. (50.8 x 35.6 cm.)

Presented in 1925 by Jonathan Edwards Woodbridge of Chester, Pennsylvania, a grandson of the subject. Por925.1

Prudence Nimmo, 1807–1903

See Prudence (Nimmo) Granbery, 1807–1903

Adolphus Wilhelm Nolting, ca. 1799–1869

Johanna Paulina Nolting, ca. 1809–1874 (Mrs. Adolphus Wilhelm Nolting)

Born in Germany about 1799, Adolphus Wilhelm Nolting was the son of J. M. W. Nolting. With his wife, Johanna Paulina Nolting, he came to Richmond where he established himself in the tobacco trade and as a commission merchant. His nephew Emil Otto Nolting later joined him in the tobacco exporting business, but sometime after 1850 he left his uncle to form a tobacco business of his own. The registers of Monumental Church record that "all seven children of Mr. A. W. Nolting" were baptized on September 24, 1846; that Charles Theodore, infant child of A. W. Nolting, was buried on July 3, 1847; that the "venerable father of Adolphus W. Nolting" was buried on November 24, 1848; and that Nolting's youngest child, Bohlen, was baptized on his first birthday, June 9, 1850. Richmond directories locate Nolting's business premises on the north side of Cary Street between Thirteenth and Fourteenth streets and his residence at the corner of Twelfth Street and Marshall. He was buried in Shockoe Cemetery on November 22, 1869; his wife was buried there on January 4, 1874.

VMHB 1 (1893–94): 343; George D. Fisher, *History and Reminiscences of the Monumental Church, Richmond, Va., from 1814 to 1878* (Richmond, 1880), pp. 452, 453, 490, 491; Mary Wingfield Scott, *Houses of Old Richmond* (Richmond, 1941), p. 249; A. Bohmer Rudd, *Shockoe Hill Cemetery, Richmond, Virginia, Register of Interments* (Washington, D.C., 1960–62), 2: 91, 107; *VMHB* 87 (1979): 241.

Portrait I. Adolphus Wilhelm Nolting

ARTIST UNIDENTIFIED

Oil on canvas: 29³/4 x 25 in. (75.6 x 63.5 cm.)

Received in 1978 as a bequest of Frances (Nolting) Hoare-Smith (Mrs. Gerald W. Hoare-Smith) of Baltimore, a great-granddaughter of the subject. Por978.1

Portrait II. Johanna Paulina Nolting

ARTIST UNIDENTIFIED

Oil on canvas: 30 x 25 in. (76.2 x 63.5 cm.)

Received in 1978 as a bequest of Frances (Nolting) Hoare-Smith (Mrs. Gerald W. Hoare-Smith) of Baltimore, a great-granddaughter of the subject. Por978.2.

Nolting Children

The three very young children depicted in the portrait are children of Adolphus Wilhelm Nolting and Johanna Paulina Nolting (qq.v.) of Richmond. The census of 1850 lists the couple's children as follows: George, aged 14; Charlotte, aged 14; William, aged 13; Harrison, aged 9; John and Pauline, both aged 7; and "Bohlin" (Bohlen) aged 1. All were born in Virginia. Charles Theodore, "infant child of Mr. A. W. Nolting," died in 1847, according to the records of the Monumental Church. Two of the children in the portrait are similar in age and appearance, and may be one or the other set of twins.

Virginia Genealogical Society, *Richmond City and Henrico County, Virginia, 1850 United States Census* (Richmond, 1977), p. 4; George D. Fisher, *History and Reminiscences of the Monumental Church, Richmond, Va., from 1814 to 1878* (Richmond, 1880), p. 490; *VMHB* 87 (1979): 241.

Nolting children

ARTIST UNIDENTIFIED

Oil on canvas: 30 x 25 in. (76.2 x 63.5 cm.)

Received in 1978 as a bequest of Frances (Nolting) Hoare-Smith (Mrs. Gerald W. Hoare-Smith) of Baltimore. Por978.3

Henry Norris, Baron Norris of Rycote, ca. 1525–1601

The subject was the son of Henry Norris, courtier and close friend of Henry VIII until, on suspicion of having had an intrigue with Anne Boleyn, he was arrested and executed. The king later restored to young Norris much of his father's estate. Norris married Marjorie Williams, daughter of John Williams, later Lord Williams of Thame; thereafter he resided at Wytham, Berkshire, a manor owned by his father-in-law, and, after the death of Lord Williams in 1559, at Rycote near Thame, Oxfordshire. Queen Elizabeth I, who had reason to be grateful to the parents of both Norris and his wife, rewarded the couple with conspicuous marks of favor. In 1561 Norris became sheriff of Oxfordshire and Berkshire; five years later the queen visited him at Rycote, knighted him, and appointed him ambassador to France. He was recalled in 1570 and as a reward for his services was created Baron Norris of Rycote. In 1592 the queen again visited Rycote, and four years later Norris was appointed lord lieutenant of Oxfordshire. He died in June 1601. William Camden, the antiquary, wrote of the subject: "Although himself of a meek and mild disposition, Norris was father of a brood of spirited, martial men"; six sons distinguished themselves as soldiers.

DNB; *Virginia House*, pp. 38–39.

ARTIST UNIDENTIFIED

Oil on canvas: 33 x 28 in. (83.8 x 71.1 cm.)

Received in 1948 as a bequest of Mr. and Mrs. Alexander Wilbourne Weddell of Richmond. Por948.74

Francis North, first Earl of Guilford, 1704–1790

Described by Horace Walpole as an "amiable, worthy man of no great genius," Francis North was born on April 13, 1704, eldest son of Francis North, second Baron Guilford, by his second wife, Alice (Brownlow) North. He matriculated at Trinity College, Oxford, in 1721 but left without taking a degree. In 1727 he took his seat in the House of Commons, but two years later, on succeeding to the title as third Baron Guilford, he withdrew to the House of Lords. An intimate friend of both George III and Queen Charlotte, North received court appointments as gentleman of the bedchamber to Frederick, Prince of Wales, in 1730, as governor to Prince George and Prince Edward in 1750, and as treasurer to Queen Charlotte in 1773. He was created earl of Guilford on April 8, 1752. He died in London on August 4, 1790. North was three times married: first, in 1728, to Lucy Montague, daughter of George Montague, second earl of Halifax; second, in 1736, to Elizabeth (Kaye) Legge, daughter of Sir Arthur Kaye, bart., and widow of George Legge, Viscount Lewisham; third, in 1751, to Catherine (Furnese) Watson,

daughter of Sir Robert Furnese, bart., and widow of Lewis Watson, second earl of Rockingham, "This last marriage, and the size of the bride, caused much amusement at the time, and George Selwyn said that the weather being hot, she was kept in ice for three days before the wedding." The subject's son, Frederick, Lord North, was prime minister during the American Revolution.

DNB; *Encyclopaedia Britannica*.

ARTIST UNIDENTIFIED. Ca. 1750

Enamel miniature: 1^3/4 x 1^1/2 in. (4.5 x 3.8 cm.)

Presented in 1929 by Dr. Hugh T. Nelson of Charlottesville. C929.2

The miniature is mounted inside the lid of an exceptionally handsome gold snuffbox. According to family tradition it was given by Lord Guilford to Thomas Nelson (q.v.), signer of the Declaration of Independence and governor of Virginia, when he was a schoolboy in England as an expression of appreciation for his having saved from drowning a member of the donor's family. Dr. Hugh T. Nelson, who presented the snuffbox to the Society, was Governor Nelson's great-great-grandson.

Portraiture, p. 119; *VMHB* 39 (1931): xiii.

William Oglesby
See The Convention of 1829–30

Ellen Elizabeth O'Neale, ca. 1811–1897
See James Madison Cutts, 1805–1863

Hierome L. Opie
See The Convention of 1829–30

William Griffin Orgain, 1815–1875
See William Allen, 1815–1875

Robert Ould, 1820–1882

Born in Georgetown, D.C., on January 31, 1820, son of Robert and Pauline (Gaither) Ould, the subject attended Jefferson College in Pennsylvania, graduated from Columbia College in Washington, D.C., in 1837, and received his law degree from the College of William and Mary in 1842. During the years preceding the Civil War he practiced his profession in Washington, D.C., served as recorder, or principal municipal judge, of Georgetown, and was appointed by President Pierce to the commission for the codification of the District laws. In 1859 he became district attorney with the avowed purpose of avenging the fatal shooting of his former law partner Philip Barton Key by Congressman Daniel Sickles; it was during these criminal proceedings that Ould first ran afoul of Edwin Stanton. When Virginia seceded he removed to Richmond, the home of his first wife, Sarah (Turpin) Ould. He was appointed to the Confederate War Department as assistant secretary of war, serving in that capacity until July 1862 when he was named commissioner for the exchange of prisoners. The personal animosity that existed between Ould and Edwin Stanton, Lincoln's secretary of war, greatly hindered Ould's work; it also was the cause for Ould's imprisonment on improvised charges after the fall of Richmond. Proved innocent, he later defended Jefferson Davis against charges of treason and conspiracy to mistreat prisoners of war. Ould was elected to one term in the state Senate in 1866 and represented the city of Richmond in the House of Delegates 1874–75. In 1878 he was elected president of the Richmond, Fredericksburg and Potomac Railroad Company. His death occurred on December 15, 1882; he was survived by his second wife, Margaret (Dorsey) Handy Ould, whom he had married on October 31, 1872. Judge Ould had children by both his marriages.

Virginia Cavalcade 14, no. 4 (1965): 10–19; *Encyclopedia of Virginia Biography*, 3: 32–33; Edson Baldwin Olds, *The Olds*

Robert Ould (Portrait II)

(Old, Ould) Family in England and America (Washington, D.C., 1915), p. 320; *Occasional Bulletin*, no. 22 (1971): 4–6 (Portrait II reproduced); CMA Archives, folio Z1n; *Biographic Catalogue*; *VMHB* 79 (1971): 241.

Portrait I

ARTIST UNIDENTIFIED

Oil on canvas: 27 x 22 in. (68.6 x 55.9 cm.)

Presented to the R. E. Lee Camp, Confederate Veterans, in 1924 by the subject's daughter, Madge Dorsey (Ould) Powers (Mrs. William Francis Powers); acquired by the Virginia Historical Society in 1946 through merger with the Confederate Memorial Association. Por946.173

Portrait II

BY EASTMAN JOHNSON. Signed. Dated December 1855

Charcoal and chalk on paper: 21 x 17 in. (53.3 x 43.2 cm.)

Presented in 1970 by Sarah (Powers) Trapnell of Richmond. Por970.8

Elizabeth Page, born ca. 1751 (later Mrs. Benjamin Harrison)

Elizabeth Page, depicted with her brother Mann Page (q.v.) in the portrait by John Wollaston, was the daughter of Mann and Ann Corbin (Tayloe) Page of Rosewell, Gloucester County. Born about 1751, she married Benjamin Harrison (1743–1807) of Brandon, Prince George County, whose first wife, Ann (Randolph) Harrison (q.v.), had died in 1767. Elizabeth (Page) Harrison died without issue; her husband married, as his third wife, Evelyn Taylor Byrd.

The Beverley Family, p. 280; *Occasional Bulletin*, no. 28 (1974): 4–5; *VMHB* 34 (1926): 386–87.

Portrait note: *see* Mann Page, 1749–1803 (Portrait II).

John Page, 1627–1692

John Page, progenitor of the Page family in Virginia, was born in 1627, son of Matthew Page of Bedfont, Middlesex, England. He came to Virginia about 1650, acquired large tracts of land, and by 1655 was representing York County in the House of Burgesses. The commissioners to suppress Bacon's rebellion reported that "Major John Page was a great loser in his estate by the rebellion." In 1681 he became a member of the colonial Council. Five years later he was appointed, with Nicholas Spencer and Philip

Ludwell, to revise and annotate the laws of the colony. Page owned the Middle Plantation on which is located the present city of Williamsburg, and he gave Bruton Parish Church, Williamsburg, the land on which it stands. He died on January 23, 1692, and is buried in Bruton Parish churchyard. His wife, Alice (Lukin) Page, bore him two sons.

Encyclopedia of Virginia Biography, 1: 136; *The Page Family*, pp. 11, 40; *Virginia Historical Portraiture*, pp. 96–97 (original portrait reproduced).

COPIED BY SARAH LANDON RIVES

Oil on canvas: 24 x 20 in. (61 x 50.8 cm.)

Received in 1966 as a bequest of the artist. Por966.21

The Society's portrait is a copy of an original at the College of William and Mary attributed to the school of Sir Peter Lely. The original, together with two other Page portraits and those of Colonel and Mrs. Archibald Cary (which were subsequently burned in the 1926 fire at the Governor's Mansion), was offered to the Virginia Historical Society in 1881 by Dr. Richard Channing Moore Page of New York City. It is not known if any of the original pictures ever came into the Society's custody.

Richmond Standard, Nov. 19, 1881, p. 1, col. 8.

Mann Page, 1749–1803
Mary (Tayloe) Page, 1758–1835
(Mrs. Mann Page)

Mann Page was born in 1749, son of Mann and Ann Corbin (Tayloe) Page of Rosewell, Gloucester County. After graduating from the College of William and Mary in 1768 and qualifying for the bar, he assumed the management of Mannsfield, a family estate in Spotsylvania County where he resided all of his adult life. He represented the county in the House of Burgesses 1772–75 and sat as a delegate in the Revolutionary Conventions of 1775 and 1776. In 1776 he succeeded George Wythe (q.v.) as a delegate to the Continental Congress; he also bore arms throughout the Revolution as a lieutenant colonel in the Spotsylvania County militia. After the war Page continued to represent his constituency in the House of Delegates almost without interruption until 1796. Thereafter he was compelled by reason of financial embarrassments to withdraw from public life and to sell a large part of the Mannsfield estate. He was a founder-member in 1772 of the Virginia Society for the Promotion of Useful Knowledge, a charter member of the Constitutional Society of Virginia, and in 1785 was elected to membership in the American Philosophical Society. He died at Mannsfield in

1803. His wife, whom he married on April 18, 1776, was Mary (Tayloe) Page, daughter of John and Rebecca (Plater) Tayloe of Mount Airy, Richmond County, who bore him three children.

The Page Family, p. 81; *Occasional Bulletin*, no. 25 (1972): 3–6 (Portrait I reproduced) and no. 28 (1974): 4–5 (Portrait II reproduced); *Antiques* 104 (1973): 558 (Portrait I reproduced), 106 (1974): 762 (Portrait II reproduced), and 116 (1979): 1131 (Portrait II reproduced).

Portrait I. Mann Page

ATTRIBUTED TO PHILIPPE ABRAHAM PETICOLAS

Miniature on ivory: 2¼ x 1½ in. (5.7 x 3.8 cm.) (oval)

Presented in 1972 by Louise (Anderson) Patten (Mrs. Clarence Wesley Patten) of Winchester. Por972.18

Portrait II. Mann Page with his sister Elizabeth Page   *See* Plate 20

BY JOHN WOLLASTON

Oil on canvas: 49 x 40 in. (124.5 x 101.6 cm.)

Received in 1973 as a bequest of Louise (Anderson) Patten (Mrs. Clarence Wesley Patten) of Winchester. Por973.16

See Elizabeth Page, born ca. 1751

Mann Page (Portrait I)

Portrait III. Mann Page

ARTIST UNIDENTIFIED

Hollow-cut silhouette: 2½ in. (6.4 cm.) in height, on paper 2¾ in. (7 cm.) in diameter (round)

Received in 1973 as a bequest of Louise (Anderson) Patten (Mrs. Clarence Wesley Patten) of Winchester. Por973.209

The subject of the silhouette bears little resemblance to the child or the young man depicted, respectively, in Portraits II and I. It may represent another member of the family.

Portrait IV. Mary (Tayloe) Page

ARTIST UNIDENTIFIED

Silhouette: 2½ in. (6.4 cm.) in height, on paper 3½ x 2½ in. (8.9 x 6.4 cm.) (oval)

Received as a bequest of Louise (Anderson) Patten (Mrs. Clarence Wesley Patten) of Winchester. Por973.208

The silhouette appears to be a modern copy.

Marianna (Keane) Palmer, b. 1799
See Hugh Payne Keane, 1807–1891

William Henry Palmer, 1835–1926

Born in Richmond on October 9, 1835, the subject was the son of William and Elizabeth Walker (Enders) Palmer. At fifteen years of age he began work as a bookkeeper for his father and later sailed as a supercargo with the ships of the Old Dominion Steamship Company. At the beginning of the Civil War he enlisted in the 1st Virginia Infantry as a private; he rose rapidly to first lieutenant, then to adjutant of the regiment; in October 1861 he was appointed assistant adjutant general of the 1st Brigade, Longstreet's Division. At the battle of Williamsburg he was put in command of the regiment with the rank of major and was there wounded. At the request of General Lee he reorganized the 1st Virginia Regiment in August 1862 and led it at Cedar Mountain, before being transferred to the staff of General A. P. Hill. He saw action at Second Manassas, Sharpsburg, Fredericksburg, Chancellorsville, and all the subsequent battles of the Army of Northern Virginia to the end at Appomattox, rising in rank to lieutenant colonel. After the surrender he was employed for five years as a commission merchant in Richmond, then organized the Southern Fertilizer Company, of which he was president until 1889. Turning to banking, Colonel Palmer became associated with the City Bank of Richmond in the early 1880s and was elected its president in 1890; in 1910 when the City Bank merged with the State Bank of Virginia to become the National State and City Bank, Colonel Palmer was elected president of the consolidated institution, retaining the office until 1920. He was president of the Virginia Fire and Marine Insurance Company and chairman of the board of the Mutual Assurance Society of Virginia. He died in Richmond on July 14, 1926, survived by four daughters and two sons. His wife, Elizabeth (Amiss) Palmer, daughter of Edwin J. Amiss and Sarah (Peck) Amiss of Montgomery County, whom he married on November 26, 1856, died in 1907. Colonel Palmer became a member of the Virginia Historical Society in 1875.

History of Virginia, 5: 91–93; *Confederate Military History*, 3: 1089; *Confederate Veteran* 34 (1926): 308; *Biographic Catalogue.*

BY WILLIAM LUDWELL SHEPPARD. Signed

Oil on canvas: 30 x 25 in. (76.2 x 63.5 cm.). Inscribed on the back: "Lt. Colonel Wm. H. Palmer, Asst. Adjt. Genl, Chief of Staff. 3d Corps A. N. V. Lt. Genl. A. P. Hill Commanding. Replica by W. L. Sheppard from original owned by Col. Palmer."

Presented to the R. E. Lee Camp, Confederate Veterans, in 1909; acquired by the Virginia Historical Society in 1946 through merger with the Confederate Memorial Association. Por946.63

William Price Palmer, 1821–1896

Born in Richmond on August 14, 1821, the subject was the son of Charles and Mary Jane Randolph (Lewis) Palmer. He attended Berkeley's Academy in Hanover County and the University of Virginia, graduating from the latter institution in 1840. At the insistence of his father he prepared himself for a medical career, uncongenial though that was to his natural inclinations, completing his medical studies at the University of Pennsylvania about the year 1844. After further training in a hospital in Baltimore, he practiced medicine in Richmond and for the Danville Railroad. An original member of the Richmond Howitzers, he served with them during the John Brown raid; subsequently, during the Civil War, he was attached to the 54th and 56th Virginia Infantry regiments as a surgeon and was senior surgeon in charge of exchanged and paroled prisoners at Camp Lee, Richmond. On the death of his father, Palmer gave up the practice of medicine to devote himself to literary, historical, and antiquarian pursuits. Keenly interested in Virginia's history, he selected, arranged, and edited the first four volumes and much of the fifth volume of the *Calendar of Virginia State Papers*, unwillingly relinquishing the undertaking for reasons of health; he also contributed

20. Mann and Elizabeth Page

articles on historical subjects to the Richmond *Times*. He was elected to the executive committee of the Virginia Historical Society in 1870; in 1891 he became a vice-president of the Society, an office he held until his death, which occurred in Richmond on March 3, 1896. Dr. Palmer was never married.

Merrow Egerton Sorley, *Lewis of Warner Hall: The History of a Family* (Columbia, Mo., 1937), p. 351; Richmond *Times*, March 4, 1896, p. 6; *Portraiture*, pp. 79–80; *VMHB* 4 (1896–97): 320 and 6 (1898–99): vi.

William Price Palmer

By HELEN RUTHERFOORD JOHNSTON. Signed

Watercolor on paper: 8¼ x 7½ in. (21 x 19.1 cm.)

Presented by the artist in 1897. Por897.1

William Watts Parker, 1824–1899

Dr. William Watts Parker was born at Port Royal, Caroline County, on May 5, 1824, son of Stafford H. Parker and Sarah B. (Pearson) Parker. He attended school in Richmond and graduated from the Richmond Medical College in 1848. For more than a decade he practiced his profession in Richmond, interrupting it in 1854–55 for a tour of the hospitals of England and France. At the beginning of the Civil War he was mustered into service as second lieutenant in the Virginia Life Guard, a unit later designated Company B, 15th Virginia Infantry, and served with it in the Peninsular campaign. In the spring of 1862 he organized Parker's Battery, leading it through the Valley campaign, Sharpsburg, Fredericksburg, Gettysburg, Chickamauga, and the Wilderness. Shortly before the surrender at Appomattox

he was promoted to major. After the war Dr. Parker returned to Richmond where he resumed the practice of his profession, becoming during the next thirty years one of the city's best-known and best-loved physicians. His charitable works were numerous: he was president of the Male Orphan Asylum for many years; he founded the Magdalen Home in 1872, the Spring Street Home in 1874, and the Richmond Home for Ladies in 1883. A charter member of the Medical Society of Virginia, he was elected to its presidency in 1890. Dr. Parker died at his home in Richmond on August 4, 1899, and is buried in Hollywood Cemetery. He was survived by his wife, Ellen Jane (Jordan) Parker, of Smithfield, whom he married on January 4, 1862; the couple had ten children.

Robert K. Krick, *Parker's Virginia Battery, C.S.A.* (Berryville, Va., 1975), pp. 346–52; *Confederate Veteran* 7 (1899): 416; *Biographic Catalogue*.

By JOHN P. WALKER. Signed. Dated 1899

Oil on canvas: 30 x 25 in. (76.2 x 63.5 cm.)

Presented to the R. E. Lee Camp, Confederate Veterans, in 1899 by the Parker Battery Association; acquired by the Virginia Historical Society in 1946 through merger with the Confederate Memorial Association. Por946.121

Cassandra Morrison (Shanks) Patton, 1807–1887

See John Thomas Anderson, 1804–1879

George Smith Patton, 1833–1864

The fourth son of John Mercer Patton and Margaret French (Williams) Patton, the subject was born in Fredericksburg on June 26, 1833. He subsequently removed with his parents to Richmond where he received his secondary education; he entered the Virginia Military Institute and graduated with the class of 1852. After two years in Richmond, during which time he taught school and studied law, he was admitted to the bar. He thereupon removed to Charleston, (West) Virginia, where he practiced his profession until the outbreak of the Civil War. In April 1861 he entered the service of the Confederate army as a captain; he rapidly attained the rank of colonel and was put in command of the 22d Virginia Infantry. Patton was wounded at the battles of Scary and Giles Court House and played a distinguished part in the battle of New Market. He fell mortally wounded at the battle of Winchester, on June 19, 1864. He married on September 8, 1855, Susan Thornton Glassell, daughter of Andrew and Susanna Thompson (Thornton) Glassell; she bore him five children; she married, second, George Hugh Smith. The World War II commander General George S. Patton, Jr., was the subject's grandson.

Memorial, Virginia Military Institute, pp. 422–24; *Virginia Genealogies*, pp. 32–34; *West Virginia History* 26 (1964–65): 178–90 (reproduces the photograph from which the portrait presumably was painted).

By MARY R. GILMER. Signed

Oil on canvas: 27 x 22 in. (68.6 x 55.9 cm.)

Acquired in 1946 through merger with the Confederate Memorial Association. Por946.133

Waller Tazewell Patton, 1835–1863

Born in Fredericksburg on July 15, 1835, the subject was the son of John Mercer Patton and Margaret French (Williams) Patton. He attended the Virginia Military Institute, graduated in 1855, and taught Latin there briefly after his graduation. Turning to the law, he was admitted to the bar in Culpeper County. Elected to the command of a company of the Culpeper Minute Men, he was present at Harpers Ferry and later, with the rank of major in the Army of the Confederacy, participated in the battle of First Manassas. With the reorganization of the company, he became colonel of the 7th Virginia Infantry, leading that regiment at Williamsburg, in the battles around Richmond, and at Second Manassas, where he was severely wounded. Returning to active duty, he served with General Longstreet in the Suffolk campaign. Soon afterward he was elected to the Virginia state Senate but declined to retire from the field; instead, he marched with Lee into Maryland and Pennsylvania. He fell at the head of his regiment in Pickett's charge at Gettysburg. He died in the College Hospital, Gettysburg, on July 21, 1863, a few days after his twenty-eighth birthday.

Memorial, Virginia Military Institute, pp. 425–30; *Biographic Catalogue*.

By MARY R. GILMER. Signed

Oil on canvas: 27 x 22 in. (68.6 x 55.9 cm.)

Presented to the R. E. Lee Camp, Confederate Veterans, in 1901 by the A. P. Hill Camp no. 2, Confederate Veterans, Culpeper; acquired by the Virginia Historical Society in 1946 through merger with the Confederate Memorial Association. Por946.176

Elisha Franklin Paxton, 1828–1863

A native of Rockbridge County, General Paxton was born on March 4, 1828, the son of Elisha and Margaret (McNutt) Paxton. He graduated from Washington College (later Washington and Lee Univer-

sity) in 1845 and from Yale University two years later and studied law at the University of Virginia. After his admission to the bar he spent several years in Ohio; in 1854 he established his law office in Lexington, Virginia. Here he married Elizabeth White, daughter of Matthew White of Lexington; four children were born of this union. Failing eyesight compelled him to resign from his profession in 1860 and to retire to Thorn Hill, his residence near Lexington. At the beginning of the Civil War he enlisted as a lieutenant in the Rockbridge Rifles; with this unit, which was reorganized as part of the 27th Virginia Infantry, he took part in First Manassas. Promoted to major, he was assigned to Stonewall Jackson's staff as assistant adjutant general and on November 1, 1862, assumed command of the Stonewall Brigade with the rank of brigadier general. General Paxton led his command in the battle of Fredericksburg and was killed at Chancellorsville on May 3, 1863. He is buried in Lexington.

Generals in Gray; Elisha Franklin Paxton, *Memoir and Memorials: Elisha Franklin Paxton, Brigadier General, C.S.A.* (n.p., 1905); CMA Archives, folio Z1n; *Biographic Catalogue*.

By JOSEPH FLECK. Signed

Oil on canvas: 27 x 22 in. (68.6 x 55.9 cm.)

Presented to the R. E. Lee Camp, Confederate Veterans, in 1924 by the subject's son; acquired by the Virginia Historical Society in 1946 through merger with the Confederate Memorial Association. Por946.96

Anna Payne, d.1832
See Richard Cutts, 1771–1845

Dolley Payne, 1768–1849
See James Madison, 1751–1836

Matthew Mountjoy Payne, 1787–1862

Born in Goochland County in 1787, the subject was the son of George and Betty McCarthy (Morton) Payne. He entered the army with the rank of first lieutenant on March 12, 1812, and thereafter served continuously for almost fifty years, excepting an eleven-month interval in 1815–16. During this time he rose to the rank of colonel. By a resolution of the Virginia General Assembly dated February 9, 1847, he was voted a sword in recognition of distinguished service during the Mexican War at Resaca de la Palma and at Palo Alto, where he was wounded. Colonel Payne resigned from the army on July 23,

1861; he died on August 1, 1862, and is buried in the cemetery of Grace Episcopal Church in Goochland County.

Portraiture, pp. 80–81; *W. & M. Quart.*, 1st ser., 6 (1897–98): 248, and 2d ser., 2 (1922): 98; *VMHB* 6 (1898–99): 428; Francis Bernard Heitman, *Historical Register and Dictionary of the United States Army* (Washington, D.C., 1903), 1: 777; VHS correspondence file, letter of Miss Juliet Lee dated July 12, 1928.

ARTIST UNIDENTIFIED

Oil on canvas: 30 x 25 in. (76.2 x 63.5 cm.)

Presented about 1895 by Margaret Henderson Lee of Richmond. PorX.3

A card attached to the back of the painting bears the inscription: "Col. Matthew Mountjoy Payne U.S.A. Loaned by Mrs. Laura Pope Martin."

William Henry Fitzhugh Payne, 1830–1904

Born at Clifton, Fauquier County, on January 27, 1830, the subject was the son of Arthur Alexander Morson Payne and Mary Conway Mason (Fitzhugh) Payne. He graduated from the Virginia Military Institute in 1849, studied law at the University of Virginia, was admitted to the bar in 1851, and practiced his profession in Warrenton. In 1856 he was elected Commonwealth's attorney for Fauquier County, a post he held until the beginning of the Civil War. Enlisting as a private, he was soon promoted to a captain in the Black Horse Cavalry and in September 1861 to major of the 4th Virginia Cavalry. Left for dead on the battlefield at Williamsburg in May 1862, he was captured, imprisoned, and in due course exchanged. Returned to duty as a lieutenant colonel, he commanded the 2d North Carolina Cavalry at Warrenton and led it at the battle of Brandy Station. At Hanover, Pennsylvania, he was again wounded and captured; after his exchange he served with General Early throughout the Valley campaign, being promoted to brigadier general on November 1, 1864. He was captured a third time and remained at Johnson's Island prison until released at the conclusion of hostilities. General Payne resumed his law practice in Warrenton after the war, was elected to one term in the Virginia House of Delegates in 1879, and later removed to Washington, D.C., to become general counsel for the Southern Railway. He died in Washington on March 29, 1904, and is buried in Warrenton. General Payne married on September 29, 1852, his cousin Mary Elizabeth Winston Payne, a daughter of William Richards Hooe Winter Payne, a congressman from Alabama; the couple had ten children.

Generals in Gray; Eminent and Representative Men, pp. 549–53; Brooke Payne, *The Paynes of Virginia* (Richmond, 1937), pp. 143–45; *Biographic Catalogue*.

BY RICHARD NORRIS BROOKE. Signed

Oil on canvas: 30 x 25 in. (76.2 x 63.5 cm.)

Presented to the R. E. Lee Camp, Confederate Veterans, in 1908; acquired by the Virginia Historical Society in 1946 through merger with the Confederate Memorial Association. Por946.156

William Ransom Johnson Pegram, 1841–1865

"Willie" Pegram, Confederate artillerist, was born on June 29, 1841, the son of General James West Pegram and Virginia (Johnson) Pegram. He entered the University of Virginia law school in 1860 but withdrew the following year on Virginia's secession from the Union. As lieutenant in the Purcell Battery, he participated in the battle of First Manassas. Rising during the course of the war to colonel, Pegram led his command at the Seven Days, Mechanicsville, Sharpsburg, Chancellorsville, Gettysburg, the Wilderness, and the defense of Petersburg. He was mortally wounded at Five Forks, dying on April 2, 1865, at the age of twenty-three. His body was reinterred after the war in Hollywood Cemetery, Richmond.

Virginia Cavalcade 23, no. 2 (1973): 12–19; *University of Virginia*, 1: 404; *The University Memorial*, pp. 714–26; *Biographic Catalogue*.

ARTIST UNIDENTIFIED

Oil on canvas: 33 x 27 in. (83.8 x 68.6 cm.)

Presented to the R. E. Lee Camp, Confederate Veterans, in 1897 by the Pegram Battalion Association; acquired by the Virginia Historical Society in 1946 through merger with the Confederate Memorial Association. Por946.227

John Pelham, 1838–1863

Gallant Pelham, the boy major of the Confederacy, was born on September 14, 1838, on his grandfather's plantation in Benton (later Calhoun) County, Alabama, the son of Atkinson and Martha (McGehee) Pelham. He entered West Point in 1856 but withdrew in the spring of 1861 to enlist in the Army of the Confederate States. Commissioned lieutenant, he was shortly promoted at J. E. B. Stuart's recommendation to captain of the Stuart Horse Artillery. His courage and ability, together with his boyish good looks, attracted widespread attention in the South and the devotion of the men in his command. Pelham's enterprise in the Seven Days battles in the summer of 1862 led to his promotion to major; at Second Manassas, Sharpsburg, and Fredericksburg he performed no less brilliantly. He was mortally wounded at the battle of Kelly's Ford on March 17, 1863, and died the same day, aged twenty-four. His body lay in state in the Capitol in Richmond before being transported for burial in Jacksonville, Alabama. Pelham achieved an almost legendary stature during his life; it was enhanced after his death by John Esten Cooke's depiction of him in *Surry of Eagle's Nest* (1894).

DAB; Philip Mercer, *The Life of the Gallant Pelham* (Macon, Ga., 1929); *SHS Papers* 26 (1898): 292; *Biographic Catalogue*.

John Pelham

By WILLIAM EDWARD TRAHERN

Oil on canvas: 30 x 25 in. (76.2 x 63.5 cm.)

Presented to the R. E. Lee Camp, Confederate Veterans, in 1898; acquired by the Virginia Historical Society in 1946 through merger with the Confederate Memorial Association. Por946.44

Philadelphia Pelham, 1654–1685

See Francis Howard, fifth Baron Howard of Effingham, 1643–1695

William Dorsey Pender, 1834–1863

Born in Edgecombe County, North Carolina, on February 6, 1834, the subject was the son of James and Sarah (Routh) Pender. He entered West Point at sixteen years of age, graduating with the class of 1854; he saw active duty with the United States Army in the Far West and engaged in Indian skirmishes on the frontier. On March 3, 1859, he married Mary Frances Shepperd, daughter of Augustine H. Shepperd of North Carolina; the couple became the parents of three sons. On the outbreak of the Civil War he offered his services to the Confederacy; elected colonel of the 3d North Carolina Volunteers and later of the 6th North Carolina Regiment, he served in the Peninsular campaign, earning promotion to brigadier general for his conduct at Seven Pines. Pender led his new command, a brigade in A. P. Hill's division, through the Seven Days, Second Manassas, the Maryland campaign, Fredericksburg, and Chancellorsville. Promoted on May 27, 1863, to the rank of major general, he led a division at Gettysburg, displacing the Union forces from Seminary Ridge in the first day; on the second day of the battle he was severely wounded. Evacuated to Staunton, Virginia, General Pender died on July 18, 1863, following the amputation of his leg. His body was interred at Calvary Church, Tarboro, North Carolina.

DAB; *Generals in Gray*; CMA Archives, folio Z1n; *Biographic Catalogue*.

By EMMA MOREHEAD WHITFIELD. Signed. Dated 1923

Oil on canvas: 30 x 25 in. (76.2 x 63.5 cm.)

Presented to the R. E. Lee Camp, Confederate Veterans, in 1924 by the subject's niece, Mrs. John W. Gordon; acquired by the Virginia Historical Society in 1946 through merger with the Confederate Memorial Association. Por946.158

Edmund Pendleton, 1721–1803

Born in Caroline County on September 9, 1721, son of Henry and Mary (Taylor) Pendleton, the subject was apprenticed at fourteen years of age to the clerk of the Caroline County court and was admitted to the bar in 1741. Four years later he was admitted to practice before the General Court. In 1751 he became a justice of the peace of Caroline County, an office he held until 1777; in 1752 he began service in the House of Burgesses that was to continue for the next twenty-two years. During the Revolutionary crisis Pendleton's conservatism was a moderating influence on the militance of Patrick Henry and his followers. He was a member of the Committee of Correspondence in 1773 and a delegate to the first Continental Congress, presided over the Virginia Revolutionary Conventions, and was elected president of the Committee of Safety. As president of the Virginia Convention of 1776 he was instrumental in framing Virginia's first constitution and in revising the legal code. In 1776 he became first Speaker of the Virginia House of Delegates; in 1778 he was elected first president of the High Court of Chancery, and the next year he became the first president of the Virginia Court of Appeals, a position he retained for the rest of his life. Thereafter, except for twice-yearly visits to Richmond to attend sessions of the court, Pendleton resided quietly at Edmundsbury, his home in Caroline County, interrupting his semiretirement to attend the 1788 convention to ratify the federal Constitution over which he was elected presiding officer. He died in Richmond on October 26,

Edmund Pendleton (Portrait II)

1803, and was buried at Edmundsbury; his remains were reinterred in 1907 in Bruton Parish Church, Williamsburg. Pendleton was married twice: his first wife, Elizabeth (Roy) Pendleton, died in childbirth in 1742 less than a year after their marriage; his second wife, Sarah (Pollard) Pendleton, whom he married June 20, 1743, lived until 1794; Pendleton left no issue.

DAB; Edward Griffith Dodson, *Speakers and Clerks of the Virginia House of Delegates, 1776–1955* (Richmond, 1956), pp. 8–9; David John Mays, *Edmund Pendleton, 1721–1803, a Biography* (Cambridge, Mass., 1952) (Portrait I, cropped, reproduced as frontispiece to vol. 1; Portrait II reproduced as frontispiece to vol. 2); *Antiques* 116 (1979): 1137 (Portrait II reproduced).

Portrait I

COPIED BY THOMAS SULLY

Oil on canvas: 30 x 25 in. (76.2 x 63.5 cm.)

Presented in 1851 by Jaquelin Plummer Taylor of Richmond. Por851.2

Sully's portrait is a copy from an original miniature (Portrait II) by William Mercer, the deaf-mute son of General Hugh Mercer of Fredericksburg. The Commonwealth of Virginia also owns two copies made from the same original: one the work of William Ludwell Sheppard and a second by William L. M. Pendleton.

Virginia Historical Reporter 1, pt. 3 (1856): 8; *Portraits and Statuary*, p. 91; *Virginia Cavalcade* 1, no. 1 (1951): 46 (Portrait I reproduced); *Portraiture*, pp. 81–82.

Portrait II

BY WILLIAM MERCER. Signed (initials)

Miniature on ivory: 1 1/2 x 1 1/4 in. (3.8 x 3.2 cm.) (oval)

Presented in 1960 by Mrs. Lewis H. Bosher, Sr., of Richmond. Por960.52

The only known life portrait, this miniature was given by the subject to his great-niece Frances (Pendleton) Taylor of Meadowfarm, Orange County. It remained in the family until it was presented to the Society by Mrs. Lewis H. Bosher, Sr., a great-greatgranddaughter of the original owner.

VMHB 69 (1961): 239; *Occasional Bulletin*, no. 1 (1960): 9, 12 (Portrait II reproduced); *Virginia Historical Portraiture*, pp. 230–31 (Portrait II reproduced).

Maria Pendleton, d. 1850
See John Rogers Cooke, 1788–1854

Philip Clayton Pendleton, 1779–1863
See The Convention of 1829–30

George Percy, 1580–ca. 1632

One of the original settlers at Jamestown and fourth president of the Council, George Percy, born on September 4, 1580, was the eighth son of Henry Percy, eighth earl of Northumberland, and Catharine (Neville) Percy, daughter of John Neville, fourth Baron Latimer. After serving in the army in the Low Countries, he sailed for Virginia in December 1606, coming ashore with the first settlers on May 24, 1607, to establish the Jamestown community. In September 1609 he succeeded Captain John Smith as president of the Council. In charge of the colony during the terrible months when sickness, famine, death, and internal dissension almost destroyed it, he has been charged with incompetence; his own sickness, severe and protracted, probably accounted for the lack of leadership that characterized his administration. When Sir Thomas Gates reached Virginia in May 1610 and relieved Percy of authority, he found only sixty of the five hundred settlers still alive. Percy again served as governor from March to May 1611 during the absence of Governor Thomas West, third Baron De La Warr. He left Virginia on April 22, 1612, and never returned. His *True Relation*, written some time after 1622, was a defense against criticism of his administration made presumably by Captain John Smith. Little is known of his later years except that he was commanding a company in the Low Countries in 1627 and died unmarried around 1632.

DAB; *Portraiture*, pp. 83–84; *Virginia Historical Portraiture*, pp. 66–67 (original portrait reproduced); *VMHB* 35 (1927): 191; Alexander Brown, *The Genesis of the United States* (Boston, 1890), 2: 964.

George Percy

COPIED BY HERBERT LUTHER SMITH. 1854

Oil on canvas: 30 x 25 in. (76.2 x 63.5 cm.)

Presented in 1854 by Conway Robinson of Richmond. Por854.2

Copied from the original owned by the duke of Northumberland, the Society's portrait was secured for Conway Robinson through the good offices of William Twopeny. Robinson's correspondence with Twopeny, together with Smith's bill for fifteen guineas, dated March 24, 1854, is preserved in the Society's manuscript collection.

VHS Mss1 R5685b 977–985.

194

Richard Perkins, 1783–1860

Son of Richard and Elizabeth (Moore) Perkins, the subject was born in Amherst County on June 12, 1783. He married in Fluvanna County on January 25, 1808, Lucy Shores, daughter of Thomas and Susannah (Bugg) Shores; they raised a family of ten children at Locust Grove, their residence in Campbell County near Lynchburg. During the War of 1812 he served as paymaster in the 3d Regiment of Virginia militia. He died on July 5, 1860, and is buried in the family graveyard at Locust Grove. His wife died in 1862.

William Kearney Hall, *Descendants of Nicholas Perkins of Virginia* (Ann Arbor, Mich., 1957), pp. 103, 164; *VMHB* 38 (1930): xvii.

Richard Perkins

ARTIST UNIDENTIFIED

Oil on canvas: 30 x 25 in. (76.2 x 63.5 cm.)

Received in 1946 as a bequest of Lucie Perkins Stone of Hollins, Virginia, a granddaughter of the subject. Por946.15.f

William K. Perrin
See The Convention of 1829–30

Edward Aylesworth Perry, 1831–1889

Confederate general and governor of Florida, Perry was a native of Richmond, Massachusetts; he was born on March 15, 1831, son of Asa and Philura (Aylesworth) Perry. After a year of study at Yale University, he removed to Alabama, where he taught school and studied law. Admitted to the bar in 1857, he began the practice of his profession in Pensacola, Florida. In 1861 he entered Confederate service as captain of Company A, 2d Florida Infantry; a year later, in May 1862, he became colonel of the regiment. Wounded at Frayser's Farm, he was promoted to brigadier general on August 28, 1862, and on his return to active duty was given command of three Florida regiments; these he led at Chancellorsville, the Overland campaign of 1864, and the Wilderness. Wounded again, he was assigned to the reserve forces in Alabama, where he served until the war's end. Returning to Pensacola, General Perry resumed the practice of law, achieving prominence in his profession and a reputation in the state for his attacks on carpetbag politics. He was elected governor of Florida in 1884; at the end of his term of office he retired from public life and died on October 15, 1889. General Perry married on February 1, 1859, Wathen Taylor, who bore him five children.

DAB; *Generals in Gray*; *Biographic Catalogue*.

By JOHN P. WALKER. Signed. Dated 1900

Oil on canvas: 30 x 25 in. (76.2 x 63.5 cm.)

Presented to the R. E. Lee Camp, Confederate Veterans, in 1900; acquired by the Virginia Historical Society in 1946 through merger with the Confederate Memorial Association. Por946.137

"William Pettet"

The portrait came to the Society as a bequest of Dr. Bernard Samuels of New York City, who identified it as "William Pettet of Northumberland County, Virginia." Efforts to identify the sitter further have been to no avail. There were Pettets and Pettits in *Northampton* County at an early date. The man depicted is about thirty years old and wears a full wig and the costume of the middle to late seventeenth century.

ARTIST UNIDENTIFIED

Oil on canvas: 30 x 25 in. (76.2 x 63.5 cm.) (oval). Inscribed on the canvas: "William Pettet."

Received in 1960 as a bequest of Dr. Bernard Samuels of New York City. Por960.51

Alonzo Lafayette Phillips, 1842–1909

The subject was born in Henrico County on June 27, 1842, the eldest son of Fleming Phillips. In April 1861 he joined the Henrico Guard, which later be-

came a part of the 15th Virginia Infantry. He participated in the battles of Bethel Church, the Seven Days, Second Manassas, and Sharpsburg. Promoted to second lieutenant on October 3, 1862, he spent the winter of 1864 in East Tennessee and North Carolina but returned to Virginia in time to fight at Drewry's Bluff. Thereafter, Phillips served with Pickett's division until the end of the war. Returning to Richmond when hostilities were over, he established a contracting company which undertook much railroad construction in the South, particularly for the Richmond, Fredericksburg and Potomac Railroad. He was active in the state militia, rising with many years' service to the rank of brigadier general. Phillips was a commander of the R. E. Lee Camp, United Confederate Veterans, and a member of the board of the Soldiers' Home. He was a member of the Richmond City Council for two terms, retiring eighteen months before his death, which occurred on October 29, 1909. Phillips was twice married: first, on December 15, 1864, to Esprella Blackburn; second, on June 26, 1895, to Ida B. Dickie. He was survived by nine children.

Richmond *Times-Dispatch*, Oct. 30, 1909, p. 2; *Confederate Military History*, 3: 1111–12; CMA Archives, folio Z1n.

By ALPHAEUS P. COLE. Signed. Dated Jan. 1926

Oil on canvas: 28 x 24 in. (71.1 x 61 cm.). Inscribed on the back: "Portrait of Gen Phillips painted from photograph by Alphaeus P. Cole. Some of the red soil of Virginia was used as pigment by the artist when painting this picture."

Presented to the R. E. Lee Camp, Confederate Veterans, in 1926; acquired by the Virginia Historical Society in 1946 through merger with the Confederate Memorial Association. Por946.228

George Edward Pickett, 1825–1875

Born in Richmond on January 25, 1825, son of Robert and Mary (Johnston) Pickett, the subject graduated from West Point in 1846. He saw action during the Mexican War from the siege of Veracruz to the capture of Mexico City and was first over the parapets of Chapultepec. From 1849 to 1856 he served in Texas; thereafter he was on duty in the Northwest, performing valuable service during the confrontation with the British in Puget Sound. Returning to Richmond on the outbreak of the Civil War, Pickett was assigned to the lower Rappahannock; promoted to brigadier general on January 14, 1862, he led his brigade through the battles of the Peninsular campaign until he was wounded at Gaines's Mill. On his return to active duty after the Maryland campaign, he was promoted to major general and was present at Fredericksburg and Suffolk. Pickett's charge at

Gettysburg, on July 3, 1863, his extraordinarily courageous assault on the Federal stronghold on Cemetery Ridge, was unsuccessful, and its cost in terms of Confederate losses was tremendous. Later Pickett commanded the Department of Virginia and North Carolina, recaptured Plymouth, North Carolina, and took part in the defense of Petersburg; he remained with his division until Lee's surrender at Appomattox. After the war he was employed as an agent of the Life Insurance Company of New York. He died in Norfolk on July 30, 1875; his remains were transferred to Hollywood Cemetery, Richmond, the following October. General Pickett was twice married: first, in January 1851, to Sally Minge of Richmond, who died after less than a year of marriage; second, on September 15, 1863, to LaSalle Corbell, by whom he had two children, only one of whom lived to maturity.

DAB; *Generals in Gray*; *Biographic Catalogue*.

George Edward Pickett (Portrait I)

Portrait I

By M. AMMEN. Signed. Dated 1899

Oil on canvas: 30 x 25 in. (76.2 x 63.5 cm.)

Presented to the R. E. Lee Camp, Confederate Veterans, in 1899 by the George E. Pickett Camp, Confederate Veterans; acquired by the Virginia Historical Society in 1946 through merger with the Confederate Memorial Association. Por946.181

Portrait II

See The Battle Abbey Murals. The Summer Mural

Anne Eliza Pleasants, 1836–1901
See Douglas Hamilton Gordon, 1817–1883

James Pleasants, 1769–1839
See The Convention of 1829–30

John Hampden Pleasants, 1797–1846
See The Convention of 1829–30

Pocahontas, ca. 1595–1617

Matoaka, nicknamed Pocahontas ("playful one"), was the daughter of Powhatan, chief of the Indian confederacy in Virginia. Born around 1595, she supposedly visited the Jamestown fort as a child and vied with the colonists' children in turning handsprings; she is likewise supposed to have interceded on behalf of Captain John Smith in 1608, saving him from a death sentence decreed by her father; the veracity of both stories has been questioned. In the spring of 1613 she was captured by Samuel Argall and brought to Jamestown; well treated by the English, she received religious instruction and was baptized into the church, adopting on this occasion the Christian name Rebecca. During her sojourn in Jamestown, John Rolfe, an English gentleman, became enamored of her; having first obtained permission from the governor, he married her in April 1614. The union was considered by both settlers and aborigines a symbol of friendship; it was in no small measure responsible for the eight years of peace that followed. In the spring of 1616 Pocahontas, her husband, and several other Indians accompanied Sir Thomas Dale to England. Entertained by the bishop of London and presented to the king and queen, she was everywhere received as a princess and conducted herself accordingly. While preparing to return to Virginia with her husband, she became ill and died at Gravesend in March 1617. The one child of the union, Thomas Rolfe, later returned to Virginia; Pocahontas has innumerable descendants.

DAB; *Portraiture*, pp. 84–86.

Portrait I

By THOMAS SULLY. 1852

Oil on canvas: 36 x 28 in. (91.4 x 71.1 cm.)

Presented by the artist in 1852. Por852.2

Begun May 17, 1852, and completed August 24, 1852, the portrait is listed in Sully's register as an "ideal portrait from an engraving."[1] Julia Sully quotes the artist as saying: "The portrait I painted and presented to the Historical Society of Virginia, was copied in part from the portrait of Pocahontas in the 'Indian Gallery', published by Daniel Rice and Z. Clark."[2] Its receipt by the Society was noted in lyrical prose, verse, and in a more straightforward manner at the Society's sixth annual meeting.[3] In March 1854 the Society's executive committee gave Robert Matthew Sully permission to copy his uncle's portrait of Pocahontas for Hugh Blair Grigsby; it gave William B. Myers permission to copy the same portrait in January 1857.[4]

1. Edward Biddle and Mantle Fielding, *The Life and Works of Thomas Sully* (Philadelphia, 1921), p. 379. 2. *Portraiture*, p. 85. 3. *Virginia Historical Register* 5 (1852): 238, 240, and 6 (1853): 49, 52. 4. VHS Archives, liber A3, pp. 28, 50.

Portrait II

By Robert Matthew Sully

Oil on canvas: 36 x 28 3/4 in. (91.4 x 73 cm.)

Pocahontas (Portrait IV)

Presented by the artist before his death in 1855. PorX.5

In a controversy publicly aired in the columns of the *Richmond Enquirer* during September 1830, the authenticity of the portraits of Pocahontas and John Rolfe that formerly hung at Turkey Island and Cobbs was debated.[1] The exchange was prompted by a report that Robert Matthew Sully had made a copy of the Pocahontas portrait. Although the provenance of the Society's portrait is unclear, it is quite possibly the same canvas that sparked the 1830 debate.[2]

1. *Richmond Enquirer*, Sept. 3, 10, 17, 28, 1830; VHS Mss2 B6386b. 2. Ella Loraine Dorsey, *Pocahontas* (Washington, D.C., 1906), pp. 47–51.

Portrait III

Copied by Anne Fletcher. 1929

Oil on canvas: 30 x 25 1/4 in. (76.2 x 64.1 cm.)

Received in 1948 as a bequest of Mr. and Mrs. Alexander Wilbourne Weddell of Richmond. Por948.103

The portrait is a copy of the Booton Rectory portrait now hanging in the National Portrait Gallery in Washington.

Virginia House, p. 61.

Portrait IV

By William Ordway Partridge. Signed

Bronze statue: 22 in. (55.9 cm.) in height, including base

Received in 1948 as a bequest of Mr. and Mrs. Alexander Wilbourne Weddell of Richmond. Por948.124

The life-sized original of this statue stands at James-town.

Virginia House, p. 36.

Camille Armand Jules Marie, Prince de Polignac, 1832–1913

A general in the Confederate army, the subject was born on February 16, 1832, at Millemont, France, the son of the Prince de Polignac, president of the Council of Ministers to Charles X of France. After completing his formal education at the College of Stanislaus in Paris and serving in the Crimean War, he resigned his commission in 1859 to study plant life in Central America. On the outbreak of the Civil War he offered his services to the Confederacy. He served on the staffs of Generals Beauregard and Bragg, and later, having been promoted to brigadier general in January 1863 and major general in April 1864, he saw action with the Army of Tennessee, distinguishing himself in the battles of Mansfield, Pleasant Hill, and other engagements of the Red River campaign. Sent by the Confederate government to secure the assistance of Napoleon III, he ran the blockade in March 1865, but hostilities ended shortly after his arrival in Europe. Thereafter he retired to his estate where he devoted himself to the study of mathematics and civil engineering. During the Franco-Prussian War in 1870–71 he emerged from retirement to lead the 1st Division; he was awarded the Legion of Honor for his services to the country. He died in Paris on November 15, 1913. He married, first, Marie Adolphine Langenberger and, second, Elizabeth Marguerite Knight; there were two children by his second marriage.

Generals in Gray; Jon L. Wakelyn, *Biographical Dictionary of the Confederacy* (Westport, Conn., 1977).

BY ELLIS MEYER SILVETTE. Signed

Oil on canvas: 30 x 25 in. (76.2 x 63.5 cm.)

Acquired in 1946 through merger with the Confederate Memorial Association. Por946.86

John Luke Porter, 1813–1893

The youngest child of Joseph and Frances (Pritchard) Porter, the subject was born in Portsmouth on September 19, 1813. He learned shipbuilding at his father's shipyard and supervised the construction of naval vessels in Washington and Pittsburgh. While engaged in work for the government at the latter place in 1846 he submitted to the Navy Department a design for an ironclad vessel; the plans were not approved. In 1852 he was again in Portsmouth, becoming in that year first president of the city's common council, and on October 1, 1859, he was commissioned naval constructor attached to the navy yard in Pensacola, Florida. When Virginia seceded from the Union, Porter offered his services to the Confederacy; he was largely responsible for reconstructing and equipping the *Merrimack*, later renamed the C.S.S. *Virginia*, as an ironclad. Appointed chief constructor of the navy, he designed numerous ironclad naval vessels, but a critical shortage both of engines and iron for armor greatly hindered his work. At the war's end he became manager of the naval department of the Atlantic Works in Norfolk, worked with the Baker Shipyards, and was superintendent of the Norfolk and Portsmouth ferry service. He died in Portsmouth on December 14, 1893, survived by six children. His wife, whom he married on December 18, 1834, was Susan (Buxton) Porter, daughter of James and Martha (Lockhart) Buxton of Nansemond County.

DAB; *W. & M. Quart.*, 1st ser., 24 (1915–16): 228–29; CMA Archives, folio Z1n; *Biographic Catalogue*.

BY JOHN P. WALKER. Signed. Dated 1924

Oil on canvas: 30 x 25 in. (76.2 x 63.5 cm.)

Presented to the R. E. Lee Camp, Confederate Veterans, in 1924; acquired by the Virginia Historical Society in 1946 through merger with the Confederate Memorial Association. Por946.188

Alfred Harrison Powell, 1781–1831
See The Convention of 1829–30

John Powell, 1882–1963

Pianist and composer John Powell was born in Richmond on September 6, 1882, son of John Henry Powell and Rebecca (Leigh) Powell. As a child he studied music with his sister Betty (Mrs. J. Smith Brockenbrough) and Frederick Hahr; he gave his first solo concert at twelve. After studying at McGuire's School in Richmond, he continued his formal education at the University of Virginia; following his graduation in 1901 he went to Vienna to study piano with Teodor Leschetizky and composition with Carl Navratil. He made his concert debut in Berlin in 1907; thereafter he appeared in Vienna, Paris, and London, winning critical acclaim. His American debut was at Carnegie Hall on February 25, 1913. In 1920 he was soloist with the New York Symphony on its European tour, and eight years later he again toured England and Europe. Keenly interested in folk music, he was indefatigable in his search for ballads and traditional airs in western Virginia; he also promoted the White Top Mountain Festival of folk music. He wove Negro and mountain melodies into his compositions; by 1929 his "Rhapsodie Nègre" for piano and orchestra had been performed more than fifty times; his Symphonie in A, or "Virginia Symphony," on which he had worked for fifteen years, received its premiere in Detroit in 1947; it was first played in Virginia on November 5, 1951, officially designated "John Powell Day" by the governor of Virginia. He was the second Virginian to be elected to the National Institute of Arts and Letters. John Powell died on August 15, 1963. His wife, whom he married on April 25, 1928, was Louise (Burleigh) Powell.

Who Was Who in America 4 (1968): 763; Pocahontas Wight Edmunds, *Virginians Out Front* (Richmond, 1972), pp. 337–74.

Portrait I

BY BERKELEY WILLIAMS, JR.

Pencil on paper: 8¾ x 5¾ in. (22.2 x 14.6 cm.)

Presented in 1978 by the artist's widow. Berkeley Williams collection, Sketchbook 6

Portrait II

BY BERKELEY WILLIAMS, JR.

Charcoal on paper: 11³/4 x 9 in. (29.9 x 24.8 cm.)

Presented in 1978 by the artist's widow. Berkeley Williams collection, Sketchbook 9

Portrait III

BY BERKELEY WILLIAMS, JR.

Charcoal on paper: 11³/4 x 9 in. (29.9 x 24.8 cm.)

Presented in 1978 by the artist's widow. Berkeley Williams collection, Sketchbook 9

Joseph Prentis, 1783–1851
See The Convention of 1829–30

Margaret Susan Prentis, 1810–1882
See Robert Henning Webb, 1795–1866

William Preston, 1816–1887

Born near Louisville, Kentucky, on October 16, 1816, General Preston was the son of William and Caroline (Hancock) Preston. He received his formal education in Kentucky and at Harvard University, received his law degree from Harvard in 1838, and was admitted to the bar in Louisville. In 1840 he married Margaret Wickliffe, the daughter of Robert Wickliffe of Lexington; she bore him five daughters and a son. After active duty as lieutenant colonel of the 4th Kentucky Infantry during the Mexican War, he entered politics; in 1850 he was elected to the lower house of the Kentucky state legislature, the following year to the upper; in 1852 he became a United States congressman, serving till 1855. Preston was a delegate to the 1856 National Democratic Convention in Cincinnati and in 1858 was appointed minister to Spain by President Buchanan. Instrumental in securing Kentucky for the Confederacy, Preston later became a member of General Albert Sidney Johnston's staff; after Johnston's death at Shiloh, Preston accepted a commission as brigadier general, seeing action at Corinth, Vicksburg, Murfreesboro, and Chickamauga. On January 7, 1864, President Davis named him minister to Mexico, but finding himself unable to reach that country, he spent the final months of the war in the Trans-Mississippi Department. Following some months of travel in Mexico, the West Indies, England, and Canada, General Preston returned with his family to Kentucky in 1866. Again in politics, he served in the Kentucky legislature 1868–69 and was a delegate to the Democratic national conventions of 1868 and

1880. General Preston died in Lexington on September 21, 1887, and is buried in Louisville.

DAB; *Generals in Gray.*

William Preston

BY H. NIEMEIER. Signed. Dated 1934?

Oil on canvas: 56 x 36 in. (142.2 x 91.4 cm.)

Acquired in 1946 through merger with the Confederate Memorial Association. Por946.205

William Radford, 1759–1803

William Radford, born in 1759, was the son of John and Ruth (Tannehill) Radford of Frederick County, Maryland. He saw military service during the American Revolution, was captured in North Carolina, sent to prison in England, but escaped and returned to Virginia. In 1783 he married Rebecca Winston (1761–1820), daughter of Geddes and Mary (Jordan) Winston of Hanover County; they became the parents of six children. After serving as undersheriff of Hanover County, he became in 1795 proprietor of the Eagle Tavern at Twelfth and Main streets, Richmond. "Col. Radford of the Eagle," according to Samuel Mordecai, chronicler of early Richmond, "was of grand dimensions, as was his house in those days, and of great resort." With his wealthy brother-in-law, Thomas Rutherfoord (q.v.), he became part owner of the Albion Mills. His death occurred in Richmond on April 3, 1803.

Richmond Portraits, p. 167; VHS Mss1 G7955a 583–636; Samuel Mordecai, *Richmond in By-Gone Days* (Richmond, 1946), p. 247.

ARTIST UNIDENTIFIED

Silhouette in India ink: 2½ in. (6.4 cm.) in height, on paper 4 x 2½ in. (10.2 x 6.4 cm.)

Presented in 1970 by Elizabeth Stuart Gray of West Point. Por970.34

The silhouette is virtually identical to the one in the Valentine Museum collection that is reproduced in *Richmond Portraits* (p. 167). Both may be recent copies of an early original.

Randolph Portraits

This chart shows the relationship of members of the Randolph family depicted in portraits owned by the Virginia Historical Society. The identity of certain of the subjects has been questioned. Although problems of identification undoubtedly exist (as do problems of attribution), in this catalogue the portraits appear under their long-standing designations and will continue to be so designated by the Society until solid evidence for reidentifying them comes to hand. Subjects of the Society's portraits are indicated in italics.

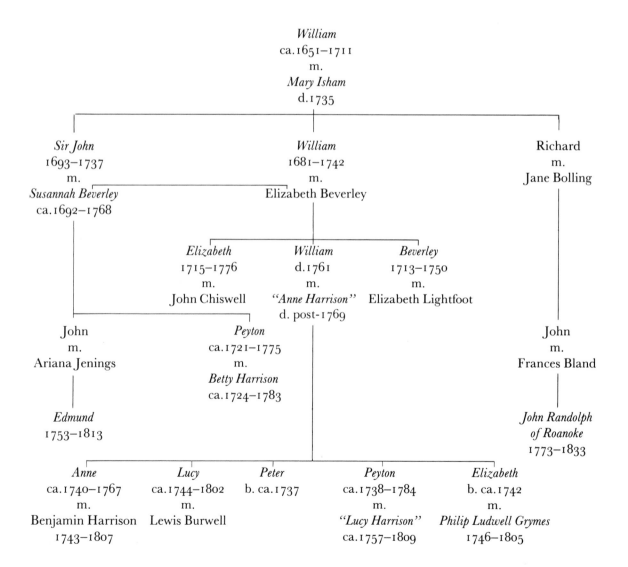

Anne Randolph, ca. 1740–1767 (later Mrs. Benjamin Harrison)

Anne Randolph, born about 1740, was one of the eight children of William Randolph III and Anne (Harrison) Randolph (qq.v.) of Wilton. She married in 1760 Benjamin Harrison (1743–1807) of Brandon, Prince George County, son of Nathaniel and Mary (Digges) Harrison. She died without issue on November 23, 1767. Her husband married, second, Elizabeth Page and, third, Evelyn Taylor Byrd.

The Beverley Family, pp. 270, 280 (where Harrison's third wife is erroneously named Elizabeth Taylor Byrd); *VMHB* 34 (1926): 386–87; Williamsburg *Virginia Gazette* (Purdie & Dixon), Nov. 26, 1767. See chart on Randolph Portraits for relationships.

By JOHN WOLLASTON

Oil on canvas: 29 x 36 in. (73.7 x 91.4 cm.)

Received in 1951 as a bequest of Kate Brander (Harris) Mayo Skipwith Williams (Mrs. Berkeley Williams; previously Mrs. Grey Skipwith, and prior to that Mrs. Edward Carrington Mayo). Por951.34

The companion piece to this portrait depicts the subject's sister Elizabeth Randolph (born ca. 1742) (q.v.), later Mrs. Philip Ludwell Grymes.

Beverley Randolph, 1713–1750

Son of William Randolph II (q.v.) of Turkey Island, Henrico County, and Elizabeth (Beverley) Randolph, the subject was born on November 12, 1713. He attended the College of William and Mary. His wife, whom he married on December 22, 1737, was Elizabeth Lightfoot, daughter of Francis Lightfoot; the couple had no children. He was commissioned justice of the peace for Henrico County on August 3, 1741, and was for a short time sheriff of the county. For the last six years of his life he represented the College of William and Mary in the House of Burgesses. He died in 1750. Portraits of the subject's brother and sister, William Randolph (d. 1761) and Elizabeth (Randolph) Chiswell (1715–1776) (qq.v.), are also in the Society's collection.

The Beverley Family, p. 118; Wassell Randolph, *William Randolph I of Turkey Island, Henrico County, Virginia, and His Immediate Descendants* (Memphis, 1949), pp. 39–40; *The Randolphs of Virginia*, p. 11; *The Randolphs* (portrait reproduced opposite p. 31); *VMHB* 25 (1917): 403. See chart on Randolph Portraits for relationships.

By JOHN WOLLASTON

Oil on canvas: 36 x 29 in. (91.4 x 73.7 cm.)

Presented in 1927 by Kate Brander (Harris) Mayo Skipwith (Mrs. Grey Skipwith; formerly Mrs. Edward Carrington Mayo; subsequently Mrs. Berkeley Williams). Por927.18

If the subject is correctly identified, the portrait must have been painted posthumously, presumably from an earlier likeness, for Wollaston did not come to Virginia until about five years after Beverley Randolph's death.

Anne Randolph, ca.1740–1767

Edmund Randolph, 1753–1813

Governor of Virginia, first attorney general of the United States, and secretary of state under Washington, Edmund Randolph was born in Williamsburg on August 10, 1753, son of John and Ariana (Jenings) Randolph and grandson of Sir John Randolph (q.v.). He attended the College of William and Mary and studied law with his father, who later, as a loyalist, withdrew to England with Lord Dunmore. Edmund Randolph was aide-de-camp to General Washington in 1775, a member of the Virginia Convention of 1776, and the same year became Virginia's first attorney general. In 1779 he was elected to the Continental Congress, serving until 1782; he was governor of Virginia 1786–88 and represented the state at the Annapolis Convention of 1786 and the Constitutional Convention of 1787, where he presented the Virginia Plan of government. Although he was critical of the Constitution and refused to sign it, he urged its ratification at the state Convention of 1788. Appointed by Washington first attorney general of the United States in 1789, he held the post until he was appointed Jefferson's successor as secretary of state on January 2, 1794. Falsely accused of a variety of diplomatic indiscretions, Randolph resigned from the cabinet on August 19, 1795; he settled in Richmond, practiced law, and in 1807 served as chief defense counsel in the trial of Aaron Burr. He likewise devoted himself to writing a *History of Virginia*, first published in its entirety in 1970 by the Virginia Historical Society. He died in Clarke County on September 12, 1813. His wife, who predeceased him by three years, was Elizabeth Nicholas, daughter of Robert Carter Nicholas. The couple married on August 29, 1776, and were the parents of a son and three daughters.

DAB; *Virginia Historical Portraiture*, pp. 271–72; *Portraiture*, pp. 91–92. See chart on Randolph Portraits for relationships.

ARTIST UNIDENTIFIED

Oil on canvas: 26½ x 21½ in. (67.3 x 54.6 cm.)

Received about 1858. Provenance unknown.
Por858.5

Moncure Daniel Conway's preface to his biography of Randolph begins: "In a room of the Virginia Historical Society there is a portrait [of Randolph] so blurred that the face is repulsive."[1] Elsewhere the same authority states: "The Virginia Historical Society picture is utterly worthless. I was told by Edmund Randolph's grandchildren, Peter V. Daniel, Jr. and Mrs. Elizabeth Cocke, that when that picture was painted Randolph's family were indignant, regarding it as almost a caricature."[2] The Society's portrait, extensively overpainted but by no means "repulsive," has long been thought to be a copy of an

Edmund Randolph

original portrait, now lost, by an unidentified artist. Another copy (the work of Flavius J. Fisher), derived from the same lost original, hangs in the Virginia State Library. Recently it has been suggested that the lost original may well have been the work of Robert Edge Pine, for Pine is known to have painted Edmund Randolph but the whereabouts of the portrait is not known.[3] Concerning the original portrait, Edmund R. Cocke of Penrith, Cumberland County, a great-grandson of the subject, wrote: "My mother was the owner of the original portrait of Randolph, but it was not a good likeness. After having had several copies made, one of which is now in my possession, she deposited the original in an institution of art and literature in Richmond called the 'Athenoeum.' The building was destroyed by fire about 1862 or 1863 and the picture lost."[4] In point of fact the Athenaeum, which also housed the collections of the Virginia Historical Society, was not destroyed by fire during the Civil War; it was demolished in 1858. The same year George Wythe Randolph, a member of the Society's executive committee, wrote: "Our collection is increasing. We have now a Peyton Randolph and Edmund Randolph."[5] The fact that the Athenaeum closed its doors and distributed its collections the same year that the Society acquired the portrait suggests that the Athenaeum's portrait and the Society's portrait are one and the same. If the original portrait was the work of Robert Edge Pine, and if, as Edmund R. Cocke stated, the original portrait was a part of the Athenaeum collection, and if the Athenaeum portrait came into the possession of the Virginia Historical Society, the value of the Society's portrait is greater than has heretofore been imagined. A thorough cleaning of the picture may be of help in determining if the Society's picture is in fact Pine's lost original.

1. Moncure Daniel Conway, *Omitted Chapters of History Disclosed in the Life and Papers of Edmund Randolph* (New York, 1888), p. v.   2. Clarence Winthrop Bowen, *The History of the Centennial Celebration of the Inauguration of George Washington* (New York, 1892), pp. 520–21.   3. Robert G. Stewart, *Robert Edge Pine, a British Portrait Painter in America, 1784–1788* (Washington, D.C., 1979), p. 76.   4. *Virginia Historical Portraiture*, p. 272.   5. Letter to Mary ("Molly") Randolph, dated May 3, 1858, Edgehill-Randolph Papers, University of Virginia.

Elizabeth Randolph, 1715–1776

See Elizabeth (Randolph) Chiswell, 1715–1776

Elizabeth Randolph, born ca. 1742 (later Mrs. Philip Ludwell Grymes)

One of the eight children of William Randolph III, builder of Wilton, and Anne (Harrison) Randolph (qq.v.), the subject is thought to have been born around 1742. She married in 1762 Philip Ludwell Grymes (1746–1805) (q.v., Grymes Children), son of Philip and Mary (Randolph) Grymes of Brandon, Middlesex County. The date of the subject's death has not been found, but it is known that she had no issue, and that her husband married second, on May 25, 1773, Judith Wormeley, daughter of Ralph Wormeley (q.v.) and Eleanor (Tayloe) Wormeley of Rosegill, Middlesex County.

The Beverley Family, pp. 270, 494. See chart on Randolph Portraits for relationships.

BY JOHN WOLLASTON

Oil on canvas: 28½ x 35 in. (72.4 x 88.9 cm.)

Received in 1947 as a bequest of Kate Brander (Harris) Mayo Skipwith Williams (Mrs. Berkeley Williams; previously Mrs. Grey Skipwith, and prior to that Mrs. Edward Carrington Mayo). Por947.71

The companion piece to this portrait, also owned by the Society, depicts the subject's sister, Anne Randolph (ca. 1740–1767) (q.v.), later Mrs. Benjamin Harrison.

George Wythe Randolph, 1818–1867

Born on March 10, 1818, at Monticello, the home of his maternal grandfather, Thomas Jefferson, the subject was the son of Governor Thomas Mann Randolph and Martha (Jefferson) Randolph. At thirteen years of age he was appointed a midshipman in the navy and spent the next six years at sea. A student at the University of Virginia 1837–39, he studied law, and after being admitted to the bar he practiced his profession first in Albemarle County and then in Richmond. He was one of the organizers of the Richmond Howitzer artillery company, a member of Virginia's peace commission to the United States early in 1861, and a delegate to the Virginia Secession Convention. During the Peninsular campaign Randolph commanded the Howitzers, was chief of artillery under Magruder, and was promoted to brigadier general on February 12, 1862. The following month he became secretary of war of the Confederate States. Discovering that the post was little more than a clerical appointment owing to President Davis's domination, Randolph resigned on November 15, 1862. Shortly thereafter he was found to have tuberculosis and went to France for the recovery of his health; there he remained until the conclusion of the war. He died on April 3, 1867, at Edgehill, near Charlottesville, survived by his wife, Mary Elizabeth (Adams) Pope Randolph, whom he had married on April 20, 1852; there were no children.

DAB; *Generals in Gray*; *Confederate Veteran* 6 (1898): 271; *Biographic Catalogue*.

BY WILLIAM LUDWELL SHEPPARD

Oil on canvas: 30 x 25 in. (76.2 x 63.5 cm.). Inscribed on the back: "Genl. George W. Randolph painted by W. L. Sheppard."

Presented to the R. E. Lee Camp, Confederate Veterans, by the Richmond Howitzer Association in 1898; acquired by the Virginia Historical Society in 1946 through merger with the Confederate Memorial Association. Por946.139

Sir John Randolph, 1693–1737
Susannah (Beverley) Randolph, ca. 1692–1768   (Lady Randolph)

Born in 1693 at Turkey Island, Henrico County, seat of his parents, William and Mary (Isham) Randolph (qq.v.), Sir John Randolph attended the College of William and Mary, entered Gray's Inn, London, in 1715, and was admitted to the bar on November 25, 1717. Returning to Virginia, he immediately became clerk of the House of Burgesses, holding that remunerative office from 1718 until 1734. Before 1721 he married Susannah Beverley, born about 1692, daughter of Peter and Elizabeth (Peyton) Beverley and sister of the wife of William Randolph II (q.v.). During the absence of the attorney general, John Clayton, in 1727, he was acting attorney general of the colony. In 1728 and again in 1732 he was sent to England to press for various concessions, among them changes in methods of raising revenues and more funds for the college library. The diplomacy with which he executed his mission was rewarded; he received a knighthood from the English and a thousand pounds from the Virginia House of Burgesses. Sir John was elected Speaker of the House of Burgesses in 1734 and shortly thereafter became treasurer of the colony; he was reelected Speaker in 1736, holding the office until his death, which occurred on March 2, 1737. Sir John and his wife resided at Tazewell Hall in Williamsburg; they had four children, one of whom, Peyton Randolph (q.v.), was Speaker of the House of Burgesses and president of the Continental Congress. Lady Randolph survived her husband by more than thirty years; she died in 1768.

DAB, *The Beverley Family*, p. 364; *Tyler's Quart.* 10 (1928–29): 203; *The Randolphs*, pp. 37, 60 (William and Mary portraits reproduced); *VMHB* 65 (1957): 253. See chart on Randolph Portraits for relationships.

Portrait I. Sir John Randolph

COPIED BY JOHN W. GÜNTHER. 1955

Oil on canvas: 30 x 25 in. (76.2 x 63.5 cm.). Inscribed on the back: "Sir John Randolph. Copy By J. W. Guenther, 1955 Williamsburg, Va."

Presented in 1956 by Langbourne Meade Williams of Rapidan. Por956.15

Portrait II. Susannah (Beverley) Randolph

COPIED BY JOHN W. GÜNTHER. 1955

Oil on canvas: 30 x 25 in. (76.2 x 63.5 cm.). Inscribed on the back: "Lady Susan, daughter of Peter Beverley of Gloucester, and wife of Sir John Randolph."

Presented in 1956 by Langbourne Meade Williams of Rapidan. Por956.16

The portraits are copies of portraits owned by the College of William and Mary. The college's portraits, the work of Edward Caledon Bruce, were copied from contemporary miniatures of the subjects.

John Randolph, 1773–1833

Congressman, orator, eccentric, John Randolph of Roanoke, as he is known, was born in Prince George County on June 2, 1773, son of John and Frances (Bland) Randolph of Bizarre, Cumberland County. He attended a variety of schools and colleges before being elected a States' Rights Democrat to the Sixth United States Congress and to the six succeeding congresses, 1799–1813. On the victory of the Jeffersonians in 1800 he was appointed, although only twenty-eight years of age, chairman of the House

Ways and Means Committee and became the recognized leader of his party. Breaking with the Jeffersonians after 1805 and opposing the War of 1812, he was defeated for reelection in 1813 but thereafter was a member of the House of Representatives 1815–17, 1819–25; he sat in the United States Senate 1825–27 and was then again in the House 1827–29. During this time he opposed the policies of Madison, John Quincy Adams, and Henry Clay, used his considerable influence to promote sectionalism, and became, by reason of his oratorical brilliance, his eccentricity, and his volatile and vitrolic temperament, one of the most conspicuous public figures of the time. He was a delegate to the Virginia Convention of 1829, and the following year accepted an appointment as United States minister to Russia, but shortly resigned the post because of ill health and increasing mental instability. He retired to Roanoke, his rustic estate in Charlotte County where for many years, when public duty permitted, he had lived in solitude. Randolph died in Philadelphia on May 24, 1833, just a few months after being elected to the Twenty-third United States Congress; he was buried at Roanoke; in 1879 his remains were removed to Hollywood Cemetery, Richmond. He was never married.

DAB; *Encyclopedia Americana*; *Biographical Directory*. See chart on Randolph Portraits for relationships.

Portrait I

BY ROBERT MATTHEW SULLY

Oil on canvas on panel: 36 x 28 in. (91.4 x 71.1 cm.)

Presented by the artist some time before his death in 1855. Por855.1

The Society's portrait is a replica of one painted from life about the year 1828. The artist's son, Robert Matthew Sully, Jr., in response to an inquiry about the portrait, stated in a letter dated December 14, 1896: "When you asked me about the history of the portrait of Jno. Randolph of Roanoke a few days ago I deferred making any positive statement at the time because I wished to talk over the matter with my mother now eighty two years old, who was perfectly familiar with all of the circumstances attending the painting of the same. The portrait was painted by my father Robert M. Sully from sittings by Mr. Randolph. It was painted for my grandfather Garland Thompson of Richmond, who it seems was at that time making a collection of notables, or rather the portraits of them. The original was painted during the winter of 1828 & 29 and a portrait of Chief Justice Marshall was painted the same winter. This also was done for my grandfather. Subsequently replicas of both of these portraits were painted by my father. The one of Judge Marshall was order[ed] from the Bar at Staunton, Va. and is probably in the court house at that place at present. The other, of

Mr. Randolph, was presented by my father, together with portraits of the Indian Chief Black Hawk, his son and the Prophet, to the Virginia Historical Society. The originals of Judge Marshall and Mr. Randolph were bequeathed by the terms of my grandfather's will, the first to his brother John Thompson of Culpeper, Va., and the latter to his brother Frank Thompson of the same county. They are in the possession of the descendants of John and Frank Thompson at the present time." The purchase of a frame for the portrait was authorized by the Society's executive committee at its meeting on May 1, 1854.

VHS Archives, liber A3, p. 29, and liber A6, p. 139.

John Randolph of Roanoke (Portrait II)

Portrait II

Attributed to Arthur J. Stansbury

Watercolor on paper: 5³/4 in. (14.6 cm.) in height, on paper 8 x 6 in. (20.3 x 15.2 cm.)

Presented in 1885 by Thomas G. Peyton of Richmond. Por885.3

Executed on lightweight paper, this watercolor portrait is either derived from or is the original for the engraving published as the frontispiece to volume 2 of Hugh A. Garland's *The Life of John Randolph of Roanoke* (New York, 1850). Before the portrait was mounted on more substantial stock, the following text, inscribed on the back, was recorded: "John Randolph of Roanoke Taken by Mr. Stansberry, Reporter to Gales & Sinton [sic] in the House of Representatives, 1829." Gales and Seaton were joint editors of the *National Intelligencer* and exclusive reporters of the United States Congress from 1812 to 1829; "Mr. Stansberry" is thought to be Arthur J. Stansbury. In light of this information it is difficult to understand why the likeness in its engraved form is captioned "John Randolph in England," or why *Harper's New Monthly Magazine*, publishing a reduced version of the sketch in 1850, stated: "This sketch is from a portrait of Randolph taken during his visit to England. It is said by those who remember him well, to present an accurate and by no means caricatured or exaggerated representation of his singular personal appearance, while walking in the streets." Although it cannot here be determined if the likeness was done by Stansbury in Washington, D.C., in 1829 or by an unidentified artist during one of Randolph's trips to England, the fact that the Society's watercolor sketch is the same height as the engraving but faces the opposite direction supports the possibility that the engraving derives from the sketch, and not vice versa.

Portraiture, pp. 92–93; *Harper's New Monthly Magazine* 2 (1850–51): 80.

Portrait III

COPIED BY CHARLES X. HARRIS. 1929

Oil on canvas: 29 x 24 in. (73.7 x 61 cm.)

Presented in 1944 by Mr. and Mrs. Alexander Wilbourne Weddell of Richmond. Por944.11

The Society's portrait is a copy of Gilbert Stuart's 1805 original that is owned by the National Gallery of Art, Washington, D.C. The copy was painted in 1929 when the original hung at Virginia House for the exhibition of Virginia historical portraiture. Other portraits of Randolph are noted, and in some instances reproduced, in William Cabell Bruce's biography, while three letters in the Society's manuscript collection throw light on the provenance of one of Chester Harding's portraits.

William Cabell Bruce, *John Randolph of Roanoke* (New York, 1922), 2: 66–71; *Portraiture*, p. 92; VHS Mss1 G8782b 3031 and Mss1 R5685b 719–730 (June 7, 17, 1875).

Portrait IV

See The Convention of 1829–30

Lucy Randolph, ca. 1744–1802

See Lucy (Randolph) Burwell, ca. 1744–1802

Maria Beverley Randolph, 1794–1845

See Maria Beverley (Randolph) DuVal, 1794–1845

Norman Vincent Randolph, 1846–1903

Born near Richmond on November 2, 1846, son of the Richmond bookseller Joseph Williamson Randolph (J. W. Randolph), the subject entered Confederate service at fifteen years of age as a private in Scott's Partisan Rangers. He remained with this command until it was disbanded late in 1863; he then served on the staff of General John B. Pegram as a volunteer aide-de-camp without rank or pay. In November 1864 he joined Mosby's Partisan Rangers and served with that unit until the end of hostilities. After the war he was employed in his father's bookselling business for some years; around 1875 he established the Randolph Paper Box Company, which he developed into a successful business. Randolph became president of the Virginia State Insurance Company, the Farmville and Powhatan Railroad, and the German-American Banking and Building Company; he was secretary and treasurer of the Virginia and North Carolina Wheel Company. Active in veterans affairs, he was one of the original members of the Society of the Army of Northern Virginia, a member of R. E. Lee Camp no. 1, and for many years president of the Lee Camp Soldiers' Home. He died at his residence on March 13, 1903. Randolph was twice married: first to Miss Reed of Baltimore; second to Janet H. Weaver of Warrenton; he was survived by his widow, a son and a daughter by his first marriage, and the three children of his second marriage.

Confederate Veteran 11 (1903): 177–78; *Confederate Military History*, 3: 1133; *Biographic Catalogue.*

By WILLIAM LUDWELL SHEPPARD. Signed

Oil on canvas: 30 x 25 in. (76.2 x 63.5 cm.)

Presented to the R. E. Lee Camp, Confederate Veterans, in 1903 by a group of the subject's friends; acquired by the Virginia Historical Society in 1946 through merger with the Confederate Memorial Association. Por946.149

Peter Randolph, born ca. 1737

Not to be confused with Peter Randolph (1717–1767) of Chatsworth, the subject was one of the eight children of William Randolph III, builder of Wilton, and Anne (Harrison) Randolph (qq.v.). He was born around 1737 and was twice married: first, to Mary Spotswood, daughter of John and Mary (Dandridge) Spotswood; second, after 1797, to Maria Taylor (Page) Byrd Bolling, daughter of John and Jane (Byrd) Page of North End, Gloucester County,

and widow of John Byrd and Archibald Bolling. Peter Randolph died without issue.

The Beverley Family, p. 270; *The Randolphs of Virginia*, p. 21; *The Randolphs* (portrait reproduced opposite p. 261). See chart on Randolph Portraits for relationships.

ARTIST UNIDENTIFIED

Oil on canvas: 35 x 30 in. (88.9 x 76.2 cm.)

Presented in 1927 by Kate Brander (Harris) Mayo Skipwith (Mrs. Grey Skipwith; formerly Mrs. Edward Carrington Mayo; subsequently Mrs. Berkeley Williams). Por927.14

Peyton Randolph, ca. 1721–1775
Betty (Harrison) Randolph, ca. 1724–1783 (Mrs. Peyton Randolph)

Speaker of the House of Burgesses and first president of the Continental Congress, Peyton Randolph was born about 1721, probably at Tazewell Hall in Williamsburg, the residence of his parents, Sir John Randolph and Susannah (Beverley) Randolph, Lady Randolph (qq.v.). He attended the College of William and Mary, studied law in London at the Middle Temple, and was admitted to the bar on February 10, 1744. After his return to Williamsburg, he was appointed in 1748 attorney general of Virginia; the same year he was elected to the House of Burgesses where he remained without interruption until 1775, serving as Speaker of that body from 1766 until the Revolution. Randolph was a member of the vestry of Bruton Parish Church, was on the board of visitors of the College of William and Mary, and was provincial grand master of the Masonic order. In 1773 he was named chairman of the Virginia Committee of Correspondence, and he presided at the Virginia Revolutionary Conventions of 1774 and 1775. Appointed by the convention to the first Continental Congress, he was elected president of congress in 1774 and again in 1775. He died in Philadelphia on October 22, 1775, and is buried in the chapel of the College of William and Mary. On March 8, 1746, he married Betty Harrison, born about 1724, daughter of Benjamin and Anne (Carter) Harrison of Berkeley, Charles City County, and sister of Benjamin Harrison, the Signer (q.v.). She died in Williamsburg on January 21, 1783. The couple had no children. Randolph's large estate passed, on his wife's death, to his nephew Edmund Randolph (q.v.).

DAB; *Virginia Historical Portraiture*, pp. 225–28 (Portraits I and II reproduced). See chart on Randolph Portraits for relationships.

21. Peyton Randolph, ca.1721–1775 (Portrait I)

Portrait I. Peyton Randolph   *See* Plate 21

BY JOHN WOLLASTON

Oil on canvas: 36¼ x 29 in. (92.1 x 73.7 cm.)

Source unknown. Por858.6

The portrait, presented by an unknown donor, was in the Society's possession as early as 1858. George Wythe Randolph, a member of the Society's executive Committee, writing to his niece Mary ("Molly") Randolph, in a letter dated Richmond, May 3, 1858, stated: "Our collection is increasing. We have now a Peyton Randolph and Edmund Randolph."

Edgehill-Randolph Papers, University of Virginia.

Peyton Randolph, ca. 1738–1784 "Lucy (Harrison) Randolph," ca. 1757–1809   (Mrs. Peyton Randolph)

Not to be confused with Peyton Randolph (ca.1721–1775) (q.v.), Speaker of the House of Burgesses and first president of the Continental Congress, this Peyton Randolph was one of the eight children of William and Anne (Harrison) Randolph (qq.v.) of Wilton. On May 5, 1775, he married Lucy Harrison, daughter of Benjamin Harrison (q.v.), the Signer, and

Betty (Harrison) Randolph

Peyton Randolph, ca.1738–1784

Portrait II. Betty (Harrison) Randolph

BY JOHN WOLLASTON

Oil on canvas: 36 x 29 in. (91.4 x 73.7 cm.)

Presented in 1927 by Kate Brander (Harris) Mayo Skipwith (Mrs. Grey Skipwith; formerly Mrs. Edward Carrington Mayo; subsequently Mrs. Berkeley Williams). Por927.19

Portrait III. Peyton Randolph

BY JOHN WOLLASTON

Oil on canvas: 36 x 30 in. (91.4 x 76.2 cm.)

Received in 1951 as a bequest of Kate Brander (Harris) Mayo Skipwith Williams (Mrs. Berkeley Williams; previously Mrs. Grey Skipwith, and prior to that Mrs. Edward Carrington Mayo). Por951.33

Elizabeth (Bassett) Harrison; she bore him four children. Peyton Randolph, who served in the Revolutionary War as an aide-de-camp to Lafayette, died on May 15, 1784 (not 1794 as is often stated). His widow remarried on October 9, 1788, Captain Anthony Singleton (1750–1795), an officer in the Continental artillery, an original member of the Society of the Cincinnati, and a silversmith; the couple became the parents of three children. Singleton died in Newport, Rhode Island, in 1795. Lucy (Harrison) Randolph Singleton died in Staunton in September 1809.

The Beverley Family, p. 270; *The Randolphs of Virginia*, p. 21; Pauline Pearce Warner, *Benjamin Harrison of Berkeley; Walter Cocke of Surry; Family Records* (Tappahannock, Va., 1962), pp. 38, 45–46; George Barton Cutten, *The Silversmiths of Virginia, together with Watchmakers and Jewelers, from 1694 to 1850* (Richmond, 1952), pp. 204–5; *VMHB* 41

207

(1933): 102–8; *The Randolphs*, p. 284 (Portrait I reproduced), p. 260 (Portrait II reproduced). See chart on Randolph Portraits for relationships.

Portrait I. Peyton Randolph

ARTIST UNIDENTIFIED

Oil on canvas: 35 x 30 in. (88.9 x 76.2 cm.)

Presented in 1927 by Kate Brander (Harris) Mayo Skipwith (Mrs. Grey Skipwith; formerly Mrs. Edward Carrington Mayo; subsequently Mrs. Berkeley Williams). Por927.13

Portrait II. "Lucy (Harrison) Randolph"

BY JOHN WOLLASTON

Oil on canvas: 36 x 30 in. (91.4 x 76.2 cm.)

Presented in 1927 by Kate Brander (Harris) Mayo Skipwith (Mrs. Grey Skipwith; formerly Mrs. Edward Carrington Mayo; subsequently Mrs. Berkeley Williams). Por927.12

If this portrait is correctly attributed to Wollaston, as it would appear to be, it cannot represent Lucy (Harrison) Randolph, who was born at just about the time that Wollaston came to Virginia.

Portrait III. Peyton Randolph

COPIED BY UNIDENTIFIED ARTIST after the original by William Bache

Silhouette, India ink on paper: 2³/₄ in. (7 cm.) in height

Acquired by purchase in 1955. Por955.21

Virginia Randolph, 1786–1852
See Virginia (Randolph) Cary, 1786–1852

William Randolph, ca. 1651–1711
Mary (Isham) Randolph, d.1735
(Mrs. William Randolph)

So numerous are the descendants of William and Mary (Isham) Randolph that the couple have been called the "Adam and Eve of Virginia." William Randolph, son of Richard and Elizabeth (Ryland) Randolph, was born in Warwickshire, England, about 1651; he came to Virginia around 1670 to join his uncle Henry Randolph, who had settled in Henrico County and was clerk of the court. William Randolph acquired large tracts of land, including Curles and Turkey Island on the James River, and by 1705 owned 10,000 acres in Henrico County alone. Around 1678 he married Mary Isham, daughter of Henry and Catherine Isham of Bermuda Hundred; they resided at Turkey Island and raised a

family of seven sons and two daughters as indicated below. William Randolph succeeded his uncle as clerk of the Henrico County court sometime before 1675; he was likewise at various times magistrate, coroner, and justice of the peace of the county. In 1685 he was elected to the House of Burgesses. He represented the county in numerous sessions thereafter, serving as Speaker of the House in 1698 and clerk in 1702; in 1696 he became attorney general of the colony. He was one of the founders and first trustees of the College of William and Mary. William Randolph died on April 11, 1711; his wife survived until 1735. The couple had nine children: William (q.v.) of Turkey Island, Thomas of Tuckahoe, Isham of Dungeness, Richard of Curles, Sir John (q.v.) of Tazewell Hall, Elizabeth who married Richard Bland of Jordans, Mary who married John Stith, Edward of Bremo, and Henry of Chatsworth.

William Randolph, ca.1651–1711

DAB; National Gallery of Art, *The Eye of Thomas Jefferson* (Washington, D.C., 1976), pp. 4–5 (Portraits I and III reproduced; Portrait I reversed); *Virginia Historical Portraiture*, pp. 128–30 (Portraits I and III reproduced); Jonathan Daniels, *The Randolphs of Virginia* (Garden City, N.Y., 1972), p. 170 (Portraits I and III reproduced); *Virginia Cavalcade* 14, no. 2 (1964): 42 (Portraits I and III reproduced). See chart on Randolph Portraits for relationships.

Portrait I. William Randolph

ARTIST UNIDENTIFIED

Oil on canvas: 35 x 27 in. (88.9 x 68.6 cm.)

Received in 1951 as a bequest of Kate Brander (Harris) Mayo Skipwith Williams (Mrs. Berkeley Williams; previously Mrs. Grey Skipwith, and prior to that Mrs. Edward Carrington Mayo). Por951.31

Portrait II. Mary (Isham) Randolph

COPIED BY WILLIAM LUDWELL SHEPPARD

Watercolor on paper: 4¼ x 3 in. (10.8 x 7.6 cm.) (oval)

Presented in 1929 by William Glover Stanard in memory of his wife, Mary Mann Page (Newton) Stanard. Por929.9

Portrait III. Mary (Isham) Randolph

ARTIST UNIDENTIFIED

Oil on canvas: 36¼ x 29¼ in. (92.1 x 74.3 cm.)

Received in 1951 as a bequest of Kate Brander (Harris) Mayo Skipwith Williams (Mrs. Berkeley Williams; previously Mrs. Grey Skipwith, and prior to that Mrs. Edward Carrington Mayo). Por951.32

Mary (Isham) Randolph (Portrait III)

William Randolph, 1681–1742

Second of the name, and eldest son of William and Mary (Isham) Randolph (qq.v.) of Turkey Island, Henrico County, the subject was born in November 1681. He attended the College of William and Mary, studied law, and in 1702 became clerk of the House of Burgesses, holding that office until 1712. In 1710 he became clerk of Henrico County, a post he held for ten years. He was a member of the House of Burgesses 1718–23 and again in 1726. William Ran-

dolph II was appointed to the colonial Council in 1728 and held that office until his death; he is consequently known as "The Councillor" to distinguish him from his nephew and contemporary William Randolph of Tuckahoe (1713–1745), son of his brother Thomas Randolph. The subject died on October 19, 1742, and is buried at Turkey Island. On June 22, 1709, he married Elizabeth Beverley (1691–1723), daughter of Peter and Elizabeth (Peyton) Beverley and sister of Susannah (Beverley) Randolph (q.v.), wife of Sir John Randolph (q.v.). The subject and his wife were the parents of seven children. The two eldest died young; the Society owns portraits of three others, William Randolph III (d.1761), Beverley Randolph (1713–1750), and Elizabeth (Randolph) Chiswell (1715–1776) (qq.v.).

The Beverley Family, pp. 117–18; Wassell Randolph, *William Randolph I of Turkey Island, Henrico County, Virginia, and His Immediate Descendants* (Memphis, 1949), pp. 32–43; *VMHB* 25 (1917): 403; *The Randolphs* (portrait reproduced opposite p. 30). See chart on Randolph Portraits for relationships.

BY JOHN WOLLASTON, copying an unidentified original

Oil on canvas: 36 x 29 in. (91.4 x 73.7 cm.)

Presented in 1927 by Kate Brander (Harris) Mayo Skipwith (Mrs. Grey Skipwith; formerly Mrs. Edward Carrington Mayo; subsequently Mrs. Berkeley Williams). Por927.17

William Randolph, d.1761
"Anne (Harrison) Randolph," died post-1769 (Mrs. William Randolph)

Third of the name, and builder of Wilton, William Randolph was the son of William and Elizabeth (Beverley) Randolph (qq.v.). Confusion surrounds the date of his birth, 1710, 1711, 1720, and 1723 all having been assigned in printed sources; if he married in 1735 as many sources suggest, the earlier birth dates are more likely. He resided first in Goochland County, but in 1747 he bought a tract of land in Henrico County on the James River known as World's End and there built Wilton. He represented Henrico County in the House of Burgesses from 1752 until his death in 1761. His wife, Anne (Harrison) Randolph, daughter of Benjamin and Anne (Carter) Harrison of Berkeley, Charles City County, died after 1769; she bore him eight children, of whom the Society owns portraits of the following: Peter, Peyton, Elizabeth, Anne, and Lucy (Randolph) Burwell (qq.v.).

The Beverley Family, p. 270; Wassell Randolph, *William Randolph I of Turkey Island, Henrico County, Virginia, and His Immediate Descendants* (Memphis, 1949), pp. 42–43; *VMHB*

25 (1917): 403 and 60 (1952): 63 (Portrait II reproduced opposite p. 59); *The Randolphs* (Portrait I reproduced opposite p. 97); Graham Hood, *Charles Bridges and William Dering, Two Virginia Painters, 1735–1750* (Williamsburg, Va., 1978), pp. 47, 51 (Portrait II reproduced). See chart on Randolph Portraits for relationships.

William Randolph, d.1761

Portrait I. William Randolph

By JOHN WOLLASTON. Ca.1755

Oil on canvas: 36 x 29 in. (91.4 x 73.7 cm.)

Presented in 1927 by Kate Brander (Harris) Mayo Skipwith (Mrs. Grey Skipwith; formerly Mrs. Edward Carrington Mayo; subsequently Mrs. Berkeley Williams). Por927.16

Portrait II. "Anne (Harrison) Randolph"

By CHARLES BRIDGES

Oil on canvas: 27 x 25 in. (68.6 x 63.5 cm.)

Presented in 1927 by Kate Brander (Harris) Mayo Skipwith (Mrs. Grey Skipwith; formerly Mrs. Edward Carrington Mayo; subsequently Mrs. Berkeley Williams). Por927.20

This curious likeness by Bridges fits so unbecomingly in the gallery of Randolph family portraits that the identity of the subject is suspect. William Randolph, builder of Wilton, commissioned Wollaston to execute a series of family portraits to adorn the walls of Wilton, and was himself painted by the artist

(Portrait I). It is surprising that he would have been content with so unflattering a portrait of his lady.

Helen (Calvert) Maxwell Read, 1750–1833 (Mrs. John K. Read)

Born in Norfolk on June 20, 1750, the subject was the daughter of Maximilian and Mary (Savage) Calvert. She married, first, in Norfolk, on April 6, 1767, James Maxwell, sailing master of the ship *Launceton*. After their marriage Maxwell continued his maritime interests; he received from his father-in-law a half interest in the vessel *Two Sisters* and during the Revolution was superintendent of the Norfolk Navy Yard and commissioner of Virginia's state navy. Mrs. Maxwell's memoirs of her early life and her recollections of Norfolk during the Revolutionary War were first published under the title "My Mother" in the first three volumes of the *Lower Norfolk County Virginia Antiquary*. She bore her husband seven children, one of whom, William Maxwell (q.v.), was a benefactor and vice-president of the Virginia Historical Society and is represented in the Society's portrait collection. After Maxwell's death in 1795, his widow married on June 25, 1796, Doctor John K. Read, a physician and sometime mayor and alderman of Norfolk; there were no children by this marriage. Doctor Read died in Goochland Courthouse on February 28, 1805. Helen (Calvert) Maxwell Read died on March 31, 1833, and is buried between her two husbands in the churchyard of St. Paul's Episcopal Church, Norfolk.

Helen Calvert Maxwell Read, *Memoirs of Helen Calvert Maxwell Read* (Chesapeake, Va., 1970) (portrait reproduced); Ella Foy O'Gorman, *Descendants of Virginia Calverts* (n.p., 1947), p. 601; Robert Armistead Stewart, *The History of Virginia's Navy of the Revolution* (Richmond, 1934), pp. 223–24; *Portraiture*, pp. 93–94.

By WILLIAM JAMES HUBARD

Oil on canvas: 30 x 25 in. (76.2 x 63.5 cm.)

Received in 1899 as a bequest of Mary Frances (Robertson) Maxwell (Mrs. William Maxwell), the subject's daughter-in-law. Por899.4

Unidentified Lady of the Redd Family

ARTIST UNIDENTIFIED

Pencil and watercolor: 2 1/2 in. (6.4 cm.) in height, on paper 3 1/4 x 2 1/2 in. (8.3 x 6.4 cm.). Inscribed: "A Lady of the Redd Family, Caroline County."

Presented in 1962 by David Silvette of Richmond. Por962.31

David Smith Redford, 1843–1899

Born in Goochland County on February 28, 1843, the subject was the son of R. S. Redford and Ann R. Redford. When he was young he moved with his parents to Richmond, where he remained for the rest of his life. At the beginning of the Civil War, Redford, eighteen years of age, enlisted in the Purcell Battery; he served with this unit throughout the war, taking part in forty-four engagements. On March 29, 1869, he married Catherine Tallon of Philadelphia; the couple had six children, five of whom lived to maturity. Redford was employed in the tobacco business; he was city agent of the American Tobacco Company from the founding of the company until his death. He was a charter member of the R. E. Lee Camp no. 1, Confederate Veterans, and a member of the executive committee of the Pegram Battalion Association. He died in Richmond on July 16, 1899.

Richmond *Times*, July 18, 1899, p. 7; *Biographic Catalogue.*

ARTIST UNIDENTIFIED

Oil on canvas: 29³/4 x 25 in. (75.6 x 63.5 cm.)

Presented to the R. E. Lee Camp, Confederate Veterans, prior to 1906; acquired by the Virginia Historical Society in 1946 through merger with the Confederate Memorial Association. Por946.184

Rebecca Ann Reger, 1831–1916

See Thomas Edward Seay, 1823–1881

David Crockett Richardson, 1845–1928

Judge Richardson, a native of New Kent County, was born on June 7, 1845, the son of Turner and Margaret Ann (Robertson) Richardson. When nine years of age he moved with his parents to Richmond. He joined Parker's Battery in 1862 as a private; wounded at Second Manassas, he returned to the battery before the battle of Fredericksburg. He saw action at Chancellorsville, Gettysburg, the Wilderness, Cold Harbor, and Chickamauga. After Appomattox, Richardson read law in the office of Johnson and Guigon and in 1870 became clerk of the police court in Richmond. Thereafter, having received his law degree from Richmond College in 1874, he became police justice. He retired in 1884 after eight years on the bench to resume private practice. Elected Commonwealth's attorney for the city of Richmond in 1896, he filled the post for ten years. Richardson was mayor of Richmond from 1908 until his resignation in 1912 to become judge of the hustings court, a position he held until January 1925 when he resigned because of poor health. Judge Richardson was at one time commander of the R. E. Lee Camp, Confederate Veterans; he became a member of the executive committee of the Virginia Historical Society in 1886 and for many years was its recording secretary. He was twice married: first, on December 4, 1874, to Alice A. Fellows; second, on February 10, 1892, to Florence B. Hechler. He had six children. Judge Richardson died on October 4, 1928. In the references cited below the judge's middle name appears variously as Crockett and Clarke.

Men of Mark in Virginia, 5: 370–72; *Encyclopedia of Virginia Biography*, 3: 316; *Confederate Veteran* 36 (1928): 426; *VMHB* 38 (1930): 64–72; CMA Archives, folio Z1n; *Biographic Catalogue*; Robert K. Krick, *Parker's Virginia Battery, C.S.A.* (Berryville, Va., 1975), p. 335.

BY JOHN P. WALKER. Signed. Dated 1924

Oil on canvas: 30¹/4 x 25 in. (76.8 x 63.5 cm.)

Presented to the R. E. Lee Camp, Confederate Veterans, in 1924; acquired by the Virginia Historical Society in 1946 through merger with the Confederate Memorial Association. Por946.165

Robert Benskin Richardson, 1831–1890

Born on December 15, 1831, the subject was the son of Henry Benskin Marshall Richardson and Eliza Taylor (Withers) Richardson of James City County. He studied medicine and during the Civil War was an assistant surgeon attached to the 10th Battalion, Virginia Heavy Artillery. He died at Marlbrook, James City County, on November 17, 1890; he and his wife, Harriet (Hankins) Richardson, are buried in the Hankins burial ground near Hickory Neck Church.

Richmond Dispatch, Nov. 18, 1890; Confederate Service Records, National Archives, microfilm roll 230; Virginia State Library, Richardson-Whitaker-Wynne-Cary family notes, sheet 4; *Biographic Catalogue.*

BY JOHN W. GÜNTHER. Signed. Dated 1925

Oil on canvas: 30 x 25 in. (76.2 x 63.5 cm.)

Presented to the R. E. Lee Camp, Confederate Veterans, in 1925; acquired by the Virginia Historical Society in 1946 through merger with the Confederate Memorial Association. Por946.119

Thomas Ritchie, 1778–1854

See The Convention of 1829–30

Amélie Louise Rives, 1832–1873 (later Mrs. Henry Sigourney)

Born on July 8, 1832, Amélie Louise Rives was the daughter of William Cabell Rives (q.v.) and Judith Page (Walker) Rives. She was born in Paris, where her father was serving as American minister to the court of Louis Philippe; she was named for Marie-Amélie, the queen consort, who was a close friend of her mother. Shortly after her birth the family returned to Castle Hill, their home in Albemarle County. Here, and in Washington, D.C., where her father was a United States senator, she remained until she was seventeen years of age. In 1849 her father, appointed minister to France a second time, again took the family to Paris, where Amélie participated in the brilliant social life of the capital. The family returned to Castle Hill in 1853. On May 10, 1854, she married Henry Sigourney of Boston, a director of the Boston, Nashua and Lowell Railroad and of the Laconia Pepperell Mills in Biddeford, Maine. The couple resided in Boston and became the parents of four children. Bound for an extended stay in Europe, Mr. and Mrs. Sigourney and three of their children died at sea on November 22, 1873, with the sinking of the steamship *Ville du Havre*. The eldest son, left behind to pursue his studies at Harvard, survived.

James Rives Childs, *Reliques of the Rives* (Lynchburg, Va., 1929), p. 585; *VMHB* 56 (1948): 238 and 75 (1967): 89–96 (portrait reproduced opposite p. 88); *The Cabells and Their Kin*, pp. 462–63; *Virginia Cavalcade* 12, no. 4 (1963): 15 (portrait reproduced).

BY LOUIS MATHIEU DIDIER GUILLAUME. Signed. Ca.1851

Pastel on paper: 22 x 18½ in. (55.9 x 47 cm.) (oval)

Presented in 1947 by the Rives estate through Sarah Landon Rives of Albemarle County. Por947.30

The back of the frame bears fragments of an elaborate framer's label, identical to one on the back of the companion portrait of the subject's sister, Ella Rives (q.v.). See that portrait for information on the two portraits and the misidentification of the companion piece.

Amélie Louise Rives, 1863–1945

See Amélie Louise (Rives) Chanler Troubetzkoy, 1863–1945

Ella Rives, 1834–1892

Younger daughter of William Cabell Rives (q.v.) and Judith Page (Walker) Rives, the subject was born on September 15, 1834. She grew up at Castle Hill in Albemarle County and in Washington, D.C., where the family resided during her father's terms in the United States Senate. When William Cabell Rives was appointed American minister to France in 1849 his family accompanied him to Paris; Ella and her sister Amélie Louise (q.v.) took an active part in the social life of the capital. In 1853 the family returned to Castle Hill. Ella never married. She died on April 12, 1892.

James Rives Childs, *Reliques of the Rives* (Lynchburg, Va., 1929), p. 578; *The Cabells and Their Kin*, p. 452.

BY LOUIS MATHIEU DIDIER GUILLAUME. Signed. Ca.1851

Pastel on paper: 22 x 18½ in. (55.9 x 47 cm.) (oval). The frame bears a framer's label: "Au Genie des Arts, 18 rue des Petits Augustins. . . ."

Presented in 1947 by the Rives estate through Sarah Landon Rives of Albemarle County. Por947.3

The subject of the portrait has been misidentified since its acquisition by the Society in 1947. The *Virginia Magazine of History and Biography*, 56 (1948): 238, identified it in the annual list of accessions as a portrait of "Mrs. David King (Ella Louise Rives) daughter of Francis Robert Rives, and a granddaughter of William Cabell Rives." Its companion piece, acquired at the same time, was correctly identified as "Mrs. Henry Sigourney (Amélie Louise Rives)," the elder daughter of William Cabell Rives. The two portraits are identical in size, treatment, and framing; each bears the elaborate label of a Parisian framer—the one on the portrait of Amélie Louise is now fragmentary. Clearly the portraits do not represent aunt and niece, as the acquisition notice states, but sisters, Ella (1834–1892) and Amélie Louise (1832–1873), only daughters of William Cabell Rives. Rives received his second appointment as American minister to France in 1849. He and his family resided in Paris until 1853, and it was doubtless during the family's sojourn in the French capital that Guillaume was commissioned to execute the two pastels. It can be assumed that the confusion in identity stemmed from the fact that both the subject and the supposed subject were named Ella. Ella Louise (Rives) King, however, was not born until 1851, just about the time that her two aunts Ella and Amélie Louise were sitting to Guillaume for their portraits. In the Society's manuscript collection is an undated letter (Mss2 R5246 a1) written from Castle Hill by Judith Page (Walker) Rives, the mother of Ella and Amélie Louise, to the artist Guillaume who by that time was in Virginia. Another letter in the same collection written from Castle Hill May 17, 1930, by Amélie Louise (Rives) Chanler Troubetzkoy (q.v.) identifies the two Guillaume portraits under discussion: "there are four (4) family portraits by

Guillaume here at Castle Hill. Two are in pastels, one of my father's sister Ella Rives in a green tulle evening gown; one of my Aunt Amélie Louise Rives, who afterward married Mr. Henry Sigourney of Boston, painted in a pale blue tulle evening gown, both slightly under life size, ¾ length (short)."

Mary Browne (Green) Rives, 1779–1860 (Mrs. Anthony Rives)

Born on June 10, 1779, the subject was the daughter of Colonel Abraham Green of Amelia County and his first wife, Elizabeth (Browne) Green. She married on May 14, 1801, Anthony Rives (1776–1844), son of Timothy and Martha (Binns) Rives. The couple resided at Chalmaria, Dinwiddie County, an estate given them on their marriage by the bride's father; they became the parents of eight children. In 1824 the family removed to Fayette County, Tennessee, but after only a short stay turned southward to Hinds County, Mississippi, where they remained, establishing themselves at Forkland plantation. Anthony Rives died in July 1844; Mary Brown (Green) Rives died in December 1860.

James Rives Childs, *Reliques of the Rives* (Lynchburg, Va., 1929), pp. 501–13 (portrait reproduced opposite p. 512); *Occasional Bulletin*, no. 26 (1973): 8–9 (portrait reproduced).

ARTIST UNIDENTIFIED

Miniature on ivory: 2¾ x 2½ in. (7 x 6.4 cm.) (oval)

Presented in 1972 by James Rives Childs of Nice, France. Por972.24

Sarah Catherine (Macmurdo) Rives, 1833–1909 (Mrs. Alfred Landon Rives)

Born in 1833, the subject was the daughter of James Brown Macmurdo and Frances (Moore) Macmurdo of Richmond and a granddaughter of Bishop Richard Channing Moore (q.v.). She married on February 1, 1859, Alfred Landon Rives (1830–1903), son of William Cabell Rives (q.v.) and Judith Page (Walker) Rives. During the Civil War her husband was for three years acting chief of the Bureau of Engineers of the Confederate States. After the war he practiced civil engineering in Richmond. He was chief engineer and general superintendent of the Mobile and Ohio Railroad 1873–83, vice-president and general manager of the Richmond and Danville Railroad 1883–86, and chief engineer and general manager of the Panama Railroad Company 1887–97. He died at Castle Hill, Albemarle County, on February 5, 1903; Mrs. Rives died at Castle Hill on October 7, 1909. The couple had three children, one of whom Amélie Louise (Rives) Chanler Troubetzkoy (q.v.), is represented in the Society's portrait collection.

Mary Browne (Green) Rives

Sarah Catherine (Macmurdo) Rives

James Rives Childs, *Reliques of the Rives* (Lynchburg, Va., 1929), p. 584; *Richmond Portraits*, p. 112; *VMHB* 56 (1948): 238.

BY LOUIS MATHIEU DIDIER GUILLAUME. Signed

Oil on canvas: 26½ x 22 in. (67.3 x 55.9 cm.)

Presented in 1947 by the Rives estate through Sarah Landon Rives of Albemarle County. Por947.32

William Cabell Rives, 1793–1868

United States senator and representative and minister to France, Rives was the son of Robert and Margaret Jordan (Cabell) Rives. He was born on May 4, 1793, attended Hampden-Sydney College and the College of William and Mary, and after graduating from the latter institution in 1809 studied law with Thomas Jefferson. In 1817 he represented Nelson County in the Virginia House of Delegates, continuing in the state legislature until 1823. On March 24, 1819, he married Judith Page Walker, daughter of Francis and Jane Byrd (Nelson) Walker (q.v.) of Castle Hill, Albemarle County; the couple resided at Castle Hill and became the parents of five children. After serving in the United States House of Representatives 1823–29, Rives became minister to France, a post he held until 1832; thereafter he represented Virginia in the United States Senate 1832–34, 1836–39, 1841–45. Again appointed minister to France, he remained abroad in that capacity from 1849 to 1853; on his return to the United States he devoted himself to writing his three-volume *History of the Life and Times of James Madison* (1859–68). Rives was a member of the Washington peace convention of 1861, a member of the Virginia Secession Convention, a member of the Provisional Confederate Congress convened in Montgomery, Alabama, and a member of the Second Confederate Congress. Poor health obliged him to resign from public life in 1862; he died at Castle Hill on April 25, 1868. Rives was elected to membership in the Virginia Historical Society in 1833; in 1848 he became the Society's third president. Portraits of his daughters, Ella Rives and Amélie Louise Rives, later Mrs. Henry Sigourney (qq.v.), are in the Society's possession.

DAB; *Biographical Directory*; *The Cabells and Their Kin*, pp. 444–52; *Virginia Cavalcade* 10, no. 2 (1960): 13 (portrait reproduced); *VMHB* 38 (1930): viii, 68 (1960): 131 (engraving reproduced), and 80 (1972): 3 (engraving reproduced); *Portraiture*, pp. 94–95.

COPIED BY SARAH LANDON RIVES

Oil on canvas: 27 x 22¼ in. (68.6 x 56.5 cm.). Inscribed on the back: "William Cabell Rives, born 1793 died 1868."

Presented by the artist in 1930. Por930.7

The artist George Cooke is known to have painted a portrait of William Cabell Rives which was shown in New York City at the exhibition of the Apollo Association in 1838. It is likely that Cooke's portrait was the original from which Charles Fenderich derived his lithographic portrait of Rives, first published in 1839 in his *Port Folio of Living American Statesmen*. The Society's portrait, painted by Sarah Landon Rives, a granddaughter of the subject, is an adaptation of the Fenderich lithograph.

Mary Bartlett Cowdry, *American Academy of Fine Arts and American Art-Union, Exhibition Record, 1816–1852* (New York, 1953), 2: 86.

John Roane, 1766–1838
See The Convention of 1829–30

Isaac Roberdeau, 1763–1829

Born in Philadelphia on September 11, 1763, the subject was the eldest child of Daniel and Mary (Bostwick) Roberdeau. After studying engineering in London he returned to the United States in 1787 and was employed by Pierre Charles L'Enfant in laying out the new federal city of Washington in 1791 and 1792. Thereafter he assisted L'Enfant at Paterson, New Jersey, and later began work on a canal intended to connect the Schuylkill and the Susquehanna rivers, an undertaking realized many years later. On the outbreak of the War of 1812 he was commissioned major in the topographical engineers and employed in the fortification of various strategic areas. At the war's end he ran the northern boundary of the United States as far as Sault Sainte Marie. Roberdeau was appointed chief of the Topographical Bureau in 1818 and removed to Washington where he resided the rest of his life, occupying a prominent position in the social life of the capital. He died at his residence in Georgetown on January 15, 1829. Roberdeau was married on November 7, 1792, to Susan Shippen Blair, daughter of the Reverend Samuel Blair and Susan (Shippen) Blair; the couple had three daughters.

DAB; Roberdeau Buchanan, *Genealogy of the Roberdeau Family, Including a Biography of General Daniel Roberdeau* (Washington, D.C., 1876), pp. 104–22; *VMHB* 30 (1922): 93 and 57 (1949): 144, 166.

BY WILLIAM GEORGE WILLIAMS

Oil on canvas: 25½ x 21 in. (64.8 x 53.3 cm.)

Received in 1920 as a bequest of Roberdeau Buchanan of Washington, D.C., a grandson of the subject. Por920.1

The donor of the portrait, in his published genealogy of the Roberdeau family, provides information on various likenesses of Isaac Roberdeau, including the one owned by the Virginia Historical Society: "The artist, Jarvis, was at this time [1826] in Washington, painting the portraits of the Cabinet; and as Colonel Roberdeau entered his studio one day, he said: 'Stand, Colonel, I will paint your portrait; the minister has disappointed me.' The portrait of Colonel Roberdeau, thus commenced, was afterwards finished by Sully. With the celebrated Gilbert Stuart, also, the Colonel was intimate; and in the well-known, full-length portrait of Washington, with his hand extended, Colonel Roberdeau's hand was his model. And besides a miniature on ivory, there is another portrait of Colonel Roberdeau, painted by an amateur, and intimate friend—Major [corrected by hand to read "Captain"] Williams, then just from West Point, and assigned to duty in the Colonel's office, and who subsequently fell fighting gallantly before Monter[r]ey. Major Williams had married Miss Peter, one of the Custis family, and this portrait hung at Arlington with the family portraits of the Custis, Lee, and Washington families, until the close of the late war, when it was removed with other things belonging to Mrs. Lee, and has recently been presented by the daughter of the artist to the Colonel's family." The Historical Society of Pennsylvania owns a miniature and a bust-length portrait of Roberdeau.

Roberdeau Buchanan, *Genealogy of the Roberdeau Family, Including a Biography of General Daniel Roberdeau* (Washington, D.C., 1876), p. 114; Nicholas B. Wainwright, *Paintings and Miniatures at the Historical Society of Pennsylvania* (Philadelphia, 1974), pp. 231–32.

Ann Hoomes (Maury) Robinson, 1852–1920 (Mrs. Poitiaux Robinson)

See Robert Henry Maury, 1816–1886 (Portrait IV)

Conway Robinson, 1805–1884

Lawyer, author, and founder-member of the Virginia Historical Society, Conway Robinson was born in Richmond on September 15, 1805, son of John and Agnes Conway (Moncure) Robinson. After a six-year apprenticeship to the clerk of two of Richmond's courts, he was admitted to the bar in 1827; he became clerk of the General Court the following year and held the post until his resignation in 1831 to engage in private practice. He ventured briefly into business, assuming the presidency of the faltering Richmond, Fredericksburg and Potomac Railroad Company in 1836 and resigning two years later after having placed the company back on a sound footing. As an attorney he became so successful that he was admitted in 1839 to the bar of the United States Supreme Court. In 1842 Robinson became reporter to the Virginia Court of Appeals. Together with John Mercer Patton he was selected in 1846 by the Virginia legislature to revise the Commonwealth's civil code and the following year to revise the criminal code; he was elected to the legislature in 1852 to adapt these revisions to the state's new constitution. Robinson's legal works include the three-volume *Practice in the Courts of Law and Equity in Virginia* (1832–39) and the seven-volume *Practice in Courts of Justice in England and the United States* (1854–74). After the Civil War he continued to practice before the Virginia Court of Appeals and the United States Supreme Court; he had resided in Washington, D.C., since 1858. Robinson's wife, whom he married on July 14, 1836, was Mary Susan Selden (Leigh) Robinson, daughter of Benjamin Watkins Leigh (q.v.); the couple had nine children, two of whom died in infancy and two of whom were killed fighting for the Confederacy. Robinson was one of the founder-members (1831) of the Virginia Historical Society; for many years he was chairman of its executive committee; he was elected recording secretary in 1856 and vice-president in 1882. His historical work *An Account of Discoveries in the West* was published by the Society in 1848. On his death, which took place in Philadelphia on January 30, 1884, the Society received from his estate a valuable collection of books and manuscripts.

DAB; *Portraiture*, pp. 96–98 (Portrait II reproduced); *Virginia Genealogies*, pp. 577–81; *Richmond Portraits*, pp. 174–78 (Portrait II reproduced); *VMHB* 20 (1912): xxiii, 35 (1927): 191, 49 (1941): 97, and 67 (1959): 201 (Portrait II reproduced).

Portrait I

By SUSAN LEIGH ROBINSON. Signed (monogram)

Oil on canvas: 24 x 20¼ in. (61 x 51.4 cm.)

Presented by the artist in 1912. Por912.1

Portrait II   *See* Plate 22

By THOMAS SULLY. Signed (monogram). Dated 1850

Oil on canvas: 24 x 20¼ in. (61 x 51.4 cm.). Inscribed on the back: "TS [monogram] 1850."

Presented in 1929 by Agnes Conway Robinson of Washington, D.C., a daughter of the subject. Por929.3

The portrait appears in Sully's list of paintings as "Portrait painted for his brother Moncure Robinson, begun Nov. 4th, 1850, finished Nov. 30th, 1850. Head. Price $100."

Edward Biddle and Mantle Fielding, *The Life and Works of Thomas Sully* (Philadelphia, 1921), p. 261; *Antiques* 116 (1979): 1134 (portrait reproduced).

215

Portrait III

Hollow-cut silhouette: $2^3/4$ in. (7 cm.) in height, on paper $3^1/2$ x $2^1/2$ in. (8.9 x 6.4 cm.)

Received in 1940 from the estate of Agnes Conway Robinson of Washington, D.C., a daughter of the subject, through Cornelia Robinson Shields of Richmond. Por940.12

The silhouette is framed in a daguerreotype case; the velvet on the inside of the front cover is stamped: "W. A. Pratt, 139 Main St., Richmond."

Elizabeth Peyton (Giles) Robinson, died ca. 1916 (Mrs. Samuel Augustine Robinson)

The subject was a granddaughter of Governor William Branch Giles (q.v.) and a daughter of Thomas Peyton Giles and Elizabeth Eppes Osborne (Branch) Giles. During the Civil War, "Lizzie" Giles was one of the reigning belles in Richmond society. She was the model for one of the figures in William D. Washington's celebrated painting *The Burial of Latané*. After her marriage to Samuel Augustine Robinson, a son of William and Frances Hunt Peyton (Turner) Robinson, the couple resided in Washington, D.C. She spent her last years in St. Louis, Missouri, where she died ca. 1916.

Eva Turner Clark, *Francis Epes, His Ancestors and Descendants* (New York, 1942), p. 224; *VMHB* 22 (1914): 24; *Virginia Genealogies*, p. 469; VHS Mss2 B4593b 4–15.

ARTIST UNIDENTIFIED

Oil on canvas: $29^1/2$ x 25 in. (74.9 x 63.5 cm.) (oval)

Presented in 1974 by Peyton (Hawes) Dunn of Washington, D.C., a granddaughter of the subject. Por974.11

A portion of the artist's signature or monogram is visible along the lower left edge of the painting.

John Robinson, 1704–1766

Speaker John Robinson was born on February 3, 1704, son of John and Catherine (Beverley) Robinson. He received his formal education at the College of William and Mary and in 1736 was elected to represent King and Queen County in the House of Burgesses. Two years later he became Speaker of the House and treasurer of the colony, both of which offices he held until his death. For many years he was second only to the governor in power and influence in the colony. At the time of his death, however, it was found that he had mismanaged public funds; the

discrepancy, a sum of more than one hundred thousand pounds, was repaid to the treasury from his estate. Robinson resided at Mount Pleasant, in King and Queen County. He was three times married: first, in 1723, to Mary Storey; second, to Lucy Moore; third, in 1759, to Susan Chiswell; he had issue by each of his three wives. Robinson died on May 11, 1766.

DAB; *Encyclopedia of Virginia Biography*, 1: 315; *VMHB* 9 (1901–2): 356, 25 (1917): 435, and 65 (1957): 253; Landon Carter, *The Diary of Colonel Landon Carter of Sabine Hall, 1752–1778* (Charlottesville, Va., 1965), 1: 113 (portrait reproduced); *Antiques* 116 (1979): 1137 (portrait reproduced).

ARTIST UNIDENTIFIED. Ca. 1755

Miniature on ivory: $1^1/2$ x 1 in. (3.8 x 2.5 cm.) (oval)

Presented in 1956 by Mrs. Marion Whiting Nelson of Falls Church, Virginia. Por956.84

The miniature appears to be derived from the Wollaston portrait now owned by Colonial Williamsburg.

Judith Robinson, 1736–1757
See Judith (Robinson) Braxton, 1736–1757

Robert Emmet Rodes, 1829–1864

Born at Lynchburg on March 29, 1829, General Rodes was the son of David and Martha (Yancey) Rodes. He graduated from the Virginia Military Institute in 1848, was a member of the faculty at the Institute for three years after his graduation, then turned to civil engineering and railroad construction, first in Virginia, then farther south. On September 10, 1857, he married Virginia Hortense Woodruff of Tuscaloosa, Alabama, who bore him a son and a daughter, the latter born posthumously. At the beginning of the Civil War he entered Confederate service as colonel of the 5th Alabama Infantry. After First Manassas he was promoted to brigadier general, leading his brigade at Williamsburg and at Seven Pines, where he was wounded. Returning to his command before he was fully recovered, he took part in the battle of Gaines's Mill; later he distinguished himself at South Mountain and Sharpsburg; at Chancellorsville he won a field promotion to major general. He commanded a division at Gettysburg, the Wilderness, and Spotsylvania and fell mortally wounded at Winchester on September 19, 1864. He is buried in Lynchburg.

Generals in Gray; *History of Virginia*, 6: 131; Rosa Faulkner Yancey, *Lynchburg and Its Neighbors* (Richmond, 1935), pp. 99–110; *Biographic Catalogue*.

ARTIST UNIDENTIFIED

Pastel on cardboard: 20 x 16 in. (50.8 x 40.6 cm.)

22. Conway Robinson (Portrait II)

Acquired in 1946 through merger with the Confederate Memorial Association. Por946.124

The photograph from which the pastel portrait was made is reproduced in Douglas Southall Freeman's *Lee's Lieutenants, a Study in Command* (New York, 1942–44), 2: xxxviii.

Alexander F. Rose
See The Convention of 1829–30

Charles Broadway Rouss, 1836–1902

Charles Broadway Rouss was born in Frederick County, Maryland, on February 11, 1836, son of Peter Hoke Rouss and Belinda (Baltzell) Rouss. The family removed in 1841 to Berkeley County, (West) Virginia, where they resided at Runnymeade, about twelve miles from Winchester. Rouss attended Winchester Academy but left it at fifteen to become a clerk in a store. In three years he established his own business which shortly became the largest commercial house in Winchester. In 1859 he married Maggie Keenan, daughter of James Keenan of Winchester; they became the parents of two sons and a daughter. At the outbreak of the Civil War, Rouss enlisted as a private in the 12th Virginia Infantry, serving as a soldier in the ranks throughout the conflict. After the war he opened a dry goods store in New York City; despite an early failure, it became a large and highly profitable business, so much so that he erected a ten-story building on Broadway to accommodate it and established as an advertising medium for his house the *Auction Trade Journal*, a monthly publication that achieved wide circulation. Although soon considered a New York millionaire, Rouss maintained close ties with Virginia. His numerous benefactions included gifts to the city of Winchester, where he and his family spent their annual vacation, a laboratory at the University of Virginia, and $100,000, one half the total sum solicited, for the construction of "a Battle Abbey of the South" to house the records of the Civil War. Although construction did not begin until a decade after Rouss's death, the Battle Abbey he envisaged became a reality; today, its walls and its purposes greatly expanded, it contains the offices, library, and galleries of the Virginia Historical Society. Rouss died in New York on March 3, 1902. He was elected to membership in the Virginia Historical Society in 1895.

Confederate Veteran 10 (1902): 131–32; Larry A. Mullin, *The Napoleon of Gotham: A Study of the Life of Charles Broadway Rouss* (Winchester, Va., 1974); *Occasional Bulletin*, no. 27 (1973): 1–4; Maria Naylor, ed., *The National Academy of Design Exhibition Record, 1861–1900* (New York, 1973), 1: 130.

Portrait I

BY A. ROSE. Signed

Oil on canvas: 27 x 22 in. (68.6 x 55.9 cm.)

Acquired through merger with the Confederate Memorial Association. Por946.123

Charles Broadway Rouss (Portrait II)

Portrait II

BY M. BUXBAUM. Signed. Dated New York, 1895

Bronze bust 26 in. (66 cm.) in height

Acquired through merger with the Confederate Memorial Association. PorX255

A marble bust of Rouss by Buxbaum was exhibited at the National Academy of Design in 1896.

Elizabeth R. (Burton) Royster (Mrs. David Royster)

The subject was the daughter of William Burton (d. 1820) of Henrico County. She married on June 2, 1800, David Royster.

Information received with the portrait; Joyce Haw Lindsay, *Marriages of Henrico County, Virginia, 1680–1808* (Richmond, 1960), p. 73; Francis Burton Harrison, *Burton Chronicles of Colonial Virginia* (Darmstadt, Ger., 1933), p. 156; *VMHB* 79 (1971): 241.

ARTIST UNIDENTIFIED

Miniature on ivory: 2½ x 1¾ in. (6.4 x 4.5 cm.) (oval)

Presented in 1970 by Charlotte Burton Picot of Richmond. Por970.25

Alexander Hawksley Rutherfoord, 1807–1886

Son of Thomas Rutherfoord (q.v.) and Sally (Winston) Rutherfoord of Richmond, the subject was born on August 30, 1807. He was employed in his father's mercantile firm and represented it from time to time in New York and in Rio de Janeiro. On April 10, 1838, he married Keziah Kitchell Clark, daughter of James Clark of Camden, South Carolina; the couple resided in Richmond and became the parents of four children. For the last eight years of his life he spent much time on his farm in Amelia County. He died on July 6, 1886, while on a visit to his son near Baltimore; his remains were returned to Richmond for burial in Hollywood Cemetery.

VHS Mss6:2 R9335:1 and Mss5:1 R9337:1; *Richmond Dispatch*, July 8, 1886, p. 1; *VMHB* 81 (1973): 237.

BY LOUIS MATHIEU DIDIER GUILLAUME. Signed

Oil on canvas: 30 x 25 in. (76.2 x 63.5 cm.)

Received in 1972 as a joint bequest of Mr. and Mrs. Alexander Rutherfoord Davenport of Los Angeles, California. Por972.4

Thomas Rutherfoord, 1766–1852

Thomas Rutherfoord was born in Glasgow, Scotland, on January 9, 1766, the son of Thomas and Janet (Mildrum) Rutherfoord. At fifteen years of age he went to Dublin as an apprentice to his elder brothers in the mercantile firm of Hawksley and Rutherfoord. In 1784, and again in 1787 and 1788, he was sent by the firm to Virginia; although the first two trips were not a financial success, the third one realized a profit; he determined to remain in Richmond and opened a business establishment on Main Street. On August 21, 1790, he married Sally Winston, daughter of Geddes and Mary (Jordan) Winston of Laurel Grove, Hanover County; she bore her husband thirteen children, one of whom, Alexander Hawksley Rutherfoord (q.v.), is represented in the Society's portrait collection. In addition to conducting a successful mercantile business, Rutherfoord speculated in tobacco and western lands, operated flour and cotton mills, and invested in Richmond

real estate, developing a tract west of the city known as Rutherfoord's Addition that extended from First Street to Belvidere. These enterprises proved so successful that by 1811 Rutherfoord was the richest man in Richmond, richer even than Joseph Gallego (q.v.), his chief competitor in the milling business. He was a director of the Richmond branch of the Bank of the United States, a member of the city council between 1816 and 1819, and in 1837 became one of the first directors of the Tredegar Iron Company. After the death of his wife in 1839, his children afforded him "all the comfort possible in my old age." His autobiographical "Narrative," written in 1845, provides a valuable commentary on the business and social life of Richmond for more than half a century. Rutherfoord died on February 3, 1852, aged eighty-six, and is buried in Shockoe Cemetery.

Richmond Portraits, pp. 182–83; *West Virginia History* 36 (1974–75): 50–62; *VMHB* 80 (1972): 238.

Thomas Rutherfoord

ARTIST UNIDENTIFIED

Oil on canvas: 30 x 25 in. (76.2 x 63.5 cm.)

Received in 1971 as a bequest of Mary (Davenport) Fleet of Richmond. Por971.26

The portrait has previously been attributed to Louis Mathieu Didier Guillaume. Since Guillaume did not come to America until after Rutherfoord's death, the portrait, if it is correctly attributed, must be a posthumous copy of an earlier likeness.

Abram Joseph Ryan, 1838–1886

The poet of the Confederacy, Father Ryan was born on February 5, 1838, in Hagerstown, Maryland, the son of Matthew and Mary (Coughlin) Ryan, recent immigrants from Ireland. He attended Niagara University in New York State, entered the novitiate of the Vincentian Fathers in Germantown, Pennsylvania, in 1854, and two years later was ordained to the priesthood. He then taught at Niagara University and at a diocesan seminary in Missouri. On September 1, 1862, he offered his services to the Confederacy as a chaplain. During the war years he devoted himself unstintingly to the wounded, the sick, and the dying, administering the last rites on the battlefield and tending those confined to pestilential hospitals and prisons. Mystical and poetic by nature, he wrote numerous poems on patriotic and battlefield themes, many of which were set to music and sung throughout the South during the war and after. A collected edition of his poems was later published (1879), going through several editions, and enjoying a considerable success. After the war Father Ryan lived in various places in the South, accepting charges in Biloxi, Mississippi; Nashville, Knoxville, and Clarksville, Tennessee; and Macon, Georgia; he served the congregation of St. Mary's Church, Mobile, Alabama, 1870–83. Father Ryan edited Catholic periodicals, made lecture tours through the United States, Mexico, and Canada for the benefit of charitable causes, and labored for the relief of southern widows and orphans. He died in Louisville, Kentucky, on April 22, 1886, and is buried in Mobile.

DAB; *Biographic Catalogue*.

By JOHN P. WALKER. Signed. Dated 1898

Oil on canvas: 58³/4 x 40 in. (149.2 x 101.6 cm.)

Presented to the R. E. Lee Camp, Confederate Veterans, before 1906; acquired by the Virginia Historical Society in 1946 through merger with the Confederate Memorial Association. Por946.206

John Caldwell Calhoun Sanders, 1840–1864

Born at Tuscaloosa, Alabama, on April 4, 1840, General Sanders was the son of Dr. Sanders, a native of Charleston, South Carolina, and his wife, a daughter of Dr. Matthew Thomson. The family removed to Clinton, Greene County, Alabama, and here the subject received his early education before entering the state university in 1858. At the beginning of the Civil War he left the university, enlisted in the 11th Alabama Infantry, and was elected captain. At Seven Pines, Gaines's Mill, and Frayser's Farm he led his company, receiving wounds in the last engagement. On his return to active duty he was given command of the regiment, led it at Sharpsburg, and shortly afterwards was promoted to colonel. Sanders fought at Fredericksburg, Chancellorsville, and Gettysburg; at Spotsylvania he took charge of General Perrin's brigade after Perrin's death and for his conduct was promoted to brigadier general on May 31, 1864. Assigned to the command of Wilcox's Brigade, composed of Alabama regiments, he participated in the operations around Petersburg and in the battle of the Crater. General Sanders was killed on August 21, 1864, in one of the battles along the Weldon railroad. He is buried in Hollywood Cemetery, Richmond.

Generals in Gray; *Confederate Military History*, 7: 443–44; Willis Brewer, *Alabama: Her History, Resources, War Record, and Public Men* (Montgomery, Ala., 1872), pp. 268–69; *Biographic Catalogue*.

By SAM HOFFMAN. Signed (under spandrel)

Oil on canvas: 30 x 25 in. (76.2 x 63.5 cm.)

Presented to the R. E. Lee Camp, Confederate Veterans, in 1899 by the subject's brother; acquired by the Virginia Historical Society in 1946 through merger with the Confederate Memorial Association. Por946.187

James Saunders
See The Convention of 1829–30

Constance Elise Schack, ca. 1852–1937
See Archibald Gracie, 1858–1912

Asenath Poston Scott, 1852–1853
See Martha Minor (Hall) Scott, 1827–1883

Frederic Robert Scott, 1830–1898

Born in County Donegal, Ireland, on October 22, 1830, son of John and Isabella (Doherty) Scott, the subject came with his parents to New York in 1850. Two years later he joined the firm of Thomas Branch and Sons of Petersburg as a clerk, remaining with the firm until 1890. On April 14, 1857, he married Sarah Frances Branch, daughter of Thomas and Sarah Pride (Read) Branch; they became the parents of nine children, eight of whom lived to maturity. On the outbreak of the Civil War he volunteered as a private in the Petersburg Rifles. He was later assigned to General Colston's brigade as quartermaster with the rank of major, then to the staff of Colonel

Cole, chief commissary of the Army of Northern Virginia. After Appomattox he resumed his business in Petersburg; in 1872 he moved to Richmond to take charge of Thomas Branch and Company's Richmond office. The same year he was elected president of the Richmond and Petersburg Railroad, holding that office until his death. He also served as president of the Petersburg Savings and Insurance Company for fifteen years and organized with John P. Branch the Merchants National Bank, of which he was vice-president. Major Scott was a director of numerous southern banks and railroads and a member of the Virginia Historical Society. He died in Richmond on May 15, 1898.

Richmond *Dispatch* (Monday Bulletin), May 16, 1898; John Scott, *Our Journal at Sea on Board the Bark "Fanny," together with Other Scott Family Papers* (Richmond, 1950), pp. 26–27, 31; CMA Archives, folio Z1n; *Biographic Catalogue.*

By ADELE WILLIAMS

Oil on canvas: 32 x 25 in. (81.3 x 63.5 cm.)

Presented to the R. E. Lee Camp, Confederate Veterans, in 1924 by the subject's son, Frederic W. Scott; acquired by the Virginia Historical Society in 1946 through merger with the Confederate Memorial Association. Por946.229

John Scott, 1781–1850
See The Convention of 1829–30

Kitty Henry Scott, 1819–1845
See Kitty Henry (Scott) Scott, 1819–1845

Kitty Henry (Scott) Scott, 1819–1845 (Mrs. Robert W. Scott)

Born at Seven Islands, Campbell County, on August 18, 1819, the subject was a daughter of Alexander Scott and his second wife, Sarah Butler (Henry) Campbell Scott, and a granddaughter of Patrick Henry (q.v.). She married on April 19, 1843, Dr. Robert W. Scott; their union, however, was of short duration, for she died on December 8, 1845. The couple had no children.

Information received with the portrait; *Virginia Genealogies*, p. 630.

By MARTHA ANN HONEYWELL. Signed

Silhouette: 2¼ in. (5.7 cm.) in height, on paper 3¾ x 3 in. (9.5 x 7.6 cm.). Inscribed: "Cut by M. Honeywell with the Mouth." Inscribed on the back: "Kitty H. Scott's when a child. S. Scott. Fauquier Co., Va.

Meadow Grove   Decb. 23th 1845. Grand-daughter of Patrick Henry."

Provenance unknown. PorX258

Martha Minor (Hall) Scott, 1827–1883 (Mrs. William Poston Scott), with Her Daughter Asenath Poston Scott, 1852–1853

Born in St. Louis, Missouri, on August 19, 1827, the subject was a daughter of Charles Rush Hall and Louise Ann (Quarles) Hall, both natives of Virginia, and a great-granddaughter of Charles and Ann (Byrd) Carter of Cleve. She married William Poston Scott, who was born in Washington County, Virginia, on December 18, 1815, son of Mitchell Scott (q.v.) and Asenath Wilder (Poston) Scott of Washington and Smyth counties. The couple spent their married life in St. Louis and had issue. William Poston Scott died there on July 21, 1868; Mrs. Scott died there on April 14, 1883. The child depicted with her mother in the portrait is Asenath Poston Scott, who was born in 1852 and died on December 12, 1853.

VHS Mss6:1 Sco865:1–5; *VMHB* 80 (1972): 238; Robert Randolph Carter, *The Carter Tree* (Santa Barbara, Calif., 1951), p. 119.

Martha Minor (Hall) Scott with her daughter, Asenath Poston Scott

By MANUEL JOACHIM DE FRANCA. Signed. Dated 1854

23. Winfield Scott

Oil on canvas: 36 x 29 in. (91.4 x 73.7 cm.)

Presented in 1971 by Mrs. C. L. Arnold of Pasadena, California. Por971.35

The date on the portrait indicates that it is a posthumous likeness of the child.

Mitchell Scott, 1790–1858

Mitchell Scott was born in Washington County in 1790, son of Charles and Elizabeth Scott. He married, on March 10, 1814, Asenath Wilder Poston, daughter of William and Sarah (Hamill) Poston; the couple had issue. Their son William Poston Scott removed to St. Louis, Missouri, where he married; a portrait of his wife, Martha Minor (Hall) Scott (q.v.), is in the Society's collection. Mitchell Scott died in Smyth County on September 8, 1858; his wife predeceased him by twelve years.

VHS Mss6:1 Sco865:1–5; *VMHB* 80 (1972): 238.

By MANUEL JOACHIM DE FRANCA. Signed. Dated 1857

Oil on canvas: 30 x 25 in. (76.2 x 63.5 cm.)

Presented in 1971 by Mrs. C. L. Arnold of Pasadena, California. Por971.36

Winfield Scott, 1786–1866

"Old Fuss and Feathers" was born at Laurel Branch, Dinwiddie County, on June 13, 1786, son of William and Ann (Mason) Scott. He attended the College of William and Mary for less than a year, studied law, and was admitted to the bar in 1806. A giant of a man, standing six feet five inches and weighing 230 pounds, he joined the army in 1808 but was shortly thereafter court-martialed and suspended from active duty for criticizing his superior officer, General James Wilkinson. During the War of 1812 he saw action in the battles of Queenstown Heights, Fort George, Chippewa, and Lundy's Lane, emerging from these engagements somewhat battered physically but with enormous popularity; he declined an appointment as secretary of war but accepted medals from Congress and the Commonwealth of Virginia. Scott participated in the Indian Wars and on June 25, 1841, became general-in-chief of the United States Army, a command he held for the next twenty years. He further distinguished himself during the Mexican War, leading his troops in the capture of Veracruz, the storming of Chapultepec, and the entry into Mexico City. In 1852 he was the Whig candidate for the presidency of the United States but was overwhelmingly defeated by Franklin Pierce. Despite his Virginian antecedents, Scott sided with the Union during the Civil War; his age, infirmities, and his disapproval of General McClellan as commander of the Army of the Potomac led to his retirement from active service on October 31, 1861. General Scott died at West Point, New York, on May 29, 1866. His wife, whom he married on March 11, 1817, was Maria (Mayo) Scott, daughter of John and Abigail (DeHart) Mayo of Richmond; she bore her husband seven children, four of whom died young.

DAB; *Encyclopedia Americana*; *VMHB* 74 (1966): 243; *Occasional Bulletin*, no. 11 (1965): 2–5 (portrait reproduced).

By MINER KILBOURNE KELLOGG. Signed

See Plate 23

Oil on canvas: 25 1/4 x 20 3/4 in. (64.1 x 52.7 cm.)

Acquired in 1965 with funds contributed for the purpose by Mr. and Mrs. Woodbury S. Ober of Orange. Por965.9

Thomas Edward Seay, 1823–1881
Rebecca Ann (Reger) Seay, 1831–1916   (Mrs. Thomas Edward Seay)

Thomas Edward Seay, son of Elisha and Susan (Toney) Seay of Fluvanna County, was born on March 3, 1823. On December 25, 1846, he married Rebecca Ann Reger, who was born at Buckhannon, (West) Virginia, on February 10, 1831, the daughter of Abraham and Leah (Brake) Reger. The couple resided in Fluvanna County and became the parents of eight children. Thomas Edward Seay died on December 21, 1881; his wife died at Atlantic City, New Jersey, on March 28, 1916; both are buried in the Seay family burial ground in Fluvanna County.

VHS Mss6:1 R2624:1 and Mss6:1 Z116:1.

Portrait I. Thomas Seay

Pencil and watercolor: 3 3/4 x 2 3/4 in. (9.5 x 7 cm.) (oval)

Presented in 1962 by the Reverend George England DeWitte Zachary of Richmond, a grandson of the subject. Por962.15

Portrait II. Rebecca Ann (Reger) Seay

Pencil and watercolor: 3 3/4 x 2 3/4 in. (9.5 x 7 cm.) (oval)

Presented in 1962 by the Reverend George England DeWitte Zachary of Richmond, a grandson of the subject. Por962.15

The two portraits are framed together behind a black glass mat decorated in gold.

Sarah Alexander Seddon, 1829–1907
See Charles Bruce, 1826–1896

Adam See, b. 1764
See The Convention of 1829–30

Raphael Semmes, 1809–1877

Admiral Semmes, born in Charles County, Maryland, on September 27, 1809, was the son of Richard Thompson Semmes and Catherine (Middleton) Semmes. He became a midshipman in the United States Navy in 1826, was commissioned lieutenant in 1837, and took part in the Mexican War. During the next twelve years he saw little active naval duty but devoted himself to writing and the practice of law. With the outbreak of hostilities in 1861 he was appointed commander in the Confederate navy. Assigned to the *Sumter*, he oversaw her conversion into a raider, and from June 1861 till the following April he sailed the Atlantic and Caribbean preying on Union merchant vessels. Forced to abandon the ship in Gibraltar, he took command of the *Alabama*, nearing completion in Liverpool; from August 1862 he cruised the seas for almost two years, destroying more than seventy Union vessels and seriously disrupting Union maritime trade; these successes earned him the gratitude of the Confederate Congress and promotion to rear admiral. On June 19, 1864, in a confrontation off Cherbourg, France, with the Union ship *Kearsarge*, the *Alabama* went down, but Semmes and most of the crew were rescued. He returned to Richmond by way of Switzerland and Mexico and was assigned to the command of the James River Squadron. After the war Semmes was forced by political pressure to resign a judgeship, a professorship, and the editorship of the *Memphis Daily Bulletin*. Settling in Mobile, Alabama, he resumed the practice of law until his death which occurred on August 30, 1877. He was survived by his wife, Anne Elizabeth (Spencer) Semmes, whom he married on May 5, 1837, and by their six children.

DAB; *Encyclopedia Americana*; *Biographic Catalogue*.

By JOHN P. WALKER. Signed. Dated 1924

Oil on canvas: 30 x 25 in. (76.2 x 63.5 cm.)

Presented to the R. E. Lee Camp, Confederate Veterans, in 1925 by the Electra Semmes Colston Chapter, U.D.C., Mobile, Alabama; acquired by the Virginia Historical Society in 1946 through merger with the Confederate Memorial Association. Por946.46

Cassandra Morrison Shanks, 1807–1887
See John Thomas Anderson, 1804–1879

Nancy Witcher (Langhorne) Shaw, 1879–1964
See Nancy Witcher (Langhorne) Shaw Astor, Viscountess Astor, 1879–1964

"Samuel Sheppard"

The silhouette is inscribed "Mr. Sam Sheppard's Likeness." Possibly it represents Samuel Sheppard who was born on February 3, 1730, son of Samuel and Mary (Kavanagh) Sheppard of Gloucester County. He married Anne Burwell of Gloucester. The couple resided in Buckingham County where they raised a family of ten children.

W. & M. Quart., 2d ser., 6 (1926): 149 and 7 (1927): 174–76.

ARTIST UNIDENTIFIED

Silhouette: 2³/₄ in. (7 cm.) in height, on paper 3 x 2¹/₄ in. (7.6 x 5.7 cm.). Inscribed: "Mr. Sam Sheppard's Likeness."

Provenance unknown. PorX248

Eliza Shipp, 1804–1862
See Benjamin Burton, 1784–1860

Frederick William Sievers, 1872–1966

Frederick William Sievers, sculptor, was born in Fort Wayne, Indiana, on October 26, 1872, son of Frederick Augustus Ferdinand Sievers and Caroline (Dieter) Sievers. He received his early education in Atlanta, Georgia, and at the Virginia Mechanics Institute in Richmond where he studied wood carving. In 1898 he went to Europe and studied at the Preparatory School of Art in Rome and at the Académie Julian in Paris; he returned to the United States and between 1905 and 1910 maintained a studio in New York City. His first public commission, 1906, was for the Confederate Monument in Abingdon; four years later his design for the Virginia Memorial at Gettysburg, one of thirty-six entries, was selected by the state commission; the monument was unveiled on June 8, 1917. This was followed by the Thomas Jonathan ("Stonewall") Jackson monument on Monument Avenue, Richmond, 1919, the Lloyd Tilghman monument at Vicksburg, Mississippi, 1925, the Matthew Fontaine Maury monument on Monument Avenue, Richmond, 1929, and the Confederate Memorial at Woodlawn National Cemetery at Elmira, New York, 1938. Sievers also executed the busts of James Madison, Zachary Taylor, Patrick

Henry, and Sam Houston in the Virginia state Capitol, and the bust of Maury in the New York Hall of Fame. He died on July 4, 1966. His wife, whom he married in 1906, was Elsie (Muegge) Sievers; the couple had a son and a daughter.

Virginia Cavalcade 12, no. 2 (1962): 4–12; *Who Was Who in America* 4 (1968): 863.

BY WILLIAM MACFARLANE JONES.
Signed (initials)

Pen and India ink on cardboard: 16³/₄ x 13 in. (42.6 x 33 cm.)

Presented by the artist in 1945. Por945.22

Amélie Louise (Rives) Sigourney, 1832–1873

See Amélie Louise Rives, 1832–1873

Lettice (Lee) Wardrop Thompson Sim, d. 1776

See Lettice (Lee) Wardrop, d. 1776

Lucy (Harrison) Randolph Singleton, ca. 1757–1809

See Peyton Randolph, ca. 1738–1784

Campbell Slemp, 1839–1907

A native of Lee County, Campbell Slemp was born on December 2, 1839, son of Sebastian and Margaret (Reasor) Slemp. He attended Emory and Henry College but was forced to withdraw before graduating because of the death of his father. On Virginia's secession from the Union he joined the Confederate army as captain of Company A, 21st Virginia Battalion. His wartime service included duty in Southwest Virginia, central Tennessee, and Kentucky, during which time he rose to lieutenant colonel of his battalion and later to colonel of the 64th Virginia Regiment, composed of infantry and cavalry. At the war's end he farmed and acquired large tracts of coal and timber lands. Turning to politics, he represented Lee County in the Virginia House of Delegates 1879–82 and was a presidential elector on the Harrison ticket in 1888 and an unsuccessful candidate for lieutenant governor of Virginia on the ticket with General William Mahone in 1889. Elected as a Republican to the Fifty-eighth United States Congress and to the two succeeding Congresses, Slemp represented his district in Washington from 1903 until his death, which took place in Big Stone Gap on Octo-

ber 13, 1907. By his wife, Nannie D. (Cawood) Slemp, formerly of Owsley County, Kentucky, whom he married in 1864, he had seven children.

Biographical Directory; *Men of Mark in Virginia*, 2: 349–50; *Biographic Catalogue.*

BY UNDERWOOD. Signed

Oil on canvas: 27 x 22 in. (68.6 x 55.9 cm.)

Presented to the R. E. Lee Camp, Confederate Veterans, in 1926; acquired by the Virginia Historical Society in 1946 through merger with the Confederate Memorial Association. Por946.92

Austin E. Smith, 1829–1862

The fourth child of Governor William ("Extra Billy") Smith (q.v.) and Elizabeth Hansborough (Bell) Smith, the subject was born in 1829. He studied law and practiced his profession in Fauquier and adjoining counties. In 1853 he removed to San Francisco, California, where he was appointed by President Buchanan naval officer of that port. Resigning from his post at the outbreak of the Civil War, he returned to Washington to settle his accounts; he was arrested and held as a prisoner of war. Released through the efforts of his father, he enlisted in the Confederate army and was assigned, with the rank of lieutenant colonel, to the staff of General Whiting. He was killed in the battle of Gaines's Mill on June 27, 1862.

Virginia and Virginians, 1: 216; John W. Bell, *Memoirs of Governor William Smith, of Virginia: His Political, Military, and Personal History* (New York, 1891), p. 135; *Biographic Catalogue.*

BY WILLIAM LUDWELL SHEPPARD. Signed. Dated 1905

Oil on canvas: 30 x 25 in. (76.2 x 63.5 cm.). Inscribed on the back: "Lt. Col. Austin E. Smith (on staff of Genl. Whiting) mortally wounded at battle of Gaines' Mill June 27th 1862."

Presented to the R. E. Lee Camp, Confederate Veterans, in 1908 by the subject's sister and brother, Mary Amelia Smith and Colonel Thomas Smith; acquired by the Virginia Historical Society in 1946 through merger with the Confederate Memorial Association. Por946.71

Edmund Kirby Smith, 1824–1893

Born at St. Augustine, Florida, on May 16, 1824, son of Joseph Lee Smith and Frances Marvin (Kirby) Smith, the subject graduated from West Point in 1845. He saw action in the Mexican War, taught at West Point 1849–52, and in 1855 was sent to Texas where he engaged in the campaigns against the Indians. On the secession of Florida from the Union he was commissioned lieutenant colonel in the Confederate army and assigned to the staff of General J. E. Johnston. Promoted to brigadier general on June 17, 1861, he received wounds at First Manassas. On his return to active duty as a major general he was assigned first to a division of Beauregard's army and later to the command of the District of East Tennessee. Smith participated in Bragg's invasion of Kentucky, then became commander of the Trans-Mississippi Department, rising in rank to full general. His was the last Confederate command in the field; he did not surrender it until June 2, 1865. After brief sojourns in Mexico and Cuba, Smith returned to the United States and became president of an insurance company, then president of a telegraph company. A man of strong religious convictions, he decided against entering the ministry because of his age. He turned instead to education, serving as president of the University of Nashville 1870–75. Thereafter he was professor of mathematics at the University of the South until his death eighteen years later on March 28, 1893. He was the last surviving full general of either army. General Smith's wife, Cassie (Selden) Smith, whom he married in Lynchburg on September 24, 1861, bore him five sons and six daughters.

DAB; Generals in Gray; Biographic Catalogue.

By JOHN P. WALKER. Signed. Dated 1923

Oil on canvas: 30 x 25 in. (76.2 x 63.5 cm.)

Presented to the R. E. Lee Camp, Confederate Veterans, in 1923; acquired by the Virginia Historical Society in 1946 through merger with the Confederate Memorial Association. Por946.197

James Power Smith, 1837–1923

Born in New Athens, Ohio, on July 4, 1837, the subject was the son of the Reverend Joseph Smith and Eliza (Bell) Smith. He graduated with the class of 1856 from Jefferson College, Pennsylvania, and attended Union Theological Seminary, which was located at that time at Hampden-Sydney, Virginia. In 1861 he entered the Army of the Confederacy as a corporal in the Rockbridge Artillery; in September 1862 he was transferred to Stonewall Jackson's staff with the rank of captain, serving in that capacity until the general's death. Thereafter, until the war's end, he was aide-de-camp to General Ewell. On October 13, 1866, Smith was ordained into the Presbyterian ministry. For three years he was pastor at Big Lick (now Roanoke), then accepted a call to Fredericksburg where he remained from 1869 to 1892. After a year of evangelistic work in Charlottes-

ville, Smith removed to Richmond where for eighteen years he edited the *Central Presbyterian*. In addition to his editorial duties he was chaplain to the Virginia State Penitentiary for twenty years, chairman of the Committee of Home Missions of East Hanover Presbytery, and chairman of the Presbyterian General Assembly's Executive Committee of Publication and Sabbath Schools; he was stated clerk of the Synod of Virginia for fifty years, 1870–1920. His devotion to the Confederate cause led him to accept assignments on the boards of the R. E. Lee Camp no. 1, the Southern Historical Society, and the Confederate Memorial Literary Society and to contribute historical monographs to the publications of these and similar organizations. Smith's wife, whom he married on April 15, 1871, was Agnes (Lacy) Smith, daughter of Major Horace Lacy of Chatham, Stafford County; they became the parents of four sons and two daughters. He died at the home of a daughter in Greensboro, North Carolina, on August 6, 1923.

Presbyterian Church in the U.S., *Minutes of the Synod of Virginia . . . August 28–30, 1923* (Richmond, 1923), pp. 161–64; *Biographic Catalogue.*

By GEORGE BAGBY MATTHEWS. Signed

Oil on canvas: 30 x 25 in. (76.2 x 63.5 cm.)

Acquired in 1946 through merger with the Confederate Memorial Association. Por946.99

Orren Randolph Smith, 1827–1913

Orren Randolph Smith, designer of the flag of the Confederate States of America, was born in Warren County, North Carolina, on December 18, 1827. As a youth he saw action in the Mexican War, receiving an honorable discharge on August 7, 1848, some months before attaining his majority. He saw further military service in Utah 1857–58 under Albert Sidney Johnston (q.v.). During the secession crisis Smith, responding to a call for a flag for the new nation, submitted the design; the "Stars and Bars," as it was called, was approved and was raised for the first time by the designer at Louisburg, North Carolina, on March 18, 1861, two months before North Carolina's secession from the Union. Smith fought throughout the war, rising to the rank of major. After the war he resided at Henderson, North Carolina. He attempted to reenlist during the Spanish-American war but was rejected because of his age. He died at Henderson on March 3, 1913, survived by a daughter.

Confederate Veteran 21 (1913): 249; *New York Times*, March 5, 1913; *History of the Stars and Bars, Designed by Orren Randolph Smith* (Raleigh, N.C., 1913).

By MARY TRAVIS BURWELL. Signed

Oil on canvas: 36 x 27 in. (91.4 x 68.6 cm.)

Presented to the R. E. Lee Camp, Confederate Veterans, in 1927; acquired by the Virginia Historical Society in 1946 through merger with the Confederate Memorial Association. Por946.136

Thomas Smith, 1836–1918

Born in Culpeper on August 25, 1836, the subject was the son of Governor William ("Extra Billy") Smith (q.v.) and Elizabeth Hansborough (Bell) Smith. He graduated from the College of William and Mary in 1856 and from the law school of the University of Virginia in 1858. He practiced his profession in Charleston, (West) Virginia, until the commencement of the Civil War, whereupon he joined the Kanawha Riflemen, as a private. He was subsequently made major of the 36th Virginia Infantry which he commanded at Fort Donelson and later became colonel. Severely wounded and taken prisoner at Cloyd's Farm, he rejoined his command in the Valley of Virginia and led it through all the engagements of that campaign till the war's end. Thereafter he practiced law in Warrenton; for six years he served as judge of the Fauquier County court, and he represented the county in the Virginia House of Delegates 1883–84. He was appointed by President Cleveland to a four-year term as United States attorney for New Mexico and at the beginning of Cleveland's second administration became for four years chief justice of the New Mexico Territory. On the expiration of his judicial term he retired from active life and resided in Warrenton until his death on June 29, 1918. He was married on October 10, 1896, to Elizabeth Fairfax Gaines, a daughter of Judge William H. Gaines of Warrenton.

Encyclopedia of Virginia Biography, 5: 601–2; *University of Virginia*, 1: 413–14; *Virginia and Virginians*, 1: 216; *Biographic Catalogue*.

By WILLIAM LUDWELL SHEPPARD. Signed

Oil on canvas: 30 x 25 in. (76.2 x 63.5 cm.). Inscribed on the back: "Col. Thos. Smith 26 Va. Infantry. Acting Brigadier Genl. In 1864."

Acquired in 1946 through merger with the Confederate Memorial Association. Por946.74

William Smith, 1797–1887

Congressman and twice governor of Virginia, "Extra Billy" Smith was born on September 6, 1797, at Marengo, King George County, the son of Caleb and Mary Waugh (Smith) Smith. He studied law in Fredericksburg and Warrenton and began practice in Culpeper in 1818. Three years later he married

Elizabeth Hansborough Bell; she bore him eleven children. In 1827 he organized a local mail coach service that prospered to such an extent that by 1834 a daily mail service was running between Washington, D.C., and Milledgeville, Georgia, bringing Smith substantial "extra" revenues from the Post Office Department and leading Benjamin Watkins Leigh (q.v.) to refer to him as "Extra Billy," a sobriquet that stuck. He represented his county in the Virginia state Senate 1836–41, was a United States congressman 1841–43, and served his first term as governor of Virginia 1846–49. After residing briefly in California, he returned to Virginia and again sat in the United States Congress 1853–61. On the outbreak of the Civil War he became colonel of the 49th Virginia Infantry and fought at First Manassas. Elected to the Confederate Congress, he attended its sessions between campaigns but resigned in 1863. Smith took part in the Peninsular campaign, the Seven Days battles, Sharpsburg, and Gettysburg; he was promoted to brigadier general on January 31, 1863, and to major general the following August. Again elected governor of Virginia, he took office on January 1, 1864, and served until the fall of the Confederacy. With the capture of Richmond he withdrew with his government to Lynchburg and then to Danville but returned to Richmond after Lee's surrender. He lived the remainder of his life at Monterosa, his estate near Warrenton, emerging once when he was eighty years of age to sit in the Virginia House of Delegates 1877–79. He died on May 18, 1887, and is buried in Hollywood Cemetery, Richmond. Portraits of two of his sons, Austin E. Smith and Thomas Smith (qq.v.), are also in the Society's collection.

DAB; *Generals in Gray*; *Biographic Catalogue*.

By JOHN P. WALKER. Signed. Dated 1900

Oil on canvas: 30 x 25 in. (76.2 x 63.5 cm.)

Presented to the R. E. Lee Camp, Confederate Veterans, in 1900 by the subject's son, Colonel Thomas Smith; acquired by the Virginia Historical Society in 1946 through merger with the Confederate Memorial Association. Por946.152

William Smith

See The Convention of 1829–30

William Pritchard Smith, 1840–1903

The subject is thought to be William Pritchard Smith, who was born in Fredericksburg on July 31, 1840. As a youth he came to Richmond where he was employed in the dry goods store of Samuel L. Price.

In July 1861 he enlisted in the 1st Richmond Howitzers and participated with that artillery command until Gettysburg, where he was captured and sustained wounds requiring the amputation of a leg and a finger. After being exchanged, he worked for a time in the Confederate Treasury Department. At the end of the war he spent several years in North Carolina, then returned to Richmond, spending the next twenty-four years with the firm of H. B. Taliaferro and Company, commission merchants. Thereafter he was associated with a variety of business enterprises in Richmond and for the last six years of his life was employed in the city treasurer's office. Colonel Smith was a member of the board of visitors of the Lee Camp Soldiers' Home and post commander of both the R. E. Lee Camp, Confederate Veterans, and of the Grand Camp of Virginia. On his death in Richmond on April 25, 1903, he was survived by five children; he is buried in Hollywood Cemetery.

Confederate Military History, 3: 1179–80; Richmond *Times-Dispatch*, April 26, 1903, p. 6, col. 4.

ARTIST UNIDENTIFIED

Pastel on cardboard: 20 x 16 in. (50.8 x 40.6 cm.)

Provenance unknown. PorX322

Charles Goodall Snead, 1840–1925

The youngest of seven sons of George Helman Snead and Oranie (Pollard) Snead, the subject was born in Fluvanna County on December 12, 1840. He attended local schools and evinced an early and abiding interest in religion; in 1859 he was chosen a delegate to the Biennial Southern Baptist Convention. At the beginning of the Civil War, Snead enlisted in the Fluvanna Artillery as fourth sergeant. He rose during four years of active duty to the rank of captain, seeing action in the Seven Days battles around Richmond, at Frederick, Maryland, and at the battle of Winchester. In February 1865 he married Sallie Miller Broaddus of Caroline County; after five years of marriage she died, leaving two daughters. At the war's end he removed to Mississippi and engaged in cotton planting with his wife's uncle, Alexander Miller. He returned nine years later to the Old Homestead, the farm where he was born, remaining there the rest of his life. In addition to farming, Captain Snead was for twenty-five years a traveling representative of a fertilizer company. He married, second, Elizabeth Mary Payne of Goochland County; the couple had seven children. For many years he was commander of the Fluvanna Camp of Confederate Veterans, county chairman of the Democratic party, deacon and teacher in the Fork Union Baptist Church, and benefactor and vice-president of the board of trustees of Fork Union Military Academy. He died on July 9, 1925, one day after the death of his wife.

Thomas Lincoln Sydnor, *Living Epistles, the Old Guard in the Present Happy Meetings* (Danville, Va., 1924), pp. 8–12; Oranie Virginia Snead Hatcher, *The Sneads of Fluvanna* (Fork Union, Va., 1959), p. 162; *Richmond Times-Dispatch*, July 11, 1925, p. 2; CMA Archives, folio Z1n; *Biographic Catalogue*.

BY MARY TRAVIS BURWELL. Signed

Oil on canvas: 30 x 24 in. (76.2 x 61 cm.)

Presented to the R. E. Lee Camp, Confederate Veterans, in 1925; acquired by the Virginia Historical Society in 1946 through merger with the Confederate Memorial Association. Por946.85

Sir George Somers, 1554–1610

Born in 1554, son of John Somers of Dorset, England, the subject took to the sea at an early age, thereafter taking part in buccaneering voyages against the Spanish between 1595 and 1602. He was knighted at Whitehall on July 23, 1603, was elected member of Parliament for Lyme Regis on February 25, 1604, and the following year became mayor of the town. Active in the formation of the Virginia Company, he was nominated admiral of the company in 1609 and organized a fleet of nine vessels to convey settlers to the colony. The fleet sailed from Plymouth on June 2, 1609; a storm dispersed the ships, and Somers's vessel was wrecked on July 25, on the Bermuda islands. Somers and his companions remained on Bermuda ten months, built two small barks, and sailed for Virginia on May 10, 1610, arriving at Jamestown on May 23. But finding the settlement in a pitiable condition, Somers resolved to embark all surviving colonists, abandon the settlement, and return to England. As he headed for open sea with all colonists aboard, he encountered Lord De La Warr arriving with food, supplies, and fresh settlers; he was persuaded to return to Jamestown. Volunteering a few days later to obtain a supply of fish and pork from Bermuda, Somers again set sail; he was carried by a current to the New England coast but finally reached Bermuda, where on November 9, 1610, he died from the effects of eating too much pork. His heart was buried in Bermuda, but his body was conveyed to England for burial at Whitchurch in Dorset. He was survived by his wife, Joanna (Heywood) Somers, a daughter of Phillip Heywood; the couple had no children.

DNB; Alexander Brown, *The Genesis of the United States* (Boston, 1890), 2: 1018–19; *Portraiture*, pp. 98–99; *Virginia Historical Portraiture*, pp. 49–52 (original portrait reproduced).

COPIED BY CHARLES X. HARRIS. 1930

Oil on canvas: 46 x 35 in. (116.8 x 88.9 cm.). Inscribed on the back: "Admiral Sir George Somers, 1554–1610 after a portrait by Paul Van Somer. Painted by C. X. Harris 1930."

Presented in 1930 by Virginia (Chase) Steedman Weddell (Mrs. Alexander Wilbourne Weddell) of Richmond. Por930.8

The original portrait, formerly the property of Winifred Bellamy of Plymouth, England, came to this country in 1929 for the exhibition of Virginia historical portraiture organized by Alexander Wilbourne Weddell under the auspices of the Virginia Historical Society. While the portrait was in Virginia, Mrs. Weddell commissioned the present copy for the Society's gallery. Shortly thereafter the original portrait was acquired by the Bermuda Historical Society, together with the companion portrait of Lady Somers.

Gilbert Moxley Sorrel, 1838–1901

Born in Savannah, Georgia, on February 23, 1838, the son of Francis Sorrel, the subject attended Chatham Academy, and at the beginning of the Civil War was a clerk in the Central Railroad Bank. As a private in the Georgia Hussars he saw active duty at Fort Pulaski and Skidaway Island, then left for Virginia where he was attached to General Longstreet's staff as a volunteer aide-de-camp with the rank of captain. He served Longstreet in every engagement of the 1st Corps from First Manassas to the Wilderness, rising in rank to lieutenant colonel. On October 27, 1864, he was appointed brigadier general and put in command of a brigade in Mahone's Division. He was wounded near Petersburg and again at Hatcher's Run; returning to his command after his recovery, he learned of Lee's surrender. Resuming his civilian life in Savannah, Sorrel became agent then manager of the Ocean Steamship Company. He was a member of the Savannah City Council 1873–75, vice-president of the Georgia Historical Society 1877–89, and for many years chairman of the board of Telfair Academy. He later spent some years in New York City as manager of the Ocean Steamship Company's office in that city, resigning in 1894 to accept the general management of the Georgia Export and Import Company in Savannah. After a year or so of failing health, he died at the residence of his brother near Roanoke on August 10, 1901. General Sorrel was survived by his wife, Kate (duBignon) Sorrel, from Milledgeville, Georgia.

Generals in Gray; Gilbert Moxley Sorrel, *Recollections of a Confederate Staff Officer* (Jackson, Tenn., 1958); *Biographic Catalogue.*

BY JOHN P. WALKER. Signed. Dated 1899

Oil on canvas: 30 x 25 in. (76.2 x 63.5 cm.)

Presented to the R. E. Lee Camp, Confederate Veterans, in 1899; acquired by the Virginia Historical Society in 1946 through merger with the Confederate Memorial Association. Por946.73

Sir Robert Southwell, 1635–1702

Sir Robert Southwell, eldest son of Robert and Helena (Gore) Southwell, was born near Kinsale, Ireland, on December 31, 1635. He prepared for a diplomatic career at Queen's College, Oxford, and Lincoln's Inn; later he traveled on the Continent and served as one of the clerks to the Privy Council. In 1665 he was knighted and appointed envoy to the court of Portugal where he was instrumental in concluding the Peace of Lisbon on February 13, 1668. He was sent as envoy extraordinary to the court of Brussels in 1671 and to the elector of Brandenburg nine years later. Thereafter for political reasons he withdrew from public life for a time, living in retirement at his estate, King's Weston, in Gloucestershire, until the accession of William and Mary in 1688. The following year he was appointed commissioner of customs, and in 1690 principal secretary of state for Ireland, an office he held for the rest of his life. Southwell was elected president of the Royal Society in 1690, holding the office until 1695. He died at King's Weston on September 11, 1702. His

Sir Robert Southwell

227

wife, described by Pepys as "a very pretty woman," was Elizabeth (Dering) Southwell, daughter of Sir Edward Dering; they were married on January 26, 1664, and became the parents of two sons and four daughters.

DNB.

ATTRIBUTED TO SIR GODFREY KNELLER

Oil on canvas: 49½ x 40 in. (125.7 x 101.6 cm.)

Presented in 1978 by the Ethyl Corporation through Floyd D. Gottwald of Richmond. Por978.11

The Society's portrait of Sir Robert Southwell was originally owned by William Byrd (1674–1744) (q.v.), second of the name, of Westover. At the tender age of seven Byrd was sent to England for schooling; he remained there, except for a brief visit to Virginia in 1696, until 1704. While in England young Byrd's education was supervised by his father's friend and sometime business associate Sir Robert Southwell. It was through Sir Robert that the young Virginian gained entrée into London's social and intellectual circles and that he was elected in 1696 to membership in the Royal Society, over which Sir Robert had lately presided, and met such prominent contemporaries as Charles Boyle, the natural philosopher, later earl of Orrery, who remained one of Byrd's lifelong friends, and whose portrait also graced the walls of Byrd's Westover gallery. Byrd probably acquired the Southwell portrait shortly after Sir Robert's death in 1702. It is based on the portrait by Kneller that now hangs in the rooms of the Royal Society in London and may well be a replica executed by the artist himself. The portrait remained at Westover until the death of Mrs. William Byrd III in 1814, when the estate was sold and the furnishings distributed. It then came into the possession of a daughter of the house, Evelyn Taylor (Byrd) Harrison, the wife of Benjamin Harrison of Brandon; their descendants owned it until it was acquired in 1977 by the Ethyl Corporation, whose chairman shortly thereafter presented it to the Society.

Alexander Spotswood, 1676–1740
Anne Butler (Brayne) Spotswood
(Mrs. Alexander Spotswood)

Alexander Spotswood, lieutenant governor of Virginia, was born in Tangier in 1676, son of Robert and Catherine (Mercer) Elliott Spotswood. In 1693 he joined the army, served in the War of the Spanish Succession, and was wounded at Blenheim. On June 23, 1719, he was appointed lieutenant governor of Virginia. During his twelve-year administration he attempted to develop a more enlightened Indian policy, to regulate the fur and tobacco trade, and to increase his own influence over the courts and the clergy. In the pursuit of these policies he aroused the antagonism of both Council and burgesses and incurred the enmity of such influential figures as William Byrd (q.v.) and Commissary James Blair (q.v.). Indefatigable in his efforts to explore the lands west of the Blue Ridge Mountains, Spotswood led various transmontane expeditions; that of 1716 is most celebrated, for its members were named by the governor "Knights of the Golden Horseshoe." Spotswood left office on September 27, 1722, retiring to his estate in Spotsylvania County where he had established extensive iron-smelting operations. Two years later he went to England; while there he married Anne Butler Brayne, daughter of Richard and Anne Brayne of St. Margaret's, Westminster; they became the parents of four children. In 1730 he returned to Virginia with his family, bearing with him a commission as deputy postmaster of the American colonies. With the outbreak of war with Spain in 1739, he was appointed major general and ordered to recruit a regiment of troops; he died at Annapolis June 7, 1740, on his way to join Baron Cathcart at the siege of Cartagena. The governor's widow married, second, on November 9, 1742, the Reverend John Thompson, rector of St. Mark's Parish, Culpeper County, and bore him two children.

DAB; *Occasional Bulletin*, no. 7 (1963): 1–3 (Portraits I and II reproduced); *VMHB* 72 (1964): 241; *Antiques* 116 (1979): 1137 (Portraits I and II reproduced).

Alexander Spotswood

Portrait I. Alexander Spotswood

ARTIST UNIDENTIFIED

Miniature: plumbago on vellum: 1¼ x 1 in. (3.2 x 2.5 cm.) (oval)

Presented in 1963 by Frances Roberdeau Wolfe of Richmond. Por963.23

Anne Butler (Brayne) Spotswood

Portrait II. Anne Butler (Brayne) Spotswood

ARTIST UNIDENTIFIED

Miniature: plumbago on vellum: 2½ x 2 in. (6.4 x 5.1 cm.) (oval)

Presented in 1963 by Frances Roberdeau Wolfe of Richmond. Por963.24

John Stagg, 1792–1842

The subject was born in Charles City County in February 1792. He married Elizabeth King Fox (1794–1842) on January 21, 1823; the couple had children. He resided in Charles City County and was a friend of Charles Carter of Shirley. He died in 1842.

Information received with the silhouette.

ARTIST UNIDENTIFIED

Silhouette: 9½ in. (24.1 cm.) in height, mounted on paper 11¼ x 7½ in. (28.6 x 19.1 cm.)

Presented in 1975 by Ella McRae Stagg of Richmond, a great-granddaughter of the subject. Por975.29

Larkin Stanard, 1760–1840

The subject was born in May 1760, son of Beverley and Elizabeth Beverley (Chew) Stanard of Roxbury, Spotsylvania County. He saw service in the Revolutionary War, first in New Jersey, later in the campaigns around Williamsburg. He married Elizabeth Perrott Chew, only daughter of Robert and Mary (Perrott) Chew; the couple resided at Stanfield, Spotsylvania County, and became the parents of twelve children. He represented his county in the Virginia House of Delegates 1798–1804. Larkin Standard died in 1840.

The Beverley Family, pp. 729, 737; Joseph Thompson McAllister, *Virginia Militia in the Revolutionary War* (Hot Springs, Va., 1913), pp. 166–67; *VMHB* 3 (1895–96): 392 and 65 (1957): 253; *W. & M. Quart.*, 1st ser., 22 (1913–14): 268–69.

ARTIST UNIDENTIFIED

Hollow-cut silhouette: 2¼ in. (5.7 cm.) in height, on paper 3½ x 2¾ in. (8.9 x 7 cm.) (oval)

Presented in 1956 by Ellen Beverley Wooldridge of Richmond. Por956.83

John Stagg

Robert Stanard, 1781–1846

See The Convention of 1829–30

William Glover Stanard, 1858–1933

For nearly thirty-five years the corresponding secretary of the Virginia Historical Society, the subject was the son of Robert Conway Stanard and Martha Virginia (Cowan) Stanard. He was born on October 2, 1858, and attended McGuire's School in Richmond, the College of William and Mary, and Richmond College. After the completion of his formal education in 1880 he was employed as a surveyor and as a reporter for the *Richmond Daily Whig*. His taste for local history and genealogy led him to contribute articles on these subjects to the Richmond *Critic* and other journals; it likewise led him to accept in October 1898 the office of corresponding secretary of the Virginia Historical Society and editor of its quarterly publication, the *Virginia Magazine of History and Biography*, both of which offices he held until his death. Over the next three decades Stanard devoted himself to developing the Society's collections of manuscripts, printed materials, and museum objects and to assisting researchers utilizing those resources. Continuing the policy of his predecessor, Philip Alexander Bruce (q.v.), under whose direction the first five volumes of the *Virginia Magazine* had been published, Stanard published in the succeeding thirty-five volumes a wealth of documentary material illustrative of Virginia's social, political, and economic development. He also wrote numerous articles on historical subjects published in his own and other journals and two volumes of enduring usefulness, *The Colonial Virginia Register* (1902) and *Some Emigrants to Virginia* (1911). In recognition of his contribution to the study of Virginia history he received an honorary doctorate from the College of William and Mary in 1915. He was a member of the Alpha chapter of the Phi Beta Kappa society and a member of the Virginia Society of the Cincinnati. William Glover Stanard died in Richmond on May 6, 1933, and is buried in Hollywood Cemetery. His wife, whom he married on April 17, 1900, was Mary Mann Page (Newton) Stanard, daughter of the Right Reverend John B. Newton; the couple had no children. Mrs. Stanard shared her husband's interest in history and was herself a writer and editor.

DAB; *VMHB* 41 (1933): supplement between pp. 188–89, and 73 (1965): 244.

Portrait I

By DAVID SILVETTE. Signed. Dated 1932

Oil on canvas: 58 x 40 in. (147.3 x 101.6 cm.)

Presented in 1932 by friends of the subject. Por932.1

William Glover Stanard (Portrait I)

Portrait II

ARTIST UNIDENTIFIED

Plaster bas-relief: 14 x 12 in. (35.6 x 30.5 cm.) (oval)

Received in 1964 from the estate of Ellen Beverley Wooldridge of Richmond, through Mrs. William Lawton Maner, Jr., of Richmond. Por964.29

—— Stansburg

See The Convention of 1829–30

William Edwin Starke, 1814–1862

Born in Brunswick County in 1814, the subject operated a stage line with his brothers before removing to Mobile, Alabama, to engage in the cotton brokerage business. He made and lost several fortunes and was residing in New Orleans at the outbreak of the Civil War. Offering his services to the Confederacy, he became aide-de-camp to General Garnett; he saw action in the campaign in western Virginia in 1861, then was put in command of the 60th Virginia Infantry with the rank of colonel; he led this command through the Seven Days battles. Promoted to brigadier general on August 6, 1862, he fought at Second Manassas and commanded the Stonewall Division during the Maryland campaign. He was killed at Sharpsburg on September 17, 1862; his body was later buried in Hollywood Cemetery, Richmond. General Starke was married, on October 4, 1834, to Louisa G. Hicks of Brunswick County.

Generals in Gray; *Confederate Military History*, 3: 663; Virginia State Library, Samuel Bassett French Papers; *W. & M. Quart.*, 1st ser., 7 (1898–99): 38; *Biographic Catalogue* (Addenda).

By J. W. KING. Signed. Dated 1862?

Oil on canvas: 23³/₄ x 19¹/₂ in. (60.3 x 49.5 cm.) (oval)

Acquired in 1946 through merger with the Confederate Memorial Association. Por946.107

J. W. King also painted a portrait of General Robert E. Lee that was exhibited in 1881 at the International Cotton Exposition in Atlanta. The portrait was the principal prize in the Richmond Howitzer Festival of 1888 and was awarded to the military company receiving the greatest number of ten-cent votes. A leaflet (VHS Rare E467.1 L4 R62) published in connection with the festival described the portrait as follows: "The portrait of Gen. Robert E. Lee, which was on exhibition at the Atlanta Exposition, possesses a historical as well as an artistic value. It was painted from life in Richmond during the civil war by the late J. W. King, who was one of the most gifted artists in the South. All of the photographic pictures of Lee and his Generals taken during the same period at the then celebrated gallery of Minnis & Cowell, in Richmond, were finished by Mr. King, whose taste and skill in colors were conceded to be of the highest order. . . . The portrait was the only one painted of Gen. Lee during the war. The artist kept it in his studio until his death, refusing to part with it at any price." In spite of the leaflet's claims, at least one other life portrait of Lee is thought to have been painted during the war years: Edward C. Bruce's portrait, a study for which is owned by the Virginia Historical Society (Robert Edward Lee, Portrait I). Nothing has been discovered about J. W. King or the present whereabouts of his portrait of Lee.

R. E. Lee Oil Painting (Life Size) to Be Voted to the Most Popular Military Company in Richmond (Richmond, 1888).

Virginia (Chase) Steedman, 1874–1948

See Alexander Wilbourne Weddell, 1876–1948

Andrew Stevenson, 1784–1857
Sarah (Coles) Stevenson, 1789–1848 (Mrs. Andrew Stevenson)

Congressman and minister to Great Britain, Andrew Stevenson was born in Culpeper County on January 21, 1784, son of the Reverend James Stevenson and Frances (Littlepage) Stevenson. After graduating from the College of William and Mary and studying law, he was admitted to the bar in 1805 and commenced the practice of his profession in Richmond. He sat in the Virginia House of Delegates 1809–16, 1818–21, part of the time as Speaker. Thereafter he was elected to the United States Congress, representing his district from March 4, 1821, until his resignation on June 2, 1834. During this period he was an active member of the Richmond Junto, and from 1827 until his resignation from Congress he was Speaker of the House. In 1834 Stevenson was nominated by President Jackson as minister to Great Britain; his appointment was not confirmed until 1836. As minister to the Court of St. James's, Stevenson and his wife took a prominent part in London's social scene; they attended Queen Victoria's coronation and marriage. Stevenson's diplomatic assignment terminated in 1841; thereafter he resided in Richmond and at Blenheim, his estate in Albemarle County. He was elected president of the Virginia Society of Agriculture in 1845; the same year he became a member of the board of visitors of the University of Virginia, becoming rector of the University in 1856. He died on January 25, 1857. Stevenson was married three times. His first wife, Mary Page (White) Stevenson, died in childbirth in 1812; the child, John White Stevenson, became governor of Kentucky; he left descendants. His second wife, Sarah (Coles) Stevenson, daughter of John and Rebecca (Tucker) Coles, of Enniscorthy, Albemarle County, was born on May 5, 1789; she and Stevenson were married on October 8, 1816; their only child died young. Sarah (Coles) Stevenson died in Virginia on January 3, 1848, seven years after she and her husband returned from abroad. Stevenson married, third, on June 28, 1849, Mary Shaaf of Georgetown, D.C., by whom he had one daughter.

DAB; *Biographical Directory*; William Bedford Coles, *The Coles Family of Virginia* (New York, 1931), pp. 123–24; *Richmond Portraits*, pp. 190–91 (Portrait I reproduced); Francis Fry Wayland, *Andrew Stevenson, Democrat and Diplomat, 1785–1857* (Philadelphia, 1949) (Portrait I reproduced as frontispiece, with background obscured); *VMHB* 78 (1970): 240 and 84 (1976): 239.

Portrait I. Andrew Stevenson

By GEORGE PETER ALEXANDER HEALY. Signed. Dated 1839

Oil on canvas on panel: 44¼ x 34¼ in. (112.4 x 87 cm.)

Presented in 1969 by Sally (Colston) Mitchell (Mrs. Mark L. Mitchell) of Cincinnati. Por969.16

Sarah (Coles) Stevenson

Portrait II. Sarah (Coles) Stevenson

BY GEORGE PETER ALEXANDER HEALY.
Ca. 1839

Oil on canvas: 44½ x 34½ in. (112.4 x 87 cm.)

Presented in 1975 by Sally (Colston) Mitchell (Mrs. Mark L. Mitchell) of Cincinnati. Por975.31

Andrew Stevenson's portrait sustained extensive fire damage before it came into the Society's possession. The artist's signature and the date, however, are still visible on the arm of the sitter's chair. The fact that Mrs. Stevenson's portrait is virtually identical in size to that of her husband suggests that Healy executed the two canvases as companion pieces. In a letter to her sisters in Virginia dated June 12, 1840, Mrs. Stevenson described her recently completed portrait. "You will be surprised to hear I have been sitting again tho' not for myself. The one that Mr. Rand exhibited in the Royal Academy has brought him so much into notice that Mr. Healy . . . made it a matter of particular favour that I would sit to him . . . therefore I consented & have given him four sittings, with which he has finished a beautiful picture 3 quarters length—he has painted me in crimson velvet, with one arm over the arm of the chair, with Mr.

Rogers richly embroidered handkerchief in that hand, and a beautiful bouquet of flowers in the other, a gold turban very like the one I sent you &c. &c. H took it yesterday to the Duke of Sussex, who thought it a good likeness and a beautiful picture. . . . I have no doubt some future day he will present it to me."[1] There can be little doubt that the portrait described in the letter and the portrait now at the Society are one and the same. Save for the fact that in the portrait Mrs. Stevenson holds handkerchief and bouquet in the same hand, the two coincide in every respect. A second, bust-length portrait of the subject by Healy also survives.[2] But where, one wonders, is the earlier portrait to which Mrs. Stevenson refers in her letter: the portrait by Rand—John Goffe Rand, the American portrait painter who worked in London between 1834 and 1840? The original, so it appears from other portions of Mrs. Stevenson's correspondence, was exhibited at the Royal Academy with such success that the artist asked to be allowed to keep it, and in return painted another portrait for Mrs. Stevenson, probably a replica of the original. The replica, so it seems, was dispatched to Virginia to the subject's sisters, who, alas, did not think it a good likeness. This may be the portrait that was destroyed by fire some twenty-five years ago, the portrait attributed, perhaps erroneously, to Healy, that depicted the subject as she appeared at her presentation at court.[3]

1. Edward Boykin, ed., *Victoria, Albert, and Mrs. Stevenson* (New York, 1957), pp. 264–65; *Occasional Bulletin*, no. 33 (1976): 3–6 (Portrait II reproduced).   2. The bust-length portrait of Mrs. Stevenson and the Society's portrait of Andrew Stevenson (Portrait I) are reproduced in *Richmond Portraits*, pp. 190–91.   3. Boykin, pp. 250, 266, 256 (illustrated on the third page of illustrations between pp. 150–51).

Robert Augustus Stiles, 1836–1905

The subject was born in Woodford County, Kentucky, on June 27, 1836, the son of the Reverend Joseph Clay Stiles and Caroline Clifford (Nephew) Stiles. As a boy of eight he removed with his family to Richmond, his father having been called to the pastorate of the United Presbyterian Church (later the Grace Street Presbyterian Church). Because his father subsequently accepted calls to churches in New York City and New Haven, Connecticut, young Stiles received much of his education in the North, graduating from Yale University in 1859. Returning to Richmond in the spring of 1861, he enlisted in the Richmond Howitzers, remaining with that command until after Chancellorsville. He was then transferred to the engineer corps; as second lieutenant he served in Early's command until shortly after Gettysburg;

he was then returned to the artillery as adjutant of Cabell's Battalion. In the spring of 1865 Stiles was assigned to the command of Chaffin's Bluff; here he remained, with the rank of major, until the retreat from Richmond. He was captured at Sayler's Creek and held prisoner at Johnson's Island until released in the autumn of 1865. After the war he studied law at the University of Virginia, was admitted to the bar, and commenced practice in Richmond. As senior partner of the firm of Stiles and Holladay, he developed a successful practice; his firm acted as counsel for the Western Union Telegraph Company in a number of important cases. On June 24, 1874, he married Lelia Caperton, daughter of Allen Taylor Caperton and Harriette (Echols) Caperton; they became the parents of three children. Stiles was the founder and first president of the Laurel Reformatory, an institution for delinquent boys conducted under the auspices of the Prison Association of Virginia. His military memoirs, *Four Years under Marse Robert*, were published in 1903. Major Stiles died at his summer home in Bon Air, a short distance from Richmond, on October 5, 1905.

Confederate Military History, 3: 1188; Richmond *Times-Dispatch*, Oct. 6, 1905; Bernard Mason Caperton, *The Caperton Family* (Charlottesville, Va., 1973), pp. 81–82; *Biographic Catalogue*.

ARTIST UNIDENTIFIED

Oil on canvas: 30¼ x 25 in. (76.8 x 63.5 cm.)

Acquired in 1946 through merger with the Confederate Memorial Association. Por946.100

Ann Wray Stith, d.1842
See David Meade, 1778–1854

Maria (Meade) Stith (Mrs. John Stith)

Daughter of Andrew and Susannah (Stith) Meade (qq.v.), and sister of David Meade (q.v.), the subject married in June 1799 John Stith, son of Robert and Mary Townshend (Washington) Stith and brother of Ann Wray (Stith) Meade, Mrs. David Meade (q.v.). It is thought that she died young. Her husband married, second, Sarah B. H. Mason, a granddaughter of George Mason (q.v.) of Gunston Hall, Fairfax County.

W. & M. Quart., 1st ser., 21 (1912–13): 270; Landon Covington Bell, *The Old Free State* (Richmond, 1927), 2: 109; Pamela C. Copeland, *The Five George Masons, Patriots and Planters of Virginia and Maryland* (Charlottesville, Va., 1975), table 9, p. 276. See chart on Meade Portraits for relationships.

ATTRIBUTED TO JEAN FRANÇOIS DEVALLÉE

Miniature on ivory: 2¼ x 1¾ in. (5.7 x 4.5 cm.) (oval)

Presented in 1966 by Flora (Allen) Penick (Mrs. Charles A. Penick) of South Boston, Virginia. Por966.8

The miniature was included in an exhibition of Virginia miniatures held at the Virginia Museum of Fine Arts during the winter of 1941–42. It was attributed in the catalogue to Jean François DeVallée and was at that time the property of Mrs. William W. Wilkinson.

Virginia Museum of Fine Arts, *An Exhibition of Virginia Miniatures* (Richmond, 1941), p. 34, item 167.

Susannah Stith, d.1815
See Andrew Meade, 1752–1795

John Ashley Stone, 1799–1852

John Ashley Stone was born on March 13, 1799, son of Caleb and Sarah (Ashley) Stone. He resided in Fluvanna County. By his wife, Susan (Pettit) Stone, he had issue. He died on December 11, 1852.

Information received with the silhouette; [William Kearney Hall], *Descendants of Nicholas Perkins of Virginia* (Ann Arbor, Mich., 1957), p. 248.

BY MARTHA ANN HONEYWELL. Signed

Silhouette: 2½ in. (6.4 cm.) in height, on paper 3¼ x 2½ in. (8.3 x 6.4 cm.). Inscribed: "Cut with the Mouth by M. A. Honeywell."

Presented in 1926 by Lucie Perkins Stone of Hollins, Virginia, a granddaughter of the subject. Por926.41

Susanna Butterfield Stowe, 1772–1852
See John Granbery, 1759–1815

Robert Mackey Stribling, 1833–1914

Born in Fauquier County on December 3, 1833, the son of Robert Mackey Stribling and Caroline Matilda (Clarkson) Stribling, the subject attended the University of Virginia 1852–53, studied medicine at the Pennsylvania Medical College, then spent four years at the Dispensary in Philadelphia. He married, first, on August 18, 1857, Mary Cary Ambler, daughter of Thomas Marshall Ambler and Lucy (Johnston) Ambler of Morven, Fauquier County; she bore him four children and died in 1868. At the outbreak of the

Civil War he was commissioned captain in the Confederate artillery; he raised a battery in Fauquier County known as Stribling's Battery, later attached, as the Fauquier Artillery, to the 38th Battalion of Virginia Light Artillery. He commanded this unit at First and Second Manassas, Williamsburg, Seven Pines, Malvern Hill, and Gettysburg, rising in rank during the course of the war to lieutenant colonel. At the end of hostilities he returned to Fauquier County, where he conducted his medical practice and resided at Mountain View, his residence near Markham. Dr. Stribling married, second, on July 28, 1870, Agnes Harwood Douthat, daughter of Robert and Mary Ambler (Marshall) Douthat of Weyanoke, Charles City County; they became the parents of three children. Stribling represented Fauquier County in the Virginia House of Delegates 1879–87. He died at Markham on March 27, 1914.

Merrow Egerton Sorley, *Lewis of Warner Hall: The History of a Family* (Columbia, Mo., 1937), pp. 124–25; Mary Frances Stribling Moursund, *Stribling and Related Families* (Austin, Tex., 1967), pp. 13–15; Hugh Milton McIlhany, *Some Virginia Families* (Staunton, Va., 1903), pp. 81–82; *Biographic Catalogue.*

By JOHN P. WALKER. Signed. Dated 1924

Oil on canvas: 30 x 25 in. (76.2 x 63.5 cm.)

Presented to the R. E. Lee Camp, Confederate Veterans, in 1925 by the subject's family; acquired by the Virginia Historical Society in 1946 through merger with the Confederate Memorial Association. Por946.178

Archibald Stuart, 1795–1855
See The Convention of 1829–30

James Ewell Brown Stuart, 1833–1864

J. E. B. ("Jeb") Stuart was born in Patrick County on February 6, 1833, the seventh of ten children born to Archibald and Elizabeth Letcher (Pannill) Stuart. After schooling in Wytheville and two years at Emory and Henry College, he entered West Point in 1850. Following his graduation he spent six years with the 1st United States Cavalry in Kansas. There he married, on November 14, 1855, Flora Cooke, daughter of Colonel Philip St. George Cooke, who bore him three children. With Virginia's secession from the Union, Stuart resigned his commission to enter the service of the Confederacy as colonel of the 1st Virginia Cavalry. After First Manassas he was promoted to brigadier general and less than a year later to major general in command of the Cavalry Corps of the Army of Northern Virginia, a command

he held until his death. Stuart's tactical brilliance earned him the devotion of his men; his integrity, coupled with his skill as an intelligence-gathering officer, won him the praise of General Lee; his flamboyant gallantry transformed him into something of a *beau ideal*, especially in the eyes of the ladies of the Confederacy. His record includes outstanding service at Second Manassas, the Maryland campaign, Fredericksburg, Chancellorsville, and Brandy Station. His absence on another assignment early in the Gettysburg campaign undoubtedly contributed to the outcome and to the heavy Confederate losses sustained there. Thereafter, during the winter and spring of 1864, though often obliged to lead dismounted cavalry, he continued to perform brilliantly. On May 11, 1864, in an attempt to prevent Sheridan from reaching Richmond, he intercepted a superior Union force at Yellow Tavern; during the battle Stuart, who had never before been touched by bullet or sword, fell mortally wounded. He died in Richmond the following day, May 12, 1864, and is buried in Hollywood Cemetery.

DAB; *Generals in Gray*; *Biographic Catalogue.*

James Ewell Brown Stuart (Portrait I)

Portrait I

By CORNELIUS HANKINS. Signed. Dated 1898

Oil on canvas: 60 x 41 in. (152.4 x 104.1 cm.)

Acquired in 1946 through merger with the Confederate Memorial Association. Por946.52

Portrait II

See The Battle Abbey Murals. The Summer Mural

Portrait III

See The Battle Abbey Murals. The Autumn Mural

Julia Sully, ca. 1833–1863 (later Mrs. Daniel McCarty Chichester)

Daughter of the artist Robert Matthew Sully and Isabella (Thompson) Sully and sister of Robert Matthew Sully, Jr. (q.v.), the subject was born around 1833. She married in Christ Church, Alexandria, on April 14, 1860, Daniel McCarty Chichester (1834–1896) of Bleak House, Fairfax County, son of William Henry Chichester and Jane Elliott (Peyton) Chichester. Her husband, a graduate of the College of William and Mary, was a lawyer; during the Civil War he was in Crutchfield's command in George Washington Custis Lee's Division; he was wounded and captured at Sayler's Creek. The subject died in Lynchburg on December 20, 1863; her two children died in infancy. Her husband married, second, in 1867, Agnes Robinson Moncure (1844–1919) and became a judge of the circuit courts of Fairfax County and Alexandria.

Virginia Genealogies, p. 108; *History of Virginia*, 6: 506; *Virginia Cavalcade*, 9, no. 1 (1959): 42–47 (portrait reproduced); *VMHB* 59 (1951): 252–53 (portrait reproduced).

Julia Sully

By **Robert Matthew Sully**. Signed. Dated 1858

Oil on canvas: 30 x 24³⁄4 in. (76.2 x 62.9 cm.)

Received in 1950 as a bequest of Julia Sully of Richmond, a niece of the subject. Por950.14

Robert Matthew Sully, Jr., 1837–1912

Son of the artist Robert Matthew Sully and Isabella (Thompson) Sully, the subject was born in Petersburg in 1837. After completing his formal education he entered the service of the Orange and Alexandria Railroad. On the outbreak of the Civil War he joined the Confederate army as a private in Company A, 17th Virginia Infantry; he later received a commission and saw active duty with the Corps of Engineers; he surrendered at Greensboro, North Carolina. On November 17, 1868, he married Elizabeth A. Williams of Lynchburg; the couple became the parents of one child, a daughter. After the war, Major Sully, resuming his career in railroading, accepted a post with the Midland Railroad as a civil engineer. He was with the Richmond and Danville Railroad 1873–76 and the Petersburg Railroad 1876–81, first as its general freight agent, later as its general superintendent. In 1881 he became superintendent of the Richmond, Fredericksburg and Potomac Railroad, a post he held for the rest of his life. He died in 1912. Also in the Society's collection is a portrait of the subject's sister, Julia Sully (q.v.).

Virginia and Virginians, 2: 656; *Virginia Cavalcade*, 9, no. 1 (1959): 42–47 (portrait reproduced); *VMHB* 59 (1951): 252–53 (portrait reproduced).

By **Robert Matthew Sully** (father of the subject). Ca.1843

Oil on canvas: 30¹⁄4 x 25 in. (76.8 x 63.5 cm.)

Received in 1950 as a bequest of Julia Sully of Richmond, a daughter of the subject. Por950.13

Lewis Summers, 1778–1843
See The Convention of 1829–30

Adrian J. Szymanski

Little has been found about Adrian J. Szymanski. He married Louisa A. Waller (1799–1858), daughter of Bowker Waller of Spotsylvania County and Philadelphia Claiborne (Chew) Waller. The couple had two daughters: Juliette Theresa, who married Dr. John May Burton (q.v.) of Madison County;

and Adrianna Louisa, who married James Gray Beverley of Spotsylvania County. Szymanski is thought to have been a dentist.

Information received with the portrait; *The Beverley Family*, p. 607-8.

ARTIST UNIDENTIFIED

Oil on canvas: 30¼ x 25¼ in. (76.8 x 64.1 cm.)

Presented in 1971 by Mrs. Erastus E. Deane and her daughter Mrs. Sterling Gibson, both of Ruckersville. Por971.27

Thomas Mann Randolph Talcott, 1838–1920

A native of Philadelphia, the subject was born on March 27, 1838, the son of Andrew and Harriet Randolph (Hackley) Talcott. Trained as an engineer, he was assistant chief engineer for the Ohio and Mississippi Railroad in 1858, assistant engineer for surveys for the railroad between Veracruz and Mexico City in 1859, and the following year was engaged in surveying for the fortification of Sandy Hook at the entrance to New York Bay. On the secession of Virginia from the Union he was commissioned first lieutenant in the engineers and assigned to the river, coastal, and harbor defenses of Virginia. Captured at Roanoke Island, he was exchanged in March 1862 and promoted to captain. The following month he was assigned to the staff of General Lee, serving with him in all the subsequent campaigns of the Army of Northern Virginia and rising in rank to colonel. After the surrender at Appomattox, Talcott again turned his attention to railroads, serving at various times as assistant engineer for the Louisville, Lexington and Cincinnati Railroad; division engineer for the Chesapeake and Ohio; general manager of the Richmond and Danville (later the Southern Railway); vice-president and general manager of the Mobile and Ohio; and assistant to the president of the Seaboard Air Line Railroad. He died at his residence in Richmond on May 7, 1920. His wife, Nannie C. (McPhail) Talcott, whom he married on June 7, 1864, survived him, as did five daughters. Colonel Talcott was elected to membership in the Virginia Historical Society in 1870.

Richmond Times-Dispatch, May 8, 1920, p. 1; *Biographic Catalogue*.

ARTIST UNIDENTIFIED

Oil on canvas: 30 x 25 in. (76.2 x 63.5 cm.)

Presented to the R. E. Lee Camp, Confederate Veterans, in 1908; acquired by the Virginia Historical Society in 1946 through merger with the Confederate Memorial Association. Por946.67

The Society has in its manuscript collection a letter to Talcott, dated October 25, 1905, from B. M. Parham, secretary of the R. E. Lee Camp, Confederate Veterans, Portrait Committee, in which Parham requested a portrait of Talcott for the Lee Camp collection. The letter concludes with the information that "the cost of most of those in our Hall was $50. each."

VHS Mss1 T1434b 554.

William Booth Taliaferro, 1822–1898

Born on December 28, 1822, at Belleville, Gloucester County, son of Warner and Frances (Booth) Taliaferro, the subject graduated from the College of William and Mary in 1841, studied law at Harvard University, was commissioned captain in the United States Army in 1847, and served in the Mexican War. He represented Gloucester County in the Virginia legislature 1850–53. On February 17, 1853, Sally Nivison Lyons, daughter of James Lyons of Richmond, became his wife; she bore him eight children. At the time of the John Brown raid Taliaferro commanded the Virginia state forces. In May 1861 he was commissioned colonel of the 23d Virginia Infantry; the following March he became brigadier general and took part in Jackson's Valley campaign until severely wounded at Groveton. Subsequently he commanded the District of Savannah, the District of East Florida, and the Seventh Military District of South Carolina. After the war General Taliaferro resumed the practice of law; he served in the Virginia state legislature 1874–79, was judge of the Gloucester County court 1891–97, and served on the boards of the Virginia Military Institute and the College of William and Mary. He was grand master of the Grand Lodge of Masons of Virginia 1876–77. General Taliaferro died at his home, Dunham Massie, Gloucester County, on February 27, 1898, and is buried in the churchyard of Ware Church. He was elected to membership in the Virginia Historical Society in 1891.

DAB; Generals in Gray; History of Virginia, 4: 562; *Biographic Catalogue*.

Portrait I

BY WILLIAM LUDWELL SHEPPARD. Signed. 1898

Oil on canvas: 30 x 25 in. (76.2 x 63.5 cm.). Inscribed on the back: "Major Genl. W. B. Taliaferro painted by Wm. L. Sheppard 1898."

Purchased by the R. E. Lee Camp, Confederate Veterans, from the artist at a cost of $57, frame included, in 1899; acquired by the Virginia Historical Society in 1946 through merger with the Confederate Memorial Association. Por946.38

Portrait II

BY SYDNEY NEWBOLD. Signed

Oil on canvas: 36 x 30 in. (91.4 x 76.2 cm.)

Presented in 1950 by the subject's daughter, Nina (Taliaferro) Sanders (Mrs. H. O. Sanders) of Gloucester County. Por950.11

Dorothea (Claiborne) Tatum, 1765–1844 (Mrs. Henry Tatum)

Daughter of Daniel Parke Claiborne and Mary Anne (Maury) Claiborne, the subject was born in Dinwiddie County on May 18, 1765. She married in 1785 Henry Tatum (1756–1830), son of Josiah and Sarah (Brooke) Tatum and a Revolutionary War veteran. The couple resided at Woodland Hill, Chesterfield County, where they raised a family "in the lap of gentility, free from all toil and traffick whatsoever." During his last years Henry Tatum suffered financial reverses and was crippled with palsy; about 1820 he sold his home in Chesterfield County, and removed to Richmond. Henry Tatum died in 1830; Dorothea (Claiborne) Tatum died in 1844 and was buried in Shockoe Cemetery, Richmond, on March 13.

Sue Crabtree West, *The Maury Family Tree* (Birmingham, Ala., 1971), pp. 266, 275–76; George Mason Claiborne, *Claiborne Pedigree: A Genealogical Table of the Descendants of Secretary William Claiborne* (Lynchburg, Va., 1900), p. 45; *VMHB* 56 (1948): 238.

ARTIST UNIDENTIFIED

Oil on canvas: 30 x 35 in. (76.2 x 63.5 cm.)

Presented in 1947 by Maria (Clopton) Jackson (Mrs. C. S. Jackson) of Portland, Oregon. Por947.31

Mary Tayloe, 1758–1835
See Mann Page, 1749–1803

Elizabeth (Fitzhugh) Conway Taylor, 1754–1823
See Elizabeth (Fitzhugh) Conway, 1754–1823

Frances Fielding (Lewis) Taylor, ca. 1802–ca. 1846 (Mrs. Archibald Taylor)

Born about 1802, daughter of Fielding and Agnes (Harwood) Lewis of Weyanoke, Charles City County, the subject married, first, Archibald Taylor of Norfolk; four children were born to the couple. Her husband died around 1833; at about the same time she inherited Belle Farm, Charles City County, where she resided with her family. She married, second, in 1840, Richard Coke (1790–1851) of Abingdon, Gloucester County, a former United States congressman; there were no children by her second marriage. She died about 1846.

Merrow Egerton Sorley, *Lewis of Warner Hall: The History of a Family* (Columbia, Mo., 1937), p. 105; Fielding Lewis Marshall, *Recollections and Reflections of Fielding Lewis Marshall* (Orange, Va., 1911), p. 52; information supplied by Ransom True.

BY WILLIAM JAMES HUBARD

Oil on canvas: 30 x 25 in. (76.2 x 63.5 cm.)

Presented in 1931 by Mrs. Fielding Lewis Taylor of Austin, Texas. Por931.13

Jaquelin Plummer Taylor, 1797–1872

Son of Robert and Frances (Pendleton) Taylor of Orange County, the subject was born on January 1, 1797. After attending school in Winchester, he came to Richmond to work in the dry goods, importing, and exporting business conducted by Edmund Taylor. On April 14, 1824, he married, in Richmond, Martha E. Richardson (1801–1881), daughter of Thomas Richardson; the couple had no children. He later managed the dry goods business for himself, achieving considerable success; he retired from business in 1841. In 1844–45 he built a row of three houses on Capitol Street, on the site of the present Virginia State Library building. He died on January 21, 1872, and is buried in the family graveyard at Meadowfarm, Orange County. Taylor became a member of the Virginia Historical Society in 1852 and was appointed treasurer of the Society in 1854.

Mary Wingfield Scott, *Houses of Old Richmond* (Richmond, 1941), pp. 239–41; Raleigh Travers Green, *Genealogical and Historical Notes on Culpeper County, Virginia* (Culpeper, Va., 1900), pt. 1, p. 74; Frederick A. Virkus, *The Abridged Compendium of American Genealogy* (Chicago, 1926–37), 2: 138; *Richmond Daily Whig*, Jan. 23, 1872, p. 3, col. 4; *VMHB* 46 (1938): 231–33 and 56 (1948): 237.

COPIED BY MARCIA SILVETTE

Oil on canvas: 20 x 16 in. (50.8 x 40.6 cm.)

Presented in 1947 by Jaquelin Plummer Taylor of Richmond, a great-nephew of the subject. Por947.27

The Society's portrait was copied from a miniature.

Richard Taylor, 1826–1879

The only son of President Zachary Taylor (q.v.) and Margaret Mackall (Smith) Taylor, the subject was born at Springfields, near Louisville, Kentucky, on January 27, 1826. He studied in Scotland and France and at Harvard University and Yale, graduating from Yale in 1845. After two years spent overseeing his father's cotton plantation in Mississippi, he established a sugar plantation of his own in Saint Charles Parish, Louisiana. In 1851 he married Louise Marie Myrthé Bringier, who bore him five children, two of whom died in childhood. He was a member of the Louisiana state Senate 1856–61. On the secession of Louisiana he was appointed colonel of the 9th Louisiana Infantry; on October 21, 1861, he became a brigadier general in the Confederate army and the following year a major general. He served in the Valley campaign under Stonewall Jackson, participated in the Seven Days battles, and in the summer of 1862 was given command of the District of West Louisiana. Prevented by his commander, General Edmund Kirby Smith (q.v.), from following up his successes on the Red River in April 1864, he resigned his command. Promoted to lieutenant general on August 15, 1864, he spent the remaining months of the war in command of the Department of East Louisiana, Mississippi, and Alabama. After the war General Taylor used his not inconsiderable influence in Washington for the release of Confederate prisoners, for the adoption of a lenient policy toward the southern states, and, as a trustee of the Peabody Education Fund, for the improvement of education in the South. His memoirs, *Destruction and Reconstruction* (1879), provide valuable insights into events and characters of the period. General Taylor died in New York on April 12, 1879; he is buried in Metairie Cemetery, New Orleans.

DAB; *Generals in Gray*; *Biographic Catalogue* (Addenda).

By JOHN P. WALKER. Signed. Dated 1930

Oil on canvas: 30 x 25 in. (76.2 x 63.5 cm.)

Acquired in 1946 through merger with the Confederate Memorial Association. Por946.127

Robertson Taylor, 1840–1924

Born in Norfolk in 1840, Robertson Taylor was a son of Walter Herron Taylor and Cornelia Wickham (Cowdery) Taylor and a brother of Robert E. Lee's aide-de-camp Walter Herron Taylor (q.v.). In 1861 he entered the Confederate army in Norfolk; he served as assistant adjutant in Mahone's Brigade, 6th Virginia Infantry, with the rank of captain. He was wounded at the battle of the Wilderness on May 6, 1864. After the war he removed to Baltimore, Maryland, where he established the firm of Taylor and Levering, importers of coffee and sugar; he later became associated with the United States Fidelity and Guaranty Company. Active in church and charitable work, he helped organize the Episcopal Church of St. Michael and All Angels and donated the property on which was built the hospital for crippled children later known as the Kernan Hospital and Industrial School. He died in Baltimore on October 15, 1924. Taylor was twice married: first, on January 24, 1866, to Baynham Baylor Tunstall, daughter of Robert Baylor Tunstall and Elizabeth Walke (Williamson) Tunstall; second, to Mae Templeman. By his first marriage he had one son, Dr. Robert Tunstall Taylor; by his second marriage he had a daughter.

Whitmore Morris, *The First Tunstalls in Virginia and Some of Their Descendants* (San Antonio, Tex., 1950), pp. 121–22; Confederate Service Records, National Archives, microfilm roll 447; *Baltimore Sun*, Oct. 16, 1924; Maryland Historical Society obituary file; *VMHB* 14 (1906–7): 438; *Biographic Catalogue*.

By CORNELIUS HANKINS. Signed. Dated 1897

Oil on canvas: 30 x 25 in. (76.2 x 63.5 cm.)

Acquired in 1946 through merger with the Confederate Memorial Association. Por946.75

Samuel Taylor, 1781–1853
See The Convention of 1829–30

Walter Herron Taylor, 1838–1916

Walter Herron Taylor was born in Norfolk on June 13, 1838. His parents were Walter Herron Taylor and Cornelia Wickham (Cowdery) Taylor. After attending Norfolk Academy and the Virginia Military Institute he embarked on a business career in Norfolk, becoming a railroad clerk in 1855 and later a member of a banking firm. Enlisting in the Confederate service early in May 1861, he was assigned to General Robert E. Lee as aide-de-camp, remaining with him in this capacity throughout the war. He was later appointed adjutant general of the Army of Northern Virginia with the rank of lieutenant colonel, served through all its subsequent campaigns, and was present with Lee at Appomattox. Out of his Civil War experience Colonel Taylor wrote two volumes, *Four Years with General Lee* (1877) and *General Lee: His Campaigns in Virginia, 1861–1865* (1906). At the conclusion of the war he returned to Norfolk where he entered the hardware business. He was a member of the Virginia state Senate 1869–73, playing a part in the development of the state's railroad system as chairman of the Senate Committee on

Roads and Internal Navigation. In 1877 he accepted the presidency of the Marine Bank of Norfolk, remaining with that institution until his death nearly forty years later. He was also for more than thirty years a member of the board of directors of the Norfolk and Western Railroad. Colonel Taylor died in Norfolk on March 1, 1916. His wife, whom he married on April 3, 1865, was Elizabeth Selden (Saunders) Taylor; she bore him eight children.

Men of Mark in Virginia, 4: 385–87; *Confederate Veteran* 24 (1916): 174; George Holbert Tucker, *Abstracts from Norfolk City Marriage Bonds (1797–1850) and Other Genealogical Data* (Norfolk, Va., 1934), p. 126; *Biographic Catalogue*.

BY THOMAS CASILEAR COLE. Signed. 1922

Oil on canvas: 46 x 32 in. (116.8 x 81.3 cm.)

Presented to the R. E. Lee Camp, Confederate Veterans; acquired by the Virginia Historical Society in 1946 through merger with the Confederate Memorial Association. Por946.45

The portrait was painted from a daguerreotype.

William Taylor, 1827–1891

Born on June 30, 1827, near Berryville, the subject was the son of William and Hannah (McCormick) Taylor. He entered the College of New Jersey (Princeton University) as a member of the class of 1847 but left in 1846 without taking a degree. On May 15, 1849, he married Gertrude McGuire (1828–1894), a daughter of Hugh Holmes McGuire and Ann Eliza (Moss) McGuire and a sister of Hunter Holmes

McGuire (q.v.); the couple resided at Springsburg, Clarke County. He was a member of the Virginia State Agricultural Society 1853 and a director of the Millwood and Berryville Turnpike Company 1859. During the Civil War he served in the Clarke Cavalry with the rank of major. After Appomattox he returned to his farm and resided there until his death which occurred on December 4, 1891. He was survived by his widow and four children.

Information received with the portrait; William Glover Stanard, *The McGuire Family in Virginia, with Notices of Its Irish Ancestry and Some Connected Virginia Families* (Richmond, 1926), pp. 51–52; Hugh Milton McIlhany, *Some Virginia Families* (Staunton, Va., 1903), pp. 216–17; VHS Mss1 T2197a 9–12.

ARTIST UNIDENTIFIED

Pencil on paper: 5¼ x 4¼ in. (13.3 x 10.8 cm.)

Acquired by purchase in 1978. Por978.19

William Penn Taylor, 1790?–1863
See The Convention of 1829–30

Zachary Taylor, 1784–1850

Twelfth president of the United States, Zachary Taylor, son of Richard and Mary (Strother) Taylor, was born in Orange County on November 24, 1784; a short time after, the family removed to Jefferson

William Taylor

Zachary Taylor (Portrait I)

County, Kentucky, where he spent his childhood and youth. Taylor's military service, which extended over forty years, began in 1808 with his commission as first lieutenant in the 7th Infantry; he fought in the Black Hawk War (1832–33) and the Seminole Wars (1837), earning in the latter both the sobriquet "Old Rough and Ready," and, for his distinguished service, command of the Department of Florida. In command of the army assigned to the Texas border in 1845, he defeated superior Mexican forces in a series of engagements that precipitated the Mexican War (1846–48); with his victories at Palo Alto, Monterrey, and Buena Vista he became a national hero and the Whig candidate for the presidency in the campaign of 1848. Inaugurated twelfth president of the United States on March 5, 1849, he served only sixteen months, dying in office on July 9, 1850. Taylor's wife, whom he married on June 18, 1810, was Margaret Mackall (Smith) Taylor; of their six children, two died in childhood; three daughters and a son, Richard Taylor (q.v.), survived.

DAB.

Portrait I.

Artist unidentified. Ca. 1847

Oil on canvas: 28 x 22¼ in. (71.1 x 56.5 cm.)

Presented in 1911 by Mr. and Mrs. Hugh Nelson of Richmond. Por911.1

It is suggested in *Portraiture in the Virginia Historical Society* that this portrait is the work of William Garl Brown. Brown is known to have visited Taylor at his western headquarters in 1847, for Taylor wrote: "Without being decided fine, I imagine the likenesses painted for me by Mr. Atwood[1] are tolerable; the one which has just been finished by a Mr. Brown from Richmond is said by those who understand or are judges of such matters to be a much better painting; Mr. B. Has nearly completed a group of officers, myself & staff in addition to several others, which I imagine will be considered a good painting by connoisseurs; he is now engaged in making a painting describing the battle ground of Buena Vista."[2] A portrait of Taylor attributed to William Garl Brown which belongs to the Louisiana State Museum is reproduced as the frontispiece to Brainerd Dyer's *Zachary Taylor* (Baton Rouge, 1946); it is remarkably like the White House portrait which is attributed to Joseph H. Bush.[3] Until further evidence comes to hand, the Society's portrait remains unattributed. It is dated 1847 on the strength of a lithographic portrait by Bufford and Company of Boston on the sheet-music cover *Grand Triumphal Quick Step* (Boston, 1847). Either the lithograph is a copy of the Society's portrait, or both are derived from a common third source. A note below the lithograph states that

it is "copied from the celebrated portrait of Gen. Taylor by permission of the Proprietors of the copyright."[4]

1. A portrait of Taylor by Jesse Atwood is reproduced in Nicholas B. Wainwright's *Paintings and Miniatures at the Historical Society of Pennsylvania* (Philadelphia, 1974), p. 186. 2. Holman Hamilton, *Zachary Taylor, Soldier of the Republic* (Indianapolis, 1941), p. 246. 3. Bush's portrait is reproduced in the *National Geographic* 127 (1965): 107. 4. A copy of the *Grand Triumphal Quick Step* is in the Society's collection of sheet music.

Portrait II

Artist unidentified

Bronze statuette: 17 in. (43.2 cm.) in height, exclusive of the base

Presented in 1961 by Jaquelin E. Taylor of Richmond. Por961.29

Littleton Waller Tazewell, 1774–1860
See The Convention of 1829–30

Alfred Tennyson, first Baron Tennyson, 1809–1892

Poet laureate and perhaps the most influential poet of the Victorian era, Alfred Tennyson was born in Somersby, Lincolnshire, on August 6, 1809, son of the Reverend George Clayton Tennyson and Elizabeth (Fytche) Tennyson. He began writing poetry at an early age, and in 1827, the year he entered Trinity College, Cambridge, several of his works appeared in print. In 1829 he won the Chancellor's Medal for his poem *Timbuctoo*, and in 1830 he published his first volume, *Poems, Chiefly Lyrical*. The death of his father in 1831 obliged him to leave the university without taking a degree, and the death two years later of his best friend Arthur Hallam caused him acute depression. His volume *Poems* (1833), which contained *The Lady of Shalott* and *The Lotos-Eaters*, was his last publication for almost a decade. With the appearance of a two-volume collection of poems in 1842 his reputation as the foremost poet of the day was established. *In Memoriam* (1850) confirmed his preeminent position. On the death of Wordsworth in 1850 he was named poet laureate; his prospects being thus improved, he married on June 13, 1850, Emily Sellwood, with whom he had been in love for fourteen years. The couple with their two sons resided on the Isle of Wight until 1869 and thereafter at Aldworth in Surrey. For much of his later life he was engaged in writing the *Idylls of the King* (1859–1889). In recognition of his contributions to English literature Tennyson was elevated to the peerage in 1884. He died on October 6, 1892, and is buried in Poets' Corner in Westminster Abbey.

DNB; *Encyclopedia Americana*; *Virginia House*, p. 69.

BY SIR LAWRENCE ALMA-TADEMA

Oil on canvas: 21³/4 x 17¹/4 in. (55.3 x 43.8 cm.). Inscribed on the original stretcher: "Alfred Tennyson   Alma Tadema." Inscribed on the back: "94. Alma Tadema."

Received in 1948 as a bequest of Mr. and Mrs. Alexander Wilbourne Weddell of Richmond. Por948.89

Charles James Terrell, 1834–1925

Dr. Terrell was born at the family home, East View, Hanover County, on September 11, 1834, the son of Dr. Nicholas Terrell and Maria (Doswell) Terrell. He was at the University of Virginia in 1854, then studied medicine at the Jefferson Medical College in Philadelphia. After his graduation he returned to Hanover County where he practiced his profession until the outbreak of the Civil War. For two years he was a lieutenant in the Ashland Artillery, a unit he helped to organize; thereafter he served as a surgeon until the end of the war, part of the time at Chimborazo Hospital, Richmond. He returned to his home in Hanover County after Appomattox and devoted the remaining years of his long life to the medical profession. Dr. Terrell was an active member of the United Confederate Veterans and was at one time surgeon general of the Confederate Veterans in Virginia. He died at the home of a daughter in Chatham on February 10, 1925; he is buried in Hollywood Cemetery, Richmond. Dr. Terrell married on November 18, 1856, Bettie Trevillian Anderson of Hanover County; he was survived by four daughters and two sons. Lewis Frank Terrell (q.v.), the subject's brother, is also represented in the Society's portrait collection.

Biographic Catalogue; *Richmond Times-Dispatch*, Feb. 12, 1925, p. 18; CMA Archives, folio Z1n.

BY CARL DAME CLARKE. Signed. Dated 1925

Oil on canvas: 30 x 25 in. (76.2 x 63.5 cm.). Inscribed on the lower right corner of the painting: "Carl D. Clarke, '25. From Photo."

Presented to the R. E. Lee Camp, Confederate Veterans, in 1925; acquired by the Virginia Historical Society in 1946 through merger with the Confederate Memorial Association. Por946.140

Lewis Frank Terrell, 1836–1864

Born in 1836, the son of Dr. Nicholas Terrell and Maria (Doswell) Terrell of East View, Hanover County, the subject graduated from the University of Virginia in 1856. After studying law in Richmond under the tutelage of Arthur A. Morson, he went to Europe to continue his professional studies. While in Paris he learned of the secession of Virginia; he returned home, offered his services to the Confederacy, and helped organize an artillery company in Hanover County, of which he was elected first lieutenant. He served throughout the Peninsular campaign; as captain and later as major, he saw action at Second Manassas, Chancellorsville, Kelly's Ford, and in the principal battles of the Army of Northern Virginia. In 1863 he was assigned to General Trimble's command as chief of artillery. When a major of artillery was needed to command at James Island, South Carolina, Terrell was recommended for the post by General Lee; subsequently he was ordered to Florida, where he contracted typhoid fever. After a short illness he died at James Island, South Carolina, on April 14, 1864, in his twenty-seventh year. A portrait of his brother, Charles James Terrell (q.v.), is also in the Society's collection.

Biographic Catalogue; CMA Archives, folio Z1n.

Lewis Frank Terrell

BY JOHN ADAMS ELDER. Signed (initials). Dated 1868

Oil on canvas: 27 x 22 in. (68.6 x 55.9 cm.). Canvas bears stencil: "From R. Wendenburg   808 Main St. Richmond, Va."

Presented to the R. E. Lee Camp, Confederate Veterans, in 1925; acquired by the Virginia Historical Society in 1946 through merger with the Confederate Memorial Association. Por946.125

William Richard Terry, 1827–1897

Born at Liberty, Bedford County, on March 12, 1827, the subject graduated from the Virginia Military Institute in 1850, then engaged in mercantile pursuits in Bedford County. On the outbreak of the Civil War he became captain of Company A, 2d Virginia Cavalry; he fought at First Manassas, and in recognition of his conduct there he was promoted to colonel of the 24th Virginia Infantry, which he led at Williamsburg, Second Manassas, and Gettysburg. On May 31, 1864, he was promoted to brigadier general in command of Kemper's Brigade, thereafter seeing action at New Bern, North Carolina, and Five Forks, where for the seventh time he was wounded in action. Following the war General Terry moved to Lynchburg as manager of the Arlington Hotel. He was a member of the Virginia state Senate 1869–77, served two terms as superintendent of the State penitentiary in Richmond, and was commandant of the Confederate Soldiers' Home in Richmond 1886–93. General Terry was paralyzed by a stroke several years before his death, which occurred in Chesterfield County on March 28, 1897, with burial in Hollywood Cemetery. He was survived by his wife Mary (Pemberton) Terry, and by two sons and three daughters.

Generals in Gray; Richmond *Times*, March 30, 1897; *Richmond Dispatch*, March 30, 1897; *Biographic Catalogue*.

By JOHN P. WALKER. Signed. Dated 1902

Oil on canvas: 30 x 25 in. (76.2 x 63.5 cm.)

Presented to the R. E. Lee Camp, Confederate Veterans, in 1902; acquired by the Virginia Historical Society in 1946 through merger with the Confederate Memorial Association. Por946.90

William Makepeace Thackeray, 1811–1863

Novelist and satirist William Makepeace Thackeray, the son of Richmond and Anne (Becher) Thackeray, was born on July 18, 1811, in Calcutta, India, where his father was a civil servant. He received his formal education in England but in 1830 left Trinity College, Cambridge, without a degree. For several years he traveled, dabbled in law, art, and journalism, and lost the greater part of a comfortable inheritance; he also became a contributor to various newspapers and periodicals. Although he achieved moderate success with such works as *The Paris Sketch-Book* (1840), *The Luck of Barry Lyndon* (1844), and *Notes of a Journey from Cornhill to Grand Cairo* (1846), it was not until the serial publication of *The Snobs of England* (1846–47) and *Vanity Fair* (1847–48) that he won widespread recognition as an author. These successes were followed closely by *Pendennis* (1848–50), *The History of Henry Esmond* (1852), and *The Newcomes* (1853–55). In 1852–53 and again in 1855–56 he visited the United States on lecture tours; his itinerary included visits to Richmond, which he pronounced "the merriest little place and the most picturesque I have seen in America." Richmonders responded with an enthusiastic welcome, and lecture rooms filled to capacity. The visit was an influential one; his next major work was *The Virginians*, published serially 1857–59. Thackeray became editor of the *Cornhill Magazine* in 1860 but died shortly afterwards, on December 24, 1863. His wife, Isabella (Shawe) Thackeray, whom he married in 1836, bore her husband three daughters, two of whom lived to maturity; Mrs. Thackeray became mentally incapacitated after only four years of marriage and never recovered.

Encyclopaedia Britannica; Sir Paul Harvey, *Oxford Companion to English Literature* (Oxford, 1933); *Virginia Cavalcade* 2, no. 2 (1952): 4–9; James Grant Wilson, *Thackeray in the United States* (London, 1904), 1: 195; *Occasional Bulletin*, no. 36 (1978): 6–7 (portrait reproduced); *VMHB* 86 (1978): 240.

William Makepeace Thackeray

ARTIST UNIDENTIFIED

Oil on panel: 15 1/2 x 13 1/2 in. (39.4 x 34.3 cm.)

Acquired by purchase in 1977. Por977.13

The Society's portrait was painted ca. 1870 from the 1856 photograph of Thackeray made by Alman of New York.

Anne Thomas, 1770–1848
See William Anderson, 1764–1839

Anne Campbell (Gordon) Thomas, 1819–1886 (Mrs. John Hanson Thomas)

Daughter of Bazil and Anna Campbell (Knox) Gordon (qq.v.) of Falmouth and sister of Douglas Hamilton Gordon (q.v.), the subject was born on October 29, 1819. She married on November 15, 1837, Dr. John Hanson Thomas (1813–1881) of Baltimore, Maryland, son of John Hanson Thomas and Mary (Colston) Thomas. Her husband, who graduated from the University of Virginia in 1832, then studied medicine at the University of Maryland and was for a short time resident physician at the Baltimore Infirmary. After his marriage he gave up the practice of medicine to become a director of the Farmers and Merchants Bank of Baltimore, soon becoming president of the bank, a post he held for forty years until ill health necessitated his retirement in 1879. Dr. Thomas served several terms on the Baltimore City Council and in the Maryland state legislature. He died at White Sulphur Springs, West Virginia, on July 15, 1881. Mrs. Thomas died in 1886. The couple had five sons and two daughters.

Armistead Churchill Gordon, *Gordons in Virginia* (Hackensack, N.J., 1918), p. 107; George Adolphus Hanson, *Old Kent: The Eastern Shore of Maryland* (Baltimore, 1876), p. 133; William McClung Paxton, *The Marshall Family* (Cincinnati, 1885), pp. 219–21; *Baltimore Sun*, July 16, 1881; *W. & M. Quart.*, 1st ser., 3 (1894–95): 68; *VMHB* 84 (1976): 239. See chart on Fitzhugh, Knox, and Gordon Portraits for relationships.

COPIED BY LOUIS P. DIETERICH

Oil on canvas: 30 x 25 in. (76.2 x 63.5 cm.). Inscribed on the back: "Annie Campbell (Gordon) Thomas, 1819–1886."

Presented in 1975 by Rosamund (Thomas) Oppersdorff (Mrs. Edward Oppersdorff) of New York City. Por975.22

The portrait is an early copy of the original by William Edward West of Baltimore.

Anne Butler (Brayne) Spotswood Thompson
See Alexander Spotswood, 1676–1740

Lettice (Lee) Wardrop Thompson, d. 1776
See Lettice (Lee) Wardrop, d. 1776

Lucas Powell Thompson, 1797–1866
See The Convention of 1829–30

David Algernon Timberlake, 1833–1901

The subject was born on March 9, 1833, son of Archibald B. Timberlake and Emily R. (Bowe) Timberlake of Hanover County. He entered the service of the Confederacy on May 9, 1861, at Ashland, as a lieutenant in Wickham's Brigade, 4th Virginia Cavalry; he was promoted to captain on October 11, 1863. His wife, whom he married on November 27, 1862, was Mary Winn Sydnor, daughter of William B. Sydnor of Meadow Farm, Hanover County. David A. Timberlake died on May 22, 1901; his remains were reinterred in Hollywood Cemetery on December 7, 1911. Mrs. Timberlake died on October 15, 1917.

William Ronald Cocke, *Hanover County Chancery Wills and Notes: A Compendium of Genealogical, Biographical, and Historical Material* (Columbia, Va., 1940), pp. 21, 145; Linwood Davis Wingfield, *History of the Wingfields of Virginia* (Richmond, 1952), pp. 87–88; *Richmond Times-Dispatch*, Oct. 17, 1917, p. 3; Virginia State Library, Sydnor Bible record 25174; *Biographic Catalogue*; Hollywood Cemetery.

BY JOHN P. WALKER. Signed. Dated 1905

Oil on canvas: 30 x 25 in. (76.2 x 63.5 cm.)

Presented to the R. E. Lee Camp, Confederate Veterans, in 1905; acquired by the Virginia Historical Society in 1946 through merger with the Confederate Memorial Association. Por946.148

Dolley (Payne) Todd, 1768–1849
See James Madison, 1751–1836

William Clayton Torrence, 1884–1953

Born in Atlanta, Georgia, on June 7, 1884, the subject was the son of John Early Torrence and Katherine Winter (Clayton) Torrence. He came to Virginia in 1903; he was bibliographer of the Virginia State Library 1906–10 and secretary of the Valentine Museum 1910–18. In 1919 he graduated from the Virginia Theological Seminary, being ordained deacon the same year and priest in December 1920.

William Clayton Torrence

James Trezvant, ca. 1813–1841
See The Convention of 1829–30

Amélie Louise (Rives) Chanler Troubetzkoy, 1863–1945 (Princess Pierre Troubetzkoy)

The popular novelist Amélie Rives was born in Richmond on August 23, 1863, daughter of Alfred Landon Rives and Sarah Catherine (MacMurdo) Rives (q.v.), granddaughter of William Cabell Rives (q.v.), and niece of Amélie Louise (Rives) Sigourney (q.v.). She grew up and spent most of her life at Castle Hill, Albemarle County, though as a young woman she made frequent trips to Europe. At an early age she became interested in drama and writing; her first story, "A Brother to Dragons," was published (anonymously) in the March 1886 number of the *Atlantic Monthly*. Her first novel, *The Quick or the Dead* (1888), published two years later, was a great success, selling 300,000 copies and becoming one of the most controversial novels of its day. This book, her most popular, was followed by such works as *Barbara Dering* (1892), *Tanis, the Sang-Digger* (1893), *A Damsel Errant* (1898), a narrative poem entitled *Seléné* (1905), and *Pan's Mountain* (1910). She later turned to the theater, writing a series of plays that enjoyed a certain success in New York during the war years and the 1920s; these included *The Fear Market* (1916), *The Prince and the Pauper* (1919); *The Sea-Woman's Cloak* (1924), and *Love-in-a-Mist* (1926). Her last novel, *Firedamp*, was published in 1930. She spent her declining years in seclusion at Castle Hill; she died on June 16, 1945. She was twice married. Her first husband, whom she married in 1888, was John Armstrong Chanler, a great-grandson of John Jacob Astor; the marriage ended in divorce. Her second husband, whom she married on February 18, 1896, was the portrait painter Prince Pierre Troubetzkoy. She had no children.

James Rives Childs, *Reliques of the Rives* (Lynchburg, Va., 1929), p. 585; *Who Was Who in America* 2 (1950): 538; *Virginia Cavalcade* 12, no. 4 (1963): 13 (Portrait II reproduced); *The Cabells and Their Kin*, p. 462; *VMHB* 56 (1948): 238; Welford Dunaway Taylor, *Amélie Rives* (New York, 1973).

Portrait I

By Antonin Carlès. Signed. Dated Paris, 1889

Marble bust: 34 in. (86.4 cm.) in height

Presented in 1947 by the Rives estate through the courtesy of Sarah Landon Rives of Albemarle County. Por947.20

For the next twenty years he was the rector of various parishes in Virginia and Maryland. In 1940 he was called from St. John's Church, Baltimore, which he had served as rector since 1934, to become corresponding secretary and director of the Virginia Historical Society. He held the post until his death thirteen years later on April 8, 1953. An indefatigable researcher in the fields of Virginia bibliography and genealogy, he wrote, among other works, *A Trial Bibliography of Colonial Virginia* (1908–10), *Winston of Virginia and Allied Families* (1927), *Virginia Wills and Administrations* (1931), and *Old Somerset* (1935); he was also, during his years at the Virginia Historical Society, editor of the *Virginia Magazine of History and Biography* and a frequent contributor to its pages. His wife, whom he married on August 1, 1912, was Elizabeth Green (Neblett) Torrence, daughter of Dr. Norman Henry Neblett and Lillian Henry (Hite) Neblett of Inglewood, Lunenburg County; the couple had three children.

Robert McIlvaine Torrence, *Torrence and Allied Families* (Philadelphia, 1938), p. 152; Protestant Episcopal Church in Virginia, Council, *Journal* (1953), p. 83; *VMHB* 61 (1953): 200.

By David Silvette. Signed. Dated 1951

Oil on canvas: 30 x 25 in. (76.2 x 63.5 cm.)

Acquired from the artist in 1951. Por951.36

George Townes, 1791–1861
See The Convention of 1829–30

Amélie Louise (Rives) Chanler Troubetzkoy (Portrait II)

Amélie Louise (Rives) Chanler Troubetzkoy (Portrait III)

Portrait II

BY PIERRE TROUBETZKOY

Oil on canvas: 40 x 30 in. (101.6 x 76.2 cm.)

Presented in 1947 by the Rives estate through the courtesy of Sarah Landon Rives of Albemarle County. Por947.33

Portrait III

BY PAUL TROUBETZKOY. Signed. Dated 1895

Bronze bust: 24 in. (61 cm.) in height

Presented in 1947 by the Rives estate through the courtesy of Sarah Landon Rives of Albemarle County. Por947.43

Henry St. George Tucker, 1780–1848

The subject was born at Matoax, Chesterfield County, December 29, 1780, son of St. George Tucker and Frances (Bland) Randolph Tucker. After graduating from the College of William and Mary in 1799 and studying law with his father, he began the general practice of law in Winchester, where his outstanding legal talents gained him a high reputation. Elected to the Virginia House of Delegates, he represented his county in the session of 1807–8. During the War of 1812 he served as a captain in the cavalry. Resuming his political career after the war, he was a member of the United States Congress 1815–19, then returning to state politics was a member of the Virginia Senate 1819–23. In 1824 Tucker was elected judge of the superior courts of chancery for the Winchester and Clarksburg districts. In 1831 he was elected president of the Supreme Court of Appeals of Virginia; for a decade he presided over the court with a distinction that won him widespread acclaim. Judge Tucker resigned in 1841 to accept the professorship of law at the University of Virginia. Declining health forced him to retire in 1845, and he died in Winchester on August 28, 1848. Despite the time-consuming obligations of the bench, Tucker wrote three treatises that were influential in their day: *Commentaries on the Laws of Virginia* (2 vols., 1836–37), *Lectures on Constitutional Law* (1843), and *A Few Lectures on Natural Law* (1844). His wife, whom he married on September 23, 1806, was Anne Eveline (Hunter) Tucker, daughter of Moses and Ann (Stephen) Dandridge Hunter; the couple had thirteen children. Judge Tucker was elected to membership in the Virginia Historical Society in 1836; later the same year he was elected to the presidency of the Society, holding the office until his death in 1848.

DAB; *Biographical Directory*; *Seldens of Virginia*, 2: 135, 164–70; *VMHB* 55 (1947): 202 and 67 (1959): 456 (portrait reproduced).

Oil on canvas: 30 x 25½ in. (76.2 x 64.8 cm.). Inscribed on the back: "Henry St. George Tucker. Copy by Rudolf V. Smutny. 4015—72nd St. Jackson Heights, N.Y."

Presented in 1946 by descendants of the subject. Por946.4

The Society's portrait is a copy of an original by William James Hubard now in the collection of Colonial Williamsburg.

John Tyler, 1790–1862
See The Convention of 1829–30

Lyon Gardiner Tyler, 1853–1935

Historian, college president, and officer of the Virginia Historical Society for forty-seven years, Lyon Gardiner Tyler was born in August 1853, son of former president John Tyler and his second wife, Julia (Gardiner) Tyler. After graduating from the University of Virginia in 1874, receiving his master's degree there, and studying law, he taught briefly at the College of William and Mary and for four years was headmaster of a school in Tennessee. He settled in Richmond in 1882, established a law practice, and wrote the first of his major historical works, *The Letters and Times of the Tylers* (1884–96), a three-volume survey of Virginia politics of 1816–40. In 1883 he helped revive the Virginia Mechanics' Institute, and five years later, as a delegate from Richmond in the state legislature, he sponsored a bill reestablishing the College of William and Mary, which for seven years had been dormant. Elected president of the college in 1888, he held that office until his retirement in 1919. Unceasing in his effort to preserve and publish Virginia's documentary resources, he founded the *William and Mary Quarterly* in 1892 and *Tyler's Quarterly* in 1920; he edited *Narratives of Early Virginia* (1907) and two monumental biographical works, *Men of Mark in Virginia* (1906–9) in five volumes and the *Encyclopedia of Virginia Biography* (1915), also in five volumes. He was a frequent contributor to periodicals and wrote numerous pamphlets and such books as *Parties and Patronage in the United States* (1891), *The Cradle of the Republic* (1900), *England in America* (1904), and *Williamsburg, the Old Colonial Capital* (1907). He served on the State Board of Education and was chairman of the board of the Virginia State Library. His death occurred at his home, The Lyon's Den, Charles City County, on February 12, 1935. Tyler was twice married: first, on November 14, 1878, to Annie B. Tucker; second, on September 12, 1923, to Sue Ruffin; he had three children by his first marriage, and two children by his second. He became a member of the Virginia Historical Society in 1883, a member of the Society's executive committee in 1888, and was elected a vice-president of the Society in 1903.

DAB (Supplement 1); *Encyclopedia of Virginia Biography*, 5: 860–61; *VMHB* 43 (1935): 257–58 and 55 (1947): 202–3.

Lyon Gardiner Tyler

By Albert Sterner. Signed. Dated 1933

Oil on canvas: 39 x 33 in. (99.1 x 83.8 cm.)

Presented in 1946 by the Pocahontas and Chanco Chapters of the Daughters of American Colonists. Por946.26

Abel Parker Upshur, 1790–1844
See The Convention of 1829–30

John Urquhart, died ca. 1845
See The Convention of 1829–30

Edward Virginius Valentine, 1838–1930
See The Battle Abbey Murals. Flanking Panels

Margaret Van Hesse, 1635–1710
See Thomas Culpeper, second Baron Culpeper of Thoresway, 1635–1689

Richard N. Venable, 1763–1838

See The Convention of 1829–30

James Alexander Walker, 1832–1901

Confederate general, lieutenant governor, and United States congressman, James Alexander Walker was born in Augusta County on August 27, 1832, the son of Alexander and Hannah (Hinton) Walker. A member of the Virginia Military Institute class of 1852, he was dismissed before graduating for challenging T. J. ("Stonewall") Jackson, a member of the faculty, to a duel. He later graduated from the University of Virginia law school, was admitted to the bar in 1856, commenced practice in Newbern, Pulaski County, and in 1859 was elected Commonwealth's attorney of Pulaski County. He entered Confederate service as captain of the Pulaski Guards and was shortly thereafter made lieutenant colonel of the 13th Virginia Infantry. He served in the Valley of Virginia, the battles of Sharpsburg and Fredericksburg, and virtually every engagement of the 2d Corps. On May 15, 1863, at the request of General Jackson, who had come to regard him highly, he was promoted to brigadier general and given command of the Stonewall Brigade, which he led at Winchester, Gettysburg, the Wilderness, and Spotsylvania. At Sayler's Creek and Appomattox he commanded Early's former division. For some years after the surrender General Walker farmed and practiced law in Pulaski County. A successful candidate for election to the Virginia legislature, he represented his county in the sessions of 1871–73; he was then elected lieutenant governor of Virginia for the term 1878–82, serving in the administration of Governor Frederick W. M. Holliday. Changing his party affiliation from Democratic to Republican, he was twice elected to the United States Congress, representing his constituency 1895–99. Unsuccessful in his attempt to win a third term, he resumed the practice of his profession. He died in Wytheville on October 21, 1901. In 1858 he married Sarah A. Poage, daughter of William and Margaret (Allen) Poage of Augusta County; she bore him six children. General Walker became a member of the Virginia Historical Society in 1894.

Generals in Gray; Virginia State Bar Association, *Proceedings* 15 (1902): 69–80; *Confederate Veteran* 9 (1901): 510; *Biographical Directory*; *Biographic Catalogue*.

By John P. Walker. Signed. Dated 1902

Oil on canvas: 30 x 25 in. (76.2 x 63.5 cm.)

Presented to the R. E. Lee Camp, Confederate Veterans, in 1902; acquired by the Virginia Historical Society in 1946 through merger with the Confederate Memorial Association. Por946.116

Jane Byrd (Nelson) Walker, 1775–1808

See Jane Byrd Nelson, 1775–1808

John George Walker, 1822–1893

Born in Cole County, Missouri, on July 22, 1822, the subject attended the Jesuit College in St. Louis and in 1846 was commissioned a lieutenant in the 1st Mounted Rifles, United States Army. He served during the Mexican War and was a member of the regular army at the time of his resignation in 1861 to enter the Army of the Confederacy. He was immediately commissioned a major in the Confederate cavalry, thereafter rising rapidly in rank to brigadier general. Walker saw action with the Army of Northern Virginia in the Maryland campaign, was promoted to major general on November 8, 1862, and rendered distinguished service at Loudoun Heights and at Sharpsburg. Transferred to the Trans-Mississippi Department, he took part in the Red River campaign; in June 1864 he was assigned to command the District of West Louisiana and at the end of the war was in command of the District of Texas, New Mexico, and Arizona. At the close of hostilities he withdrew to Mexico. Later he was American consul general at Bogotá, Colombia, and a special commissioner of the Pan-American Convention. He died at Washington, D.C., on July 20, 1893, and is buried in Winchester.

Generals in Gray; *Confederate Military History*, 9, pt. 2: 223–25.

By Ellis Meyer Silvette. Signed

Oil on canvas: 30 x 25 in. (76.2 x 63.5 cm.)

Acquired in 1946 through merger with the Confederate Memorial Association. Por946.132

Maggie Lena (Mitchell) Walker, 1867–1934 (Mrs. Armistead Walker)

Black businesswoman and community leader, Maggie Walker was born in Richmond on July 15, 1867, daughter of William and Elizabeth (Draper) Mitchell. She completed high school at the age of sixteen, taught school for three years, and in 1899 became executive secretary of a black burial society, the Independent Order of Saint Luke, a group organized to provide low-cost cooperative insurance to cover funeral expenses. In ten years she increased the membership from 700 to 20,000, and by the time of her death the order had 53,000 members and assets of over $300,000. To help publicize the order

Maggie Lena (Mitchell) Walker

and the virtues of thrift and regular saving that it promoted, she established in March 1902 the *Saint Luke Herald*, a weekly magazine. The following year the Saint Luke Penny Savings Bank opened its doors in Richmond with Mrs. Walker as its president; now known as the Consolidated Bank and Trust Company, it is the oldest black bank in the nation. As president of the Council of Colored Women, she did much to help such organizations as the Girls' Industrial School at Peaks, Virginia, the Community House in Richmond, and the Piedmont Tuberculosis Sanitorium at Burkeville. She was a member of the board of the National Association for the Advancement of Colored People and of the Virginia Union University and was a director of the National Training School for Women and Girls. She died on December 15, 1934. Mrs. Walker's husband, whom she married on September 14, 1890, was Armistead Walker, son of Armistead and Mary Walker; the couple had two sons.

Wendell Phillips Dabney, *Maggie L. Walker and the I. O. of Saint Luke: the Woman and Her Work* (Cincinnati, 1927); Sadie Iola Daniel, *Women Builders* (Washington, D.C., 1931), pp. 28–52; Writers' Program, Virginia, *The Negro in Virginia* (New York, 1940), pp. 292–93; *Richmond Times-Dispatch*, Dec. 16, 1934; *VMHB* 83 (1975): 237; *Occasional Bulletin*, no. 32 (1976): 11–12 (portrait reproduced).

By P. BENEDUCE. Signed. Dated 1934

Plaster bust: 12 1/2 in. (31.8 cm.) in height

Acquired by purchase in 1973. Por973.212

Reuben Lindsay Walker, 1827–1890

A native of Albemarle County, General Walker was born on May 29, 1827, the son of Meriwether Lewis Walker and Maria (Lindsay) Walker. He graduated from the Virginia Military Institute in 1845, turned to civil engineering, then farmed in New Kent County. On the outbreak of hostilities in 1861 he entered Confederate service as captain of the Purcell Battery and led it at First Manassas. Rising in rank to brigadier general, he served as chief of artillery of A. P. Hill's Division and finally of the 3d Corps; he participated in sixty-three battles and engagements, including Sharpsburg, Fredericksburg, Chancellorsville, Gettysburg, the Wilderness, Spotsylvania, and Cold Harbor. He surrendered with Lee at Appomattox, after which he turned again to agricultural pursuits. In 1872 he removed to Selma, Alabama, where for two years he was superintendent of the Marine and Selma Railroad. In 1876 he was back in Virginia in the employ of the Richmond and Danville Railroad. Thereafter he was superintendent of the Richmond street railways, construction engineer for the Richmond and Alleghany Railroad, and in charge of the construction of an addition to the Virginia State Penitentiary. He again left Virginia in 1884 to superintend the erection of the Texas state Capitol, remaining in Austin for that purpose until 1888. He died on June 7, 1890, at his farm in Fluvanna County and is buried in Hollywood Cemetery, Richmond. General Walker was twice married: first, in 1848, to Maria B. Eskridge of Staunton, who bore him four sons; second, to Sally Elam, a daughter of Dr. Albert Elam of Chesterfield County and a granddaughter of Governor James Pleasants; she survived him, as did their five children.

DAB; *Generals in Gray*; *Richmond Dispatch*, June 8, 1890, p. 3; *VMHB* 10 (1902–3): 95–96; *Biographic Catalogue*.

ARTIST UNIDENTIFIED

Oil on canvas: 30 x 25 in. (76.2 x 63.5 cm.)

Presented to the R. E. Lee Camp, Confederate Veterans, in 1897; acquired by the Virginia Historical Society in 1946 through merger with the Confederate Memorial Association. Por946.134

Richard Peyton Walton, 1819–1892

Dr. Richard Peyton Walton was born in Cumberland County on March 31, 1819, son of Thomas

Hobson Walton and Anne (Brackett) Hatcher Walton. He studied medicine at the University of Pennsylvania Medical School, graduating in the class of 1841. Returning to Cumberland County, he married in 1842 Mary Jemima Woodson, daughter of Charles Lewis Woodson and Linton Grayson (Powell) Woodson; he resided at Morning Side, five miles west of Cartersville, and developed a thriving medical practice. At the beginning of the Civil War he enlisted as a surgeon in the Black Eagle Company from Cumberland County, which later became a part of the 18th Virginia Infantry; during the last years of the war he was assigned to the General Hospital in Farmville. Dr. Walton remained in Farmville for several years after the war before returning to his home in Cumberland to resume his practice. In 1885 he sold Morning Side and removed to Norfolk, where he opened a dispensary in connection with his medical practice. He died in Norfolk in October 1892, survived by his wife and eight children.

Henry Morton Woodson, *Historical Genealogy of the Woodsons and Their Connections* (Memphis, Tenn., 1915), pp. 316–17; Wyndham Bolling Blanton, *Medicine in Virginia in the Nineteenth Century* (Richmond, 1933), pp. 11, 306, 418; CMA Archives, folio Z1n; *Biographic Catalogue*.

BY JOHN P. WALKER. Signed. Dated 1924

Oil on canvas: 30¼ x 25 in. (76.8 x 63.5 cm.)

Presented to the R. E. Lee Camp, Confederate Veterans, in 1924 by Charles Cortlandt Walton II; acquired by the Virginia Historical Society in 1946 through merger with the Confederate Memorial Association. Por946.98

Lettice (Lee) Wardrop, d. 1776 (Mrs. James Wardrop)

Granddaughter of Richard and Letitia (Corbin) Lee of Westmoreland County and daughter of Philip and Elizabeth (Lawson) Sewell Lee of Blenheim, Prince Georges County, Maryland, the subject entered into matrimony three times. Her first husband was James Wardrop, a Scot with business interests in New York City and Upper Marlboro, Maryland, who died in 1760. Her second husband was Dr. Adam Thompson, a physician of New York City and Upper Marlboro, Maryland; there were two daughters born of this union; Dr. Thompson died in 1767. Her third husband, whom she married in 1775, was Colonel Joseph Sim, a prominent planter of Prince Georges County, Maryland, a member of the Privy Council of Maryland, and a member of the Maryland Convention of 1775. The subject died on April 3, 1776; her third husband survived her by seventeen years.

Lee of Virginia, pp. 96, 100; *Portraiture*, p. 58; Effie Augusta Gwynne Bowie, *Across the Years in Prince George's County* (Richmond, 1947), pp. 519–22; VHS Mss2 Si415b; *VMHB* 49 (1941): 97–98.

ATTRIBUTED TO JOHN WOLLASTON. Ca. 1755

Oil on canvas: 47½ x 37½ in. (120.7 x 95.3 cm.)

Received in 1940 as a bequest of Alice C. Strong of New York City. Por940.13

The attribution to John Singleton Copley (printed in the *Virginia Magazine of History and Biography* and in *Portraiture in the Virginia Historical Society*) is untenable. The portrait appears to be the work of John Wollaston.

George Washington, 1732–1799

Martha (Dandridge) Custis Washington, 1732–1802 (Mrs. George Washington)

Pater patriae and first president of the United States, George Washington was born at Wakefield, Westmoreland County, on February 22, 1732, the eldest son of Augustine and Mary (Ball) Washington. At seventeen he helped survey Fairfax property west of the Blue Ridge; he commanded Virginia troops during the French and Indian War, was aide-de-camp to General Braddock in 1755, and in 1758 led a successful expedition against Fort Duquesne. On January 6, 1759, he married Martha (Dandridge) Custis who was born in New Kent County on June 2, 1732, the daughter of John Dandridge (q.v.) and Frances (Jones) Dandridge and the widow of Daniel Parke Custis; although the couple had no children, Washington acted as father to his wife's children by her first marriage, Martha Parke Custis ("Patsy") and John Parke Custis ("Jackie"). The family resided at Mount Vernon, the Fairfax County property that Washington inherited from his brother Lawrence in 1752. Washington was a member of the House of Burgesses 1758–74, a delegate to the Virginia Revolutionary Convention of 1774, a member of the first and second Continental Congresses, and on June 15, 1775, was unanimously chosen commander of the Continental Army. He commanded the army for six years; on October 19, 1781, he accepted the surrender of the British at Yorktown. After resigning his commission in 1783, he retired to Mount Vernon to devote himself to agrarian pursuits. His retirement, however, was of short duration; in 1787 he was called on to preside over the convention charged with framing the federal Constitution. Unanimously elected first president of the United States, he was inaugurated on April 30, 1789; unanimously reelected for a second term but declining nomination for a third term, he retired to private life on March 3, 1797. George Washington died on December 14, 1799; Mrs. Washington died on May 22, 1802; they are buried at Mount Vernon.

DAB.

Portrait I. George Washington

COPIED BY THOMAS SULLY. 1856

Oil on canvas: 30½ x 25 in. (77.5 x 63.5 cm.)

Presented in 1857 by William Barret of Richmond. Por857.2

Painted between June 6 and July 5, 1856, the portrait is a copy of an original by Gilbert Stuart.

Portraiture, p. 105; Edward Biddle and Mantle Fielding, *The Life and Works of Thomas Sully* (Philadelphia, 1921), p. 311; VHS Archives, liber A3, p. 49.

Portrait II. George Washington   *See* Plate 24

BY CHARLES WILLSON PEALE

Oil on canvas: 22½ x 19¼ in. (57.2 x 48.9 cm.)

Presented in 1889 by R. B. Kennon of South Gaston, North Carolina. Por889.5

Gustavus A. Eisen, *Portraits of Washington* (New York, 1932), 2: 379.

Portrait III. George Washington

COPIED BY AN UNIDENTIFIED ARTIST

Oil on canvas: 50 x 40 in. (127 x 101.6 cm.)

Received from the Southern Society of New York City in 1901 through Howard R. Bayne. Por901.2

The portrait is a copy of an original by Gilbert Stuart.

Portraiture, p. 105; VHS Archives, liber A6, p. 247.

Portrait IV. George Washington

BY CHARLES PEALE POLK

Oil on canvas: 32 x 28 in. (81.3 x 71.1 cm.)

Presented in 1902 by Anthony M. Keiley of Alexandria, Egypt. Por905.10

The donor of the portrait, a longtime citizen of Richmond, an officer of the Society, and a judge of the International Court at Cairo, wrote on January 2, 1902, that he had lent the Society "long ago, a portrait which I bought in Petersburg, said to be that of Washington, painted by a young Frenchman, who visited the United States in or about 1795, perhaps earlier, and who gave the canvas to the father of a Mr. Rambaut, who I knew in P[etersburg] in my youth, from whose daughter Mary, now Mrs. Mary Morrison, a widow, I bought it. . . . I want the Historical Society to have an unchallengable title to it and write this to serve for a deed of gift." Although

Judge Keiley's recollection of the artist appears to have been inaccurate, the letter was produced more than thirty-five years later as proof of ownership when the Society sought to recover the canvas, which was in the custody of the Westmoreland Club and had hung for so long in the club that it was thought to be its property. The portrait was recovered by the Society in 1939.

Portraiture, pp. 104–5; *VMHB* 39 (1931): 345–46 and 48 (1940): 88; VHS Archives, liber A6, p. 264 and liber A9, pp. 103–4.

George Washington (Portrait V)

Portrait V. George Washington

COPIED BY R. ORLANDI. Signed

Marble statue: 39½ in. (100.3 cm.) in height, including the base

Presented in 1922 by W. D. Judkins of New York. Por922.1

The statue is a greatly reduced copy of Antonio Canova's monumental work commissioned by the

24. George Washington (Portrait II)

General Assembly of North Carolina in 1815. Unveiled in Raleigh on Christmas Eve, 1821, the original statue was lost in the fire that destroyed the Capitol ten years later. The Society's near-contemporary copy was found in Lausanne, Switzerland.

Portraiture, pp. 134–35; *Occasional Bulletin*, no. 20 (1970): 4–8 (portrait reproduced).

Portrait VI. George Washington

COPIED BY ALICE MATILDA READING

Oil on canvas: 29¼ x 24 in. (74.3 x 61 cm.)

Presented in 1934 by Mr. and Mrs. J. Collins Lee of Hartford, Connecticut. Por934.16

The portrait is a copy of an original by Gilbert Stuart.

Portrait VII. George Washington

BY FREDERICK WILLIAM SIEVERS. Signed. Dated 1934

Plaster plaque: 24 in. (61 cm.) in diameter (round)

Presented by the artist in 1935. Por935.10

The plaque bears likenesses in relief of George Washington, Thomas Jefferson, and Patrick Henry.

VHS Archives, liber A7, p. 479, and liber A8, p. 2.

Portrait VIII. George Washington

ARTIST UNIDENTIFIED

Cameo: ¾ x ½ in. (1.9 x 1.3 cm.)

Presented in 1957 by C. S. Sherwood, Jr., of Portsmouth. Por957.22

Portrait IX. George Washington

BY CHARLES CALVERLEY. Signed. Dated 1887

Relief in bronze: 21 x 16½ in. (53.3 x 41.9 cm.). Inscribed: "From Houdon's Bust. By C. Calverley, Sc. 1887."

Presented in 1971 by Seldon T. Williams of Southbury, Connecticut. Por971.53

Below the relief is the inscription: "Copyright 1877 By W. S. Barlow, N.Y. The bust from which I modeled this medallion has carved upon it the following inscription C. Calverley Sc. This bust is from the living face of Washington by Houdon Oct 1785. Permission was granted to Clark Mills in 1849 by Col. Washington at Mount Vernon to take a copy of the original Bust in Bronze, Clark Mills Sc."

Portrait X. Martha (Dandridge) Custis Washington

BY CHARLES WILLSON PEALE

Oil on canvas: 30 x 25 in. (76.2 x 63.5 cm.)

Presented about 1854 by Catherine Power (Lyons)

Martha (Dandridge) Custis Washington

Chevallié (Mrs. Jean Auguste Marie Chevallié) of Richmond. Por857.3

The portrait appears to be a replica of Peale's portrait in the Independence Hall collection. Rembrandt Peale examined it during his visit to the Society's rooms in 1858 and pronounced it "an original by his father and a good likeness."

Portraiture, pp. 105–7; *Virginia Historical Portraiture*, pp. 223–24 (portrait reproduced); *Portraits and Miniatures*, pp. 243, 362 (Independence Hall portrait reproduced); VHS Mss1 R5685b 812.

"Henry Washington"

The portrait was given to the Society in 1951 as a likeness of Henry Washington (1765–1812) of Westmoreland County and Alexandria. The firm attribution to Charles Bird King, the probable date of its execution, and the fact that the portrait depicts a young man in his twenties makes the identification impossible.

Andrew J. Cosentino, *The Paintings of Charles Bird King, 1785–1862* (Washington, D.C., 1977), p. 162 (portrait reproduced); *VMHB* 22 (1914): 437.

BY CHARLES BIRD KING. Signed. Ca.1815

Oil on canvas: 30 x 25 in. (76.2 x 63.5 cm.)

Presented in 1951 by Sydney Horace Lee Washington of Cambridge, Massachusetts. Por951.14

John Augustine Washington, 1821–1861

Great-grandson and namesake of General Washington's brother and the last member of the family to own Mount Vernon, the subject was born in Jefferson County, (West) Virginia, on May 3, 1821, son of John Augustine Washington and Jean Charlotte (Blackburn) Washington. He attended schools in Westmoreland County, Bristol, Pennsylvania, and Alexandria before entering the University of Virginia in 1838. After his graduation in 1841 he resided at Mount Vernon, which had been bequeathed to him as the eldest son and which he attempted to farm and keep in repair. Eventually, however, the expense of maintaining the estate and of entertaining the large number of visitors who appeared on his doorstep became more than he could accept. He sold the property to the Mount Vernon Ladies' Association in 1858; two years later he removed with his family to Waveland, an estate he had acquired in Fauquier County. At the beginning of the Civil War he offered his services to the governor of Virginia; he was appointed aide-de-camp to General Robert E. Lee with the rank of colonel and was killed a few months later on September 13, 1861, while on active duty near Cheat Mountain, (West) Virginia. Colonel Washington's wife, Eleanor Love (Selden) Washington, daughter of Wilson Cary Selden of Exeter, Loudoun County, whom he married on February 16, 1843, bore him seven children.

Seldens of Virginia, 1: 347–53; *The University Memorial*, pp. 57–61; *Biographic Catalogue*.

By JOHN P. WALKER. Signed. Dated 1909

Oil on canvas: 30 x 25 in. (76.2 x 63.5 cm.)

Presented to the R. E. Lee Camp, Confederate Veterans, in 1909; acquired by the Virginia Historical Society in 1946 through merger with the Confederate Memorial Association. Por946.170

Reade Macon Washington, 1796–1856

Son of Warner and Sarah (Rootes) Washington of Clarke County, Reade Macon Washington was born in 1796. He inherited Audley, near Berryville, and lived there until 1837 when he moved to Pittsburgh, Pennsylvania. He married at Chambersburg, Pennsylvania, Elizabeth Sterrett Crawford (1802–1876); the couple had issue. He died in 1856.

Information received with the portrait; VHS Mss File 31-11-1-W; *VMHB* 59 (1951): 253–54, 266.

ARTIST UNIDENTIFIED

Oil on canvas: 30½ x 25 in. (77.5 x 63.5 cm.) (oval)

Received in 1950 as a bequest of Mary Elizabeth (Washington) Engels of Pittsburgh, a granddaughter of the subject. Por950.4

Washington Family

The Society owns ten hollow-cut, bust-length silhouettes identified only as "members of the Washington family." They are uniformly framed, six in one frame, four in the other, and according to Alexander Wilbourne Weddell (*Portraiture*, p. 126) they were "found in a trunk belonging to Mrs. Robert E. Lee, and were given [to the Society] by General G. W. C. Lee."

ARTIST UNIDENTIFIED

Ten hollow-cut silhouettes: approximately 2½ in. (6.4 cm.) in height

Presented by George Washington Custis Lee. Por892.10

David Watson, 1834–1864

Born in Louisa County on November 25, 1834, the son of Dr. James Watson and Susan Dabney (Morris) Watson, the subject graduated from the University of Virginia in 1855, then returned to farm Westend, his widowed mother's Louisa County estate, which she shortly thereafter conveyed to her two children. On the secession of Virginia from the Union, Watson enlisted in the 1st Regiment of Virginia Artillery, seeing action with that unit in the Peninsular campaign. On April 30, 1862, he became captain of the 2d Company of the Richmond Howitzers, leading his command at Seven Pines and through the Maryland campaign. After the battle of Fredericksburg he was promoted to major; he participated in the battles of Chancellorsville and Gettysburg and fell, mortally wounded, at Spotsylvania, dying three days later on May 13, 1864.

The University Memorial, pp. 570–78; Robert Angus Murdock, "An Architectural and Historical Study of Westend" (photocopy of typescript at VHS); *Biographic Catalogue*.

By CARTER. Signed

Oil on canvas: 30 x 25 in. (76.2 x 63.5 cm.)

Presented to the R. E. Lee Camp, Confederate Veterans, in 1900 by the Confederate Veterans of Louisa County; acquired by the Virginia Historical Society in 1946 through merger with the Confederate Memorial Association. Por946.168

Joseph Prentis Webb, 1843–1892
See Robert Henning Webb, 1795–1866

Robert Henning Webb, 1795–1866
Margaret Susan (Prentis) Webb, 1810–1882 (Mrs. Robert Henning Webb), with Her Son Joseph Prentis Webb, 1843–1892

Robert Henning Webb, eldest son of Daniel and Mary Darden (Gardner) Webb of Hill's Point, Nansemond County, was born on December 18, 1795. He studied medicine and practiced his profession in Suffolk. He was a member of the Virginia state legislature for the session 1829–30 and was surveyor of the port of Suffolk in 1838 and 1853. His first wife, whom he married on August 8, 1822, was Mary Prentis Jones, daughter of Matthias Jones; his second wife, whom he married on January 22, 1834, was Margaret Susan Prentis, daughter of Joseph and Susan Caroline (Riddick) Prentis of Suffolk. Webb and his second wife had four children; their only child to reach maturity was Joseph Prentis Webb (the child depicted in his mother's portrait), who was born on October 30, 1843, married Annie Jordan Darden on January 27, 1881, and died on December 27, 1892. Dr. Robert Henning Webb died on July 22, 1866; his wife died on March 24, 1882; both are buried at Cedar Hill Cemetery in Suffolk.

Fillmore Norfleet, *Suffolk in Virginia* (Richmond, 1974), pp. 100–101, 106, 159 (both portraits reproduced); Fillmore Norfleet, *Bible Records of Suffolk and Nansemond County, Virginia* (Suffolk, Va., 1963), pp. 49–50, 115, 168; *VMHB* 64 (1956): 96, 101.

Portrait I. Robert Henning Webb

By Oliver Perry Copeland. 1843

Oil on canvas: 30 x 25 in. (76.2 x 63.5 cm.). Inscribed on the back: "Dr. R. H. Webb. Painted by O. P. Copeland 22nd Feby 1843 Aged 47 years."

Received in 1978 from the estates of Robert Henning Webb and Blanche (Miller) Webb of Charlottesville, through their son Dr. Joseph Prentis Webb II. Por978.7

Portrait II. Margaret Susan (Prentis) Webb with her son, Joseph Prentis Webb

By Oliver Perry Copeland. 1844

Oil on canvas: 30 x 25 in. (76.2 x 63.5 cm.). Inscribed on the back: "Mrs. Margaret S. Webb & Joseph Prentis Webb Aged 33 years & Infant 4 months. painted by O. P. Copeland Feb 22 1884 [*sic*] Suffolk Va."

Margaret Susan (Prentis) Webb with her son, Joseph Prentis Webb

Received in 1978 from the estates of Robert Henning Webb and Blanche (Miller) Webb of Charlottesville, through their son Dr. Joseph Prentis Webb II. Por978.8

Both portraits have recently been relined. Below the reproduction of Mrs. Webb's portrait in Norfleet's *Suffolk in Virginia* (p. 159), it is stated that the date 1844 is inscribed on the reverse. The portrait's present inscription and the erroneous date may be recent additions, not transcriptions.

William Augustine Webb, 1824–1881

Son of Commodore Thomas Tarlton Webb and Harriet (Davis) Webb, the subject was born in Norfolk on July 27, 1824. At ten years of age he accompanied his father on a cruise to the West Indies on the sloop of war *Vandalia*. He was appointed midshipman in the United States Navy on January 26, 1838, and rose in rank to lieutenant. He was a member of Commodore Perry's expedition to Japan and assisted in the laying of the Atlantic cable. At the outbreak of the Civil War he was in New York, having just returned from a cruise; he resigned his commission on May 17, 1861, and offered his services to the Confederate navy. In the action in Hampton Roads he commanded the gunboat *Teaser*; on May 13, 1863, he was promoted to commander, thereafter being assigned to the ironclad *Atlanta*. As he was attempting to take her from Savannah to Charleston, the vessel ran aground and was shortly afterwards captured by the enemy; Commodore Webb was taken prisoner. After his exchange he was ordered to England to take command of one of the cruisers under construction there; while he was waiting for the ship to be completed, the war ended. With the return of peace he settled in Goochland County with his family, remaining there until his death which occurred on December 1, 1881. Commander Webb's wife was Elizabeth Anne (Fleming) Webb, daughter of Tarleton and Rebecca (Coles) Fleming, whom he married in Goochland County on March 6, 1849; she bore him seven children.

Biographic Catalogue; CMA Archives, folio Z1n; Virginia State Library, Samuel Bassett French Papers.

BY JOHN P. WALKER. Signed. Dated 1924

Oil on canvas: 30¼ x 25 in. (76.8 x 63.5 cm.)

Presented to the R. E. Lee Camp, Confederate Veterans, in 1925 by the subject's daughters, Elizabeth (Webb) Vaughan, Virginia (Webb) Dickins, and Harriet Coles Webb; acquired by the Virginia Historical Society in 1946 through merger with the Confederate Memorial Association. Por946.79

Alexander Watson Weddell, 1841–1883

Penelope Margaret (Wright) Weddell, 1840–1901 (Mrs. Alexander Watson Weddell)

Born in Tarboro, North Carolina, on May 20, 1841, Alexander Watson Weddell was the son of James Weddell (q.v.) and Margaret (Ward) Weddell. The family moved to Petersburg some years before the Civil War. Weddell attended Hampden-Sydney College and later the University of Virginia, which he left on the outbreak of the Civil War to enlist in the Confederate army. He was commissioned a second lieutenant in the Ragland Guards, a Petersburg company that subsequently became Company G, 41st Virginia Infantry. He saw active duty with the unit until after the battle of Seven Pines when he was invalided out; thereafter he was private secretary to the Confederate secretary of state, Judah P. Benjamin (q.v.). After the war he studied law, but after having been admitted to the bar he decided to enter the ministry and was in due course ordained into the Protestant Episcopal church. He served the congregation of Emmanuel Church, Harrisonburg, until 1875 when he accepted a call to St. John's Church, Richmond. His ministry in Richmond was a fruitful

one but of short duration; he died on December 6, 1883. He was survived by his wife, Penelope Margaret (Wright) Weddell, a daughter of David Minton Wright and Penelope Margaret (Creecy) Wright (qq.v.) of Norfolk, whom he married on January 31, 1866. One of the couple's children was Alexander Wilbourne Weddell (q.v.), the Society's great benefactor.

VHS Mss3 P9465a (Sect. 1, A. W. Weddell); *Virginia House*, p. 73; Virginia Armistead Garber, *The Armistead Family, 1635–1910* (Richmond, 1910), pp. 249–56.

Portrait I. Alexander Watson Weddell

BY JULIAN LAMAR. Signed

Oil on panel: 27 x 21¾ in. (68.6 x 55.3 cm.)

Received in 1948 as a bequest of Mr. and Mrs. Alexander Wilbourne Weddell of Richmond. Por948.95

Portrait II. Penelope Margaret (Wright) Weddell

BY DOUGLASS EWELL PARSHALL

Oil on canvas: 32½ x 24 in. (82.6 x 61 cm.) (oval). Inscribed on the back: "Penelope M. Wright 1857 aetat 17."

Received in 1948 as a bequest of Mr. and Mrs. Alexander Wilbourne Weddell of Richmond. Por948.96

The portrait was copied from a daguerreotype.

Alexander Wilbourne Weddell, 1876–1948

Virginia (Chase) Steedman Weddell, 1874–1948 (Mrs. Alexander Wilbourne Weddell)

Diplomat and president and benefactor of the Virginia Historical Society, Alexander Wilbourne Weddell was born in Richmond on April 6, 1876, son of the Reverend Alexander Watson Weddell and Penelope Margaret (Wright) Weddell (qq.v.). After receiving his formal education at George Washington University, he entered the diplomatic service. His numerous overseas assignments included Beirut in 1916, Athens 1917–20, Calcutta 1920–24, and Mexico City 1924–28. He was the American ambassador to Argentina 1933–39 and ambassador to Spain 1939–42. Weddell also represented his country at various international conferences. He married on May 31, 1923, Virginia (Chase) Steedman, daughter of Edwin Eli Chase and Virginia (Atkinson) Chase of St. Louis, Missouri, and the widow of James Harrison Steedman. Mr. and Mrs. Weddell were active in the civic and cultural life of Richmond; they gave

25. Alexander Wilbourne Weddell (Portrait IV)

generous support to such organizations as the Richmond Academy of Arts, the Virginia Museum of Fine Arts, and the Virginia Historical Society. In 1926, using materials from Warwick Priory in England, they began the construction of Virginia House, in Windsor Farms, Richmond; three years later the house with its contents was conveyed to the Virginia Historical Society, the donors retaining a life interest in the property. Virginia House was the setting for an exhibition in 1929 of Virginia portraits organized by Weddell under the auspices of the Virginia Historical Society; a sumptuous catalogue, *A Memorial Volume of Virginia Historical Portraiture, 1585–1830* (1930), compiled under Weddell's direction, was published. Among other books written or edited by Weddell are *Richmond, Virginia, in Old Prints* (1932), *Introduction to Argentina* (1939), *Portraiture in the Virginia Historical Society* (1945), and *A Description of Virginia House* (1947). Mr. and Mrs. Weddell were killed in a train accident on January 1, 1948; they left no children. Weddell became a member of the Virginia Historical Society in 1901; he was elected to the Society's executive committee in 1930, and from 1943 until his death he was the Society's president.

Who Was Who in America 2 (1950): 564; *VMHB* 56 (1948): 119–23; VHS Mss6: 1 W4127: 1–2; *Virginia House*, pp. 40, 47, 50–51, 68.

Portrait I. Alexander Wilbourne Weddell

By JOHN C. JOHANSEN. 1923

Oil on canvas: 46¹/₂ x 32¹/₂ in. (118.1 x 82.6 cm.)

Received in 1948 as a bequest of Mr. and Mrs. Alexander Wilbourne Weddell of Richmond. Por948.88

Portrait VI is the companion piece to this portrait.

Portrait II. Alexander Wilbourne Weddell

By MARGARET FOOTE HAWLEY. Signed. Dated 1924

Miniature on ivory: 3³/₄ x 3 in. (9.5 x 7.6 cm.) (oval)

Received in 1948 as a bequest of Mr. and Mrs. Alexander Wilbourne Weddell of Richmond. Por948.27

Portrait III. Alexander Wilbourne Weddell

By DAVID SILVETTE. Signed. Dated 1932

Oil on canvas: 60 x 36¹/₄ in. (152.4 x 92.1 cm.)

Received in 1948 as a bequest of Mr. and Mrs. Alexander Wilbourne Weddell of Richmond. Por948.121

Portrait IV. Alexander Wilbourne Weddell

See Plate 25

By PHILIP A. DE LASZLO. Signed. 1937

Oil on canvas: 35³/₄ x 25³/₄ in. (90.8 x 65.4 cm.)

Received in 1948 as a bequest of Mr. and Mrs. Alexander Wilbourne Weddell of Richmond. Por948.105

The portrait was painted in London in 1937, a few months before the artist's death; it was the last portrait he undertook.

Portrait V. Alexander Wilbourne Weddell

By ALFRED JONNIAUX. Signed. 1945

Oil on canvas: 30 x 25 in. (76.2 x 63.5 cm.)

Received in 1948 as a bequest of Mr. and Mrs. Alexander Wilbourne Weddell of Richmond. Por957.47

Portrait VI. Virginia (Chase) Steedman Weddell

By JOHN C. JOHANSEN. Signed. Dated 1923

Oil on canvas: 46¹/₂ x 32¹/₂ in. (118.1 x 82.6 cm.)

Received in 1948 as a bequest of Mr. and Mrs. Alexander Wilbourne Weddell of Richmond. Por948.87

Portrait I is the companion piece to this portrait.

Portrait VII. Virginia (Chase) Steedman Weddell

By ALFRED JONNIAUX. Signed. 1936

Oil on canvas: 29¹/₂ x 24³/₄ in. (74.9 x 62.9 cm.)

Received in 1948 as a bequest of Mr. and Mrs. Alexander Wilbourne Weddell of Richmond. Por948.58

Virginia (Chase) Steedman Weddell (Portrait VII)

The portrait was painted in Buenos Aires in 1936 during Weddell's ambassadorship to the Argentine.

Portrait VIII. Virginia (Chase) Steedman Weddell

BY COUNTESS EDGERLY-KASYBSKA. Signed. Dated 1937

Oil on ivory: 10 1/2 x 3 1/2 in. (26.7 x 8.9 cm.)

Received in 1948 as a bequest of Mr. and Mrs. Alexander Wilbourne Weddell of Richmond. Por948.72.

The subject is depicted in the hall of the American Embassy in Buenos Aires.

Portrait IX. Virginia (Chase) Steedman Weddell

BY ALFRED JONNIAUX. Signed. 1945

Oil on canvas: 29 1/2 x 24 1/2 in. (74.9 x 62.2 cm.)

Received in 1948 as a bequest of Mr. and Mrs. Alexander Wilbourne Weddell of Richmond. Por948.62

Archibald Weddell, 1772–1850

Archibald Weddell, great-grandfather of the Society's president and benefactor Alexander Wilbourne Weddell (q.v.), was born in West Calder, Scotland, on June 28, 1772. He married in 1803 Henrietta Laurie (1779–1837), daughter of Alexander and Agnes (Reid) Laurie; the couple had five children, one of whom, James Weddell (q.v.), came to the United States and is represented in the Society's portrait collection. In 1823 the family was residing in Brickfield near Leith, Scotland. Archibald Weddell died on January 6, 1850.

VHS Mss6: 2 W4125: 1; *Virginia House*, p. 73.

ARTIST UNIDENTIFIED

Oil on canvas: 28 3/4 x 24 1/2 in. (73 x 62.2 cm.)

Received in 1948 as a bequest of Mr. and Mrs. Alexander Wilbourne Weddell of Richmond. Por948.93

James Weddell, 1807–1865

Son of Archibald Weddell (q.v.) and Henrietta (Laurie) Weddell, the subject was born in East Calder, Scotland, on March 19, 1807. He came to the United States at an undetermined date, married at Tarboro, North Carolina, on February 26, 1835, Margaret Wilbourne Ward (1819–1881). Later the family removed to Petersburg where they resided in a house on Sycamore Street that later was used by William Gordon McCabe (q.v.) for his boys' school. Two of the couple's sons were killed in the Civil War;

a third, Alexander Watson Weddell (q.v.), became rector of St. John's Church, Richmond. James Weddell died in Petersburg on March 13, 1865.

VHS Mss6: 2 W4125: 1 and Mss6: 1 W4127; *Virginia House*, p. 73; *Portraiture*, pp. 66, 142.

BY WILLIAM GARL BROWN. 1866

Oil on canvas: 30 x 24 3/4 in. (76.2 x 62.9 cm.) (framed as an oval). Inscribed on the back: "Wm. Garl Browne, Pinx. A.D. 1866."

Received in 1948 as a bequest of Mr. and Mrs. Alexander Wilbourne Weddell of Richmond. Por948.94

David Addison Weisiger, 1818–1899

Born on December 23, 1818, at The Grove, the Chesterfield County home of his parents, Daniel and Signora Tabb (Smith) Weisiger, the subject as a young man became a commission merchant in Petersburg. At the beginning of the Mexican War he enlisted as a second lieutenant in Company E, 1st Regiment of Virginia Volunteers, which saw action in Mexico in 1847 and 1848. After his return to Petersburg he devoted himself to the commission business until he was again called to arms in 1861. Entering the Confederate army as colonel of the 12th Virginia Infantry, he served in the vicinity of Norfolk until the spring of 1862 when his regiment became a part of the Army of Northern Virginia. He led his command at Seven Pines and the Seven Days and received wounds at Second Manassas that disabled him for nearly a year. At the Wilderness he was placed in command of Mahone's Brigade, later received promotion to brigadier general, and led his command in all its subsequent engagements, distinguishing himself particularly at the battle of the Crater. General Weisiger was paroled at Appomattox; he returned to Petersburg where he became cashier of the Citizens Bank. Subsequently he moved to Manchester, across the river from Richmond, where he was employed as a bookkeeper for a firm dealing in railroad supplies; later he was associated with Hunter, Sims and Company, dealers in hardware, in Richmond. He retired from the firm around 1893 and at about the same time moved across the James River to Richmond, where he remained until his death, which occurred on February 23, 1899. He was buried at Blandford Cemetery, Petersburg. General Weisiger married, first, in 1843, Rebecca McIndoe, who lived but a short time; second, Alice Barksdale of Halifax County, by whom he had one son; third, Louise Christine (Bland) Harrison, who survived him.

Generals in Gray; *Biographic Catalogue*; VHS Mss1 W4354a98.

By William Ludwell Sheppard. Signed

Oil on canvas: 30 x 25 in. (76.2 x 63.5 cm.)

Presented to the R. E. Lee Camp, Confederate Veterans, by the subject's widow before 1903; acquired by the Virginia Historical Society in 1946 through merger with the Confederate Memorial Association. Por946.113

which occurred on September 14, 1852, caused nationwide mourning.

DNB; *Encyclopedia Americana*; *Encyclopaedia Britannica*.

ARTIST UNIDENTIFIED

Relief in ormolu: 7 in. (17.8 cm.) in height, mounted on a backing 12 x 9 in. (30.5 x 22.9 cm.)

Presented in 1944 by Alexander Wilbourne Weddell of Richmond. Por944.7

Arthur Wellesley, first Duke of Wellington, 1769–1852

The duke of Wellington, hero of Waterloo, was born in Dublin, Ireland, on April 29, 1769, son of Garret Wesley, second Baron Mornington and first earl of Mornington. After his formal education he attended the military academy at Angers, France, then took a seat in the Irish Parliament and managed his family estates. In 1793 he obtained a commission as major in the 33d Regiment of foot. After service with the regiment in India 1797–1805, during which time he displayed great military ability and rose to the rank of major general, he became chief secretary for Ireland. On April 10, 1806, he married Catherine Pakenham, daughter of Edward Michael Pakenham, 2d Baron Longford, by whom he had issue. Two years later Wellesley was promoted to lieutenant general and sent to aid Spain and Portugal in their efforts to resist Napoleon. His campaign was successful; in honor of his victory at Talavera he was named Baron Douro and Viscount Wellington. He repulsed the French attempt to capture Lisbon, invaded Spain, fought a decisive battle near Salamanca, and entered Madrid. In 1813 he pursued the French across Spain and entered France; shortly after his victory at Toulouse, Napoleon abdicated. Elevated to a dukedom, Wellington, after brief diplomatic missions in Madrid and Paris, became the British delegate to the Congress of Vienna. Upon Napoleon's escape from Elba, he was put in command of the English troops that had been dispatched to Brussels. On June 18, 1815, Wellington, with the tardy assistance of the Prussians, defeated the French decisively at Waterloo; he entered Paris on July 7. "The Soldier of Europe" became commander in chief of all the allied troops in France, and the recipient of innumerable honors. In 1819 he reentered politics; he was British minister to the Congress of Verona 1822 and prime minister from 1828 until his resignation two years later. At first opposed to parliamentary reform, he later used his influence to assure its passage by the House of Lords in 1832; thereafter he served in the cabinet under Sir Robert Peel and in 1846 helped Peel to carry the repeal of the Corn Laws. His death,

John Spotswood Wellford, 1783–1846

The subject was born in Fredericksburg on March 30, 1783, son of Robert and Catherine (Yates) Thornton Wellford. He owned an extensive dry goods business and was involved in other commercial enterprises, including an iron mine in Spotsylvania County. A pioneer in the production of iron on a large scale, he established furnaces as early as 1830 and did much to promote the industry in the state. During the Mexican and Seminole wars his firm was a supplier of shot to the government. He was twice married: first, in 1807, to Fanny Page Nelson, daughter of William and Lucy (Chiswell) Nelson; second, on March 16, 1820, to Janet Henderson, daughter of Alexander Henderson of Fredericksburg. His first wife bore him three children; his second wife bore him seven. He died on December 23, 1846.

[Edward Lloyd Lomax], *Genealogy of the Virginia Family of Lomax* (Chicago, 1913), pp. 54–56 (portrait reproduced, p. 53); *The Beverley Family*, p. 166.

ARTIST UNIDENTIFIED

Oil on canvas: 36 x 27½ in. (91.4 x 69.9 cm.)

A bequest of Edward Lloyd Lomax of Fredericksburg. Received in 1966 from his son Edward Lloyd Lomax of Redwood City, California. Por966.3

Ann Mary Wetzel, 1759–1834
see Ann Mary (Wetzel) Aulick, 1759–1834

Joseph Wheeler, 1836–1906

Confederate general and congressman from Alabama, "Fighting Joe" Wheeler was born near Augusta, Georgia, on September 10, 1836, the son of Joseph and Julia Knox (Hull) Wheeler. He graduated from West Point in the class of 1859, saw two years' service in the regular army, then resigned his commission on April 22, 1861, to join the Army of the Confederacy as a first lieutenant. He was shortly afterwards promoted to colonel of the 19th Alabama Infantry, which he led through the Shiloh campaign, and on July 18, 1862, he became chief of cavalry of the Army of Mississippi. For the next two and a half years he was in charge of the cavalry in the western theater of operations, rising in rank to lieutenant general and taking part in two hundred engagements and eight hundred skirmishes. After the war he was for several years a commission merchant in New Orleans; he removed to Wheeler, Alabama, in 1868 to practice law and plant cotton. He was elected to the United States Congress in 1881, but the election was contested by W. M. Lowe, and Wheeler was forced to relinquish his seat, only to be appointed to the office shortly afterward to fill the vacancy occasioned by Lowe's death. He was elected to the Forty-ninth Congress and to the seven succeeding congresses, 1885–1900. Appointed major general of volunteers by President McKinley, Wheeler commanded a cavalry division during the Spanish-American War. He retired as a brigadier general of the regular army on September 10, 1900. He died in Brooklyn, New York, on January 25, 1906, and was buried in Arlington National Cemetery. General Wheeler married on February 8, 1866, Daniella (Jones) Sherrod; they became the parents of two sons and five daughters.

DAB; *Generals in Gray*; *Biographic Catalogue*.

BY B. NEBEL. Signed

Bronze statuette. 29½ in. in height. (74.9 cm.)

Acquired in 1946 through merger with the Confederate Memorial Association. Por946.230

Elijah Veirs White, 1832–1907

Born in Montgomery County, Maryland, on August 29, 1832, the son of Stephen Newton White and Mary (Veirs) White, the subject received his education at Lima Seminary in New York State and at Granville College in Ohio. He took part in the slavery conflicts in Kansas 1855–56 and three years later participated in checking John Brown's raid. Having bought a farm in Loudoun County, he resided in Virginia until the outbreak of the Civil War, whereupon he enlisted in the Confederate army and served as a scout under Ashby until the autumn of 1861. White then organized an independent company which became the nucleus of the 35th Battalion of Virginia Cavalry. As major and later as colonel of this unit, known as The Comanches, he led it at such engagements as Malvern Hill, Brandy Station, Gettysburg, the Wilderness, and Five Forks; he also

employed it effectively in scouting operations. During the final months of the war White and Mosby operated together in Loudoun County and the Valley of Virginia. After the war he returned to his home in Loudoun where he farmed, acted as sheriff of the county, and ministered to the Baptist congregation. He helped establish the People's National Bank of Leesburg in 1885 and became its president in 1887, retaining that office until his death which occurred in Leesburg on January 11, 1907. Colonel White was twice married: first to Elizabeth Gott; second to Margaret B. Banes; he was the father of nine children.

Men of Mark in Virginia, 2: 413–14; *History of Virginia*, 6: 409–11; *Confederate Military History*, 3: 1252–55; CMA Archives, folio Z1n; *Biographic Catalogue*.

BY JOHN P. WALKER. Signed. Dated 1924

Oil on canvas: 30 x 25 in. (76.2 x 63.5 cm.)

Presented to the R. E. Lee Camp, Confederate Veterans, in 1925 by the subject's son; acquired by the Virginia Historical Society in 1946 through merger with the Confederate Memorial Association. Por946.91

Peter Johnston White, 1848–1933

Born in Albemarle County on July 24, 1848, son of Peter J. White and Martha (Adams) White, the subject joined the Confederate States Army at an early age, serving in Fitzhugh Lee's 5th Virginia Cavalry Regiment. At the close of the war he resumed his education, attending Pinewood Academy near Scottsville for two years, then devoting himself to the study of architecture at the Maryland Institute in Baltimore 1867–72. Thereafter he practiced his profession in Richmond until his retirement in 1921; he planned and superintended the construction of such buildings as Blanchard's warehouse, the P. H. Mayo tobacco factory on Seventh Street, the Morris block of residences on Harrison Street, near Franklin, and several of the houses near the Commonwealth Club. On December 15, 1874, at the Broad Street Methodist Church he married Fannie Hopkins Mosely of Prince Edward County. White was active in Confederate organizations; in 1909 he was elected commander of the R. E. Lee Camp, and he also served on the camp's Portrait Gallery Committee and was a member of the board of the Soldiers' Home. For more than fifty years he was a member of Centenary Methodist Church. He died at his home, 103 South Third Street, Richmond, on September 8, 1933, survived by his widow and by a grandson, Orrin Banks White, Jr.

Richmond Times-Dispatch, Sept. 9, 1933, pp. 1, 3; Andrew Morrison, *The City on the James: Richmond, Virginia* (Richmond, 1893), p. 56; *Biographic Catalogue*.

By John P. Walker. Signed. Dated 1929

Oil on canvas: 27 x 22 in. (68.6 x 55.9 cm.)

Acquired in 1946 through merger with the Confederate Memorial Association. Por946.202

Robert White, 1833–1915

Robert White, colonel in the Confederate army and twice attorney general of West Virginia, was born in Romney, (West) Virginia, on February 7, 1833, eldest son of John B. White and Frances (Streit) White. After his early schooling he worked in the office of his father, who was county clerk, studied law in Lexington with Judge Brockenbrough, was admitted to the bar in 1854, and began the practice of his profession in Romney. During the Civil War he served as colonel of the 22d Virginia Cavalry and took part in numerous engagements. After the war he returned to Romney, formed a legal partnership with John J. Jacob, later governor of the state, and developed a thriving practice. He removed to Wheeling on his election to the office of attorney general, a post he held for two four-year terms, 1877–85. Thereafter he served in the state legislature in 1885 and again in 1891, was solicitor for the city of Wheeling, president of the state bar association, and, as a partner in the firm of White and Allen, was counsel for the Baltimore and Ohio Railroad Company and other large corporations. He died at his residence near Wheeling on December 12, 1915. His wife, who survived him, was Ellen E. (Vass) White, daughter of James Cummings Vass of Richmond; the couple were married in 1859 and had six children.

Wheeling Intelligencer, Dec. 13, 1915.

By Adele Williams. Signed

Oil on canvas: 32 1/4 x 26 in. (81.9 x 66 cm.)

Acquired in 1946 through merger with the Confederate Memorial Association. Por946.72

Williams Carter Wickham, 1820–1888

The subject was born in Richmond on September 21, 1820, son of William Fanning Wickham and Anne (Carter) Wickham and grandson of the celebrated Richmond lawyer John Wickham. He attended the University of Virginia, studied law, and was admitted to the bar in Hanover County in 1842, withdrawing from active practice after several years to devote himself to agriculture. He was elected to represent Hanover County in the Virginia House of Delegates for the 1849–50 term; in 1859 he became presiding justice of the Hanover County court; he

served in the state Senate 1859–61. As a member of the Convention of 1861 he opposed secession, but when the measure was approved, he offered his services to the Confederacy as captain of the Hanover Dragoons. He took part in the battle of First Manassas, was promoted to lieutenant colonel of the 4th Virginia Cavalry in September 1861, and to colonel the following August. Attached to Stuart's Cavalry Corps, he led his command at Williamsburg, Sharpsburg, Upperville, Fredericksburg, and Chancellorsville. Although he was elected to the Second Confederate Congress he continued in active duty as brigadier general through the Gettysburg campaign, Yellow Tavern, the Wilderness, Spotsylvania, and the Valley campaign. Wickham resigned his commission on November 9, 1864, to take his seat in Congress, where he remained until the war's end. He later became affiliated with the Republican party; he was chairman of the board of supervisors of Hanover County from 1871 until his death, and for the last five years of his life was again a member of the Virginia state Senate. In 1865 he was elected president of the Virginia Central Railroad, and later of the Chesapeake and Ohio Railway. He declined the secretaryship of the navy offered him by President Hayes in 1880 and also declined the Republican nomination for governor of Virginia the following year. He died in Richmond on July 23, 1888. General Wickham married at Hayfield, Caroline County, on January 11, 1848, Lucy Penn Taylor, daughter of Henry Taylor and granddaughter of John Taylor of Caroline; they became the parents of two sons and a daughter. General Wickham was elected to membership in the Virginia Historical Society in 1875.

Generals in Gray; *National Cyclopedia*; *Encyclopedia of Virginia Biography* 3: 45; *Biographic Catalogue*.

By Cornelius Hankins. Signed. Dated 1897

Oil on canvas: 30 x 25 in. (76.2 x 63.5 cm.)

Presented to the R. E. Lee Camp, Confederate Veterans, in 1897; acquired by the Virginia Historical Society in 1946 through merger with the Confederate Memorial Association. Por946.88

Edmund Randolph Williams, 1871–1952

Born in Richmond on May 1, 1874, the subject was the son of John Langbourne Williams and Maria Ward (Skelton) Williams and a grandson of John Williams (q.v.). He attended McGuire's School in Richmond and the University of Virginia School of Law, from which he graduated in 1893. After two years on the staff of the *American and English Encyclopedia of Law* in Northport, New York, he returned to

Edmund Randolph Williams

Richmond where he formed with William Wirt Henry (q.v.) a law partnership that continued until the death of Henry in 1900. On November 1, 1901, he and Henry Watkins Anderson (q.v.) joined with Beverley B. Munford and Eppa Hunton, Jr., to form the law firm that continues, with various name changes, to the present time. During the course of a long and successful professional career he was also, from time to time, president of the Richmond Traction Company, director of various railroad companies, general counsel of the Richmond, Fredericksburg and Potomac Railroad, and director of the First and Merchants National Bank. A lifelong communicant of St. Paul's Episcopal Church, he was its senior warden for many years; he was also chancellor of the Diocese of Virginia, a trustee for the schools of the diocese, and president of the Children's Home Society of Virginia. He was appointed by the governor to the first board of trustees of the Virginia Museum of Fine Arts in 1934, serving on its executive committee from 1935 until 1947. Williams became a member of the Virginia Historical Society in 1896; he was elected to the executive committee in 1926 and held office as president of the Society from 1948 until his death, which occurred on June 9, 1952. His wife, whom he married on November 22, 1900, was Maud Lathrop (Stokes) Williams; the couple had four children.

Virginia State Bar Association, *Proceedings* 63 (1952): 157–59; *Who Was Who in America* 3 (1960): 920; Thomas Benjamin Gay, *The Hunton Williams Firm and Its Predecessors* (Richmond, 1971), 1: 26–35; *VMHB* 54 (1946): 171.

By Alfred Jonniaux. Signed

Oil on canvas: 36 x 28 in. (91.4 x 71.1 cm.)

Presented in 1945 by friends of the subject. Por945.17

John Williams, 1793–1860

Born in Lappan, County Monaghan, Ireland, on March 26, 1793, the subject was the son of Mathew and Margaret (Bell) Williams. He came to Richmond in 1816 and in partnership with Marcus Jacob operated an importing and exporting business on the south side of Main Street between Fourteenth and Fifteenth streets. On October 10, 1820, he married Sianna Armistead Dandridge, a niece of Martha Washington and daughter of William and Susanna (Armistead) Dandridge of Woodlawn and Windsor, just west of Richmond; the couple became the parents of five children. Williams was later treasurer of the Richmond and Petersburg Railroad and owned a sawmill at the falls of the James River near Thirteenth Street. An active member of the Episcopal church, he was superintendent of the Sunday school at Monumental Church from 1828 to 1835 and a founder, vestryman, warden, and treasurer of St. James's. He died on April 23, 1860.

Richmond Portraits, pp. 209–10 (portrait reproduced); Carrington Williams, *The Family of Walter Armistead Williams and Alice Marshall Taylor Williams* (Richmond, 1968), pp. 26–33 (portrait reproduced, p. 30); VHS Mss 6: 4 W6767: 2; *VMHB* 70 (1962): 237.

John Williams

By Louis Mathieu Didier Guillaume.
Signed

Oil on canvas: 30 x 25 in. (76.2 x 63.5 cm.) (oval)

Presented in 1961 by John Skelton Williams of Richmond. Por961.36

Rose Adèle (Cutts) Douglas Williams, 1835–1899
See Rose Adèle (Cutts) Douglas, 1835–1899

Jacob Williamson
See The Convention of 1829–30

Eugenius M. Wilson
See The Convention of 1829–30

Sallie Browne (Cocke) Wilson, 1840–1909   (Mrs. Samuel Mazyck Wilson)

Daughter of General Philip St. George Cocke and Sally Elizabeth Courtney (Bowdoin) Cocke of Belmead, Powhatan County, the subject was born on January 31, 1840. She married on January 31, 1866, Samuel Mazyck Wilson, a native of Charleston, South Carolina, who attended the University of Virginia in 1834, was a lawyer, and was later president of the Seaboard and Roanoke Railroad. The couple had two children: a son, Philip St. Julien Wilson, and a daughter, Mazyck Wilson, who married W. B. Shields. After the death of her husband she resided at 211 East Franklin Street, Richmond. She died on December 20, 1909, and is buried in Hollywood Cemetery.

Portraiture, p. 108 (portrait reproduced); Leonie Doss Cocke, *Cockes and Cousins* (Ann Arbor, Mich., 1967—), 1: 155; *VMHB* 52 (1944): 77.

By Louis Mathieu Didier Guillaume.
Signed

Pastel on paper: 24 x 20 in. (61 x 50.8 cm.) (oval)

Received in 1943 as a bequest of Mazyck (Wilson) Shields (Mrs. W. B. Shields) of Bremo, Virginia, daughter of the subject. Por943.12

Henry Alexander Wise, 1806–1876

United States congressman, governor of Virginia, and Confederate general, Henry Alexander Wise

Henry Alexander Wise

was a native of Drummondtown, Accomack County, on the Eastern Shore of Virginia. He was born on December 3, 1806, to John and Sarah Corbin (Cropper) Wise. After graduating from Washington College, Pennsylvania, in 1825, he studied law in Winchester under Judge Tucker, practiced for two years in Nashville, Tennessee, then returned in 1830 to practice in his native county. Elected as a Jacksonian Democrat to the United States Congress, he served as a representative from 1833 until his resignation in 1844. He was then minister to Brazil 1844–47. Wise was nominated Democratic candidate for governor of Virginia in 1854; he defeated the Know-Nothing candidate and served as governor of the Commonwealth 1856–60. After the secession of Virginia, Wise offered his services to the Confederate government, and although without military experience and no longer young, he was appointed brigadier general on June 5, 1861. The Wise Legion, which he recruited in the western part of Virginia, fought in the West Virginia campaign, in North Carolina, in the defense of Charleston, and during the last year of the war in the defense of Petersburg and Richmond. After the war Wise practiced law in Richmond. His book *Seven Decades of the Union*, a review of the life and career of President Tyler, was published in 1872. He died in Richmond on September 12, 1876, and is buried in Hollywood Cemetery. Governor Wise married three times: first, on October 8, 1828, to Ann Eliza Jennings; second, in November 1840, to Sarah Sergeant of Philadelphia; third, in November 1853, to Mary

Elizabeth Lyons of Richmond. He was survived by his third wife, two sons, and three daughters.

DAB; Generals in Gray; Biographical Directory; Biographic Catalogue.

BY LYELL CARR. Signed. Dated 1907

Oil on canvas: 30 x 25 in. (76.2 x 63.5 cm.)

Acquired in 1946 through merger with the Confederate Memorial Association. Por946.82

Lewis Warrington Wise, 1844–1917

Son of Tully Robinson Wise and Margaret Douglas Pettitt (Wise) Wise, the subject was born in Washington, D.C., on November 4, 1844. Entering Confederate service at a very early age, he was attached to the Wise Legion, commanded by his uncle General Henry Alexander Wise (q.v.); later as sergeant major of the 46th Virginia Infantry he saw action in North Carolina and Virginia. He was wounded at the battle of the Crater and was captured at Sayler's Creek in the final days of the war. With the return of peace he resumed his studies, graduating from the Virginia Military Institute with the class of 1867. Thereafter he settled in Richmond, where until about 1875 he engaged in the tobacco business. Later he removed to Durham, North Carolina, and still later became the eastern representative of the Southern Pacific Railroad in New York. On November 26, 1896, he married Martha (Allen) Wilson, widow of Nathaniel Macon Wilson and daughter of William Coates Allen of Richmond. Afterwards he returned to Richmond where he resided until his death on April 5, 1917. The Society also owns a portrait of the subject's brother, Peyton Wise (q.v.).

Jennings Cropper Wise, *Col. John Wise of England and Virginia (1617–1695): His Ancestors and Descendants* (Richmond, 1918), p. 152; *Richmond Times-Dispatch*, April 7, 1917, p. 8; *Biographic Catalogue.*

BY JOHN P. WALKER. Signed. Dated 1908

Oil on canvas: 30 x 25 in. (76.2 x 63.5 cm.)

Acquired in 1946 through merger with the Confederate Memorial Association. Por946.81

Peyton Wise, 1838–1897

Born in Accomack County on February 9, 1838, son of Tully Robinson Wise and Margaret Douglas Pettitt (Wise) Wise, the subject received his education in Washington, D.C., then studied law in Philadelphia. The secession crisis interrupted his studies; he returned to Virginia and entered Confederate service as second lieutenant of Company H, 46th Virginia Infantry, under the command of his uncle General

Henry Alexander Wise (q.v.). He saw action in West Virginia, the Peninsular campaign, and Roanoke Island; during the reorganization of 1862 he was promoted to major and the following year to lieutenant colonel of the 46th Regiment, which he commanded for most of the remainder of the war. Severely wounded before Petersburg, he was subsequently captured; paroled but not exchanged, he was unable to undertake further military duty. He settled in Richmond after the war and entered the tobacco business, operating under the firm name of Peyton Wise and Company and later, in partnership with his brother James M. Wise, as Wise Brothers. For some years he was tobacco inspector for Richmond's tobacco exchange. In 1870 Governor Walker appointed him ranking major general of the state militia. He retired from mercantile life in 1888, thereafter devoting himself to such organizations as the YMCA and the R. E. Lee Camp no. 1, Confederate Veterans. He was chairman of the local committee for the Confederate reunion of 1896 and one of the organizers of the Jefferson Davis Monument Association. He died on March 29, 1897. Wise married on November 25, 1869, Laura Mason Chilton, daughter of General Robert Hall Chilton, C.S.A. A portrait of the subject's brother, Lewis Warrington Wise (q.v.), is also in the Society's collection.

Jennings Cropper Wise, *Col. John Wise of England and Virginia (1617–1695): His Ancestors and Descendants* (Richmond, 1918), p. 152; Richmond *Times*, March 18, 1897; *Confederate Military History*, 3: 1280–81; *Biographic Catalogue.*

ARTIST UNIDENTIFIED

Oil on canvas: 30¼ x 25 in. (76.8 x 63.5 cm.)

Presented to the R. E. Lee Camp, Confederate Veterans, in 1897; acquired by the Virginia Historical Society in 1946 through merger with the Confederate Memorial Association. Por946.93

Archibald Logwood Wooldridge, ca. 1792–1854

Born about 1792, the subject was the son of William Wooldridge of Chesterfield County. He was one of the incorporators, with his brother Abraham, of the Midlothian Coal Mining Company in 1835 and of the Chesterfield Coal Mining Company in 1837. He also had an interest in the Huguenot Springs, a watering place in Powhatan County. Dr. Wooldridge was twice married: first, to Elizabeth Perrott Stanard, daughter of Larkin Stanard (q.v.) and Elizabeth Perrott (Chew) Stanard of Stanfield, Spotsylvania County; second, to his first wife's niece, Julia Ann Stanard (1809–1839), daughter of Beverley Chew Stanard and Mary Bolling (Fleming) Stanard; he had three children by his second wife. He died in 1854.

The Beverley Family, pp. 740, 743; Virginia Museum of Fine Arts, *An Exhibition of Virginia Miniatures* (Richmond, 1941), p. 43, item 278; *VMHB* 64 (1956): 238.

ARTIST UNIDENTIFIED

Miniature on ivory: 2¼ x 2 in. (5.7 x 5.1 cm.) (oval)

Presented in 1955 by Ellen Beverley Wooldridge of Richmond. Por955.4

Wormeley Portraits

This chart shows the relationship of members of the Wormeley family depicted in portraits owned by the Virginia Historical Society. Subjects of the Society's portraits are indicated in italics.

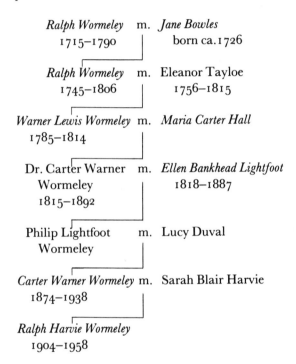

Ralph Wormeley   m.   *Jane Bowles*
1715–1790   born ca.1726

Ralph Wormeley   m.   Eleanor Tayloe
1745–1806   1756–1815

Warner Lewis Wormeley   m.   *Maria Carter Hall*
1785–1814

Dr. Carter Warner   m.   *Ellen Bankhead Lightfoot*
Wormeley   1818–1887
1815–1892

Philip Lightfoot   m.   Lucy Duval
Wormeley

Carter Warner Wormeley   m.   Sarah Blair Harvie
1874–1938

Ralph Harvie Wormeley
1904–1958

Carter Warner Wormeley, 1874–1938

Son of Philip Lightfoot Wormeley and Lucy (Duval) Wormeley, the subject was born in Richmond on October 12, 1874. After working briefly with the Virginia-Carolina Chemical Company in Alabama, he returned to Richmond where he turned to journalism, first with the *Richmond Journal*, later, for about ten years, with the Richmond *News-Leader*. Around 1923 he became director of advertising and publicity for the Commonwealth of Virginia. His sprightly newspaper column, "Assembly Spotlight," and his verse-portraits of public figures were widely read and admired in the state; in 1936 his friends in the

General Assembly voted him Virginia's official "poet laureate," by act of the legislature. "Bishop" Wormeley, as he was called, "knew everybody of consequence in Virginia, was witty at the expense of most of them, and probably never made an enemy in the lot." He died on August 24, 1938, survived by his wife, Sarah Blair (Harvie) Wormeley, and a son, Ralph Harvie Wormeley (q.v.).

Richmond Times-Dispatch, Aug. 25, 1938; VHS Mss1 W8945b 1124–1128. See chart on Wormeley Portraits for relationships.

BY ELLIS MEYER SILVETTE. Signed

Oil on canvasboard: 20 x 16 in. (50.8 x 40.6 cm.)

Received in 1958 from the estates of Carter Warner Wormeley and Ralph Harvie Wormeley of Richmond. Por958.31

Ellen Bankhead (Lightfoot) Wormeley, 1818–1887 (Mrs. Carter Warner Wormeley)

Daughter of Philip and Sally Sevigné (Bernard) Lightfoot of Port Royal, the subject was born on May 29, 1818. She married on October 5, 1836, Dr. Carter Warner Wormeley (1815–1892), son of Warner Lewis Wormeley and Maria Carter (Hall) Wormeley (qq.v.). The couple resided at Manskin Lodge, King William County, where they raised a family of nine children. Her husband was an ardent supporter of the Confederacy and, although a civilian, spent some time in Northern prisons. Mrs. Wormeley died on June 7, 1887.

Merrow Egerton Sorley, *Lewis of Warner Hall: The History of a Family* (Columbia, Mo., 1937), pp. 278, 281; VHS Mss1 W8945b 1120–1123; *VMHB* 37 (1929): 84 and 67 (1959): 234. See chart on Wormeley Portraits for relationships.

ARTIST UNIDENTIFIED

Oil on canvas: 30¼ x 25 in. (76.8 x 63.5 cm.)

Received in 1958 from the estates of Carter Warner Wormeley and Ralph Harvie Wormeley of Richmond. Por958.33

Ralph Wormeley, 1715–1790
Jane (Bowles) Wormeley, born ca. 1726 (Mrs. Ralph Wormeley)

Son of John and Elizabeth Wormeley of Rosegill, Middlesex County, Ralph Wormeley was born on October 5, 1715, and received his formal education in England. He represented Middlesex County in the House of Burgesses between 1742 and 1764.

Ralph Wormeley, 1715–1790 (Portrait I)

Jane (Bowles) Wormeley

During the American Revolution his sympathies were probably with Britain, but he remained discreetly quiet during the hostilities. In June 1781 Rosegill was attacked by a tory privateer; the estate was robbed of thirty-six slaves and much valuable property. Wormeley died on August 19, 1790. He was twice married: first, on November 4, 1736, to Sarah Berkeley, daughter of Edmund Berkeley of Barn Elms, Middlesex County, after whose death, on December 2, 1741, he married as his second wife, Jane Bowles, daughter of James Bowles of Maryland. He had one daughter by his first marriage and six children by his second; his eldest son, Ralph Wormeley (1745–1806) (q.v.), inherited Rosegill and is represented in the Society's portrait collection.

VMHB 36 (1928): 385–87 (Portrait II reproduced) and 67 (1959): 234; Frances Berkeley Young, *The Berkeleys of Barn Elms* (Hamden, Conn., 1964), p. 35. See chart on Wormeley Portraits for relationships.

Portrait I. Ralph Wormeley

BY JOHN WOLLASTON

Oil on canvas: 50 x 40 in. (127 x 101.6 cm.)

Deposited in 1951 by John Chauncey Williams of Fauquier County; presented in 1958 by the estate of John Chauncey Williams. Por951.20

Portrait II. Ralph Wormeley

ATTRIBUTED TO JOHN WOLLASTON

Oil on canvas: 30 x 24³/4 in. (76.2 x 62.9 cm.)

Presented in 1958 by the estates of Carter Warner

Wormeley and Ralph Harvie Wormeley of Richmond. Por958.28

This portrait, thought to be by Wollaston, is a bust-length version of his three-quarter-length portrait (Portrait I).

Portrait III. Jane (Bowles) Wormeley

BY JOHN WOLLASTON

Oil on canvas: 50 x 40 in. (127 x 101.6 cm.)

Deposited in 1951 by John Chauncey Williams of Fauquier County; presented in 1958 by the estate of John Chauncey Williams. Por951.21

Ralph Wormeley, 1745–1806

Ralph Wormeley, fifth of the name in Virginia, was born in April 1745, son of Ralph and Jane (Bowles) Wormeley (qq.v.) of Rosegill, Middlesex County. He was sent to England for his formal education, entering Eton on September 12, 1757, and later studying at Trinity Hall, Cambridge. He returned to Virginia in 1765 and in 1771 was appointed to the colonial Council, holding that appointment until the outbreak of the American Revolution. Because of his loyalist sympathies, he was confined for a time to his father's lands in Berkeley and Frederick counties and was required to post a large bond of security; in 1778, however, he was permitted to return to Rosegill, where he remained until the war's end. He

26. Ralph Wormeley, 1745–1806 (Portrait I)

represented Middlesex County in the House of Delegates for the sessions of 1788, 1789, and 1790 and was a delegate to the Convention of 1788. After his father's death in 1790 he inherited Rosegill and a large estate. A man of academic tastes, he assembled a large library, many volumes from which are now in the collection of the Virginia Historical Society. He died on January 19, 1806. On November 19, 1772, he married Eleanor Tayloe, daughter of John Tayloe of Mount Airy, Richmond County; she bore him seven children.

VMHB 18 (1910): 373–75, 37 (1929): 82–84, 66 (1958): 237, and 67 (1959): 234; *Antiques* 116 (1979): 1133 (Portrait I reproduced). See chart on Wormeley Portraits for relationships.

Portrait I   *See* Plate 26

By ROBERT EDGE PINE. Signed. Dated 1763

Oil on canvas: 50 x 40 in. (127 x 101.6 cm.)

Deposited in 1951 by John Chauncey Williams of Fauquier County; presented in 1957 by the estate of John Chauncey Williams. Por951.22

Portrait II

By JOHN WOLLASTON. Ca.1755

Oil on canvas: 26¼ x 25¼ in. (66.7 x 64.1 cm.)

Presented in 1958 by the estates of Carter Warner Wormeley and Ralph Harvie Wormeley of Richmond. Por958.30

The society acquired, along with the portrait, the velvet jacket in which the youthful subject is depicted.

Ralph Harvie Wormeley, 1904–1958

The subject was born on May 16, 1904, son of Carter Warner Wormeley (q.v.) and Sarah Blair (Harvie) Wormeley. He resided in Richmond and was employed by the Chesapeake and Ohio Railway Company as a claims examiner. He died on May 27, 1958, survived by his mother and by his wife, Belle (Sturman) Wormeley; he is buried in Hollywood Cemetery.

Richmond Times-Dispatch, May 28, 1958, p. 6; VHS Mss1 W8945b 525–529. See chart on Wormeley Portraits for relationships.

By ANNE FLETCHER. Ca. 1914

Oil on canvas: 20 x 16 in. (50.8 x 40.6 cm.)

Received in 1958 from the estates of Carter Warner Wormeley and Ralph Harvie Wormeley of Richmond. Por958.32

The subject is shown as a child about ten years of age.

Warner Lewis Wormeley, 1785–1814
Maria Carter (Hall) Wormeley (Mrs. Warner Lewis Wormeley)

Born at Rosegill, Middlesex County, on March 24, 1785, son of Ralph Wormeley (q.v.) and Eleanor (Tayloe) Wormeley, the subject was the last of his line to be educated in England and to reside at Rosegill. He died on December 31, 1814, at twenty-nine years of age. His wife, whom he married on December 3, 1807, was Maria Carter (Hall) Wormeley, daughter of Elisha and Caroline (Carter) Hall of Fredericksburg; she bore her husband four children. On November 25, 1819, she married, as her second husband, James H. Caldwell, a manager of theaters in Virginia and Louisiana, by whom she had three children.

Virginia Historical Portraiture, pp. 344–46 (Portrait I reproduced); *VMHB* 37 (1929): 84 and 68 (1960): 243; *W. & M. Quart.*, 1st ser., 22 (1913–14): 137. See chart on Wormeley Portraits for relationships.

Portrait I. Warner Lewis Wormeley

ARTIST UNIDENTIFIED

Oil on canvas: 40¾ x 32 in. (103.5 x 81.3 cm.)

Received in 1958 from the estates of Carter Warner Wormeley and Ralph Harvie Wormeley of Richmond. Por958.29

Warner Lewis Wormeley (Portrait II)

Portrait II. Warner Lewis Wormeley

ATTRIBUTED TO JAMES PEALE

Miniature on ivory: 3 x 2 1/2 in. (7.6 x 6.4 cm.) (oval)

Received in 1959 from the estates of Carter Warner Wormeley and Ralph Harvie Wormeley of Richmond. Por959.5

Portrait III. Maria Carter (Hall) Wormeley

ARTIST UNIDENTIFIED

Miniature on ivory: 2 3/4 x 2 1/4 in. (7 x 5.7 cm.) (oval)

Received in 1959 from the estates of Carter Warner Wormeley and Ralph Harvie Wormeley of Richmond. Por959.6

David Minton Wright, 1809–1863
Penelope Margaret (Creecy) Wright, 1816–1889 (Mrs. David Minton Wright)

David Minton Wright, youngest son of David and Mary (Armistead) Wright of Nansemond County, was born on April 21, 1809. He received his early education at Captain Patrick's Military Academy in Middletown, Connecticut, studied medicine under Dr. William Warren of Edenton, North Carolina, and graduated from the University of Pennsylvania. On April 21, 1833, he married Penelope Margaret Creecy, born July 11, 1816, daughter of Joshua Skinner Creecy (q.v.) and Mary (Benbury) Creecy of Edenton, North Carolina. The couple resided in Norfolk, where Dr. Wright earned a distinguished reputation for the zeal with which he practiced his profession and for his service during the yellow fever epidemic of 1855. During the Federal occupation of Norfolk, Dr. Wright, a noncombatant, shot and killed a Union officer; passions ran high during the trial, for it was felt that there had been ample provocation for the shooting. The verdict, however, was a foregone conclusion; Dr. Wright was executed by the military authorities on October 23, 1863. Dr. and Mrs. Wright had nine children; their eldest daughter, Penelope, married the Reverend Alexander Watson Weddell (qq.v.). Mrs. Wright died in Norfolk on May 11, 1889.

Virginia House, pp. 50, 68; Virginia Armistead Garber, *The Armistead Family, 1635–1910* (Richmond, 1910), pp. 249–56.

Portrait I. David Minton Wright

BY WILLIAM GARL BROWN. 1866

Oil on canvas: 27 1/4 x 22 in. (69.2 x 55.9 cm.). Inscribed on the back: "Wm. Garle Browne Pinx A.D. 1866."

Received in 1948 as a bequest of Mr. and Mrs. Alexander Wilbourne Weddell of Richmond. Por948.59

Portrait II. David Minton Wright

COPIED BY ADELE WILLIAMS. 1929

Oil on canvas: 30 x 25 in. (76.2 x 63.5 cm.) (oval)

Received in 1948 as a bequest of Mr. and Mrs. Alexander Wilbourne Weddell of Richmond. Por948.85

The portrait is copied from a miniature. Portrait IV is its companion.

Portrait III. Penelope Margaret (Creecy) Wright

ARTIST UNIDENTIFIED. 1833

Miniature on ivory: 2 3/4 x 2 1/4 in. (7 x 5.7 cm.) (oval)

Received in 1948 as a bequest of Mr. and Mrs. Alexander Wilbourne Weddell of Richmond. Por948.31

It is stated in Garber's work that "the Weddells have lovely miniatures of David Minton Wright and his beautiful wife, Penelope Creecy, painted for each other when he was a medical student in Philadelphia and she was seventeen." The miniature of David Wright has not been found; it is assumed, however, that Portrait II was copied from it.

Virginia Armistead Garber, *The Armistead Family, 1635–1910* (Richmond, 1910), p. 249.

Portrait IV. Penelope Margaret (Creecy) Wright

COPIED BY ADELE WILLIAMS. 1929

Oil on canvas: 30 x 25 in. (76.2 x 63.5 cm.) (oval)

David Minton Wright (Portrait I)

Received in 1948 as a bequest of Mr. and Mrs. Alexander Wilbourne Weddell of Richmond. Por948.84

This portrait is copied from Portrait III; its companion is Portrait II.

Jordan Armistead Wright, 1808–1834

The third son of David and Mary (Armistead) Wright of Nansemond County, the subject was born on November 5, 1808 (a second source, Garber, gives 1802). On July 16, 1832, he married Harriet Eliza Pugh; one daughter was born of the union. He died at the early age of twenty-six on August 1, 1834. Family tradition asserts that General Lafayette, who met young Wright on his visit to Norfolk in 1824, pronounced him the handsomest man he had encountered in America. Whether or not the Society's miniature portrait of Wright substantiates this view is a matter of opinion.

Virginia Historical Portraiture, pp. 390–91 (portrait reproduced); Virginia Armistead Garber, *The Armistead Family, 1635–1910* (Richmond, 1910), pp. 249, 256–57.

ARTIST UNIDENTIFIED

Miniature on ivory: 3¼ x 2½ in. (8.3 x 6.4 cm.) (oval)

Received in 1948 as a bequest of Mr. and Mrs. Alexander Wilbourne Weddell of Richmond. Por948.32

Jordan Armistead Wright

Marcus Joseph Wright, 1831–1922

Marcus Joseph Wright, Confederate general and editor of Confederate archives, was born in Purdy, Tennessee, on June 5, 1831, the son of Benjamin and Martha Ann (Hicks) Harwell Wright. He studied law and became clerk of the common law and chancery court in Memphis. As lieutenant colonel of the 154th Tennessee Militia Regiment, he entered Confederate service with this unit in April 1861; after acting as military governor of Columbus, Kentucky, and seeing action at Belmont and Shiloh, he was promoted to brigadier general on December 13, 1862. He led his brigade at Chickamauga and in the Chattanooga campaign and was active in the defense of Atlanta; early in 1865 he was assigned to command the District of North Mississippi and West Tennessee. After the war he resumed his law practice in Memphis, serving also as assistant purser of the United States Navy Yard. On July 1, 1878, General Wright was appointed agent for the collection of Confederate archives, an enormous task to which he devoted himself for almost forty years, until his retirement in June 1917. During the same period he published books and pamphlets and contributed articles to periodical publications. His work was a substantial aid to the War Department in its preparation of the monumental series (128 volumes) *The War of the Rebellion: A Compilation of the Official Records of the Union and Confederate Armies* (1880–1901). He died in Washington, D.C., on December 27, 1922, and is buried in Arlington Cemetery. General Wright was twice married: first to Martha Spencer Elcan of Memphis; second to Pauline Womack of Alabama; he was survived by his second wife and by four of his five children. General Wright became a member of the Virginia Historical Society in 1894.

DAB; *Generals in Gray*; *Biographic Catalogue*.

ARTIST UNIDENTIFIED

Oil on canvas: 30 x 25 in. (76.2 x 63.5 cm.)

Presented to the R. E. Lee Camp, Confederate Veterans, in 1915; acquired by the Virginia Historical Society in 1946 through merger with the Confederate Memorial Association. Por946.108

Penelope Margaret Wright, 1840–1901
See Alexander Watson Weddell, 1841–1883

Stephen Wright, 1763–1851

Born in Norfolk County on December 24, 1763, the subject was the son of Captain Nathaniel Wright and Ann (Phripp) Wright. In 1780 he participated in the defense of Norfolk, Portsmouth, and the adjacent area, and the following year he was present at the surrender of Cornwallis at Yorktown. Shortly thereafter he sailed for the West Indies aboard the ship *Scorpion*; it was captured by the British, and Wright and the ship's officers were incarcerated in a prison ship in Bermuda until 1783. After his return to Norfolk he married, on June 18, 1795, Abba Connor, daughter of Colonel Charles Connor; the couple resided on Craney Island, Norfolk County, and later in the borough of Norfolk. Wright was for many years the presiding justice of the county court and colonel of the county militia. He died on December 25, 1851.

Portraiture, pp. 124–26 (silhouette reproduced); *American Beacon* (Norfolk), Dec. 27, 1851, p. 2, col. 1; *VMHB* 53 (1945): 149 and 54 (1946): 172.

Stephen Wright

ARTIST UNIDENTIFIED

Silhouette: 9 in. (22.9 cm.) in height, mounted on paper 11 x 8 in. (27.9 x 20.3 cm.)

Presented in 1945 by Elizabeth Wright Weddell of Richmond, a great-great-great-niece of the subject. Por945.14

The subject's name is inscribed below the silhouette.

268

George Wythe, 1726–1806

Professor of law and signer of the Declaration of Independence, George Wythe, a native of Elizabeth City County, was born in 1726, son of Thomas and Margaret (Walker) Wythe. Left an orphan at an early age, he received little formal education; he studied law and in 1746 was admitted to the bar in Spotsylvania County. Entering politics as a member of the House of Burgesses, Wythe represented Williamsburg 1754–55, the College of William and Mary 1758–61, and Elizabeth City County 1761–68. He was mayor of Williamsburg in 1768 and became clerk of the House of Burgesses the following year, retaining the office until 1775. As a delegate to the Continental Congress he supported the resolutions for independence and was one of the Virginia signers of the Declaration of Independence. With Jefferson and Pendleton he was charged with revising the laws of the Commonwealth; he was Speaker of the House of Delegates 1777–78 and in 1778 became one of the three judges on the High Court of Chancery. When the board of visitors of the College of William and Mary established a professorship of law in 1779, the first chair of law in an American college, Wythe was invited to accept the post; he held the professorship until 1790, exercising during those years an important influence on the development of jurisprudence in the nation. He was a delegate to the convention to ratify the federal Constitution in 1788 and the same year was made sole chancellor of the state, holding that office until 1801 when three districts were formed; thereafter he presided over the Richmond district. A resident of Richmond during the last years of his life, he died there on June 8, 1806, poisoned, it is thought, by his great-nephew George Wythe Sweeney, the principal beneficiary of his will. Wythe survived long enough to disinherit his murderer, but in the trial that followed Sweeney was acquitted for lack of evidence. Wythe married, first, on December 26, 1747, Ann Lewis, daughter of Zachary and Mary (Waller) Lewis of Spotsylvania County, who died the next year; he married, second, in 1755, Elizabeth Taliaferro, daughter of Richard and Elizabeth (Eggleston) Taliaferro of Williamsburg and James City County. He survived his second wife by nineteen years; their only child died in infancy.

DAB; *Portraiture*, pp. 108–10; Edward Griffith Dodson, *Speakers and Clerks of the Virginia House of Delegates, 1776–1955* (Richmond, 1956), p. 13; *VMHB* 48 (1940): 80.

COPIED BY EUGENIE DELAND SAUGSTAD. Signed

Oil on canvas: 19½ x 13½ in. (49.5 x 34.3 cm.) (oval)

Presented by the artist in 1939. Por939.11

John Trumbull's group portrait *The Declaration of*

Independence at the Yale University Art Gallery includes, at the extreme left, a portrait of Wythe. The Society's portrait is a copy of J. F. Wear's copy of Trumbull's original likeness. Another portrait of Wythe by Mrs. Saugstad is owned by the Commonwealth of Virginia.

William Hugh Young, 1838–1901

Born in Booneville, Missouri, on January 1, 1838, son of Hugh F. Young, a native of Augusta County, Virginia, Young removed to Texas with his parents as a child. He attended Washington College in Tennessee, McKenzie College in Texas, and the University of Virginia 1859–61. Returning to Texas in the late summer of 1861, he raised a company which became a part of the 9th Texas Infantry; after Shiloh he was made colonel of the regiment and thereafter led his command at Perryville, Murfreesboro, Vicksburg, Chickamauga, and the Atlanta campaign. Promoted to brigadier general on August 15, 1864, he saw action during the evacuation of Atlanta; at Allatoona, Georgia, he was wounded and taken prisoner. Confined in hospitals and in Johnson's Island prison, he was not released until July 25, 1865. After the war he resided in San Antonio, Texas, where he engaged in the practice of law and the real estate business; he died there on November 28, 1901, and is buried in the Confederate Cemetery.

Generals in Gray; *Confederate Military History*, 11: 266–67; *Biographic Catalogue* (Addenda).

BY ELLIS MEYER SILVETTE. Signed

Oil on canvas: 33 x 27¼ in. (83.8 x 69.2 cm.). Inscribed on the back: biographical information about the subject and "Painted by Ellis M. Silvette at Richmond, Va. from a daguerre type."

Acquired in 1946 through merger with the Confederate Memorial Association. Por946.163

Felix Kirk Zollicoffer, 1812–1862

General Zollicoffer was born in Maury County, Tennessee, on May 19, 1812, son of John Jacob Zollicoffer and Martha (Kirk) Zollicoffer. He attended Jackson College, Columbia, Tennessee, for one year, then at sixteen years of age embarked on a career in journalism, entering a newspaper office in Paris, Tennessee. In 1834 he became editor of the Columbia *Observer* and the following year was ap-

pointed official printer to the state; during the Seminole War of 1836 he served as a lieutenant. Zollicoffer's political influence was greatly increased by his appointment in 1842 to the editorial staff of the Nashville *Republican Banner*; he served as adjutant general and state comptroller 1845–49 and senator in the state legislature 1849–52. He was appointed editor of the *Republican Banner* in 1850 and was instrumental in securing Tennessee for the Whig candidate, General Winfield Scott (q.v.), in the presidential campaign of 1852. Himself a successful candidate for the United States Congress, he represented his district in Washington 1853–59. He was a member of the Washington peace conference in 1861, but on the outbreak of hostilities accepted a commission as brigadier general in the Confederate army. In command of East Tennessee, he moved his army to Mill Spring, Kentucky, late in 1861; he was killed in action at Fishing Creek, Kentucky, on January 19, 1862. General Zollicoffer's wife, Louisa Pocahontas (Gordon) Zollicoffer, bore him eleven children, five of whom died in infancy.

DAB; *Generals in Gray*; *Biographical Directory*; *Biographic Catalogue*.

BY CORNELIUS HANKINS. Signed. Dated 1929

Oil on canvas: 30 x 25¼ in. (76.2 x 64.1 cm.)

Acquired in 1946 through merger with the Confederate Memorial Association. Por946.185

Unidentified Colonial Gentleman

The donor of this handsome eighteenth-century portrait identified the subject as "Governor Johnson of Virginia." Since Virginia had no governor of that name during the colonial period, the identity of the subject remains a mystery. The portrait, however, is almost certainly the work of Charles Bridges, the English artist who painted in Virginia between 1735 and 1745, and for that reason is appropriately retained in the collection of the Virginia Historical Society despite the anonymity of the subject.

Graham Hood, *Charles Bridges and William Dering, Two Virginia Painters, 1735–1750* (Charlottesville, Va., 1978), pp. 78–79 (portrait reproduced); *Portraiture*, pp. 110–11; VHS Archives, liber A7, pp. 265–66.

BY CHARLES BRIDGES. Ca. 1740

Oil on canvas: 29 x 24½ in. (73.7 x 62.2 cm.)

Presented in 1929 by Herbert L. Pratt of New York City. PorX252

The Battle Abbey Murals: The Four Seasons of the Confederacy

By CHARLES HOFFBAUER. Signed.
Dated 1913–1920

The headquarters building of the Virginia Historical Society is a large neoclassical building situated on the Boulevard in the near west end of Richmond. The building was constructed in 1912–13 by the Confederate Memorial Association in memory of those who had died for the Confederate cause. Just as the fallen soldiers of William the Conqueror's army had been honored at Battle Abbey in southern England, so, according to the Association's spokesmen, the Confederate dead were to be honored at Richmond's Battle Abbey. Although the building was never intended to be a place of religious pilgrimage, as was the original, the name Battle Abbey persisted, and remains to this day the building's accepted though still unofficial designation. Soon after the completion of the building, a French artist, Charles Hoffbauer, was commissioned to execute a series of murals for the building's south gallery. Interrupted in his labors by the outbreak of World War I, Hoffbauer hastened to France where he served throughout the war as a private in the trenches. Following the armistice, Hoffbauer returned to Richmond and, to the amazement of the Association's officials, obliterated all traces of his earlier work, explaining that his view of warfare was now quite different as a result of his front-line experiences. His new murals, representing *The Four Seasons of the Confederacy*, were unveiled on the last day of January 1921. Battle Abbey housed, in addition to Hoffbauer's murals, a collection of captured Confederate battle flags returned by the United States War Department, the extensive portrait collection assembled by the R. E. Lee Camp, Confederate Veterans, and much later, the Richard D. Steuart collection of Confederate weapons and military equipment. In the early 1940s the Association's dwindling membership produced grave financial difficulties. These were resolved in 1946 by an agreement whereby Battle Abbey and its collections passed into the custody of the Virginia Historical Society. A decade later a large addition to the building was constructed to house the Society's administrative offices, library, and galleries. The building, still popularly referred to as Battle Abbey, has been the headquarters of the Virginia Historical Society since 1959.

THE SPRING MURAL

The Spring Mural depicts Thomas Jonathan ("Stonewall") Jackson (q.v.) reviewing his troops at an undesignated place in the Shenandoah Valley.

THE SUMMER MURAL   *See* Plate 27

This mural, which confronts the visitor as he enters the gallery, is the dominant composition in the series. Although no such meeting of Confederate commanders ever took place, Hoffbauer succeeded in creating a striking group portrait in which every likeness bears the stamp of authenticity. The officers in the group are, left to right: John Bell Hood (q.v.), Wade Hampton (q.v.), Richard Stoddert Ewell (q.v.), and John Brown Gordon (q.v.); Thomas Jonathan ("Stonewall") Jackson (q.v.) and Fitzhugh Lee (q.v.), both on horseback; Ambrose Powell Hill (q.v.), standing with hands on his sword hilt; Robert E. Lee (q.v.), the central figure, with James Longstreet holding binoculars, on his other side; Joseph Eggleston Johnston (q.v.), George Edward Pickett (q.v.), and Pierre G. T. Beauregard (q.v.), all mounted, and James Ewell Brown ("Jeb") Stuart (q.v.), leaning against his mount.

THE AUTUMN MURAL

James Ewell Brown ("Jeb") Stuart (q.v.) is portrayed in the Autumn Mural leading his cavalrymen on a foray through the Virginia woods.

THE WINTER MURAL

The Winter Mural, in stark contrast to the group portrait of Lee and his commanders, depicts the misery of an artillery battery in retreat through the snow, its equipment shattered, its men on the verge of exhaustion. There is no identifiable portrait in the mural.

FLANKING PANELS

The panel at the left of the Spring Mural depicts the naval engagement between the Confederate ram *Virginia-Merrimack* and the Federal ships *Cumberland* and *Congress*. The panel at the right shows the arrival of a hospital train. The figure in the foreground is a portrait of the sculptor Edward Virginius Valentine. The Autumn Mural is flanked at the left by a panel showing John S. Mosby (q.v.) on a midnight raid and on the right by a panel entitled *The Coast Artillery, Confederate Marines*.

27. The Battle Abbey Murals. The Summer Mural

The Convention of 1829–30

By George Catlin. 1829–30   *See* Plate 28

Oil on panel: 24½ x 33 in. (62.2 x 83.8 cm.)

Acquired in 1957. Pic957.39

During the winter of 1829–30 Richmond was crowded with a host of political luminaries, come to take part in a convention to revise the state constitution. Also in the capital were such artists as Chester Harding, Robert Matthew Sully, James W. Ford, and George Catlin, eager to execute portraits of the delegates and well aware that this would probably be the last meeting of the political giants of an earlier generation—Madison, Monroe, and Marshall. George Catlin, who later achieved fame as a painter of the Indians of western America, resolved to record the likenesses of all the delegates in a single composition, a painting he intended to have engraved and, as a print, to distribute widely and profitably. To this end he issued invitations to the delegates "to call . . . at my painting Room at Mrs. Duval's and allow me to make a sketch of your head for my picture of the Convention."[1] In due course Catlin completed a preliminary watercolor study, copied the composition onto a wooden panel, and prepared a pen-and-ink key identifying each of the 101 figures in the painting. The proposed engraving, however, was never published. Both the watercolor study and the pen-and-ink key eventually found their way into the collection of the New-York Historical Society. The panel painting, after passing through many hands and twice crossing the Atlantic, came into the custody of the Virginia Historical Society in 1949 and became its property in 1957. Despite the opinion of one writer that "Catlin made that august convention a crowded parliament of gnomes with huge heads and warped dwarf bodies,"[2] his miniature portraits are in fact accurate likenesses, painted from individual life studies. Of many of the delegates his miniatures are the only surviving portraits.

1. VHS Mss1 H7185a 941–942. 2. Loyd Haberly, *Pursuit of the Horizon: A Life of George Catlin* (New York, 1948), p. 34.

Occasional Bulletin, no. 23 (1971): 11–15 (painting reproduced); *New-York Historical Society Quarterly* 32 (1948): 69–77 (watercolor and key reproduced); *Antiques* 116 (1979): 1128 (painting reproduced).

Alphabetical list of persons depicted in *The Convention of 1829–30*

Mark Alexander (5)
William Anderson (82)
Briscoe Gerard Baldwin (87)
John Strode Barbour (8)
Philip Pendleton Barbour (19)
Fleming Bates (94)
John Baxter (85)
Thomas M. Bayly (90)
Andrew Beirne (79)
Elisha Boyd (27)
Samuel Branch (29)
—— Briggs (100)
William H. Brodnax (71)
William Byars (43)
Benjamin William Sheridan Cabell (31)
Alexander Campbell (80)
Edward Campbell (96)
William Campbell (58)
Henley Chapman (75)
Augustine Claiborne (38)
Samuel Claytor (32)
John Bacon Clopton (59)
Gordon Cloyd (49)
John Coalter (30)
Samuel Coffman (83)
John Rogers Cooke (78)
Philip Doddridge (15)
William Donaldson (65)
George Coke Dromgoole (68)
Edwin Steele Duncan (73)
William Henry Fitzhugh (10)
James Mercer Garnett (21)
John B. George (70)
William Branch Giles (3)

William Osborne Goode (23)
William Fitzhugh Gordon (28)
John Williams Green (86)
Thomas Griggs, Jr. (74)
Hugh Blair Grigsby (62)
Peachy Harrison (53)
Richard H. Henderson (77)
Waller Holladay (54)
Chapman Johnson (17)
John Winston Jones (60)
Thomas Robinson Joynes (56)
John Laidley (47)
Benjamin Watkins Leigh (35)
William Leigh (63)
Richard Logan (7)
George Loyall (61)
William McCoy (50)
Andrew McMillan (42)
John Macrae (26)
James Madison (2)
John Marshall (20)
Joseph Martin (89)
John Young Mason (6)
Thomas Massie, Jr. (25)
John P. Mathews (13)
Charles Fenton Mercer (9)
Fleming Bowyer Miller (24)
James Monroe (1)
Richard Channing Moore (97)
Samuel McDowell Moore (92)
Charles Stephen Morgan (81)
Richard Morris (33)
William Naylor (51)
Augustine Neale (67)

Philip Norborne Nicholas (91)
William Oglesby (76)
Hierome L. Opie (57)
Philip Clayton Pendleton (11)
William K. Perrin (39)
James Pleasants (93)
John Hampden Pleasants (98)
Alfred Harrison Powell (55)
Joseph Prentis (64)
John Randolph (34)
Thomas Ritchie (99)
John Roane (4)
Alexander F. Rose (95)
James Saunders (72)
John Scott (40)
Adam See (14)
William Smith (66)
Robert Stanard (44)
—— Stansbury (101)
Archibald Stuart (12)
Lewis Summers (22)
Samuel Taylor (46)
William Penn Taylor (69)
Littleton Waller Tazewell (16)
Lucas Powell Thompson (48)
George Townes (88)
James Trezvant (36)
John Tyler (52)
Abel Parker Upshur (45)
John Urquart (37)
Richard N. Venable (18)
Jacob Williamson (84)
Eugenius M. Wilson (41)

Numerical list of persons depicted in *The Convention of 1829–30*

1. James Monroe, 1758–1831
2. James Madison, 1751–1836
3. William Branch Giles, 1762–1830
4. John Roane, 1766–1838
5. Mark Alexander, 1792–1883
6. John Young Mason, 1799–1859
7. Richard Logan, 1789?–1869
8. John Strode Barbour, 1790–1855
9. Charles Fenton Mercer, 1778–1858
10. William Henry Fitzhugh, 1792–1830
11. Philip Clayton Pendleton, 1779–1863
12. Archibald Stuart, 1795–1855
13. John P. Mathews
14. Adam See, b.1764
15. Philip Doddridge, 1773–1832
16. Littleton Waller Tazewell, 1774–1860
17. Chapman Johnson, 1779–1849

18. Richard N. Venable, 1763–1838
19. Philip Pendleton Barbour, 1783–1841
20. John Marshall, 1755–1835
21. James Mercer Garnett, 1770–1843
22. Lewis Summers, 1778–1843
23. William Osborne Goode, 1798–1859
24. Fleming Bowyer Miller, 1793–1874
25. Thomas Massie, Jr., 1783–1864
26. John Macrae, 1791–1830
27. Elisha Boyd, 1767–1841
28. William Fitzhugh Gordon, 1787–1858
29. Samuel Branch, d.1847
30. John Coalter, 1769–1838
31. Benjamin William Sheridan Cabell, 1793–1862
32. Samuel Claytor
33. Richard Morris, 1778–1833

70. John B. George, 1795?–1854
71. William H. Brodnax, 1786–1834
72. James Saunders
73. Edwin Steele Duncan, 1789–1858
74. Thomas Griggs, Jr., 1780–1860
75. Henley Chapman, 1779–1864
76. William Oglesby
77. Richard H. Henderson, 1781–1841
78. John Rogers Cooke, 1788–1854
79. Andrew Beirne, 1771–1845
80. Alexander Campbell, 1786–1866
81. Charles Stephen Morgan, 1799–1859
82. William Anderson, b.1788
83. Samuel Coffman
84. Jacob Williamson
85. John Baxter

86. John Williams Green, 1781–1834
87. Briscoe Gerard Baldwin, 1789–1852
88. George Townes, 1791–1861
89. Joseph Martin, 1785–1850
90. Thomas M. Bayly, 1775–1834
91. Philip Norborne Nicholas, 1776–1849
92. Samuel McDowell Moore, 1796–1875
93. James Pleasants, 1769–1839
94. Fleming Bates, 1778–1831
95. Alexander F. Rose
96. Edwin Campbell, born ca.1785
97. Richard Channing Moore, 1762–1841
98. John Hampden Pleasants, 1797–1846
99. Thomas Ritchie, 1778–1854
100. —— Briggs
101. —— Stansbury

274

28. Convention of 1829–30

INDEX OF ARTISTS
AND THEIR SUBJECTS

The index of artists is arranged alphabetically by the surname of the artist. Under the artist's name are to be found, alphabetically by the subject's surname, the examples of his or her work in the Society's collection. Life dates of subjects appear in the main body of the text; they are supplied in this index only when needed to distinguish between two persons of the same name. A single asterisk (*) preceding a subject's name indicates that the portrait is illustrated in black-and-white; a double asterisk (**) indicates that the illustration is one of the color plates.

Abbot, Scaisbrook Langhorne, 1908–
  *Elizabeth Dabney (Langhorne) Lewis

? Alonzo, C.
  Armistead Churchill Gordon

Alma-Tadema, Sir Lawrence, 1836–1912
  Alfred Tennyson, first Baron Tennyson

Ammen, M.
  *George Edward Pickett

Anderson, ——
  Benjamin Watkins Leigh (Portrait III)

Andrews, Eliphalet Frazer, 1835–1915
  Robert Edward Lee (Portrait II)

Andrews, Marietta (Minnigerode), 1869–1931
    (Mrs. Eliphalet Frazer Andrews)
  *Robert Carter, 1663–1732 (copy of original portrait)
  Burton Norvell Harrison
  Robert Edward Lee (Portrait II)

Augusta, George Victor
  *Samuel Merrifield Bemiss

Bailey, Helen Schuyler (Smith) Hull, 1920–
  Philip Alexander Bruce (copy of original portrait by Pierre
    Troubetzkoy)
  Robert Alexander Lancaster

Banks, James Francis, 1900–
  *John Lamb (copy of original portrait by Charles Hoffbauer)

Barlow, Florence
  John Hunt Morgan

Barney, Alice (Pike), 1860–1931 (Mrs. Albert
    Clifford Barney)
  *Constance (Cary) Harrison (Mrs. Burton Norvell Harrison)

Beale, Mary, 1632–1697
  *Sir Edmund Andros
  **Philadelphia (Pelham) Howard, Lady Howard of Effingham

Beneduce, P.
  *Maggie Lena (Mitchell) Walker (Mrs. Armistead Walker)

Bennett, J.
  Samuel D. Buck

Bogle, James, ca. 1817–1873
  James Monroe (copy of original portrait by Gilbert Stuart)

Boileau, Philippe, 1864–1917
  *Anne Eliza (Pleasants) Gordon (Mrs. Douglas Hamilton
      Gordon) (Portrait III)
  *Elizabeth Iris Southall (Clarke) Gordon
      (Mrs. Douglas Huntly Gordon) (Portrait IV)

Boteler, Alexander Robinson, 1815–1892
  Thomas Jonathan Jackson (Portrait VII)

Boudon, David, b. 1748
  *David Meade, 1778–1854 (Portrait I) (attributed)

Brewster, George Thomas, 1862–1943
  Rawley White Martin

Bridges, Charles
  Anne (Harrison) Randolph (Mrs. William Randolph)
  Unidentified Colonial Gentleman

Brodnax, John
  Hunter Holmes McGuire (Portrait II)

Brooke, Richard Norris, 1847–1920
  William Henry Fitzhugh Payne

Brown, William Garl, 1823–1894
  **Thomas Jonathan Jackson (Portrait I)
  William Henry Fitzhugh Lee (Portrait II)
  James Weddell
  *David Minton Wright (Portrait I)

Brown, William Henry, 1808–1883
  John Marshall (Portraits II, III)
  Richard Channing Moore (Portrait I)

Bruce, Edward Caledon, 1825–1901
  **Robert Edward Lee (Portrait I)

Bryce, Virginia (Keane), 1861–1935 (Mrs.
    Clarence Archibald Bryce)
  Clarence Archibald Bryce
  Hugh Payne Keane (Portrait II)

Burwell, Mary (Travis), b. 1869 (Mrs. T. Norman
    Burwell)
  George Ainsley Barksdale
  Orren Randolph Smith
  Charles Goodall Snead

Buxbaum, M.
  *Charles Broadway Rouss (Portrait II)

Calverley, Charles, 1833–1914
  George Washington (Portrait IX)

Cardelli, Peter, d. 1822
  *James Madison (Portrait II)

Carlès, Antonin
  Amélie Louise (Rives) Chanler Troubetzkoy, Princess Pierre
    Troubetzkoy (Portrait I)

Carr, Lyell, 1856–1912
  *Henry Alexander Wise

Carregi, I.
  Ellen Anderson Gholson Glasgow (Portrait I)

Carson, Kate Montague
  Theodore Myers Carson

Carter, ——
  David Watson

Cartwright, Isabelle Branson, 1885–
  John Summerfield Griffith (copy of original portrait by
    Miriam Fort Gill)

Catlin, Bessie A.
  Nathaniel Harrison Harris

Catlin, George, 1796–1872
  **"The Convention of 1829–30"

Charoux, Siegfried Joseph, 1896–1967
  *Nancy Witcher (Langhorne) Shaw Astor, Viscountess Astor
    (Portrait I)

Chefdebien, Louis
  *Jane Byrd Nelson (later Mrs. Francis Walker) (attributed)

Clarke, Carl Dame, 1904–
  Elijah Lewis Clarke
  Charles James Terrell

Coffin, William Haskell, 1876–1925
  James Conner

Cole, Alphaeus Philemon, b. 1876
Alonzo Lafayette Phillips

Cole, Thomas Casilear, 1888–
Walter Herron Taylor

Cooke, George, 1793–1849
**Patrick Henry (Portrait V) (attributed)
*Francis Taliaferro Brooke (attributed)

Copeland, Oliver Perry, 1816–1876?
*Margaret Susan (Prentis) Webb (Mrs. Robert Henning
Webb)
Robert Henning Webb

Corner, Thomas Cromwell, 1865–1938
David Gregg McIntosh

Cox, W. B.
*Robert Edward Lee (Portrait VI) (attributed)

Davidson, Jo 1883–1952
Nancy Witcher (Langhorne) Shaw Astor, Viscountess Astor
(Portrait II)

de Franca, Manuel Joachim, 1808–1865
*Martha Minor (Hall) Scott (Mrs. William Poston Scott)
Mitchell Scott

de Laszlo, Philip A., 1869–1937
**Alexander Wilbourne Weddell (Portrait IV)

DeVallée, Jean François
Maria (Meade) Stith (Mrs. John Stith) (attributed)

Dieterich, Louis P., 1841–1922
Douglas Huntly Gordon (Portrait II)
Anne Campbell (Gordon) Thomas (Mrs. John Hanson
Thomas) (copy of original portrait by William Edward
West)

Dodge, Edward Samuel 1816–1857
Edward R. Chambers (attributed)
Henrietta Lucy Chambers (attributed)
Martha Eppes (Chambers) Laird (Mrs. Thomas Harvey
Laird) (attributed)

Doyle, Alexander, 1857–1922
Robert Edward Lee (Portrait III)

Drummond, Samuel, 1765–1844
Hugh Payne Keane (Portrait I)

Dunlop, Anna Mercer, 1883–
Andrew Meade (copy of original portrait by John Durand)

Durand, John
**Lucy (Randolph) Burwell (Mrs. Lewis Burwell) (attributed)
*Susannah (Stith) Meade (Mrs. Andrew Meade)

Edouart, Auguste, 1789–1861
*Douglas Hamilton Gordon (Portrait I)

Edgerly-Kasybska, Countess
Virginia (Chase) Steedman Weddell (Mrs. Alexander
Wilbourne Weddell) (Portrait VIII)

Elder, John Adams, 1833–1895
Jessup Lightfoot Allen (attributed)
John Allen
*William Allen, 1855–1917
*Lewis Frank Terrell

Everett, Edith (Leeson), 1882–1965 (Mrs. Joseph
William Everett)
Archer Anderson (Portrait I)
**Nancy Witcher (Langhorne) Shaw Astor, Viscountess Astor
(Portrait III)
*George Llewellyn Christian

Ezekiel, Moses Jacob, 1844–1917
Robert Edward Lee (Portrait V)

Fairfax, William Henry, 1804–1837
Octavius Fairfax

Field, Robert, ca. 1769–1819
George Washington Parke Custis (Portrait II)

Fisher, Flavius Joseph, 1832–1905
James Dearing

Fleck, Joseph
Elisha Franklin Paxton

Fletcher, Anne, 1876–1955
John Young Mason (Portrait II) (copy of original portrait by
Thomas Sully)
Pocahontas (Portrait III) (copy of original portrait)
Ralph Harvie Wormeley

Ford, James Westhall, 1805?–1868
*Charles Stephen Morgan (Portrait I)

Forster, John Wycliffe Lowes, 1850–1938
*Archer Anderson (Portrait II)
**Jubal Anderson Early (Portrait II)
Archibald Gracie, 1859–1912

"Fox, Charles J.," see Resnikoff, Irving

Franca, Manuel Joachim de, see de Franca, Manuel
Joachim

Frazee O.,
Jefferson Davis (Portrait II)

Freeman, Lloyd
Turner Ashby
Samuel Horace Hawes

Frymire, Jacob, 1765?–1822
*Ann Mary (Wetzel) Aulick (Mrs. Charles Aulick)

Galt, Alexander, 1827–1863
Sarah Alexander (Seddon) Bruce (Mrs. Charles Bruce)
(Portrait III)
*Ellen Carter (Bruce) Morson (Mrs. James Marion Morson)
(Portraits I, II)

Gibson, Charles Dana, 1867–1944
*Hetty (Cary) Harrison (Mrs. Fairfax Harrison) (Portraits II,
III)

Gilmer, Mary R.
William Claiborne (copy of original portrait)
George Smith Patton
Waller Tazewell Patton

Gould, Walter, 1829–1893
*John Tayloe Lomax

Granbery, George, 1794–1815
John Granbery (Portrait I)
Susanna Butterfield (Stowe) Granbery (Mrs. John
Granbery) (Portrait II)
Two daughters of John and Susanna Granberry (Portraits
III, IV)

Granbery, Virginia
Prudence (Nimmo) Granbery (Mrs. Henry Augustus Thaddeus Granbery)

Günther, John W.
Sir John Randolph (copy of original portrait)
Susanna (Beverley) Randolph (wife of Sir John Randolph) (copy of original portrait)
Robert Benskin Richardson

Gutmann, Bernhard, 1869–1936
Thomas Taylor Munford

Guillaume, Louis Mathieu Didier, 1816–1892
*Frances Augusta (Jessup) Allen (Mrs. William Allen)
William Allen, 1815–1875 (attributed)
George Washington Bolling
*Benjamin Franklin (Portrait I) (copy of original portrait by Charles P. A. Vanloo)
*Thomas Jefferson (Portrait I) (copy of original portrait by Gilbert Stuart)
*George Mason (copy of original portrait)
John Singleton Mosby (Portrait I)
Amélie Louise Rives (later Mrs. Henry Sigourney)
Ella Rives
*Sarah Catherine (Macmurdo) Rives (Mrs. Alfred Landon Rives)
Alexander Hawksley Rutherfoord
*John Williams
Sally Browne (Cocke) Wilson (Mrs. Samuel Mazyck Wilson)

Hallwig, Paul
Annie (Fielding) Early (Mrs. Charles Early)

Hankins, Cornelius, 1863–1946
Matthew Calbraith Butler
Thomas Henry Carter
John Baytop Cary
Nathan Bedford Forrest
John Brown Gordon
William Wirt Henry
Thomas Carmichael Hindman
Bradley Tyler Johnson
Fitzhugh Lee (Portraits I, II)
Hunter Holmes McGuire (Portrait I)
*William Mahone
Dabney Herndon Maury
Young Marshall Moody
*James Ewell Brown Stuart
Robertson Taylor
Williams Carter Wickham
Felix Kirk Zollicoffer

Harding, Chester, 1792–1866
*William Branch Giles (Portrait I)

Hare, Channing Weir, 1899–
*Arthur Graham Glasgow

Harris, Charles X., b. 1856
Christopher Gale (copy of original portrait)
François Joseph Paul, marquis de Grasse-Tilly (copy of original portrait by Jean Baptiste Mauzaisse)
James I, king of England, Scotland, and Ireland (copy of original portrait by Frans Pourbus)
*John Murray, fourth earl of Dunmore (copy of original portrait by Sir Joshua Reynolds)
John Randolph (Portrait III) (copy of original portrait by Gilbert Stuart)
Sir George Somers (copy of original portrait by Paul Van Somer)

Hawley, Margaret Foote, 1880–1963
Alexander Wilbourne Weddell (Portrait II)

Haynes, C. Younglove
Henry Clay

Headley, Samuel Tardrew
Norborne Berkeley, Baron de Botetourt (copy of original portrait)

Healy, George Peter Alexander, 1813–1894
Ellen Elizabeth (O'Neale) Cutts (Mrs. James Madison Cutts) (Portrait III)
*James Madison Cutts (Portraits I, II)
*Rose Adèle (Cutts) Douglas (Mrs. Stephen Arnold Douglas) (Portraits II, III)
*Robert Mercer Taliaferro Hunter
Andrew Stevenson
*Sarah (Coles) Stevenson (Mrs. Andrew Stevenson)

Henderson, David English, 1832–1887
Judith Frances Carter Bassett (later Mrs. Charles Tunis Mitchell)

Herman, H. Starr
David Kirkpatrick Este Bruce (Portrait I)

Hesselius, John, 1728–1778
*Elizabeth (Fitzhugh) Conway (Mrs. Francis Conway)
Henry Fitzhugh, 1614–1664 (copy of original portrait)
*Henry Fitzhugh, 1687–1758
Henry Fitzhugh, 1723–1783
Sarah (Battaile) Fitzhugh (Mrs. Henry Fitzhugh)
*William Fitzhugh (copy of original portrait)
**Grymes Children

Hix, W. P.
Joseph Brevard Kershaw

Hoffbauer, Charles, 1875–1957
**The Battle Abbey Murals

Hoffman, Sam
John Caldwell Calhoun Sanders

Honeywell, Martha Ann
Richard Channing Moore (Portrait II)
Kitty Henry (Scott) Scott (Mrs. Robert W. Scott)
John Ashley Stone

Hubard, William James, 1807–1862
Robert Randolph DuVal (attributed)
Sallie Dandridge (Cooke) DuVal (Mrs. Robert Randolph DuVal) (attributed)
India Charlotte (Goddin) Hallowell (Mrs. Joshua C. Hallowell) (attributed)
Joshua C. Hallowell (attributed)
Helen (Calvert) Maxwell Read (Mrs. John K. Read)
Frances Fielding (Lewis) Taylor (Mrs. Archibald Taylor)

Hudson, Thomas, 1701–1779
**Robert Carter, 1728–1804 (attributed)

Ingham, Charles Cromwell 1796–1863
*Virginia (Randolph) Cary (Mrs. Wilson Jefferson Cary)

Jackson, ——
William Logan Dunn

Jarvis, John Wesley, 1781–1839
*Robert Selden Garnett

Janssen, Cornelius, 1593–1664?
**Sir Dudley Digges

Johansen, John Christen, 1876–1964
Alexander Wilbourne Weddell (Portrait I)
Virginia (Chase) Steedman Weddell (Mrs. Alexander Wilbourne Weddell) (Portrait VI)

Johnson, Eastman, 1824–1906
*Robert Ould (Portrait II)

Johnston, Helen (Rutherfoord), 1864–1944 (Mrs. George Ben Johnston)
*William Price Palmer

Jones, Carroll N.
*Edwin Cox
**John Melville Jennings

Jones, William Macfarlane, 1868–1951
Frederick William Sievers

Jonniaux, Alfred, 1882–
Henry Watkins Anderson
Alexander Wilbourne Weddell (Portrait V)
*Virginia (Chase) Steedman Weddell (Mrs. Alexander Wilbourne Weddell) (Portraits VII, IX)
*Edmund Randolph Williams

Kajiwara, Takuma, 1876–1960
Lorraine Farquhar Jones

Kalide, Theodor 1801–1863
Thomas Jefferson (Portrait III)

Kellogg, Miner Kilbourne, 1814–1889
**Winfield Scott

King, Charles Bird, 1785–1862
Anna (Payne) Cutts (Mrs. Richard Cutts) (copy of original portrait by Gilbert Stuart)
"Henry Washington"

King, J. W.
William Edwin Starke

Kneller, Sir Godfrey, 1646–1723
**William Byrd (Portrait II) (attributed)
*Francis Howard, fifth Baron Howard of Effingham (Portraits I, II) (attributed to the School of Kneller)
*Sir Robert Southwell (attributed to the School of Kneller)

Lamar, Julian, 1893–
Alexander Watson Weddell

Laszlo, Philip A. de, *see* de Laszlo, Philip A.

Liddell, C.
Thomas Culpeper, second Baron Culpeper (copy of original portrait)

Lightfoot, Nan (Lemmon) (Mrs. John B. Lightfoot, Jr.)
Patrick Henry (Portrait IV)

Linding, Herman M., 1880–
Thomas Ball

Linen, George, 1802–1888
Anna Campbell (Knox) Gordon (Mrs. Bazil Gordon) (Portrait III)
Martha Bickerton (Greenhow) Maury (Mrs. Robert Henry Maury)
*Robert Henry Maury
Children of Robert Henry Maury

Longacre, James Barton, 1794–1869
Benjamin Watkins Leigh (Portrait I)

Lossing, Benson John, 1813–1891
*George Washington Parke Custis (Portrait I)

Lutyens, Robert, 1901–
*David Kirkpatrick Este Bruce, (Portrait II)

Marschall, Nicola 1829–1917
John Cabell Breckinridge

Martin, John Blennerhassett, 1797–1857
*John Buchanan
Ariana McCartney (Gunn) Cunningham (Mrs. Edward Cunningham)
Edward Cunningham
*James Gibbon
*Moses Drury Hoge (Portrait I)

Matthews, George Bagby, 1857–1944
George William Bagby
John Jeter Crutchfield
James Taylor Ellyson
James Power Smith

Mercer, William, 1773–1850
*Edmund Pendleton (Portrait II)

Myers, William Barksdale, 1839–1873
*John Marshall (Portrait I) (copy of original portrait by Henry Inman)
*Gustavus Adolphus Myers (Portraits II, III)

Nebel, B.
Joseph Wheeler

Neilson, Raymond Perry Rodgers, 1881–1964
**Ellen Anderson Gholson Glasgow (Portrait II)

Newbold, Sydney
William Booth Taliaferro (Portrait II)

Nichols, Melvin N.
Douglas Southall Freeman

Nicholson, Hugh
Elizabeth Iris Southall (Clarke) Gordon (Mrs. Douglas Huntly Gordon) (Portrait III)

Niemeier, H.
*William Preston

Noce, Barin Della
Constance Elise (Schack) Gracie (Mrs. Archibald Gracie)

Orlandi, R.
*George Washington (Portrait V)

Otis, Bass, 1784–1861
William Branch Giles (Portraits II, III)

Parshall, Douglass Ewell, 1899–
Penelope Margaret (Wright) Weddell (Mrs. Alexander Watson Weddell)

Partridge, William Ordway, 1861–1930
*Pocahontas (Portrait IV)

Peale, Charles Willson 1741–1827
*Louis Antoine Jean Baptiste, chevalier de Cambray-Digny
*Conrad Alexandre Gérard
**Marie Joseph Paul Yves Roch Gilbert du Motier, marquis de Lafayette
*Arthur Lee
*Anne César, chevalier de la Luzerne
*Daniel Morgan
**George Washington (Portrait II)
*Martha (Dandridge) Custis Washington (Mrs. George Washington) (Portrait X)

Peale, James, 1749–1831
*Warner Lewis Wormeley (Portrait II) (attributed)

Pepoon, Willis, 1860–1940
William Green (copy of original portrait)

Pereira, C. Bernard
Douglas Huntly Gordon (Portrait I)

Peticolas, Philippe Abraham, 1760–1841
*Mann Page (Portrait I)

Pine, Robert Edge, 1730?–1788
**Ralph Wormeley, 1745–1806 (Portrait I)

Polk, Charles Peale, 1767–1822
George Washington (Portrait IV)

Pratt, Matthew, 1734–1805
**James Balfour
**Mary Jemima Balfour (Mrs. James Balfour)
*Custis Children

Price, B. E. L.
Thomas Jefferson (Portrait IV)

Randall, William George
Bryan Grimes (copy of a portrait by William Garl Brown)

Reading, Alice Matilda, 1859–1939
Elizabeth Collins Lee
Elizabeth (Collins) Lee (Mrs. Richard Bland Lee) (copy of
original portrait)
Henry Lee (copy of original portrait)
Richard Bland Lee (copy of original portrait)
George Washington (Portrait VI) (copy of original portrait)

Resnikoff, Irving
George Bolling Lee
George Washington Custis Lee
Mary Tabb (Bolling) Lee (Mrs. William Henry Fitzhugh
Lee) (Portraits V, VI)
Robert Edward Lee, 1869–1922

Ridgeway, Marion Patterson
Barnard Elliott Bee

Rives, Sarah Landon 1874–1957
John Page (copy of original portrait attributed to the School
of Sir Peter Lely)
William Cabell Rives (copy of original lithograph portrait)

Robinson, Susan Leigh, 1854–1922
Conway Robinson (Portrait I)

Rose, A.
Charles Broadway Rouss (Portrait I)

Rouillon, Emilie
Harriet Hopkins

Ryland, Robert Knight b. 1873
Evelyn Russell Early

Saint-Mémin, Charles Balthazar Julien Févret de,
1770–1852
*Andrew Nicolson

Saugstad, Eugenie DeLand, b. 1872
George Wythe (copy of original portrait)

Saunders, George Lethbridge, 1807–1863
Charles Bruce (Portrait I)
*Sarah Alexander (Seddon) Bruce (Mrs. Charles Bruce)
(Portrait II)

Sheppard, William Ludwell, 1833–1912
James Markham Marshall Ambler
Thomas Alexander Brander
William Byrd (Portrait I) (copy of original portrait)
*Ambrose Powell Hill
William Henry Palmer
George Wythe Randolph
Mary (Isham) Randolph (Mrs. William Randolph) (Portrait
II) (copy of original portrait)
Norman Vincent Randolph
Austin E. Smith
Thomas Smith
William Booth Taliaferro (Portrait I)
David Addison Weisiger

Shuman, S. T.
*Joseph Eggleston Johnston

Sievers, Frederick William, 1872–1966
Patrick Henry (Portrait II)
Thomas Jonathan Jackson (Portrait III)
Thomas Jefferson (Portrait II)
George Washington (Portrait VII)

Silvette, David, 1909–
*James Branch Cabell
Josiah Jordan Leake
*William Glover Stanard (Portrait I)
*William Clayton Torrence
Alexander Wilbourne Weddell (Portrait III)

Silvette, Ellis Meyer, 1876–1940
James Christian Hill
William Gordon McCabe (Portraits I, II)
Camille Armand Jules Marie, Prince de Polignac
John George Walker
Carter Warner Wormeley
William Hugh Young

Silvette, Marcia
Joseph Dupuy Eggleston
William McKendree Evans
Jacquelin Plummer Taylor (copy of original portrait)

Smith, Duncan, 1877–1934
*Joseph Bryan (Portrait I) (copy of original portrait by W.
Funk)
Thomas Nelson (copy of original portrait by Mason
Chamberlin)

Smith, Herbert Luther, 1811–1870
*George Percy (copy of original portrait)

Smutny, Rudolf V.
James Bruce (copy of original portrait by John Neagle)
Henry St. George Tucker (copy of original portrait by
William James Hubard)

Stansbury, Arthur J., 1781–1845
*John Randolph (Portrait II) (attributed)

Sterner, Albert Edward, 1863–1946
*Lyon Gardiner Tyler

Stevens, Hugo
*Eppa Hunton, 1904–1976 (Portraits I, II)

Strait, Clara Barrett
*Wade Hampton

Stuart, Gilbert, 1755–1828
*Richard Cutts

Sully, Lawrence, 1769–1804
  *Nathaniel Darby (attributed)

Sully, Robert Matthew, 1803–1855
  *Black Hawk
  Pocahontas (Portrait II)
  John Randolph (Portrait I)
  *Julia Sully (later Mrs. Daniel McCarty Chichester)
  Robert Matthew Sully, 1837–1912

Sully, Thomas, 1783–1872
  *Patrick Henry (Portrait I)
  James Madison (Portrait I) (copy of original portrait by
      Gilbert Stuart)
  *Gustavus Adolphus Myers (Portrait I)
  Edmund Pendleton (Portrait I) (copy of original portrait by
      William Mercer)
  Pocahontas (Portrait I)
  **Conway Robinson (Portrait II)
  George Washington (Portrait I) (copy of original portrait by
      Gilbert Stuart)

Swain, William, 1803–1847
  *Hugh Blair Grigsby (Portrait I)

Taylor, W. Irving
  Hugh Blair Grigsby (Portrait II)

Thompson, Cephas, 1775–1856
  *John Durburrow Blair
  **John Rogers Cooke, 1788–1854
  **Maria (Pendleton) Cooke (Mrs. John Rogers Cooke)
  William Maxwell

Toole, John, 1815–1860
  Benjamin Burton
  Eliza H. (Shipp) Burton (Mrs. Benjamin Burton)
  *John May Burton

Trahern, William Edward
  Moses Drury Hoge (Portrait II)
  *John Pelham

Troubetzkoy, Paul, 1866–1938
  *Amélie Louise (Rives) Chanler Troubetzkoy, Princess Pierre
      Troubetzkoy (Portrait III)

Troubetzkoy, Pierre 1864–1936
  *Amélie Louise (Rives) Chanler Troubetzkoy, Princess Pierre
      Troubetskoy (Portrait II)

Trumbull, John, 1756–1843
  *Thomas Jefferson (Portrait IV) (attributed)

Underwood, ——
  Campbell Slemp

Vallée, Jean François de, see DeVallée, Jean François

Van Court, ——
  Clifford Cabell Early (Portrait I)

Ver Bryck, William, 1823–1899
  Richard Channing Moore (Portrait III) (copy of original
      portrait by Henry Inman)

Von Jost, Alexander, 1889–
  George Munford Betts

Walker, John P., 1855–1932
  Richard Heron Anderson
  William S. Archer
  Judah Philip Benjamin
  Joseph Virginius Bidgood
  Robert Semple Bosher

  Reuben Beverley Boston
  Charles William Penn Brock
  David Andrew Brown
  John Thompson Brown
  Joseph Bryan (Portrait II)
  George M. Cayce
  John Randolph Chambliss
  Roger Preston Chew
  John Rogers Cooke, 1833–1891
  Montgomery Dent Corse
  John Cussons
  Wilfred Emory Cutshaw
  John Warwick Daniel
  Jefferson Davis (Portrait I)
  Varina Ann Jefferson Davis
  Joseph Coleman Dickerson
  Henry Thompson Douglas
  Jubal Anderson Early (Portrait I)
  John Echols
  Richard Stoddert Ewell
  John Charles Featherston
  Samuel Garland
  Edward S. Gay
  Robert Hobson Gilliam
  Lewis Ginter
  Don Peters Halsey
  Henry Heth
  Eppa Hunton, 1822–1908 (copy of original by Uhl)
  Thomas Jonathan Jackson (Portrait II)
  Edward Johnson
  Albert Sydney Johnston
  *John William Jones
  William Edmondson Jones
  James Lawson Kemper
  John Landstreet
  James Henry Lane
  John E. Laughton
  George Washington Custis Lee (Portrait I)
  Robert Edward Lee, 1807–1870 (Portrait IV)
  Robert Edward Lee, 1843–1914
  William Henry Fitzhugh Lee (Portrait I)
  John McCausland
  William McComb
  John Bankhead Magruder
  John Bowie Magruder
  Charles Marshall
  *Matthew Fontaine Maury
  William Lewis Moody
  William Augustine Morgan
  William Watts Parker
  Edward Aylesworth Perry
  John Luke Porter
  David Crockett Richardson
  Abram Joseph Ryan
  Raphael Semmes
  Edmund Kirby Smith
  William Smith
  Gilbert Moxley Sorrell
  Robert Mackey Stribling
  Richard Taylor
  William Richard Terry
  David Algernon Timberlake
  James Alexander Walker
  Richard Peyton Walton
  John Augustine Washington
  William Augustine Webb
  Elijah Veirs White
  Peter Johnston White
  Lewis Warrington Wise

Warburg, Eugene, 1825–1859
*John Young Mason (Portrait I)

Waugh, Beverley
*John Marshall (Portrait IV)

Wegner, Harry M. 1850–1932
James Gordon (copy of original portrait by John Hesselius)
John Gordon (copy of original portrait by John Hesselius)
Daniel Harvey Hill (copy of original portrait)
Edward Wilson James

Weisz, Eugen, 1890–1954
*Fairfax Harrison

White, Cherry (Ford) (Mrs. John K. White)
Giles Buckner Cooke

Whitfield, Emma Morehead, 1874–1932
Robert Lewis Dabney
John Wotton Gordon
Richard Griffith
Robert Daniel Johnston (copy of original portrait)
William Dorsey Pender

Wickliffe, Mary McPherson
Lafayette McLaws

Wilkins, Emma C., b. 1870
William Jones (copy of original portrait)

Williams, Adele, 1868–1952
Samuel Scott Dunlap
Edmund Christian Minor
Frederic Robert Scott
Robert White
David Minton Wright (Portrait II) (copy of original portrait)
Penelope Margaret (Creecy) Wright (Mrs. David Minton Wright) (Portrait IV) (copy of original portrait)

Williams, Berkeley, 1904–1976
John Powell (Portraits I, II, III)

Williams, William George, 1801–1846
Isaac Roberdeau

Williams, Winslow
*Wyndham Bolling Blanton

Williamson, William G.
Thomas Jonathan Jackson (Portraits V, VI)

Wollaston, John
Elizabeth (Randolph) Chiswell (Mrs. John Chiswell)
*David Meade
*Susanna (Everard) Meade (Mrs. David Meade)
**Mann Page (Portrait II)
*Anne Randolph (later Mrs. Benjamin Harrison)
*Betty (Harrison) Randolph (Mrs. Peyton Randolph)
Beverley Randolph
Elizabeth Randolph (later Mrs. Philip Grymes)
Lucy (Harrison) Randolph
**Peyton Randolph, ca. 1721–1775 (Portraits I, III)
*William Randolph, 1681–1742 (copy of original portrait)
*William Randolph, d. 1761
Lettice (Lee) Wardrop, d. 1776 (Mrs. James Wardrop)
*Jane (Bowles) Wormeley (Mrs. Ralph Wormeley) (Portrait III)
*Ralph Wormeley, 1715–1790 (Portraits I, II)
Ralph Wormeley, 1745–1806

Wood, Joseph, ca. 1778–1830
**Dolley (Payne) Todd Madison (Mrs. James Madison) (Portrait V)
**James Madison (Portrait III)

Wooldridge, Julia Stanard, 1869?–1938
Judith (Robinson) Braxton (copy of original portrait)

Three thousand copies of this book have been printed in Linoterm Baskerville on Mohawk Superfine paper. The book was designed, typeset, and printed by The Stinehour Press and The Meriden Gravure Company. Five copies are specially bound in full leather.